Variations in
Organization
Science

Variations in
Organization
Science

In Honor of Donald T. Campbell

Joel A.C. Baum / Bill McKelvey

Editors

SAGE Publications
International Educational and Professional Publisher
Thousand Oaks London New Delhi

For information:

SAGE Publications, Inc.
2455 Teller Road
Thousand Oaks, California 91320
E-mail: order@sagepub.com

SAGE Publications Ltd.
6 Bonhill Street
London EC2A 4PU
United Kingdom

SAGE Publications India Pvt. Ltd.
M-32 Market
Greater Kailash I
New Delhi 110 048 India

Printed in the United States of America

Library of Congress Cataloging-in-Publication Data

Main entry under title:

Variations in organization science: In honor of Donald T. Campbell/
    edited by Joel A.C. Baum and Bill McKelvey.
        p. cm.
    Includes bibliographical references and index.
    ISBN 0-7619-1125-1 (cloth)   ISBN 0-7619-1126-X (paper)
    1. Organization. 2. Organizational behavior. 3. Organizational sociology.
    I. Campbell, Donald Thomas, 1916-1996. II. Baum, Joel A. C. III. McKelvey, Bill.
    HD58.7 .V37 1999
    302.3'5—dc21   98-58085

99 00 01 02 03 10 9 8 7 6 5 4 3 2 1

Acquiring Editor: Harry Briggs
Editorial Assistant: Mary Ann Vail
Production Editor: Astrid Virding
Editorial Assistant: Nevair Kabakian
Typesetter/Designer: Marion Warren
Indexer: Teri Greenberg
Cover Designer: Candice Harman

Contents

Part II: Multilevel Coevolution

Part III: Process-Level Analysis and Modeling

Part IV: Methodology and Epistemology

Foreword

During Don Campbell's lifetime, I never used the name of Campbell. Instead, after our 1983 marriage, I continued using the name acquired after my first marriage, long before one's surname became a feminist issue. I did this chiefly because Frankel had been my professional name for a number of years by the time we met. Moreover, Don often spoke of his longtime custom of advising his female graduate students to keep their maiden names when they married. ("Given the high rate of divorce among psychologists, I warned them that they could find themselves saddled professionally with the surname of a person they no longer even liked," he would say, then he'd add, with a twinkle: "None of them took my advice, and all of those to whom I gave that advice have stayed married!") But, the strongest reason for eschewing the Campbell name was, I must now confess, a perverse pride: I didn't want to trade on his renown in any way. All this points to the fact that it was not simple marrying a man whose fame was so great.

But what a joy it was! He was not merely a famous man, but a great one, a true original whose value and role in the intellectual world were unique and irreplaceable. (I can say that, because I had nothing to do with his success, which was achieved long before we met.) One reason, at least, was not hard to discern: Donald T. Campbell was, quite simply, the best academic I have ever encountered—and I have encountered quite a few.

During the 15 years we were together, I had ample opportunity to contemplate the qualities that made him that. It was not sheer brilliance, though he was indeed, as one admirer said, "the last of the polymaths." Nor was it drive and ambition, though he certainly had plenty of those qualities, as well. It was not his creativity or his enormous capacity for work, though he was well above the norms in those regards (even though he complained of needing more sleep than most people and insisted he had never been able to work long hours). It was not even his immense talent for collaboration with other scholars. It was all these things in magical combination with special qualities of personality and character that made Don one of the few major figures in any field—perhaps the only one—who seems to have had no enemies, even among longtime intellectual adversaries.

Intellectual disagreements were never rancorous, but always friendly, treated as opportunities to learn from another's work. Indeed, sometimes Don was said to "suffer fools gladly"—and, oddly, this was consistent not only with his kindly disposition but also with his fallibilist epistemology, which taught him that all of us are fools, and that you never know where a good idea might come from.

Thus, in his teaching, he gave only three grades: A, B, or Incomplete, for his faith in everyone's capacity to learn and contribute was limitless.

Chip Reichard wrote (in one of Don's many obituaries) that he wondered whether there was anyone Don ever met that he did not encourage. I, having seen him in action more times than I can count, have wondered the same thing. He had a great gift for finding what was positive and original in the work of others, and letting them know how much he valued it. More than one discouraged scholar carried on through years of adversity because of Don's help and support, and if they faltered at last and abandoned the struggle, he mourned the loss to the intellectual world. He wanted everyone to love that world as he did, and his influence on students was nothing short of seductive in many cases.

Early in his life, Don Campbell decided to be a scientist and an intellectual, though what sort of intellectual he did not discover until later. To him, no other life could possibly have been as rewarding or as noble as the life of the mind. He used to joke wryly that he was lucky to have stumbled into academe, because he surely would have been a failure had he tried to earn a living at anything else. I doubted that proposition the first time I heard it, and my subsequent years of watching assured me that his talents as a diplomat and a salesman would have earned him a living anywhere. Still, he believed it, and his generosity was such that he wished everyone in the world could share his pleasure in the intellectual enterprise.

Since Don's death in 1996, I have had letters and messages from many people whose lives he had touched in some way. Each of them is special, a touching tribute to the love people felt for Don in return for the love he gave. That is not so very surprising: What really astounded me was to learn of the enormous variety of intellectual projects and interests my husband had engaged in over his 50-year career, many of which I learned of only after his death. Now, after 15 years as both colleague and wife, after the innumerable meetings we attended together the world over, and after reading substantial portions (though not nearly all) of his immense scholarly output, I am still learning about interests he shared, even projects he had undertaken, often with people whose names were unfamiliar.

I cannot say that I had *no* idea that Don had contact with specialists in studies of organizations. It seemed to me peripheral to what I knew he was actively involved in, but I do remember a meeting in New York City several years ago, one that was organized by Joel Baum. (I went to New York with Don, but not to the meeting, I confess. Don had told me it was about management, a field in which I regard myself as a hopeless case.) What I didn't suspect, though, was that Donald T. Campbell's influence on the field of organization science merited a volume in his memory. I am sure he would be grateful, and as always a little surprised, to learn that so distinguished a group of colleagues has accorded him this honor.

On occasions such as this one, Don used to elaborate his thesis that the more honors one has received, the more of them one is likely to receive in the future. With each honorary degree or award, he would say, with the self-deprecating twinkle he showed on such occasions, that here was another case of "autocorrelated error." On the other hand, his was the only C.V. I've ever seen that had a section titled "Books Dedicated to Me," and despite the many other honors he received, that list was the achievement of which he was proudest. I know, therefore, that the present volume would please and gratify him, and I thank the editors, and whoever else is responsible, for honoring his memory in the way he valued most.

—Barbara Frankel Campbell

Acknowledgments

Shortly after his death in 1996, we confessed to each other the great influence Don Campbell had had on each of us.

Bill first met Don—in print—in 1965 when Don's "Variation and Selective Retention in Socio-Cultural Evolution" appeared in a book titled *Social Change in Developing Areas*. At this time, Bill was a PhD student at MIT studying personal, group, organizational, and social change and Third World industrial development. Bill's first draft of anything evolutionary appeared in 1970 and led more than a decade later to an enthusiastic selectionist theory application to organizational growth and survival, competition grouping, and dominant competence as elements in the creation of organizational species—all summarized in Bill's book, *Organizational Systematics* (1982). Although the book ostensibly was about organizational taxonomy, the required development of a theory of speciation based on selectionist evolutionary theory brought Bill, accompanied by Howard Aldrich, face to face with Don in 1980, not long after he had moved to the Maxwell School at Syracuse University. Their conversation dwelt mainly on the "evolution of evolution" in the study of organizations and in teasing out the genetic algorithm connecting Amos Hawley, Armen Alchian, and Don to early contributors and to students of organizational evolution such as Sid Winter, Herbert Kaufman, Jack

Hirshleifer, Karl Weick, Howard Aldrich, Jerry Salancik, Mike Hannan, John Freeman, Marion Blute, and, eventually, Bill.

Joel first encountered Don in 1988 while a PhD student at the University of Toronto. Don quickly became excited about Joel's dissertation (itself inspired by Bill's *Organizational Systematics*), and they began to correspond, keeping each other informed about their ideas on organizational evolution. When Joel began plans with Jitendra Singh for their 1992 conference on organizational evolution in New York City, Don was the first invited, along with Jim March, as a "pioneer" in the field of organizational evolution. After writing his organizational whole-part competition essay for that conference, Don encouraged Joel to work with him on fleshing out the significance of that phenomenon. Although they never did work together on it, Joel's chapter in this volume pursues that question directly.

We also lamented the failure in organization science to acknowledge its intellectual debt to Don and wondered what we could do to begin a correction. We quickly decided that, whatever we did, we should not do it alone. We decided to organize a conference and to publish its proceedings to celebrate, examine, and build Don's legacy. We were thrilled by the enthusiasm of everyone we approached about our plans. One of our earliest supporters was Jerry Salancik—a Campbell student himself—who quickly committed himself to the project a short time before his death. Three others who supported and influenced the volume you are holding, but, for one good reason or another, are not represented directly in it are Rebecca Henderson, Anjali Sastri, and Karl Weick. Barbara Frankel Campbell, at a difficult time in her own life, promptly compiled and provided us with a detailed record of Don's publications and achievements, enabling us all to explore his intellectual legacy more thoroughly. We also owe a debt of gratitude to all the conference and volume participants, who carefully read, debated, and commented on one another's work, completed thoughtful revisions (often several), and generally met (and kept quiet about) the fast-paced deadlines we set.

The conference itself, held November 7-9, 1997, at the Rotman School of Management, University of Toronto, was made possible by generous grants from Paul Halpern, Interim Dean of the Rotman School, and John Mamer, Interim Dean of UCLA's Anderson Graduate School of Management. We are most grateful to them for their financial support of the conference, and also to the universities that sponsored their faculty members' travel to the conference. Finally, thanks to Harry Briggs and Sage Publications for supporting our vision and allowing us to present it to you.

—JB, Toronto
—BM, Los Angeles

Chapter 1

Donald T. Campbell's Evolving Influence on Organization Science

BILL McKELVEY
JOEL A. C. BAUM

Donald T. Campbell was born November 20, 1916, and he died May 6, 1996. During the 80 years of his life, he earned a PhD from the University of California, Berkeley (1947), produced 240 publications, and received 19 honors and awards. He held 10 positions at various institutions, but mostly he was at Northwestern University. After retiring in 1982, he married his second wife, Barbara Frankel, and produced the last 78 of his works.

The year 1905 was a good one for Albert Einstein—he published his first paper on the theory of relativity, and he won the Nobel Prize for another paper that year on the photoelectric effect. The year 1959 was a good one for Campbell—his first paper on the multitrait-multimethod idea appeared, as did his first one on epistemology. The quasi-experiment idea first appeared in 1963. These three papers (Campbell, 1959: Campbell & Fiske, 1959; Campbell & Stanley, 1963) started the streams of research that led to most of his many honors and awards.

Before he retired in 1982, Campbell's ratio of epistemology to all other publications was 11%; after retirement, it was 61%. Campbell is particularly unusual because he is a bench scientist who achieved significant recognition later in life for epistemological contributions. He published 50 bench scientist–type papers before his first "knowledge process" paper, the beginning of his writing on epistemology (Campbell, 1959). Most bench scientists never turn to philosophical writing. Most would say, "I ignore all that philosophy stuff. I just try to do good science." Usually, this means hypotheses are tested for possible refutation—reflecting a vague Popperian influence. Occasionally, Nobel Prize winners become drawn into the philosophical fray in their later years be-

AUTHORS' NOTE: Discussions with Howard Aldrich and Martin Evans helped us sharpen this introduction. Citations in this chapter follow temporal order.

cause their more pivotal contributions are often what philosophers point to in their writings, Bohr, Mach, Schrödinger, and Einstein being typical.[1] Needless to say, philosophers never become bench scientists in their later years.

In a short introduction to Campbell's "Comment: Another Perspective on a Scholarly Career" (1981a), Brewer and Collins (1981) say, "this chapter provides a glimpse of the fits, starts, and blind alleys that characterize the life of a working scientist and intellectual" (p. 454). Campbell agrees with this, saying one page later, "It will enable me to exemplify the blind-variation-and-selective-retention (BVSR) epistemology . . . by illustrating with my own career the inevitable wastefulness of scientific exploration, the chancy indirectness of discovery, and the further chanciness of recognition." We leave the following quandary to the reader. Campbell's own BVSR theory suggests that the change in the ratio of epistemology to other writings results from selection—the epistemology papers are more essential to his intellectual survival. Alternatively, it could be a life-cycle effect—some famous scientists are drawn toward epistemology for other reasons.

Campbell's Interests

The Brewer and Collins volume, titled *Scientific Inquiry and the Social Sciences*, was created by some of Campbell's students in honor of his retirement. It is clear from this book that Campbell's primary interests are (a) the natural selection model of knowing, that is, evolutionary epistemology; (b) multimethod perspectives; (c) ontological entitivity and multilevel units of analysis; (d) a Gestalt psychological approach to pattern matching particularly relevant to cross-cultural research; (e) the contextual basis of perception, whether experiential or cultural; and (f) methods of knowing and stimulus cue utilization. As a seventh category, we would add the significant body of Campbell's work devoted to program evaluation, out of which grew his interest in quasi-experimental design. All these themes continued into the 1990s.

Brewer and Collins (1981) note "Campbell's remarkable facility in moving across levels of gen-

erality, from the abstract to the concrete" (p. 7). Surely nothing is more abstract than his combination of scientific realism, evolutionary epistemology, and hermeneutics. Oppositely, we note his interest in the triangulation of multiple operational measures. What is unique about Campbell, the bench scientist, is his contribution to all the major epistemological themes philosophers define as the desiderata of effective science. Campbell worries about the quality and appropriate use of specific operational measures—that is, measurement reliability and validity. He studies the upward and downward causality and entitivity of metaphysical concepts. He wonders whether evolutionary epistemology will tilt his science toward operationalism and naïve realism. His focus on experiments and quasi-experiments aims at the heart of philosophers' concerns about avoiding explanations and theories based on what might be accidental regularities. He worries about the tension between the goal of objectivity in science and the individual interpretations of scientists and the social construction of knowledge by scientific communities. Finally, he studies the root problem of philosophy, how to know which theories are more or less truthful, and how sciences systematically move toward more truthful theories and winnow out mistakes.

Although Campbell's interests and most of his contributions cover much of the broad table of social science, our particular interest, honored in this book, focuses on his seminal contribution to organization science. His interests in quasi-experiments and triangulating multiple methods have been brought to the study of organizations by the many psychologists and social psychologists taking positions in business schools and applying their disciplines to the study of firms (see Evans, this volume). Even so, out of the vast sweep and number of Campbell's works, we believe that a single chapter stands out as having the most pervasive influence on organization science—"Variation and Selective Retention in Socio-Cultural Evolution" (Campbell, 1965).[2] Granted that triangulation and quasi-experiments could improve bench-level organization science, the countering of the intentions and rational decisions by the visible hand of managerial elites (Chandler, 1977) with the invisible hand of emergent forces and consequent emergent behavior, processes, functions, and structure surely ranks as a major turning point in organization science.

Campbell's Influence in Organization Science

Organization science is a receptive soil to Campbell's seed. Early evolutionary tilling stems from the influence in social science of Hawley's (1950) book, *Human Ecology*, and Alchian's (1950) classic article, "Uncertainty, Evolution, and Economic Theory." These are followed by Friedman's (1953) use of natural selection theory to justify the idea that firms behave "*as if* they were seeking rationally to maximize their expected returns" (p. 22). Then comes Winter's (1964) investigation of some differential equation models of selection processes. Other evolutionary insertions into economics come from Penrose (1952), Dunn (1971), Farrell (1979), and Hirshleifer (1977). More narrowly in organization theory, perhaps early sensitizing stems from Haire's (1959) use of the biological metaphor in his growth and development model. Possibly, the idea emerges from Buckley's (1967) book on general systems theory—he mentions Campbell's evolutionary ideas and cites his 1959 article. The most direct early uses are by Aldrich (1972) in his article "Organizational Boundaries and Inter-Organizational Conflict" and by Kaufman (1975) in his article "The Natural History of Organizations." This is followed quickly by Aldrich and Pfeffer (1976), Hannan and Freeman (1977), Aldrich (1979), Weick (1979), McKelvey (1982), and Nelson and Winter (1982).

Organization science benefits primarily from four key Campbellian ideas about scientific inquiry. Dominating is the focus on selectionist evolutionary explanations of emergent order and differential survival. Having much less effect are the other themes: evolutionary epistemology, multimethod triangulation perspectives, and experiments and quasi-experiments. This is unfortunate. As Donaldson (1995) observes, the first theme adds to paradigm proliferation in organization science, but if the other three themes were stronger in organization science, paradigm proliferation would diminish. Why? Because the scientific basis for winnowing out less truthful theories, terms, and entities would improve considerably. Coupled with the integration of those that are left into broader, more compelling theories, this would result in fewer but more fruitful theories having more influence and practical impact.

McKelvey (this volume) develops the scientific realist basis of *Campbellian realism* to show that Campbell's particular synthesis of the second, third, and fourth themes presents us with a strong nomic[3] and experimentally driven objectivist epistemology that is, nevertheless, sensitive to Kuhnian (1962) historical relativism and the dynamics of changing beliefs among scientific communities. Campbell accomplishes this by recognizing that the following sequence is possible, if not actually followed in most scientific communities: (a) individual scientists develop idiosyncratic interpretations of the phenomena they study, (b) individual interpretations are socially constructed into a more coherent view held by the scientific community (in the manner of the hermeneuticists' coherence theory), and (c) the community view slowly becomes a more correct view of the phenomena as the less accurate idiosyncratic interpretations and social constructions are winnowed out via the BVSR process. Key elements of Campbellian realism are the following:

1. Objectivist belief in the potential realness of measurable, detectable, and metaphysical terms;
2. Semantic relativist interpretation and social construction do not thwart an objective, though fallible, search for increased verisimilitude, given that the more incorrect idiosyncratic interpretations of individual scientists and social constructions of a scientific community are winnowed out by the BVSR process;
3. The selectionist process of knowledge development winnows out the more fallible terms, theories, and entities over time;
4. This selectionist process does not favor either metaphysical or operational terms;
5. The true/false dichotomy of truth is replaced by degrees of verisimilitude;
6. More truthful theories remain as the more fallible theories are selectively winnowed out—

thus, successful theories tend to be more truth-like;

7. The truthlikeness of knowledge is probable and consists of both observable and metaphysical terms;

8. Theories consist of some lawlike statements having predictive elements capable of being tested experimentally;

9. Theories preferably are based on model behavior capable of being tested as to representation of real-world phenomena;

10 Verisimilitude is defined in terms of the content of models;

11. A process of convergent realism exists in which increased verisimilitude reduces errors of measurement and prediction and vice versa; and

12. The relationship between theory and prediction and organizations and how they behave is independent of the realness of terms and entities.

If we compare psychology and organization science, we are forced to conclude that psychology much more reflects the influence of the second, third, and fourth of Campbell's themes, whereas organization science shows much more of his first and ambivalence toward the other three—though evolutionary psychology is gaining attention. Campbell was a psychologist, so perhaps he had more influence on psychology than on organization science. Possibly, this is a life versus social science thing. Because of psychologists' renewed interest in the biological basis of human behavior (Barkow, Cosmides, & Tooby, 1992; Bates & Wachs, 1994; Plomin, 1994; Nicholson, 1997; Pinker, 1997), perhaps they more easily fall in step with Campbellian realism. Organization science seems buffeted much more by multiparadigmaticism and the tendency in current social science to hear much more loudly from the subjectivist, relativist, and postmodernist kinds of postpositivisms than from the normal science postpositivisms embedded in Campbellian realism.

Campbellian Realism

Our honoring of Campbell's life and work is surely a celebration of Campbellian realism as well. This is especially important to organization science given its multiparadigmatic disarray and the pull by elements in the field toward postmodernism.[4] The 15 or more different paradigms (Donaldson, 1995) are based on partly different theories but also reflect the longtime division between objectivists and subjectivists (Natanson, 1963). The plurality of perspectives seems to have led to an overabundance of discourse and a paucity of explanation in organization science.[5] Presaging, but also stimulated by, Pfeffer's Presidential Address to the Academy of Management (Pfeffer, 1993), many authors have remarked on the "problem" the multiple paradigms create for organization science (Hartman, 1988; Aldrich, 1992; Donaldson, 1995; Pfeffer, 1995; Van Maanen, 1995a, 1995b; McKelvey, 1997). Pfeffer's basic argument, that multiparadigmaticism is characteristic of low-status sciences, still stands unrefuted:

> Without working through a set of processes or rules to resolve theoretical disputes and debates, the field of organizational studies will remain ripe for either a hostile takeover from within or from outside. In either case, much of what is distinctive, and much of the pluralism that is so valued, will be irretrievably lost. (1993, p. 620)

Although cognizant of the potentially divisive effects of ethnocentric disciplines or subdisciplines, Campbell (1969a) suggested that a

> fish-scale model of omniscience represents the solution . . . [the] slogan is collective comprehensiveness through overlapping patterns of unique narrownesses. Each narrowness is in this analogy a "fish scale." . . . Our only hope of a comprehensive social science, or other multiscience, lies in a continuous texture of narrow specialties which overlap with other narrow specialties. (p. 328)

But this works only when each of the "scales" has scientific credibility in its own right. Based on scientific realist epistemology, in which an objective reality is accepted as the ultimate criterion variable, and the translation of Popper's (1935/1959) notion of "falsificationism" into incremental falsification and incremental corroboration,

McKelvey (1997) argues that multiple paradigms, or more fallible scales, persist when a field has no objective means of carrying out studies leading to the incremental corroboration or refutation of key elements of the paradigms—hence paradigm proliferation. In this light, organization science is in great need of epistemological and methodological elaboration aimed at developing better methods of providing such tests. This would be unnecessary if it were avowedly Campbellian realist.

Organizational epistemology surely is *not* Campbellian realist. At best, it is confused; at worst, it is in danger of becoming an anti-science (or alternative science or parascience), as defined by Holton (1993), metascience (Fuller, 1993), or nonscience (Wolpert, 1992). Organization scientists continue to debate among normal science and postmodernism (positivist and relativist approaches loosely defined) (Brown, 1992; Hassard, 1993; Pfeffer, 1993, 1997; Burrell, 1996; Donaldson, 1996), even though philosophers abandoned both two decades ago (Suppe, 1977). Consequently, those in the field who are trying to avoid anti-science have lost their traditional philosophical basis of legitimacy without having found a suitable replacement. During this period of epistemological confusion and weakness, normal science in organization science has been under attack by subjectivists, interpretists, phenomenologists, social constructionists, critical theorists, and postmodernists (see the authors listed in note 4 as well as Daft and Lewin [1990]), decrying positivism while arguing that organization science needs a different approach, one more relevant to social sciences—see for example Burrell and Morgan (1979), Perrow (1994), and Reed (1996).

Recently, Hunt (1994) shows how incorrect are the anti–normal science scholars in their accusations against positivism. By today's understanding, organization scientists have always been much more *realist* than *positivist* (Miner, 1980; Godfrey & Hill, 1995). Organization researchers practice a logic-in-use, which holds that there is

enough of an objective reality "out there" that repeated attempts by various researchers, using a variety of generally approved methods of "justification

logic" eventually will discover the approximate truth of theories by successively eliminating errors. (McKelvey, 1997, p. 363)

Campbellian realism brings to the social sciences in general, and to organization science in particular, a vision of science and method rooted in scientific realism and evolutionary epistemology—both of which show the strong influence of the noted philosophers Karl Popper (1935/1959, 1963, 1972, 1956/1983) and Stephen Toulmin (1953, 1961, 1972). Given the abandonment of positivism by current philosophers, the misconceptions of positivist epistemology by social science postpositivists, and lack of a coherent replacement epistemology that conforms to the expectations of normal science and higher status sciences, the field of organization science is in great need of a new organizational epistemology.

Buried within Campbell's second theme of evolutionary epistemology is the concern about coevolutionary change and the conflation of upward (reductionist) and downward (contextualist) causation (explanation). Traditional organization theory, since the time of Max Weber, generally has studied organizations with little attention paid to the coevolutionary competitive context of organizational niches—that is, contextual causation. Although there were earlier related treatments (e.g., Aldrich, 1972; Kaufman, 1975; Aldrich & Pfeffer, 1976), it was Hannan and Freeman's (1977) seminal article on population ecology that introduced niche theory into the mainstream of organization science. Since then, various authors have developed organizational population ecology, which has focused mainly on organizational foundings and failures and population regulation (for a recent review, see Baum, 1996).

What is missing is a development of coevolutionary effects among firms in niches. Some progress was made recently in the volume edited by Baum and Singh (1994a). Parallel to the development of population ecology, organization science has seen the rise of competitive strategy, dominated until a few years ago by industrial organization economists and game theorists (Porter 1980; Besanko, Dranove, & Shanley, 1996). Economists study the competitive context of firms but frequently treat firms as "black boxes," ignoring the extension of their analytical approaches inside firms—exceptions being game theory (Rasmusen, 1994), agency theory (Besanko et al., chap. 16), and transaction cost economics (Williamson, 1975; Groenewegen 1996) (see also Barney and Ouchi [1986] for an overview of organizational economics). Thus, reductionist explanations starting from within firms have suffered. Consequently, as it stands in the late 1990s, organization science needs further development of theory and research that brings the competitive perspectives of economics and strategic management inside organizations, while not letting go of the rich understanding of organizational functioning gained by organization theorists. The emerging stream of research on the microdynamics of interfirm rivalry, through which firms (re)define their market positions and interrelationships (e.g., Chen & MacMillan, 1992; Miller & Chen, 1994; Chen & Hambrick, 1995; Baum & Korn, 1996, in press; Chen, 1996; Stuart & Podolny, 1996; Korn & Baum, in press) reinforces other recent work on asymmetric competitive dynamics (e.g., Baum & Mezias, 1992; Barnett, 1993, 1997; Barnett, Greve, & Park, 1994; Baum & Singh, 1994a, 1994b; Baum, 1995; Podolny, Stuart, & Hannan, 1996; Baum & Haveman, 1997) and interorganizational learning (e.g., Darr, Argote, & Epple, 1995; Miner & Haunschild, 1995; Haunschild & Miner, 1997; Ingram & Baum, 1997a, 1997b; Baum & Ingram, 1998) which, taken together, appear to hold real promise as a basis for realizing a general coevolutionary approach to competitive interfirm dynamics.

The second theme contains additional scientific dynamics—a stretching of analysis in two directions. One stretch moves toward increasingly micro and macro levels of, respectively, reductionist and contextualist explanation. The second moves from assumptions of uniform underlying phenomena—particles, molecules, or microstates—such as the rational actor assumption in economics (Hogarth & Reder, 1987) to the stochastic assumption, say, that each actor has stochastically idiosyncratic perceptions and behaviors. Over the 100 years from the discovery of Brownian motion in 1828, to Boltzmann's statistical mechanics of 1870, to the acceptance of the implications of quantum and relativity theories circa 1930, physicists have shifted from the uniformity to the stochastic assumption. Over the past 100 years, biologists also shifted from the notion of uniform genetic processes to a view recognizing that the stochastic elements characterizing the basic processes of cell replication are at the root of adaptive evolution (Williams, 1966; Maynard Smith, 1975; Dawkins, 1976; Kauffman, 1993; Eldredge, 1995). The emergence of complexity theory in many sciences also gives witness to this shift (Nicolis & Prigogine, 1989; Cramer, 1993; Kaye, 1993; Cowan, Pines, & Meltzer, 1994; Belew & Mitchell, 1996; Arthur, Durlauf, & Lane, 1997). The shift in these disciplines did not come easily. For one thing, it takes a century. Boltzmann committed suicide from feelings that his work was not recognized. It takes the circuitous route from Gibbs (1902), who "popularized" Boltzmann in English in the United States, via Fisher in England, to finally and slowly affect the Germans. Fisher (1930) and Wright (1931) also were instrumental in fostering the shift in biology with their stochastic modeling of genetic improvements on adaptive landscapes.

The organization science life cycle is a couple of centuries behind other sciences such as physics, biology, and economics. Consequently, organization scientists are only just now coming to terms with the essential idiosyncrasy of their microstate phenomena. Assumptions and observations of idiosyncratic phenomena are endemic to the work of ethnomethodologists, interpretists, radical humanists, and postmodernists (Burrell & Morgan, 1979; Lincoln, 1985; Reed & Hughes, 1992; Cannella & Paetzold, 1994; Alvesson & Deetz, 1996; Chia, 1996). To date, the two assumptions of uniformity and stochasticity in organization science are at the heart of the paradigm debate—uniformity assumptions of the normal science aspects of the field versus the idiosyncratic assumptions of the relativists (Perrow, 1994). McKelvey (1997) observes that the assumptions promulgated by the social science postpositivists (Lincoln, 1985; Chia, 1996) are remarkably similar to underlying assumptions held by other disciplines, as demonstrated by Schwartz and Ogilvy (1979).[6] The fact is that the microstate assumptions of the physical and life sciences have evolved such that they are now similar to microstate assumptions held by relativists, postmodernists, and complexity theorists.

The scientific realist roots that McKelvey (this volume) highlights as essential to fully understanding Campbellian realism clearly put (preferably formalized) models at the center of science. In this, scientific realists (Bhaskar, 1975/1997; Aronson, Harré, & Way, 1994; De Regt, 1994) are joined by those espousing the semantic conception of theories (Beth, 1961; Suppes, 1962; Suppe, 1977, 1989; van Fraassen, 1980; Lloyd, 1988; Thompson, 1989). Campbell was so broadly familiar with both the biological and scientific realist literatures that it is inconceivable to us that he was not aware of scientists' acceptance of the changing microstate assumptions and the recognition of the centrality of models. There is even evidence of this. Campbell (1994) cites an earlier work (Campbell, 1983) that cites Haldane's *Causes of Evolution* (1932). Haldane, along with Fisher, was an early contributor to mathematical modeling in genetics. In the 1994 chapter, Campbell also cites Williams (1966), one of the strongest advocates of the role of genetic mutations in fostering evolutionary changes in species. Admittedly, 1994 is late in Campbell's career. Although the 1983 citation of Haldane is much earlier, still, it is just after he retired. Excepting these citations, we find little if any evidence in his work that Campbell addressed these issues directly in his epistemology or methodological writings, strange as this might seem.

The most obvious telltale clue would be evidence that Campbell was familiar with agent-based adaptive learning models. These are modeling methods that draw specifically on idiosyncratic microstate assumptions and have been used heavily by the "upward causation" theorists in biology (Fisher, 1930; Maynard Smith, 1975; Kauffman, 1993). Examples of these modeling approaches are *spin glass* (Mézard, Parisi, & Virasoro, 1987; Fischer & Hertz, 1993; Kauffman, 1993), *simulated annealing* (Arts & Korst, 1989), *cellular automata* (Kauffman, 1993; Weisbuch, 1993), *neural networks* (Freeman & Skapura, 1992), and *genetic algorithms* (Holland, 1975; Mitchell, 1996). We give mostly recent references, but in biology they have been in the literature in computational form for more than two decades. These are so-called "particle" or "nearest neighbor" models, in which very simple-minded "agents" adopt a neighboring agent's attributes to reduce energy or gain fitness. Prerequisite to the use of these models is the need to view organizational process-level behavior as coevolving discrete random events in a multilevel micro- and macrocoevolutionary context.

Volume Themes and Contributions

Our short history of Campbell's influence across the seven broad topic categories and the four narrower themes relevant to organization science suggests that by the time in his life that he had fleshed out the essential features of Campbellian realism, he no longer had the time to elaborate on all its implications. Because he was a psychologist, there is no reason to expect that he would have more specifically developed the implications of his brand of scientific realism and selectionist evolutionary epistemology as they might pertain to organization science. Our volume is titled *Variations in Organization Science: In Honor of Donald T. Campbell* because we wish to give current organization scientists opportunities to honor his many contributions by producing "variations" that stem from the 240 papers that he did write, the additional implications of Campbellian realism he did not elaborate, and further applications of his perspective to organization science (Campbell's full curriculum vitae is presented in the appendix to this volume). One key strength of Campbellian realism is that it very much reflects what might be called "normal science" in psychology and organization science. The "bench science"–type chapters in this volume all measure up reasonably well in terms of the tenets summarized by McKelvey. The chapters are not particularly self-conscious about this, and there is certainly room for improvement. They are not as far along in terms of nomic necessity and lawlike statements as Campbell's realism calls for, nor are models as central in some of the chapters as Campbellian realism calls for, though some are model-centered.

Blind-Variation-Selection-and-Retention

This heading—Campbell's favorite phrase—covers five chapters that variously tease out further implications of BVSR processes *inside* firms. Organization science has progressed from the early applications of BVSR in population ecology studies to greater emphasis on intrafirm BVSR processes, as indicated by the decreasing number of population-level studies, going from Carroll (1988), to Singh (1990), to Baum and Singh (1994a), to this volume. Now, with both population and intrafirm level studies, organization science sets up the debate that Eldredge (1995) points to in biology. Earlier in the natural selection theory life cycle, emphasis was on ecological forces affecting speciation. Later, as genetics developed, along with more powerful microscopes, lab techniques, and modeling approaches, the intrabody microstate origins of adaptive change became strong elements of modern biology. The chapters in this section suggest that a similar process is beginning in the study of firms—with the potential for a similar debate.

- Aldrich and Kenworthy couple Campbell's BVSR model with his writings on creativity, experimentation, playfulness, clique selfishness, and altruism to create two *Campbellian antinomies*, or apparent contradictions, that help explain why most organizational foundings are simple reproductions of existing forms rather than innovative creations.
- Miner and Raghavan challenge contemporary organization theorists' taken-for-granted assumption (reinforced by Campbell's BVSR framework) that interorganizational imitation produces homogeneity. Their review of models from a variety of fields reveals that imitation can indeed produce convergence to a single routine, but it also can produce stable mixes of routines and oscillatory patterns of routines over time.
- Rao and Singh build on Campbell's idea that new mutations represent failed forms to explore how new organizational forms are built *with* the ruins of existing organizational forms rather than *on* the ruins of old organizational forms. Their chapter chronicles and clearly typifies the *variety in variation* in organizational populations.

- Romanelli critiques the ubiquitous practice of interorganizational copying by exploring the possibility raised by Campbell that a substantial cost to variety and innovation may arise from an overemphasis on copying. By fostering a belief in prescience (i.e., ability to know outcomes in advance), copying limits organizations' experimentation with their own variations and fundamentally and detrimentally reduces the ability of an organization to advance.
- Miller explores how BVSR processes and whole-part competition *within* organizations are engendered by success. Perceived success shapes managerial attributions and attitudes, and it transforms corporate cultures, structures, and information processing behavior, which, in turn, push strategies toward extreme conservatism or boldness, toward simplicity and inertia, and toward insularity.

Multilevel Coevolution

Although we usually talk in terms of "evolutionary theory," as Kauffman says, "the true and stunning success of biology reflects the fact that organisms do not merely evolve, they *coevolve* both with other organisms and with a changing abiotic environment" (1993, p. 237). Roughgarden's (1976) initial definition and application of coevolution has been extended from the ecological-level analyses of populations to coevolution at all levels. Thus, Kauffman applies it at the chromosome, gene, cell, and organ levels of analysis, in addition to the species/population level. Kauffman's book is the epitome of modern biological analysis: multilevel *and* coevolutionary. Campbell's interest in the levels of analysis problem—and implications for causal analysis—is obvious (Campbell, 1974, 1981b, 1990, 1994). He does not appear, however, to have pursued multilevel *coevolutionary* analysis. Coevolutionary analysis in firms began with several chapters in the Baum and Singh (1994a) book (chapters by Baum and Singh, Rosenkopf and Tushman, and Van de Ven and Garud). The first two of these chapters follow Roughgarden's population ecology application, whereas the Van de Ven and Garud chapter shows coevolution at two levels—technical and institutional. Three of these authors, along with two new additions, continue their coevolutionary perspective in this volume: coevolution of organizational parts and wholes and competitive contexts. This is a significant step forward in evolutionary applications in organizations and obviously a conflation of Campbell's multilevel and evolutionary perspectives.

- Baum elaborates Campbell's rationale for expecting individuals and face-to-face groups to undermine the efficacy of organizational selection. He formalizes several aspects of whole-part coevolutionary competition in organizations using Kauffman's (1993) *NK*[*C*] model of coupled fitness landscapes, and he derives some novel approaches to the problem of shared control in organizations that focus on *tuning* the structure of coevolution within themselves.
- Anderson draws on the idea that BVSR occurs through a *nested hierarchy*, which Campbell helps to popularize, to examine how the range of variation in the population of venture capital funds shapes and constrains variation in firms that receive venture capital funding.
- Ingram and Roberts examine empirically the idea that organizational components may experience evolution independently of entire organizations. Their dynamic analysis of new drug introductions in the U.S. pharmaceutical industry robustly supports their model, in which firms are conceived as bundles of routines that comprise productive capabilities, which are, in turn, associated with specific product offerings.
- Rosenkopf and Nerkar advance theories of technological evolution by conceptualizing technology as hierarchies of systems, products, and components and by applying Campbell's evolutionary concepts to these hierarchies. Their case study of the optical disc industry illuminates *cross-level* phenomena of downward causation and whole-part coevolutionary competition, as well as *within-level* phenomena of interdependent components and products.
- Van de Ven and Grazman explore how new organizational forms emerge and evolve in a lineage by the crossing and joining of existing organizational units, resources, and competencies. They ground their framework, in which organizations evolve as entities nested within evolving systems at higher and lower levels, by constructing 150-year genealogies of management, strategy, structure, and institutional arrangements of health care delivery organizations in Minneapolis-St. Paul.

Process-Level Analysis and Modeling

As mentioned earlier, although Campbell (1994) writes of multilevel evolutionary processes and shows some minimal awareness of the use of microstate modeling in biology, in all his writing he never quite gets to coevolutionary microstate analysis at the basic process levels of sociocultural systems or firms. We think this is a life-cycle thing. By the time Campbell evidenced appreciation of this kind of analysis, he was at retirement age—well past the time when most scientists turn their energies to the nitty-gritty of their discipline—cell counts and gene sequence analyses in biology, item analysis and experimental treatment protocols in psychology, and for both sciences, empirical research, number crunching, and mathematical and computational modeling. Campbell was 31 years old at the time he received his PhD degree and started as an assistant professor at Ohio State University. His research at the time involved such bench scientist things as indirect assessment, effect of ordinal position of responses, social distance scales, operational delineation, galvanic skin response, bias estimates, trait judgments, and response sets—very definitely the nitty-gritty of psychology at the time. Suppose Campbell is 31 and starting as an assistant professor in 1998, and suppose he were to focus more specifically on firms? What kinds of research would he do? We imagine it would look much like the chapters in this section.

- Madsen, Mosakowski, and Zaheer develop a multilevel model of intrafirm BVSR processes that produces firms' dynamic capabilities and heterogeneity. Their empirical analysis of the foreign exchange trading industry from 1973 to 1993 reproduces the model, showing how prior performance and experience influence the current stock of change capabilities, which, in turn, shape future performance and behavior.
- Pentland adopts a process-oriented approach and empirically grounds a method for characterizing organizations as structured patterns of action to enable organizations to be modeled as *networks of action* that transform inputs and create value rather

than networks of individuals, groups, subunits, or divisions.

- Lomi and Larsen use cellular automata models to represent the recombinant processes hierarchical social systems use to reproduce themselves. Their modeling is designed to illustrate how *levels* are connected without imposing any a priori aggregation rules to explore evolution unfolding at different levels of action in organizational systems.
- McKelvey proposes an explanation for why firms like General Motors cannot seem to adapt, based on propositions from Prigogine's self-organization theory and Kauffman's complexity catastrophe theory. Four organizational forces—adaptive tension, self-organization, interdependency effects, and coevolution—are illustratively modeled using Kauffman's Boolean network and *NK[C]* models. Campbellian realism and model-centered science are, thus, illustrated.

Epistemology and Methodology

Campbell wrote about these two topics often and well, dating back to 1959. Although our "ratio analysis" shows his epistemological work to be mostly a late career activity, his interest in multimethod triangulation and quasi-experiments dominates his midcareer attention. Thus, his methodological ideas had matured into stability by the time of his retirement, whereas the epistemological writing started slowly but kept growing throughout his life. Quite possibly, Campbell's longtime interest in bench science measurement and experiments kept objectivism at the forefront as he searched for an improved epistemology. Starting in 1959, his early epistemology focuses on BVSR and the evolution of knowledge. Then, in 1969, we see the first evidence of his "corrigible, hypothetical and critical realism" (Campbell, 1969b, 1988). Attention to cultural relativism emerges in 1972, with multilevel analysis beginning in 1974. His move into semantic relativism and hermeneutics shows up by 1986 (models of language) and 1991 (coherence theory and hermeneutics). As noted earlier, Campbellian realism includes scientific realism, selectionist epistemology, and hermeneutics. Over the years, Campbell slowly evolved toward an objective epistemology that also attends to the concerns of interpretists and social constructionists

and to the dynamics of how sciences change over time.

- Evans traces Campbell's influence on methodologies in organization science by exploring the influence of two well-known bodies of work—construct validity and quasi-experimentation—and one less familiar set of ideas: the analysis of case studies.
- Hendrickx keys in on Campbell's eventual addition of hermeneutics to his development of selectionist evolutionary epistemology. Using Campbell's (1994) essay on individual versus group selection, she shows that a hermeneutic reading of the text indicates that Campbell's fundamental concern centers *not* on whether "groups are real" but rather on whether his use of BVSR necessarily implies the selection and retention of selfish individuals at the expense of sociocultural (group) solidarity and altruism.
- McKelvey's examination of Campbell's intense interests in scientific realism and evolutionary epistemology reveals a basis—*Campbellian realism*—for an objective organization science that denies neither the epistemological dynamics of historical relativists nor the sociology of knowledge developed by interpretists and social constructionists, and demonstrates that the current "paradigm war" between organizational positivists and relativists is philosophically uninformed and dysfunctional.

Looking to the Future

Given the growing rapprochement of organization theory and competitive strategy, especially as indicated by the development of the "resource-based" or "competence-based" views of strategy, which focus on idiosyncratic resources internal to firms (Teece, 1984; Rumelt, 1987; Barney, 1991; Reevis-Conner, 1991; Lado & Wilson, 1994; Pfeffer, 1994; Heene & Sanchez, 1996; Porter, 1996), there is a growing recognition that organization science needs further development of theories that deal specifically with the rapprochement. Specifically, what are needed are theories that deal with both micro- and macrocoevolutionary multilevel applications of the effects of competitive context (contextualism) and microstates (reductionism). Some starts have been made in this direction in Baum and Singh (1994a), and in recent papers by

Sorenson (1997), Levinthal (1997), Rivkin (1997), and McKelvey (1998, in press), among others, on the microdynamics of interfirm rivalry, asymmetric competitive dynamics, and interorganizational learning (as noted previously), as well as new work in this volume. These are only bare beginnings. More theoretical and methodological "variations" clearly are called for if organization science is to improve its standing as a science and contribute more meaningfully to the competitive positioning, managing, and designing of organizations. Some new variations appear as chapters in this book.

There are four facets to our future vision. One goal is to foster the development of an explicit organizational epistemology that is up to date in terms of recent developments in the philosophy of science and is relevant in that it specifically focuses on the epistemological peculiarities of organization science. A second goal is to stimulate the development of methods that will be more successful in the incremental refutation or corroboration of key elements of the conflicting paradigms in organization science. A third goal focuses on fostering the development of micro- and macrocoevolutionary approaches and multilevel applications of selectionist competitive context perspectives. Our fourth goal is to speed up the rapprochement of organization theory and competitive strategy by encouraging authors to try to be as innovative and far reaching in their ideas as a young Don Campbell might be if he were starting his career in the late 1990s.

Besides celebrating Campbell's many contributions, we hope this volume will stimulate organization scientists to offer various new extensions to the Campbellian themes, thereby speaking directly to the needs of the field, perhaps as we have characterized them. Our view of the field suggests that this is indeed a timely and worthwhile goal.

Notes

1. Mach was appointed to the first chair for philosophy at the University of Vienna, and then Boltzmann held it. Bohr, Schrödinger, and Einstein carried on philosophical arguments for years over the "reality" of the entities constituting quantum theory in their debates about the "Copenhagen interpretation" (Bitbol, 1996). Einstein was named (on the signature page of

the Vienna Circle's first publication about logical positivism [Neurath, Carnap, & Hahn, 1929/1973]) along with Russell and Wittgenstein as having significant impact on the development of logical positivism.

2. Psychologists would likely see his 1959 article with Donald W. Fiske, "Convergent and Discriminant Validation by the Multitrait-Multimethod Matrix" as having the most pervasive influence in psychology.

3. Nomic (necessity) is a requirement imposed by philosophers to protect against explanations responding to "accidental regularities" by insisting that all explanations be based on theories that include at least some laws of the "counterfactual conditional" kind, that is, "If A then B." For example, a theory purporting to explain why all General Motors products are cars is based on what most people would consider an accidental regularity—"all General Motors products are cars."

4. For evidence of the "pull," see recent books by Reed and Hughes (1992), Hassard and Parker (1993), Chia (1996), Clegg, Hardy, and Nord (1996), Burrell (1997), Bentz and Shapiro (1998), Hassard and Holliday (1998), and McKinlay and Starkey (1998).

5. Discourse refers to "modes of argument that are more generalized and speculative than normal scientific discourse. . . . Discourse seeks persuasion through argument rather than through prediction" (Alexander, 1988, p. 80).

6. In a nutshell, the common assumptions refer to elements such as, that systems are increasingly complex and diverse; order is not only the result of hierarchy—as in holography, many parts may contain information about the whole; phenomena are indeterminate/probabilistic rather than being exactly predictable; there is multiple causality—multiple levels and directions, as well as coevolutionary processes; structure emerges from the self-organization of stochastic idiosyncratic microstates; and science has subjective processes in its discourse.

References

Alchian, A. A. (1950). Uncertainty, evolution and economic theory. *Journal of Political Economy, 58,* 211-222.

Aldrich, H. E. (1972). Organizational boundaries and interorganizational conflict. *Human Relations, 24,* 279-293.

Aldrich, H. E. (1979). *Organizations and environments.* Englewood Cliffs, NJ: Prentice Hall.

Aldrich, H. E. (1992). Incommensurable paradigms? Vital signs from three perspectives. In M. Reed & M. Hughes (Eds.), *Rethinking organization: New directions in organization theory and analysis* (pp. 17-45). London: Sage.

Aldrich, H. E., & Pfeffer, J. (1976). Environments of organizations. *Annual Review of Sociology, 2,* 79-105.

Alexander, J. C. (1988). The new theoretical movement. In N. Smelser (Ed.), *Handbook of sociology* (pp. 77-101). Newbury Park, CA: Sage.

Alvesson, M., & Deetz, S. (1996). Critical theory and postmodernism approaches to organizational studies. In S. R. Clegg,

C. Hardy, & W. R. Nord (Eds.), *Handbook of organization studies* (pp. 191-217). Thousand Oaks, CA: Sage.

Aronson, J. L., Harré, R., & Way, E. C. (1994). *Realism rescued.* London: Duckworth.

Arthur, W. B., Durlauf, S. N., & Lane, D. A. (Eds.). (1997). *The economy as an evolving complex system* (Proceedings Vol. 27). Reading, MA: Addison-Wesley.

Arts, E., & Korst, J. (1989). *Simulated annealing and Boltzmann machines.* New York: Wiley.

Barkow, J. H., Cosmides, L., & Tooby, J. (1992). *The adapted mind: Evolutionary psychology and the generation of culture.* Oxford, UK: Oxford University Press.

Barnett, W. P. (1993). Strategic deterrence among multipoint competitors. *Industrial and Corporate Change, 2,* 249-278.

Barnett, W. P. (1997). The dynamics of competitive intensity. *Administrative Science Quarterly, 42,* 128-160.

Barnett, W. P., Greve, H,. & Park, D. Y. (1994). An evolutionary model of organizational performance. *Strategic Management Journal, 15*(Special issue), 11-28.

Barney, J. B. (1991). Firm resources and sustained competitive advantage. *Journal of Management, 17,* 99-120.

Barney, J. B., & Ouchi, W. G. (Eds.). (1986). *Organizational economics.* San Francisco: Jossey-Bass.

Bates, J. E., & Wachs, T. D. (Eds.). (1994). *Temperament: Individual differences at the interface of biology and behavior.* Washington, DC: American Psychological Association.

Baum, J.A.C. (1995). The changing basis of competition in organizational populations: The Manhattan hotel industry, 1887-1990. *Social Forces, 74,* 177-205.

Baum, J.A.C. (1996). Organizational ecology. In S. R. Clegg, C. Hardy, & W. R. Nord (Eds.), *Handbook of organization studies* (pp. 77-114). Thousand Oaks, CA: Sage.

Baum, J.A.C., & Haveman, H. A. (1997). Love thy neighbor? Differentiation and agglomeration in the Manhattan hotel industry. *Administrative Science Quarterly, 42,* 304-338.

Baum, J.A.C., & Ingram, P. (1998). Survival-enhancing learning in the Manhattan hotel industry, 1898-1980. *Management Science, 44,* 996-1016.

Baum, J.A.C., & Korn, H. J. (1996). Competitive dynamics of interfirm rivalry. *Academy of Management Journal, 39,* 255-291.

Baum, J.A.C., & Korn, H. J. (in press). Dynamics of dyadic competitive interaction. *Strategic Management Journal.*

Baum, J.A.C., & Mezias, S. J. (1992). Localized competition and organizational mortality in the Manhattan hotel industry, 1898-1990. *Administrative Science Quarterly, 37,* 580-604.

Baum, J.A.C., & Singh, J. V. (Eds.). (1994a). *Evolutionary dynamics of organizations.* New York: Oxford University Press.

Baum, J.A.C., & Singh, J. V. (1994b). Organizational hierarchies and evolutionary processes: Some reflections on a theory of organizational evolution. In J.A.C. Baum & J. V. Singh (Eds.), *Evolutionary dynamics of organizations* (pp. 3-20). New York: Oxford University Press.

Belew, R. K., & Mitchell, M. (Eds.). (1996). *Adaptive individuals in evolving populations* (Proceedings Vol. 26). Reading, MA: Addison-Wesley.

Bentz, V. M., & Shapiro, J. J. (1998). *Mindful inquiry in social research.* Thousand Oaks, CA: Sage.

Besanko, D., Dranove, D., & Shanley, M. (1996). *The economics of strategy.* New York: Wiley.

Beth, E. (1961). Semantics of physical theories. In H. Freudenthal (Ed.), *The concept and the role of the model in mathematics and natural and social sciences* (pp. 48-51). Dordrecht, The Netherlands: Reidel.

Bhaskar, R. (1997). *A realist theory of science.* London: Verso. (Original work published 1975)

Bitbol, M. (1996). *Schrödinger's philosophy of quantum mechanics.* Dordrecht, The Netherlands: Kluwer.

Brewer, M. B., & Collins, B. E. (Eds.). (1981). *Scientific inquiry and the social sciences.* San Francisco: Jossey-Bass.

Brown, C. (1992). Organization studies and scientific authority. In M. Reed & M. Hughes (Eds.), *Rethinking organization: New directions in organization theory and analysis* (pp. 67-84). London: Sage.

Buckley, W. (1967). *Sociology and modern systems theory.* Englewood Cliffs, NJ: Prentice Hall.

Burrell, G. (1996). Normal science, paradigms, metaphors, discourses and genealogies of analysis. In S. R. Clegg, C. Hardy, & W. R. Nord (Eds.), *Handbook of organization studies* (pp. 642-658). Thousand Oaks, CA: Sage.

Burrell, G. (1997). *Pandemonium: Towards a retro-organization theory.* Thousand Oaks, CA: Sage.

Burrell, G., & Morgan, G. (1979). *Sociological paradigms and organizational analysis.* London: Heinemann.

Campbell, D. T. (1959). Methodological suggestions from a comparative psychology of knowledge processes. *Inquiry, 2,* 152-182.

Campbell, D. T. (1965). Variation and selective retention in socio-cultural evolution. In H. R. Barringer, G. I. Blanksten, & R. W. Mack (Eds.), *Social change in developing areas: A reinterpretation of evolutionary theory* (pp. 19-48). Cambridge, MA: Schenkman.

Campbell, D. T. (1969a). Ethnocentrism of disciplines and the fish-scale model of omniscience. In M. Sherif & C. W. Sherif (Eds.), *Interdisciplinary relationships in the social sciences* (pp. 328-348). Chicago: Aldine.

Campbell, D. T. (1969b). A phenomenology of the other one: Corrigible, hypothetical and critical. In T. Mischel (Ed.), *Human action: Conceptual and empirical issues* (pp. 41-69). New York: Academic Press.

Campbell, D. T. (1972). Herskovits, cultural relativism, and metascience. In M. J. Herskovits, *Cultural relativism* (pp. v-xxiii). New York: Random House.

Campbell, D. T. (1974). "Downward causation" in hierarchically organized biological systems. In F. J. Ayala & T. Dobzhansky (Eds.), *Studies in the philosophy of biology* (pp. 179-186). London: Macmillan.

Campbell, D. T. (1981a). Comment: Another perspective on a scholarly career. In M. B. Brewer & B. E. Collins (Eds.), *Scientific inquiry and the social sciences* (pp. 454-486). San Francisco: Jossey-Bass.

Campbell, D. T. (1981b). Levels of organization, selection, and information storage in biological and social evolution. *The Behavioral and Brain Sciences, 4,* 236-237.

Campbell, D. T. (1983). The two distinct routes beyond kin selection to ultra-sociality: Implications for the humanities and social sciences. In D. L. Bridgeman (Ed.), *The nature of prosocial development: Interdisciplinary theories and strategies* (pp. 11-41). New York: Academic Press.

Campbell, D. T. (1986). Science's social system of validity-enhancing collective belief change and the problems of the social sciences. In D. W. Fiske & R. A. Shweder (Eds.), *Metatheory in social science: Pluralisms and subjectivities* (pp. 108-135). Chicago: University of Chicago Press.

Campbell, D. T. (1988). Descriptive epistemology: Psychological, sociological, and evolutionary. In D. T. Campbell, *Methodology and epistemology for social science: Selected papers* (E. S. Overman, Ed., pp. 435-486). Chicago: University of Chicago Press.

Campbell, D. T. (1990). Levels of organization, downward causation, and the selection-theory approach to evolutionary epistemology. In G. Greenberg & E. Tobach (Eds.), *Theories of the evolution of knowing* (T. C. Schneirla Conference Series, Vol. 4, pp. 1-17). Hillsdale, NJ: Erlbaum.

Campbell, D. T. (1991). Coherentist empiricism, hermeneutics, and the commensurability of paradigms. *International Journal of Educational Research, 15,* 587-597.

Campbell, D. T. (1994). How individual and face-to-face-group selection undermine firm selection in organizational evolution. In J.A.C. Baum & J. V. Singh (Eds.), *Evolutionary dynamics of organizations* (pp. 23-38). New York: Oxford University Press.

Campbell, D. T., & Fiske, D. W. (1959). Convergent and discriminant validation by the multitrait-multimethod matrix. *Psychological Bulletin, 56,* 81-105.

Campbell, D. T., & Stanley, J. C. (1963). Experimental and quasi-experimental designs for research on teaching. In N. L. Gage (Ed.), *Handbook of research on teaching* (pp. 171-246). Chicago: Rand McNally.

Cannella, A. A., & Paetzold, R. L. (1994). Pfeffer's barriers to the advance of organization science: A rejoinder. *Academy of Management Review, 19,* 331-341.

Carroll, G. R. (Ed.). (1988). *Ecological models of organizations.* Cambridge, MA: Ballinger.

Chandler, A. D., Jr. (1977). *The visible hand.* Cambridge, MA: Belknap Press of Harvard University Press.

Chen, M.-J. (1996). Competitor analysis and interfirm rivalry: Toward a theoretical integration. *Academy of Management Review, 21,* 100-134.

Chen, M.-J., & Hambrick, D. (1995). Speed, stealth, and selective attack: How small firms differ from large firms in competitive behavior. *Academy of Management Journal, 38,* 453-482.

Chen, M.-J., & MacMillan, I. C. (1992). Nonresponse and delayed response to competitive moves: The roles of competitor dependence and action irreversibility. *Academy of Management Journal, 35,* 539-570.

Chia, R. (1996). *Organizational analysis as deconstructive practice.* Berlin: Walter de Gruyter.

Clegg, S. R., Hardy, C., & Nord, W. R. (Eds.). (1996). *Handbook of organization studies.* Thousand Oaks, CA: Sage.

Cowan, G. A., Pines, D., & Meltzer, D. (Eds.). (1994). *Complexity: Metaphors, models, and reality* (Proceedings Vol. 19). Reading, MA: Addison-Wesley.

Cramer, F. (1993). *Chaos and order: The complex structure of living things* (D. L. Loewus, Trans.). New York: VCH.

Daft, R. L., & Lewin, A. Y. (1990). Can organization studies begin to break out of the normal science straitjacket? An editorial essay. *Organization Science, 1,* 1-9.

Darr, E. D., Argote, L., & Epple, D. (1995). The acquisition, transfer and depreciation of knowledge in service organizations: Productivity in franchises. *Management Science, 42,* 1750-1762.

Dawkins, R. (1976). *The selfish gene.* New York: Oxford University Press.

De Regt, C.D.G. (1994). *Representing the world by scientific theories: The case for scientific realism.* Tilburg, The Netherlands: Tilburg University Press.

Donaldson, L. (1995). *American anti-management theories of organization.* Cambridge, UK: Cambridge University Press.

Donaldson, L. (1996). *For positivist organization theory.* Thousand Oaks, CA: Sage.

Dunn, E. S. (1971). *Economic and social development.* Baltimore, MD: Johns Hopkins University Press.

Eldredge, N. (1995). *Reinventing Darwin.* New York: Wiley.

Farrell, M. J. (1970). Some elementary selection processes in *Review of Economic Studies, 37,* 305-319.

Fischer, K. H., & Hertz, J. A. (1993). *Spin glasses.* New York: Cambridge University Press.

Fisher, R. A. (1930). *The genetical theory of natural selection.* Oxford, UK: Oxford University Press.

Freeman, J. A., & Skapura, D. M. (1992). *Neural networks: Algorithms, applications, and programming techniques.* Reading, MA: Addison-Wesley.

Friedman, M. (1953). *Essays in positive economics.* Chicago: University of Chicago Press.

Fuller, S. (1993). *Philosophy of science and its discontents* (2nd ed.). New York: Guilford.

Gibbs, J. W. (1902). *Elementary principles in statistical mechanics.* New Haven, CT: Yale University Press.

Godfrey, P. C., & Hill, C.W.L. (1995). The problem of unobservables in strategic management research. *Strategic Management Journal, 16,* 519-533.

Groenewegen, J. (Ed.). (1996). *Transaction cost economics.* Boston: Kluwer.

Haire, M. (1959). Biological models and empirical histories of the growth of organizations. In M. Haire (Ed.), *Modern organization theory* (pp. 272-306). New York: Wiley.

Haldane, J.B.S. (1932). *The causes of evolution.* New York: Harper.

Hannan, M. T., & Freeman, J. (1977). The population ecology of organizations. *American Journal of Sociology, 83,* 929-984.

Hartman, E. (1988). *Conceptual foundations of organization theory.* Cambridge, MA: Ballinger.

Hassard, J. (1993). Postmodernism and organizational analysis: An overview. In J. Hassard & M. Parker (Eds.), *Postmodernism and organizations* (pp. 1-23). Thousand Oaks, CA: Sage.

Hassard, J., & Holliday, R. (1998). *Organization representation: Work and organizations in popular culture.* Thousand Oaks, CA: Sage.

Hassard, J., & Parker, M. (Eds.). (1993). *Postmodernism and organizations.* Thousand Oaks, CA: Sage.

Haunschild, P. R., & Miner, A. S. (1997). Modes of interorganizational imitation: The effects of outcome salience and uncertainty. *Administrative Science Quarterly, 42,* 472-500.

Hawley, A. (1950). *Human ecology.* New York: Ronald Press.

Heene, A., & Sanchez, R. (Eds.). (1996). *Competence-based strategic management.* New York: Wiley.

Hirshleifer, J. (1977). Economics from a biological viewpoint. *Journal of Law and Economics, 20,* 1-52.

Hogarth, R. M., & Reder, M. W. (Eds.). (1987). *Rational choice: The contrast between economics and psychology.* Chicago: University of Chicago Press.

Holland, J. H. (1975). *Adaptation in natural and artificial systems.* Ann Arbor: University of Michigan Press.

Holton, G. (1993). *Science and anti-science.* Cambridge, MA: Harvard University Press.

Hunt, S. D. (1994). On the rhetoric of qualitative methods: Toward historically informed argumentation in management inquiry. *Journal of Management Inquiry, 23,* 221-234.

Ingram, P., & Baum, J.A.C. (1997a). Chain affiliation and the failure of Manhattan hotels, 1898-1980. *Administrative Science Quarterly, 42,* 68-102.

Ingram, P., & Baum, J.A.C. (1997b). Opportunity and constraint: Organizations' learning from the operating and competitive experience of industries. *Strategic Management Journal, 18*(Summer special issue), 75-98.

Kauffman, S. A. (1993). *The origins of order: Self-organization and selection in evolution.* New York: Oxford University Press.

Kaufman, H. (1975). The natural history of human organizations. *Administration & Society, 7,* 131-149.

Kaye, B. (1993). *Chaos & complexity.* New York: VCH.

Korn, H. J., & Baum, J.A.C. (in press). Chance, imitative and strategic antecedents to multimarket contact. *Academy of Management Journal.*

Kuhn, T. S. (1962). *The structure of scientific revolutions.* Chicago: University of Chicago Press.

Lado, A. A., & Wilson, M. C. (1994). Human resource systems and sustained competitive advantage: A competency-based perspective. *Academy of Management Review, 19,* 699-727.

Levinthal, D. A. (1997). Adaptation on rugged landscapes. *Management Science, 43,* 934-950.

Lincoln, Y. S. (Ed.). (1985). *Organizational theory and inquiry.* Newbury Park, CA: Sage.

Lloyd, E. A. (1988). *The structure and confirmation of evolutionary theory.* Princeton, NJ: Princeton University Press.

Maynard Smith, J. (1975). *The theory of evolution* (3rd ed.). Harmondsworth, UK: Penguin.

McKelvey, B. (1982). *Organizational systematics: Taxonomy, evolution and classification.* Berkeley: University of California Press.

McKelvey, B. (1997). Quasi-natural organization science. *Organization Science, 8,* 351-380.

McKelvey, B. (1998). Complexity vs. selection among coevolutionary microstates in firms: Complexity effects on strategic organizing. *Comportamento Organizacional E Gestão, 4,* 17-59.

McKelvey, B. (in press). Avoiding complexity catastrophe in coevolutionary pockets: Strategies for rugged landscapes. *Organization Science.*

McKinlay, A., & Starkey, K. (1998). *Foucault, management, and organization theory.* Thousand Oaks, CA: Sage.

Mézard, M., Parisi, G., & Virasoro, M. A. (1987). *Spin glass theory and beyond.* Singapore: World Scientific.

Miller, D., & Chen, M.-J. (1994). Sources and consequences of competitive inertia: A study of the U.S. airline industry. *Administrative Science Quarterly, 39,* 1-23.

Miner, A. S., & Haunschild, P. R. (1995). Population level learning. In B. Staw & L. Cummings (Eds.) *Research in Organizational Behavior* (Vol. 17, pp. 115-166). Greenwich, CT: JAI.

Miner, J. B. (1980). *Theories of organizational behavior.* Hinsdale, IL: Dryden.

Mitchell, M. (1996). *An introduction to genetic algorithms.* Cambridge, MA: MIT Press.

Mone, M. A., & McKinley, W. (1993). The uniqueness value and its consequences for organization studies. *Journal of Management Inquiry, 2,* 284-296.

Natanson, M. (Ed.). (1963). *Philosophy of the social sciences.* New York: Random House.

Nelson, R. R., & Winter, S. G. (1982). *An evolutionary theory of economic change.* Cambridge, MA: Belknap Press of Harvard University Press.

Neurath, O., Carnap, R., & Hahn, H. (1973). Wissenschaftliche Weltauffassung, Der Wiener Kreis, Wien, Artur Wolf, 1929. In M. Neurath & R. S. Cohen (Eds.), *Empiricism and sociology* (pp. 301-318). Dordrecht, The Netherlands: Reidel (Original work published 1929)

Nicholson, N. (1997). Evolutionary psychology: Toward a new view of human nature and organizational society. *Human Relations, 50,* 1063-1078.

Nicolis, G., & Prigogine, I. (1989). *Exploring complexity: An introduction.* New York: Freeman.

Penrose, E. T. (1952). Biological analogies in the theory of the firm. *American Economic Review, 42,* 804-819.

Perrow, C. (1994). Pfeffer slips. *Academy of Management Review, 19,* 191-194.

Pfeffer, J. (1993). Barriers to the advancement of organizational science: Paradigm development as a dependent variable. *Academy of Management Review, 18,* 599-620.

Pfeffer, J. (1994). *Competitive advantage through people.* Boston: Harvard Business School Press.

Pfeffer, J. (1995). Mortality, reproducibility, and the persistence of styles of theory. *Organization Science, 6,* 681-686.

Pfeffer, J. (1997). *New directions for organization theory: Problems and prospects.* New York: Oxford University Press.

Pinker, S. (1997). *How the mind works.* New York: Norton.

Plomin, R. (1994). *Genetics and experience: The interplay between nature and nurture.* Thousand Oaks, CA: Sage.

Podolny, J., Stuart, T. E., & Hannan, M. T. (1996). Networks, knowledge, and niches. *American Journal of Sociology, 102,* 659-689.

Popper, K. R. (1959). *The logic of scientific discovery.* New York: Harper & Row (Original work published 1935)

Popper, K. R. (1963). *Conjectures and refutations.* London: Routledge & Kegan Paul.

Popper, K. R. (1972). *Objective knowledge: An evolutionary approach.* Oxford, UK: Oxford University Press.

Popper, K. R. (1983). *Realism and the aim of science.* Totowa, NJ: Rowman and Littlefield. (Original work published 1956)

Porter, M. E. (1980). *Competitive strategy.* New York: Free Press.

Porter, M. E. (1996, November-December). What is strategy? *Harvard Business Review,* pp. 61-78.

Rasmusen, E. (1994). *Games and information* (2nd ed.). Cambridge, MA: Basil Blackwell.

Reed, M. (1996). Organizational theorizing: A historically contested terrain. In S. R. Clegg, C. Hardy, & W. R. Nord (Eds.), *Handbook of organization studies* (pp. 31-56). Thousand Oaks, CA: Sage.

Reed, M., & Hughes, M. (Eds.). (1992). *Rethinking organization: New directions in organization theory and analysis.* London: Sage.

Reevis-Conner, K. (1991). A historical comparison of resource-based theory and five schools of thought within industrial organizational economics: Do we have a new theory of the firm?" *Journal of Management, 17,* 121-154.

Rivkin, J. (1997, August). *Imitation of complex strategies.* Paper presented at Academy of Management, Boston.

Roughgarden, J. (1976). Resource partitioning among competing species—A coevolutionary approach. *Theoretical Populations Biology, 9,* 388-424.

Rumelt, R. P. (1987). Theory, strategy, and entrepreneurship. In D. J. Teece (Ed.), *The competitive challenge* (pp. 137-158). Cambridge, MA: Ballinger.

Schwartz, P., & Ogilvy, J. (1979). *The emergent paradigm: Changing patterns of thought and belief* (Analytic Report 7, Values and Lifestyle Program). Menlo Park, CA: SRI International.

Singh, J. V. (Ed.). (1990). *Organizational evolution.* Newbury Park, CA: Sage.

Sorenson, O. (1997). *The complexity catastrophe in the evolution of the computer industry: Interdependence and adaptability in organizational evolution.* Unpublished doctoral dissertation, Sociology Department, Stanford University.

Stuart, T. E., & Podolny, J. M. (1996). Local search and the evolution of technological capabilities. *Strategic Management Journal, 17*(Special issue), 21-38.

Suppe, F. (1977). *The structure of scientific theories* (2nd ed.). Urbana: University of Illinois Press.

Suppe, F. (1989). *The semantic conception of theories & scientific realism.* Urbana-Champaign: University of Illinois Press.

Suppes, P. (1962). Models of data. In E. Nagel, P. Suppes, & A. Tarski (Eds.), *Logic, methodology, and philosophy of science: Proceedings of the 1960 International Congress* (pp. 252-261). Stanford, CA: Stanford University Press.

Teece, D. J. (1984). Economic analysis and strategic management. *California Management Review, 26,* 87-110.

Thompson, P. (1989). *The structure of biological theories.* Albany: State University of New York Press.

Toulmin, S. (1953). *The philosophy of science: An introduction.* London: Hutchinson.

Toulmin, S. (1961). *Foresight and understanding.* London: Hutchinson.

Toulmin, S. (1972). *Human understanding* (Vol. 1). Princeton, NJ: Princeton University Press.

Van Fraassen, B. C. (1980). *The scientific image.* Oxford, UK: Clarendon.

Van Maanen, J. (1995a). Fear and loathing in organization studies. *Organization Science, 6,* 687-692.

Van Maanen, J. (1995b). Style as theory. *Organization Science, 6,* 133-143.

Weick, K. E. (1979). *The social psychology of organizing* (2nd ed.). Reading, MA: Addison-Wesley.

Weisbuch, G. (1993). *Complex systems dynamics: An introduction to automata networks.* Reading, MA: Addison-Wesley.

Williams, G. C. (1966). *Adaptation and natural selection: A critique of some current evolutionary thought.* Princeton, NJ: Princeton University Press.

Williamson, O. E. (1975). *Markets and hierarchies: Analysis and antitrust implications.* New York: Free Press.

Winter, W. G. (1964). Economic "natural selection" and the theory of the firm. *Yale Economic Essays, 4,* 225-272.

Wolpert, L. (1992). *The unnatural nature of science.* Cambridge, MA: Harvard University Press.

Wright, S. (1931). Evolution in Mendelian populations. *Genetics, 16,* 97-159.

Part I

Blind-Variation-Selection-and-Retention

Chapter 2

The Accidental Entrepreneur

Campbellian Antinomies and Organizational Foundings

HOWARD E. ALDRICH
AMY L. KENWORTHY

> The great heterogeneity and the tremendous numbers of variations make almost inevitable the "accidental discovery" of any strongly adaptive form.
>
> —*Donald T. Campbell (1965, p. 37)*

In the fall of 1994, Steven was in his second and final year of the MBA program at the Stanford Graduate School of Business, and things were going well. Over the summer, he had worked as an intern at McKinsey, and the company had offered him a permanent job for the following year, after graduation. He also was engaged to be married, and he and his fiancée were making coast-to-coast trips nearly every week to see each other and plan the wedding. As a break from his regular class work in the fall, he had arranged with two friends to take an independent studies course with Associate Dean Parker to develop a business plan for a new venture. The venture involved an innovation in the marketing of insurance products, using a Web site that allowed consumers to comparison shop between identical features of the policies they were considering. In his previous job, as an analyst at an investment banking firm, Steven had been involved in mergers and acquisitions in the insurance industry, and he had learned something about its practices. He thought he saw a way of creating a better

AUTHORS' NOTE: The authors shared equally in the challenging task of adequately contextualizing organizational emergence using Donald Campbell's ideas in one short chapter. We wish to acknowledge the helpful comments of Ted Baker, Bill Barnett, Jennifer Cliff, Bill Gartner, Lisa Keister, Alessandro Lomi, Tammy Madsen, Bill McKelvey, Anne Miner, Hugh O'Neill, and Elaine Romanelli.

product, but for the moment it was just something to do as an intellectual challenge.

When the team members turned in their project, they were surprised when the dean told them that they were not yet finished. He said the idea had some promise and that they ought to shop the idea around to get reactions from possible funding sources. The dean's positive feedback piqued Steven's curiosity, and he followed up on an introduction to some New York City funding sources that the dean arranged. The investors were impressed and were ready to commit some funding up front, although not enough to guarantee the start-up's survival for more than a year or two. In spite of this reasonably good news, when the spring semester began, Steven's two colleagues dropped out of the project, with one deciding to take a job with a consulting firm and the other deciding to pursue more graduate work. Undaunted, Steven persisted in developing the plan, but now he needed to assemble a new team. He turned to an old college roommate and longtime friend who was a computer wizard, bringing him on to serve as the management information systems expert. Through his fiancée, he found the second person for his team—a person in his late twenties who was a marketing whiz and bored at his current job.

As the new team worked on the project, Steven finally decided to tell McKinsey that he was going to continue planning the new venture, rather than going to work for them. They were quite generous in their response, saying that they would wait for him if he wanted to pursue the idea further, and to check back with them if he changed his mind. In June, 1995, he graduated from Stanford, in July he was married, and in August he received his first measure of money from the investors, out of the $2.1 million they had pledged. He found a site in Alexandria, Virginia, hired his first employees, and launched the firm.

We draw several lessons from this story. First, entrepreneurship often happens when people are on their way to something else. Activities coalesce, and people find they have become entrepreneurs. Second, truly innovative start-ups are often the result of creative experimentation with new ideas by outsiders to an industry. Experience guides the choice of a domain for exploration, but indiffer-

ence to industry routines and norms gives an outsider the freedom to break free of the cognitive constraints on incumbents. Third, nascent entrepreneurs often encounter discouraging events along the way, but many persist and find ways around the obstacles. In their persistence, they often have a little help from their friends, acquaintances, and work associates. Fourth, regardless of their ambitions and skills, the fate of nascent entrepreneurs ultimately is still subject to external selection forces, such as demand, trends in technological regimes, and the actions of outsiders with legitimacy and money.

Our Objectives and Plan

Our goals in this chapter are rather modest: We want to pay homage to Donald Campbell and his work, and we want to draw on his ideas to build a simple model of innovative entrepreneurship. We pay homage to Campbell because of his influence on the field of evolutionary organizational studies. We try to invoke the spirit of Campbell by approaching the problem in a way we think he would appreciate, making liberal use of quotations from his work and creating an eclectic mix of ideas from diverse sources. In developing our model of innovative entrepreneurship, we draw on Campbell's ideas from his writings on evolutionary epistemology, creativity and experimentation, playfulness, altruism and clique selfishness, and more generally from his blind-variation-and-selective-retention (BVSR) model. We use the term "nascent entrepreneur" to refer to persons thinking about starting a new firm and involved in activities that could result in a new organization, distinguishing them from "entrepreneurs" who actually have created an operating entity (Reynolds & White, 1997).[1] We focus on explaining the degree to which nascent entrepreneurs, in creating new ventures, remain faithful to, or depart from, the established order of things.

Our chapter is structured as follows. First, using a strategy often adopted by Campbell, we list six empirical facts and puzzles characterizing entrepreneurship, choosing those that have a reasonable degree of empirical support. Second, for the sake of readers who may not be familiar with Campbell's work, we review his BVSR model. Third, we link the six puzzles to Campbell's BVSR model through a discussion of a reproducer-innovator continuum of organizational foundings. Fourth, drawing on Campbell's writings, we create two Campbellian antinomies (apparent contradictions) to explain why people fall at various points along the reproducer-innovator continuum. Finally, using the Campbellian antinomies and the reproducer-innovator continuum, we return to the six puzzles and interpret them using the BVSR model.

Six Empirical Facts and Puzzles Regarding Entrepreneurship

Our six facts and puzzles are drawn from a review of the entrepreneurship literature, with some based on extrapolations from existing work and others more firmly grounded in replicated studies. We chose them because they resonate with themes in Campbell's writings and because they represent the kinds of data that energized him in his debates with critics and doubters. The facts and puzzles reveal significant gaps in our understanding of organizational foundings as well as answering a question organizational and entrepreneurship theorists might well pose: "If we're so smart, why can't we find the one right way?"

1. In science, the arts, and even many spheres of everyday life, we find strong evidence of creative human endeavor (National Endowment for the Arts, 1997). In contrast, among entrepreneurs and the new ventures they create, we mostly find mundane replications of existing organizational forms (Aldrich & Fiol, 1994; Gartner, 1985; Low & Abrahamson, 1997).

2. Entrepreneurship is often discussed as an isolated, solo event, but research on entrepreneurship suggests that many people are implicated in the founding of new ventures (Reynolds & White, 1997). Some are founding team members, some are investors and employees, and others play a variety of supporting roles.

3. Some people appear much better at creating new firms and ensuring their survival than others,

as they own multiple firms and have been involved in multiple start-ups (Starr & Bygrave, 1992; Starr, Bygrave, & Tercanli, 1993). The knowledge of these habitual entrepreneurs, however, has proven very difficult to codify.

4. The gestation period of start-ups is lengthy and fraught with delays, in spite of the good intentions of the founders and the cost of procrastination. The average time for building a start-up is about 1 year, but the range is substantial (Reynolds & White, 1997). In the computer software industry, Van de Ven, Angle, and Poole (1989) found the process took about 4 years.

5. The more activities people engage in, the greater the chances of their starting, *but* also the greater their chances of quitting the process altogether (Carter, Gartner, & Reynolds, 1996; Gatewood, Shaver, & Gartner, 1995). The highest likelihood of persisting in "thinking about" starting a business, but not actually starting it, occurs among people who are less active than other nascent entrepreneurs.

6. Venture capital firms make their living from their investments and devote great effort to screening new business ventures, yet only a small portion of the firms they fund are successful (Gifford, 1997; Gorman & Sahlman, 1989). A great many fail, and of those that survive, many of them achieve, at best, an average rate of return on the capital invested. Venture capital firms appear unable to find a predictive template.

Two intriguing themes run through these puzzles. First, most entrepreneurs create organizations that look pretty much like all the other organizations in their population. Only a few create organizations that depart, in significant ways, from the current order of things. Second, the behaviors involved in getting any new venture up and running appear surprisingly difficult to master and codify, even for experienced hands.

BLIND-VARIATION-AND-SELECTIVE-RETENTION (BVSR)

One of Campbell's seminal contributions, especially for organization theory, was his selection model based on the analogy between "natural selection in biological evolution and the selective propagation of cultural forms" (Campbell, 1965, p. 26). There are three major components to this model (Campbell, 1965, p. 27, emphasis ours):

1. The occurrence of *variations*: heterogeneous, haphazard, "blind," "chance," "random," but in any event variable (e.g., the mutation process in organic evolution and exploratory responses in learning).
2. Consistent *selection* criteria: selective elimination, selective propagation, and selective retention of certain types of variations (e.g., differential survival of certain mutants in organic evolution, differential reinforcement of certain responses in learning).
3. A mechanism for the *preservation*, duplication, or propagation of the positively selected variants (e.g., the rigid duplication process of the chromosomegene system in plants and animals, memory in learning).

Campbell believed that the three conditions listed above, taken together, resulted in "evolution in the direction of better fit to the selective system" (Campbell, 1965, p. 27). Campbell went so far as to state that *no* fit or order would occur if any of the three components were missing. This proposition was based on his belief that (a) the possibility of all three components occurring simultaneously was minimal and (b) changes in environmental fit or order were, correspondingly, rare (Campbell, 1974b). One explanation for his "rare occurrence" belief is the tension he posited between variation and retention processes. He explained, "variation and retention are at odds in most exemplifications of the model. Maximizing either one jeopardizes the other. Some compromise of each is required" (Campbell, 1974b, p. 143).

Campbell used aspects of his selection theory to explain vision (1956b), problem solving (1956a), creative thought (1960), and sociocultural evolution (1965, 1979). Much of this work was done using what Campbell called his BVSR dogma (Campbell, 1960, 1974a, 1982a, 1990b), summarized as follows:

1. A blind-variation-and-selective-retention process is fundamental to all inductive achievements, to all genuine increases in knowledge, and to all increases in fit of system to environment.
2. The many processes that shortcut a fuller blind-variation-and-selective-retention process are in themselves inductive achievements, containing wisdom about the environment achieved originally by blind-variation-and-selective-retention.
3. In addition, such shortcut processes contain in their own operation a blind-variation-and-selective-retention process at some level, substituting for overt locomotor exploration or the life-and-death winnowing of organic evolution.

Although Campbell's BVSR dogma may appear somewhat tautological in nature (fit selects the learning that leads to further fit), it is a useful tautology (Scriven, 1959). Among other things, it leads us to ask interesting questions.

Why use the term "blind," as opposed to "random," to describe the generation of variations? Campbell did not want to confuse the statistically precise process of randomization with less precise variation mechanisms. Additionally, he wanted to capture the "accidental" nature of variation. Thus, he wrote:

"Deliberate" or "intelligent" variations would do as well as "blind," "haphazard," "chance," "random," or "spontaneous" ones. They might be better insofar as they could be pre-selected. But they might be worse in that they could be restricted to the implications of already achieved wisdom and would not be likely to go beyond it. One of the services of terms like "blind" and "haphazard" in the model is that they emphasize that elaborate adaptive social systems . . . could have emerged, just as did termite societies, without any self-conscious planning or foresightful action. It provides a plausible model for social systems that are "wiser" than the individuals who constitute the society, or than the rational social science of the ruling elite. It provides an anticipation of powerful "inadvertent" social change processes in our own day which may be adaptive in unforeseen or unwanted ways (Campbell, 1965, p. 28)

In Campbell's BVSR model, the cycle of variation, selection, and retention is repeated endlessly, as systems move toward greater fit with their environments. Most of the observed changes are rather small, serving mainly to perpetuate the existing order rather than displace it. We turn now to a closer consideration of the degree to which entrepreneurial outcomes also reflect a bias toward reproduction rather than innovation.

Figure 2.1. Organizational Founding Continuum

Innovator/Reproducer Continuum

The six puzzles we listed focus on the *behaviors* exhibited by individuals engaged in entrepreneurial endeavors and the *type* of entrepreneurial endeavors created. We will return to the issue of behaviors in a subsequent section. For the moment, we focus on the nature of the foundings themselves. Although the popular press portrays the typical entrepreneur as someone like Bill Gates of Microsoft, in fact the overwhelming majority of entrepreneurs are people starting small "reproducer" organizations. Reproducer organizations are defined as those organizations started in an established industry that are only minimally, if at all, different from existing organizations in the population. Most start-ups are reproducers. In contrast, the number of entrepreneurs creating innovative new firms that could potentially open up new niches or even entirely *new* industries is very small. As we saw in the example of Steven and insurance sold over the Web, innovation can, and does, happen. We will use the term "innovator" organizations to refer to this type of organizational founding, regardless of whether the venture actually succeeds.

As shown in Figure 2.1, the continuum of organizational foundings has "reproducer" organizations at one end and "innovator" organizations at the other.[2] Using Campbell's BVSR model, we attempt to explain why new ventures are found along the length of the continuum but mostly cluster at the reproducer end. First, we define the terms *reproducer* and *innovator*, using organizational knowledge to differentiate between them. Second, we use two Campbellian antinomies to explore why people fall at various points on the continuum. Following that discussion, in the next section we

return to the puzzles and interpret them through the lens of Campbell's BVSR environment.

Organizational knowledge is defined as "the patterns of cognitive associations developed by the organization's members," or the behavioral outcomes that result from patterns of cognitive associations (Fiol & Lyles, 1985, p. 805). We define "innovators" as those entrepreneurs who, through the development of new knowledge and consequent new organizational form, either transform an existing industry or create a new one. In the language of Anderson and Tushman (1990), innovative entrepreneurs have created competence-enhancing or competence-destroying innovations by departing from current knowledge. Although Anderson and Tushman do not label it, the implicit baseline in their scheme of organizational innovation is the *absence* of innovation. We extend their scheme by explicitly including a category of "reproducers," defined as those entrepreneurs who bring little or no incremental knowledge to the industries they enter. Reproducers create organizations in established industries by copying the received form and thus do not challenge the status quo.

Using the distinction between reproducer and innovator as developing incremental or new organizational knowledge, respectively, we can expand the reproducer-innovator continuum into the form of a ledger. We have labeled the ledger "Campbellian Antinomies," as shown in Table 2.1. In the ledger, we present two antinomies we have gleaned from the relevant 40-plus papers (of more than 200) that Campbell authored. We have listed only a subset of them in the reference section, to save space.

We use the term "Campbellian antinomies" to honor Campbell's influence over the ledger, as all the concepts and terms are his, and to represent the inherent paradoxes between the reproducer and

TABLE 2.1 Campbellian Antinomies

Reproducer	Innovator
Constructing Incremental Organizational Knowledge	Creating New Organizational Knowledge
Obedience to cultural routines, norms, habits	Creativity/experimentation & play/make-believe
Altruism	Egoism

innovator sides of the ledger. The term *antinomy*, defined as "a contradiction between two apparently equally valid principles or between inferences correctly drawn from such principles" (*Webster's New World Dictionary,* 1966, p. 39), describes the tension facing nascent entrepreneurs who could be reproducers or innovators. The two antinomies are (a) obedience to cultural routines, norms, and habits versus creativity/experimentation and play/make-believe; and (b) altruism versus egoism.

We selected these antinomies for two reasons. First, we believe that the contradictions represented by both antinomies clearly relate to the process of organizational founding. Second, the antinomies inform many of the behavioral and biological evolutionary processes to which Campbell devoted many of his papers.

Obedience to Cultural Routines, Norms, and Habits

Campbell was very clear about the overwhelming effects of culture and cultural routines on evolutionary processes. In describing the relationship of individuals to groups, he repeatedly mentioned the pressures toward conformity and cultural rigidity inherent in social processes. He wrote, "the social glue that holds . . . groups together has structure-maintenance requirements that limit and bias the portrait of the world such social groups sustain" (Campbell, 1979, p. 184). Campbell sometimes used the scientific community as an example of a self-perpetuating community constrained by social processes that often stifle individual variations. "Social processes in science can be seen as increasing or ensuring objectivity through providing a curb to individual 'subjective' biases or delusions. The 'objective' or the 'real' becomes that which can

be seen also by others. The logical positivist requirements of 'intersubjectivity' or 'intersubjective verifiability' make explicit this social role" (Campbell, 1979, pp. 181-182).[3]

He described the role of the individual in the social system of science as follows:

Not only is science conducted in the context of the elaborate social system of science, but its products "scientific knowledge" or "scientific truths" (or even more relativistically, "the accepted theories of physics as of May 11, 1977") are *social products*, incompletely specifiable in the beliefs of any one scientist or the writings in any one book. This remains true even for specialized areas and restricted topics. No matter how small the area, scientific knowledge is achieved in spite of minor disagreements, ignorances, and misunderstandings on the part of every one of its leading participants. This is analogous to the situation in a language, where, for the vast bulk of the working vocabulary, all speakers have some idiosyncratic usages and no one speaker adequately represents the language; where each individual speaker is soon replaced, yet the language persists as a coherent whole in spite of this. So too, each individual scientist is as replaceable as is any one cell in the body. The major innovations in any one epoch are independently invented by several persons, as sociology-of-science studies show. (Campbell, 1979, pp. 182-183)[4]

Campbell stressed the pervasiveness of cultural routines, and individuals' obedience to such routines, in his discussion of habits. Habits are the bedrock upon which evolutionary processes have been built, and in his discussion of the "evolutionary puzzle of instinct," also called the "Baldwin effect," Campbell noted that

Baldwin . . . proposed that for such instincts, learned adaptive patterns . . . preceded the instincts. The adaptive pattern being thus piloted by learning, any mutations that accelerated the learning, made it more certain to occur, or predisposed the animal to certain component responses would be adaptive and selected[,] no matter which component responses or in what order affected. The habit thus provided a selective template around which the instinctive components could be assembled. . . . In the habit-to-instinct evolution, the once-learned goals and subgoals become innate at a more and more specific response-fragment level. (Campbell, 1974a, pp. 425-426; reprinted in 1982a, p. 93)

We see in this discussion the importance of contextualizing learning as a "habit-to-instinct" cycle, structured by the environment. Learned adaptive patterns do not occur in isolation but rather are a result of the sociocultural environment in which the individual (i.e., animal) is immersed. Campbell used this argument to drive home his point about the constraints placed on individuals by their environments. If learning is grounded in a set of environmentally conditioned "learned adaptive patterns," then individual initiatives are severely fettered.

In contrast to the cultural conformity induced by social processes, Campbell identified creativity, experimentation, play, and make-believe as behaviors through which individuals "disobey" ingrained cultural routines, norms, and habits. The tension between conformity and creativity can be seen in the following quotation: "There is, perhaps, always a potential conflict between the freedom to vary, which makes advance possible, and the value of retaining the cultural accumulation" (Campbell, 1965, p. 35). We turn now to a description of these "deviant" behaviors.

Creativity/Experimentation and Play/Make-Believe

Why should we experiment? What value does creativity or make-believe have for organizational foundings? Campbell argued that the more "movement" or "experimental activity" in which an individual engages, the greater is the likelihood that innovative knowledge will result. Campbell believed that all creative thought has a BVSR component (Campbell, 1990a, p. 9) and that creativity is "a prime example of such a short-cut process using fallible vicarious selectors. Not at all do I deny the importance of creative thought. But I insist upon an explicit model for how it operates and require that this model fit in with radical selection theory" (Campbell, 1994, p. 31).[5]

The following quotations, on the importance of creativity/experimentation and play/make-believe, are taken from Campbell (1982a):

Truth is brought about through the "fundamental process of experimentation." The highest functions of thought are thus to be looked upon as experimental. (p. 92)

Play is a generalized native impulse toward the exercise of specific and useful activities. It is itself a functional character which has arisen by the selection, among the individuals of a very great number of animal forms, of variations toward the early and artificial use of their growing powers. It is a natural and powerful tendency in vigorous and growing young; in fact, it is an impulse of extraordinary strength and persistence, and of corresponding utility. (p. 90)

On the psychological side, a corresponding advance has been made in the interpretation of the state of "make-believe," which accompanies and excites to the indulgence of play. Make believe . . . leads to a sort of sustained imagination of situations, treated as if real—a playful "dramatization"—in which the most important principles of individual and social life are tentatively and experimentally illustrated. Play thus becomes a most important sphere of practice, not only on the side of the physical powers, but also in intellectual, social, and moral lines. (pp. 90-91)

Playfulness and experimentation are thus natural impulses that have been wired into humans because of their utility. The full expression of these tendencies is opposed, however, by another set of impulses—humans' tendencies to defer to the beliefs of others. Indeed, obedience to cultural routines can be powerful enough to intimidate individuals with dissenting beliefs. Campbell (1993) called unwarranted deference to others' beliefs "conformity-induced pseudo-confirmation" and noted the consequent loss of innovation:

Tremendously important in the establishment of both common-sense and scientific knowledge is consensual validation, the confirmation of observations by other persons. . . . There are two aspects to this process: On one hand, each person must describe the world as uniquely seen from his own particular point of vantage. On the other hand, each must take seriously the reports of others as to what they see. . . . These two essentials run counter to each other. Insofar as systematic biases have been observed. . . [there is] a tendency to contaminate one's reports in the direction of agreement with what others are reporting and thus to fail to report what is uniquely available from one's own perspective. The agreement achieved represents *pseudo-confirmation*. (1993, p. 37)

Thus, we see the reproducer/innovator tension: Individuals are torn between following the path of acceptance (i.e., least resistance) or the path of deviance, experimentation, and innovative risk.

How powerful are conformity-inducing forces? Campbell often noted the tension between "doubt" and "trust" in social systems, arguing that trust in the existing order played a critical role in stabilizing the system (Campbell, 1978; 1991b). The greater the propensity to doubts about current practices, the more likely individuals are to deviate and thus potentially destabilize the order. Although he could cite no experimental evidence in his favor, Campbell estimated the ratio of "trust to doubt" at about 99 to 1 (Campbell, 1987, p. 157). He arrived at that estimate using his own playful shortcut through the thicket of inductive logic thrown up by more data-driven theorists.

An alternative path to the nonconformist, innovative creation of new organizational knowledge is found via ignorance of existing cultural norms. Circumstances may occur where individuals simply do not know what the prevailing conformity-inducing forces dictate. We mentioned at the beginning of this chapter that *entrepreneurship often happens when people are on their way to something else.* For individuals who are outsiders to an industry or community of practice, the serendipitous, accidental emergence of a new organization will occur without knowledge of existing norms and practices. If an individual were ignorant of the norms, rules, and practices that dictate organizational forms within an industry or population, then conformity would be purely accidental. For these individuals, and the organizations they found, ignorance or blindness to (seen as deviance from) the norms of the population would be the root cause for creative, innovative organizational emergence (Cliff, 1997).

Altruism

Campbell's second antinomy is the tension between altruism and egoism. He believed that all individuals experience a tension between innate altruistic tendencies toward the social community or "in-group" and a set of opposing tendencies involving egoistic/nepotistic drives. Campbell's (1986a) article proposed that this tension or conflict, at its most fundamental level, exists between cultural and biological behavioral tendencies.

> Previously (1975) my acceptance of the individual selectionist point of view for us vertebrates (but not for social insect cooperators) led me to dramatize self-denying altruism as a purely cultural product. Now, due to Axelrod, I am ready to credit our biological-dispositional inheritance with containing what some biologists call a "facultative polymorphism" on the selfish/cooperative dimension. Just as all male macaques have innate repertoires for both dominance and submission available for use in male-male encounters, so too biology may give us both cooperative and opportunistic-cheating proclivities, which may be differentially developed depending upon conditions (e.g., rural vs. urban) or cultures, but which remain ambivalently available in all of us. This facultative polymorphism could be the product of individual-level selection. (Campbell, 1986a, p. 795)

These inherent ambiguities, given the cultural pressures for "altruistic conformity" and the overwhelming majority of individuals who do, in fact, behave altruistically, result in unevenly distributed benefits/outcomes. Those who cooperate get less, whereas those who compete get more:

> While group selection no doubt occurs, its effects are undermined by individual selection. For example, individuals may sometimes have genes that lead to effective, group-survival-enhancing, self-sacrificial altruism. The chances of survival of the group as a whole are improved because of their presence. But the net benefits of this group-selection are greatest for non-altruists. For the altruists, their group-selection gains are reduced by the risks they run. No such costs, but only the benefits, accrue to non-altruists. Thus the relative frequency of non-altruists increases in the group in future generations. . . . I summarize the problem by the phrase "genetic competition among the cooperators." (Campbell, 1994, p. 24)

The tension between "what's best for the group as a whole" (altruism) and "what's best for the individual" (egoism) is not unidimensional. Campbell argued that conformity to group norms is a form of self-preservation. He used the term *clique selfishness* to describe this in-group protective behavior: "If we turn the phrase from 'reciprocal altruism' to 'clique selfishness,' we note that the internally altruistic groups are exploiting unorganized persons, or organized out-groups. . . . Each in-group can plausibly accuse the other group of clique selfishness and use this accusation to mobilize their own in-group solidarity. (Campbell, 1991b, p. 107).

The positive value that clique selfishness has for group maintenance and survival results in a rather high level of psychological ambiguity, as tendencies supporting both cooperative and competitive behaviors persist within individuals:

> To abbreviate a much longer argument (cf. Campbell, 1982a, 1983) for human complex social coordination that is achieved in spite of (rather than through eliminating) genetic competition among the cooperators, moral norms curbing ruthless intelligent individual optimization are rational selfish individual preferences as to how others behave. If the social organization is intact and if the collective goods are substantial, it is also rational to conform to such norms oneself if that is necessary for maintaining group membership. We probably have innate ambivalence (facultative polymorphism) on this score: an available repertoire of cooperative group solidarity and another one of individual optimization at the expense of the group. (Campbell, 1986b, pp. 360-361)

Having argued for the presence of altruistic tendencies in humans and their social systems, we next review the other side of the ledger—the pressure producing facultative polymorphism for individuals engaged in innovative, self-seeking behaviors—the "maximize my own benefits first and foremost" mind-set.

Egoism

An ongoing conflict exists between a social system's best interests and the interests of its members (Campbell, 1985). This conflict will be particularly salient when the individual is a creative, entrepreneurial member interested in challenging the dominant paradigm.

Even though the primary message of my chapter requires a continual ongoing conflict between behaviors that optimize organized groups and behaviors that optimize an individual's personal and nepotistic interests (which I pose as a conflict between the products of biological and cultural evolution), I do not want to deny that our biological history. . . has been increasingly social. (Campbell, 1994, p. 29)

Based on this apparent dichotomy, with each of the poles having deleterious effects (pure egoism leads to destruction, and pure altruism, as mentioned in the section above, results in nonadaptation and eventual extinction), Campbell argued against promoting pure egoism:

> In all social communities, narcissistic people with competitive egocentric pride are a problem. Cooperative people who defer to the majority, who get along and go along with others, and who hold the team together, get preferential treatment even if they are less competent. (Campbell, 1979, p. 194)

For Campbell, egoism, or "competition among the cooperators," results in secrecy and self-serving behaviors.

Campbell illustrated his point with an example of competition among scientists to be the first to report an innovative discovery:

> Our predicament as social animals who must achieve our sociality without inhibition of genetic competition among the cooperators (Campbell, 1975), and as social animals with a fundamental disposition to individual and clique selfishness, puts us in a special predicament insofar as public belief assertion is concerned. Were science designed only to guide our own behavior, then the value neutrality of our scientific conclusions would be complete. The model of the world best-suited to implementing our own values would also have the validity optimal for guiding others with different values. However, the fact that we are in varying degrees in competition with those others provides a motive to keep our knowledge, of our beliefs, private. This motive to achieve secrecy is inevitably characteristic of applied science, social or physical, industrial or national. (Campbell, 1982b, p. 335)

Competition for primacy thus drives scientists underground in their laboratory practices, but recognition for their achievements requires disclosure to the world. Disclosures, in turn, allow other scientists to learn about the discovery, and the shared knowledge—if replicated and validated—creates a new baseline for subsequent work.

Selection Rules: Campbellian Antinomies and Entrepreneurship Puzzles

Thus far, the quotations we have used from Campbell represent four different levels of analysis: individual, group, community, and population. In the following discussion of relationships among Campbell's antinomies, the BVSR environment, and our six entrepreneurial puzzles, we employ the *firm* as the unit of selection. Entrepreneurial variations in behaviors and activities, if successful, create a bounded entity that stands or falls as a unit. Campbell noted that

If, after all of this internal, structural selection an adult, fertile phenotype is produced, this phenotype is then subject to an *external* natural selection. Of all these many selective systems, only this last can involve an improvement in the fit of the organism to the environment, an increase in the "knowledge" which the genome carries in the external world. (Campbell, 1979, p. 185)

Selection of an entity does not imply that all of its components, taken in isolation, are viable. This is particularly significant to our discussion, given the underlying tension between variation and selection pressures.

To understand differences across entrepreneurial foundings with respect to variation and selection, we must first appreciate the complexity of the BVSR environment. Campbell believed that the environment was fluid and dynamic, and within this environment, adaptive and maladaptive organizational forms coexist.

The "wisdom" produced by biological and social evolution is retrospective, referring to past environments. It is only adaptive to the extent that these environments remain stable. Yet the rigid preservation systems essential for the process of evolution, also

provide for a retention of these systems long beyond their usefulness. (Campbell, 1965, p. 35)

We see, therefore, that at any given moment, both adaptive and maladaptive firms inhabit local environments—the enigma is that we cannot tell which is adaptive until the environment selects out maladaptive firms. The simultaneous existence of adaptive and maladaptive organizations is one of the inherent complexities of the BVSR environment:

Evolutionary theory—biological or cultural—does not automatically produce a "Panglossian" picture of perfect rationality or adaptedness. Indeed its theoretical resources can be assembled to understand and predict systematic dysfunction, and it may well be this potentiality that might most modify economic theory were the merger to be carried further. (Campbell, 1986b, p. 358)

One aspect of BVSR environmental selection we have ignored to this point is the required level of persistence on the part of nascent entrepreneurs (Gartner, Bird, & Starr, 1992). Campbell noted that environmental complexity and uncertainty imply a minimal chance of success for most new entities. Even highly focused, intentional behavior by motivated nascent entrepreneurs must contend with environments that reveal their structures only grudgingly. Repeated trials, over the lives of many nascent entrepreneurs, may be the only way to learn what environments have to offer:

There is bound to be a lot of the purely fortuitous or non-transferably specific in the life or death of a single biological individual or social system or culture item. For a systematic selective criterion to make itself felt above this "noise level," there must be numerous instances involved, and a high mortality rate. (Campbell, 1965, p. 31)

Persistence does not guarantee selection, but it keeps variations alive long enough for them to experience many different selection environments.

We now turn to an examination of the six entrepreneurial puzzles listed at the beginning of this chapter. Our goal is to provide interpretations of the puzzles, using Campbell's BVSR dogma and his antinomies, linking Campbell's theories to the literature on entrepreneurship. Our interpretations are not meant to be exhaustive or conclusive in nature. Instead, we hope that they will serve as a catalyst for further theoretical and empirical explorations. We repeat the puzzles, in greatly simplified form, for ease of exposition.

Puzzle #1: Most new organizations merely reproduce existing forms, rather than creating new ones. Campbell's description of the cultural routines, norms, and habits that restrict creative human activity may, in fact, be more relevant during the period of organizational founding than during succeeding periods. The tension between retaining cultural accumulation and an individual's "freedom to vary" often is resolved by forceful adoption of existing processes. Not only is it easier for entrepreneurs to follow accepted "recipes for success," but resource providers also frequently require it (Aldrich & Fiol, 1994; Suchman, 1995). Such recipes provide templates for the mundane reproduction of existing organizational forms. As Romanelli points out (this volume), to the extent that entrepreneurs blindly assume that copying from existing organizations will work, they fail to explore alternatives that might be more effective.

Innovation requires the ability to challenge, and often disregard, dominant cultural routines. Challenging the dominant paradigm is an overwhelming obstacle for many entrepreneurs. For example, resource requirements for founding, via loans or venture capital funding, may result in coercive isomorphism (DiMaggio & Powell, 1983) in which a new firm is forced to adopt a taken-for-granted form.

In-group pressures are a related reason we might observe a disproportionate number of reproducer organizations over innovator organizations. Individuals following the safer, more supported, in-group routes establish organizations in existing accepted industries. By contrast, we would expect to see innovator firms being established by individuals engaged in the less accepted, egoistic/nepotistic practices. Because they do not know the norms of a population well enough to be conceptually constrained by them, perhaps only outsiders can make radical breaks with tradition.

Finally, as described in the chapter by Miner and Raghavan in this volume, heterogeneous organizational copying or imitation may differentiate between reproducer and innovator organizations. Miner and Raghavan argue that copying and then implementing an eclectic mix of routines from other organizations might result in either increased *or* decreased adaptation. Using their terms, we believe that most firms are founded via simplistic imitation practices, resulting in reproducer organizations, but that foundings created using an extraordinary mix of routines occasionally may blossom into innovative organizations (see Gartner, Mitchell, & Vesper, 1989).

Puzzle #2: Most new ventures, even small ones, involve more than just the nascent entrepreneur during the start-up process. The altruism/egoism antinomy sheds light on this puzzle. The practitioner literature typically portrays entrepreneurial ventures as one-person foundings, but recent research suggests otherwise (Reynolds & White, 1997). Even though entrepreneurs may start their journey working alone, most successful entrepreneurial ventures require cooperative input from a variety of individuals. Entrepreneurs who try to manage their organizational founding as a single-person venture, rather than trading on their in-group status, forgo an array of potentially valuable resources. Campbell's discussion of the security/protection resulting from in-group membership highlights the value of maintaining a cooperative network during organizational foundings.

Involving other people in a founding, however, carries some costs. The more people involved, the greater the pressures on nascent entrepreneurs to follow well-understood routines and practices. What might have become a radically innovative approach to producing or selling a product/service may be so diluted by multiple contributions that it devolves into a replication of the familiar. Nascent entrepreneurs thus face a dilemma: Cooperative behavior facilitates resource acquisition and boundary construction, but egoistic/nepotistic behavior may be necessary to preserve the radical nature of the proposed venture. Because most new ventures involve groups rather than solo individuals (Reynolds & White, 1997), they face pressures pushing them toward the "reproducer" end of our continuum.

Puzzle #3: Habitual entrepreneurs are highly visible icons in many industries, yet their valuable knowledge has been difficult to codify and diffuse. Why is success not contagious? First, success across multiple start-ups requires repeated acquisition of tacit knowledge about local environments. Such knowledge is needed for an understanding of the influential customs, routines, norms, and habits that guide local environmental selection criteria. Deep understanding of tacit knowledge has the potential to mask egoistic drives as altruistic tendencies. Certainly, one of Campbell's strongest propositions relates variation to environmental fit (if there is fit, selection will follow), and one aspect of fit is local adaptation. Campbell argued that the peculiarities of language often obscure tacit knowledge, impeding people's efforts to transmit their local knowledge (Campbell, 1991a). Thus, successful entrepreneurs may not possess the language to codify their approach. If every speaker has an idiosyncratic usage and no two speakers use the same language pattern, then every speaker is constrained by the fit between her or his communication and the interpretations of others.

Second, the altruism/egoism antinomy may also shed light on this puzzle. Highly competitive business environments display what Campbell described as "the problem of competition among the cooperators." Why would successful entrepreneurs share their templates for success when they know full well that others replicating the templates would instantly become direct competitors? Our biologically (and culturally) determined competitive drives may be strong enough to inhibit codification of knowledge by successful entrepreneurs.

Puzzle #4: In spite of the best-laid plans, the gestation period of start-ups is lengthy and fraught with delays. Constructing a new entity takes a long time because nascent entrepreneurs make a lot of mistakes, pursue many blind alleys, and repeatedly retrace their steps. Why are mistakes and blind alleys so common? The direction in which "adaptive" lies, on the reproducer/innovator continuum,

is not readily apparent to most nascent entrepreneurs, so they are vulnerable to the social conformity pressures spelled out by Campbell's antinomy. Lacking strong evidence to the contrary, the path well traveled looks pretty good to nascent entrepreneurs, and they do what others have done. Because of local differentiation, however, much of what once worked no longer does.

Luckily for many nascent entrepreneurs, pressures for obedience to traditions and habits have not completely driven out tendencies toward experimentation and playfulness. Some deviant behaviors actually work. The result, over time, is a mix of start-ups containing mostly conformists or near-conformists, who eventually got it right, plus a few innovative deviants whose activities were rewarded. In the BVSR model, emergence as a coherent entity ultimately depends, of course, on fitness, and fitness is the interactive product of what nascent entrepreneurs offer and what local environments accept.

In addition, the process is lengthy only if some nascent entrepreneurs doggedly persist in their intentions to start a new firm. Discouraged entrepreneurs who give up quickly are of interest primarily if continuing entrepreneurs learn something by observing the dropouts, but learning from others is difficult without insider information. Environmental complexity and uncertainty create situations that take time for founders to learn and unravel. Repeated trials are required, over weeks and months, and may be the only way to place oneself in a position to be selected (Gartner et al., 1992).

Puzzle #5: The more activities people engage in, the greater the chances of their starting, *but* also the greater their chances of quitting the process altogether. Experimentation and persistence pay off for nascent entrepreneurs, although the payoff may be an early exit rather than a start-up. Campbell praised the virtues of experimentation by claiming that the "highest functions of thought" are experimental. In uncertain environments, playfulness and experimentation within the dark corners of an industry may reveal secrets not available to culturally obedient founders.[6] We can also see, in Campbell's writings, the value of persistence. Those entrepreneurs who actively pursue organizational founding, regardless of what they do, will have a better chance of creating a firm than those entrepreneurs who remain relatively inactive.

With respect to the type of activities engaged in, the dynamic nature of the environment allows entrepreneurs to design any number of alternative paths to success. What works at one time may not work at another. Moreover, the degree of constraint between start-up activities is remarkably low. In one study of correlations between indicators of 14 different start-up activities, 60 of the 91 possible correlations were below 0.2 (Carter et al., 1996; Gatewood et al., 1995). Apparently, nearly anything goes, and effective mixes of activities exist in many different combinations.

Puzzle #6: Venture capital firms appear unable to find a predictive template for picking firms in which to invest.

This puzzle captures Campbell's overall message for those interested in organizational foundings. There is no predictive template that will guarantee success. Given the composition of the environment, containing both adaptive and maladaptive organizations, coupled with its fluidity, any template that would guarantee success would (a) apply only to the local environment (local culture-specific) and (b) be applicable at only one point in time (what is adaptive today may be maladaptive tomorrow). Venture capitalists would *seem* to be well placed to design a predictive template because they are in the business of designing them for evaluating business plans. They have not been able to do this for their own investments because no such generic template exists. Campbell's BVSR model explains why. The environment is far too fluid and contains complex antinomies that obviate any potential for developing "*the* right answer" or "*the* template for success."

Summary and Conclusions

Based on his BVSR dogma, Campbell's message to organizational and entrepreneurship theorists is clear: There is no *one right way* to found an organization, nor is the path necessarily straight.

The fluidity and dynamism of the environment create a situation in which success (i.e., founding) results from the interaction between organizational configuration and local environmental selection mechanisms. Because selection mechanisms are neither instantaneous nor perfect, adaptive and maladaptive firms coexist in every local environment. Only through post hoc analysis of what worked can we begin to understand the environmental selection mechanisms in place during any given period. Our understanding of what worked, however, will be constrained by the language in which we communicate and the vision derived from our past experiences.

We have used the terms *reproducer* and *innovator* to label differences among entrepreneurs and the types of organizations they found. Stated simply, reproducer organizations are severely constrained by the boundaries and institutional norms imposed by existing organizations, and they are dangerous models because they are a mix of adaptive and maladaptive forms. Innovator organizations face not only legitimization issues but also rigorous selection forces that may be impossible to overcome. The activities in which nascent entrepreneurs engage, as outlined in the Campbellian antinomies ledger, provide one overarching message for potential success: *Do something.*

Implications

Evolutionary theorists have not paid enough attention to entrepreneurship and the reproducer/innovator continuum (Aldrich & Fiol, 1994). Instead, evolutionary research has focused primarily on monumental discontinuities that occur only once or twice during a population's life cycle (Anderson & Tushman, 1990). Researchers need to turn their attention to nascent entrepreneurship and the founding process at the organizational level of analysis, not only to understand more about the processes and activities leading to organizational emergence but also to complement existing population-level theories.

More dynamic analyses of firm emergence and the founding process would strengthen all aspects of organization theory. We need methods for tracking founding processes, and thus we must find nascent entrepreneurs when they are just beginning to construct their ventures. One way of tackling this empirically is through random-digit dialing surveys of the entire adult population. Currently, the multi-university Entrepreneurship Research Consortium (ERC) is conducting such a longitudinal survey in an attempt to capture what happens during the gestation period when nascent entrepreneurs are only *thinking* about organizational foundings.

Epilogue

As for Steven, the entrepreneur with whom we began our story, over the fall of 1995, he continued to develop his firm. He mostly hired software engineers, but he also employed a few marketing specialists and salespeople. As the company grew, and as he searched for insurance companies as clients for his site, the tens of thousands of dollars per month from his investors no longer seemed like enough to sustain the firm through its early years of planned losses. On one of his trips to California, to look for strategic partners, the Intuit Corporation learned about his firm and asked if he was interested in being acquired. Over a period of several months, Steven and his partners hashed out the advantages of remaining independent and hoping for an early IPO (initial public offering) versus being acquired. Eventually, the choice became clear—be acquired or risk losing everything. In June of 1996, Steven and his partners sold the firm to Intuit for $8 million. His investors were handsomely rewarded for their 9 months of support.

Notes

1. Our chapter applies Campbell's ideas to entrepreneurship as a method of organizational emergence. For a discussion of Campbell's ideas as they relate to variation among existing organizations, see Romanelli's chapter in this volume.

2. Our reproducer/innovator continuum parallels March's (1991) exploiter/explorer discussion of organizational learning.

3. As McKelvey notes in his chapters in this volume, Campbell, in his later years, moved beyond logical positivism and

supported the scientific realist school (critical realism) that replaced positivism.

4. For a complete listing of the supporting cites provided by Campbell, see his 1979 article.

5. For a complete description of Campbell's BVSR dogma, as applied to creative thought, see Campbell (1990a).

6. We thank Bill Barnett for suggesting the expression "dark corner" to refer to unexplored but potentially profitable niches in a market.

References

Aldrich, H. E., & Fiol, M. C. (1994). Fools rush in? The institutional context of industry creation. *Academy of Management Review, 19*(4), 645-670.

Anderson, P., & Tushman, M. (1990). Technological discontinuities and dominant designs: A cyclical model of technological change. *Administrative Science Quarterly, 35,* 604-633.

Campbell, D. T. (1956a). Adaptive behavior from random response. *Behavioral Science, 1*(2), 105-110.

Campbell, D. T. (1956b). Perception as substitute trial and error. *Psychological Review, 63*(5), 330-342.

Campbell, D. T. (1960). Blind variation and selective retention in creative thought as in other knowledge processes. *Psychological Review, 67*(6), 380-400.

Campbell, D. T. (1965). Variation and selective retention in socio-cultural evolution. In H. R. Barringer, G. I. Blanksten, & R. W. Mack (Eds.), *Social change in developing areas: A reinterpretation of evolutionary theory* (pp. 19-48). Cambridge, MA: Schenkman.

Campbell, D. T. (1974a). Evolutionary epistemology. In P. A. Schilpp (Ed.), *The philosophy of Karl R. Popper* (pp. 413-463). La Salle, IL: Open Court.

Campbell, D. T. (1974b). Unjustified variation and selective retention in scientific discovery. In F. J. Ayala & T. Dobzhansky (Eds.), *Studies in the philosophy of biology* (pp. 139-161). London: Macmillan.

Campbell, D. T. (1975). On the conflicts between biological and social evolution and between psychology and moral tradition. *American Psychologist, 30,* 1103-1126.

Campbell, D. T. (1978). Qualitative knowing in action research. In M. Brenner, P. Marsh, & M. Brenner (Eds.), *The social contexts of method* (pp. 184-209). London: Croom Helm.

Campbell, D. T. (1979). A tribal model of the social system vehicle carrying scientific knowledge. *Knowledge, 2,* 181-201.

Campbell, D. T. (1982a). The "blind-variation-and-selective-retention" theme. In J. M. Broughton & D. J. Freeman-Moir (Eds.), *The cognitive-developmental psychology of James Mark Baldwin: Current theory and research in genetic epistemology* (pp. 87-96). Norwood, NJ: Ablex.

Campbell, D. T. (1982b). Experiments as arguments. *Knowledge: Creation, Diffusion, Utilization, 3*(3), 327-337.

Campbell, D. T. (1983). The two distinct routes beyond kin selection to ultrasociality: Implications for the humanities and social sciences. In D. L. Bridgeman (Ed.), *The nature of prosocial development: Interdisciplinary theories and strategies* (pp. 11-41). New York: Academic Press.

Campbell, D. T. (1985). Altruism: Biology, culture, and religion. *Journal of Social and Clinical Psychology, 3*(1), 33-42.

Campbell, D. T. (1986a). The agenda beyond Axelrod's *The evolution of cooperation. Political Psychology, 7*(4), 793-796.

Campbell, D. T. (1986b). Rationality and utility from the standpoint of evolutionary biology. *Journal of Business, 59*(4), S335-S364.

Campbell, D. T. (1987). Selection theory and the sociology of scientific validity. In W. Callebaut & R. Pinxten (Eds.), *Evolutionary epistemology: A multiparadigm program* (pp. 139-158). Dordrecht, The Netherlands: D. Reidel.

Campbell, D. T. (1990a). Epistemological roles for selection theory. In N. Rescher (Ed.), *Evolution, cognition, and realism: Studies in evolutionary epistemology* (pp. 1-19). Lanham, MD: University Press of America.

Campbell, D. T. (1990b). Selection theory and the sociology of scientific validity. In W. Callebaut & R. Pinxten (Eds.), *Evolutionary epistemology: A multiparadigm program* (pp. 139-158). Dordrecht, The Netherlands: D. Reidel.

Campbell, D. T. (1991a). Coherentist empiricism, hermeneutics, and the commensurability of paradigms. *International Journal of Educational Research, 15*(6), 587-597.

Campbell, D. T. (1991b). A naturalistic theory of archaic moral orders. *Zygon, 26*(1), 91-114.

Campbell, D. T. (1993). Systematic errors to be expected of the social scientist on the basis of a general psychology of cognitive bias. In P. D. Blanck (Ed.), *Interpersonal expectations: Theory, research, and applications* (pp. 25-41). New York: Cambridge University Press.

Campbell, D. T. (1994). How individual and face-to-face-group selection undermine firm selection in organizational evolution. In J.A.C. Baum & J. V. Singh (Eds.), *Evolutionary dynamics of organizations* (pp. 23-38). New York: Oxford University Press.

Carter, N. M., Gartner, W. B., & Reynolds, P. D. (1996). Exploring start-up sequences. *Journal of Business Venturing, 11*(3), 151-166.

Cliff, J. (1997). *Building on experience: A cross-level, learning-based approach to the design of new firms.* Unpublished manuscript, College of Commerce and Administration, University of British Columbia, Vancouver.

DiMaggio, P. J., & Powell, W. W. (1983). The iron cage revisited: Institutional isomorphism and collective rationality in organizational fields. *American Sociological Review, 48*, 147-160.

Fiol, C. M., & Lyles M. A. (1985). Organizational learning. *Academy of Management Review, 10*(4), 803-813.

Gartner, W. B. (1985). A conceptual framework for describing the phenomenon of new venture creation. *Academy of Management Review, 10*(4), 696-706.

Gartner, W. B., Bird, B., & Starr, J. (1992). Act as if: Differentiating entrepreneurial from organizational behavior. *Entrepreneurship: Theory and Practice, 16*(3), 13-32.

Gartner, W. B., Mitchell, T. R., & Vesper, K. H. (1989). A taxonomy of new business ventures. *Journal of Business Venturing, 4*(3), 169-186.

Gatewood, E. J., Shaver, K. G., & Gartner, W. B. (1995). A longitudinal study of cognitive factors influencing start-up behaviors and success at venture creation. *Journal of Business Venturing, 10*(5), 371-392.

Gifford, S. (1997). Limited attention and the role of the venture capitalist. *Journal of Business Venturing, 12*(6), 459-482.

Gorman, M., & Sahlman, W. A. (1989). What do venture capitalists do? *Journal of Business Venturing, 4*(4), 231-248.

Low, M. B., & Abrahamson, E. (1997). Movements, bandwagons, and clones: Industry evolution and the entrepreneurial process. *Journal of Business Venturing, 12*(6), 435-457.

March, J. G. (1991). Exploration and exploitation in organizational learning. *Organization Science, 2*, 71-87.

National Endowment for the Arts. (1997). National Medal of Arts press release [Announcement posted on the World Wide Web]. Retrieved from the World Wide Web: http://arts.endow.gov/Community/News/Medals98.html

Reynolds, P., & White, S. (1997). *The entrepreneurial process: Economic growth, men, women, and minorities.* Westport, CT: Quorum.

Scriven, M. (1959, August 2). Explanation and prediction in evolutionary theory. *Science*, pp. 477-482.

Starr, J. A., & Bygrave, W. D. (1992). The second time around: The outcomes, assets and liabilities of prior start-up experience. In S. Birley & I. C. MacMillan (Eds.), *International perspectives on entrepreneurship research* (pp. 340-363). Amsterdam: Elsevier.

Starr, J., Bygrave, W., & Tercanli, D. (1993). Does experience pay? Methodological issues in the study of entrepreneurial experience. In S. Birley & I. C. MacMillan (Eds.), *Entrepreneurship research: Global perspectives* (pp. 125-155). Amsterdam: Elsevier.

Suchman, M. (1995). Managing legitimacy: Strategic and institutional approaches. *Academy of Management Review, 20*(3), 571-610.

Van de Ven, A. H., Angle, H. L., & Poole, M. S. (1989). *Research on the management of innovation.* New York: Harper & Row.

Webster's new world dictionary. (1966). Cleveland, OH: World.

Chapter 3

Interorganizational Imitation

A Hidden Engine of Selection

ANNE S. MINER
SRI V. RAGHAVAN

In this chapter, we argue that repeated interorganizational imitation acts as a selection engine to change the nature and mix of routines enacted in a population of organizations. Organizational researchers have often assumed that interorganizational imitation and vicarious learning generate homogeneity among practices, in which a single organizational routine "takes over" a population over time (DiMaggio & Powell, 1983; Meyer & Rowan, 1977). This idea can produce predictions both that a group of organizations will converge to the most effective or efficient routine (Griliches, 1957; Mansfield, 1968) and that they will converge to a ceremonially desirable but technically irrelevant routine (Meyer & Rowan, 1977). For the most part, scholars have assumed that imitation's important role in the dynamics of population level change is to *retain* or sustain existing routines, practices, and divisions against the forces of change.

Theorists in several disciplines and an increasing number of organizational researchers also have pointed out, however, that imitation and vicarious learning can generate change, at least in principle (Baum, in press; Boyd & Richerson, 1985; DiMaggio, 1988; Lumsden & Wilson, 1981; Zucker, 1988). In this chapter, we draw together work from varied literatures to develop the idea that imitation can produce selection. We review aspects of a deliberately varied set of papers that contain representations of one of three distinct imitation "modes" (Haunschild & Miner, 1997). We claim that these papers imply that a large and plausible set of factors moderate the impact of imitation and interorganizational learning, so that in some cases imitation produces new mixes of routines in populations of organizations. Furthermore, the work taken as a whole implies that imitation and learning can either increase or decrease the adaptive potential of the new mixes.

Our chapter builds on Donald Campbell's work in two ways. Campbell's (1960, 1969) early work emphasized variation-selection-retention processes as general models for change in social systems.

AUTHORS' NOTE: We appreciate the contributions to this work made by Howard Aldrich, Joel Baum, Pamela Haunschild, Eric Larsen, William McKelvey, and Elaine Romanelli.

Drawing on this tradition, Miner and Haunschild (1995) advocated a general V-S-R model as a good starting place for examining how the mix of organizational routines in a population of organizations changes over time. They defined the systematic change in the nature and mix of routines *that arises from shared experience* as a population-level learning outcome. Such systematic change represents the main focus of this chapter, with imitation serving as the way experience is shared.

Campbell also devoted substantial attention specifically to the process of selection. Much of his work focused on individual-level actions and processes, such as the evolution of individual beliefs about the world (Campbell, 1990), although he also tackled the contested issue of group selection (Campbell, 1994). He also called attention to increasingly sophisticated treatments of dynamic selection processes over time (e.g., Boyd & Richerson, 1985; Lumsden & Wilson, 1981). Over the years, he developed an interest in selection at all levels of analysis: "For me, what is important is a very general 'selection theory' and its call to examine what is actually being selected for at each level of individual, subgroup and firm-level selection of courses of action" (Campbell, 1994 p. 37). We follow Campbell's lead by beginning to consider quite detailed aspects of the fruits of selection processes, and links between imitation and selection. This chapter, then, shares with the work of Miller (this volume) and Romanelli (this volume) a focus on imitation and its outcomes. Those chapters deal with the important topic of how imitation and vicarious learning affect the focal organization that imitates other organizations. Our chapter complements those by exploring the impact of repeated imitation by many organizations, over time, on mixes of routines in the whole organizational population.

To foreshadow the results of our review, we find convincing arguments that features of (a) the imitator, (b) the practice imitated, (c) the exact sequence of steps involved in imitation, and (d) features of the imitation context can all moderate imitation's impact so that it can produce either a mix of routines or convergence. This claim holds true even for the seemingly crude, simple form of imitation in which organizations enact whatever routine the majority of other organizations now carry out. The work we review highlights many different ways in which imitation can produce new mixtures of routines, as well as oscillation, rather than the traditional S-curve convergence to a single routine (Rogers, 1995). We underscore five factors that influence both the degree of mix and its adaptive value: (a) ambiguity, (b) noise and error, (c) sequential imitation, (d) use of multiple imitation modes, and (e) neighborhoods of interaction. Two other contextual factors—the degree of correlation between organizational traits and the stability of context—should have far-reaching consequences for the adaptive impact of iterated imitation. We suggest that this work extends the theoretical frameworks of population-level learning, evolutionary change, and neoinstitutional theory. We conclude by asking whether it is appropriate to see imitation as a potentially fundamental engine of selection in organizational systems, along with competition and complexity.

Theoretical Context and Concepts

By focusing on change in a population in the mix of routines arising from experience, we examine a "population-level learning" outcome (Miner & Haunschild, 1995). Population-level learning represents an emerging framework for organizational analysis rather than a formal theory. It emphasizes change in the "nature and mix of organizational routines in a population of organizations arising from experience" as a population-level learning outcome. Recent work has tackled the question of population-level learning *processes* (Miner, Kim, Holzinger, & Haunschild, 1998). Overall, the population-level learning framework emphasizes two distinguishable types of processes: (a) iterated vicarious learning and imitation by individual organizations, and its impact at the population level (Baum, in press); and (b) fully population-level processes that contain a collective element that goes beyond aggregation of interorganization-level imitation and vicarious learning (Anderson, 1998; Lant & Phelps, 1998). This chapter falls squarely in the first category. It focuses on the implications of iterated imitation by organizational "adopters" on the nature and mix of routines in a population of organizations.

We structure our investigation of imitation and vicarious learning by exploring three specific "modes" of imitation: (a) *frequency imitation* (copying the most common organizational routine), (b) *trait imitation* (copying the routine of some organization based on a trait of that organization such as size, prestige, or similarity to self), and (c) *outcome imitation* (copying routines that appear to have good consequences for other organizations) (Haunschild & Miner, 1997). For this investigation, we make no assumptions about the motivation of such imitation or vicarious learning, only exploring the long-term impact on the population-level mix of routines if organizations repeatedly follow a given imitation mode.

The processes that could produce these modes include both "mindless" imitation and vicarious learning that involves making inferences. For example, an organization that automatically adopted, without reflection, whatever was most popular at trade shows would manifest frequency imitation, but so would an organization that consciously used a particular marketing approach because it first observed that all the marketers in that country used it and then concluded that the approach met the key preferences of consumers in that country. Some of the models we review do assume cognition (as when the potential adopter calculates a mean or updates a prior expectation); however, we focus on whether a crucial determinant of which routine is imitated is (a) the overall frequency of a routine, (b) its link to organizations with some distinct trait, or (c) its observed outcome.

Research Questions and Investigation Strategy

Research Questions

We began with three underlying sets of research questions:

1. What do models of imitation imply about the effect of repeated imitation on the resulting mix of routines, and what factors drive it?

2. What do models of imitation imply about whether the imitation process produces a more "adaptive" mix of routines over time?

3. Is there illustrative empirical evidence that a given imitation mode actually occurs in the material world and on moderators of its strength?

Investigation Strategy

We observed that scholars in many different fields have considered many different formal or implicit models that include at least one of the three imitation modes. To deepen our understanding of whether or how careful modeling implies that imitation can create variation, we selected a small set of models from several different literatures, intentionally seeking diversity in style and purpose. We were curious to see whether scholars in different fields, working with relatively little contact with one another, came up with similar factors.

We asked the following questions of each paper. For formal and implicit models of imitation, we stressed the following. First, if organizations repeatedly follow the imitation process described, will this result in a single routine overtaking the population of organizations, a new mix of routines, or an oscillating pattern of routines? What factors will tend to enhance the chances of a new mix or oscillation? Second, if organizations repeatedly follow the imitation process described, will the resulting mix of routines (including convergence to a single routine) enhance the survival and prosperity of the whole population? What factors will enhance the chances of a mix that enhances survival/prosperity? For primarily empirical papers, we stressed the following: Does this article provide empirical evidence that (a) this mode actually occurs in the material world, and that (b) one or more specific factors moderate its chances of occurring?

We reviewed both "formal" models (typically mathematical representations) and "implicit" models (typically verbal presentations of an argument about imitation or vicarious learning). We included a small but varied set of empirical papers partly to double-check our intuition that all three imitation modes occur in varied settings in the world, and also to check for evidence moderating effects may occur. The Investigation Results section describes the results of our review, organized by imitation mode. Across all imitation modes, we summarize 33 papers in our tables. For each imitation mode, we first describe what we see as the papers' implications for whether repeated imitation in this mode enhances the degree of variety in the population mix of routines, and factors that increase the chances it will do so. Then, we discuss whether the papers imply that this entire process will produce a more "adaptive" mix of routines, and the factors that can enhance that result. Finally, we comment on aspects of the illustrative empirical work. At the end of our review, we propose four broad categories of factors that moderate imitation's impact on variety of routines and the mix's adaptive potential or overall value. The papers do not represent a random sample of articles with either formal models or empirical data related to imitation and vicarious learning, and certainly not a complete sample of related work. Even so, taken as a group, they suggest some regularities.

Levels of Analysis

We have emphasized papers focused on *organizational* imitation and vicarious learning but have included several papers that treat individual human beings as the potential adopter, for two reasons. First and foremost, the logic of whether an imitation process will produce diversity or convergence does not depend on the actual nature of the potentially adopting unit. If repeated imitation of some other social actor by a risk-averse imitator will produce convergence to a single routine, this finding does not depend on whether the potential adopter is a person or an organization. Second, in many cases, even interorganizational imitation will involve action by individuals or coalitions of individuals using one of the processes described.

Resulting Mixes of Routines

Many complex mixes can result from repeated interorganizational imitation. For this review, we made a judgment and classified each paper in terms of whether repeated use of the rule in question would most likely lead to one of three broad outcomes: (a) *convergence toward a single routine*

over time, (b) creation of *a mix of routines*, or (c) *oscillation*. Classification in the tables of a possible outcome as "single routine" does not mean the whole population quickly arrives at total domination by one routine, but that repeated imitation will tend to move one routine closer and closer to domination. We classified potential outcomes as "a mix" when we judged that repeated use of the rule in question would create or keep recreating a mix that predictably contains more than one of the candidate routines. Finally, we labeled the potential outcome as "oscillation" when we inferred that repeated imitation would produce a systematic pattern of ongoing shifts from one routine's tendency to dominate toward another routine's domination, or from one mix to another.

Assessing the Value of a New Mix of Routines

In considering how selected mixes of routines may enhance the survival and prosperity of the population of organizations, we faced the relentlessly thorny problem of defining collective welfare and/or adaptation over time. As Sober (1984) notes, "If we are to avoid the fallacies that have preyed upon evolutionary theory in the past, a precise vocabulary is needed for the scientific study of adaptation" (p. 5). Our default definition was that a new mix is "adaptive" if it contains a higher percentage of a routine that is "valued" from the perspective of the paper describing the process. Thus, convergence to one routine might be seen as "adaptive" if it is viewed as a better routine than the ones it replaces. As we will discuss later, this definition ignores issues of epistasis or complementarity between routines, which may further complicate patterns. In addition, it assumes that a routine can be permanently assigned a value in some stable metric. We believe this to be a reasonable starting place for initial comparisons of different processes and outcomes. In some cases, the author(s) state or imply some other, specific outcome as being valuable, and we classified the model as having "adaptive" outcomes accordingly. For example, some of the work considers the case in which there are two equivalent routines available for adoption, with neither really superior. In that instance, we would consider the outcome "adaptive" if the population ends up with a mix of both routines and avoids the inappropriate domination by one of the equivalent routines.

Implications of Models

In trying to characterize a model's implications for change in the mix of routines, we sometimes could rely on very explicit models and reasoning presented by the authors. In other cases, especially in the empirical papers we present, we had to make more aggressive inferences about what repeated imitation would produce. We caution the reader, then, not to assume that our table represents the authors' own views on convergence or adaptation. We hope our summaries will encourage others to examine the models directly, and we welcome suggestions for alternative interpretations of their implications. Finally, we have used the following conventions in boiling down what are often complex, nuanced models with their own terminology into our summary tables.

1. The organization that does or does not imitate is called the "adopter."
2. The entity (or entities) whose experience is being used in the imitation/learning process is the "model" or "models."
3. The practice, action, strategy, product, or item that may be adopted is called the "routine."

Investigation Results

Frequency-Based Imitation

Frequency-based imitation occurs when an organization uses the proportion of other organizations using a given routine as the basis for adopting the routine itself (Haunschild & Miner, 1997). Most presentations of this rule posit that increased frequency increases the chances of adoption. In some models, frequency also can tend to decrease adoption chances, as when "snob" appeal leads to the avoidance of a routine (Biddle, 1991; Dosi, Ermoliev, & Kaniovsky, 1994). Table 3.1a provides a short summary of eight formal and two implicit models and studies that invoke frequency imita-

tion, and Table 3.1b summarizes five primarily empirical papers that examine the occurrence of frequency-based imitation in some way.

We first consider some of the implications of these papers for whether repeated frequency-based imitation will lead to a single routine, a mix, or an oscillating pattern. The third and fourth columns of each table indicate our interpretation of how the type of frequency imitation described in the focal paper will affect the mix of routines and what factors—if any—should moderate that outcome. Next, we consider some implications of these papers concerning whether iterated imitation will produce adaptive change or not for the population as a whole. The fifth and sixth columns of each table display our speculation on that topic. Finally, we discuss the evidence from the five illustrative empirical papers concerning the existence of frequency-based imitation and empirical evidence of moderators of its effect.

As noted, we extrapolate from papers that articulate these issues in terms of individual-level "adopters" to the organizational level of analysis. For example, consider a model implying that when individuals use "frequency of prior adopters" to pick products, the population of consumers will converge toward everyone using the same product. In the interorganizational context, this work would imply that if organizations use the simple frequency of prior adopters of a new technology, compensation policy, or organizational form to determine their own technology, policy, or form, the population of organizations will converge toward all organizations using the same technology, compensation policy, or organizational form.

Convergence or Mix

Table 3.1a indicates that even frequency-based imitation—which intuitively seems most likely to produce convergence to one routine—can produce mixed and oscillating patterns of routines in populations of organizations. In Abrahamson and Rosenkopf's (1993) model of bandwagon adoption by organizations, for example, firms adopt a new practice or technology "T" based both on their assessment of the innovation's value and on a "bandwagon" pressure factor that is proportional

TABLE 3.1a Formal and Implicit Models of Frequency-Based Imitation

Author(s) and Year of Publication	Model Type	Mix	Contingency Factors for Mix	Adaptive Consequences	Contingency Factors for Adaptive Consequences	Selected Model Features and Assumptions	Selected Implications of the Author(s)	Adopter Heterogeneity
Abrahamson and Rosenkopf (1993)	Formal	Stable mix or single routine	Ambiguity levels of routine's technical efficiency	Beneficial or maladaptive	Ambiguity levels of routine's technical efficiency	• Equal bandwagon impetus from all firms • No information flows from early adopters	Minor organizational differences cause major bandwagon pressures	Organizational goals are heterogeneous
Bell (1997)	Formal	Convergence to patches of preferences	• Production returns to scale of product • Market structure	Beneficial or maladaptive	• Production returns to scale of product • Market structure	• Adopters change their preferences based on most frequently used product in local neighborhood • Two products and three alternate technologies • Adopters function in an endowment or a production economy	• Adopters form clusters of same preferences over time • Average preferences evolve so as to reflect the relative availability of goods or to minimize the per unit cost of production	Initial preferences can vary
Biddle (1991)	Formal	Oscillation	Snob factor in demand decisions	Beneficial or maladaptive	• Efficacy of copied practices • Strength of snob effects	Individual demand affected by aggregate demand levels	Diffusion of information and bandwagon effects play a role in adoption decisions	
Boyd and Richerson (1985) "frequency dependent bias"	Formal	Stable mix or single routine	• Weights given to the models whose routines were copied • Weight given to one's *own* behavior • Variance in the models available for imitation	Beneficial or maladaptive	• Prior population experience • Strength of the frequency rule	• Routine selection based on frequency of prior adoptions • Competing routines are not compared	Identical routine adoption patterns leads to weak biases	• Differences in prior adoptions • Differences in the weights attributed to the models whose routines are copied

Dosi, Ermoliev, and Kaniovsky (1994) (first model)	Formal	Stable mix or single routine	Imperfect information in acquisition process	Indeterminate		• Adopters sample prior adopters and with some probability pick most common product • Products equivalent but varied mixes/ monopoly can arise	Informational imperfections foster variety	• Adopters are risk averse • Adopters exhibit different learning strategies
Farrell and Saloner (1985)	Formal	Stable mix or single routine	• Completeness of information about other adopters' preferences • Communication between adopters	Beneficial or maladaptive	• Completeness of information about other adopters' preferences • Communication between adopters	Incomplete information regarding firms' eagerness to adopt	• Symmetric and asymmetric inertia occurs because of information flow constraints • Inertia precludes adoption even though adoption is warranted	Differences in eagerness to adopt an innovation
Henshel and Johnston (1987)	Formal	Single routine		Beneficial or maladaptive	Accuracy of predictions	Rational behavior among discerning voters	Forecasts and predictions can be self-fulfilling	Voters differ in their choice of candidate
Herbig (1991)	Implicit	Stable mix or single routine or oscillation	Interaction of routine's perceived value and prior frequency	Beneficial or maladaptive	Interaction of routine's perceived value and prior frequency	Innovation adoption/ rejection decisions are discontinuous and not gradual	The longer the resistance to innovation adoption/ rejection, the greater the internal disruption to the firm	Differences in levels of commitment to a given innovation
Meyer and Rowan (1977)	Implicit	Single routine or mix	Link between ceremonial and technical routines	Beneficial or maladaptive	• Efficacy of acquired procedures and practices • Relationship of ceremonial to technical routines	• Institutionalized products, services, techniques, and routines are adopted by organizations ceremoniously • Conformity to ceremonial rules may conflict with efficiency concerns	• Environments that have institutionalized greater number of rational myths, generate more formal organization • Incorporation of institutionalized myths results in greater legitimacy and survival prospects	Differences in the need among adopters for organizational legitimacy

TABLE 3.1b Empirical Studies on Frequency-Based Imitation

Author(s) and Year of Publication	Study Type	Evidence	Mix	Contingency Factors for Mix	Adaptive Consequences	Contingency Factors for Adaptive Consequences	Selected Implications of the Author(s)
Burns and Wholey (1993)	Field study using survey data (organization level)	Prior adopters of matrix management systems in hospitals determined likelihood of future adoptions	Stable mix or single routine	Time period	Beneficial or maladaptive	Efficacy of prior adoptions	Task diversity and imitation both influence adoption with little effect on disadoption
Haunschild and Miner (1997)	Field study using secondary data (organization level)	Number of other firms using a given investment banking firm during the prior 3 years affects the acquiring firms' choice of investment banker in the current year	Single routine or mix	Uncertainty about nature of routine and performance of models	Beneficial or maladaptive	Uncertainty strengthens frequency as a determinant of investment banker choice	Frequency imitation is one of three modes seen
Hershey, Asch, Thumasathit, Meszaros, and Waters (1994)	Field study (individual level)	Willingness to accept vaccination increased as more subjects were told of others' vaccinations	Stable mix or single routine	• Level of free riding • Degree of perceived immunity from disease for the population	Beneficial or maladaptive	• Level of free riding • Degree of perceived immunity from disease for the population	Bandwagon effects compete with free-riding processes
Narduzzo and Warglien (1996) "popularity rule"	Experimental study (individual level)	Stable domination of one product over others in four out of six aggregate choices	Single routine		Beneficial or maladaptive		• Process can produce unjustified dominance of one product • Adopters use majority choice rules • Role of chance
Wade (1995)	Field study using primary and secondary data (organization level)	Number of prior entrants increases chances of new entrance event	Single routine or stable mix	Period (effect reverses after inflection point)	Beneficial or maladaptive	Period effect dynamics	Imitators' (second sources) entrance influenced by prior entrants (curvilinear) but also by community traits

to the degree of ambiguity about the innovation and the number of prior adopters. In their model, they show that over time, this "rule" may or may not produce a convergence to T in the population. Less ambiguity about a routine's value can decrease bandwagon pressures, as noted in our table. In addition, the authors argue that (a) increases in the difference between the adopters' assessment of returns to a particular innovation can cause decreases in the extent of the innovation's bandwagon pressure, and (b) lower average assessments of the innovation will decrease the tendency toward convergence. The process in their article can produce homogeneity among early imitators that stops, creating a new mix.

Boyd and Richerson (1985) models of "frequency dependent bias" in cultural evolution also imply that the degree of convergence may vary after frequency imitation. For example, if the potential adopter picks out subsets of models (others to imitate) before making the frequency determination, this can reduce the degree to which frequency imitation encourages convergence. Biddle (1991) models what happens if adopters use the proportion of previous adopters who have used vanity license plates to make their own adoption choices. In his work, high frequencies of vanity plate adoption do not always lead to an increased demand for such plates. The model predicts that after a certain frequency, "snob effects" set in, and adoptions of the vanity license plates decline.

Sharif and Ramanathan's (1982) work follows in the line of formal models of the diffusion of innovations in marketing and other fields. They add explicit consideration of two features: (a) after a routine has been adopted, it may later be rejected by the adopter; and (b) there may be a group of permanent nonadopters who consciously disapprove of the innovation. Their simulations produce some patterns in which one routine dominates the population but also some outcomes that include mixtures of disapprovers and adopters, as well as temporary dominance of adopters followed by mixes of rejecters and disapprovers.

Adaptive Consequences

The fifth and sixth columns give our interpretations of how the type of frequency imitation in each paper affects the adaptive potential, or value, of the resulting nature and mix of routines. The papers imply that both beneficial and maladaptive mixes can result from very plausible processes of repeated frequency-based imitation. One simple version of this contingency perspective is that if the population converges to a "better" routine than that used before, it is an adaptive outcome. Hershey, Asch, Thumasathit, Meszaros, and Waters's (1994) study of vaccination choices, for example, takes it for granted that convergence to all subjects choosing vaccination is good for the population. Hershey and colleagues find that individual adopters' tendencies to be "free riders" and the apparent structure of the context—that is, do they believe the vaccine makes one unable to transmit the disease to others?—moderate the impact of the proportion of others who have chosen to be vaccinated. Whether the actual final mix is the "good" outcome of all being vaccinated or not depends both on the preference structure of potential adopters and on the structure of the context.

Boyd and Richerson (1985) call attention to the powerful value of frequency-based imitation when two subpopulations exist, each of which has "learned" over time that routine A or B works in its local environment (so that the appropriate routine characterizes most members of each subpopulation). In that case, if "newcomers" to a subpopulation use the frequency rule, it increases the chances they will adopt a "good" routine and enhances the proportion of "good" routines in the subpopulation. The papers underscore, however, that frequency imitation also can produce "runaway" convergence toward dominance of a poor routine (e.g., Abrahamson & Rosenkopf, 1993; Boyd & Richerson, 1985; Meyer & Rowan, 1977).

In addition, the papers point to a variety of factors that will influence whether repeated frequency-based imitation produces a greater presence of "good" routines or a better distribution from the perspective of the population as a whole. For example, in Farrell and Saloner's (1985) model of technology adoption decisions, incomplete information creates excess inertia, so that "a new technology is not adopted even when the adoption is favored by both firms" (p. 80). Communication between the potential adopters, however, can alter the situation. Where preferences of the firms are the same, communication in the form of a "straw vote" will eliminate excess inertia, and where preferences vary, it can increase inertia. Or, for example, in Henshel and Johnston's (1987) model of voting behavior, if predictions are made in accordance with the majority preference of the voters, then the preferred candidate gets elected, but this does not necessarily occur.

Finally, Bell's (1997) model of choice assumes that potential adopters must choose between two products that have different production costs, under varied market structures. The adopters repeatedly use the frequency of prior adopters in their own immediate "neighborhood" to determine their own preferences in an ongoing set of market processes. Bell shows that this "local" frequency-based imitation of preferences often produces "patches" of similar adopters (but an overall mix), and that the consumers come to prefer the most available product. If organizations continually adjust their own preferences to match those of a set of closely associated organizations, Bell's model would imply that under certain conditions a group of organizations will come to prefer the most available routines.

Empirical Illustrations

Table 3.1b lists five varied empirical studies that provide data about frequency-based imitation. The literature on the diffusion of innovation, of course, contains many studies indicating (both statistically and through self-reports) that frequency-based imitation occurs at the individual level of analysis (Rogers, 1995). An increasing number of empirical papers also provide evidence that organizations use frequency imitation (e.g., Fligstein, 1985; Palmer, Jennings, & Zhou, 1993; Kraatz, 1995). The papers noted here provide evidence of frequency imitation in the adoption of hospital matrix management design (Burns & Wholey, 1993), entry into technological communities (Wade, 1995), and the use of investment bankers (Haunschild & Miner, 1997). Three of the papers have special interest because they suggest that frequency-based imitation may occur in the presence of other decision rules (including other imitation rules; see Hershey et al.,

1994; Narduzzo & Warglien, 1996; Haunschild & Miner, 1997).

If a paper provides evidence of a frequency effect but no evidence of moderating variables, we typically judged the likely "outcome" to be convergence. The papers, however, provide varied empirical evidence for moderating effects of frequency-based imitation. For example, in Hershey and colleagues's (1994) study, the proportion of others who already had chosen vaccination tended to increase subjects' willingness to be vaccinated themselves. The individual preferences of the adopter and the nature of the context, however, could affect the strength of this pattern. If subjects believed there is "herd immunity," in which there is a decreased chance of infection for others when a large number of people are immunized, they appeared to be less likely to be influenced by the prior proportion of adopters. Haunschild and Miner's (1997) study shows that the degree of uncertainty (both about the target of an acquisition and about the record of the investment banker being chosen) increases the effect of frequency, implying that reducing uncertainty in this case would weaken the impact of frequency-based imitation. Finally, Wade's (1995) study of second source entrants into technological communities showed a curvilinear relationship in which frequency's initial positive impact has an inflection point within the values of the study, so that at some point, frequency decreases the chances of a second source entry.

Trait-Based Imitation

Trait-based imitation occurs when an organization imitates a practice executed by other organizations having some specific trait (e.g., size, prestige, location, or similarity to the potential adopter) (Haunschild & Miner, 1997). The decisive factor in adoption is not the number of prior adopters or features of the routine being adopted, but some specific feature of the imitated organization that makes it the model. Tables 3.2a and 3.2b offer summaries of models and illustrative empirical work that address this type of imitation. Again, we first consider their implications for whether imitation will produce a mix of routines, then speculate on their implications about adaptive or beneficial

TABLE 3.2a Formal and Implicit Models of Trait-Based Imitation

Author(s) and Year of Publication	Model Type	Mix	Contingency Factors for Mix	Adaptive Consequences	Contingency Factors for Adaptive Consequences	Selected Model Features and Assumptions	Selected Implications of the Author(s)	Adopter Heterogeneity
Boyd and Richerson (1985) "indirect bias"	Formal	Stable mix or single routine or oscillation	• Error in imitation • Covariance of indicator trait and routine	Beneficial or maladaptive	• Link between indicator trait and value of routine • Relative selection strength on indicator or routine	• Adopter picks model using "indicator" trait (e.g., prestige), copies other routine • Adopter uses "blending rule" with models	• Runaway processes can occur when indicator traits override fitness criteria • Weak indicator variable biases result in maximization of beneficial routines • Trait imitation can enhance adaptation	Adopters may attribute different weights to the models that are copied
DiMaggio and Powell (1983)	Implicit	Single routine or possible mix	Organizational uncertainty regarding the means/ends links for routine	Beneficial or maladaptive	• Actual value of routines linked to trait • Organizational ability to learn and adjust • Overall value of diversity in population	Organizational and population-level factors affect homogeneity of population-level routines	• Mimetic processes are one of three main forces • Institutional processes can produce homogeneity and change	Organizations start in many diverse forms
Mezias and Lant (1994)	Simulation	Stable mix (of organizations and possibly traits)	• Probability of environmental changes • Magnitude of environmental change • Carrying capacity of environment for organizations	Beneficial or maladaptive	• Very high/low probability of environmental change and imitation • Very high/low magnitude of environmental change and imitation	• Fixed and mimetic organizations exist • Organizations imitate at founding or later • Aspiration-driven search by organizations	• Mimetic organizations can survive • Success depends on environmental change and search	Two types of organizations

TABLE 3.2b Empirical Studies on Trait-Based Imitation

Author(s) and Year of Publication	Study Type	Evidence	Mix	Contingency Factors for Mix	Adaptive Consequences	Contingency Factors for Adaptive Consequences	Selected Implications of the Author(s)
Bascom (1948)	Ethnographic study (individual level)	Size of yams was considered a sign of prestige	Single routine		Beneficial or maladaptive		N/A
Baum (in press)	Field study of change in organizational population	Prior increases in diversity enhance the degree of heterogeneity in a core trait, and prior decreases reduce heterogeneity in a core trait	Stable mix or oscillation	Available models/ fragmented context	Beneficial or maladaptive	Indeterminate	
Burns and Wholey (1993)	Field study using survey data (organization level)	Adoption by high-*prestige* hospitals enhances chances of others adopting	Single routine		Beneficial or maladaptive	Task diversity and imitation will influence adoption (have little effect on disadoption)	
Handy and Handy (1924)	Ethnographic/case study (individual level)	• Individuals who had acquired tattoos were considered prestigious • Copying based on prestige	Stable mix		Maladaptive		N/A
Haunschild (1993)	Field study using secondary data (organization level)	Acquisition numbers related to acquisitions completed by *interlock* partners	Single routine or stable mix		Beneficial or maladaptive	• Network characteristics • Efficacy of partner acquisitions	Social networks are an important source of acquisition information
Haunschild and Miner (1997) "trait imitation"	Field study using secondary data (organization level)	*Large firms* that use a given investment banker during the prior 3 years determine whether the acquiring firm uses them in the current year	Single routine or stable mix	Uncertainty about nature of routine	Beneficial or maladaptive	Uncertainty strengthens trait (size) as a determinant of investment banker choice.	Trait imitation among one of three imitation modes in the population
Walker (1971)	Study of state government adoption programs	State governments tend to adopt innovations made by *high-status* states	Single routine		Beneficial or maladaptive		

outcomes. We then comment on the illustrative empirical work.

Convergence or Mix

The models clearly imply that trait-based imitation can produce convergence to a single routine, mixtures of routines, or oscillation in the population as a whole. DiMaggio and Powell (1983), for example, observe that prior work by Meyer and Rowan (1977) seemed to imply that repeated imitation of successful organizations will produce organizations with externally similar traits but with internal variation. This would produce convergence of external traits but mixes of internal traits in the population. In contrast, DiMaggio and Powell (1983) predicted that imitating successful organizations will produce convergence in both external traits and internal practices.

The papers also underscore that trait-based imitation may fail to generate convergence at all, over time. For example, the degree of error in the imitation process can enhance the possibility that iterated trait-based imitation will avoid convergence and produce a mix of routines (Boyd & Richerson, 1985). Mezias and Lant's (1994) simulation model of mimetic organizations implies that medium probabilities and magnitude of environmental change should reduce the chances of trait-based imitation leading to domination of a single routine, because these factors will reduce the number of mimetic organizations imitating apparently successful organizations.

Another contextual factor that can prevent trait-based imitation from producing simple convergence is the nature and degree of covariance between the indicator trait (size, prestige, similarity) and the routine that is imitated. In some cases, trait-based imitation can produce more variation in the routine being implemented than there is in the original indicator trait. For example, if organizations used an indicator trait with relatively little variation (say, profitability in a very successful population of organizations), but there was a great deal of possible variation in the routine they adopted (say, manufacturing procedures), the resulting mix could have a higher level of variation in manufacturing processes than in organizational profitability (Boyd & Richerson, 1985).

Adaptive Consequences

The papers imply that repeated trait-based imitation can produce both beneficial and maladaptive mixes of routines in the population. In the most intuitive case, if the indicator trait really is associated with a valuable routine, repeated imitation will produce useful convergence to the valuable routine in the population (Boyd & Richerson, 1985; DiMaggio & Powell, 1983). For example, if successful firms adopt a production practice that really is more efficient and others imitate that practice based on the overall success of the firms (rather than knowledge of the production practice's direct outcome), then the industry as a whole will become more efficient. At the same time, if the routine copied from the "successful" organizations has no genuine value, or is in fact harmful, repeated trait-based imitation will not enhance an adaptive mix of routines and can decrease the adaptive value of the mix. The empirical papers by Bascom (1948) and Handy and Handy (1924) embody this type of perceived outcome of individual-level trait-based imitation.

The papers also imply additional contingencies that affect trait-based imitation's impact. DiMaggio and Powell (1983) argue that misguided or inaccurate trait-based imitation can still generate useful population-level change if the adopters can learn from their own experience after imitation, for example. We think that Mezias and Lant's (1994) simulation implies that trait-based imitation may produce mixes of routines when (a) the probability or (b) the magnitude of environmental change is unusually high or low. In those circumstances, mimetic organizations successfully find "good" routines by imitating others, presumably enhancing the presence of these good routines.

Finally, the degree and nature of covariance between indicator traits and the adopted routine can have complex contingent effects on the value of the resulting mix of routines. As often noted, the use of an easily observed (and actually correlated) indicator trait to choose action may be a very efficient and low-cost method of discovering valuable routines. The repeated use of this rule can in some cases produce a better mix of routines than other available imitation rules (Boyd & Richerson, 1985). If, however, individual adopters have different preferences about the indicator trait—for example, some organizations imitate larger organizations and others imitate middle-sized organizations—these preferences themselves may change over time. This can lead either to the increased presence of "good" routines or to "runaway" processes. If organizations get (a) their preferences about what size makes an organization admirable and (b) their own size-determining activities from the same models, this can produce such runaway processes (Boyd & Richerson, 1985, p. 260).

Empirical Illustrations

The empirical papers suggest that trait-based imitation does occur and reveal some factors that moderate its impact. In addition, one paper argues that mimetic processes will enhance the degree of heterogeneity in routines over time and finds supporting evidence (Baum, in press). A large body of studies in the literature on diffusion of imitation document individual-level imitation based on prestige (Rogers, 1995), and recent work supports organizational imitation based on traits. The papers noted here provide evidence of trait-based imitation based on status in states' adoption of policies and programs (Walker, 1971), imitation based on prestige in the adoption of matrix management designs in hospitals (Burns & Wholey, 1993), imitation based on interlock links in the domain of acquisition practices (Haunschild, 1993), and imitation based on size in the use of investment bankers (Haunschild & Miner, 1997). The Haunschild and Miner (1997) article also finds that uncertainty about the transaction involved enhances the impact of size of the model, implying that reducing such uncertainty would reduce the power of trait-based imitation in this context. Burns and Wholey (1993) find that prestige influences matrix adoption in one period but not in another.

Finally, Baum (in press) directly examines change in the core characteristics in a population of child care organizations over time, arguing that the effects of ecological and institutional processes are highly particularistic and contradictory, promoting homogeneity on some core features and, at the same time, diversity on others. His results show that the level of prior changes in the diversity of an organizational feature increases the degree of heterogeneity in that feature. Baum argues that this result supports the prediction that trait-based imitation can produce variation as well as homogeneity.

Outcome-Based Imitation

Outcome-based imitation occurs when an organization imitates a practice based on that practice's apparent outcome when implemented by other organizations (Haunschild & Miner, 1997). Here, the adopter does not look to the overall frequency of the routine or the properties of its prior implementers, but to apparent consequences of the routine itself. Once more, we consider whether this imitation mode can produce both convergence and mixes, we examine the possibility of beneficial or maladaptive outcomes, and we examine illustrative empirical studies.

Convergence or Mix

Tables 3.3a and 3.3b summarize papers containing some form of outcome-based imitation. They imply that it can generate convergence to a single routine, movement to a mix of routines, or oscillation. As in the case of other models, several contingency factors moderate the evolution of either convergence or a stable mix. In Arthur and Lane's (1994) model, potential adopters must choose between two new products. The adopters have some public information about the products, and they supplement this by getting additional information sequentially from prior adopters on their perceptions of the product's effectiveness, which they process using Bayesian updating. In the case where the adopters have the same public information and the products perform identically well, at least two factors can produce ("inappropriate") convergence to a single product rather than a mix of the equal products: (a) risk aversion on the part of the adopters and (b) unanticipated product effectiveness.

TABLE 3.3a Formal and Implicit Models of Outcome-Based Imitation

Author(s) and Year of Publication	Model Type	Mix	Contingency Factors for Mix	Adaptive Consequences	Contingency Factors for Adaptive Consequences	Selected Model Features and Assumptions	Selected Implications of the Author(s)	Adopter Heterogeneity
Arthur and Lane (1994)	Formal	Stable mix or single routine	• Adopter level of risk aversion • Unexpected value of routine • Stopping rule for sampling • Change order of prior adopters	Beneficial or maladaptive	• Adopter level of risk aversion • Unexpected value of routine • Stopping rule for sampling • Change order of prior adopters	• Adopters sequentially pick one of two products • Risk-averse adopters update prior expectations based on information from sample of prior adopters	• Adopters learning from prior adopters induces information feedback	• Homogenous distribution of information across adopters • Can produce domination even when products are equal
Kapur (1995)	Formal	Stable mix	• Number of lag periods through which adoption proceeds, and the availability of information	Beneficial or maladaptive	• Accurate perception of prior adoption outcomes	• For each firm, gains from switching to new technique is independent of other firms' choices • Adoption entails identical sunk costs and presence of uniform prior beliefs about sunk costs for all firms	• Firm-level heterogeneity is not essential for diffusion • Delayed adoption is facilitated by information about prior adoption outcomes	
Lane and Vescovini (1996)	Formal	Stable mix or single routine	• Which heuristic used to assess results of prior adopters • Difference in true value of routines • Adopter risk aversion • Sample size of prior adopters	Beneficial or maladaptive	• Which heuristic used to assess prior adopters' results (best is "max" rule) • Difference in true value of routines • Risk aversion of adopter • Sample size of prior adopters	• Risk-averse adopters sequentially pick one of two different products • Adopters update prior expectations using information from sample of prior adopters • May use Bayesian rule, or one of four heuristics	• Most adaptive rule is "max" rule • Bayesian optimization does not always lead to selection of best routine • More information may not produce convergence to best routine	
Ziegler (1985)	Implicit	Single routine or mix	• Characteristics of routine (e.g., legal protection) • Value of routine	Beneficial or maladaptive	• Value of routine • Cost of transgression of norms	Imitative entrepreneurs copy tacit, technical routines they have seen work, then leave original firms to start new firms ("fissioning process")	Skill development and lack of compensation motivate imitative entrepreneurs to use fissioning process	

TABLE 3.3b Empirical Studies on Outcome-Based Imitation

Author(s) and Year of Publication	Study Type	Evidence	Mix	Contingency Factors for Mix	Adaptive Consequences	Contingency Factors for Adaptive Consequences	Selected Implications of the Author(s)
Argote, Beckman, and Epple (1990)	Field study using secondary data (organization level)	New shipping firm start-ups learning from experiences of earlier firms	Single routine or mix	Number of new firms	Beneficial or maladaptive	Number of new firms	No vicarious learning after founding period
Connell and Cohn (1995)	Field study using secondary data (organization level)	Prior strike success enhanced chances of future strikes	Stable mix or oscillation	• Period • Context	Beneficial or maladaptive	Significance of prior successes to future successes	Strikes that occur in short bursts of imitation produce potential for large concentrated peaks
Haunschild and Miner (1997) "outcome imitation"	Field study using secondary data (organization level)	• Low premiums paid by other firms in using an investment banker would increase the likelihood of the focal firm's choice of that investment banker • High premiums also enhance likelihood	Single routine or stable mix	Uncertainty for high premium effect	Beneficial or maladaptive	Uncertainty	Outcome imitation is one of three modes in population
Narduzzo and Warglien (1996) "max," "mean," and "min" rules	Experiment (individual)	Self-report of three rules: (a) Pick product with the highest value for prior adopters, (b) pick product with the highest single outcome, or (c) pick product with the least bad outcome • Resulted in convergence in four of six trials	Single routine or stable mix	• Chance • Rule(s) used • Sequence of rules used	Beneficial or maladaptive	• Chance • Rule(s) used • Sequence of rules used	• Process can produce unjustified long-term dominance of one product • Adopters use multiple choice rules • Role of chance

Lower adopter risk aversion or less product surprise make it more likely a mix might emerge when the two products are of equal value.

In Kapur's (1995) article, firms delay adoption of a new technology hoping that they will be able to make better adoption decisions after looking at the outcomes of the prior adopters. The firms end up in a series of "wars of attrition" among the potential adopters at each stage. As in several of the models, if routines have lower expected benefit, the model predicts a greater tendency toward a mix and away from convergence.

Adaptive Consequences

The papers imply that outcome-based imitation can produce both beneficial and maladaptive mixes of routines over time. Lane and Vescovini's (1996) article, for example, explores a similar setting to the Arthur and Lane (1994) context, in which potential adopters learn about results from a sample of prior adopters. They examine several different rules of thumb the adopter might use to evaluate prior adopter information. In addition to Bayesian updating, the potential adopter may use one of three different "outcome" rules: the "max rule" (pick the product that produced the single highest value in your sample of prior adopters), the "mean rule" (choose the product associated with the highest mean value in your sample of prior adopters), and the "min rule" (choose the product linked to the highest minimum value in your sample of prior adopters).

Lane and Vescovini (1996) argue that the choice of rule has a major impact on the value of the ultimate outcome. For example, Bayesian optimization can produce substantial market share for an inferior product. At the same time, to their surprise, if all the adopters use the max rule, the proportion of adopters who choose the superior product will move toward 1, no matter how small the difference between the two products. In addition, more information can lead to smaller rather than greater market shares for the better product in this model. In short, the specific choice of heuristic or rule used to evaluate prior adopter outcomes can affect the adaptive value of the resulting mix. More information can affect it too, but in this model, more information does not necessarily generate a better

match between the actual value of the routines and distribution of adopters, in spite of expectations that it should do so.

Empirical Illustrations

The empirical papers provide evidence suggesting that organizational outcome-based imitation occurs. Argote, Beckman, and Epple (1990) provide data on vicarious learning in shipyards, Connell and Cohn (1995) give evidence that successful strikes were more likely to be imitated (under certain conditions), and Haunschild and Miner (1997) find that acquiring firms are more likely to use investment bankers who had apparently (a) produced exceptionally good outcomes in prior deals (lower premiums) and (b) produced exceptionally bad outcomes (very high premiums). In the Haunschild and Miner article, only extreme outcomes seem to have an effect, and both ends of the extreme produce imitation. Their results also show an interaction effect between two different types of uncertainty and the tendency to pick investment bankers who apparently generated very bad outcomes. Uncertainty reduces the coefficient for these negative outcomes. This implies that the tendency to imitate a practice generating a "bad" outcome would be reduced by uncertainty.

Narduzzo and Warglien's (1996) experimental study provides experimental evidence that individuals use all three of the outcome rules of thumb (max rule, mean rule, and min rule). This article also provides important empirical evidence for the power of chance itself in this type of outcome-based imitation. The authors found that with the same initial conditions, one product tended to become prevalent in four out of six experiments, shares oscillated in a fifth, and a 50-50 split eventually occurred in the sixth run. Additionally, they found that adopters sometimes used more than one rule. They imply that the actual distribution of routines (and their appropriateness) is related to the mix of rules used by the adopters.

Factors Influencing Distributions of Routines and Adaptive Outcomes

Taken together, the papers imply that at least four broad factors can moderate the impact of the

TABLE 3.4 Some Factors That May Enhance the Degree of Variety in the Mix of Routines After
Iterated Imitation

Features of adopters

Frequency mode	Individual adopter preferences: snob value
	Individual adopter preferences: unequal weights on models used
	Individual adopter preferences: want to be free rider
	Different original preferences among adopters
Trait mode	Adopter gives varied weights on models imitated
	Adopter groups models
	Adopter's goals are clear and certain
Outcome mode	Adopter lack of risk aversion
	Adopters imitate only "extremely good" and "extremely bad" routines
	Adopters use varied evaluation rules for outcomes (e.g., pick routine with least bad results for prior adopters; pick routine with best high value for prior adopters)

Features of candidate routines

Frequency mode	Low value of routine
	Routine easy to evaluate
Trait mode	Clarity, certainty in outcomes of routine
Outcome mode	Routines very similar to one another

Process

Frequency mode	Probabilistic use of frequency rule
	Accidental order of prior adopters visible to adopter
Trait mode	Errors in imitation
Outcome mode	Stopping rule when sampling prior adopters' outcomes (e.g., sample one more if prior three all the same, at certain levels of risk aversion)
	Accidental order in which prior adopters are sampled for their outcomes
	Adopters sample fewer prior adopters (in some settings)

Structure of imitation/learning context

Frequency mode	Communication between potential adopters about shared preferences
	Incompleteness of information on what other adopters prefer
	Early (or late) time period (depends on setting)
	Level of perceived collective impact of routine (e.g., immunization)
	Clarity of link between routine and its outcome
	Not constant returns to scale in production combined with localized imitation processes
Trait mode	Large or small number of visible models (depending on process)
	Middle-level values of probability of change in the environment
	Middle-level values of magnitude of change in the environment
Outcome mode	Routine (product) is about as effective as originally expected
	Increased numbers of new organizations entering population
	Time period

three imitation modes on the resulting mix of routines and their adaptive potential:

1. Features of the adopters (e.g., risk aversion, preference for snob appeal),
2. Features of the routines (e.g., easy to evaluate, actually has value),
3. Features of the imitation process itself (e.g., degree of error in imitation, accidental order of sequential sample of prior adopters), and

4. Structure of the imitation context (e.g., no communication between potential adopters, preferences about indicator traits can itself evolve).

Table 3.4 reviews selected factors that appear to enhance the chances that repeated use of each mode will produce a mix of routines rather than convergence, and Table 3.5 lists factors that may enhance the prospects of a more adaptive or valuable mix of routines after iterated imitation.

TABLE 3.5 Some Factors That May Enhance the Prospects of More "Valuable" Distribution of Routines in Population After Iterated Imitation

Features of adopters

Frequency mode	*Lower adopter risk aversion* may produce mix of two equivalent routines rather than unwarranted dominance of one
Trait mode	*Ability of adopter to learn* can enhance long-term value of traits acquired through imitating prestigious actors
Outcome mode	*Adopter's lack of risk aversion* when sampling prior adopter outcomes produces mix of two equivalent routines rather than unwarranted dominance of one
	Adopter's use of the "max rule" in assessing outcomes of prior adopters (pick product/routine that had the highest individual value for any prior adopter) will enhance chances that the market will be dominated by superior product (routine)
	Use of multiple criteria to evaluate outcomes of prior adopters may produce mix of two equivalent routines rather than unwarranted dominance of one

Features of candidate routines

Frequency mode	*Clarity about impact of routine* can reduce bandwagon pressure toward adoption of unvalued routine
Trait mode	*High correlation of indicator trait with valuable routines* can enhance presence of valuable routine
Outcome mode	*Routine (product) is about as effective as originally expected* means sequential sampling of prior adopter outcomes produces mix of two equivalent routines
	Greater differences between two available routines can enhance chances that outcome imitation will produce dominance of a superior routine rather than unwarranted dominance of one

Process

Frequency mode	
Trait mode	*Imitation of similar other* can enhance chances of adoption of routines appropriate to adopter
Outcome mode	*Particular stopping rule* in sampling prior adopter outcomes produces mix of two equivalent routines rather than unwarranted dominance of one
	Adopter's ethically marginal imitation of routine from prior user may enhance presence of good technical routine but simultaneously enhance presence of poor ethical routines
	Large number of new firms entering industry may enhance presence of valuable routine when vicarious learning occurs only during founding process

Structure of imitation/learning context

Frequency mode	*Decreasing returns for production* can enhance chances consumer will prefer goods that are available
	A population's prior history that led to a frequent routine being more common makes frequency imitation an effective strategy for newcomers
	More complete information about another adopter could make it more likely firms will converge on new technology in which both would be better off
	Higher uncertainty enhances adoption of valuable routine
Trait mode	*If strength of selection processes over time on indicator trait* is greater than selection on the routine adopted, this can enhance presence of valuable routine
	Imitation based on prestige rather than trial and error can speed up adoption of valuable routine
Outcome mode	*Adoption in period similar to context of successful prior adoptions* may enhance chances that valuable routines will be produced through outcome imitation
	Uncertainty may enhance chances that a bad routine will not be dominant

Two features of these tables stand out. First, although the three rules may well vary in their intrinsic tendencies to produce convergence, the features of adopters, routines, process, and context can affect the impact of all three imitation modes. Second, although any one of our interpretations of these papers may be off the mark, the tables as a whole provide formidable evidence that imitation represents a potentially nuanced engine of change. Although for modeling purposes we need to focus on a small subset of factors that will affect the ultimate patterns generated by imitation, the actual results of interorganizational imitation will be determined by combinations of the factors listed in

Tables 3.4 and 3.5. Clearly, many combinations of such factors are not only possible but also likely to occur.

Discussion

We began our study with the question of whether and how imitation and vicarious learning may operate as engines of repeated imitation. Specifically, we wanted to know if selection can systematically produce change in the nature and mix of organizational routines in a population of organizations (beyond reducing the current level of variety). We also wanted to explore whether the direction of such change might be toward more "adaptive" mixes for the population as a whole. In this discussion, we first consider whether our work suggests that imitation can act as an important engine of selection. We then discuss several broad factors moderating imitation's impact that we see as especially promising for further work. After considering some limitations of our study, we discuss selected implications for the population-level learning, evolutionary, and neoinstitutional theoretical frameworks. We close by asking whether imitation should be added to competition and complexity as a fundamental selection mechanism.

Do Imitation and Vicarious Learning Act as Selection Forces?

Tables 3.4 and 3.5 suggest that features of the adopter, the routine, the process, and the context all can influence an imitation mode's tendency to produce a systematically new mix of routines and the nature of the new mix. The tables also document a surprisingly large number of sensible, plausible factors that can affect the degree of variety in and the nature of the mix of selected routines. We find the evidence here compelling in showing that imitation may work as a selective force.

We considered whether the rich array of theoretical factors that can turn imitation into a selection device may be an artifact of the rules for academic publishing. For example, an analytic paper that shows formally that repeated frequency-based imitation—absent any complications whatsoever—will produce convergence would not be publishable because of its simplicity and intuitive finding. Perhaps the many proposed features that turn imitation from a force for convergence to a force producing new mixes arise because academics are rewarded for generating "interesting" models. The contingency factors explicated in these models are plausible and common features of everyday life, however, rather than rare or exotic variables. In many cases, existing research documents (a) that individuals and organizations vary on the dimensions involved (e.g., risk aversion, choice of imitation rules) and (b) that processes and contexts vary in terms of the proposed structural features (e.g., sequence of sampling of prior adopters, degree of communication, level of ambiguity).

In addition, the illustrative empirical papers present credible evidence that all three imitation modes we have considered do occur in the real world. Although there is perhaps more detailed empirical evidence historically about individual-level imitation and vicarious learning, an increasing number of specifically organizational studies has confirmed the existence of more than one mode of interorganizational imitation and vicarious learning (Haunschild & Miner, 1997).

On balance, then, we find the evidence convincing that interorganizational imitation and vicarious learning operate as an important engine of selection among organizational routines, practices, products, and activities. Furthermore, we argue that interorganizational imitation and learning not only "select" through producing convergence from a variety of routines toward a single routine, but also (a) sometimes produce a mix of routines or oscillating patterns and (b) sometimes can produce systematic movement toward more adaptive or valued mixes, and in other cases produce movement away from such mixes.

What Factors Determine the Impact of Imitation/Vicarious Learning Selection?

Tables 3.4 and 3.5 highlight many features of the potential adopter, the routine, the process, and the context that can affect imitation and learning's selective impact. Each can play a moderating role within a specific model. Are there common factors running across models and imitation modes? Our initial reflection on this highlights five broad factors that affect both the tendency to produce a new mix of routines and the adaptive value of the new mix:

1. Ambiguity about the nature or impact of a routine,
2. Noise or error in the imitation system,
3. Sequential imitation and learning,
4. The imitator's use of multiple imitation modes, and
5. Neighborhoods of interaction.

These include, then, factors related to the imitator, the routine, the process, and the context.

Additionally, we see two broad structural features that stand out as crucial influences, primarily on whether selection through imitation influences the adaptive value of new mixes of routines: (a) the degree of correlation between an indicator trait and an imitated routine, coupled with the overall level of correlation among the impacts of organizational traits, and (b) the long-term stability of the system within which imitation takes place. All of these represent especially promising areas for further work, as we discuss briefly below.

Ambiguity

Institutional theory and many of the models here imply that ambiguity concerning the imitation context, the nature, and the actual impact of a target routine plays an important role in imitation processes and outcomes. Much theory and some evidence suggests that ambiguity about the overall context and about the actual value or consequences of a focal routine will generate imitation itself as an activity (DiMaggio & Powell, 1983; Miner & Haunschild, 1995; Rogers, 1995; Zucker, 1988). It is often assumed that this imitation, then, will produce more convergence. Precise modeling of the role of ambiguity, however, suggests that its ultimate impact may not always follow our intuition. For example, in Abrahamson and Rosenkopf's (1993) models, ambiguity's impact on the tendency toward convergence is nonlinear and can depend on how the organizations assess the prob-

able value of the routine. Narduzzo and Warglien's (1996) individual-level study of imitators suggests an even more extreme possibility: that high ambiguity may prompt the imitator to combine different modes of imitation as time goes on, which—as we discuss below—could lead to new mixes of routines implemented by the imitator. It is possible, then, that ambiguity may well prompt imitation without producing convergence.

Error, Noise, and Incomplete Information

Scholars have long noted that errors or noise in imitation can introduce variety into the population (Aldrich, 1979). Several of the models described here underscore the potentially powerful role of error and information imperfections of many sorts. Imperfections in the imitation process may include both direct errors (as when an imitated routine perceived to produce good results actually produced bad results), noise (as when a routine is implemented in a somewhat different way), and information incompleteness (as when an adopter lacks a complete sample of the outcomes for all prior adopters). Taken as a whole, the models imply that these imperfections in imitation processes represent a powerful influence on whether imitation produces new mixes and avoids convergence (Arthur & Lane, 1994; Boyd & Richerson, 1985; Dosi, Ermoliev, & Kaniovsky, 1994).

The net consequences of error, however, again may not always follow our intuition. For example, imperfect imitation can produce more variation in the mix of routines, reducing the movement toward convergence and serving as a variation source. In terms of adaptive value, it may be a double-edged sword. In outcome-based imitation, for example, accurate imitation of a routine that does indeed have positive value increases the presence of this valuable routine in the population. If variation within the population has a higher-level collective value, however, some imperfection has value for the population as a whole. In at least one model, more complete information reduced the chances of a good fit between the mix of routines and the actual value of the routines (Lane & Vescovini, 1996).

Sequential Imitation and Learning

Early neoinstitutional theorists raised the general theme of the link between imitation and timing (Tolbert & Zucker, 1983). Several of the papers described here demonstrate that recent work points to even more nuanced impacts of timing and the nature of sequential imitation processes (Arthur, 1989). Some models imply that imitation may produce different mixes of routines and/or degrees of convergence because of accidental sequences when organizations sample the behaviors or reported outcomes of behavior by other organizations (Dosi et al., 1994). These models tend to suggest an important role for chance in whether imitation leads to one outcome or another.

In one model, the consequences of imitation based on sequential sampling appear to violate long-held assumptions about the value of more complete information. In the Lane and Vescovini (1996) model, more information reduced rather than increased the probability that a "good" routine (product) would dominate under certain circumstances, for example. These authors also argue that in some sequential sampling settings, Bayesian optimization performs less well than simple rules of thumb. Thus, the existence and nature of sequential imitation can alter the probability that imitation will generate (a) convergence to a specific routine, (b) convergence at all, and (c) the proportion of valuable routines in the resulting mix.

Use of Multiple Imitation/Learning Modes

The models reviewed tended to focus on the repeated use of one imitation mode, consistent with the enormous literature on the diffusion of innovations. Haunschild and Miner (1997), however, suggest the possibility that organizations may use more than one imitation rule (although their data could not rule out different organizations using different rules). Other empirical work supports the occurrence of the use of multiple modes at the individual level of analysis (Narduzzo & Warglien, 1996; Wilkening, 1952). Haunschild and Miner speculate that if organizations use multiple rules over time, or across different routines—for example, using frequency-based imitation for accounting procedures but outcome-based imitation for sales approaches—this would produce new combinations of routines within the adopting organization.

Neighborhoods of Interaction

An important factor that shapes the nature of the collection of models being imitated is "proximity," in the sense of "nearness" to the potential adopter. The degree to which imitation/learning produces a mix can depend not only on how many models are imitated but also on how they are clustered (Bell, 1997; Boyd & Richerson, 1985). If imitation occurs only among local neighborhoods but other interactions occur in a broader population, this may produce non-obvious mixes of routines in the population as a whole (Bell, 1997). If imitation processes themselves produce neighborhoods, which in turn determine later models for imitation, the entire process may produce dynamic patterns of change in the imitated routines not easily predictable at the beginning of the process. This conceptual notion underscores the importance of continuing empirical research on the specific networks within which interorganizational imitation occurs.

In addition to these five factors that moderate the tendency for imitation to produce convergence and to produce valuable new mixes of routines, we see two major contextual features that have especially important implications for the adaptive impact of repeated imitation.

Correlation Between Routines

Intuition, along with several models, highlights that the adaptive value of trait-based imitation depends on whether the indicator trait (such as profitability) really does have a positive, stable relationship with the imitated trait (such as a new manufacturing procedure). If a new procedure does in fact increase profits, there will be a correlation and adopting the new procedure may enhance the adopter's profits too. From this perspective, a positive correlation between these two organizational traits increases the chances that the iterated imitation will produce a higher presence of the valuable routine in the population.

As we observed in the discussion of trait-based imitation, however, repeated imitation over time can produce higher-level change in which the nature of the correlation between indicator and imitated trait changes over time. Cultural evolutionists have long noted that the iterated imitation process itself may affect the level of correlation between indicators and other traits (e.g., Boyd & Richerson, 1985). Not only does the correlation of routines affect the short-term collective impact of repeated imitation, but the imitation system also may have important long-term feedback loops that affect collective survival and prosperity. These can include "runaway" processes in which maladaptive routines spread through the population (Boyd & Richerson, 1985).

Finally, if the effect of routines depends on the presence of other routines, what counts may not be just individual, independent routines, but specific bundles of routines. If adopters use several imitation modes at different times or in different parts of the organization, this may produce new bundles made out of practices that had value in other contexts but represent very bad new combinations (Kauffman, 1993). Levels of correlation between routines in terms of their impact could thus create situations in which imitation produces sudden, sharp changes in the adaptive value of new mixes of routines.

Stability of Context

As we discussed earlier, the value of frequency-based imitation rests heavily on the past history of the imitation context. If a population of organizations has over time experimented with many routines in a way that enhances the chances that a valuable routine will flourish, then frequency is in fact a valid signal of the value of the routine (Boyd & Richerson, 1985). This is true even using a very simple definition of what is an adaptive change in the mix of routines. The prior history plays a crucial role in determining the link between the selection factor (frequency, trait) and the potential value of the adopted routine. Frequency-based imitation presumably is less costly and perhaps more rapid than outcome-based imitation and perhaps trait-based imitation in some cases (Romanelli, this

volume). Under stability, then, we could speculate that frequency-based imitation represents a better strategy for members of the population to follow than the other imitation modes.

Many theorists, however, argue that exogenous shocks or even coevolutionary change processes will alter the relative value of routines, in which case all three imitation modes can systematically generate maladaptive mixes of routines. That is, imitating what worked in the past may be a very bad strategy if the current context rewards different routines. For example, imitating buggy maker routines as automobiles began to replace buggies might represent a poor strategy. This in turn implies that the impact of iterated imitation in a given model will depend crucially on the nature and pace of exogenous change processes.

Campbell explored implications that this may have for what sort of variation provides the best long-term source for change in the collectivity (Campbell, 1960, 1994; Romanelli, this volume). Interestingly, this shift also could change whether a particular imitation mode represents a "good" general strategy, in the sense that the population will prosper if many organizations follow it. For example, at a certain point in technological evolution, frequency-based imitation might reinforce a less efficient technology while outcome-based imitation increased the presence of a new, genuinely valuable technological routine. Thus, the degree of stability in the context not only will moderate the value of imitation in general but also may determine which imitation mode is most likely to produce adaptive population-level consequences when applied repeatedly.

Limitations of This Study

To conduct our review, we sought work from a variety of fields. Our sample of studies is not random and does not reflect the relative frequency of different types of models. It includes work of varying theoretical origins, quality, and style of scholarship. It is not possible, then, to draw conclusions about how frequently different factors appear even in academic models, or how likely they are to occur in the material world. Because we sought a varied group of literatures, our review does not capture the richness or depth of some of the literature we have sampled. In addition, important detailed features of individual models may be only partially included or oversimplified. We invite readers to extend our initial review both in interpreting the models and in considering their implications. The empirical work we discuss generally provides evidence supporting the existence of the three imitation modes but does not test predictions about their impact on mixes of routines. Important recent empirical work seeks to test the proposition that imitation can produce change (Baum, in press), but this remains a crucial area for field research.

We also did not address the important question of the relative speed in reaching new mixtures or convergence. This is important not only in terms of anticipated resulting mixes but also in terms of the adaptive advantages of using different rules. Rapid change to a new mix may or may not have long-term advantage to a population, for example. In general, we would anticipate the usual trade-off in terms of rapid change: Rapid movement to a new mix with more valuable routines would have adaptive advantage in the presence of competing populations. Slow movement to any change in mix might have value through preventing runaway shifts to harmful routines with little time to change course even if the collective consequences of the new routine become evident. The issue of speed of change in the mix of routines remains an important area for further work.

Implications

We propose that iterated imitation and vicarious learning play a decisive—and non-obvious—role in the selection of mixes of routines in populations of organizations. We first consider implications of this claim for the population-level learning framework, then discuss briefly its possible links to evolutionary and neoinstitutional theory. We conclude with a comment on the general notion of basic selection engines.

Population-level learning represents an emerging framework for organizational analysis rather than a formal theory. Miner and Haunschild (1995) focused attention on the key population-level learning *outcome* of change in the nature and mix of organizational routines in a population of organizations arising from shared experience. More recent work has tackled the question of population-level learning *processes*. This work distinguishes two types of processes: (a) the aggregate impact of iterated organization-level learning over time and (b) fully population-level processes (as when a whole industry imitates a collective routine of another industry). Our chapter falls in the first category because it focuses on the implications of iterated imitation by individual "adopters" on the nature and mix of routines in a population of adopters.

The papers reviewed here tend to support Miner and Haunschild's (1995) argument that iterated imitation and vicarious learning may represent a more powerful and systematic engine for population-level change than we have tended to assume in organizational studies. Specifically, it supports the important claim that imitation/learning can produce systematic change and can support variation rather than producing simple replication. Even "mindless" frequency-based imitation and trait-based imitation, for example, can result in new, varied mixes of routines when affected by such factors as copying error, neighborhoods of interaction, and correlations between routines. Our examination may be conservative, and creative cognition could produce additional variety even beyond the level we have presented here. For example, none of the models we described permits the adopter to deduce a principle from the outcomes of a routine for prior adopters, and then create a novel routine based on that principle. Such a process would represent vicarious learning and could add truly new routines to the population (Dickson, 1998). Of course, some work suggests that strong inertia occurs even in cognitive "routines" such as assumptions and taken-for-granted beliefs, making the actual contribution of cognitive processes to variety in routines an important empirical question.

The work here also raises the important possibility that iterated organization-level imitation/learning eventually may produce population-level contours that shape future population-level dimensions that then shape ongoing organizational interaction (and future imitation). Anderson (1998), for example, argued that organizational interaction influenced collective performance standards in the United States cement industry, which in turn influenced not only population prosperity but also future organizational interaction. Once institutionalized, the performance standards had an effect that did not arise from the simple aggregation of individual imitation events and that influenced later actions by members of the population. Explicating and examining these types of change arising from shared experience represents an important frontier for population-level learning research.

Evolutionary theories of organizations have considered several of the key issues raised here (Aldrich, 1979; McKelvey & Aldrich, 1983). Baum and Singh (1994) argue that some forms of interorganizational imitation serve as replication engines, sustaining continuity within a group of organizations. They also note that interorganizational processes including imitation can produce variety and that "the features of organizational inheritance suggest evolutionary effects and levels of organizational diversity and variation that are strikingly different from those expected with purely genetic transmission" (p. 7). In general, however, organizational work to date in the evolutionary framework has tended to assume that imitation represents primarily a replication system (McKelvey & Aldrich, 1983). In the context of organizational evolutionary theory and that of some cultural evolutionists, this chapter's substantive focus primarily considers *horizontal transmission*, because we emphasize imitation across organizations rather than between generations of organizations. We hope the chapter contributes to evolutionary theory by highlighting the potentially diverse consequences of horizontal imitation. Our argument amounts to a claim that horizontal imitation represents an engine of both interaction and transmission. Dynamic interactions between generations of learning organizations represent an important issue for future work.

Our investigation does differ from evolutionary or ecological approaches that assume that the primary determinant of the nature and mix of routines

in population of organizations will be the birth and death of whole organizations. Whether organizational birth and death may produce greater changes in the nature and mix of population routines than does interorganizational imitation and learning seems to us an open empirical question. Finally, we note that traditional evolutionary approaches in organizational research do not typically contemplate the adopters and observers as developing *representations* or theories about the world. The deeper development of cognitive models of vicarious organizational learning may generate predictions distinct from those of prior organizational evolutionary research.

Neoinstitutional Theory

Critics of early neoinstitutional theory have argued that its emphasis on imitation limited its ability to account for variation and change (Zucker, 1988). The models here clearly show that with plausible moderators, imitation can produce convergence, stable mixes of routines, and some unstable temporal patterns that do not "settle down" at all with time. Some neoinstitutional theory suggests that ambiguity and uncertainty support imitation as a way to decide what to do (DiMaggio & Powell, 1983), and empirical data generally support that claim. Uncertainty and ambiguity, however, may moderate the effects of frequency- and trait-based imitation, and of extremely high or low routines, in different ways. This suggests a much more nuanced potential impact of uncertainty and ambiguity: They may produce imitation without producing homogeneity. The outcome would depend on the specific processes of imitation and vicarious learning involved. In general, our review supports neoinstitutionalist suggestions that paying attention to imitation may not mean attending solely to homogeneity, stability, and inertia but also may illuminate more subtle change processes (DiMaggio & Powell, 1991).

Engines of Social Selection

Finally, we return to the broader issue of whether imitation and vicarious learning should be added to the candidate list for important engines of selection. In general, much theory seems to assume that *competition* represents the most important, if not the only, force for selection over organizations and routines. One of the most fundamental assumptions of modern capitalism is that organizations will compete, with some surviving and some failing. This implies that a powerful determinant of the mix of routines in a population will be the competitive process, perhaps coupled with chance. The assumption that competition ultimately drives selection underlies much evolutionary theory in biology as well. This very basic viewpoint has been challenged by some complexity theorists who offer alternative models of the origins of order (Kauffman, 1993). Our addition to the candidate list for major selection engines is more modest. We simply suggest that in social systems, we may need to explore whether imitation and vicarious learning may represent a selection engine with much more complex and powerful implications than have been assumed up until this time.

In considering this issue, one might ask if models of organizational competition do not implicitly already involve imitation. For example, organizations may observe their competitors and try to imitate their successful routines as a part of the competitive process. Competition, however, does not necessarily involve imitation at all. A group of organizations can feel the effects of new competitors through reduced demand without even knowing the nature of that competition, and they can fail to respond or can respond in ways that have nothing to do with the actions of these unseen competitors. The focal organizations may change their own behavior in response to the reduced demand but base all their actions on their own experience. Competitive interaction therefore does not necessarily involve imitation. By the same token, imitation does not necessarily involve competition. A group of organizations completely sheltered from competition may engage in imitation and vicarious learning of many different types, for example. We argue that the constructs are distinct and can be considered separately from each other.

Imitation, then, represents a distinct potential engine of selection not already subsumed under work on competition. The question remains, of course, whether imitation really matters as an en-

gine of selection of routines enacted in populations of organizations. Campbell called for a very general theory of selection at all levels of analysis, drawing on variation-selection-retention models. We think the many plausible contingency factors that can moderate the population effects of interorganizational imitation suggest that it may be premature to develop such a general theory. At the same time, the many plausible models of three simple imitation modes that generate varied outcomes make it seem very likely that imitation does work as a force for the selection of routines. If organizations also draw inferences by observing others, interorganizational imitation could produce even more complex outcomes. Taken as a whole, then, we believe that prior investigations imply that imitation represents a powerful, ubiquitous, and non-obvious engine of selection of routines in populations of organizations. Only further empirical research can answer the question of exactly how powerful and how ubiquitous an engine it is, and we look forward to learning the results of such work.

References

Abrahamson, E., & Rosenkopf, L. (1993). Institutional and competitive bandwagons: Using mathematical modeling as a tool to explore diffusion of innovation. *Academy of Management Review, 18*(3), 487-517.

Aldrich, H. E. (1979). *Organizations and environments.* Englewood Cliffs, NJ: Prentice Hall.

Anderson, P. (1998, June). *How does the mix of routines in a population change? Technology choice in the American cement industry.* Paper presented at the Carnegie-Wisconsin Conference on Knowledge Transfer and Levels of Learning, Carnegie Mellon University, Pittsburgh, PA.

Argote, L., Beckman, S. L., & Epple, D. (1990). The persistence and transfer of learning in industrial settings. *Management Science, 36,* 140-154.

Arthur, W. B. (1989). Competing technologies, increasing returns, and lock-in by historical events: The dynamics of allocation under increasing returns. *Economic Journal, 99,* 116-131.

Arthur, B. W., & Lane, D. A. (1994). Information contagion. In W. B. Arthur (Ed.), *Increasing returns and path dependence in the economy* (pp. 69-98). Ann Arbor: University of Michigan Press.

Bascom, W. R. (1948). Ponapae prestige economy. *Southwestern Journal of Anthropology, 4,* 211-221.

Baum, J.A.C. (in press). Competitive and institutional isomorphism in organizational populations. In D. L. Jones & W. W. Powell (Eds.), *Frontiers in institutional analysis*. Chicago: University of Chicago Press.

Baum, J.A.C., & Singh, J. V. (1994). Organizational hierarchies and evolutionary processes: Some reflections on a theory of organizational evolution. In J.A.C. Baum & J. V. Singh (Eds.), *Evolutionary dynamics of organizations* (pp. 3-20). New York: Oxford University Press.

Bell, A. M. (1997). *Locally interdependent preferences in a general equilibrium environment* (Working paper No. 97-WO2). Department of Economics and Business Administration, Vanderbilt University.

Biddle, J. (1991). A bandwagon effect of personalized license plates? *Economic Inquiry, 29*, 375-388.

Boyd, R., & Richerson, P. J. (1985). *Culture and the evolutionary process*. Chicago: The University of Chicago, Burns Press.

Burns, L. R., & Wholey, D. (1993). Adoption and abandonment of matrix management programs: Effects of organizational characteristics and interorganizational networks. *Academy of Management Journal, 38*, 106-138.

Campbell, D. T. (1960). Blind variation and selective retention in creative thought of knowledge processes. *Psychological Review, 67*, 380-400.

Campbell, D. T. (1969). Variation and selective retention in socio-cultural evolution. *General Systems, 14*, 69-85.

Campbell, D. T. (1990). Epistemological roles for selection theory. In N. Rescher (Ed.), *Evolution, cognition and realism* (pp. 1-19). Lanham, MD: University Press of America.

Campbell, D. T. (1994). How individual and face-to-face-group selection undermines firm selection in organizational evolution. In J.A.C. Baum & J. V. Singh (Eds.), *Evolutionary dynamics of organizations* (pp. 23-38). New York: Oxford University Press.

Connell, C., & Cohn, S. (1995). Learning from other people's actions: Environmental variation and diffusion in French coal mining strikes, 1890-1935. *American Journal of Sociology, 101*, 366-403.

Dickson, P. (1998). *A general theory of competitive rationality*. Unpublished manuscript, A. C. Nielsen Center for Marketing Research, School of Business, University of Wisconsin–Madison.

DiMaggio, P. J. (1988). Interest and agency in institutional theory. In L. G. Zucker (Ed.), *Institutional patterns and organizations: Environment and culture* (pp. 3-21). Cambridge, MA: Ballinger.

DiMaggio, P. J., & Powell, W. W. (1983). The iron cage revisited: Institutional isomorphism and collective rationality in organizational fields. *American Sociological Review, 48*, 147-160.

DiMaggio, P. J., & Powell, W. W. (1991). Introduction. In W. W. Powell & P. DiMaggio (Eds.), *The new institutionalism in organizational analysis* (pp. 1-38). Chicago: University of Chicago Press.

Dosi, G., Ermoliev, Y., & Kaniovsky, Y. (1994). Generalized urn schemes and technological dynamics. *Journal of Mathematical Economics, 23*, 1-19.

Farrell, J., & Saloner, G. (1985). Standardization, compatibility and innovation. *Rand Journal of Economics, 16*(1), 70-83.

Fligstein, N. (1985). The spread of the multidivisional form among large firms, 1919-1979. *American Sociological Review, 50*, 377-391.

Griliches, Z. (1957). Hybrid corn: An exploration in economics of technological change. *Econometrica, 25*, 501-522.

Handy, E.S.G., & Handy, W. C. (1924). Samoan house building, canoeing and tattooing. *Bernice P. Bishop Museum Bulletin, 15*, 270-271.

Haunschild, P. R. (1993). Interorganizational imitation: The impact of interlocks on corporate acquisition activity. *Administrative Science Quarterly, 38*, 564-592.

Haunschild, P. R., & Miner, A. S. (1997). Modes of interorganizational imitation: The effects of outcome salience and uncertainty. *Administrative Science Quarterly, 42*, 472-500.

Henshel, R. L., & Johnston, W. (1987). The emergence of bandwagon effects. *Sociological Quarterly, 28*(4), 493-511.

Herbig, P. A. (1991). A cusp catastrophe model of the adoption of an industrial innovation. *Journal of Product Innovation Management, 8*, 127-137.

Hershey, R. L., Asch, D. A., Thumasathit, T., Meszaros, J., & Waters, V. V. (1994). The roles of altruism, free riding, and bandwagoning in vaccination decisions. *Organizational Behavior and Human Decision Processes, 59*(2), 177-187.

Kapur, S. (1995). Technological diffusion with social learning. *The Journal of Industrial Economics, 43*, 173-195.

Kauffman, S. A. (1993). *The origins of order: Self-organization and selection in evolution*. New York: Oxford University Press.

Kraatz, M. (1995, August). *The role of interorganizational networks in shaping strategic adaptation: Evidence from liberal arts colleges*. Paper presented at the Academy of Management meetings, Vancouver.

Lane, D., & Vescovini, R. (1996). Decision rules and market share: Aggregation in an information contagion model. *Industrial and Corporate Change, 5*(1), 127-146.

Lant, T., & Phelps, C. (1998, June). *The coevolution of learning in competitive groups*. Paper presented at the Carnegie-Wisconsin Conference on Knowledge Transfer and Levels of Learning, Carnegie Mellon University, Pittsburgh, PA.

Lumsden, C. J., & Wilson, O. E. (1981). *Genes, mind and culture: The coevolutionary process*. Cambridge, MA: Harvard University Press.

Mansfield, E. (1968). *Industrial research and technological innovation, an econometric analysis*. New York: Norton.

McKelvey, B., & Aldrich, H. E. (1983). Populations, natural selection, and applied organizational science. *Administrative Science Quarterly, 28*, 101-128.

Meyer, J., & Rowan, B. E. (1977). Institutionalized organizations: Formal structure as myth and ceremony. *American Sociological Review, 83*, 340-363.

Mezias, S. J., & Lant, T. K. (1994). Mimetic learning and the evolution of organizational populations. In J.A.C. Baum &

J. V. Singh (Eds.), *Evolutionary dynamics of organizations* (pp. 179-198). New York: Oxford University Press.

Miner, A. S., & Haunschild, P. (1995). Population level learning. *Research in Organizational Behavior, 17*, 115-166.

Miner, A. S., Kim, J., Holzinger, I., & Haunschild, P. (1998, June). *Fruits of failure: Organizational failure and population level learning.* Paper presented at the Carnegie-Wisconsin Conference on Knowledge Transfer and Levels of Learning, Carnegie Mellon University, Pittsburgh, PA.

Narduzzo, A., & Warglien, M. (1996). Learning from the experience of others: An experiment on information contagion. *Industrial and Corporate Change, 5*(1), 113-126.

Palmer, D., Jennings, P. D., & Zhou, X. (1993). Late adoption of the multidivisional form by large U.S. corporations: Institutional, political and economic accounts. *Administrative Science Quarterly, 38*, 100-131.

Rogers, E. (1995). *Diffusion of innovations* (4th ed.). New York: Free Press.

Sharif, M. N., & Ramanathan, K. (1982). Polynomial innovation diffusion models. *Technological Forecasting and Social Change, 21*, 301-323.

Sober, E. (1984). *The nature of selection.* Chicago: The University of Chicago Press.

Tolbert, P. S., & Zucker, L. G. (1983). Institutional sources of change in the formal structure of organizations: The diffusion of civil service reform, 1880-1935. *Administrative Science Quarterly, 28*, 22-39.

Wade, J. (1995). Dynamics of organizational communities and technological bandwagons: An empirical investigation of community evolution in the microprocessor market. *Strategic Management Journal, 16*(Summer), 111-133.

Walker, J. L. (1971). Innovation in state policies. In H. Jacob & K. N. Vines (Eds.), *Politics in the American states: A comparative analysis* (pp. 358-381). Boston: Little, Brown.

Wilkening, E. A. (1952). *Acceptance of improved farm practices in three coastal plain counties* (Technical Bulletin #98). Raleigh: North Carolina Agricultural Experimental Station.

Ziegler, C. A. (1985). Innovation and the imitative entrepreneur. *Journal of Economic Behavior and Organization, 6*, 103-121.

Zucker, L. G. (1988). Where do institutional patterns come from? In L. G. Zucker (Ed.), *Institutional patterns and organizations: Environment and culture* (pp. 23-52). Cambridge, MA: Ballinger.

Chapter 4

Types of Variation in Organizational Populations

The Speciation of New Organizational Forms

HAYAGREEVA RAO
JITENDRA V. SINGH

In his seminal essay, Campbell (1965a) stated that

> for an evolutionary process to take place there need to be variations (as by mutation, trial, etc.), stable aspects of the environment differentially selecting among such variations and a retention-propagation system rigidly holding on to the selected variations. *The variation and retention system(s) are inherently at odds. Every new mutation represents a failure of reproduction of prior selected forms.* Too high a mutation jeopardizes the preservation of already achieved adaptations. There arise in evolutionary systems mechanisms for curbing the variation rate. The more elaborate the achieved adaptation, the more likely are mutations to be deleterious and, therefore, the stronger are inhibitions on mutation. (pp. 306-307; italics added)

In this chapter, we take Campbell's idea that new mutations represent failed forms as a point of departure. We explore how new organizational forms are built *with* (the ruins of) existing organizational forms rather than *on* (the ruins of) old organizational forms. We use the notion of building with the ruins of existing forms, noted elsewhere by Stark (1996), to emphasize recombination and bricolage (Douglas, 1986), that is, the recombination of existing stock repertoires of structures, technologies, and ideas. By doing so, we aim to unpack sources of variation in organizational populations.

We begin by focusing on organizational speciation (Lumsden & Singh, 1990; Rao & Singh, in press)—the creation of new forms—as one important source of variation in organizational populations. We review different approaches toward the

AUTHORS' NOTE: We thank Howard Aldrich, Joel Baum, Paul DiMaggio, Dick Scott, and Sid Winter for helpful suggestions.

classification of organizational forms and briefly discuss how different theories of organization rely on diverse classification approaches when defining forms. We suggest that new organizational forms and species entail discontinuities in the core features of organizations. Thereafter, we distinguish between strong and weak speciation and note how speciation differs from imitative entrepreneurship. We draw on *cultural-frame institutional* models to explore how new forms are built with the ruins of existing forms by entrepreneurs primarily through recombination of organizing elements from extant organizational forms. Finally, we advance a typology of variations in organizational forms and conclude this chapter by highlighting the role of institutional selection in the creation of new organizational forms.

Speciation of New Organizational Forms as a Source of Variation

The rise of new forms can be viewed properly as an organizational counterpart to the biological phenomenon of speciation (Lumsden & Singh, 1990; Rao & Singh, in press). Speciation is an important form of variation by which new organizational assemblages come into existence, and it plays a vital role in the evolution of organizational diversity. New organizational forms are novel recombinations of goals, authority relations (including governance structures), technologies, and client markets. Novel organizational forms matter because they instantiate organizational diversity. The ability of societies to respond to social problems may even hinge on the diversity of organizational forms, and, in the long run, in a fluid environment, diversity can be maintained or increased by the rise of new forms (Hannan & Freeman, 1989, p. 3). Moreover, new forms are consequential motors of evolution—indeed, an important piece of organizational change, at the macrolevel, consists of the replacement of existing organizational forms by new organizational forms (Aldrich, 1998; Schumpeter, 1950). Furthermore, because new organizational forms are structural incarnations of beliefs, values, and norms, they emerge in tandem with new institutions and foster cultural change in so-

cieties (Scott, 1995; Stinchcombe, 1965). For these reasons, where new organizational forms come from is one of the central questions of organizational theory (see Singh, 1993).

What Are New Organizational Forms?

McKelvey (1982) asserts that classification is an essential precondition for the rigorous understanding of speciation and, by implication, variation in organizational populations. There is considerable disagreement, however, on how to define organizational forms (or organizational species). The multiple definitions of organizational forms in the literature are premised on different approaches to classification. We first review approaches to classification and then discuss the definition of organizational forms.

A system of classification needs to recognize sharp discontinuities among the objects classified, show high homogeneity within classes, be stable, and show relationships between objects and their ancestors (see McKelvey, 1982, pp. 35-65). There are two types of classifications—special and general. *Special classifications* group objects together on the basis of a small number of attributes of interest to researchers. For example, a health care researcher can classify hospitals into hospitals attached to medical schools and hospitals devoid of connections to medical schools. Special classifications have high predictive validity but pertain to a very small portion of organizations. One approach for generating special classifications is *essentialism*, under which entities are organized on the basis of a small set of essential, unchanging taxonomic characters. An alternative is *nominalism*, under which entities are grouped according to attributes of interest for research purposes.

In contrast, a *general classification* aspires to group organizations on the basis of all attributes, with different weights given to different attributes. General classifications aim to identify homogeneous populations, present a framework for describing diversity, aid in the handling of complex sets of variables, and serve as a matrix for organizing research findings (McKelvey, 1982, pp. 15-17). One example of general classification is *numerical* classification, which attempts to group entities on the basis of most, if not all, known attributes. Finally, *evolutionist* classification holds that organizational species are polythetic groups of competence-sharing populations isolated from one another because their dominant competencies are not easily learned or transmitted.

Essentialist and Nominalist Approaches

Numerous contingency researchers, organizational economists, and ecologists have relied on essentialist typologies, wherein a very few key, unchanging taxonomic characters are used as the basis for classifications. In some cases, ecological researchers have also used nominalist approaches, wherein the definition of forms changes according to the research question.

Thus, *contingency researchers* have described organizational forms as structural arrangements to organize intraorganizational task interdependencies to cope with environmental contingencies (e.g., Thompson, 1967). Some contingency researchers identify different forms as discrete alternatives to decision makers seeking to reduce uncertainty (Galbraith & Kazanjian, 1986). Others take more of a gestalt view, identifying different archetypal authority structures in organizations, ranging from the simple bureaucracy to the machine bureaucracy to the ad-hocracy, that bundle together with other elements like strategy and technology in gestalt-like wholes (e.g., Burns & Stalker, 1961; Mintzberg, 1990).

Organizational economists have also identified different types of governance arrangements as responses to problems of uncertainty. Agency theorists have focused on how ownership and management are combined in organizations, ranging from partnerships to nonprofit firms, to address uncertainties in the principal-agent relationship (Fama & Jensen, 1983). Transaction cost economists have emphasized how transaction costs are minimized by hierarchical arrangements ranging from the holding company to the multidivisional firm (Williamson, 1975). In recent years, transaction cost theorists have begun to distinguish among a variety of hybrid forms that commingle elements of markets and hierarchy (Williamson, 1985).

Empirical research by *organizational ecologists* also leans on essentialist typologies and, in some cases, nominalist ideas. Hannan and Freeman (1977, 1989) posed the influential question of why there are so many different kinds of organizations and considered various approaches to defining organizational forms. They rejected a "forms as genes" metaphor in favor of a simpler, more pragmatic definition. The approach they took rested on an isomorphism between forms and populations (or the duality of niches and forms). Thus, organizational forms inhabit populations of organizations, and populations were defined as aggregates of organizations that were similar in some respect; that is, they had some unitary character (e.g., restaurants, trade unions). Moreover, ecological research also acknowledges distinctions within populations; for example, a population of restaurants (see Freeman & Hannan, 1983) would comprise both specialist and generalist restaurants, or a population of labor unions would contain both craft and industrial labor union forms (Hannan & Freeman, 1987). Ecologists have also drawn on nominalist ideas and tied the definitions of populations to research questions (e.g., mutual banks as a population).

Numerical and Evolutionist Approaches

Early on, there also was an interest in numerical approaches to organization. For example, Haas, Hall, and Johnson (1966) studied 75 organizations and used 99 characteristics as the basis of comparison. Pugh, Hickson, and Hinings (1969) used 16 characteristics to factor analyze 46 organizations. Since then, students of strategic groups have used different criteria to isolate the existence of subgroups in industries. Numerical approaches have fallen into disfavor because of poor weights given to characteristics, the lack of a good way to discriminate between trivial and significant differences, and arbitrary choices made by researchers.

McKelvey (1982) favored evolutionist approaches to classification and defined an organizational species as a polythetic group of competence-sharing populations isolated from others because its dominant competencies are not easily learned or transmitted. Although this is a useful beginning, the construct of dominant competencies may not give us sufficient leverage to define new forms concretely. One might ask, what are dominant competencies, and how does one identify them? McKelvey (1982) defines them as unit operations, workplace interdependencies, control systems, internal differentiation, and vertical and horizontal layering. Put simply, dominant competencies consist of all techno-administrative capabilities and constitute a comprehensive catchall list. We believe that, in spite of the strength of this view of dominant competencies in focusing interest on more genetic aspects of organizational form, there may be a need for a more precise and concrete notion of how one form might differ from another.

Core and Peripheral Features and Organizational Forms

A useful starting point for understanding discontinuities between organizational forms is the distinction between core and peripheral properties of organizational forms. Core features include goals, authority relations, technologies, and markets (Hannan & Freeman, 1984; Scott, 1995), and they vary in the ease with which they can be changed. At one extreme, goals are the innermost core feature of organizational forms and are the hardest to modify. At the other extreme, markets are relatively less deep in the core and are easier to change. Peripheral features refer to all other attributes.

Organizational forms constitute polythetic groupings, in that members of the form share common core characteristics but may differ with respect to peripheral features. Hence, one form or species differs from another primarily according to core characteristics of the form. The core features listed by Scott define a four-dimensional space in which new organizational forms appear or disappear over time. An advantage of focusing on core features is that they provide a parsimonious list of the dimensions on which an organizational form can differ from incumbent forms. The four features also can show how an organizational form is connected to ancestor forms. Moreover, the four core features also direct attention to the processes by which discontinuities in the bundling of goals,

authority, technology, and marketing strategies arise.

Elsewhere (Rao & Singh, in press), we have discussed the early automobile and biotechnology industries as exemplars of new organizational forms. The early American automobile industry, for example, was a new organizational form that constituted a strong departure from its precursor, the horse carriage industry. In contrast to the horse carriage industry, the automobile industry's goal was to develop horseless vehicles of transportation. Moreover, automobile firms used a completely different set of technologies based on steam, gasoline, and electric power to provide customers with horseless carriages. Furthermore, early automobile firms also differed from the horse carriage industry in the structure of authority: Unlike horse carriage firms that were one-man operations, early automobile firms were assemblers that put together bought-out components. Finally, early automobile firms also catered to a different class of customers: The early purchasers of automobiles were physicians who needed mobility and auto enthusiasts (Flink, 1970).

Some other instances of new organizational forms include the multidivisional form (Williamson, 1975), health maintenance organizations (HMOs), biotechnology firms, and firms engaged in electronic commerce on the World Wide Web, such as the bookstore Amazon.com. The multidivisional form, at the time of its origin earlier in this century (Chandler, 1972), was novel primarily in terms of authority relations, although the various divisions functioning as independent companies were able to address broader scope than the precursor functional form organization. In contrast, HMOs represent a relatively radical departure in health care delivery in large part because of the salience of the cost containment goal, although differences undoubtedly are involved in authority relations and markets served as well. Earlier, the cost containment goal usually was not the primary objective in health care provision. Biotechnology firms represent novelty primarily in the use of new technologies such as recombinant DNA and hybridoma applied to both new and existing markets (diseases, crops, bioremediation) and novel alliance-based structural arrangements with universities for research and development. Electronic commerce firms are novel mainly in the use of Web-based commerce and have a virtual existence and novel authority relations.

Weak and Strong Speciation

It should be clear from the examples above that not all new organizational forms are equivalent. Arguably, a new form differs strongly from preexisting forms when it is different from the precursor form in terms of all four core features—goals, authority relations, technology, and served markets. We think it is useful to characterize such new forms as examples of *strong speciation*. Naturally, distinctions between new and old forms weaken when differences exist only in terms of markets or technologies, for example. *Weak speciation* occurs when the new form differs from existing ones on only one or two less core dimensions. Strategic groups in an industry, wherein served markets or technologies typically serve as mobility barriers and impede homogeneity across groups, can illustrate weak speciation. For example, in the hotel industry, luxury hotels differ from budget hotels on the dimensions of customer base (market served) and the technology of service.

We think this definition of organizational forms as novel recombinations of goals, authority relations, technologies, and markets provides a useful template for thinking about new organizational forms. The distinction between strong and weak speciation suggests that boundary dynamics play a central role in the rise of new organizational forms. When segregating mechanisms are uniformly stronger than blending mechanisms, strong speciation is the outcome, but when blending mechanisms weaken segregating pressure, then weak speciation is the outcome.

Hannan and Freeman (1989, pp. 45-65) proposed that segregating mechanisms separate organizations into distinct forms (they reify differences) and identified four main forces driving the segregation of organizational forms. First, technological factors create differences between organizational forms; gaps between organizational forms appear because certain combinations of goals, control structures, marketing strategies, and modes of production are inconsistent technologically. Second, closure of social networks segregates organizational forms through inbreeding; that is, sets of organizations hire employees from the same educational or training institutions or hire each other's employees. Inbreeding yields the development and diffusion of idiosyncratic language, culture, knowledge, and practices throughout any circumscribed organizational population and so separates it from other populations. Third, successful collective action on behalf of a group of organizations, such as organizations in some industry creating a lobbying association or organizations in some region working together on some legal issue that threatens all of them, creates distinctions between those engaged in collective action and those not so engaged. Fourth, various institutional processes erect boundaries between organizational forms. Powerful institutional actors may endorse the claim of a particular organizational form in disputes with other forms. In another institutional segregation process, organizational forms may become taken for granted as the natural way to effect some kind of collective activity. In both cases of institutionally driven segregation, arbitrary differences between organizations become transformed into differences with real social consequences, so that nominal classifications become substantive (Hannan & Freeman, 1989, p. 57).

Blending mechanisms, however, may also weaken segregating pressures and lead to weak speciation (Hannan & Freeman, 1989, pp. 57-60). First, random or unintentional drift in established organizations can erase boundaries between organizational forms. Such random drift results from the accumulation of many small, unintended changes in procedures or routines, and it is accelerated by personnel turnover. Second, planned recombination of existing routines and structures into new packages also can cause the blending of organizational forms. Recombination of routines and structures can be brought about through imitation of similar or superior organizations through merger and acquisition, or through participation in joint ventures, joint operating agreements, and other strategic alliances that open organizations to novel external influences. Third, deinstitutionalization can erase distinctions between organizational forms; this is the converse of institutionalization creating distinctions between forms.

Research on hybridization suggests that weak speciation can arise when blending mechanisms dominate. Stark (1996) analyzed the inducements for entrepreneurs to construct hybrid organizations and institutions. He concluded that entrepreneurs build new organizations with the ruins of existing organizational forms, rather than on the ruins of these forms (Stark, 1996, p. 995). He contended that entrepreneurs mate different ideological principles to deal with uncertainty and hedge against unforeseen evaluation contingencies. In particular, Stark (1996) found that the boundaries between forms of enterprise in the countries he studied are blurred by cross-ownership, which functions as a form of hedging against technical and market uncertainties.

Another example of how blending mechanisms lead to weak speciation is provided by Haveman and Rao (in press) in their account of hybridization in the California thrift industry. They reported that entrepreneurs built new hybrid forms of savings and loan associations that combined elements of two or more existing organizational forms to deal with technical and institutional uncertainty. They argued that the new forms created through deliberate recombination increased diversity in the population.

Speciation Versus Imitative Entrepreneurship

Our analysis of weak and strong speciation suggests that a noteworthy aspect of speciation is that it represents the first instance of the creation of a new form (Lumsden & Singh, 1990). Thus, it is very different from imitative entrepreneurship, wherein potential founders emulate a new form that already exists. The large literature on density dependence in the founding process refers more to the imitation of the first instance of a form (Hannan & Carroll, 1992; Hannan & Freeman, 1989) than to the speciation of the form itself. There is a crucial difference between the first instance of a new form, the act of speciation, and the emulation of a new form, imitative entrepreneurship. Building the institutional context and institutional entrepreneurship, including but not limited to acquiring legiti-

macy, is a more crucial issue for speciation. Because the first instance of a new form represents an innovation, it requires successful integration into the prevalent social order for it to be viable. This echoes Campbell's (1965b) observation that variation and retention are at odds, and that evolutionary systems possess mechanisms to curb variations so as not to undermine the prevalent social structures.

Our speciation versus imitative entrepreneurship distinction echoes Aldrich and Kenworthy's (this volume) distinction between reproducer and innovator forms. A growing literature suggests that imitation is also central in the building of new organizations. Aldrich and Kenworthy suggest that most new organizations are "reproducers" that copy existing forms because entrepreneurs use simple imitation rules. At one extreme of reproduction, organizations create branches that account for 25% of all new foundings (Aldrich, Kalleberg, Marsden, & Cassell, 1989). At the other extreme of reproduction, organizations can create subsidiaries and business units in different lines of business. In both cases, resource constraints are fewer because the parent firm provides support, and the pre-organizing period is also shorter because of the availability of templates for copying (Aldrich, 1998).

Imitative entrepreneurship ensues when actors engage in frequency-based imitation and copy actions taken by large numbers of individuals. Alternatively, actors can engage in trait-based imitation, wherein they imitate a subset of models based on specific traits. In some cases, similarity of traits can be the basis on which role models are chosen. Finally, actors can also copy models on the basis of outcomes (Haunschild & Miner, 1997).

It is important to note that imitation by itself need not lead to homogeneity. Miner and Raghavan (this volume) show that all four copying rules need not necessarily produce convergence to a single routine. Several types of factors can influence whether imitation leads to convergence or not, and what patterns results. These include (a) features of the imitating agents (e.g., the weights they give to the other agents they imitate), (b) processes agents use while imitating (e.g., how to weigh choices made by multiple others), (c) the context in which the imitation occurs (e.g., the degree of heterogeneity in prior adoptions, starting variance of routines in the population, or number of competitors present), and (d) the nature of the link between routines and their observed outcomes (e.g., ambiguous or not). Lomi and Larsen (this volume) extend these ideas when they show that if individual agents have spatial extension, population-level heterogeneity will emerge even in the absence of any individual difference in identities or strategies. Their emphasis on the granularity and spatial extension of the organizational world implies that the structure and dynamics of social networks mediate the extent of homogeneity within a population.

An Institutional Perspective on Organizational Speciation

It is only recently that organizational theorists have begun to analyze the origins of new organizational forms. The *random variation* perspective is premised on biological evolutionary models and holds that realized variations in organizational forms are random. Proponents of this view suggest that new forms arise when search routines lead to modifications of operating routines (Nelson & Winter, 1982), or when a small group of competence-sharing organizations is isolated and finds a favorable resource environment (McKelvey, 1982). Despite its appeal, the random variation perspective is of limited use because it is difficult empirically to identify competencies and routines. Another major drawback is that this perspective is silent on the specific processes that generate variations and on the content of variations. A third drawback is that variations may be outcomes of systematic rather than random processes—a point developed by institutional theorists of organizations (DiMaggio & Powell, 1991; Meyer & Rowan, 1977).

The *constrained variation* perspective asserts that conditions in the environment predictably foster or diminish variations in organizational forms. Its different versions emphasize creative destruction through technological innovation (Schumpeter, 1950; Tushman & Anderson, 1986); environmental imprinting, wherein social conditions at the time of founding limit organizational inventions

(Kimberly, 1975; Stinchcombe, 1965); and depiction of existing organizations as producers of new organizational forms (Brittain & Freeman, 1982; Lumsden & Singh, 1990). A key premise common to all versions of the constrained variation perspective is that the existence of unfilled ecological niches—that is, places unoccupied by other organizational forms—is an important precondition for the birth of new organizational forms. Proponents of the constrained variation perspective differ, however, with respect to the antecedents of resource spaces. On one hand, models of creative destruction hold that the demise of existing organizations frees up resources for new organizations. On the other hand, models of environmental imprinting stress the importance of political upheavals and entrepreneurs' access to wealth and power, labor markets, and the protective role of the state (see Aldrich, 1979, 1998). By contrast, those who portray existing organizations as producers of new organizations hold that interrelations among existing organizations influence the branching of new resource spaces (Carroll, 1985) and the ability of existing organizations to exploit new resource spaces (Romanelli, 1989). Although the constrained variation perspective usefully emphasizes the primacy of resource spaces, its drawback is that resources do not preexist as pools of free-floating assets, but have to be mobilized through opportunistic and collective efforts (Van de Ven & Garud, 1989). Another drawback is that the constrained variation perspective elides how entrepreneurs imbue formal structures with norms, values, and beliefs during the process of resource mobilization.

The *cultural-frame institutional* perspective complements the constrained variation perspective and proposes that new organizational forms arise when actors with sufficient resources see in them an opportunity to realize interests that they value highly. A core premise is that the creation of all new organizational forms requires work on an institutional agenda wherein the theory and values underpinning the form are legitimized by institutional entrepreneurs (DiMaggio, 1988; Scott, 1995). In this perspective, institutional projects can arise from either organized politics or social movements. Organized politics can resemble social movements to the extent that resources and interests are not fixed and the rules governing inter-action are contested (Fligstein, 1996a, p. 5; Have-man & Rao, 1997; Rao, 1998). Cultural-frame institutional accounts of speciation suggest that human agency and interests play a central in the birth of new forms. Human agency is centrally involved in the speciation process in the guise of "foolish" (March & Olsen, 1976), though intend-edly rational, entrepreneurs.

Entrepreneurs, Recombination, and New Forms

Entrepreneurs devise new recombinations of core features—goals, authority, technology, and marketing strategies. They create forms at different locations in the four-dimensional space where each of the core features is a dimension. Although indi-vidual entrepreneurial sagas of either heroism or failure may well get written at one level, the real contribution of entrepreneurs is to broaden the search for new organizational forms into regions of the form space that might otherwise have gone unexplored.[1] Sometimes this entrepreneurial search in form space can hit one of the "hot points" in the space, and this results in speciation (the current plethora of experimentation on viable ways to do commerce on the World Wide Web illustrates well this notion).

The emphasis on foolish though intendedly rational entrepreneurs echoes Campbell's (1965b) emphasis on "blind" variation. In his numerous writings, Campbell (1988) observed that "Being a purposeful problem solver, or a sub-cultural tradi-tion of purposeful problem solvers, does not make one clairvoyant or prescient" (p. 173) and declared that increasing knowledge or adaptation of neces-sity involves exploring the unknown, going beyond existing knowledge and adaptive recipes. This of necessity involves unknowing, non-preadapted fumbling in the dark (see Romanelli, this volume).

It is also important to say more about the process by which entrepreneurs arrive at variations in forms. Institutional analysts of organizations em-phasize recombination of existing templates by entrepreneurs as the source of variation. Swidler (1986) portrays entrepreneurs as users of existing repertoires who select from a menu of cultural items and design structures that recombine estab-lished ones. New forms, as Stark (1996) points out, are built with the ruins of existing forms rather than on the ruins of existing forms. Douglas (1986, p. 67) summarizes the process of building with the ruins of existing arrangements as follows:

> Like so much bric-a-brac, these proto-theoretical pieces lie around to be pressed into service. . . . Levi-Strauss (1962) invented the image of the thinker as bricoleur, the amateur craftsman who turns the broken clock into a pipe rack, the broken table into an um-brella stand, the umbrella stand into a lamp, and anything into something else. The bricoleur uses everything there is to make transformations within a stock repertoire of furnishings. . . . Bricolage [is] a form of institutional thinking to problems of . . . choice.

The creation of new forms through recombina-tion implies that structure shapes action and in turn, action shapes structure (DiMaggio & Powell, 1991; Friedland & Alford, 1991). Douglas (1986) notes: "People are tempted out of their niches by new possibilities of exercising or evading control. Then they make up new institutions, and the insti-tutions make new labels, and the label makes new people" (p. 108). Preexisting routines are, there-fore, the building blocks with which entrepreneurs build new forms.

Perhaps a quite clear, if somewhat abstract, il-lustration of recombination is shown in Bruderer and Singh's (1996) genetic algorithm–based ap-proach to modeling firm evolution. In their view, organizational forms can be conceptualized as or-dered bit strings of 1s and 0s, corresponding re-spectively to the presence and absence of certain features. Recombination occurs through the com-bined effects of the crossover and mutation opera-tions. Whereas the mutation operation involves changes akin to random error, the crossover opera-tion involves half of one bit string combining with half of another bit string to create a new bit string representing a different form. Of course, not all recombinations survive the forces of selection. Given the shape of the fitness landscape, some recombinations that have higher fitness than others not only survive but also eventually spread through the population as others imitate their success. The role of recombination is to generate more variations in the population of forms. Together with selection, this enables search for regions of the form space with higher fitness values.

The notion of recombination of preexisting routines by entrepreneurs implies that builders of new forms shortcut natural selection pressures because of what Campbell (1965b) labeled as vicarious selection. For Campbell (1965b), vicarious selection meant that knowledge functions as a selector vicariously anticipating selection by the environment. Once "fit" knowledge has been retained in the form of preexisting templates, the templates can accelerate or catalyze selection, and thus can be said to anticipate, or to vicariously represent, the naturally selected configuration. Thus, anticipatory selectors select possible actions of the system in function of the system's goal (ultimately survival) and the situation of the environment. By eliminating dangerous or inadequate actions before they are executed, the vicarious selector forgoes selection by the environment and thus increases the chances for survival of the system. The organization of vicarious selectors is a "nested hierarchy": A retained selector itself can undergo variation and selection by another selector, at a higher hierarchical level. This allows the development of multilevel cognitive organization, leading to ever more intelligent and adaptive systems.

How retained knowledge is stored and organized, and the different criteria that determine which pieces of knowledge will be selected and which ones will be eliminated, influence the content and trajectory of variation. From an institutional perspective, each routine or piece of knowledge is connected with values, beliefs, and master logics. As a result, when rival bands of entrepreneurs select different pieces of knowledge, values, and beliefs and combine them into a form, there may be conflict between competing coalitions of entrepreneurs (Friedland & Alford, 1991).

A Typology of Recombination

As discussed above, processes of recombination play a central role in generating variation among organizational forms, and entrepreneurs often are active agents generating such variations. We think that not all recombinations are identical. We also believe it is useful to distinguish between different types of recombinations and the institutional challenges involved in creating instances of different recombinations. We turn next to this question.

Recombinations involve pieces of different existing organizational forms (Bruderer & Singh, 1996). Most generally, recombination involves working with primitive entities called *organizing elements,* These are stable subassemblies that provide the raw materials for form creation. These may be routines, capabilities, templates for structure or governance, decision-making processes, or other elements of an organizational form.

A simple typology of recombination can be useful in focusing attention on the quite different organizing demands that are placed by different kinds of recombinations. Salancik and Leblebici (1988) argue that several possible forms can be created by rearranging transactions in different ways, and they urge researchers to pay attention to the grammar of organizing. Thus, recombination of existing arrangements is the source of diversity.

A useful way to extend Salancik and Leblebici's (1988) idea is to delineate how a recombination of existing forms may occur under different circumstances. Entrepreneurs may delete existing organizing elements from extant organizational forms or add new organizing elements. Alternatively, they can both add and delete organizing elements or neither add nor delete organizing elements. In the last case, when neither addition nor deletion of organizing elements is involved, the new organization emulates the preexisting organizational form and is, therefore, a case of imitative entrepreneurship. Table 4.1 demonstrates all these four possibilities.

The upper left-hand cell of the matrix refers to the case of imitative entrepreneurship. Once a new form has been created, other instances of the same organizational form, including the mutations that may occur in the copying process, belong here. Thus, all followers of Borders, the recombination of a mega-bookstore and coffee shop, or all imitators of Amazon.com, an e-commerce role model in bookselling (and more generally, retailing on-line),

TABLE 4.1 A Recombination Typology of New
Organizational Forms

	No addition of organizing elements	*Addition of new organizing elements*
No deletion of organizing elements	Imitative entrepreneurship (followers of Borders)	Partial enlargement (hospitals entering managed care)
Deletion of organizing elements	Partial contraction of elements (point-to-point airlines)	Radical recombination (health maintenance organizations or HMOs)

belong here. Although mutation may, on occasion (though with low probability), lead to the creation of major variations in form, this usually is not the case. The upper right-hand cell of the matrix involves the addition of some organizing elements but not the deletion of existing organizing elements. We refer to this cell as the partial enlargement mode of recombination. Examples of such recombination are leading business schools getting actively involved in executive education (including executive MBA programs) or, more recently, hospitals getting involved in the managed care business. The lower left-hand cell involves the deletion of some elements and no addition of new elements. We refer to this cell as the partial contraction mode of recombination. An example of such a recombination may be no frills, cut-rate airlines. Such airlines compete primarily on price (e.g., Southwest Airlines or the late, departed People Express) and do not have the service, in-flight, or baggage handling elements that usually are part of a regular, full-service airline. Finally, the lower right-hand cell involves both the addition and deletion of organizing elements. We refer to this cell as radical recombination. We believe the institutional demands from such recombinations are the most taxing. An illustration of such a recombination may be health maintenance organizations (HMOs). On one hand, HMOs add the elements that come with a profit orientation and greater cost consciousness, such as preventive care and careful review of referrals to specialists. On the other hand, routine access to high-tech diagnostic procedures and the avail-

ability of significant discretion to physicians typically are curtailed in HMOs.

We believe the organizing challenges are likely to be the greatest in the last of these cells, although even imitative entrepreneurship is unlikely to be entirely trivial. It is also likely that radical recombination will see most of the category-killer innovations that are often accompanied by significant profit streams, provided that the organizing challenges are successfully met. In the next section, we suggest how the institutional tasks of entrepreneurs might differ across the four cells of this typology. Accordingly, we focus on institutional selection.

Institutional and Competitive Selection

Until this point, we have, by choice, focused rather exclusively on the process of variation in the creation of new organizational forms. It should be clear, however, that selection also plays an important role in the retention of organizational forms with higher fitness. Indeed, we believe that for new organizational forms, the burden of selection pressures may lie more in the realm of *institutional selection* than in the realm of *competitive selection*.

Stinchcombe (1968) asserts that the entrepreneurial creation of new forms "is pre-eminently a political phenomenon" (p. 194) because support has to be mobilized for the goals, authority structure, technology, and clients embodied in the new form. As a result, all new organizational forms face external and internal liabilities of newness (Stinchcombe, 1965). Externally, new forms require the endorsement of the state and of capital and personnel markets; internally, the task is one of developing to routines to coordinate work. Below, we briefly identify how external liabilities of newness are likely to vary across the four cells of our typology.

Because imitative entrepreneurship entails the reproduction of an existing form, the emergence of many new organizations generally entails only the reproduction of preexisting blueprints (Delacroix & Rao, 1994). Such organizations are likely to be isomorphic to a normative order linked to a broad conception of the state (Meyer & Rowan, 1977). Civil authorities, in particular, are likely to grant recognition to such organizations on a nearly automatic basis because of existing precedents and place minimal restrictions on their domain, structure, and evaluation protocols. In such cases, recognition by civil authorities has spillover effects on personnel and financial markets (Delacroix & Rao, 1994). The average magnitude of this spillover can, perhaps, be inferred from its most extreme manifestations. Melville (cited in Smelser, 1963, p. 222) observes that the government's perfecting of credit mechanisms contributed to the rapid birth of "bubble companies" in England in the 1720s. Indeed, the generalization has been advanced that wherever a high level of legitimacy is imparted to organizations by secure government and stable laws, there ensues an increased likelihood that speculative crazes will succeed and absurd organizations will be founded. In this connection, Mottram (cited in Smelser, 1963, p. 163) compares politically stable England with unstable France and notes that

> In France . . . during seventy years the material organization of the State suffered changes between empires, a kingdom and three republics. . . . Thus arises the contrast, that while the handling of credit instruments and speculative machinery was more widely developed in Great Britain, yet the financial history of the Kingdom contains far more frequent and serious commotions. . . . That of France has been marked by greater stability and far less general consequences arising from credit upheavals.

The case of recombination through partial contraction resembles imitative entrepreneurship in several respects. State endorsement may not be problematic to the extent that the new form is eliminating some elements from preexisting blueprints. Consequently, it is more likely that such forms will be specialists and prone to fare well when there is concentration among generalists (Carroll, 1985). Because forms in this cell represent leaner versions of existing forms, financial markets and consumers may also welcome them as low-cost options. Because such forms represent deviations from preexisting forms, they can more readily draw on the stock of institutional understandings (e.g., mail order computer manufacturers).

In the case of recombination through partial enlargement, external liabilities of newness are likely to ensue because the new form needs to be intelligible. In some instances, legislative barriers may prevent some types of enlargement (for example, full-service banks combining commercial and investment banking were prohibited by provisions of the Glass-Steagall Act). In other cases, regulators themselves may encourage existing forms to add elements by conferring new powers; for example, credit union regulators enabled credit unions to expand beyond the literal definition of common bond and become like banks. Even when permitted by the state, however, a new form created by the addition of new elements to a preexisting form may not be intelligible to financial markets. Zuckerman (1997) suggests that the boundaries of for-profit firms have to correspond to the pattern of specialization of financial analysts on Wall Street. When diversified firms combine and add elements unfamiliar to their analysts, they are penalized and forced to spin off operations. Similarly, prospective donors and philanthropists may be confused about nonprofit firms that pursue multiple causes and therefore may be reluctant to support them.

In sharp contrast, radical recombination involves new forms that embody new beliefs, values, goals, systems of authority, technology, and products available to consumers. Such new forms find it harder to draw on existing institutional understandings and often have to establish new understandings and new cognitive frames. Because entrepreneurs are trying to convince others to go along with their view, the formation of new industries and forms resembles social movements (Fligstein, 1996b, pp. 663-664). Accordingly, entrepreneurs have to establish a "need" for a new form by stating grievances and discrediting existing arrangements, and they must mobilize support for an organizational solution. Social movement theorists suggest that for collective action to be mobilized, entrepreneurs need to create bridges between the macrolevel potential and the microlevel tasks of recruitment (McAdam, McCarthy, & Zald, 1988). Snow, Rochford, Worden, and Benford (1986) suggest that frames are intermediate mechanisms that enable entrepreneurs to create a bridge between macrolevel potential for collective action and the microlevel tasks of recruiting individual participation in a social movement. Frames consist of explanations that provide a cognitive impetus to collective action, include exhortations that create moral foundations, and may also comprise structural and behavioral solutions (Snow et al., 1986). Frames define the interests of aggrieved constituencies, diagnose their problems, identify threats, assign blame, provide a prognosis, and enable collective attribution processes to operate (Snow & Benford, 1992). When entrepreneurs construct frames, like other social actors, they strategically select rules from a menu and assemble them into an institutional logic (Swidler, 1986) and can devise new combinations. When different coalitions of issue entrepreneurs champion incompatible frames, however, they collide like tectonic plates, and interorganizational conflict ensues. Hence, which frame or institutional rule should be chosen to define and organize an activity is a political question (DiMaggio, 1991; Friedland & Alford, 1991). In such cases, state endorsement becomes critical for the new form to take hold and proliferate.

For example, in the history of nonprofit consumer watchdogs, the first one, Consumers Research, was set up to rate products for their value and to promote rational purchasing. It split as a result of ideological conflict precipitated by a bitter strike. A rival organization, Consumers Union, sprang up to champion the idea that consumers were, in the ultimate sense, workers. Consumers Union rated not only products but also working conditions in the plants that produced them in a bid to improve the lot of the consumer-worker's quest for a decent wage. As these two organizations and their supporters struggled with each other to define the meaning and design of consumer watchdogs, the legitimacy of the organizational form was in question. Consumers were torn between competing visions, newspapers criticized both organizations for disorder, and congressional committees on un-American Activities investigated Consumers Union. Only after Consumers Union disavowed labor-related advocacy did state surveillance decline and nonprofit consumer watchdogs flourish.

Conclusion

The contribution of this chapter consists of showing the differences in variation among organizational populations. It began by chronicling variety in the definitions of organizational form, identified two types of speciation, and then detailed how new forms arose out of recombination. In doing so, it highlighted the salience of institutional entrepreneurs in reducing external liabilities of newness for new organizational forms. Two directions for future research stem from our discussion.

One fruitful line of research consists of analyzing internal liabilities of newness in the speciation process. For example, recombination through partial enlargement can generate internal coordination problems. In such cases, can firms reduce internal liabilities of newness by isolating the new added elements from the rest of the organization? Similarly, does recombination through partial contraction spawn internal coordination issues that trigger external image issues? For example, no-frills airlines that subcontracted all components found that externalizing maintenance compromised safety and undermined their reputations (e.g., ValueJet). Likewise, are external liabilities of newness facing radical recombinations diminished when there is lateral entry by preexisting firms (e.g., horse carriage firms becoming auto producers)? The study of these and related questions is essential for understanding the viability of variations in organizational populations.

Another trajectory for future research is to look at how selection pressures impinge on new forms and on elements of forms. By focusing on new forms and external selection pressures, our analysis has elided the issue of how selection pressures can also operate on elements of forms. It is useful to ask how selection processes play out at the level of the entire organization as a unit versus on organizing elements themselves. We think the answer to this question depends on the distinction between external selection pressures as opposed to internal *contrived selection forces*. Whereas the former may be the outcome of competition and institutional pressures in input or output markets, the latter often result from the decisions of managers about what kind of internal ecology they want their organization to represent. It is our view that external selection pressures are more likely to be prominent at the level of the entire organization, whereas internal selection forces are likely to dominate over organizing elements. One example of such internal competitive selection occurs when internal benchmarking against multiple comparable manufacturing plants is used as a disciplining force to raise productivity. Similarly, internal institutional pressures that lead to reproduction in the hiring of personnel can constrain variation and impede innovation.

Organizing elements also can be exposed to the outside environment directly and also may be subject to external selection pressures. For example, boundary spanning units (such as investor relations departments) are more likely to be exposed to environmental influences and therefore can be selected by external pressures. Similarly, internal selection forces, when applied to numerous organizing elements that have direct impacts on performance, may accrete to selection pressures on the organization as a unit. Future research needs to systematically differentiate across institutional and competitive selection pressures, define when they stem from internal and external sources, and delineate the scope conditions under which they impinge on new forms and organizing elements of forms.

Note

1. It is worth noting that entrepreneurs also engage in imitative entrepreneurship, as noted earlier. Their more profound contributions to the economy occur, however, when they help create new organizational forms. It also is worth noting that, infrequently, imitative entrepreneurship might itself introduce variation in organizational forms because of imperfect imitation or adaptation to local conditions. Such mutation rates, however, are likely to be low.

References

Aldrich, H. E. (1979). *Organizations and environments.* Englewood Cliffs, NJ: Prentice Hall.

Aldrich, H. E. (1998). *Organizations evolving.* Thousand Oaks, CA: Sage.

Aldrich, H., Kalleberg, A., Marsden, P., & Cassell, J. (1989). In pursuit of evidence: Strategies for locating new businesses. *Journal of Business Venturing, 4,* 367-386.

Brittain, W. J., & Freeman, J. (1982). Organizational proliferation and density dependent selection. In J. R. Kimberly & R. H. Miles (Eds.), *The organizational life cycle* (pp. 291-338). San-Francisco: Jossey-Bass.

Bruderer, E., & Singh, J. (1996). Organizational evolution, learning and selection: A genetic algorithm based model. *Academy of Management Journal, 39,* 1322-1349.

Burns, T., & Stalker, G. M. (1961). *The management of innovation.* London: Tavistock.

Campbell, D. T. (1965a). Ethnocentric and other altruistic motives. In D. Levine (Ed.), *Nebraska Symposium on Motivation* (pp. 283-311). Lincoln: University of Nebraska Press.

Campbell, D. T. (1965b). Variation and selective retention in socio-cultural evolution. In H. R. Barringer, G. I. Blanksten, & R. Mack (Eds.), *Social change in developing areas* (pp. 19-49). Cambridge, MA: Schenkman.

Campbell, D. T. (1988). A general "selection theory" as implemented in biological evolution and in social belief-transmission-with-modification in science [A commentary on Hull]. *Biology and Philosophy, 3,* 171-177.

Carroll, G. R. (1985). Concentration and specialization: The dynamics of niche width in organizational populations. *American Journal of Sociology, 90,* 1262-1283.

Chandler, A. (1972). *Strategy and structure: Chapters in the history of American industrial enterprise.* Cambridge, MA: MIT Press.

Delacroix, J., & Rao, H. (1994). Externalities and ecological theory: Unbundling density dependence. In J.A.C. Baum & J. V. Singh (Eds.), *Evolutionary dynamics of organizations* (pp. 255-268). New York: Oxford University Press.

DiMaggio, P. (1988). Interest and agency in institutional theory. In L. G. Zucker (Ed.), *Institutional patterns and organizations: Culture and environment* (pp. 3-21). Cambridge, MA: Ballinger.

DiMaggio, P. (1991). Constructing an organizational field as a professional project: U.S. art museums 1920-1940. In W. W. Powell & P. DiMaggio (Eds.), *The new institutionalism in organizational analysis* (pp. 267-292). Chicago: University of Chicago Press.

DiMaggio, P. J., & Powell, W. W. (1991). Introduction. In W. W. Powell & P. DiMaggio (Eds.), *The new institutionalism in organizational analysis* (pp. 1-38). Chicago: University of Chicago Press.

Douglas, M. (1986). *How institutions think.* Syracuse, NY: Syracuse University Press.

Fama, E., & Jensen, M. (1983). Separation of ownership and control. *Journal of Law and Economics, 26,* 301-323.

Fligstein, N. (1996a). How to make a market: Reflections on the attempt to create a single market in the European Union. *American Journal of Sociology, 102,* 1-33.

Fligstein, N. (1996b). Markets as politics: A political cultural approach to market institutions. *American Sociological Review, 61,* 656-673.

Flink, J. J. (1970). *America adopts the automobile, 1895-1910.* Cambridge, MA: MIT Press.

Freeman, J. (1986). Entrepreneurs as organizational products: Semi-conductor firms and venture capital firms. In G. Libecap (Ed.), *Advances in the study of entrepreneurship, innovation, and economic growth* (pp. 33-58). Greenwich, CT: JAI.

Freeman, J., & Hannan, M. T. (1983). Niche width and the dynamics of organizational populations. *American Journal of Sociology, 88,* 1116-1145.

Friedland, R., & Alford, R. R. (1991). Bringing society back in: Symbols, practices, and institutional contradictions. In W. W. Powell & P. J. DiMaggio (Eds.), *The new institutionalism in organizational analysis* (pp. 232-263). Chicago: University of Chicago Press.

Galbraith, J., & Kazanjian, R. (1986). *Strategy implementation: Structure, systems and process.* St. Paul: West.

Haas, J. E., Hall, R., & Johnson, N. (1966). Towards an empirically derived taxonomy of organizations. In R. V. Bowers (Ed.), *Studies on behavior in organizations* (pp. 157-180). Athens: University of Georgia Press.

Hannan, M. T., & Carroll, G. R. (1992). *Dynamics of organizational populations.* New York: Oxford University Press.

Hannan, M. T., & Freeman, J. (1977). The population ecology of organizations. *American Journal of Sociology, 82,* 929-964.

Hannan, M. T., & Freeman, J. (1984). Structural inertia and organizational change. *American Sociological Review, 49,* 149-164.

Hannan, M. T., & Freeman, J. H. (1987). The ecology of organizational founding: American labor unions, 1936-1985. *American Journal of Sociology, 92,* 910-943.

Hannan, M. T., & Freeman, J. (1989). *Organizational ecology.* Cambridge, MA: Belknap.

Haunschild, P. R., & Miner, A. S. (1997). Modes of interorganizational imitation: The effects of outcome salience and uncertainty. *Administrative Science Quarterly, 42,* 472-500.

Haveman, H., & Rao, H. (1997). Structuring a theory of moral sentiments: Institutional-organization co-evolution in the early thrift industry. *American Journal of Sociology, 6,* 1606-1651.

Haveman, H., & Rao, H. (in press). Hybrid forms and institutional change in the early California thrift industry. In W. Powell & D. Jones (Eds.), *Bending the bars of the iron cage: Institutional dynamics and processes.* Chicago: University of Chicago Press.

Kimberly, J. R. (1975). Environmental constraints and organizational structure: A comparative analysis of rehabilitation organizations. *Administrative Science Quarterly, 20,* 1-19.

Lumsden, C., & Singh, J. (1990). The dynamics of organizational speciation. In J. V. Singh (Ed.), *Organizational evolution: New directions* (pp. 145-163). Newbury Park, CA: Sage.

March, J. G., & Olsen, J. (1976). *Ambiguity and choice in organizations.* Bergen, Norway: Universitatsforlaget.

McAdam, D., McCarthy, J. D., & Zald, M. N. (1988). Social movements. In N. J. Smelser (Ed.), *Handbook of sociology* (pp. 695-737). Newbury Park, CA: Sage.

McKelvey, B. (1982). *Organizational systematics: Taxonomy, evolution, classification.* Berkeley: University of California Press.

Meyer, J. W., & Rowan, B. (1977). Institutionalized organizations: Formal structure as myth and ceremony. *American Journal of Sociology, 83,* 340-363.

Mintzberg, H. (1990). *Structuring in fives.* Englewood Cliffs, NJ: Prentice Hall.

Nelson, R. R., & Winter, S. G. (1982). *An evolutionary theory of economic change.* Cambridge, MA: Belknap.

Pugh, D., Hickson, D., & Hinings, C. R. (1969) An empirical taxonomy of the structures of work organizations. *Administrative Science Quarterly, 14,* 115-126.

Rao, H. (1998). Caveat emptor: The construction of non-profit consumer watchdog organizations. *American Journal of Sociology, 103,* 912-961.

Rao, H., & Singh, J. (in press). Organizational speciation as new path creation: Institution building activity in the early automobile and bio-tech industries. In R. Garud & P. Karnoe (Eds.), *Path as process.* Mahwah, NJ: Lawrence Erlbaum.

Romanelli, E. (1989). Organizational birth and population variety: A community perspective on origins. In B. Staw & L. L. Cummings (Eds.), *Research in organizational behavior* (Vol. 11, pp. 211-246). Greenwich, CT: JAI.

Salancik, G. R., & Leblebici, H. (1988). Variety and form in organizing transactions. In N. DiTomaso & S. Bachrach (Eds.), *Research in the sociology of organizations* (pp. 2-40). Greenwich, CT: JAI.

Schumpeter, J. A. (1950). *Capitalism, socialism, and democracy.* New York: Harper.

Scott, W. R. (1995). *Organizations and institutions.* Thousand Oaks, CA: Sage.

Singh, J. (1993). Review essay on density dependence. *American Journal of Sociology, 99,* 464-473.

Smelser, N. J. (1963). *Theory of collective behavior.* New York: Free Press of Glencoe.

Snow, D. A., & Benford, R. D. (1992). Master frames and cycles of protest. In A. Morris & C. Mueller (Eds.), *Frontiers in social movement theory* (pp. 133-155). New Haven, CT: Yale University Press.

Snow, D. A., Rochford, E. B., Worden, S. K., & Benford, R. D. (1986). Frame alignment processes: Micromobilization and movement participation. *American Sociological Review, 51,* 464-481.

Stark, D. (1996). Recombinant property in Eastern European capitalism. *American Journal of Sociology, 101,* 993-1027.

Stinchcombe, A. L. (1965). Social structure and organizations. In J. G. March (Ed.), *Handbook of organizations* (pp. 142-193). Chicago: Rand McNally.

Stinchcombe, A. L. (1968). *Constructing social theories.* Chicago: University of Chicago Press.

Swidler, A. (1986). Culture in action: Symbols and strategies. *American Sociological Review, 51,* 273-286.

Thompson, J. D. (1967). *Organizations in action.* New York: McGraw-Hill.

Tushman, M. L., & Anderson, P. (1986). Technological discontinuities and organizational environments. *Administrative Science Quarterly, 31*, 439-465.

Van de Ven, A. H., & Garud, R. (1989). A framework for understanding the emergence of new industries. In R. Rosenbloom & R. Burgelman (Eds.), *Research in techno-* *logical innovation, management and policy* (pp. 195-225). Greenwich, CT: JAI.

Williamson, O. E. (1975). *Markets and hierarchies: Analysis and antitrust implications.* New York: Free Press.

Williamson, O. E. (1985). *The economic institutions of capitalism.* New York: Free Press.

Zuckerman, E. (1997). *Mediating the corporate product: Securities analysts and the scope of the firm.* Unpublished manuscript, Graduate School of Business, Stanford University.

Chapter 5

Blind
(But Not Unconditioned)
Variation

Problems of Copying in
Sociocultural Evolution

ELAINE ROMANELLI

Throughout both the theoretical and practical worlds of modern organizations, we discover a pervasive belief that successful change in one organizational or social system can be accomplished through copying the attributes or practices of another organization or system. In the academic world, researchers have observed a profound similarity of organizational routines and structures over broad numbers and classes of organizations (Hannan & Freeman, 1984; Stinchcombe, 1965) and have attributed much of this homogeneity to imitation processes, including direct learning and imitation by organizational actors (e.g., Levitt & March, 1988; Haunschild & Miner, 1997; Miner & Haun-schild, 1995; Miner & Raghavan, this volume), interlocking directorates (e.g., Mizruchi, 1996; Palmer, 1983) and other forms of institutional diffusion (Abrahamson, 1991; DiMaggio & Powell, 1983; Tolbert & Zucker, 1983), and various forms of institutional coercion by external actors (e.g., venture capitalists, professional associations, regulatory bodies) in exchange for critical resources and legitimacy (e.g., Hannan & Freeman, 1984, 1989; Pfeffer & Salancik, 1978). Although scholars are not universally sanguine about the excellence of all imitated routines or structures, the idea that such processes *are* a prevalent source of change in organizations is itself broadly accepted.

AUTHOR'S NOTE: This chapter was prepared for Variations in Organization Science: A Conference in Honor of Donald T. Campbell, University of Toronto, 1997. The author is grateful to Howard Aldrich, Joel Baum, and Amy Kenworthy for comments on an earlier draft and the Global Entrepreneurship Studies Program at the Georgetown School of Business for support of this research.

In the popular organizational literature, we find a similar, albeit more prescriptive, concept of copying in the idea of "benchmarking." Benchmarking, from the literature on total quality management (Imai, 1986), refers to processes by which actors in one organization analyze systems and routines of another organization for potential adoption in the first organization. The idea has pervaded management thinking. From the *Harvard Business Review* editors, who exhort authors to identify company "best practices" that can improve the efficiency or profitability of other organizations, to business reporters who examine (and typically despair of) regional abilities to emulate the growth and vitality of Silicon Valley, experts agree that imitation—of the right things—is an effective route to improved organizational (or even regional) performance.[1]

Copying, or "borrowing" as it was termed by Campbell (1969, 1974b), represents a potentially very efficient means for introducing new practices, or variations, into an organization's activities and routines. Through copying, organizations may avoid some of the costs of pure trial-and-error learning, such as costs associated with the number of trials needed to improve fit, risks of catastrophic error, and loss of time to reach a more effective novel solution. Copying may also extend an organization's repertoire of potentially effective variations, that is, trials that actors might not have discovered through examination of solely their own systems and processes. In other words, Why reinvent the wheel? seems a fair question to ask of any organization that can copy the proven attributes or practices of other organizations.

Copying, however, is not the only way that novel variations can be introduced, and it may not be an unmitigated good for organizational development. Copying, especially as it provides a ready-made rationale for expending resources on certain trials rather than others, will tend to limit an organization's search for other trials. Variations that might have developed from the organization's own, idiosyncratic system of knowledge and routines, and that might have proved more efficient or effective than the copied routines, may be less likely to be discovered. Because copying itself may become a broadly legitimate mode of learning, as described in Miner and Raghavan's (this volume) review and classification of copying routines, the chances for an organization to introduce and try essentially new variations may become severely limited. Can we invent anything new at all? seems another fair question to ask of organizations interested in improving fit.

In this chapter, I explore the pros and cons of copying as an efficient or effective process for learning and development in organizations. Building on the ideas of Donald T. Campbell, who argued, in his lifetime of work on sociocultural evolution, that blind-variation-and-selective-retention stands as the sole useful explanation for the astonishing "fit" we seem to observe between the workings of social systems and the purposes they have been created to serve, I explore the possibility of unintended consequences and perhaps substantial costs to variety and innovation that may develop from overemphasis on copying.

Blind-Variation-and-Selective-Retention: The Basic Ideas

Campbell's ideas about variation, selection, and retention as the principal means of sociocultural evolution are today well known and (largely uncritically) accepted in modern organization theory. For any human system, actors discover better ways of doing things primarily through trial-and-error learning. Trials are variations in the established ways of doing things. Variations that improve the "fit" of the system—that is, its ability to survive or achieve its ends more efficiently or effectively—will be selected "for" and retained by the system; those which either fail to improve the system or detract from its achievement of ends will be selected "against" and not retained.

The keys to the effectiveness of this system for development-with-improvement lie, first, in the ability of the system to generate multiple variations, for which the outcomes in terms of efficiency or effectiveness are not known, and second, in the existence of consistent selection criteria and mechanisms for retention. Selection and retention are critical to development because, *assuming variation*, if there is no way for a system to determine whether a variation improves the fit of the system to its environment, or if there is no way for the system to retain a useful variation, then there is no way for a system to improve. Variations will simply multiply. Some useful and some not useful variations will be retained; some useful and not useful variations will be discarded. The history of any social system will be profoundly random and not in any way tend toward improvement or development.

Campbell argued passionately that random development is not what we observe in social systems. Certain kinds of systems, such as educational systems for transmitting knowledge over generations, and even scientific systems for generating new knowledge, which were special concerns of Campbell's (e.g., Campbell, 1974a, 1974b; Campbell & Paller, 1989), reveal remarkable similarity and persistence over time and across societies. Certain features of these systems have developed repeatedly and persisted in different societies. In many cases, such as the innovation of a new technology, the organization of cities, and the establishment of trade, the developments occurred in isolation from one another and without obvious possibility for one system to have learned from another. The repeated and often isolated development of particular ways of doing things argues strongly, according to Campbell, for the existence of selective and retentive mechanisms, even though they may be difficult to see or specify. Especially for sociocultural evolution, "where we do not understand the environment, or selective system, as well as we do the environments relevant to the forms of wings or eyes," Campbell reasoned that where we "find convergent evolution on a common form, we could argue a common advantageous selective system" (Campbell, 1969, p. 78).

But what of variation? Although selection and retention guarantee the identification and preservation of forms or processes that improve a system's fit either internally or with environments, they can operate only in the presence of variations. Campbell (1974b) defined variation as "a heterogeneity of alterations on an existing form" (p. 143).

Three characteristics of variations are necessary, according to Campbell, for development or improvement of a social system. First, variations must be blind; the outcome of a variation (i.e., its ability to improve fit), must not be known in advance. Second, variations must be multiple. Finally, most variations must fail, either failing to improve or actively detracting from the social system's ability to survive. Selection, in other words, is a "choosing" device, one that systematically eliminates variations, from the ones presented, that are less able to improve fit.

These ideas—blind and multiple variations with failures—form the basis for my exploration in this chapter of the pros and cons of copying as a source of variation in social systems. In the following section, I explore each of these ideas in detail to expose Campbell's reasoning about the importance of each of the characteristics. Although sometimes subtle, the arguments are critical to understanding the achievement of a rich "heterogeneity of alterations."

Characteristics of Effective Variation

The Concept of Blind Variation

Blind variation requires only that the outcome of a variation, that is, its ability to improve or detract from an organization's or any social system's fit, not be known (or even be presumed to be known) by organizational actors in advance of trial. The principle of blind variation is simple and, according to Campbell, fundamental to organizational improvement or development. Blind variation is the only way in which novel solutions can be discovered.

Why? To understand this principle, and also its subtlety, consider its main alternative, that an actor might be able to identify, analytically, a new organizational routine or attribute that could improve the organization's outcomes. Implicitly, this actor employs a mental version of the variation and selection model, analyzing and comparing the outcomes of imagined alternatives and selecting the most efficient or effective routine or characteristics. Assuming retention, as the rational actor gained experience with the system, other alternatives might be identified, either through rational deduction or observation of other systems, and the same mental comparison of assessment and selection could be conducted. Organizations might thus avoid costs of actual trials for an indefinite time.

Campbell discussed at length the problems, and also the seductiveness, of this rational approach to variation, selection, and retention. Most explicitly, in response to an argument by Richards (1977), who hailed the efficiency of this conceptual approach, Campbell (1977a) rejected the "notion of direct, unwasteful, prescient problem solving in which a properly gifted or tutored scientist goes directly to the new or more appropriate conceptualization. . . . While there may often be presumptive procedures that turn out to be appropriate and thereby reduce the waste, it can never be entirely eliminated" (Campbell, 1977a, p. 502). Moreover, some waste—such as investment in failed trials—can be beneficial. "A nonprescient variation in heuristics will usually lead to waste but occasionally to unanticipated breakthroughs" (Campbell, 1977a, p. 505).

To be sure, Campbell acknowledged that many *potential* novel solutions to problems can be identified "intelligently," through both the observation of other systems and rational analysis of their effectiveness. He emphasized, however, that such processes are beneficial mainly for *discovery* of potentially useful variations and insisted that "the value of a new conceptualization cannot be judged until after the conceptualization is generated" (Campbell, 1977a, p. 503). Thus, it was not observation, rational analysis, or copying per se that Campbell inveighed against. Rather, it was the easily associated idea that, through such activities, the outcomes of a variation could be effectively known or predicted. To rely on "wise, designed, prescient, informed, foresighted, clairvoyant, intelligent [or] preadapted" variations, according to Campbell (1974b, p. 147), will fundamentally prevent organizational improvement or development. Three problems, he argued, attend the efficacy of unblind or prescient variation and selection.

First, belief in an ability of human actors, even highly intelligent and well-schooled actors, to know or predict the outcomes of a variation supposes that the actors are sufficiently knowledgeable about selection criteria to be able to replace, analytically, the actual processes of selection and retention. Campbell argued that such knowledge is

impossible. Organizational environments are complex and dynamic. Although rationally generated selection criteria may yield some optimization with respect to the specific criteria, they will also insidiously limit consideration of other criteria or other combinations of criteria. In most cases, analytical selection criteria will develop only from existing understandings of the environment, based on past experience of fit with existing organizational routines and practices. If actual selection criteria differ from those that are understood, other variations that might prove, in practice, to improve the organization's fit will not be discovered.

Second, belief in rational analysis as an efficient alternative to pure trial-and-error learning fundamentally restricts both the range and the number of variations that will be tried in practice. Not only will fewer alternatives be considered, but through rational analysis, fewer will be tried. In the extreme, rational analysis will produce trial of only a single alternative, the one believed, through analysis, to be best for the presumed selection criteria. Because selection depends on the presentation of multiple trials, selection itself will be analytically thwarted.

Finally, Campbell argued that belief in and reliance on rational analysis as the mechanism of variation and selection subtly induces its own proof. Except insofar as the variation may prove grossly inferior to the existing routine or practice, the variation will tend to be retained regardless of actual improvement. Explanations generated in support of the trial will be used to explain its success. Campbell (1977a) rejected the belief "that the one formulation that historically proved to be more correct was necessarily most intelligent or rational *in its generation*. . . . The correct solutions were often suggested for *wrong* reasons" (Campbell, 1977a, p. 502).

Thus, Campbell argued throughout several papers (e.g., Campbell, 1969, 1974b, 1982) that any of several adjectives—chance, random, contingent, aleatory, fortuitous, spontaneous, haphazard, happenstance, and blind—are acceptable as modifiers of the variation process because the developmental process, that of selection and retention, will still work. As long as the modifier does not in any way suggest a foreknowledge of the outcomes of variation, selective processes will still accept or reject the variations as they improve or do not improve the system's fit. Thus, evolution may occur.

At the other extreme, Campbell (1974b) also explored whether, if development cannot occur rationally, blind variations need be random. This he also rejected. Randomness, he argued, assumes several properties—equiprobability, unrestrainedness, and statistical independence among successive variations—that he considered unnecessary. It is useful to consider these arguments briefly because they specify the rather broad and unrestricted availability of blind variations that social systems may present for selection.

Equiprobability. According to this property of *random* variation and selective retention, all variations, for any social system, must be equally likely. Equiprobability in system variations ensures the broadest and richest presentation of trials for selection to operate on, and thus the greatest potential for novel solutions to be discovered. Equiprobability, of course, is not what we observe in either social or organic systems. In social systems, whether because of institutionalized understandings about right and appropriate forms of activity (Zucker, 1977) or formal control systems—what Campbell (1969) termed "vicarious selectors"—that systematically dispose a system toward some but not other variations, actors tend to develop predilections for certain responses or variations. Campbell argued, however, that such restrictions do not constrain a system *only* to the most likely responses. Especially when the actors face a problem that is outside their historical, adapted ken, repeated frustration in solving the problem using historically successful methods may induce them to try low-probability variations. For evolution to occur, it need only be possible for social systems to reach beyond the set of most likely responses.

Unrestrainedness. Second, and extending this idea, any system may not be capable of evolving into any other system; thus, variation need not be unrestrained. As Campbell discussed, for evolution to occur according to a variation-selection-retention model, it is not important for an octopus to be able

to evolve into a giraffe, or a textbook publisher into a pharmaceutical research organization. In fact, as in biological evolutionary theory (e.g., Gould, 1990; Dawkins, 1996a, 1996b), an essential characteristic of selection processes is that they cannot select for a feature that reduces the survival likelihood of the system. Selection works in one direction only—the direction of improvement. Even when better-adapted features can be observed in other systems, if evolution toward those features would require the adoption of intermediary, maladapted features that would not promote survival, then selection will not favor evolution toward the improvements. Although social systems may be more able than organisms to withstand, or to survive, maladaptive trials, evolution toward any other observable social system need not be assumed as a feature of a variation-selection-retention model.

Statistical independence. Finally, statistical independence as a property of random variations over successive trials, though desirable, also is unnecessary. Here again, idiosyncratic learning over the history of an organization's trials of variations may predispose actors to future trial or avoidance of certain kinds of variations. Campbell (1969) discussed, in particular, the development of "vicarious selectors" that function to eliminate trial of variations that would be fundamentally detrimental to the fit or survival of the system, or even to anticipate certain kinds of variations that might prove beneficial. Through past trial-and-error learning, organizations may evolve control systems, such as employment or accounting systems, that systematically predispose an organization toward trial of certain variations and avoidance of others. Path dependence and positive feedback loops in social systems (Arthur, 1988, 1989, 1990) represent vicarious selectors in social systems. Campbell emphasized that the vicarious selectors, though they do restrain a social system to certain directions of evolution, must only themselves be subject to selection processes for evolution to occur.

Thus, so long as any regularity of exploration and experimentation is independent of any *fore-knowledge* of the correct response, from among multiple blind trials, selection and retention processes will continue to operate. In other words, variations may be differentially likely to occur, restricted to certain forms, and not independent of one another over successive trials. Campbell (1974b) cautioned only, and strongly, that actors should not conclude from these conditions that a "trial-and-correction" relationship among successive variations was acceptable. Correction of a trial also implies prior knowledge of a variation's effective outcomes. New variations need not be blind with respect to the outcomes of previous variations; they merely must be blind with respect to their own outcomes.

Campbell settled on the concept of *blind (but not necessarily random) variation* as a clear expression of the single essential requirement of sociocultural evolution as a variation-and-selective-retention process, that is, that the variations may be predicated on no a priori understanding or knowledge of the adaptive outcomes the variations may or may not produce. He later suggested the concept of *unjustified variation* to express, more clearly, the dangers of presuming any foreknowledge of outcomes in the trial of a variation.

The Requirement for Multiple Variations

The fundamental and essential point to be grasped here is that selection does not operate by comparing any one variation, even a blind variation, to some hypothetical best routine or template of excellence or selection. No such template exists or can be known. What we understand as "best" is in fact only a relative construct, reflecting the emergence of one variation, *from among those that were tried*, as better improving the system's fit. Selection essentially "chooses," from among the presented variations, which of them most improves the system's fit. Campbell regularly defined selection in terms of a "systematic elimination." Thus, selection can work only if multiple, in a sense competing, variations are presented.

Although straightforward, the requirement for trial of multiple variations under the same selective criteria can be difficult in complex organizations. When a social system possesses multiple similar systems—for example, organizational forms within a population, or subunits within an organi-

zation—that also are relatively stable, then multiple variations can be tried against presumed-to-be similar selection criteria. Selection can identify the variation that best improves the system's fit, and this variation can be retained and diffused over other similar systems. When a variation either affects all of a social system, however, or acts within a context of changing selection criteria, the presentation of multiple variations becomes highly problematic. In effect, only one trial can occur at a time.

Campbell emphasized that selection can still operate even under this quite restrained notion of multiple variations, as long as (a) comparison with the previous system is fairly assessed, and (b) the system remains open to other, future trials. Organizations can sequentially try alternative variations until selection reveals a system-improving variation.

The Need for Multiple Failures

If selection is a process of systematic elimination, then there must of course be failures among the multiple variations tried. Selection cannot operate if failures are not presented. This is true even in situations where only one variation can be presented at a time.

For most actors, however, the very idea of generating potential failures is fraught with difficulty. Trials are costly and involve risk, and actors in social systems typically are not rewarded for even the most creative failures. Thus, actors are motivated to discover and "find" successful variations. Selection cannot operate if it is systematically denied the opportunity to choose or eliminate failed variations.

Campbell (1977b, 1981; Tavris, 1975) explored this problem in several discussions or papers about what he called the "experimenting society." Novel solutions can be found only by taking steps into the unknown. Novel solutions can be revealed only after they have been tried. According to Campbell, human actors need to understand variations as the trials that they are, and evaluate them against outcomes instead of, more commonly, assuming them as solutions to be defended. In other words, failure must be possible.

Here Campbell (1977b; Tavris, 1975) argued that the political nature of social systems, even though it may tend the system generally toward conservative trials, nevertheless can be helpful for honestly monitoring the outcomes of trials. Social systems, especially formal organizations, comprise numerous individuals and subsystems whose interests may conflict. Rival parts of the system, either those with alternative trials that directly compete or those whose well-being might be affected negatively by successful change in another part of the system, will be self-interestedly motivated to discover failures in other parts of the system. Although Campbell was skeptical of the ability of politics in social systems to do much more than trade competing justifications for preferred variations, he nevertheless explored its ability to challenge prejustified trials and thus to identify failed variations.

In later works, Campbell (e.g., 1990, 1994) explored an opposite problem of social systems comprising multiple and competing parts. Individuals and subunits in organizations may tend to implement trials and optimize the fit of their subunits to the detriment of the overall fit of the system or organization. A significant problem, discussed at length by Baum (this volume), develops from the fact that subunits can evolve faster that the overall system. Subunits, evolving at different paces, both compared with one another and with respect to the overall system, may regularly undermine the possibility for the overall system to evolve into an integrative, adapted unit.

Here, Campbell suggested the existence or development of "vicarious selectors." Vicarious selectors are themselves systems that operate, usually in a controlling fashion, across the many subparts of an organization or larger system. Vicarious selectors may reduce the risk of catastrophic organizational failure by excluding from trial those variations that might produce such an outcome. They may even incline the system toward certain variations that may more likely improve its effectiveness and survival. Vicarious selectors, according to Campbell, are themselves the product of selection processes, of trial-and-error learning.

It must be emphasized, however, that vicarious selectors can only partly solve the problem of organizational actors confronting potential failure. Vicarious selectors, though they may usefully restrict and direct the sorts of variations that will be possible, must still permit sufficient numbers of variations, for which outcomes are unknown. Catastrophic failure, in addition to breakthrough innovation, must be possible, or selection does not work. Indeed, as Campbell often argued, the occurrence of breakthrough innovation may depend on the possibility of catastrophic failure.

Sources of Blind Variations

Campbell was insistently agnostic about the relative usefulness of different sources or kinds of variation for any social system. As long as variations are blind, numerous, and able to fail, selection and retention will work regardless of the source of the variation. Campbell discussed three sources, which I briefly review here.

Diffusion or borrowing between social groups. A distinguishing feature of human social systems is that actors within them may observe the characteristics and practices of other social systems, evaluate their relationship to effective outcomes, and try them within their own systems. In other words, actors in human systems can copy the characteristics of other systems. As long as the copied routine or practice is approached as a trial, and not as a proven solution—that is, as long as it may fail—selection will work.

Selective propagation of temporal variations. All variations, however, need not be imported from outside the social system and, as I will argue in the next section of this chapter, probably they had better not all be borrowed. Variations may arise spontaneously in a variety of ways. Mistakes in the application of a routine practice or procedure may give rise to new outcomes that reveal a more effective practice. Actors in the system may creatively identify a new routine, or change in an existing routine, that might result in better outcomes. Threats to the ongoing effectiveness of the original system may be especially productive of such creativity. Or a new routine may be forced on an organization, either by regulatory bodies or institutional monitors such as professional associations. As long as the variation is blind and subject to failure, selection will operate.

Rational selection. Finally, Campbell admitted, if a bit reluctantly, the possibility that actors within a social system might analyze the contributions of routines or attributes to the system's outcomes and then devise potential improvements. Campbell was especially leery of humans' assumptions about their own prescience under these conditions. First, we may be led to assume outcomes for variations that have not been tried, and then never examine the outcomes. Second, if outcomes prove beneficial, we may overemphasize our analytical and predictive capacities. In principle, however, as long as the variation is blind and thus subject to failure, rational deduction is as good as any other method for identifying potential variations.

Fundamentally, Campbell was uninterested in sources of variation. He explored them in many papers to distinguish characteristics of the sources from the properties of variation that can produce system development. Campbell cared only that a system try many variations, on a more or less regular basis, and that the variations be blind and open to failure. It is a mistake, he believed, to assume that properties of variation are reflected in the sources of variation.

The Problem of Organizational Copying

As presented thus far, it is difficult to see any problem with copying per se. As above, Campbell acknowledged copying as a potentially effective means for introducing variation into an organizational system. As long as the copied variation does not know its own outcome, and as long as the variation is presented multiple times, in the company of failed variations, copying may be an excellent and highly efficient mechanism for introducing variation into a social system.

As I discussed at the outset of this chapter, however, the pervasive practice of copying the apparently improving attributes and practices of other organizations, though it may potentially gen-

erate great efficiencies, is fraught with difficulty. The problems lie both in the difficulty of meeting the above conditions faithfully and in subtle pressures, born of assumptions and processes attendant to copying, to forgo the requirements of blind variations with multiple failures.

The Problem of Prescience

At its best, or at least its most rational, learning through copying requires (a) collection of data about how the routine or practice actually works, (b) identification and assessment of the outcomes produced by the routine or practice, and (c) some determination about whether the environment surrounding the routine or practice is similar to that of the observing organization. Perhaps in this learning exercise, which is much more elaborate than the purely mental exercise I discussed above, actors also explore and analyze the processes, outcomes, and environments of multiple, alternative routines and practices. In this scenario, assuming some heterogeneity of variations, we might go so far as to characterize copying as the human contribution, in organizational settings, to selection and retention.

The scenario is attractive and fundamentally underlies the pervasive prescription for "benchmarking" in modern strategy. In fact, this form of copying is precisely intended by the original benchmarking literature from total quality management (Imai, 1986). In its original argument, benchmarking was explicitly restrained to analysis of very specific processes in organizations—such as warehousing systems, order-taking systems, customer response systems, or distribution systems—where very detailed and analytically specific relationships between features of a particular routine or process and its direct outcomes could be assessed directly. Then, assuming similar selection criteria for the copying organization, the routine could be copied with good expectation that the same positive outcomes would result. Although *in practice,* benchmarking has been distorted somewhat to mean imitation of virtually any attributes or processes exhibited by a more successful organization—that is, what Miner and Raghavan (this volume) term "outcome-based copying"—*in the-*

ory benchmarking is as good a *source* for system variations as any other.

And what could be more efficient? The observing organization acquires the trial-and-error experience of another organization without ever investing resources in its own trial. What could be less risky? The chosen routine or practice, from among those observed, has demonstrated its ability to improve an organization's environmental fit.

The problem, of course, is prescience. Especially in this most rational of approaches to learning through copying, prescience is not only a difficult-to-avoid outcome of copying, it is also in fact a sought-after objective. Learning in this manner is highly costly. Organizational actors do not invest resources in such learning without an expectation that new routines or practices, ones that will improve performance, will be discovered. They will tend to try, analytically, to determine which, from several potential variations, will best improve system fit. Given discovery of improvement after trial, actors will tend to have confidence that the outcomes were the best that could be achieved. This conclusion will be based not on actual results from multiple trials with failures, but rather on comparison with presumed results of other variations *that were never tried*. Actors will tend to rely on the pretrial analysis which indicated that the one trial would be best.

Moreover, as long as there occurs no immediate and dramatic decline in system performance—decline that can be traced clearly to the change that was introduced—actors may always rationalize that the system would have functioned worse if the change had not been introduced, almost whatever the results of the trial. Gould (1990) explored this problem as one of historical reasoning in evolutionary theory. Given an observed evolutionary trajectory, if a change is introduced, and if the system subsequently performs better than before the change was introduced, we may tend to conclude that the change, a variation, produced the better performance. As Gould pointed out, however, we can never replay the tape of history to ascertain the validity of this argument. We can never know whether the system would have performed either less well or much better if the change had not been introduced. In the end, when only a single change is introduced, we have only a hypothesis that it was efficacious. Selection has had no chance to work. In sum, as Campbell discussed numerous times, if the variation is not tried blindly, then, no matter the reason for believing in its outcomes, selection will not operate or will operate only in cases of the extreme failure of a trial.

The Problem of Multiple Variations With Failures

Not all copying processes, of course, require the kind of costly investments that attend the kind of learning that I have been describing. Miner and Raghavan (this volume) describe three modes of learning through copying—frequency-based, outcome-based, and trait-based—at the population level, which may suggest a less assiduous analytical process. In effect, organizations may copy the practices of other organizations because (a) they are prevalent in the population and thus presumed to be effective; (b) they are associated, even if only coincidentally, with positive outcomes; or (c) they exhibit desirable characteristics independent of any presumed or demonstrated relationship to performance.

Although these forms of copying may not trap individual organizational actors in the kind of commitment or rationalization that may result from substantial investments of resources in learning, population-level imitation largely merely shifts the danger of prescience from actors in the individual organization to population-level actors. As best practices in some organizations are identified (and often widely reported in various business press outlets and management journals), they will tend to be adopted less critically by actors in other organizations. Except in the case of clear failures from trial of the practices, successes will tend to be discovered because in fact they were presumed.

The result of such population-level imitation, however, is a severe restriction on the number and range of variations that will likely be tried for both individual organizations and the population. Fewer variations will be tried because greater knowledge is assumed about the relative benefits of alternative, untried variations. Selection processes will be limited to those already-assumed-effective variations. Individual organizations will discover a good-enough way of doing things. New variations will not be tried. Thus, at the population level, forms and practices also will tend to converge on good-enough ways of doing things. Miner and Haunschild (1995) point out the substantial danger of suboptimal convergence if such population-level learning occurs too quickly. Just as at the organizational level, if actors in a population quickly imitate practices that appear "best" at any one time, the number of new trials will decline and the possibility for other, potentially better practices will decline. There will no longer be grist for the selection mill.

Some new trials, of course, probably will occur. Most examinations of copying, in fact, rely on the assumption of randomly produced variations in the larger system—the population. Some organizations may happen upon a variation that, for whatever reason, is tried and shown to be effective. Any prevalent reliance on copying, however, tends to limit the likelihood of such development. As individual organizations follow the increasingly prevalent practice of copying, though novel solutions may occasionally be discovered, populations will at best oscillate from one form, or one set of best practices, to another (Miner & Raghavan, this volume).

There is also, however, a potentially more pernicious influence of copying on the production of multiple variations. With respect to multiple variations, the problem of prescience restricts the number of variations likely to be observed or tried primarily with respect to *external* possibilities. Copying, however, may also limit the tendencies of individual organizations to experiment with variations on their own existing, and importantly idiosyncratic, systems, routines, and practices. Internally generated variations will not possess the kind of legitimacy held by variations that are observed, analyzed, and socially validated in the external environment.

Thus, copying presents a conundrum of contradictions. Copying offers the possibility of efficient learning but also fundamentally and subtly works against the discovery of variations that are more effective and more idiosyncratic within individual

organizations. Copying, because it seems so efficient and requires substantial investments in learning, may preclude trial of other potentially more efficacious variations that the system might "naturally" have produced. Copying, because it requires, for effective learning, a similar environment, may lead to inappropriate attention to change of the selective system itself.

Overcoming the Problems of Copying

Two kinds of solutions to the many problems of organizational copying can be identified. First, we might directly exhort organizations, as Campbell did, to remember that variations are trials and that, as such, they must be open to error or failure. Campbell did not argue merely for a wait-and-see attitude toward assessing or learning the outcomes of a variation; rather, he suggested a far more active collection and monitoring of data about outcomes produced by existing systems, routines, or practices as well as about outcomes of alternatives, whether the alternatives are tried contemporaneously or serially. Analytically, we should be able to know something (if not everything) about outcomes generated by any existing system or routine. Experiments, or variations, should be explicitly designed and implemented to be amenable to comparison with the existing system or routine for the extent to which they yield improvements in outcomes. Most important of all, Campbell suggested that observers be open to discovery of unanticipated novel improvements from a variation.

We should not forget, in this volume about variations, that Campbell was first and fundamentally an experimental psychologist. First in his investigations of human cognition and later in his considerations of evolution in large social systems and even science itself, Campbell was a systematic observer of complex and hard-to-observe developmental processes and scholar of valid and reliable methods of systematic observation. *Experimental and Quasi-Experimental Designs for Research* (Campbell & Stanley, 1966) remains standard reading for doctoral students in the social sciences. Campbell was not solely interested, however, in good research by scholars. In both the book on method and the original article (Campbell & Stanley, 1963) that formed the basis for the book, Campbell was concerned with how we might learn, to very practical ends, what methods of teaching might improve students' learning.

Second, we might consider whether organizations are the appropriate level for considering the pros and cons of copying for introducing variation into the systems and processes of organizations. Organizations represent but one sort of social system for which blind-variation-and-selective-retention is important to development. As discussed at the outset of this chapter, copying has been advanced as an efficient mechanism for introducing variation at the organizational subunit, industry, and even regional levels of national economies. I have concentrated on organizations mainly because, by focusing on one level (and any level could have been chosen), we can most clearly examine the pros and cons of copying.

The existence of multiple and interdependent levels in social systems, however, raises a question about whether it is necessary for individual organizations in a social system to carry the burden, for society, of blind-variation-and-selective-retention. Perhaps, over the multitude of organizations copying one another, and because of the very difficulties I have described for faithful copying to occur, sufficient variation in attributes and practices will emerge for selection to operate. Perhaps, as Schumpeter (1934) might have argued, the detrimental convergence on a particular set of socially agreed-upon practices will itself create problems that will, in time, engender some low-probability trials that will dramatically demonstrate a new and better attribute or practice. For our economy and our society, these are comforting speculations.

Copying systems may, in the end, only guarantee that they will be the failures upon which selection eventually will operate. If this is true, then, no matter the broad benefit to society of such failures, copying, for the given system, will not have produced a better fit with the environment. Perhaps actors in such systems might reduce the chances of such a fate if they will remember that blind variations in rather great numbers within the system, and with most suffering failure, is the only route to sociocultural evolution.

Conclusions

In this chapter, I have cast a perhaps excessively critical eye on the prevalent, seemingly legitimate, and perhaps selected-for practice of organizations to learn about and to copy the attributes and practices of other organizations. No credible argument against the use of copying can be offered. The *potential* benefits of copying are simply too evident. Moreover, to argue for abandonment would fundamentally cut off a source of variation in the evolution of social systems and thus would be neither true to the way in which actors in systems behave nor fair to the premises of the blind-variation-and-selective-retention model, which, as developed by Campbell, does not care about the sources of blind variations. Copying as a source of blind variation is as legitimate as any other mechanism in organizations that will produce the necessary variation on which selection criteria can operate.

It is fair to ask, however, of any variation-producing mechanism whether it leads to a reduction in the production of other variations, and if so, to guard against this outcome. As I have argued, and as Campbell recognized, any variation-selecting system that engenders a belief in our ability to know in advance—that is, to be prescient about—the outcomes of variation fundamentally and detrimentally reduces the ability of a system to develop. Copying quietly seduces such belief. The result may be not variations in a system's attributes and practices—variations that are subject to selection—but rather merely occasional change that, because of its singular instance, is never subjected to selective processes.

Note

1. During the last year, while this chapter was being prepared, virtually every major news publication, including *Forbes*, *Fortune*, *Business Week*, and *The Wall Street Journal*,

and even National Public Radio, has examined the attempts of regions throughout the United States to copy attributes of Silicon Valley. It is intriguing and perhaps instructive to note that all prognostications are for the likely failure of the copying regions.

References

Abrahamson, E. (1991). Managerial fads and fashions: The diffusion and rejection of innovations. *Academy of Management Review, 16*, 586-612.

Arthur, W. B. (1988). Self-reinforcing mechanisms in economics. In P. W. Anderson, K. J. Arrow, & D. Pines (Eds.), *The economy as a complex evolving system* (pp. 9-31). Redwood City, CA: Addison-Wesley.

Arthur, W. B. (1989). Competing technologies, increasing returns, and lock-in by historical events: The dynamics of allocation under increasing returns. *Economic Journal, 99*, 116-131.

Arthur, W. B. (1990). Positive feedbacks in the economy. *Scientific American, 262*, 92-99.

Campbell, D. T. (1969). Variation and selective retention in socio-cultural evolution. *General Systems, 14*, 69-85.

Campbell, D. T. (1974a). Evolutionary epistemology. In P. A. Schilpp (Ed.), *The philosophy of Karl R. Popper* (The Library of Living Philosophers, Vol. 14, pp. 413-463). La Salle, IL: Open Court.

Campbell, D. T. (1974b). Unjustified variation and selective retention in scientific discovery. In F. J. Ayala & T. Dobzhansky (Eds.), *Studies in the philosophy of biology* (pp. 139-161). London: Macmillan.

Campbell, D. T. (1977a). Discussion comment on "the natural selection model of conceptual evolution." *Philosophy of Science, 44*, 502-507.

Campbell, D. T. (1977b). Keeping the data honest in the experimenting society. In H. W. Melton & J. H. David (Eds.), *Interdisciplinary dimensions of accounting for social goals and social organizations* (pp. 37-42). Columbus, OH: Grid, Inc.

Campbell, D. T. (1981). Introduction: Getting ready for the experimenting society. In L. Saxe & M. Fine (Eds.), *Social experiments: Methods for design and evaluation* (pp. 13-18). Beverly Hills, CA: Sage.

Campbell, D. T. (1982). The "blind-variation-and-selective-retention" theme. In J. M. Broughton & D. J. Freeman-Moir (Eds.), *The cognitive-developmental psychology of James Mark Baldwin: Current theory and research in genetic epistemology* (pp. 87-96). Norwood, NJ: Ablex.

Campbell, D. T. (1990). Levels of organization, downward causation, and the selection-theory approach to evolutionary epistemology. In G. Greenberg & E. Tobach (Eds.), *Theories of the evolution of knowing* (pp. 1-17). Hillsdale, NJ: Lawrence Erlbaum.

Campbell, D. T. (1994). How individual and face-to-face-group selection undermine firm selection in organizational evolution. In J.A.C. Baum & J. V. Singh (Eds.), *Evolutionary dynamics of organizations* (pp. 23-38). New York: Oxford University Press.

Campbell, D. T., & Paller, B. T. (1989). Extending evolutionary epistemology to "justifying" scientific beliefs: A sociological rapprochement with a fallibilist perceptual foundationalism. In K. Hahlweg & C. A. Hooker (Eds.), *Issues in evolutionary epistemology* (pp. 231-257). Albany: State University of New York Press.

Campbell, D. T., & Stanley, J. C. (1966). *Experimental and quasi-experimental designs for research.* Chicago: Rand McNally.

Dawkins, R. (1996a). *The blind watchmaker: Why the evidence of evolution reveals a universe without design.* New York: W. W. Norton.

Dawkins, R. (1996b). *Climbing Mount Improbable.* New York: W. W. Norton.

DiMaggio, P., & Powell, W. W. (1983). The iron cage revisited: Institutional isomorphism and collective rationality in organizational fields. *American Sociological Review, 48*, 147-160.

Gould, S. J. (1990). *Wonderful life: The Burgess shale and the nature of history.* New York. W. W. Norton.

Hannan, M. T., & Freeman, J. (1984). Structural inertia and organizational change. *American Sociological Review, 49*, 149-164.

Hannan, M. T., & Freeman, J. (1989). *Organizational Ecology.* Cambridge, MA: Harvard University Press.

Haunschild, P. R., & Miner, A. S. (1997). Modes of interorganizational imitation: The effects of outcome salience and uncertainty. *Administrative Science Quarterly, 42*, 472-500.

Imai, M. (1986). *Kaizen: The key to Japan's competitive success.* New York: Random House.

Levitt, B., & March, J. G. (1988). Organizational learning. *Annual Review of Sociology, 14*, 319-340.

Miner, A. S., & Haunschild, P. R. (1995). Population level learning. In L. L. Cummings & B. Staw (Eds.), *Research in organizational behavior* (Vol. 17, pp. 115-166). Greenwich, CT: JAI.

Mizruchi, M. (1996). What do interlocks do? An analysis, critique, and assessment of research on interlocking directorates. *Annual Review of Sociology, 22*, 271-298.

Palmer, D. (1983). Broken ties: Interlocking directorates and intercorporate coordination. *Administrative Science Quarterly, 28*, 40-55.

Pfeffer, J., & Salancik, G. R. (1978). *The external control of organizations.* New York: Harper & Row.

Richards, R. J. (1977). The natural selection model of conceptual evolution. *Philosophy of Science, 44*, 494-501.

Schumpeter, J. (1934). *The theory of economic development: An inquiry into profits, capital, credit, interest, and the business cycle.* Cambridge, MA: Harvard University Press.

Stinchcombe, A. L. (1965). Social structure and organization. In J. G. March (Ed.), *Handbook of organizations* (pp. 142-193). Chicago: Rand McNally.

Tavris, C. (1975, September). The experimenting society: To find programs that work, government must measure its failures—a conversation with Donald T. Campbell. *Psychology Today*, pp. 46-56.

Tolbert, P. S., & Zucker, L. G. (1983). Institutional sources of change in the formal structure of organizations: The diffu-sion of civil service reform, 1880-1935. *Administrative Science Quarterly, 28*, 22-39.

Zucker, L. G. (1977). The role of institutionalization in cultural persistence. *American Sociological Review, 42*, 726-743.

Chapter 6

Selection Processes Inside Organizations

The Self-Reinforcing Consequences of Success

DANNY MILLER

Donald T. Campbell's legacy to organizational science is manifold. Some of his very greatest contributions show how random variation and selective-retention processes shape organizational forms and practices and mold firms to their environments. Unlike many organizational ecologists, however, Campbell casts aside the evolutionism that has selective forces inevitably improving fit. Instead, he suggests that

> one must examine ALL of the selective and retentive forces at work, *not just those that would predict improved adaptation*. Where we find "clearly" effective organizational form, then selection, at that level of organization, for that level of efficacy, is probably the best explanation. But this must not lead us into thinking that ALL selection processes lead to optimal organizational form. There are also selection forces at all other organizational levels. Those at the individual and group levels may lead to firm-level dysfunction, and may be parasitic or entropic in effect. (Campbell, 1994, p. 23)

This chapter embraces and explores these ideas. First, like Campbell (1965, 1990b, 1991, 1994), it investigates selection forces within the organization as opposed to those beyond its boundaries—the former have been underemphasized by the organizational ecology literature, and Campbell did well to draw attention to them. Second, this analysis examines information- and belief-based selection forces. These "vicarious" selectors take the form of efforts at rationality that substitute presumed knowledge, with all its fallibility, for "real selective factors" that operate by extinguishing entities (Campbell, 1960, 1970, 1990a, 1991). A third Campbellian theme that is central to this analysis is that the selective forces that enhance adaptation at the local (e.g., executive, group, or departmental) level may circumvent adaptation at the organizational level (Campbell, 1965, 1982, 1994).

Most evolutionists have concentrated on the selection forces of punishment or failure. This analysis, however, will examine selective-retention forces that come from success. Success may drive some of Campbell's most potent internal selectors by shaping thought, behavior, and structure (1970, 1991), but the consequences of success may engender exactly the kinds of conflict that Campbell (1965, 1982, 1994) has noted between the adaptive responses of subsystems and the viability of the larger organization. A company's success, it will be argued, can have a dramatic impact by "selecting in" certain ideas, people, groups, and practices, and "selecting out" others. For example, it may benefit the empowered and punish others, it may reinforce established practices while inhibiting new ones, and it may replace diversity and variation with simplicity and stability.

It will be argued that once set into motion, the outcomes and processes engendered by success will be self-perpetuating, further exacerbating the conflict that Campbell (1965, 1994) identified between subunit adaptations and the survival of the larger entity (see also Baum, this volume). These processes can override external influences, at least until very critical conditions are reached. In fact, in successful organizations, there will be a natural tendency for internal selective-retention processes to dominate external ones.

On the Wings of Success

Successful organizations, like temples, are places of worship—worship of heroes, ideologies, and recipes. The potential for superstition, idolatry, intolerance, and extremism is thus ever present. Here, with Campbell's help, I wish to look inside the temple, to review the research and speculate further on what happens when managers take their firms to be successful.

Turning the Tables: Success as a Predictor

Over the past four decades, scholars of management have been much preoccupied with explaining organizational performance. They have analyzed managerial factors such as leadership, organizational aspects such as culture and structure, and

strategic elements such as strategy content, process, and fit with environment. The results have been mixed, with one set of findings contradicting another (see reviews by Meyer & Zucker, 1989, and Scott, 1995). This may be because most studies of performance are cross-sectional rather than longitudinal. In many cases, what are believed to be the causes of good performance—strong cultures (Deal & Kennedy, 1982), decisive leadership, precise controls (Simons, 1995), and simple, focused strategies (Rommel, 1995; Treacy & Wiersema, 1995)—might actually be its *effects*. Here I explore not the determinants of good performance but rather its consequences. Among them are some of the very managerial, organizational, and strategic factors that have been viewed as contributors to success. To sharpen my arguments, I will occasionally contrast outcomes from success with those from failure. This chapter nevertheless is about the former. The consequences of failure are too complex to be explored properly here and already have benefited from insightful analyses elsewhere (Ocasio, 1995; Sitkin, 1992).

Actual Versus Perceived Success?

Because "success" or "good performance" affects organizations largely through the perceptions of top decision makers, it is ultimately a subjective construct. In the business organizations that are the subjects of this analysis, success is defined by most executives in financial terms—sales or market share growth and/or profitability—and success often will be gauged relative to the performance of significant competitors. Certainly, perceived success is likely to increase with the level and duration of superior performance in an executive's chosen indicators (Sitkin, 1992); however, the indicators and thresholds of success vary among industries, firms, and even individual managers. Thus, in the discussion that follows, "organizational success" will always refer to *perceived* good performance along the indicators most valued by a firm's key executives. Later in the chapter, I will discuss the relationship between objective indicators and perceived success.

Early Intimations About the Evolutionary Impetus of Success

Twenty years ago, Miller and Friesen (1977) derived a rough taxonomy of business organizations. They wanted to find the most common types or "configurations" in a diverse sample of major companies. After dividing their sample into high and low performers, they identified a few prevalent but very different successful types, along with a few common but again highly varied unsuccessful types. What they found was surprising: Instead of the successful types being very distinct from the unsuccessful ones, almost every successful type had a similar unsuccessful counterpart. The differences between the successful and unsuccessful members of the pairs were subtle but interesting. First, the unsuccessful types seemed simpler and more extreme: For example, among bureaucracies, the unsuccessful type was more bureaucratic and inertial than the successful one, but for innovative and entrepreneurial companies, the unsuccessful firms were more innovative and took greater risks than the high performers. Second, less information processing took place within the unsuccessful types—less scanning of the environment, less careful analysis in making decisions. The operating themes, goals, central skills, and even the structures and strategies of the successful and unsuccessful members of each of the pairs, however, were similar.

Could it be, then, that successful companies ultimately *evolved into* their unsuccessful twins? To answer this question, Miller and Friesen (1984) began to study organizations over time. They found that different types of companies evolved in different ways—bureaucracies tended to become more bureaucratic, whereas entrepreneurial enterprises became more entrepreneurial. This "momentum" was especially common among companies that were doing well. Such firms extended their current practices whenever these appeared to pay off. Only serious reversals of fortune interrupted this propensity of thriving companies to become more extreme, less nuanced versions of their former selves (Miller, 1990, 1993, 1994; Miller & Friesen, 1984). In short, success may have a major effect on the way organizations evolve, yet past performance has not often been used as a predictor variable in research on organizations (Miller, 1994; Milliken & Lant, 1991). This research begins to speculate more systematically about the evolutionary processes that occur in organizations as a result of their past success.

The Evolutionary Terms of the Analysis

According to Campbell (1965, 1982, 1994), the evolutionary model applies not only to the emergence of biological forms and species but also to the development of cultures, social organizations, and even knowledge. The three components of the well-known model are variation, selection, and retention.

First, there need to be variations upon which selection can operate. These may be haphazard, heterogeneous, chance, random, blind, or whatever. In organic evolution, mutations are the variations of interest. In learning, exploratory trial-and-error responses are central. Across organizations, variations occur among competencies, structural forms, or routines, and within organizations, the province of interest here, there are differences among managers and departments; among routines, skills, and specialties; and among competitive tactics (at an instant and over time). It is these latter differences, whatever their source, that will be "operated upon" by the selective criteria that emerge from success.

The second aspect of the model—consistent selection criteria—acts by selectively eliminating, propagating, or retaining certain variations. In biology, there are different rates of survival for particular mutants, and in learning, there occurs a differential reinforcement of responses. Among organizations, selection may operate via the differential survival of particular structural forms. Within organizations, selection may occur via the hiring, promotion, reward, and empowerment (or expulsion or demotion) of particular individuals, groups, or departments. Internal selection also may operate via the more exclusive support—or extinction—of particular rituals, goals, routines, information, decision criteria, policies, and tactics. As we shall see, after success, internal selection criteria may fail to reflect external adaptive requirements because parochial interests become too powerful. In addition, internal selection not only reduces variation within an organization but also can impair managers' ability to perceive important variations in the external environment.

The third component of Campbell's model is a mechanism for the retention or "the preservation, duplication, or propagation of the positively selected variants" (1965, p. 27). In biology, this can be the duplication process of the chromosome-gene system of plants and animals. In learning, it is memory. Within organizations, it is the rules, policies, structures, systems, and routines that regularize behavior.

Categories of Post-Success Behavior

Campbell (1965, 1982, 1994) maintains that selective forces operating at the individual, group, and departmental levels can importantly shape the way an organization sees and responds to its environment. I believe that past success will engender or augment a number of such forces.

First, I will examine the impact of success on *managerial cognitions, attributions, and attitudes*. Success, it will be argued, causes managers to focus on and attribute merit to fewer concerns or practices, usually those that had been prized to begin with. The differential reinforcement of certain beliefs and responses in real or imagined learning is a fundamental selective mechanism that is associated with myopic learning, political opportunism, and managerial overconfidence.

Perceived success also can transform the *culture* of an organization into one of greater intolerance and homogeneity. Here, internal selection takes the form of channeling a preponderance of status and clout to departments and people with the "right" skills, while other parties become less influential. Skewed organizational *structures* also arise that accord disproportionate power to a corporate elite. At the same time, routines and systems may be embraced that institutionalize the winning strategy

and enforce its rigorous implementation; these routines and systems act as important retention mechanisms.[1]

Finally, success is expected to have important consequences for *strategy process and content*. Extremes begin to develop in decision making: extremes of complacency in the case of conservative companies, or of risk taking in entrepreneurial firms. In addition, strategies become more simple—more focused on a few critical elements—and also more inertial, or less apt to change. These developments make an organization insensitive and unresponsive, increasing the likelihood that internal and local selection processes will encumber effective adaptation of the whole organization to its external environment (Campbell, 1994).

Having proposed some consequences of success, I examine their interactions and moderating conditions. A theme of this research is that many of the outcomes of success reinforce each other and are self-perpetuating. They therefore reduce variation, narrow the criteria for selection, and augment the mechanisms of retention. Table 6.1 summarizes some consequences of success.

Managerial Consequences

Campbell's random variation, selective-retention model can help us understand how managers learn and make inferences about their environments, and how they go wrong under conditions of success. Campbell (1960, p. 380; 1990b; 1994, pp. 30-31) believes that the creative thought and wisdom of managers arise largely from an inductive, trial-and-error process by which they learn about their environments. The related "solutions" and problem solving, however, are not "based on 'reality' directly, but only on incomplete memory and simplified extrapolation. Even where wise, the wisdom reflects past realities, not the current or future ones directly relevant to group survival" (Campbell, 1994, p. 31). I will argue that perceived success further distorts this fallible process. It impinges on the cognitions, attributions, and attitudes of managers, engendering myopia and supersti-

TABLE 6.1 Consequences of Perceived Success

Managerial	Organizational	Strategic
Myopic learning	Monolithic culture	Extremes of action or inaction
Opportunism	Skewed structure	Simple strategy
Overconfidence	Restricted information processing systems	Inertial strategy Unresponsive to environment

tion, inspiring opportunism, and promoting overconfidence.

1. Myopic Learning

The "incomplete memory" and "simplified extrapolations" noted by Campbell (1994) very much influence how managers learn from their successes. According to Milliken and Lant (1991), "managers must attempt to figure out why the organization achieved the performance outcomes it did" (p. 130). Administrators try to learn about why they succeed or fail. Such learning, however, is by no means an unbiased activity; rather, it is myopic (Levinthal & March, 1981, 1993). March and his associates describe a process they call "superstitious learning" (Levitt & March, 1988; March, 1991). Managers, they claim, attribute outcomes to the events that preceded them, but these events are chosen from a small set of possibilities, a set that is constrained by selective attention and long-established prejudices (Levinthal & March, 1993; Weick, 1984). When outcomes are positive, therefore, managers ascribe them to internal acts on which they already had focused (Bettman & Weitz, 1983; Brockner, 1992; Salancik & Meindl, 1984; Staw, McKechnie, & Puffer, 1983). In the process, they may single out things of no, or even of negative, consequence. In this way, myopic learning induces managers to give more and more credit to fewer policies and practices that they continue to exploit—especially if there are too few negative results to broaden managers' range of concerns (Levinthal & March, 1993; Sitkin, 1992). Thus, for example, the managerial elite at General Motors and Ford attributed virtually all good re-

sults to stifling financial controls, even though the obsessive application of these controls ultimately was very harmful (Halberstam, 1986; Wright, 1979).

Myopic learning is more likely to occur after success than after failure. When managers mistakenly credit a practice or skill for good performance, they receive little information to tell them they are wrong (Lant & Montgomery, 1987). Success, then, underwrites comfortable illusions (Sitkin, 1992). On the other hand, failure, although it may be ignored or rationalized for a while (Staw, Sandelands, & Dutton, 1981), ultimately forces remedial search (Ocasio, 1995). Although this process will be biased, the shock and urgency of a crisis eventually will force more realistic evaluations. Starbuck and Milliken (1988), for example, tell of how the administrators at NASA began to scrutinize their systems only after the *Challenger* tragedy. A paucity of accidents had prevented them from learning about their safety problems earlier.

Proposition 1: The set of concerns and variations that top managers attend to and learn from will decrease with the perceived level of past success.

2. Opportunism and the Politics of Attribution

Managers are likely to attribute success to their own policies because this attribution flatters them, highlights their good judgment, and enhances their status (Alvesson, 1994; Miller & Ross, 1975; Milliken & Lant, 1991; Salancik & Meindl, 1984). Even where success is due to random fluctuations or windfalls in the market, opportunistic managers are wont to credit the soundness of their own policies and decisions. Moreover, powerful managers wield the influence to credit success to the practices, actions, and departments with which they are most closely identified. In other words, managers tend not to credit just any behavior contemporaneous with good results, but especially those practices and skills that they themselves have developed or promoted, or are most closely identified with (Kiesler & Sproull, 1982). In that way, executives are able to benefit personally from the good performance of their enterprises.

Proposition 2: The selective preference leaders have for the policies and practices that they personally have created, publicly backed, or are identified with (vis-à-vis all other policies and practices) will increase with the perceived level of past success.

3. Overconfidence

Most managers are eager to "put a face" to success, and usually it is that of the CEO and perhaps those of other members of top management (Salancik & Meindl, 1984). Only the most well grounded and resolute leaders can remain objective following the resulting admiration (Kets de Vries & Miller, 1992). Indeed, fine records give many executives the impression that they, their policies, and their routines are invincible (Sitkin, 1992). This is doubly true when there are too few past experiences of failure to arm managers with a sobering humility (Starbuck & Milliken, 1988).[2]

Overconfidence can be self-reinforcing: It leads managers to ascribe *future* success to their own abilities and policies rather than, say, to chance (Miller & Ross, 1975; Salancik & Meindl, 1984). These growing opportunities for self-flattery build confidence still further.

Proposition 3A: Overconfidence in current selection-retention mechanisms will increase with the perceived level of past success.

Overconfidence can lead to complacency. In their well-known research, Kahneman and Tversky (1979) and Tversky and Kahneman (1986) found that decision makers use targets or reference points in evaluating choices. People are shown to be risk averting when expected outcomes are above their reference points, a condition that often prevails when a firm is perceived to have an excellent track record. Thus, after success, managers tend to become more reluctant to take new or different actions: They become complacent and favor the exploitation of current activities over the exploration of new ones (see also Levinthal & March, 1993, p. 102; Sitkin, 1992; Sitkin & Pablo, 1992). Thus variation, an important vehicle for further learning and adaptation, is reduced.

Proposition 3B: Variation-reducing complacency will increase with the perceived level of past success.

Organizational Consequences

4. Monolithic Culture

Campbell (1982, 1994, p. 29) argued that regular face-to-face contacts among members of a group increase the chances of "ingroup solidarity, homogeneity of belief, and discipline." He believed this especially to be the case under conditions of external threat. I will argue, however, that success also can produce these reactions—to the benefit of a small group, department, or set of actors, and at the expense of the adaptiveness of the whole organization, which ultimately "becomes organized around purposes that are contrary to the larger group's collective interests" (Campbell, 1994, p. 30).

Perceptions of success come to influence beliefs about a firm's central competencies and skills, the composition of its top management team, managerial consensus, and the tolerance for dissent. In all cases, there is a tendency toward specialization, homogeneity, and intolerance.

Many of the cultural outcomes brought about by success occur in part via Campbell's (1965, 1991, 1994) processes of selection that take place *within* an organization. These processes reinforce the priorities, competencies, and practices favored by the elite while extinguishing most others (Burgelman, 1991). Scholars of self-organizing systems call this the phenomenon of "them that has gets" (Masuch, 1985; Waldrop, 1992, p. 36). The following case of "competency traps" is illustrative.

A Celebration of Competency

The managerial attributions and opportunistic reactions described above suggest that certain practices and parties associated with success become the source of *competency credos*. These beliefs by top managers about the competencies of their organization serve as powerful internal selection forces (Campbell, 1965, 1991, 1994; Levinthal & March, 1993, p. 102; Meyer & Starbuck,

1991). Such credos identify and celebrate the distinctive skills and talented parties of an organization and thus guide resource allocation, strategic priority setting, routines, and reward and information systems. If, as suggested, success reinforces past beliefs, then beliefs about competency are no exception (Miller, Droge, & Vickery, 1997).

Because they direct attention and resources toward favored practices and parties, competency credos can be self-fulfilling. They cause the skills and constituencies they celebrate to be funded and developed, while degrading others. In so doing, they contract a firm's range of talents. Levinthal and March (1993, p. 102), for example, talk about the "mutual positive feedback between experience and competence." Firms concentrate on what they believe they are good at, thereby becoming ever better at it and worse at other things. Competency credos and the skills they engender also ensure that any subsequent success will be attributed to the favored competency. The ability to reevaluate the wisdom of engaging in particular activities is thereby reduced.

The "scientists" who controlled Cray Research, for example, credited research and development for their firm's success, whereas the engineer-dominated top management team at Digital Equipment applauded design quality. As a result, the firms put more attention and resources into these respective areas, providing generous budgets and talented people. This sharpened the skills or departments further and increased their role in creating success. It also drew attention and resources away from other areas that then became even weaker because the best employees were driven away (Miller, 1990). In short, the mere ascription of competency, whether warranted or not, may actually increase the truth of that ascription as it makes a skill, initially celebrated, even stronger.

Proposition 4: A firm's celebrated competencies and skill set will narrow with the perceived level of past success.

Internal selection processes such as those identified by Campbell shape not only the celebrated competencies of a firm but also the composition and stability of its top management team, the homogeneity of goals and beliefs among its managers, and the tolerance of ideological differences (Campbell, 1994).

The Top Management Team

The narrowing worldviews, sharper preferences, and overconfidence of successful leaders may come to be reflected in the increasing *homogeneity* and *stability* of their top management teams (Hambrick, 1993). If CEOs celebrate a single function, they are apt to accord its managers the most representation and influence on the top management team. At Digital Equipment, for example, engineers dominated the top team; at Ford, GM, and ITT it was the finance people (Miller, 1990). It is as though chief executives, confident of which skills made their enterprises great, made sure to stack their top teams with the possessors of those skills. Most of the managers on the teams also shared very similar beliefs (Halberstam, 1986; Wright, 1979).

As long as companies are doing well, the composition of the top management team is unlikely to change very much. After all, winning teams rarely alter their rosters (Carroll, 1984; Hambrick, 1993; Helmich, 1978; Keck & Tushman, 1993). Team stability, along with the homogeneous backgrounds and beliefs of top managers, can contribute greatly to the inertia and insularity of successful organizations (Tushman & Romanelli, 1985; Wiersema & Bantel, 1992).

Proposition 5: The homogeneity and stability of the top management team will be positively related to the perceived level of past success.

Intolerance

According to Campbell (1982, p. 435):

It is the common circumstance of modern social organizations . . . that they are made up of many separate face-to-face groups [each of which] tends to become an ingroup whose solidarity tends to be motivated by treating other units as outgroups. Given human nature . . . such occurrences are not occasional, isolated instances, but are unavoidable, universal tendencies. If they fail to produce major problems for large organizations it is because other factors keep them in check, not because they are absent.

Success, I believe, will amplify these problems by diminishing intergroup respect and tolerance, as well as by removing the necessity for intergroup understanding, communication, and collaboration to address common threats. Success, as noted above, reinforces top managers' convictions about which skills and parties make an organization successful. In celebrating some groups and degrading others, top managers may foster intolerant cultures and promote homogeneous beliefs within favored departments (Campbell, 1982; Martin & Meyerson, 1988; Sitkin, 1992, pp. 235-236). This may drive out those with different perspectives, further increasing consensus among those who are left and perpetuating a cycle of closure (Chatman, 1991; Janis, 1972; Schneider, 1987). As Campbell (1982) has argued, in-group solidarity is almost always accompanied by out-group hostility.

Uniformity of belief breeds intolerance, especially when it is enforced by a like-minded elite. One of the most destructive aspects of focused, homogeneous cultures is their impatience with dissent and alternative viewpoints (Campbell, 1982; Martin, 1990, 1992; Turner, 1990). When almost everyone agrees, opposing viewpoints go unheard and unimagined (Asch, 1956; Janis, 1972). Managers may come to take offense at or even make taboo any challengers or subunits that question their policies.

> *Proposition 6:* Homogeneity of belief and intolerance for opposing or critical viewpoints will vary directly with the perceived level of past success.

5. Skewed Structures

Campbell's (1965, 1991, 1994) internal selection forces may also shape the structure of organizations, especially in the context of success. After success, organizational structures are apt to get more skewed and specialized—more designed to institutionalize and implement a celebrated recipe. Structures do this via the way power and rewards are distributed, the way tasks are routinized, and the way information is processed.

Centralization

Success allows those in power to get even more power. It builds and enhances the reputations of the top managers, who usually are accorded credit for organizational success (Pfeffer, 1981). It also gives these administrators more slack resources to allocate the way they see fit (Cyert & March, 1963), and it makes top managers more credible and influential (Mintzberg, 1983). In short, with reputation comes power, and with power comes the ability to further enhance reputation. Powerful managers, for example, can shape organizational goals and appraisal and information systems to make themselves and their companies look good (Scott, 1995). The same reasoning suggests that more power also will go to those departments that are given the most credit for success (Martin, 1992).

> *Proposition 7:* Centralization of power in the CEO, the top management team, and the dominant function or department will increase with the perceived level of past success.

Routines

If success encourages managers to believe that they have found the right approach, then there will be much effort devoted to establishing routines, programs, policies, and special positions to implement and institutionalize this approach—to enhance its consistency and reliability (Campbell, 1994; Hannan & Freeman, 1984). Success, in other words, reinforces and thus stabilizes behavior, and stable behavior can be programmed most easily by retention mechanisms such as routines, formal policies, reward and information systems, and rituals (Levinthal & March, 1993; Nelson & Winter, 1982). Success also generates rules to ensure behavioral repetition, which in turn creates stable social arrangements (Campbell, 1982; Drazin & Sandelands, 1992; Scott, 1995). Again, these rules facilitate the routinization of dominant organizational preoccupations. This process will be more thorough and will meet with less resistance in successful firms where there is consensus among the powerful concerning goals and means.

Proposition 8: The specialization of routines to serve a dominant goal, skill, or practice will increase as a function of the perceived level of past success.

Reward and Selection Systems

When upper-echelon executives believe that they have found the formula for success, they make that formula very explicit and design selection, promotion, and reward systems accordingly (Campbell, 1994; Chatman, 1991; Schneider, 1987). This ensures that only the "right" kinds of people will be recruited, retained, and promoted. The resulting homogeneity in the skills and outlooks of personnel, especially of top-level personnel, then reinforces existing hiring and advancement standards (Campbell, 1994; Schneider, 1987).

> *Proposition 9:* Targeting of reward systems to reinforce only the most prized achievements and skills will increase with the perceived level of past success.

6. Restricted Information Processing Systems

According to Campbell (1994, p. 36):

> Management information systems . . . produce "proxy variables" that are componentially (and/or factorially) complex, with not all of the components that determine scores relevant to the variable the indicator is intended to monitor. Once any such proxy variable becomes used in managerial control, "irrelevant" components that will produce the desired score come to dominate, and validity is undermined.

This process can be made more pernicious by a firm's success. Success reduces the incentive to search and narrows the scope of search (Cyert & March, 1963; Levinthal & March, 1981). This often is reflected in firms' information processing systems. After success, companies tend to do less scanning of their markets, they monitor fewer external contingencies, and they consider a narrower range of factors and criteria in making decisions (Aguilar, 1967; Miller, 1994; Walsh, 1995; Wilensky, 1971).

The information systems of successful firms are targeted to pick up, pass upward, and take into account only very specific kinds of information: those directly reflecting the goals, primary skills, and market factors that are established preoccupations (Starbuck, 1985). This targeting and specialization of information gathering, dissemination, and processing systems leads a company to focus on "good news"—for example, on feedback about what it does well—while neglecting potentially important information that is external, qualitative, or peripheral to the current strategy (Ashton, 1976; Wilensky, 1971). Indeed, success gives some top managers the power to decide how success itself will be measured, thus perhaps leading to the further specialization of intelligence systems. Campbell (1994) argues that the selection of the proxy variables used in information systems is often made to serve the interests of a powerful individual or subgroup.

> *Proposition 10A:* The sensitivity and scope of information processing systems will diminish with the perceived level of past success.
>
> *Proposition 10B:* The targeting and routinization of information systems to focus on a dominant goal, skill, or function will increase with the perceived level of past success.

Strategic Consequences

The forces of selective retention initiated by success may also have an important impact on a firm's decision-making practices, its strategies, and its ability to adapt to its environment.

7. Extremes in Action and Inaction

Earlier arguments suggest that success will induce overconfidence in existing policies and practices. This can lead to extremes of action or inaction, depending on the initial preferences of those in power. The rationale is simply that success reinforces "more of the same" (March, 1991; Milliken & Lant, 1991). In a study of the histories of 36 major companies, Miller (1994) found that during periods that followed success, decision-making styles tended to be more "extreme" than during periods following poor or mediocre performance. For example, after success, companies that had been conservative in their approach to decision making tended to become still more conservative. Firms that had been entrepreneurial, on the other hand, became reckless. Similarly, companies that did a good deal of product innovation accelerated the pace after success, whereas firms that engaged reluctantly in adaptation stopped changing entirely.

> *Proposition 11:* Extremes of conservatism and risk taking both will increase with the perceived level of past success.

8. Simple Strategies

As argued above, the learning processes following success tend to "focus attention and narrow competence" (Levinthal & March, 1993, p. 96). Indeed, the strategies of successful companies can be distinguished in large part by their simplicity. In their research on the U.S. domestic airline industry, Miller and Chen (1996) found that the most successful airlines began to focus more narrowly in the way they competed. They tended to concentrate on their favorite tactics: altering prices, *or* manipulating their route structures, *or* marketing aggressively. The more successful the company, the greater its tendency to concentrate on just one or two kinds of competitive actions in its day-to-day rivalry. In effect, companies with the best financial returns narrowed and focused the repertoire of actions that they used in competing. Firms with poorer performance were far more likely to employ a broader range of actions—a wider repertoire (Miller & Chen, 1996).[3] Success, then, appears to cause several related kinds of strategic "simplification": first, a preoccupation with fewer kinds of day-to-day market-oriented actions; and second, focus by top executives on fewer competencies, and collaterally, an allocation of human and financial resources to fewer activities.

> *Proposition 12:* The simplicity of business strategies—their concentration on a few kinds of day-to-day competitive actions and competencies, and a correspondingly skewed allocation of re-

sources—will increase with the perceived level of past success.

9. Strategic Inertia

Success may also promote strategic inertia (Amburgey, Kelly, & Barnett, 1993; Amburgey & Miner, 1992; Lant, Milliken, & Batra, 1992). The rationale seems to be "don't fix it if it ain't broke" (Sitkin, 1992; Sitkin & Pablo, 1992). Certainly, sticking to the old ways of doing things poses the least personal risk for most managers, and their past success provides them with a good excuse to pursue this course. Thus, fine performance gives managers a strong incentive to remain with the central elements of the status quo (Lant & Montgomery, 1987). Miller and Chen (1994) found that after success, companies are far less likely to alter the kinds of decisions they use to compete on a day-to-day basis: They stick closely to a very stable repertoire of actions. Moreover, thriving organizations are loath to embark on any significant reorientations (Amburgey et al., 1993; Miller & Chen, 1994; Miller & Friesen, 1984; Tushman & Romanelli, 1985). Spender (1990) has referred to "recipes" that many successful companies and even industries follow. The term *recipe* very much connotes a formula that always yields the same predictable results. In following these recipes, successful firms develop conventional modes of behavior that do not change until there is a good deal of pressure to do so.

Inertia can endure even beyond the period of success. Indeed, the work on organizational stagnation shows that many firms resist making significant changes until after they have been hurt (Hedberg, Nystrom, & Starbuck, 1976; Starbuck, Greve, & Hedberg, 1978). Pain, it seems, is the doctor most organizations heed. It is important to emphasize that I am not claiming that success will prevent all change; rather, it will induce companies to pursue changes that build on and extend an existing core theme or skill (Tushman & Romanelli, 1985). For example, the strategic simplification to which I have referred *is* a kind of change.

> *Proposition 13:* Inertia and momentum in strategy and competitive methods will increase with the perceived level of past success.

10. Unresponsiveness to the Environment

Campbell (1965, 1982, 1991, 1994) has argued that the selective-retention forces operating at the subsystem level can hinder adaptation of the overall system. That is exactly what happens as a result of the processes discussed until now. The resulting homogeneous beliefs and cultures, targeted structures and systems, and simple and inertial strategies can erode a successful firm's fit with its environment. The environment keeps changing, but the organization does not. Also, managers confident that they are doing the right thing fail to monitor closely the needs of customers or the actions of competitors (Janis, 1972). And homogeneous and intolerant cultures ensure that challenges to the status quo will be rare and will go unheeded. Finally, simple strategies are so focused that they are apt to miss emergent contingencies in the environment (Miller, 1993).

Miller (1994) found that the fit of an organization with its environment was more likely to deteriorate after periods of success than after periods of failure. Specifically, a company's structure, processes, and strategy were the least likely to match the levels of environmental uncertainty after years of good performance. In another study, Miller (1992) found internal fit and external fit to be negatively correlated: Those companies that achieved tight complementarity among their elements of strategy and structure were the most apt to adopt practices that were inappropriate to their external environments.

> *Proposition 14:* The fit of an organization with its environment will weaken as a function of the perceived level of past success.

Chains and Networks of Causality

Propositions 1 to 14 are not independent. Collectively, they suggest that there are chains or networks of causality that link managerial, organizational, and strategic outcomes of success. For example, the overconfidence born of success can generate strategic inertia (Amburgey & Miner, 1992), managerial complacency can atrophy intelligence activities and systems (Daft, Sormunen, &

Parks, 1988), and myopic learning can isolate firms from their markets (Levinthal & March, 1993).

Conversely, restricted and specialized information systems induce myopic learning, simplify managerial worldviews, and cause organizations to be unresponsive to their environments (Starbuck, 1985). Moreover, specialized routines funnel managerial perceptions (March & Simon, 1958), narrow skills (March, 1991), and thus encourage simple strategies (Miller & Chen, 1996). Simple strategies in turn give rise to targeted information systems and dedicated routines (Perrow, 1986). They also focus managerial attention and specialize the organization so that further strategic simplicity becomes more likely. In these and countless other ways, managerial, organizational, and strategic outcomes of success reinforce one another.

The reciprocal nature of some of these causal links is especially interesting. For example, whereas simple strategies may give rise to specialized routines and systems, the latter in turn reinforce the former by directing attention and resources. Indeed, such causal reciprocity supports a configurationist viewpoint that envisions mutual reinforcement among cognitive, ideological, structural, and strategic elements of organizations (Meyer, Tsui, & Hinings, 1993; Miller, 1996). This self-perpetuating aspect of the consequences of success enables internal selection and retention processes to dominate external ones, thereby exacerbating the potential conflict Campbell (1965, 1994) identified between subunit adaptations and the survival of the larger entity.

> *Proposition 15:* To the extent that success produces any one of the managerial, organizational, or strategic outcomes identified above, the other outcomes also become more likely.

Moderating Contingencies

The above propositions will be moderated by a number of important factors. Managerial moderators pertain to qualities of top managers and their teams, environmental moderators describe conditions in the environment, and organizational moderators apply to the culture, structure, or strategy of an organization. In fact, many of the managerial and organizational moderators are the very outcomes of success already discussed (Masuch, 1985). In other words, the outcomes of success themselves serve as potent internal selectors.

Managerial Moderators

Three classes of moderators may operate at the managerial or top management team level: managers' discretion to act, their incentive to react to success, and their attributions about success.

The Discretion to Act

Significant *managerial discretion* over organizational outcomes is necessary for perceptions of performance to have consequences for action (Hambrick & Finkelstein, 1996). The effects of performance will be smaller when top managers lack discretion over the routines, strategies, and systems that translate perceptions into action (Hambrick & Finkelstein, 1996).

A CEO's discretion, naturally, is influenced by his or her *power*. When power resides largely with CEOs, their perceptions of performance alone can produce the effects previously discussed. Where power is distributed diffusely, CEO perceptions may have little impact on organizational outcomes. This will be especially true if there is a lack of *consensus* about performance and practices among those in power (Ocasio, 1995, p. 317; Sitkin, 1992).

The Incentive to React to Success

If company success is seen by executives to lead to personal benefits such as money, power, or recognition, it will increase managers' incentives to celebrate and sustain the practices and parties thought to create success (Miller et al., 1997). Managers also are more apt to react to success if they are at critical stages in their careers, for example, if they are up for a major promotion or monetary settlement.

Attributions Regarding Success

Managers are more likely to react to success if they attribute it to valued firm policies and skills

(Miller & Ross, 1975). This may depend in part on their job tenure and their cohorts on the top management team. Because leaders with *short tenures* may not identify with past policies, they are less likely to take credit for success or to be rendered complacent or overconfident by it (Hambrick & Fukutomi, 1991; Miller, 1991). Similarly, *heterogeneous and participative top management teams* in which divergent views are discussed openly may preserve a healthy skepticism even after success (Keck & Tushman, 1993; Wiersema & Bantel, 1992).

> *Proposition 16:* Propositions 1 through 15 are likely to be better supported where top managers have much discretion, have an incentive to react to success, and attribute success to their own actions.

It is noteworthy that the above moderating factors as well as their determinants are themselves influenced by success. Specifically, success makes managers more powerful, thereby increasing their discretion to act. It also rewards managers with money, reputation, and long tenures, giving them an incentive to react to success by preserving the practices associated with it. Finally, by lengthening tenures and fostering top management team homogeneity, success elicits convergent attributions that preserve the status quo. The moderators of the above propositions, it seems, are themselves shaped by success (Masuch, 1985). I will return to this issue later.

Environmental Moderators

Uncertainty, heterogeneity, and competition in the environment also can moderate the propositions.

Uncertainty

Campbell (1965, 1990b, 1994) maintains that random variation is essential for learning, and environmental uncertainty is an important source of such variation. Uncertainty may be defined as the rate and unpredictability of change in the environment. Typically, it is manifested in new product introductions, technological change, shifts in patterns of demand or competition, new market entrants, and so on. Executives in uncertain environments witness cataclysms befalling competitors, new technologies upsetting the industry, and shifting customer tastes. They are therefore more likely to be aware of the precarious nature of success and the continual need to adapt (Keck & Tushman, 1993). Uncertainty also can shake managers' beliefs in a single formula and promote greater vigilance and variation (Ocasio, 1995; Sitkin, 1992).

Companies operating in stable environments, on the other hand, are more apt to be influenced by their past success. According to Milliken and Lant (1991), managers in stable environments "because of the paucity and redundancy of experience in such contexts . . . do not have as many opportunities to learn about the role of the environmental context. . . . As a result they are less likely to be vigilant" (p. 146).[4]

Heterogeneity

The heterogeneity or diversity of the environment may also open managers' minds to different ways of doing things and make them less confident about their methods and skills. A diverse mix of rivals acquaints managers with assorted modes of rivalry, and these rivals present a variety of potential role models that can shake worldviews (Miller & Chen, 1994). A heterogeneous group of customers also can serve as an important source of information for managers—the diversity of challenges and complaints that they present can be useful antidotes to myopia, complacency, and simplicity (Miller & Chen, 1996).

Competition, Scarcity, and Hardship

Competition mandates alertness; it forcibly broadens managers' perspectives by presenting challenges that are impossible to ignore (Miller & Chen, 1996). This is especially true where firms have little control over their markets and are fairly matched with their competitors. Continual challenge, even in the face of success, prevents managers from becoming too complacent and organizations from becoming too monolithic or insular.

Proposition 17: Propositions 1 through 15 are likely to be better supported where firms operate in stable and predictable, homogeneous, and noncompetitive environments.

These environmental moderators of the relationship between success and its outcomes may have the least impact in successful organizations. There, as I have argued, managers tend to remain insulated from their environments. Complacency and overconfidence attenuate search, information systems become narrowly specialized, and groupthink blinds decision makers to important challenges. Thus, many successful firms may fail to recognize the environmental uncertainty, diversity, and competition that might forestall the effects of success (Miller, 1990). It is a catch-22.

Organizational Moderators

It is reasonable to believe that the negative outcomes of success will be less likely to occur when top management teams remain curious and heterogeneous, where corporate cultures value experimentation and diversity, where tolerance prevails, where power is not too centralized, where information systems are broadly targeted, and where routines are flexible (Miller, 1990, 1993; Ocasio, 1995; Sitkin, 1992). The arguments behind many of the propositions already support these contentions.

Again, however, there is a catch. The likelihood of the above moderating conditions obtaining is itself reduced by success. Success, as was argued, leads to complacency, cultural homogeneity, intolerance, centralization, myopic systems, and imprisoning routines; in other words, many of the organizational consequences of success serve as positive moderators of the relationship between success and *themselves*, and so again can be self-reinforcing. They also strengthen the relationship between success and its *other* consequences. This can initiate a vicious circle (Masuch, 1985). Thus, although Proposition 15 suggested that the outcomes of success reinforce each other directly, these outcomes also can serve to strengthen their own ties with success. For example:

1. The uniform and intense values engendered by success increase the likelihood that success will be attributed to those values, the influence of which will increase with more success.
2. The complacency induced by success leaves managers unaware of the threats confronting them, further contributing to complacency.
3. The focused information systems brought about by success will ensure that what is monitored will take on still greater importance in the light of success, and will be scrutinized by still more targeted information systems.

Proposition 18: Propositions 1 through 15 are apt to be better supported once some initial reactions to success already have occurred; for example, the consequences of success predicted are more likely to occur where managers are confident and complacent, where cultures are homogeneous and intolerant, where power is centralized, and where routines, reward and information systems, and strategies are narrowly targeted.

Perceived Versus Actual Success

My concern has been with managerial *perceptions* of success; it is these rather than objective indicators of performance that lead most directly to managerial action. Certainly, the most salient and relevant indicators of success vary among industries, firms, and managers. That is not to imply, however, that there is no connection between objective indicators and perceptions of success. This connection may itself be an important area of study. On average, one would expect that perceived success will increase with (a) the length of time a firm has been successful, (b) the margin by which it beats its most salient competitors, and (c) the stability and consistency of superior performance.

Different performance records, of course, are apt to have varying impacts on managerial perceptions and reactions. For example, dramatic success over 2 or 3 years can be especially convincing and lead to more focusing and risk taking to capitalize on a winning strategy. By contrast, less dramatic but longer-term success may have a slower impact on managerial attitudes and strategy, but by reducing perceived threats it may lead to more complacency

and inertia (Miller, 1990). Perhaps, too, the relationships between actual and perceived performance are nonlinear: Moderate success along valued indicators may have almost no impact on managerial perceptions, whereas substantial success may have very significant consequences.

There are also cases in which objective performance will have a less clear influence on managerial perceptions. Some firms, for example, are exceedingly profitable but do not grow very rapidly, or vice versa. It is difficult to predict managers' reactions to such mixed results. Another case in which the propositions may not hold occurs when unprotected organizations have been objectively successful for a very long time, say more than 5 years. In such instances, managers no doubt will perceive this success, but likely will have avoided its traps. Their long track records show that they and their firms have reacted to success very differently from what has been predicted here. Such firms represent ideal sites for further research.

Some Cautions

It is useful to close with some cautions. The propositions about the impact of success cannot simply be reversed to predict the effects of failure. It is true that where poor performance *severely* threatens managers, it may evoke some defensive reactions that resemble the outcomes of success. These may include inertia, insularity, and intolerance of opposing viewpoints (Ocasio, 1995; Staw, 1976; Staw et al., 1981). But we must not make too much of such parallels because failure also engenders reevaluation, soul searching, risk taking, experimentation, consultation, and reorientation—reactions that almost never follow success (Ocasio, 1995; Sitkin, 1992). Failure can be both informative and bracing, if not immediately, then eventually (Sitkin, 1992; Starbuck & Milliken, 1988).

It is tempting to conclude with a list of recommendations for how managers can avoid some of the traps of success. In fact, the lengthy analysis of moderating variables suggests a large assortment of potential remedies. These include participative and diverse cultures, fresh and heterogeneous top management teams, close and broad contact with the environment, frequent questioning and experimentation, and even the encouragement of debate, change, and small failures (Ocasio, 1995; Sitkin, 1992). It would be misleading, however, to suggest that these conditions will be easy to achieve in successful firms. Success itself, it was noted, might prevent this.

Afterword

Certainly, Campbell's thinking has taken us well beyond the pure evolutionism of most ecologists. By examining the effects of success, this chapter has tried to build on Campbell's ideas concerning internal selective-retention processes, the conflict between subsystem and system adaptation, and the notion of vicarious selection via mental mediation rather than extinction. These ideas of Campbell's also hold promise for exploring organizational behavior under conditions of failure or equivocality, and for gaining insights into the resulting changes in routines, decision making, power allocation, and strategy. I would encourage others to look into these issues.

Notes

1. Whereas the managerial factors I discuss are mostly cognitive, cultural factors are mostly normative and structural factors mostly regulative (Scott, 1995).

2. Perceived success can exacerbate leaders' vulnerabilities. In their study of "neurotic corporations," for example, Kets de Vries and Miller (1992) found the greatest examples of CEO hubris in companies that had been very successful. Their past triumphs so emboldened some executives that confidence turned into narcissism and arrogance, and independent thought into iconoclasm and obsessionality.

3. Some might argue that simple strategies are what created success in the first place. Porter (1980), for example, stresses that firms must distinguish themselves from the competition by differentiating their offerings or attaining unique mastery over costs. This requires considerable concentration of effort as firms rarely have the resources to do *all* things particularly well. Similarly, advocates of the resource-based view of the firm stress the importance of developing special talents or resources that cannot be copied easily by rivals (Barney, 1991; Prahalad & Hamel, 1990). This again can demand concentration of effort and attention. In short, some scholars maintain that simple

strategies are associated with success because they cause success (Rommel, 1995; Treacy & Wiersema, 1995).

That is not what Miller and Chen (1996) found in their research. They showed that the simplicity of a strategy was associated with past but not subsequent performance. In fact, in challenging and uncertain environments, strategic simplicity was negatively associated with future performance (Miller & Chen, 1996). Whereas Miller, Lant, Milliken, and Korn (1996) found that strategic simplicity could be of benefit in the stable furniture industry, this was not true in the dynamic software business.

4. Uncertainty may actually enhance the effects of success where it is associated with more managerial discretion (Hambrick & Finkelstein, 1996). Under uncertainty, leaders have to respond more actively to challenges in their environments, and this gives them greater influence. In addition, uncertainty creates ambiguity, thereby allowing managers to take credit for good performance when in fact they do not deserve it (Miller et al., 1997). I suspect, however, that although uncertainty gives managers power and the capacity for opportunism, it also presents great challenges that induce caution and humility.

References

Aguilar, F. J. (1967). *Scanning the business environment.* New York: Macmillan.

Alvesson, M. (1994). Talking in organizations: Managing identity and impressions in an advertising agency. *Organization Studies, 15,* 534-563.

Amburgey, T. L., Kelly, D., & Barnett, W. P. (1993). Resetting the clock: The dynamics of organizational change and failure. *Administrative Science Quarterly, 38,* 51-73.

Amburgey, T. L., & Miner, A. S. (1992). Strategic momentum: The effects of repetitive, positional and contextual momentum on merger activity. *Strategic Management Journal, 13,* 335- 348.

Asch, S. E. (1956). Studies of independence and conformity. *Psychological Monographs, 70*(9, Whole No. 416).

Ashton, R. H. (1976). Deviation-amplifying feedback and unintended consequences of management accounting systems. *Accounting, Organizations, and Society, 1,* 289-300.

Barney, J. (1991). Firm resources and sustained competitive advantage. *Journal of Management, 17,* 99-120.

Bettman, J., & Weitz, B. (1983). Attributions in the boardroom: Causal reasoning in corporate annual reports. *Administrative Science Quarterly, 28,* 165-183.

Brockner, J. (1992). The escalation of commitment to a failing course of action. *Academy of Management Review, 17,* 39-61.

Burgelman, R. A. (1991). Intraorganizational ecology and strategy making and organizational adaptation. *Organization Science, 2,* 239-262.

Campbell, D. T. (1960). Blind variation and selective retention in creative thought as in other knowledge processes. *Psychological Review, 67,* 380-400.

Campbell, D. T. (1965). Variation and selective retention in socio-cultural evolution. In H. Barringer, B. Blanksten, & R. Mack (Eds.), *Social change in developing areas: A reinterpretation of evolutionary theory* (pp. 19-48). Cambridge, MA: Schenkman.

Campbell, D. T. (1970). Natural selection as an epistemological model. In R. Naroll & R. Cohen (Eds.), *A handbook of method in cultural anthropology* (pp. 51-85). Garden City, NJ: Natural History Press.

Campbell, D. T. (1982). Legal and primary-group social controls. *Journal of Social and Biological Structures, 5*(4), 431-438.

Campbell, D. T. (1990a). Epistemological roles for selection theory. In N. Rescher (Ed.), *Evolution, cognition, realism* (pp. 1-19). Lanham, MD: University Press of America.

Campbell, D. T. (1990b). Levels of organization, downward causation, and the selection theory approach to evolutionary epistemology. In G. Greenberg & E. Tobach (Eds.), *Theories of the evolution of knowing* (pp. 39-55). Hillsdale, NJ: Lawrence Erlbaum.

Campbell, D. T. (1991). Autopoetic evolutionary epistemology and internal selection. *Journal of Social and Biological Structures, 14*(2), 166-173.

Campbell, D. T. (1994). How individual and face-to-face-group selection undermine firm selection in organizational evolution. In J.A.C. Baum & J. V. Singh (Eds.), *Evolutionary dynamics of organizations* (pp. 23-38). New York: Oxford University Press.

Carroll, G. R. (1984). Dynamics of publisher succession in newspaper organizations. *Administrative Science Quarterly, 29*, 93-113.

Chatman, J. A. (1991). Matching people and organizations: Selection and socialization in public accounting firms. *Administrative Science Quarterly, 36*, 459-484.

Cyert, R. M., & March, J. G. (1963). *A behavioral theory of the firm.* Englewood Cliffs, NJ: Prentice Hall.

Daft, R., Sormunen, J., & Parks, D. (1988). Chief executive scanning, environmental characteristics, and company performance. *Strategic Management Journal, 9*, 123-139.

Deal, T., & Kennedy, A. (1982). *Corporate cultures.* Reading, PA: Addison-Wesley.

Drazin, R., & Sandelands, L. (1992). Autogenesis: A perspective on the process of learning. *Organization Science, 2*, 230-249.

Halberstam, D. (1986). *The reckoning.* New York: Avon.

Hambrick, D. C. (1993). *Top management groups: A conceptual integration and reconsideration of the "team" label.* Unpublished manuscript, Columbia Business School.

Hambrick, D. C., & Finkelstein, S. (1996). *Strategic leadership.* Minneapolis: West.

Hambrick, D. C., & Fukutomi, G. (1991). The seasons of a CEO's tenure. *Academy of Management Review, 16*, 719-742.

Hannan, M. T., & Freeman, J. (1984). Structural inertia and organizational change. *American Sociological Review, 49*, 149-164.

Hedberg, B.L.T., Nystrom, P., & Starbuck, W. H. (1976). Camping on seesaws: Prescriptions for a self-designing organization. *Administrative Science Quarterly, 21*, 41-65.

Helmich, D. L. (1978). Leader flows and organizational process. *Academy of Management Journal, 21*, 463-478.

Janis, I. L. (1972). *Victims of groupthink.* New York: Free Press.

Kahneman, D., & Tversky, A. (1979). Prospect theory: An analysis of decisions under risk. *Econometrica, 47*, 262-291.

Keck, S. L., & Tushman, M. (1993). Environmental and organizational context and executive team structure. *Academy of Management Journal, 36*, 1314-1344.

Kets de Vries, M., & Miller, D. (1992). *The neurotic organization.* New York: HarperCollins.

Kiesler, S., & Sproull, L. (1982). Managerial response to changing environments: Perspectives on problem sensing from social cognition. *Administrative Science Quarterly, 27*, 548-570.

Lant, T. K., Milliken, F., & Batra, B. (1992). The role of managerial learning and interpretation in strategic persistence and reorientation. *Strategic Management Journal, 13*, 585-608.

Lant, T. K., & Montgomery, D. B. (1987). Learning from strategic success and failure. *Journal of Business Research, 15*, 503-518.

Levinthal, D. A., & March, J. G. (1981). A model of adaptive organizational search. *Journal of Economic Behavior and Organization, 2*, 307-333.

Levinthal, D. A., & March, J. G. (1993). The myopia of learning. *Strategic Management Journal, 14*, 95-112.

Levitt, B., & March, J. G. (1988). Organizational learning. *Annual Review of Sociology, 14*, 319-340.

March, J. G. (1991). Exploration and exploitation in organizational learning. *Organization Science, 2*, 71-87.

March, J. G., & Simon, H. A. (1958). *Organizations.* New York: Wiley.

Martin, J. (1990). Deconstructing organizational taboos. *Organization Science, 1*, 339-359.

Martin, J. (1992). *Cultures in organization: Three perspectives.* New York: Oxford University Press.

Martin, J., & Meyerson, D. (1988). Organizational culture and the denial, channeling and acknowledgement of ambiguity. In L. Pondy (Ed.), *Managing ambiguity and change* (pp. 93-125). Chichester, UK: Wiley.

Masuch, M. (1985). Vicious circles in organizations. *Administrative Science Quarterly, 30*, 14-33.

Meyer, A. D., & Starbuck, W. H. (1991). *Organizations and industries in flux: The interplay of rationality and ideology.* Unpublished manuscript, University of Oregon.

Meyer, A. D., Tsui, A. S., & Hinings, C. R. (1993). Guest co-editors' introduction: Configurational approaches to organizational analysis. *Academy of Management Journal, 36*, 1175-1195.

Meyer, M., & Zucker, L. (1989). *Permanently failing organizations.* Newbury Park, CA: Sage.

Miller, D. (1990). *The Icarus Paradox: How exceptional companies bring about their own downfall.* New York: HarperCollins.

Miller, D. (1991). Stale in the saddle: CEO tenure and the match between organization and environment. *Management Science, 37*, 34-52.

Miller, D. (1992). Environmental fit versus internal fit. *Organization Science, 2*, 159-178.

Miller, D. (1993). The architecture of simplicity. *Academy of Management Review, 18*, 116-138.

Miller, D. (1994). What happens after success: The perils of excellence. *Journal of Management Studies, 31*, 85-102.

Miller, D. (1996). Configurations revisited. *Strategic Management Journal, 17*, 505-512.

Miller, D., & Chen, M.-J. (1994). Sources and consequences of competitive inertia. *Administrative Science Quarterly, 39*, 1-23.

Miller, D., & Chen, M.-J. (1996). The simplicity of competitive repertoires. *Strategic Management Journal, 17*, 419-439.

Miller, D., Droge, C., & Vickery, S. (1997). Celebrating the essential. *Journal of Management, 23*, 147-168.

Miller, D., & Friesen, P. H. (1977). Strategy making in context: Ten empirical archetypes. *Journal of Management Studies, 14*, 253-280.

Miller, D., & Friesen, P. H. (1984). *Organizations: A quantum view.* Englewood Cliffs, NJ: Prentice Hall.

Miller, D. T., & Ross, M. (1975). Self-serving biases in the attribution of causality: Fact or fiction. *Psychological Bulletin, 82*, 213-225.

Milliken, F. J., & Lant, T. K. (1991). The effects of an organization's recent performance history on strategic persistence and change. *Advances in Strategic Management, 7*, 129-156.

Mintzberg, H. (1983). *Power in and around organizations.* Englewood Cliffs, NJ: Prentice Hall.

Nelson, R., & Winter, S. G. (1982). *An evolutionary theory of economic change.* Cambridge, MA: Harvard University Press.

Ocasio, W. (1995). The enactment of economic adversity: A reconciliation of theories of failure induced change and threat-rigidity. *Research in Organizational Behavior, 17*, 287-331.

Perrow, C. (1986). *Complex organizations: A critical essay.* New York: Random House.

Pfeffer, J. (1981). *Power in organizations.* New York: Pitman.

Porter, M. E. (1980). *Competitive strategy.* New York: Free Press.

Prahalad, C. K., & Hamel, G. (1990, May-June). The core competence of the corporation. *Harvard Business Review*, pp. 79-91.

Rommel, H. (1995). *Simplicity wins.* New York: McGraw-Hill.

Salancik, G. R., & Meindl, J. (1984). Corporate attributions as strategic illusions of management control. *Administrative Science Quarterly, 29*, 238-254.

Schneider, B. (1987). The people make the place. *Personnel Psychology, 14*, 437-453.

Scott, W. R. (1995). *Institutions and organizations.* Thousand Oaks, CA: Sage.

Simons, R. L. (1995). *Strategy and control.* Boston: Harvard University Press.

Sitkin, S. B. (1992). Learning through failure: The strategy of small losses. *Research in Organizational Behavior, 14*, 231-266.

Sitkin, S. B., & Pablo, A. L. (1992). Reconceptualizing the determinants of risk behavior. *Academy of Management Review, 17*, 9-38.

Spender, J. C. (1990). *Industry recipes.* London: Blackwell.

Starbuck, W. H. (1985). Acting first and thinking later: Theory versus reality in strategic change. In J. M. Pennings and Associates (Eds.), *Organizational strategy and change* (pp. 336-372). San Francisco: Jossey-Bass.

Starbuck, W. H., Greve, A., & Hedberg, B.L.T. (1978). Responding to crises. *Journal of Business Administration, 9*, 111-137.

Starbuck, W. H., & Milliken, F. J. (1988). Challenger: Fine-tuning the odds until something breaks. *Journal of Management Studies, 25*, 319-340.

Staw, B. M. (1976). Knee-deep in the big muddy: A study of escalating commitment to a chosen course of action. *Organizational Behavior and Human Performance, 16*, 27-44.

Staw, B. M., McKechnie, P., & Puffer, S. (1983). The justification of organizational performance. *Administrative Science Quarterly, 28*, 582-600.

Staw, B. M., Sandelands, L., & Dutton, J. (1981). Threat-rigidity effects in organizational behavior: A multilevel analysis. *Administrative Science Quarterly, 26*, 501-524.

Treacy, M., & Wiersema, F. (1995). *The discipline of market leaders.* New York: HarperCollins.

Turner, B. (1990). The rise of organizational symbolism. In J. Hassard & D. Pym (Eds.), *The theory and philosophy of organizations* (pp. 233-268). London: Routledge.

Tushman, M. L., & Romanelli, E. (1985). Organizational evolution: A metamorphosis model of convergence and reorientation. In L. Cummings & B. Staw (Eds.), *Research in organizational behavior* (pp. 171-222). Greenwich, CT: JAI.

Tversky, A., & Kahneman, D. (1986). Rational choice and the framing of decisions. *Journal of Business, 59*, S251-S278.

Waldrop, M. M. (1992). *Complexity: The emerging science at the edge of order and chaos.* New York: Simon & Schuster.

Walsh, J. P. (1995). Managerial and organizational cognition. *Organization Science, 6*, 280-320.

Weick, K. E. (1984). Small wins: Redefining the scale of social problems. *American Psychologist, 39*(1), 40-49.

Wiersema, M. F., & Bantel, K. (1992). TMT demography and corporate strategic change. *Academy of Management Journal, 35*, 91-121.

Wilensky, H. (1971). *Organizational intelligence.* New York: Free Press.

Wright, P. (1979). *On a clear day you can see General Motors.* New York: Avon.

Part II

Multilevel Coevolution

Chapter 7

Whole-Part Coevolutionary Competition in Organizations

JOEL A. C. BAUM

Organizations start up and fail at high rates, suggesting a node of selection at the organization level. Based on this observation, for roughly 20 years now, a substantial group of organization theorists have been developing cultural evolutionary models of organizational selection (for a review, see Baum, 1996). Noting that selection processes operate at other levels of organization, Campbell (1994) recently cautioned against neglecting the possibility that evolution "at individual and face-to-face group levels may lead to firm-level dysfunction" (p. 23) as a result of "ongoing conflict between behaviors that optimize organized groups and behaviors that optimize an individual's personal and nepotistic interests . . . a conflict between products of biological and cultural evolution" (p. 29). This ongoing "competition among the cooperators" at different levels within an organizational hierarchy results in an ambivalent so-ciality and weakly integrated organization (Campbell, 1994).

My aim here is, first, to further develop the rationale for expecting individuals and face-to-face groups to (consciously or unconsciously) undermine the efficacy of organizational selection, and outline some implications of such evolutionary conflicts for organizations. Then, after briefly reviewing several largely unsuccessful attempts to address whole-part competition by aligning fitness across organizational levels, I use Kauffman's (1993) $NK[C]$ coupled fitness landscape model to formalize some aspects of coevolutionary whole-part competition in organizations. Finally, I outline several alternative, and potentially more tractable, approaches to managing whole-part coevolutionary competition in organizations. Specifically, I identify strategies that *tune the structure of whole-part coevolution* to render it more effective by

AUTHOR'S NOTE: My interest in and basic understanding of this topic both resulted from conversations with Don Campbell. I regret not taking him up on his offer several years ago to write this together. Surely the results would have been far superior. A version of this chapter was presented at *How History Matters: Path-Dependent Processes in Organizations*, a symposium jointly sponsored by the Business Policy and Strategy, Organization and Management Theory, and History divisions of the Academy of Management, Boston, August, 1997, and at the *Variations in Organization Science* workshop at the University of Toronto, November, 1997. I am most grateful to Whitney Berta, Corinne Coen, Bill McKelvey, Brian Silverman, and Mayer Zald for comments on earlier versions.

raising access to high-fitness local maxima, and either speeding the pace of evolution at the organization level or slowing its pace at individual and face-to-face-group levels.

Levels of Organizational Evolution

Organizational evolution is frequently conceived as taking place simultaneously at multiple hierarchical levels (e.g., individual, face-to-face group, organization, population, community); the levels nested one within the other, wholes composed of parts at lower levels of organization, and are themselves parts of more extensive wholes (e.g., Aldrich, 1979; Baum & Singh, 1994a; Carroll, 1984; Csanyi, 1989; Hodgson, 1993). Hierarchical thinking also has a long history in the larger organization and strategic management literature (e.g., Andrews, 1971; Cyert & March, 1963; March & Simon, 1958; Thompson, 1967). Each level at which elements of an organization are either retained or eliminated represents a "node of selection" (Baum & Singh, 1994a; Campbell, 1974, 1990, 1994). Agents at all these levels try to optimize *fitness*, where fitness is a complex function of the agent and its environment. Agents that have the highest fitness are selected. Agents' evolution can be seen as a path-dependent exploration of possible configurations (variations) with different degrees of fitness. Agents are semiautonomous units that seek to maximize some measure of "goodness" by searching possible configurations over time. This exploration can be visualized as movement through a *fitness landscape*, where configurations correspond to points in a two-dimensional (horizontal) space and fitness corresponds to the configuration's value on the third (vertical) dimension (Kauffman, 1993; Wright, 1931, 1932). Local fitness maxima correspond to "peaks" in the landscape, local minima to "valleys."

What is best for an agent at one level is not, however, likely best for an agent at another level. Thus, agents at different levels enter into competition, the agents at each level trying to direct activity to favor their own well-being. This competition between individuals and groups at various levels of

aggregation very much complicates organizational evolution.

In general, evolution is faster and more effective at lower levels of organization. The reason for this is that variation, selection, and retention processes unfold more quickly at lower levels of organization (Ashby, 1956; Baum & Singh, 1994a; Ghemawat, 1991; McKelvey, 1994, 1998). Furthermore, the variety of possible configurations that evolution can explore is much smaller for organizational subsystems than for global organizational systems, because global variety is the product of the possible varieties for each subsystem (Glance, Hogg, & Huberman, 1997). This is analogous to Simon's (1962) argument that evolutionary integration of subsystems is limited to small assemblies because the probability of discovering the right configuration is far lower for large assemblies. Individual and group fitness therefore increase more quickly than organizational fitness, leading to "suboptimization" rather than global optimization (Machol, 1965, pp. 1-8). If an individual or group can choose competitive moves that give larger immediate rewards than corresponding cooperative moves, competitive moves will be selected, even though their contributions to organizational fitness will be lower than those of cooperative moves.

Even if we assume that, by some unlikely combination of events, an organization reaches a cooperative configuration with high global fitness, this configuration would be eroded constantly by the ongoing "competition among the cooperators" (Campbell, 1983, 1991, 1994). Even though cooperation may lead to increased fitness for the group, it is unstable because it can be invaded easily by egoist strategies. Even being near a global optimum does not preclude the inherently faster process of suboptimization from continuing, and, whatever the collective benefits of cooperation, competitive moves will in general still provide organizational components (individuals and subgroups) gains in relative fitness. The problem is that everybody benefits from cooperation, but that noncooperators benefit more, because they reap the additional resources produced by synergy, while investing nothing in return. Thus, whereas groups of cooperators outcompete groups of noncooperators, noncooperators outcompete cooperators *within* groups (Wilson & Sober, 1994). This is the classic "free rider" problem. Because evolution never stops, variation will sooner or later produce free riders in an otherwise optimized social system, and it is the latter who will be selected, not the faithful cooperators, resulting in the erosion and eventual collapse of the cooperative system (Campbell, 1994; Glance & Huberman, 1993, 1994; Glance et al., 1997). What is optimal at the individual level can be far from optimal for the group.

Shared Control in Human Groups

The above scenario assumes that individuals are free to develop either cooperative or competitive behavior. If, however, actions are somehow preselected by a control system vicariously anticipating the possibly lethal effects of selfish individual-level selection, the system can achieve greater fitness. Such "vicarious selectors" are the most basic form of an anticipatory control system (Campbell, 1969). They shortcut purely blind variation and selection by eliminating dangerous or inadequate actions before they are executed and by making different selections under different circumstances. Once established, selection processes will act primarily on the control system, rather than on the system itself (Campbell, 1969).

The most direct control on behavior in a biological system is the knowledge stored in its genes. Genes dictate particular actions in particular circumstances, and preclude other actions. One way to solve the problem of cooperation, then, would be to have a configuration of individuals whose genes predispose them to cooperate. As long as the genes of different individuals in a group can vary independently, however, we should expect the evolution of deviant genes that predispose their carriers to selfishness and defection, through genetic competition among the cooperators (Campbell, 1983, 1994). The fully cooperative configuration can be achieved only if the genes for the whole group are constrained to remain virtually identical. This form of "shared control" configuration is found in the social insects: bees, ants, and termites (see Campbell, 1983, 1994). The different members of an ant colony are genetically very similar,

and there is no independent evolution of genes, because only the colony's queen is capable of reproducing her genes. This creates a highly cooperative ultrasocial system, because each worker has the best chances to further the retention and replication of (shared) genes by helping the colony as a whole to achieve a maximal production of offspring by the queen. "Free-rider genes" cannot survive because "rebel workers" are unable to reproduce (Campbell, 1983; Dawkins, 1976).

In almost all other species of animals (including humans, of course), groups are comprised of mixes of nonrelatives and genetic relatives of varying degrees, and groups' members are able to reproduce their genes. Any cooperative arrangement is thus always open to possible erosion. The conclusion that seems to follow from this observation is that we should not see much cooperation in human social groups, yet human groups create some of the most extensive cooperative ultrasocial systems (e.g., Campbell, 1983). This can be explained by the evolution of shared cognitive controls in addition to the genetic one (Boyd & Richerson, 1985, 1990, 1992; Campbell, 1983; Huberman & Hogg, 1995; Sober & Wilson, 1998; Wilson & Sober, 1994). The most typically human control mechanism can be found in culture: knowledge or beliefs shared among individuals through communication. A belief, element of knowledge, or pattern of behavior that is transmitted from one individual to another one can be said to "replicate." In analogy to genes, such cultural replicators (Csanyi, 1989; Hull, 1988) have been called "memes" (Dawkins, 1976) or "culturgens" (Lumsden & Wilson, 1981). Nelson and Winter (1982) and McKelvey (1982) have drawn a similar analogy for elements of organizing and management competence, which they label "routines" and "comps," respectively. Thus, human groups and organizations persist and thrive because within them, individual competition is suppressed by group- and organization-level rules, morality, and custom (Boyd & Richerson, 1992; Campbell, 1991; Sober & Wilson, 1998).

To achieve shared control, in addition to replication of knowledge, a constraining or isolating mechanism is needed that keeps copies of a piece of knowledge carried by different individuals virtually identical. One such mechanism is found in what Boyd and Richerson (1985) call *conformist transmission.* Unlike biological reproduction, where genetic information is transmitted from one or two parents to offspring, in cultural reproduction information can be transmitted from several individuals (parents) to the same individual (multiple parenting). In their dual-inheritance model, Boyd and Richerson (1985) show that, under a range of plausible conditions, it is optimal for learners to adopt majority or plurality beliefs when several competing beliefs are transmitted by different individuals. In relatively small groups, this leads quickly to homogeneity on all cultural traits. Organization theorists have similarly conceived organizational inheritance as a strong homogenizing force (DiMaggio & Powell, 1983) that is *frequency dependent* (e.g., Abrahamson, 1991), varying with the rarity or commonness of organizational practices; *path dependent* (e.g., Arthur, 1989, 1990; Hodgson, 1993), sensitive to the effect of self-reinforcing positive feedback on small fortuitous events; and *reputation dependent* (e.g., Han, 1994; Haveman, 1993; Korn & Baum, in press), with large and successful organizations providing the most attractive models for imitation.

Cultural-Group Selection

The positive feedback inherent in conformist transmission implies that small differences in initial distributions of beliefs between different groups will be intensified: If only slightly more individuals initially share a belief, it may be sufficient for that belief to come to dominate all others. Thus, small variations between groups tend to be reinforced, whereas variations within groups tend to be erased. Although the resulting homogeneities within groups and sharp differences between groups need not be interpreted as the products of adaptive selection, they do, however, provide the possibility for cultural-group selection: The group whose set of beliefs is most beneficial will have a higher global fitness and tend to replace groups with less adaptive beliefs (e.g., Fligstein, 1987). In this context, "beneficial" implies beliefs that promote a synergistic or cooperative pattern of interaction within the group. The more groups vary in

fitness, the stronger such group selection becomes. The group selection is of culturally transmitted beliefs and customs and social-organizational structures—not of genes (Campbell, 1994; Sober & Wilson, 1998). Such *cultural* organized-social-group selection makes possible the social norms, behaviors, and organizational forms that potentially lead group and organizational members to override their own individual fitness maximization. Thus, the often functional forms of human groups can be seen as adaptations that have evolved because groups expressing them outcompete other groups (Sober & Wilson, 1998; Wilson & Sober, 1994).

Groups of individuals who are regularly in face-to-face contact quickly develop an in-group solidarity and the power to discipline, reward, and punish in the service of collective group interests. As Campbell (1986) notes:

> We are all responsive to signs of approval and disapproval coming from those whom we see face-to-face on a regular basis. We all have a dread of ostracism at some underlying level, if not consciously. . . . There results . . . a tendency for every face-to-face aggregation in the organization to become an "in-group," with both those in other buildings at higher, equal-status, or lower echelons and those transient others, such as customers, becoming "out-groups." The clique interests of primary groups lead to solidarity in furthering the comfort of in-group members, often at the expense of the interests of the larger group of which the face-to-face groups are a part. (p. S362)

Members of the same face-to-face group often share a feeling of high regard, friendship, and trust that is based not on any prior experience but merely on the fact that they are members of the same group; exploitation within such groups is often avoided even when opportunities are experimentally provided without any chance of detection (Boyd & Richerson, 1992; Wilson & Sober, 1994).

Axelrod (1984) explains the human tendency to form such localized reciprocally cooperative cliques in purely selfish individual terms: Given long-lived individuals who encounter one another again and again, and who have the capacity to identify and remember each other, such cliques are likely to emerge. Sober and Wilson (1998; Wilson

& Sober, 1994) offer an alternative, group-selection-based explanation for the evolution of in-group altruism. Altruistic behaviors *lower* an individual's relative within-group fitness while *raising* the fitness of the individual's group relative to other groups. Evolution of social norms, and rewards and punishments to reinforce them, promotes group-beneficial behaviors that would be altruistic in their absence by overwhelming costs naturally associated with the behavior. Compared to altruistic behavior, which is personally costly to perform without any associated rewards and punishments, the personal cost of *imposing* rewards and punishments is low. The imposition of rewards and punishments thus constitutes a class of behavior that can benefit entire groups at little or no individual cost. Rewards and punishments, therefore, can evolve more easily by group selection than altruistic behaviors because they are less strongly opposed by selfish, individual within-group selection. Conceptualizing rewards and punishments as products of group selection thus helps to explain how human groups, comprising nonrelatives, can become highly cooperative, ultrasocial systems.

Such in-group solidarity and altruism, however, also tends to be associated with out-group hostility. This follows from the fact that selection takes place at the group level, where relative fitness of one group with respect to others is the dominant criterion (LeVine & Campbell, 1972). When different groups use similar tools and resources, a competitive configuration obtains (Hannan & Freeman, 1977, 1989; McPherson, 1983). Competitive between-group selection favors the evolution of within-group altruism (Sober & Wilson, 1998). In practice, in-group solidarity, then, becomes "clique selfishness" as each individual cares most about the behavior of his or her own group: Whatever the consequences for other groups, the action that will be preferred is the one best for this group.

Indeed, a ubiquitous problem for organizations is the tendency for those who work closely together in face-to-face settings to establish primary group solidarity, treating as out-groups (a) the customers they are supposed to serve, (b) rival face-to-face groups in other divisions of the organization, and (c) higher management located in other buildings or cities (Heylighen & Campbell, 1995). For exam-ple, one baby foods company had a conventional sales force compensation plan in which sales targets were negotiated annually. Higher-level targets then became the base level for the next year's negotiations. The national sales manager noticed that salespeople in Florida routinely made their targets. It was clear to him that they had figured out a way to increase sales. They denied this and refused to reveal their secret. With much effort, the sales manager finally uncovered their secret: Baby food could be sold to nursing homes. This insight proved valuable to the entire company. In keeping their discovery (a face-to-face-group level adaptation) a secret, the Florida sales force had, however, behaved rationally in the light of the reward system (Tushman & O'Reilly, 1997, p. 148). Thus, face-to-face-group solidarity often works against, rather than for, the purposes of larger collectives.

Shared Control in Complex Organizations

Competition between organizations and the individuals and face-to-face groups composing them, which tends to be won at individual and face-to-face-group levels, poses a fundamental obstacle to the emergence of integrated, cooperative systems at the organizational level.[1] Development of a shared control, which aligns fitness across organizational levels and restricts independent evolution at suborganizational levels, provides one possible mechanism for overcoming this obstacle (Boyd & Richerson, 1985, 1992; Sober & Wilson, 1998; Wilson & Sober, 1994). Although agency theorists maintain that the right set of incentives is capable of aligning individual, group, and organizational interests, achievement of shared control in organizations remains illusive. Keeping interests coaligned remains one of the major unsolved problems in organization theory and strategic management (Barney, 1997; Campbell, 1994, Milgrom & Roberts, 1992). Some well-worn organizational adaptations that attempt to align fitness across organizational levels include enlarging the shadow of the future, superordinate goals and common enemies, and efficient organizational boundaries and nexus of contracts, discussed in the following sections.

Enlarging the Shadow of the Future

Mutual cooperation can be stable if the future is important relative to the present (Hill, 1990). As Axelrod (1984, pp. 130-131) has noted, organizational hierarchies (consciously or unconsciously) are especially effective at concentrating and sustaining interactions between specific individuals:

> A bureaucracy is structured so that people specialize, and so that people working on related tasks are grouped together. This organizational practice increases the frequency of interactions, making it easier for workers [working on related tasks] to develop stable cooperative relationships. Moreover, when an issue requires coordination between different branches of the organization, the hierarchical structure allows the issue to be referred to policy makers at higher levels who frequently deal with each other on just such issues. By binding people together in a long-term, multilevel game, organizations increase the number and importance of future interactions, and thereby promote the emergence of cooperation of groups too large to interact individually.

A related approach is creation of stock option programs, internal career and promotion systems, retirement benefit packages, and other incentives that increase individuals' financial stakes in the future of their organization. In organizations, where relations are less fluid and transactions more varied (than in markets), however, the *quality* of relationships is critical in determining the quality of transactions across them (e.g., Granovetter, 1985; Hill, 1990). As Barnard (1968) argued, therefore, the solution resides in organizations creating a social context of identification, trust, and commitment that fosters convergence of individual, group, and organizational fates. Increasing organizational members' nonfinancial stakes (i.e., identification, trust, and commitment) can lead individual and organizational fates to converge. Consequently, organizations make frequent use of processes of choice, visibility, and irrevocability to promote individual psychological commitment (Tushman & O'Reilly, 1997, pp. 132-141).

Superordinate Goals and Common Enemies

Evolution (both cultural and biological) has produced organization-optimizing (group solidarity) mechanisms that become active in intergroup conflict (Heylighen & Campbell, 1995). Given our long history of living in small groups, it is not surprising that we have evolved mechanisms that lead us to easily become "team players" when placed in competition with other groups (e.g., Hogg & Abrams, 1988; LeVine & Campbell, 1972; Sherif, Harvey, White, Wood, & Sherif, 1961). Between-group competition favors psychological mechanisms that blur the distinction between group and individual welfare. Groups of individuals who identify so strongly with their group that they do not consider the possibility of profiting at the expense of their fellows will be superior in competition with less civic-minded groups. Consequently, increasing the efficacy of organization-level selection by increasing the threat of out-group competition can be a powerful stimulus for organization-level optimizing behaviors (LeVine & Campbell, 1972). Perceptions of out-group hostility are open to manipulation by organizational leaders and their competitors, and can be used to resolve conflict temporarily. Identifying a common enemy is the negative side of superordinate goals: Groups in conflict may temporarily resolve their differences and unite to combat a common enemy.

Efficient Organizational Boundaries and Nexus of Contracts

Economists have been interested in organizational control since Berle and Means (1932) first observed the increasing separation of ownership and control of large firms. The general concern is with the degree to which managerial discretion impedes profit maximization. Managers are viewed as avoiding courses of action that could potentially threaten their positions in favor of pursuing sales and asset growth through mergers and diversification, whereas owners would act in a more risk-neutral manner. Transaction cost economics (TCE) and agency theory are the dominant economic approaches to interest alignment.

TCE views firms and markets as alternative ways to govern transactions (Williamson, 1975, 1985). Transaction costs (or control losses) measure the degree of (mis)alignment of transactor interests. Internal organization is adaptive (better aligns transactor interests) compared to markets when (a) transactions are complex, (b) transactions are repeated, and (c) transactions involve significant dedicated assets. In this view, organizations create shared control by efficiently locating their boundaries to "minimize" transaction costs, which indicates optimally aligned transactor interests. In principle, the problem can be solved with strict management, but in practice worker monitoring is always imperfect, and employee effort can vary widely within the acceptable range. Moreover, for internal monitoring and incentives to be effective in restricting self-interested individual behaviors in specific areas that are considered important, such areas must be few for both cost and practicality considerations:

> When the balloon of opportunistic behavior has been poked in one place by the blunt instrument of rational (i.e., hierarchical) control, it readily yields but reemerges elsewhere in ways that may make it more difficult and costly to detect and curtail. In focusing attention on the relatively few activities or outcomes that lend themselves more easily to observation, measurement, and evaluation, rational controls give rise to opportunism by enhancing any negative feelings . . . toward the organization. Heightened opportunism, in turn, induces opportunistic individuals to "game the system" in other important but less accessible areas. (Ghoshal & Moran, 1996, p. 24)

Thus, use of rational controls shifts voluntary compliance to compulsory compliance and encourages more difficult to detect opportunistic behavior; monitoring measurable behaviors leads to shirking on unmeasurable ones. The cost of removing controls escalates until it is no longer an option. "By then, the most promising individuals within the firm . . . will be more likely those who are most skilled at furthering their own interests, with the most guile" (Ghoshal & Moran, 1996, p. 27).

Agency theorists advance related arguments based on the premise that principals (e.g., owners who supply capital to firms) and agents (e.g., managers who have decision-making authority within the firm) have divergent interests (Jensen & Meckling, 1976). The firm is seen as a governance structure made up of contracts and claims on assets and cash flows. Incentive contracts that make executive pay contingent on future firm performance are the preferred solution to the problem of divergent interests that arises in large firms. To motivate agents to act in their best interest, principals design compensation contracts that make agents' compensation contingent on firm performance. The principal-agent relation is further mediated by boards of directors, which monitor managers when optimal incentive contracts cannot be written; financial markets, which efficiently weed out poor governance structures; and ultimately the market for corporate control, which permits competing groups of managers to bid for control.

Agency theorists assert that corporate control is efficiently allocated and optimal governance ensured by efficient capital markets. Managers' wealth is tied to share price to align manager and shareholder interests. Boards of directors are elected by shareholders to monitor managers and ratify their most important decisions. Failing these (and other) interest alignment tactics, if management drives the share price down far enough through its actions, others will buy control of the firm, compensating shareholders with an acquisition premium and being rewarded themselves with a gain in value of the firm. "Thus capital markets ensure that the structure of the nexus of contracts that survives is the one that minimizes agency costs and maximizes shareholder wealth" (Davis & Thompson, 1994, p. 145). The functionalist logic of agency theory, however, is undermined by risk-bearing consequences of incentive compensation (Beatty & Zajac, 1994), limited monitoring effectiveness of boards of directors (Davis & Thompson, 1994), and impediments to and regulation of the market for corporate control (Davis & Thompson, 1994), making it unlikely that the governance structures we observe are the "efficient outcome of competition."

TABLE 7.1 Different Coevolutionary Configurations

Configuration	Supercompetitive	Competitive	Partly Competitive	Independent	Synergistic
Change in fitness (ΔF)	$\Delta F < -A$	$\Delta F = -A$	$-A < \Delta F < 0$	$\Delta F = 0$	$\Delta F > 0$
Sum ($\Delta F + A$)	Negative	Zero	Positive	Positive	Positive
Difference ($D = A - \Delta F$)	Increased $D > 2A$	Increased $D = 2A$	Increased $2A > D > A$	Constant $D = A$	Decreased $D < A$

SOURCE: Adapted from Heylighen and Campbell (1995, p. 187).
NOTE: ΔF is the changes in fitness for a coevolving system when the initial system's change in fitness has the positive value A.

Whole-Part Coevolutionary Competition and Organizational Suboptimization

Of course, there are many more adaptations designed to align the interests of organizations and their members (see, e.g., Barney, 1997; Milgrom & Roberts, 1992). Thus far, however, no general solution has been found to the problem of shared control. One basic limitation of current strategies is that they are undermined by faster and more effective evolution at individual and face-to-face-group levels, and their equal (or greater) effectiveness at fostering local face-to-face-group solidarity relative to global organizational solidarity.[2] This occurs because alignment strategies, although generally recognizing the *reactiveness* of performance measurement, fail to account for the faster pace of evolution at lower levels of organization. Rapid adaptation to organizational incentives and controls by face-to-face groups and individuals— especially high-ranking organizational officials and other individuals who can significantly enhance their status and wealth by committing the organization to certain risky or otherwise undesirable actions—to achieve their own selfish preferences decreases their informativeness. As a result, the organization's ability to discriminate good from bad individual and/or group performance declines because the organization-level side effects of lower-level actions go undetected for some period of time, preventing organization-level adaptation and typifying the "fugitive nature of control" (Meyer, 1994, p. 569).

Whole-part competition in organizations is thus a *coevolutionary* problem. That is, the organization and its parts do not merely evolve, they coevolve, both with each other and with a changing organizational environment (Baum & Singh, 1994b). In a coevolutionary process, the fitness landscape of one agent is altered as other agents make their own adaptive moves. Well-known examples of coevolution include "arms races" (D'Aveni, 1994), the "Red Queen" (Barnett & Hansen, 1996; Van Valen, 1973), and the "tragedy of the commons" (Hardin, 1968). These examples feature *complex* behavior produced by nonlinear, positive feedback that pressures agents to continually adapt just to maintain their fitness relative to others. Heylighen and Campbell (1995) describe five different classes of coevolution, the characteristics of which are summarized in Table 7.1.

As the table shows, depending on the form of coevolution, an increase in fitness by one agent alters the fitness of the other agent (ΔF) in the system in different ways. *Independent* configurations represent a null case where the global system is the aggregate of its independent parts: An increase in one agent's fitness does not affect the other's fitness. In the zero-sum, *purely competitive* configuration, the increase in one agent's fitness results in an equal decrease in the other's fitness. In the negative-sum, *supercompetitive* configuration, the increase in one agent's fitness results in a larger decrease in the other's fitness. In the *partly competitive* configuration (i.e., where some resources are shared and others are not), the increase in one agent's fitness results in a smaller decrease in the other's fitness. Finally, and in contrast, in the *synergistic* configuration, an increase in one part's fitness results in the other's fitness being increased as well. Heylighen and Campbell (1995) speculate that the partly competitive configuration is the most common.

Turning to fitness difference implications of the different configurations, all competitive configurations raise the fitness difference between agents with respect to the initial change, A, and only the synergistic configuration diminishes it. A larger fitness difference means that smaller moves result in greater gains/losses in relative fitness—the fitness landscape becomes steeper. This produces a net increase in selective pressure, which speeds up *local optimization* while lowering the likelihood of *global optimization*. Thus, at the agent level, competition can either facilitate or impede optimization, depending on the shape of the fitness landscape. This illustrates the general principle of suboptimization (Machol, 1965, pp. 1-8), which states that suboptimization—that is, optimizing the outcome for each subsystem (e.g., individual or face-to-face group)—does not generally lead to an optimal outcome for the global system (e.g., organization); the prisoners' dilemma is a classic example. For an aggregate of *independent* agents, suboptimization equals global optimization; however, when agents are interdependent, this is not the case. Only the synergistic and partly competitive configurations increase global fitness.

These insights from evolutionary theory—that coevolutionary competition between organizations and their components tends to be won at individual and face-to-face-group levels and that suboptimization does not generally result in global optimization—help to explain the inefficacy of prevailing incentive-based interest alignment strategies. They also suggest potential alternatives to tackling the whole-part competition problem. Complexity theory provides a rich theoretical framework for understanding such complex, coevolutionary systems. In the next section, therefore, I examine more formally how the structure of coevolutionary interaction influences its global effectiveness using a model of coupled fitness landscapes called the *NK[C]* model (Kauffman, 1993, chap. 6).[3]

NK[C] Models of Whole-Part Coevolution on Coupled Fitness Landscapes

Here, following Kauffman (1993, chap. 6), I conceive *coevolution* as a process that couples the *NK* fitness landscapes of different agents. My aim is to specify conditions under which agents composing a coevolving system are able to adapt successfully, as a means of advancing propositions about how to tune the structure of a coevolutionary system to increase its global effectiveness. The analysis is based on simulation results obtained and presented by Kauffman (1993, chap. 6). In this section, I introduce Kauffman's *NK[C]* model, which couples the fitness landscapes (and fitness) of coevolving agents. In the next section, I examine the results of Kauffman's (1993) simulations and their implications for creating effective coevolving whole-part systems in organizations.

In the *NK[C]* model, N refers to the number of traits of an agent; K refers to internal complexity, the number of traits that are interdependent; and C refers to external complexity, the number of traits of one agent that coevolve with the traits of another agent. Each trait, K, makes a fitness contribution that depends on that trait and on K other traits among the N that compose the agent. Thus, K reflects how richly interconnected are the components of the agent. Each trait (N) can take two or more states A (or in geneticists' terms, alleles). The set of possible genotypes (i.e., combinations of traits) is A^N. Each genotype has a fitness, and the distribution of fitness values over the range of genotypes constitutes a fitness landscape (Kauffman, 1993; Wright, 1931, 1932).

To model a coevolutionary system, we need to couple the fitness landscapes of agents in the system, such that adaptive moves by one agent interact (more or less profoundly) with the fitness landscapes of other agents in the system. A natural way to couple different agents' landscapes is to assume that each trait of agent$_1$ depends on K other of its *own* traits and on C other traits of agent$_2$ (Kauffman, 1993, p. 244). Thus, C represents the number of agent$_2$'s traits that might coevolve with a given trait of agent$_1$. More generally, in a system comprising S interacting agents, each trait in agent₁ will depend on K of its own traits, and on C traits in each of the other S agents with which its fitness landscape is coupled. In a system of S agents, the interactions can be represented as a web of such couplings.

In the $NK[C]$ model, adaptive evolution is represented as a hill-climbing process. Agents are semiautonomous units that seek to maximize some measure of "goodness" over time. Mutations move an agent to neighboring points in the landscape, representing neighboring genotypes. Evolutionary success is a matter of exploring possibilities in which various combinations of traits are tested. Over time, as each agent attempts to move uphill on its own fitness landscape, it also alters the landscapes (and fitness) of other agents in the system. Adaptive moves by one agent can either increase or decrease the fitness of each other agent in the system, depending on how such moves alter other agents' landscapes.

Adaptive behavior depends on the distribution of the fitness values or *ruggedness* of an agent's fitness landscape and the speed at which the coevolutionary system in which it interacts reaches equilibrium. In the simplest case, agents quickly climb to and cluster around one (of perhaps many) fitness peaks. In more complex cases, agents may spread widely—for example, following the web of ridges across the landscape (Kauffman, 1993, chap. 3)—and equilibrium remain elusive.

The speed at which a coevolutionary system stabilizes depends on C and K (Kauffman, 1993, pp. 249-254). The lower the value of C, the faster the system reaches an equilibrium state. Conversely, the speed at which agents encounter equilibria increases as K increases. Thus, raising internal (lowering external) complexity speeds the process of achieving stable equilibria.

K's influence on the speed of a coevolutionary system derives from its effects on the *ruggedness* of fitness landscapes—the result of an increasing number of constraints as K increases relative to N. For $K = 0$, each trait makes an independent fitness contribution, and the fitness landscape is highly correlated about a single, global peak—the fitness value for neighboring genotypes is similar, and any

move toward increased fitness leads to the global optimum. Behavior in such systems is path *independent*—when disturbed by innovative behavior or by the environment, the system always returns to the same behaviors; systems are "stuck" (Arthur, 1988, 1989). For $K = N - 1$, the landscape is fully uncorrelated and has many local peaks and ridges—the fitness value for neighboring genotypes varies widely, and moves toward increased fitness are not predictive of outcomes for other moves (Kauffman, 1993). Behavior is reigned by ambiguity and incompatibility in which an order has yet to emerge; *history does not matter.*

More generally, as K increases, the number of peaks (local optima) increases, the steepness of peaks increases, the level of fitness at any given optima decreases, and the predictability of finding a better-than-average fitness peak diminishes. The falling height of accessible fitness peaks make it more likely that agents will become trapped on suboptimal peaks, which Kauffman terms a "complexity catastrophe" (Kauffman, 1993, p. 35). Systems for which $0 < K << N - 1$ are characterized by complex patterns of behavior that lie between order and chaos and show great adaptability to changing environmental conditions (Kauffman, 1993; Waldrop, 1992). Complex behavior enables the system to maximize benefits of stability while retaining a capacity to change by admitting both *path dependence* (i.e., historical forces that shape *future* organizational evolution) and *path creation* (i.e., the enactment of *novel* approaches that break from the past) processes (Garud & Jain, 1996; Kauffman, 1993). Behavior is irregular, uncertain, and sensitive to initial conditions, making it difficult to predict and plan ahead. Change tends to be small most of the time, but occasionally large-scale change will occur (Bak & Chen, 1991). The system's output is point-by-point unpredictable; nevertheless, the overall behavior of the system does have a pattern that can be identified, and there are boundaries that set limits to behavior (Kauffman, 1993).

Thus, Kauffman's $NK[C]$ framework affords a dynamic model of coupled fitness landscapes whose ruggedness and richness of coupling can be *tuned*. Increasing K tunes the landscape toward more ruggedness (increased numbers of less-fit local optima) and increased likelihood of agents becoming stranded on local (sub)optima—a complexity catastrophe. Increasing C prolongs the "coupled dancing" (Kauffman, 1993) in which agents' moves alter one another's fitness landscapes, preventing stabilization.[4]

Kauffman's *NK[C]* Model Simulations of Coevolutionary Dynamics

Kauffman (1993, chap. 6) presents a series of simulations carried out using the *NK[C]* model. In the analyses, Kauffman assumed that each agent acts in turn, in the context of the current state of the other agent. On its turn, each agent tries a random mutation and moves to that mutant variant if the variant is fitter; if the variant is not fitter, the agent does not move. Thus, any move by an agent is at least transiently beneficial for that agent, but may increase or decrease the fitness of coevolving agents.[5]

Kauffman's Figure 6.2 (1993, p. 246) shows eight agents coevolving over 2,500 generations, with $N = 24$, $K = 13$, and $C = 1$. Thus, each of the 24 traits composing each agent depends on 13 other of its own traits and one trait in each of the seven other agents. In the simulation, over eight generations, each agent in turn tries a random mutation and moves to that new genotype only if it is fitter than the current genotype in the context of the current genotypes of the other seven agents. The first major result is that *Nash equilibria* arise.[6] For the first several hundred generations, the mean fitness for all agents in the system increases, rapidly at first and then more slowly. Increasingly long intervals with no change start to occur as the waiting time for agents to find fitter variants increases with their increasing fitness levels. Several bursts of change are incited by occasional changes in a single agent, but by 1,600 generations, Nash equilibrium is found. As Kauffman (1993, p. 245) points out, however, it is not self-evident that Nash equilibria should occur because each two-alleled agent has 2^N (here, 2^{24}) genotypes among which it

is evolving, and an S-agent system has the *product* of these genotypes in its joint strategy space. Given this result, Kauffman next examines how values of K and C influence waiting time to encounter a Nash equilibrium.

Kauffman's Figure 6.3 (1993, p. 247) shows the proportion of 100 coevolving pairs that have found a Nash equilibrium for K values of 2, 8, and 16 combined with C values of either 1 or 8. The main conclusion is that as K increases relative to C (increasing the ruggedness of fitness landscapes), the waiting time to reach a Nash equilibrium *decreases*. This result

> reflects the increased number of local optima in *NK* landscapes as K increases for fixed N. When $K > C$, Nash equilibria are found rapidly. When $K < C$, Nash equilibria are still found, but the mean waiting time becomes very long. In short, for a pair of agents that are coevolving, $K = C$ is a crude line separating these two regimes. (Kauffman, 1993, p. 246)

Thus, complex coupling among coevolving agents delays Nash equilibria.[7]

So far, Kauffman's simulations have assumed that coevolving agents are on landscapes of equal ruggedness. It is of interest, however, to consider how coevolution proceeds when pairs of agents are on different landscapes. Kauffman's Figure 6.4 (1993, p. 248) gives results for simulations in which 200 pairs of agents, with various combinations of values for K (2, 4, 8, 12, and 16) and C (1, 8, and 20), are simulated for 250 generations, after which time some fraction of pairs reach Nash equilibria and the rest are still coevolving. This figure reveals several noteworthy features (Kauffman, 1993, p. 249), summarized in Table 7.2. A key overall result of Kauffman's *NK[C]* model simulations is that K acts as a force toward increased complexity and complexity catastrophe, whereas C acts as a force away from catastrophe.

All the foregoing results are based on mutating one trait at a time in each coevolving agent; however, agents may make more than one move in any iteration. Kauffman (1993, p. 251) shows that as the number of genes mutated simultaneously increases, the number of local optima declines, so the

TABLE 7.2 Features of Coevolutionary Competition

1. For all values of K, the fraction of pairs reaching Nash equilibria in 250 generations decreases as C increases. Conversely, for all values of C, the fraction of pairs reaching Nash equilibria in 250 generations increases as K increases. Thus, as in Figure 6.3 (Kauffman, 1993, p. 247), high K leads to more rugged landscapes and Nash equilibria are encountered more rapidly.
2. When $C > 1$, the fitness at Nash equilibria is greater than the corresponding pre–Nash equilibria fitness when the agents are still coevolving.
3. As C increases, the pre–Nash equilibria fitness of both coevolving agents declines; for high values of C, a single move by one entity lowers fitness for the other entity more sharply.
4. When C is high, high-K agents have higher mean pre–Nash equilibria fitness than low-K agents—a $K = 4$ entity does better against a $K = 2$ entity than does a $K = 2$ entity, while a $K = 8$ entity would fare even better, and so on.
5. When C is high, a low-K entity achieves higher mean pre–Nash equilibria fitness if it is paired with a high-K entity— a $K = 2$ entity does better against a $K = 4$ entity than against a $K=2$ entity, would fare even better against a $K=8$ entity, and so on. Thus, when C is high, increasing the value of K by one entity increases the fitness for *both*.
6. At Nash equilibria, fitness of low-K agents is higher than for high-K agents at each level of C.

SOURCE: Adapted from Kauffman (1993, Figure 6.4, p. 248).

probability of achieving Nash equilibria also declines. This suggests that the optimal mutation rate for maintaining fitness in coevolving systems may be quite low.

Managing Whole-Part Coevolutionary Competition in Organizations

In the remainder of this chapter, I outline alternative, and potentially more tractable, approaches to managing whole-part coevolutionary competition in organizations. Specifically, I identify strategies that *tune the structure of whole-part coevolution* to render it more globally effective by raising access to high-fitness local maxima, and either speeding the pace of evolution at the organization level or slowing its pace at individual and face-to-face-group levels. Kauffman's (1993) results, reviewed above, suggest the four basic strategies, summarized in Table 7.3, for tuning the structure and speed of whole-part coevolutionary competition in organizations to increase its effectiveness. Some more specific operationalizations of these four strategies, also listed in Table 7.3, include the strategies outlined in the following sections.

TABLE 7.3 Strategies for Managing Whole-Part Coevolutionary Competition in Organizations

Strategy	Rationale	Operationalization
Strategy 1.0: Raise organization or component K when C is high	When C is high (and the likelihood of Nash equilibria is low), high-K (low-K) agents achieve higher mean pre–Nash equilibria fitness if paired with low-K (high-K) agents	Strategy 1.1: Employ multiple, inconsistent, changing performance measures Strategy 1.2: Continually, incrementally, reorganize Strategy 1.3: Adopt cumulative organizational performance criteria
Strategy 2.0: Lower organization K when C is low	When C is low (and the likelihood of Nash equilibria is high), lowering K increases access to local optima with high fitness peaks at Nash equilibria	Strategy 2.1: Adopt comparable performance measures
Strategy 3.0: Balance organization K and C	As implied by Strategies 1 and 2	Strategy 3.1: Match organizational structure to diversification strategy
Strategy 4.0: Lower C	When C is low (and the likelihood of Nash equilibria is high), K can be lowered, increasing access to local optima with high fitness peaks at Nash equilibria	Strategy 4.1: Increase internal differentiation Strategy 4.2: Decentralize to coordinate

Strategy 1.1: When C Is High, Increase Component K by Employing Multiple, Inconsistent, Changing Performance Measures

White (1992) suggests that control is best achieved through multiple, inconsistent performance measures. Meyer (1994, p. 574) makes a related argument, suggesting that the velocity with which performance measures change affects organizational performance outcomes: "Internal control and hence stability may be a function of an organization's ability to shift its performance measures."

Multiple, inconsistent (i.e., orthogonal), and changing performance criteria slow the speed of evolution by increasing the number of configurations an individual or group needs to explore to hit upon the optimum. Changing, orthogonal performance criteria also increase the difficulty of optimizing because search is local (Cyert & March, 1963) and path dependent (March, 1994). Considerations that are close in time and close in cognitive and organizational distance dominate those that are more distant. When such "exploitative" search (i.e., the identification, routinization, and extension of known good ideas) leads to locally positive outcomes, it is likely to dominate "exploratory" search (i.e., experimenting with new options from which new possibilities can be learned) that ultimately may lead searchers to globally better results (March, 1991). Moreover, the historical path of trials, in which the outcomes in a particular evaluation regime depend not only on that regime but also on previous regimes and the ways in which they have been experienced, also makes some outcomes unrealizable in the future—including some previously realized (March, 1994). As a result, individuals and groups may become "stranded" at one (of many) local (rather than global) maxima, increasing the fitness of organizations relative to individuals and face-to-face groups. In a recent simulation study derived from game-theoretic logic, Erev (1998) shows how managers can limit the degree of suboptimization by shifting back and forth between individual and team-based performance criteria for subordinates.

Although these suggestions might appear to undermine possibilities for organization-level adaptation, as Meyer (1994, p. 572) demonstrates cogently, this need not be the case: First, if organizational performance is (plausibly) considered to be an uncertain, moving target, then multiple, inconsistent, regularly changing measures can facilitate organizational adaptation because "as one approaches asymptotically the upper limits of performance on a given dimension, the dimension loses salience and performance on another dimension increases correspondingly in significance." Second, if organizational performance is considered a fixed target, but a target can be approached only indirectly, then multiple, inconsistent, regularly changing measures can also facilitate organizational adaptation.

> The principle of indirection is best understood by example: consider a sailboat tacking against the wind and current, first in one direction, and then another. Each time, the course shifts ninety degrees more or less, but the Euclidean distance between the boat and its destination decreases at every turn. The analogy . . . can be generalized from two to several dimensions. One can improve on one dimension of performance and then another, each time moving closer to optimization on all dimensions simultaneously but at no time moving directly toward the performance target. (Meyer, 1994, p. 572)

Strategy 1.2: When C Is High, Increase Component K by Continually, Incrementally Reorganizing

The emergence of face-to-face-group solidarity makes cooperation a more likely outcome for hierarchically structured organizations than flat, structureless organizations (Abrahamsson, 1993; Glance & Huberman, 1994). As indicated above, however, face-to-face-group solidarity often becomes "clique selfishness": Whatever the consequences for other groups, the action that will be preferred is the one best for this group. Although Kauffman, Macready, and Dickenson (1994) provide evidence that such clique selfishness is not always harmful to organizational performance (see Strategy 4.2), in an organization faced with the problem of producing a collective good, continually, incrementally reorganizing face-to-face groups can result in cooperation that spreads beyond of the boundaries of local, face-to-face groups.

Supporting this idea, in a recent simulation study, Glance and Huberman (1994) found that "fluid" organizations, in which individuals move between groups or start new groups of their own, display higher levels of cooperation than is attainable by organizations with either a fixed structure or no structure at all. Globally, fluidity translates into a mixing and merging of organizational members, which provides an incentive for free riders to cooperate. By fostering diffusion of common beliefs and values and increasing the likelihood of future interaction, fluidity also increases opportunities for cooperation and lowers the risk of conflict. Glance and Huberman show that a combination of ease of starting new groups and difficulty of moving between groups enables an organization to restructure itself to overcome outbreaks of defection or an initial bias toward defection in the organization, producing the highest levels of cooperation. Thus, an enclave of cooperation within the organizational hierarchy can initiate a widespread transition to cooperation within the entire organization. This combination of ease of starting new groups and difficulty of moving between groups, however, also causes the structure to become very dilute and disconnected—in the extreme, all individuals want to be on their own—lowering overall organizational effectiveness. Organizational effectiveness, they show, is highest when barriers to moving between groups are relatively low and when it is moderately difficult to start new groups. Organizations operating within this range of fluidity display less cooperativeness over time than more fluid organizations, but overall performance is enhanced by their having higher levels of clustering.

Oticon, a Danish designer and manufacturer of hearing aids, is an example of a pure project-based organization attempting to solve complex problems (Tushman & O'Reilly, 1997). Since the early 1990s, Oticon has relied almost entirely on the use of temporary projects for the organization of

work; mobile computer workstations and cellular phones substitute for offices, and interaction and learning through face-to-face communication with other employees and customers is strongly encouraged.

Strategy 1.3: When C Is High, Increase Component K by Adopting Cumulative Organizational Performance Criteria

The agency theory notion of protecting shareholders' interests through incentive compensation for executives, in which pay is made contingent on *future* organizational performance, through stock options and partnerships, has achieved taken-for-granted status (Davis & Thompson, 1994). Such incentives attempt to mitigate suboptimal use of organizational resources by organizational members who do not bear the full cost of their actions. Because future organizational performance cannot be measured directly, however, current market-based value of a publicly traded organization's shares (assuming efficient stock markets) is used as a proxy for its economic value. Alternatively, compensation is based on accounting measures of organizational performance (e.g., return on assets). Use of such measures to evaluate managerial effectiveness (especially in North America) has produced a range of negative side effects including postponed maintenance and other decisions that raise short-term shareholder returns at the expense of long-term organizational effectiveness. Barney (1997) recently concluded that "Far from reassuring stockholders that their interests are being cared for, reliance on accounting measures of performance assures shareholders that their interests are *not* paramount in strategies or operations of a diversified firm's divisions" (p. 424).

Individuals who have the potential to significantly enhance their status and wealth by committing their firms to certain actions will be inclined to pursue those actions—even if they involve substantial risk. For example, when Archie McCardell was president of International Harvester (IH), he had a management bonus contract that substantially increased his income if certain of IH's accounting performance ratios equaled the industry average. In the light of these incentives, McCardell adopted some accounting method changes that inflated IH's reported accounting performance above industry averages. McCardell received his bonus, but IH was bankrupt within 2 years (Hamermesh & Christensen, 1981).

A more recent example is "Chainsaw" Al Dunlap, who has become a widely known "corporate killer" for his downsizings of Sunbeam Corporation and Scott Paper Company, accompanied by simultaneous increases in their growth, sales, and stock performance. In April 1994, Dunlap became CEO of Scott Paper; he went on to lay off 11,200 of the company's 29,000 workers, as well as closing plants and shutting down the headquarters building. By the end of his 18-month tenure, Scott's stock had increased 220%; Dunlap made about $100 million and Scott's other shareholders made more than $6 billion. Dunlap then sold Scott to Kimberly-Clark. In July 1996, Dunlap was elected chairman of Sunbeam. Upon announcement of his appointment, Sunbeam's market value jumped 59%. At Sunbeam, he cut half of the company's 12,000 workers and promised to close two thirds of the company's plants while doubling sales. After 6 months of losses, Dunlap was fired in June 1998. In August 1998, Sunbeam was fighting Dunlap's claim on a $27 million severance package, the U.S. Securities and Exchange Commission was investigating irregularities in the company's accounting practices during Dunlap's tenure, and the company's market value had declined more than 50% since Dunlap's departure.

As Gary Hamel (1997) points out,

It's really a no-brainer to raise short-term shareholder returns. Find a 59-year-old CEO, give that person a ton of share options, and set a mandatory retirement age of 62. Voila!—the share price will zoom. The CEO will get rid of underperforming businesses, repurchase shares, and slash away at corporate bloat . . . senior executives, near retirement age or not, have been behaving in precisely this way for some time. That should be no surprise, given the increasing alignment between top management's compensation criteria and short-term gains in share price. Neither should it be surprising that in 1996, U.S. companies repurchased more than $170 billion of their own shares—a

record. Nor that between 1980 and 1995, the top 100 companies in the U.S. got rid of more than 25% of their employees.

While such actions may succeed in raising share price, they do not create new wealth. They do not yield new revenue streams, they do not take the company into new markets, and they do not create fundamentally new value for customers. . . . Companies that don't do more than excise the things that destroy wealth will soon run out of room for improving share price. . . . What do you do once you've trimmed away all the fat and given all the excess cash back to shareholders? Any savvy corporate turnaround artist will be on the beach when the day of reckoning arrives. (p. 74)

Nicholas Leeson's role in the failure of Barings Bank in 1993 reinforces the point that it is not only *senior* executives who can "bet the firm."

Recent runaway (parasitic) executive compensation has exposed factors not considered in the logic of agency theory. Although organizational performance historically has depended strongly on the efforts of a few executives, because of the broader scope of markets—a result of factors including globalization, deregulation, new sources of financial capital, and advances in manufacturing technology, communications, and transportation—today's executives have much greater leverage than their predecessors. These developments raise the stakes of poor organizational performance, making it crucial for organizations to bid for the most talented executives (Frank & Cook, 1995). Although it was once almost universal practice to promote business executives from within, in today's market, executives who do not receive their due can simply move to another organization. This rise in employer competition for the services of executives has made it more likely they will be paid their economic value as determined by the marketplace. The greater mobility of executives has been accompanied by explosive growth in their salaries. In 1990, *Fortune* 200 CEOs earned an average of 150 times the salary of the average U.S. production worker (up from 35 times in 1974). Intense competition forces organizations to participate in the market for key executives because failure to pay high salaries can mean losing top candidates to rival bidders. In Japan and Germany, where inter-firm bidding for executive talent remains far less common, CEOs earned 16 times and 21 times the average worker's salary, respectively. Executive incomes have thus grown as structural changes have made them more valuable and competition for them has intensified (Frank & Cook, 1995).

Consistent with these observations, Boyd and Richerson's (1985) cultural evolutionary models indicate that conditions for organization-level selection are best when shifts of key individuals from organization to organization are low. Organization-to-organization exchange of executives undermines market-based executive performance criteria by disconnecting the interests of individuals and organizations, making it possible for executives (and especially turnaround gurus) to "out-evolve" their organizations: Hiring executives based on *individual* reputations for innovations in their original organizations usually takes place long before the efficacy of their innovations has been demonstrated (i.e., the organization-level side effects of executives' actions will not have had time to surface). The situations that create executive reputations are far from providing opportunities for validating superior ability. One way to overcome this is to base hiring of outside executives on their organization's, not their own, reputation for effectiveness (Campbell, 1994). Another is risk-reward pay schemes, which condition payouts from stock options on *future* performance. For example, *performance vesting* grants executives stock options that can be exercised only if their firms' share prices reach values specified by the board of directors 5 (or more) years hence; otherwise, the options are forfeited (e.g., Citigroup Inc.). *Premium-priced options* compensate executives with stock options from which they profit only on the gain above future target share prices set by their board of directors (e.g., Monsanto Co.).

Strategy 2.1: When C Is Low, Lower Own K by Adopting Comparable Performance Measures

Consider the implications of the transformation from a functional (F-form) to multidivisional (M-form) design for organizational control. A typical F-form design groups organizations by activity, concentrates production in large facilities, and disperses its sales force geographically. In contrast, a typical M-form design groups production, sales, and staff activities together by product, and sometimes by geographic region. Under the F-form, subunits are interdependent (the outputs of one subunit are inputs for another) and the performance of each subunit (function) is described *uniquely*, usually in terms of some function-specific output measure(s) such as sales per employee or production speed. Under the M-form, subunits are independent (each subunit is self-contained) and the performance of each subunit (division) is described *similarly*, in terms of some accounting measure(s) such as sales or return on assets. In other words, the F-form yields *noncomparable* functional performance outcomes, whereas the M-form yields *comparable* divisional performance outcomes. Meyer (1994, p. 563) concludes that this is *the* principal advantage of M-form organizations: "The principal advantage of multiunit compared to unitary organizations . . . is comparability of performance measures. One cannot, after all, allocate capital or bonuses efficiently among units whose performance is described by different and noncommensurable metrics."

Beyond this basic benefit, from an evolutionary standpoint, comparability of performance measures can be seen to simplify the optimization problem for complex organizational systems by lowering the range of possible configurations for evolution to explore at the organizational level relative to the subunit level. The adoption of comparable performance measures thus strengthens evolutionary processes at the organizational level by "simultaneously improving the processes by which organizations seek out or generate new options (exploration) and improving their capabilities for implementing options that prove effective (exploitation)" (March, 1994, p. 47).[8] In terms of the $NK[C]$ model, adoption of comparable performance measures lowers the organization's K. When C is low (and the likelihood of Nash equilibria is high), this can help the organization balance K and C, as well as increasing the organization's access to high fitness peaks at Nash equilibria.

Strategy 3.1: Balance K and C by Matching Organizational Structure to Diversification Strategy

Different diversification strategies require distinctly different internal organizational arrangements; as a result, firm performance is not the consequence of diversification strategy alone, but of the *fit* between strategy and internal structure (Hill, Hitt, & Hoskisson, 1992). Realization of benefits of *related* diversification, which arise from *scope economies* (i.e., the value of joint production is greater than the value of separate production), requires a *cooperative* internal arrangement (Hill et al., 1992, pp. 504-505) to coordinate the activities of otherwise independent divisions so that skills can be transferred and resources shared. Strategic and operating decisions of interdependent divisions must be shared with the corporate office as well as with other divisions. Interdivisional cooperation should be reinforced by reward and incentive systems emphasizing corporate rather than divisional outcomes. Performance ambiguities resulting from the interdependencies must be resolved by assessing division performance over a range of subjective and objective nonfinancial performance criteria (e.g., ability to innovate, degree of cooperativeness with other divisions, labor productivity, capacity utilization, market share, growth) and by resource allocation by corporate office on the basis of these criteria (Gupta & Govindarajan, 1986; Hill & Pickering, 1986).

By comparison, realization of benefits of *unrelated* diversification, which derive from *governance economies* (i.e., information and control advantages of internal governance over markets), requires a *competitive* configuration (Hill et al., 1992, pp. 505-507). Each division must have autonomy with regard to operating decisions so that divisions can be evaluated as autonomous independent units and division managers can be held accountable for divisional profit performance. Incentive systems for divisional managers must be linked to divisional rather than overall corporate returns. The corporate office should exercise control over divisions by setting market-based targets for rate of return and by monitoring financial outcomes. Resources must be allocated by corporate office to high-yield uses on a competitive basis. For unrelated diversified firms, interdivisional integration creates unnecessary performance ambiguities, information processing requirements, and corporate bureaucracy.

From an evolutionary standpoint, matching related (unrelated) diversification strategies with cooperative (competitive) internal structures can be seen to balance K and C: Cooperative (high C) internal structures are more effective for related (high K) diversification strategies, whereas competitive (low C) structures are more effective for firms with unrelated (low K) diversification strategies.

Strategy 4.1: Lower C by Increasing Internal Differentiation

The most productive way to foster cooperation is to increase the division of labor, each individual focusing on a different subtask while contributing to a common goal. Such differentiated action is easier because tasks that are smaller (a) require less coordination and information exchange, (b) limit the potential for competition, and (c) create possibilities for synergistic complementarity. Such action is also potentially more productive because, by lowering C and K, specialization also raises the likelihood of Nash equilibria, stopping arms races that pressure individuals to follow every move of their competitors, while increasing individuals' access to high fitness peaks at Nash equilibria. Extension of the division of labor, however, also requires extension of cooperation and resource sharing, and thus the need for shared social control (Heylighen & Campbell, 1995).

As described above, conformist transmission (Boyd & Richerson, 1985), combined with mutual monitoring (Axelrod, 1984) and cultural-group selection (Campbell, 1994; Sober & Wilson, 1998), can produce shared controls that foster cooperation and group-beneficial behavior in small face-to-face groups with close contacts. When groups become larger, however, not all members are in direct contact with one another, shared controls based on reciprocal monitoring become difficult to maintain, and self-optimizing behavior can emerge. Thus, as groups grow in size, the balance shifts in favor of within-group (versus between-group) selection. This can be addressed with two additional mechanisms (Campbell, 1982, 1991):

1. Making the belief so strong that it is internalized, effectively controlling behavior even in the absence of other group members; and
2. Developing a centralized, hierarchically superior control system whose task it is to reach an explicitly formulated goal by rewarding actions that contribute to reaching that goal and punishing those that deviate from it.

Because hierarchical control relies on explicit rules, it typically suffers less diversification of belief than internalized control (Heylighen & Campbell, 1995). Hierarchical control can, however, arise in two very different ways, with very different implications for organizational fitness (Sober & Wilson, 1998). On one hand, some individuals may "escape" social controls and succeed in establishing their dominance over others. In this case, hierarchy is a product of *within-organization* competition and likely should not be interpreted as "functional" at the organizational level. Although hierarchical structures make it possible to gather extensive and expert knowledge, the knowledge is removed from the practical situations to which it is applied, concentrating power and making it possible for leaders to selfishly optimize at the expense of the organization (see Strategy 1.3). Even if individual optimizing by leaders creates a heavy parasitic load, the arrangement may be so group-beneficial that there is a net-group benefit (Heylighen & Campbell, 1995). On the other hand, it is common for functional organizational systems to become more hierarchical and differentiated as they increase in size (Abrahamsson, 1993; Simon, 1962). If this stratification results from *between-organization* selection, then the hierarchy does not signify selfish within-organization competition and may benefit the organization.

Strategy 4.2: Lower C by Decentralizing to Coordinate

It is generally assumed that coordination among subtasks or agents to optimize some overall performance criterion is best achieved by hierarchical coordinating and steering structures that attempt to ensure that change is always beneficial for overall organizational performance. Turchin (1977), for example, argues that a system formed by an integration of a variety of subsystems, together with a command-and-control structure to guide the actions of the subsystems, will be more fit than a simple aggregation of subsystems without hierarchical control. Although, intuitively, it seems obvious that if subsystems collaborate systematically through planning and coordination, they will be more effective than if they behave haphazardly, contrary to this intuition, the opposite may be true in some cases: Coordination among subtasks to optimize *difficult* problems characterized by many conflicting constraints may often be achieved better by partitioning the overall problem into selfishly optimizing subgroups.

Supporting this idea, in a recent simulation study, Kauffman and colleagues (1994) found that for difficult optimization problems, enhanced solutions could be found by partitioning the total problem into subtasks, each of which is then optimized selfishly, with no attention paid to the effects of actions on the problems facing neighboring subtasks. Subtask boundaries permit constraints from other subtasks to be ignored, helping each subtask to avoid becoming trapped on poor local optima. Overall good performance arises as a collective emergent behavior of the interacting, co-evolving subgroups. Such "coevolutionary problem solving" is not useful for simple problems but becomes increasingly valuable as landscapes become less rugged (i.e., as K increases relative to N). For $N = 120$ and $K = 4$, for example, the fitness landscape is sufficiently correlated that good optimization requires that any candidate change be beneficial for the overall system—the entire problem is solved best in its entirety (Kauffman et al., 1994). When conflicting constraints increase ($N = 120$ and $K = 8$, or higher), however, their results show that the overall system progressively achieves higher performance if it is partitioned into subtasks (Kauffman et al., 1994). The increasing advantage reflects the increasing danger, as K increases (relative to N), of becoming trapped on very poor local optima when the entire problem is treated as a single unit. Thus, it is not surprising that organizations effective at solving difficult problems with many conflicting constraints typically are divided into departments, profit centers, and other quasi-independent suborganizations (e.g, Oticon's pure project-team organizational form). Kauffman and colleagues' (1994) results provide a theoretical foundation for such decentralization.

Critical Values and Adaptive Tension

Kauffman's *NK[C]* model is fundamentally about complexity effects and emergent structure. From a complexity perspective, organizational suboptimization is seen as a reflection of emergent structures at the edge of chaos. At the organization level, natural complexity effects are arrested so that suboptimization remains and is reinforced by face-to-face-group dynamics. Consequently, the implications of the strategies for critical values and levels of adaptive tension within whole-part systems are important to consider.

Two fundamental constraints facing adaptive evolution emerge from Kauffman's *NK[C]* model. One is that in landscapes containing some fitness peaks having clearly superior adaptive advantage, if selection forces are too weak to hold members of a population high up on the peaks, the apparent order in the population is due to the typical properties of the majority of the population still spread around the valley. That is, "adapting systems exhibit order not *because* of selection but *despite* it" (Kauffman, 1993, p. 35). The second is that given (a) that as peaks proliferate, they become less differentiated from the general landscape; and (b) that in precipitous rugged landscapes, adaptive progression is trapped on the many suboptimal "local" peaks, then even in the face of strong selection forces, the fittest members of the population exhibit characteristics little different from the entire population (1993, p. 35).

Kauffman labels these *complexity catastrophes* because either one or the other must inevitably happen if the complexity of the agents under selection increases. The first occurs because, for a system with a sufficiently large number of parts (N),

the fitness loss resulting from mutation of any part is small, and the likelihood of mutation is greater than the strength of selective pressures that might restore the loss. As a result, selection becomes too weak a force to hold adapting agents at adaptive peaks. Thus, when N exceeds a critical value, selection forces can neither reach nor remain upon adaptive peaks. Inevitably, adaptive search turns up poorer solutions as N increases (Kauffman, 1993, p. 53). The second occurs because as K increases relative to N, the number of conflicting constraints increases, the number and steepness of adaptive peaks increases, the level of fitness at any given peak and the probability of finding a better than average fitness peak fall, and the likelihood that agents will become trapped on suboptimal fitness peaks rises (Kauffman, 1993, p. 52). In this case, the falling height of accessible peaks thwarts the selection process.

Complexity thus imposes an upper bound on adaptive progression via selection when either the number of parts (N) or constraints (K) exceeds a critical value (Kauffman, 1993, p. 36). In Kauffman's view, therefore, adaptive evolution takes place in a narrow band of complexity between the "the edge of chaos" and the "edge of catastrophe." Move over the catastrophe edge, and selection stops; move over the chaos edge, and order stops. The implications of the four strategies for critical values and adaptive tension are summarized in Table 7.4. As the table shows, invoking Strategies 1 and 3 risks complexity catastrophe, whereas invoking Strategy 2 avoids complexity catastrophe. Strategies 2 and 4 risk nonadaptiveness, however, because they may move the system away from the edge of chaos, where complex patterns of behavior show the greatest adaptability to changing environmental conditions (Kauffman, 1993; Waldrop, 1992).

Conclusion

Units of organizational evolution are nested and overlapping, so that some units (individuals and groups) are integral parts of other adapting units (organizations). The structure of relations among them arises from the interaction among the various

TABLE 7.4 Critical Value Implications of Whole-Part Coevolution Management Strategies

Strategy 1.0: Raise organization or component K when C is high	Increases K relative to N, raising adaptiveness but potentially risking complexity catastrophe
Strategy 2.0: Lower organization K when C is low	Lowers K relative to N, avoiding complexity catastrophe but raising the risk of nonadaptiveness
Strategy 3.0: Balance organization K and C	Risks nonadaptiveness if K is lowered relative to N and complexity catastrophe if K is raised relative to N
Strategy 4.0: Lower C	Risks nonadaptiveness if K is lowered relative to N (following Strategy 3)

nested units responding to a shifting environment and their own internal, historical dynamics. The problem is that all groups, at all levels, demonstrate "clique selfishness" and that lower-level units typically out-evolve those at higher levels. These features of organizational evolution complicate it considerably (March, 1994); the same two individuals may either compete or cooperate, depending on the level at which their interaction takes place (Heylighen & Campbell, 1995).

Here, drawing on theories of biological and cultural evolution, I sketched out how the inherently faster pace of evolution at individual and face-to-face-group levels undermines the emergence of integrated, cooperative organization-level systems, and explains the inefficacy of interest alignment strategies that organizations typically employ. I then used Kauffman's (1993) $NK[C]$ model to formalize some aspects of coevolutionary whole-part competition in organizations and to derive four alternative "structure-tuning" strategies for managing whole-part coevolutionary competition in organizations.

My theoretical analysis and derived strategies might easily be rejected on the basis that the concepts and models on which they were based were developed originally by biologists. Before rushing to dismiss, however, consider the plausibility of the two basic claims on which my analysis relies: (a) organizations can be better managed by understanding the links between biological evolutionary selection and social interaction, and (b) complexity competes with selection theory as an explanation of coevolutionary order.

Largely absent from my analysis has been any discussion of the relationship between whole-part coevolution and welfare. Some evolutionary views are tied to the income and welfare benefits of capitalism (e.g., Nelson & Winter, 1982). Although I do not believe that this view is satisfactory, the main reason for my silence is that neither I, nor anyone else that I know of, has theorized a selection function that embodies the social and political economy of organizational communities as I have portrayed them here. Although institutional, sociocultural, and sociocognitive processes are all making their way into models of the evolutionary dynamics of organizations, how they intersect with the evolutionary framework remains to be fully explored.

Notes

1. Here I assume the feasibility of organization-level selection. For a discussion of the conditions favoring effective selection at the organization level, see Campbell (1994, pp. 33-35).

2. Granovetter's (1985) observation that economic action is embedded in social ties that can facilitate (or derail) exchange is in much the same spirit.

3. McKelvey (1998, this volume) explores the implications of $NK[C]$ models for *inter*firm coevolution.

4. Increases in S also slow equilibria and increase instability, but that is another paper.

5. In addition to these *random dynamics*, Kauffman (1993) also examined two more adaptive mutation strategies: *fitter dynamics*, in which each agent examines in turn all its single-mutant variants and chooses at random one of the fitter variants, and *greedy dynamics*, in which each agent in turn chooses the fittest single mutant variant. The main results are the same for all strategies (Kauffman, 1993, p. 249).

6. In assuming that each agent is able at each moment to mutate a single trait, Kauffman constrains the range of alternative moves locally accessible to the agent. Thus, use of the term

"Nash equilibria" is used here with respect to the mutant search range, *not* with respect to all possible moves.

7. Consistent with this conclusion, Kauffman (1993, pp. 246-247) also reports that in simulations where N increases for fixed K and C, the waiting time to Nash equilibrium increases as the density of local optima decreases.

8. Of course, this approach is not incompatible with employing multiple, inconsistent, changing performance measures, because the same measures can be applied to every individual and group.

References

Abrahamson, E. (1991). Managerial fads and fashions: The diffusion and rejection of innovations. *Academy of Management Review, 16*, 586-612.

Abrahamsson, B. (1993). *Why organizations?* Newbury Park, CA: Sage.

Aldrich, H. E. (1979). *Organizations and environments.* Englewood Cliffs, NJ: Prentice Hall.

Andrews, K. R. (1971). *The concept of corporate strategy.* Homewood, IL: Irwin.

Arthur, B. (1988). Self-reinforcing mechanisms in economics. In P. W. Anderson, K. J. Arrow, & D. Pines (Eds.), *The economy as an evolving complex system* (pp. 9-31). Redwood City, CA: Addison-Wesley.

Arthur, B. (1989). Competing technologies, increasing returns, and lock-in by historical events: The dynamics of allocation under increasing returns. *Economic Journal, 99*, 116-131.

Arthur, B. (1990, February). Positive feedbacks in the economy. *Scientific American*, pp. 92-99.

Ashby, W. R. (1956). *Design for a brain.* New York: Wiley.

Axelrod, R. (1984). *The evolution of cooperation.* New York: Basic Books.

Bak, P. & Chen, K. (1991, January). Self-organized criticality. *Scientific American*, pp. 26-33.

Barnard, C. (1968). *The functions of the executive.* Cambridge, MA: Harvard University Press.

Barnett, W. P., & Hansen, M. T. (1996). The Red Queen in organizational evolution. *Strategic Management Journal, 17*(Summer special issue), 139-158.

Barney, J. B. (1997). *Gaining and sustaining competitive advantage.* New York: Addison-Wesley.

Baum, J.A.C. (1996). Organizational ecology. In S. Clegg, C. Hardy, & W. Nord (Eds.), *Handbook of organization studies* (pp. 77-114). Thousand Oaks, CA: Sage.

Baum, J.A.C., & Singh, J. V. (1994a). Organizational hierarchies and evolutionary process: Some reflections on a theory of organizational evolution. In J.A.C. Baum & J. V. Singh (Eds.), *Evolutionary dynamics of organizations* (pp. 3-20). New York: Oxford University Press.

Baum, J.A.C., & Singh, J. V. (1994b). Organizational-environment coevolution. In J.A.C. Baum & J. V. Singh (Eds.), *Evolutionary dynamics of organizations* (pp. 379-402). New York: Oxford University Press.

Beatty, R. P., & Zajac, E. J. (1994). Managerial incentives, monitoring and risk-bearing: A study of executive compensation, ownership and board structure in initial public offerings. *Administrative Science Quarterly, 39*, 313-335.

Berle, A. A., & Means, G. C. (1932). *The modern corporation and private property.* New York: Macmillan.

Boyd, R., & Richerson, P. J. (1985). *Culture and the evolutionary process.* Chicago: University of Chicago Press.

Boyd, R., & Richerson, P. J. (1990). Culture and cooperation. In J. J. Mansbridge (Ed.), *Beyond self-interest* (pp. 111-132). Chicago: University of Chicago Press.

Boyd, R., & Richerson, P. J. (1992). Punishment allows the evolution of cooperation (or anything else) in sizable groups. *Ethology and Sociobiology, 13*, 171-195.

Campbell, D. T. (1969). Variation and selective retention in socio-cultural evolution. *General Systems, 16*, 69-85.

Campbell, D. T. (1974). "Downward causation" in hierarchically organized biological systems. In F. Ayala & T. Dobzhansky (Eds.), *Studies in the philosophy of biology* (pp. 179-186). Berkeley: University of California Press.

Campbell, D. T. (1982). Legal and primary-group social controls. *Journal of Social and Biological Structures, 5*, 431-438.

Campbell, D. T. (1983). The two distinct routes beyond kin selection to ultrasociality: Implications for the humanities and social sciences. In D. L. Bridgeman (Ed.), *The nature of prosocial development: Theories and strategies* (pp. 11-41). New York: Academic Press.

Campbell, D. T. (1986). Rationality and utility from the standpoint of evolutionary biology. *Journal of Business, 59*, S355-S364.

Campbell, D. T. (1990). Levels of organization, downward causation, and the selection-theory approach to evolutionary epistemology. In G. Greenberg & E. Tobach (Eds.), *Theories of the evolution of knowing* (pp. 1-17). Hillsdale, NJ: Lawrence Erlbaum.

Campbell, D. T. (1991). A naturalistic theory of archaic moral orders. *Zygon, 26*, 91-114.

Campbell, D. T. (1994). How individual and face-to-face-group selection undermine firm selection in organizational evolution. In J.A.C. Baum & J. V. Singh (Eds.), *Evolutionary dynamics of organizations* (pp. 23-38). New York: Oxford University Press.

Carroll, G. R. (1984). Organizational ecology. *Annual Review of Sociology, 10*, 71-93.

Csanyi, V. (1989). *Evolutionary systems and society: A general theory.* Durham, NC: Duke University Press.

Cyert, R. M., & March, J. G. (1963). *A behavioral theory of the firm.* Englewood Cliffs, NJ: Prentice Hall.

D'Aveni, R. A. (1994). *Hypercompetition: Managing the dynamics of strategic maneuvering.* New York: Free Press.

Davis, G. F., & Thompson, T. A. (1994). A social movement perspective on social control. *Administrative Science Quarterly, 39*, 141-173.

Dawkins, R. (1976). *The selfish gene.* New York: Basic Books.

DiMaggio, P. J., & Powell, W. W. (1983). The iron cage revisited: Institutional isomorphism and collective rationality in organizational fields. *American Sociological Review*, *48*, 147-160.

Erev, I. (1998, June). *On the nontrivial relation between individual and organizational learning.* Paper presented at the INFORMS International Conference, Tel Aviv, Israel.

Fligstein, N. (1987). The intraorganizational power struggle: The rise of finance presidents in large firms: 1919-79. *American Sociological Review*, *52*, 44-58.

Frank, R., & Cook, P. (1995). *The winner-take-all society.* New York: Oxford University Press.

Garud, R., & Jain, S. (1996). The embeddedness of technological systems. In J. Baum & J. Dutton (Eds.), *Advances in strategic management* (Vol. 13, pp. 389-408). Greenwich, CT: JAI.

Ghemawat, P. (1991). *Commitment: The dynamic of strategy.* New York: Free Press.

Ghoshal, S., & Moran, P. (1996). Bad for practice: A critique of the transaction cost theory. *Academy of Management Review*, *21*, 13-47.

Glance, N. S., Hogg, T., & Huberman, B. A. (1997). Training and turnover in organizational evolution. *Organization Science*, *8*, 84-96.

Glance, N. S., & Huberman, B. A. (1993). The outbreak of cooperation. *Journal of Mathematical Sociology*, *17*, 281-302.

Glance, N. S., & Huberman, B. A. (1994). Social dilemmas and fluid organizations. In K. Carley & M. Prietula (Eds.), *Computational organization theory* (pp. 217-239). Hillsdale, NJ: Lawrence Erlbaum.

Granovetter, M. (1985). Economic action and social structure: The problem of embeddedness. *American Journal of Sociology*, *91*, 481-510.

Gupta, A. K., & Govindarajan, V. (1986). Resource sharing among SBUs: Strategic antecedents and administrative implications. *Academy of Management Journal*, *29*, 695-714.

Hamel, G. (1997, June 23). How killers count. *Fortune*, pp. 70-84.

Hamermesh, R. G., & Christensen, E. T. (1981). *International Harvester (A)* (Harvard Business School Case no. 9-388-096). Boston: Harvard Business School.

Han, S.-K. (1994). Mimetic isomorphism and its effects on the auditor services market. *Social Forces*, *73*, 637-664.

Hannan, M. T., & Freeman, J. (1977). The population ecology of organizations. *American Journal of Sociology*, *83*, 929-984.

Hannan, M. T., & Freeman, J. (1989). *Organizational ecology.* Cambridge, MA: Harvard University Press.

Hardin, G. (1968). The tragedy of the commons. *Science*, *162*, 1243-1248.

Haveman, H. A. (1993). Follow the leader: Mimetic isomorphism and entry into new markets. *Administrative Science Quarterly*, *38*, 593-627.

Heylighen, F., & Campbell, D. T. (1995). Selection of organization at the social level: Obstacles and facilitators of metasystem transitions. *World Futures: The Journal of General Evolution* (Special issue on "The Quantum of Evolution: Toward a Theory of Metasystem Transitions"), 181-212.

Hill, C.W.L. (1990). Cooperation, opportunism, and the invisible hand: Implications for transaction cost theory. *Academy of Management Review*, *15*, 500-513.

Hill, C.W.L., Hitt, M. A., & Hoskisson, R. E. (1992). Cooperative vs. competitive structures in related and unrelated diversified firms. *Organization Science*, *3*(4), 501-521.

Hill, C.W.L., & Pickering, J. F. (1986). Divisionalization, decentralization, and performance of large United Kingdom companies. *Journal of Management Studies*, *23*, 26-50.

Hodgson, G. M. (1993). *Economics and evolution.* Cambridge, UK: Polity.

Hogg, M., & Abrams, D. (1988). *Social identifications.* London: Routledge.

Huberman, B. A., & Hogg, T. (1995). Communities of practice: Performance and evolution. *Journal of Computational and Mathematical Organization Theory*, *1*, 73-92.

Hull, D. (1988). *Science as a process.* New York: Oxford University Press.

Jensen, M. C., & Meckling, W. H. (1976). The theory of the firm: Managerial behavior, agency costs, and ownership structure. *Journal of Financial Economics*, *3*, 305-350.

Kauffman, S. A. (1993). *The origins of order: Self-organization and selection in evolution.* New York: Oxford University Press.

Kauffman, S. A., Macready, W. G., & Dickenson, E. (1994). *Divide to coordinate: Coevolutionary problem solving.* Unpublished manuscript, The Santa Fe Institute.

Korn, H. J., & Baum, J.A.C. (in press). Chance, imitative, and strategic antecedents to multimarket contact. *Academy of Management Journal.*

LeVine, R. A., & Campbell, D. T. (1972). *Ethnocentrism: Theories of conflict, ethnic attitudes, and group behavior.* New York: Wiley.

Lumsden, C. J., & Wilson, E. O. (1981). *Genes, mind, and culture: The coevolutionary process.* Cambridge, MA: Harvard University Press.

Machol, R. E. (1965). *The system engineering handbook.* New York: McGraw-Hill.

March, J. G. (1991). Exploration and exploitation in organizational learning. *Organization Science*, *2*, 71-87.

March, J. G. (1994). The evolution of evolution. In J.A.C. Baum & J. V. Singh (Eds.), *Evolutionary dynamics of organizations* (pp. 39-49). New York: Oxford University Press.

March, J. G., & Simon, H. A. (1958). *Organizations.* New York: Wiley.

McKelvey, B. (1982). *Organizational systematics.* Los Angeles: University of California Press.

McKelvey, B. (1994). Evolution and organization science. In J.A.C. Baum & J. V. Singh (Eds.), *Evolutionary dynamics of organizations* (pp. 314-326). New York: Oxford University Press.

McKelvey, B. (1998). Complexity vs. selection among coevolutionary firms: Factors affecting Nash equilibrium fitness levels. *Comportamento Organizacional E Gestão*, *4*, 17-59.

McPherson, J. M. (1983). An ecology of affiliation. *American Sociological Review*, *48*, 519-532.

Meyer, M. W. (1994). Measuring performance in economic organizations. In N. J. Smelser & R. Swedberg (Eds.), *The handbook of economic sociology* (pp. 556-578). Princeton, NJ: Princeton University Press.

Milgrom, P. R., & Roberts, J. (1992). *Economics, organization, and management.* Englewood Cliffs, NJ: Prentice Hall.

Nelson, R. R., & Winter, S. G. (1982). *An evolutionary theory of economic change.* Cambridge, MA: Harvard University Press.

Sherif, M., Harvey, O. J., White, B. J., Wood, W. R., & Sherif, C. W. (1961). *Intergroup conflict and cooperation: The robber's cave experiment.* Norman, OK: The University Book Exchange.

Simon, H. A. (1962). The architecture of complexity. *Proceedings of the American Philosophy Society, 106,* 467-482.

Sober, E., & Wilson, D. S. (1998). *Unto others: The evolution and psychology of unselfish behavior.* Cambridge, MA: Harvard University Press.

Thompson, J. D. (1967). *Organizations in action.* New York: McGraw-Hill.

Turchin, V. (1977). *The phenomenon of science: A cybernetic approach to human evolution.* New York: Columbia University Press.

Tushman, M. L., & O'Reilly, C. A. (1997). *Winning through innovation.* Boston: Harvard Business School Press.

Van Valen, L. (1973). A new evolutionary law. *Evolutionary Theory, 1,* 1-30.

Waldrop, M. M. (1992). *Complexity: The emerging science at the edge of order and chaos.* London: Penguin.

White, H. C. (1992). *Identity and control: A structural theory of social action.* Princeton, NJ: Princeton University Press.

Williamson, O. E. (1975). *Markets and hierarchies: Analysis and antitrust implications.* New York: Free Press.

Williamson, O. E. (1985). *The economic institutions of capitalism.* New York: Free Press.

Wilson, D. S., & Sober, E. (1994). Reintroducing group selection to the human behavioral science. *Behavioral and Brain Sciences, 17,* 585-654.

Wright, S. E. (1931). Evolution in Mendelian populations. *Genetics, 16,* 97-159.

Wright, S. E. (1932). The roles of mutation, inbreeding, crossbreeding, and selection in evolution. *Proceedings of the Sixth International Congress of Genetics, 1,* 356-366.

Chapter 8

Venture Capital Dynamics and the Creation of Variation Through Entrepreneurship

PHILIP ANDERSON

One of Donald Campbell's most enduring legacies is a theory describing the process of sociocultural evolution. More than any other figure, he restored evolutionary theory to prominence in the social sciences. Before Campbell, social evolutionary theories aimed principally to describe the course of evolution, not the process by which evolution occurs. Campbell clarified a set of basic mechanisms that must be common to any evolutionary theory. This allowed scholars to examine how a behavior or structure of behavior evolves, without committing to a specific point of view about the trajectory of progress.

Campbell (1965) set forth three requirements for any sociocultural evolutionary process. As long as variations arise, they are subjected to consistent selection criteria, and positively selected variants are preserved and propagated, evolution will occur. These three mechanisms are very general; their operation in social life does not depend on finding a social analogue to every important feature of biological evolution. Campbell (1965) showed how evolution through variation, selection, and retention can occur in a variety of ways, such as the selective survival of social structures, selective borrowing and imitation, selective promotion of individuals who propagate some variation, or selective repetition of behaviors that seem to be associated with success.

In addition, Campbell (1974b) clarified and popularized the idea that natural selection occurs through a nested hierarchy of selective systems. External selection results from encounters between an organism and its environment; this kind of selection drives evolution both directly and indirectly. At the highest level, the survival or death of entire organisms (especially mutants) alters the distribution of different types of organisms. Additionally, indirect effects arise because it is economical for organisms to develop vicarious selective

AUTHOR'S NOTE: The assistance of Jesse Reyes of Venture Economics and David Ben Daniel of the Johnson Graduate School of Management is gratefully acknowledged. The Amos Tuck School at Dartmouth College funded the empirical research reported here.

systems. These reinforce successful behaviors and extinguish unsuccessful ones, so that trial-and-error-adaptation can proceed without failures killing the subject. (In the context of evolutionary epistemology, Campbell quotes the memorable phrase of Popper [1966]: "the development of error-eliminating controls . . . makes it possible, ultimately, for our hypotheses to die in our stead" [p. 25].)

Indirect selection mechanisms emerge and become established because they lower the cost of exploration and selection. For example, most animals have evolved taste and smell mechanisms that transmit pain signals when the animal encounters a noxious substance. Such mechanisms originally were mutations. They became ubiquitous because they provide a powerful adaptive advantage: Animals that possessed the mutation were able to avoid ingesting harmful substances. Taste and smell allow animals to probe their environment through trial and error instead of eating a substance and finding out through death or injury that it was, in retrospect, harmful.

Indirect selective systems evolve as the outcome of external variation, selection, and retention. Organisms that acquire an effective vicarious selector are able to propagate more as a result, so the indirect mechanism eventually diffuses throughout the population. Each indirect selective system then constitutes an environment within which even more indirect selective systems can evolve, leading to a nested hierarchy.

For example, business organizations usually generate revenues from customers to survive, so external selection occurs when organizations are unable to generate enough sales to cover their costs. Through variation, selection, and retention, organizations develop internal, vicarious selective systems that allow them to generate sales campaigns and terminate unsuccessful ones before reaching the point of bankruptcy. It would be expensive to run every unsuccessful sales campaign to the point where it has lost enough money to demonstrate conclusively that it is a failure; hence, organizations develop even more indirect selective mechanisms (e.g., test marketing procedures) that allow them to gauge whether a prospective sales campaign is likely to succeed without incurring the full expense of a failure. Organizations that de-

velop such mechanisms are more likely to survive, succeed, and be imitated, so these mechanisms diffuse. They create the basis for even more indirect mechanisms. For example, it would be expensive to test market every possible sales campaign, so organizations develop internal procedures for screening proposals, allowing only the most promising to move forward to the next stage. In this way, ever more indirect selection mechanisms pyramid atop one another, as long as they continue to provide a selective advantage.[1]

Selective systems constitute a nested hierarchy because each system is the outcome of trials at the next higher level. For example, the configuration of a modern wolf's taste and smell mechanism results from the differential survival of wolves who retain effective subsystems bequeathed them by ancestors, and of wolves who benefit from favorable mutations. Campbell (1974a) suggests that to explain a process, we need to take into account downward causation, because the function of any process is an outcome of a selective system at a higher level. For example, why have the jaws of soldier ants become so specialized for killing enemies that such ants can no longer feed themselves? An explanation requires both upward causation (how mechanical principles of levers confer survival advantages on ants with such jaws) and downward causation (why ants gain selective advantages by belonging to groups whose division of labor includes full-time soldiers).

This chapter investigates how the range of variation among firms receiving venture capital funding is influenced by the evolution of the venture capital industry. An exploratory study suggests that the degree of heterogeneity in the population of venture capital funds is related to the degree of variation in the funding such firms provide to entrepreneurs. Building on Campbell's model, I suggest that understanding the degree of variation among entrepreneurs is explained in part by downward causation. Venture capital is an indirect selection system for some entrepreneurs, particularly those founding high-technology businesses. Consequently, I argue that greater dispersion in the demography of venture capital firms and funds, combined with the rise of specialists in the venture capital industry, helps explain why venture capitalists funded a greater variety of portfolio companies in 1994 than they did in 1980.

Downward Causation and Entrepreneurship

Campbell's model has stimulated scholars who study the evolution of organizations and groups of organizations to examine how variations among organizations arise, are selected, and are preserved and propagated. This chapter focuses on the variation process. One of the most fertile sources of organizational variation is entrepreneurship. An entrepreneur is a person who puts together a new combination of resources, who seeks out unexploited opportunities (Schumpeter, 1934). By this definition, entrepreneurship can take place within existing organizations. Often, however, entrepreneurs found organizations as vehicles for novel resource combinations because no existing structure is appropriate for the synthesis they are introducing to the world. Likewise, the founders of new organizations often are entrepreneurs[2] because organizations that are differentiated from rivals via new resource combinations enjoy selective advantages.

In recent years, empirical research into the factors governing the rate of organizational foundings has increased dramatically (see Baum, 1996, for a recent review). To understand organizational evolution, however, we must know something in addition to why more or fewer organizations are started in a particular period. We also need to understand why more or fewer *kinds* of organizations are started, or why the range of variation among newly founded organizations is greater or lesser at a given time (Aldrich & Fiol, 1994; Astley, 1985).

The evolution of a population (or community) is expressed through changes in the distribution of characters among its members (Mayr, 1982). For example, a population may start with 50% red-eyed flies and 50% black-eyed flies but through evolution end up with 99% red-eyed flies and 1% black-eyed flies. Such a change in the distribution of characteristics may occur through differential entry and exit (Hannan & Freeman, 1989) or through selective imitation and learning (Miner & Haunschild, 1995; see also Romanelli's chapter in this volume). A wave of organizational foundings can increase or reduce variation in the population, depending on the dispersion of characters within the entering cohort and the degree to which that dispersion resembles the dispersion among surviving incumbent firms. Studies of founding rates per se, therefore, do not tell us how much variation is introduced into an evolving group of organizations.

Understanding the rate of variation among newly founded organizations, however, is distinctively important, because entrepreneurial innovations occur disproportionately among new firms. If firms are inertial (see Hannan and Freeman, 1989, for a thorough discussion), then variations are most likely to arise and take hold among organizations that are influenced little by their own history. In addition, newly founded firms typically are less complex than firms that have accumulated many cycles of mutual adaptation and adjustment among their subunits. Other things equal, the more complex a system is, the stronger are the selection pressures maintaining it (Campbell, 1975). Mutations that must fit into a complex internal ecology tend to be maladaptive, because they are subject to a broader range of adaptive behavior. Consequently, mutations might not only arise more readily in younger firms, but they also might be more easily preserved long enough to confer selective advantage.

This chapter focuses on understanding why the range of variation among recently founded firms is greater or lesser. Its thesis is that variation among such organizations is partly driven by downward causation, by indirect selective systems that have evolved to lower the cost of exploration and mutation. I argue that an important subset of organizational foundings (especially in the United States) is influenced by a higher-level selective system that has not received as much empirical attention as it deserves. This system is the evolving institution of professional venture capital.

Venture Capital as Vicarious Selector

Access to capital has long been one of the major factors constraining entrepreneurs who wish to start organizations. In societies where access to capital is limited, organization founders are dispro-portionately channeled into businesses that pro-duce high cash flows relative to the initial invest-ment required. Even where start-up funding is relatively easy to obtain, it may be attracted more to some sectors or regions than to others, changing the distribution of entrepreneurial start-ups that would otherwise prevail. Differential capital flows can be an important evolutionary force driving the distribution of characteristics among organiza-tions.

Historically, entrepreneurs have found it diffi-cult to tap into debt markets until they are able to legitimate their businesses and create a stable flow of revenues. Consequently, the principal sources of start-up funding in the United States have long been personal savings, loans, or investments from private individuals ("angels"), and, to a lesser ex-tent, loans from lending institutions, including those financed by governments.

Shortly after World War II, the first venture capital funds were started (see Henderson, 1989, for a history). These channeled money from wealthy individuals and families into newly founded enterprises. Their distinctive hallmarks were a limited partnership structure and limited life (in contrast to the organization of bank trust depart-ments, which traditionally have managed money for wealthy people), professional management, and a willingness to back entrepreneurs who were not personally known to the investors.

The amount of money, number of funds, and number of firms backed by venture capital contin-ued to grow throughout the last half of the 20th century, principally in the United States. A historic shift in the locus of wealth fueled this growth. Government regulations and increased affluence channeled a considerable portion of national sav-ings into professionally managed pension funds, whose investments are subject to regulation. With huge amounts of capital to place and constant pressure to show superior returns, pension fund managers often contracted with others to manage portions of their investment portfolios. Because young, privately held firms typically need more oversight and mentoring, pension funds sought intermediaries to select and manage investments in such enterprises. Pension funds thus supplanted wealthy individuals as the primary investors in venture capital.

In Campbell's terms, the institution of venture capital is an indirect, vicarious selective system. It has succeeded because it allows investors (princi-pally pension funds) to lower the costs of search and selection. The investor does not have to depend on or wait for external selection to drive the ulti-mate success or failure of a venture. Rather, venture capitalists invest in companies that look as if they will succeed, that emit indirect signals proven in the past to be predictors of success. Much more often than not, they earn returns on their invest-ments either when another firm acquires the ven-ture or when the venture's shares are sold on open exchanges in an initial public offering. Venture capitalists distribute to their investors the proceeds from acquisitions and the shares of firms that have become publicly traded.[3] Consequently, like most vicarious selectors, they optimize achievement of a subgoal, not adaptation per se. Their job is to maximize returns to the fund from acquisitions or public offerings, and these are not perfectly corre-lated with the venture's long-run earnings or sur-vival chances.

As Campbell predicted, vicarious selective sys-tems begat other vicarious selective systems. For example, a cottage industry of publications and conferences has sprung up, advising venture capi-talists on how to select selective systems for evalu-ating ventures. Another niche has emerged consist-ing of firms that advise investors which venture capital fund to choose, selecting the selector of the selective system, as it were.

The great majority of newly founded enterprises neither seek nor receive professional venture capi-tal funding. In fact, venture-financed companies account for a minority of firms that close an initial public offering on a listed American exchange. In a number of industries, however, particularly those characterized by rapid technological change, ven-ture capital is an important selective system that winnows potential new foundings before they offer products for sale, the point that most organizational studies select to mark a founding (with several exceptions, e.g., Schoonhoven, Eisenhardt, & Ly-man, 1990). Venture investors provide not only financial capital but also social capital (Janeway,

1986), lending their prestige and connections to new ventures. Particularly for firms whose technologies must mesh with those of other firms, credibility and access to potential alliance partners may be more valuable than money.

Campbell (1974a) urges us to take downward causation into account when explaining the evolution of a social structure or process. Following this dictum, I investigate how the evolution of the venture capital industry has influenced the rate of variation within the population of newly founded firms receiving venture capital. Under what circumstances is venture capital channeled toward a narrower or broader set of firms?

The Evolving Structure of the U.S. Venture Capital Industry

A firm enters the venture capital industry when it successfully closes a private placement in a fund it is raising. A professional venture capital firm is an enterprise that can raise enough money to support a venture capital fund. The typical life span of a fund is 10 years; when the fund's life ends, its assets are redistributed to its investors (the limited partners). The venture capital firm is the general partner in its funds, responsible for making investments, monitoring them, disposing of them, and returning either money or ownership shares to the limited partners. Partnership is and always has been the predominant organizational form for venture capital firms. A venture capital partnership derives revenues principally from two sources: management fees and a share of the investment returns from its funds. A typical fund might give the general partner 20% of the fund's returns plus a fee equaling 1% per year of the money remaining under management.

Because the amount of money in a fund dwindles as investments are cashed out, most venture capital firms must raise a new fund every 3-5 years to maintain the fee levels needed to support their partners and employees. Firms whose funds have earned high returns for their investors have tended to enhance their profits by expanding the amount of money under management, rather than raising fees. A successful venture capital firm in the late

1990s might raise an initial fund of $25-$50 million, a second fund of $50-$90 million several years later if the first fund was successful at that point, a third fund of $100-$150 million if the second fund appears to be successful, and so on. The size of funds has risen dramatically over time. A $2 million fund would have been substantial in the early 1980s; by the late 1990s, the largest funds raised hundreds of millions of dollars.

Funds can specialize on any of three dimensions: industry, geography, or stage of investment. Some funds are raised with the intention of placing investments only in a particular sector, such as biotechnology or specialty retailing. Some are targeted at specific geographic regions, such as the Rocky Mountains or Silicon Valley. Some focus on "seed" investments, specializing in getting new enterprises off the ground with their initial venture capital funding. Others focus on subsequent rounds of venture funding, additional infusions of capital that typically occur closer to the time when a portfolio company is acquired or makes an initial public offering.

Funds also specify to their limited partners what their minimum and maximum investments are. These parameters, plus the firm's investment policies, dictate whether the fund will make relatively fewer, larger investments or spread its capital across relatively more, smaller placements.

Over the years, a number of secular trends in the U.S. venture capital industry have persisted.

- The number of firms grew through the mid-1980s, peaking in 1986 (see Figure 8.1). After a steep decline through 1993, the number of firms rebounded to near its historic high in the late 1990s.
- The number of funds followed the same pattern of growth, decline, and renewed growth (see Figure 8.1). The average number of funds per firm has grown (see Figure 8.2) according to a skewed distribution. On the high end, successful firms have been able to raise capital on the strength of their track record, and these manage more funds simultaneously. The low end principally comprises newer firms that have raised only one fund, plus unsuccessful firms that are unable to raise a second fund. If a firm is successful enough to raise a second fund, it usually is able to raise a third;

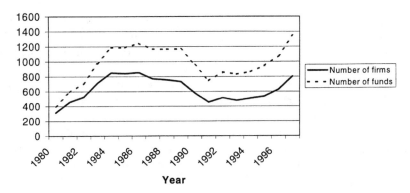

Figure 8.1. Number of U.S. Venture Capital Firms and Funds

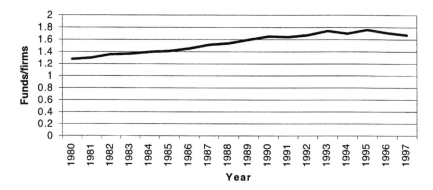

Figure 8.2. Average Number of Funds per Firm

however, even successful firms may dissolve because of disagreements among their principals.

- The amount of money flowing from limited partners into venture capital was largely stable during the mid-1980s, declined briefly in the early 1990s, then shot upward in the late 1990s (see Figure 8.3). The average fund size, in contrast, has tended upward (see Figure 8.4), reflecting the fact that the most successful funds have dramatically increased the amount of money in each of their subsequent funds. When a venture capital firm's early funds succeed, it has been able to raise enormous amounts of money (by historical industry standards) for subsequent funds.

The size of the average investment has grown, but not in proportion to the size of the average fund. Firms that raise larger funds typically do not increase their number of employees proportionally, so they have more money per partner under management. Because partners have a finite capacity for monitoring and mentoring firms, they put more money into approximately the same number of investments, instead of increasing the number of investments and maintaining the same average level of investment.

Within these secular trends, however, the industry has bifurcated into a set of generalist firms, which invest in a relatively large number of sectors, regions, and stages, and a set of specialist firms, which select a narrower range of companies to fund. Size and age are correlated with specialism: Generalists tend to be larger and older than specialists. The founding and failure rates of specialists tend to be higher than those of generalists, even

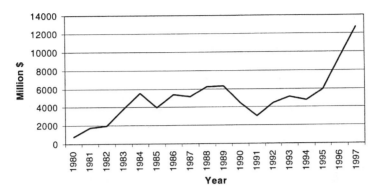

Figure 8.3. Inflows Into Venture Capital

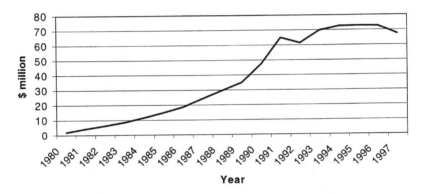

Figure 8.4. Average Fund Size

controlling for age and size. Over time, however, specialists have accounted for a growing proportion of the number of firms and the amount of money invested in venture capital (see Figure 8.5), because entries have outpaced exits more among the population of specialists.

Propositions

My aim is to identify how shifts in the population of venture capital funds translate into a wider or narrower range of variation in the portfolio companies that receive venture capital funding from year to year. I argue that variation in entrepreneurship is strongly linked to the presence of younger, specialist venture capital firms. This is somewhat paradoxical, because *individually*, generalist firms invest in a wider range of sectors, regions, and stages than do specialist firms. One might therefore conclude that a population composed largely of generalists would finance a broader range of portfolio companies.

Population-level heterogeneity is not, however, a simple function of individual-level breadth. As long as specialists specialize in different things, a population of individually focused investors can support a variegated population of portfolio companies. I suggest that generally speaking, they do. Specialist firms tend to be different from one another, whereas generalist firms tend to resemble one another more closely. If most generalist firms invest in the same few sectors, then as a group, they support less variation.

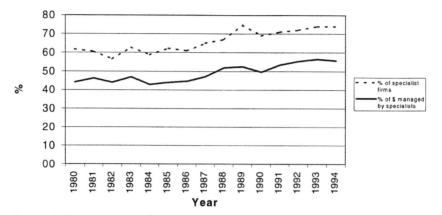

Figure 8.5. Trends in Specialism Versus Generalism

Why would specialist firms tend to diverge from one another and from generalist firms?

- *Ecological crowding.* Generalist firms generally are older, are larger, and have a track record of success; this is why they are generalists. Younger, smaller specialists without such an extensive track record have difficulty competing for the best deals against generalists. Consequently, they tend to invest in sectors where they will not run into direct competition with generalists. Carroll (1985) refers to this as resource partitioning.
- *Network centrality and social capital.* Generalist firms usually are more central than specialist firms in the industry's social network. They also have more social capital (Coleman, 1988). Many venture capital investments are syndicated: A lead investor invites other venture capitalists to join in a round of financing. Generalists are more likely to become involved in such syndications because of their network centrality and social capital. Consequently, a higher proportion of their investments flows into the same portfolio companies that other generalists are funding. As a consequence, the investment patterns of generalists are much more similar than are the investment patterns of specialists.
- *Reputational capital and indirect selection.* To raise large funds, generalists seek sizable amounts of capital from large investors, principally pension funds. Such pension funds typically look to these investments as a way of participating in "hot" industry sectors, such as semiconductors, the Internet, or biotechnology. It is difficult to raise a large

fund without promising investors that their money will be placed into these sectors. Conversely, when large investors place money with specialist venture capital funds, they expect the specialists to diversify the investors' portfolios; therefore, specialists who receive funding from the same sources as generalists are subject to an indirect selection mechanism: They are successful in fund-raising only if they can sell a different investment concept than their generalist competitors offer.

If a greater range of variation among portfolio companies is supported by the presence and health of specialist venture capital firms, coexisting with generalists that are typically larger, better capitalized, and older, the following propositions are suggested:

Hypothesis 1: The greater the coefficient of variation (standard deviation divided by the mean) in fund size in a given year, the greater the variation in portfolio companies funded that year.

Hypothesis 2: The greater the coefficient of variation in minimum investment size in a given year, the greater the variation in portfolio companies funded that year.

Hypothesis 3: The greater the coefficient of variation in fund age in a given year, the greater the variation in portfolio companies funded that year.

Hypothesis 4: The greater the ratio of specialists to generalists in a given year, the greater the variation in portfolio companies funded that year.

Hypothesis 5: The greater the ratio of capital invested by specialists to capital invested by generalists in a given year, the greater the variation in portfolio companies funded that year.

Data and Methods

Venture Economics, a unit of Thomson Publishing Corporation, has gathered data on venture capital funds since 1976. Venture funds voluntarily submit data on investments in return for reports summarizing industrywide data. Because this is the same data that must be reported to limited partners on a quarterly basis, the reporting firms have a strong incentive to be accurate. The data used in this study are drawn from Venture Economics' database, compiled for calendar years 1980-1996. Although a few venture capital firms do not report their results to Venture Economics, Thomson estimates that reporting firms account for well more than 90% of all venture capital that is invested.

Funds were designated as specialist funds if

- at least 80% of the cumulative capital invested by the end of a given year was directed toward one industry sector, or
- at least 80% of the cumulative capital invested by the end of a given year was directed toward firms in California or toward firms in New England (but not both), or
- at least 80% of the cumulative capital invested by the end of a given year was directed toward first-round funding.

With respect to the second measure, it was not possible to identify the geographic location of each portfolio company, but with the help of regional directories, it was possible to ascertain whether a portfolio company was headquartered in California, Massachusetts, Rhode Island, Connecticut, New Hampshire, Vermont, or Maine. Because firms headquartered in California (especially Silicon Valley) and New England (especially the Route 128 area in Massachusetts) account for well more than two thirds of venture capital investments, I used a pattern of investing in one or the other as a proxy for geographic specialization.

TABLE 8.1 Means for Variables Across All Years

	Specialists	*Generalists*
Number of firms	408.6	214.7
Fund size	$23.8 million	$62.9 million
Minimum investment	$156,500	$654,975
Firm age	2.3 years	5.7 years
Total funds	$2,077.3 million	$2,103.8 million

With respect to the third measure of specialization, it is possible for firms to specialize in late-round financing as well as seed financing, but such specialization would be difficult to detect. It may not be clear at the time of investment whether a round of funding is late, because firms that run into unexpected snags may need more rounds of funding, turning a presumptive late-stage financing into a middle-stage financing. Furthermore, a large proportion of assets entrusted to venture capitalists is naturally placed into later rounds, because these typically are the rounds where capital needs are highest, to fund going concerns. As a result, I limited my identification of specialization by stage to first-round investments, because a seed-funding specialist can be identified without ambiguity.

Table 8.1 summarizes the means of the variables I use to examine the five hypotheses. The dependent variables I examined are two measures of variation:

- *Funding variation:* This is the coefficient of variation of the investments made during a given year. A high value indicates that venture capitalists are funding a wide range of capital requirements.
- *Industry variation:* Venture Economics has established a proprietary set of industry codes, analogous to four-digit Standard Industrial Classification codes. Venture Economics assigns each portfolio company to the industry that accounts for the majority of its sales or prospective sales, based on information supplied by the venture capital firms and independent sources. This measure is the numbers equivalent (Adelman, 1969), which is simply the multiplicative inverse of the standard Herfindahl-Hirschman index (Hirschman, 1964). It indicates the degree to which investments are concentrated in a few sectors, dividing 1 by the square of the share of capital in each sector. The minimum value of this index is 0, which would be

attained if all venture capital were devoted to one industry; it increases monotonically toward one as the share of capital devoted to different sectors goes toward equality.

Fifteen years of data are used for each analysis,[4] relating the industry structure to the amount of variation in venture capital investment for a given year. Because the number of data points in the time series is small, this is an exploratory analysis. I am able to establish whether the data are consistent with the hypotheses, but there is not enough information to rule out chance as an explanation for the associations I observe.

Results

Table 8.2 summarizes the data used to explore the five hypotheses. Figure 8.6 shows graphically how trends in key variables are associated with the first measure of variation I explored, the coefficient of variation in the size of investments. Figure 8.7 shows graphically how the same trends are associated with the second measure of variation, a numbers equivalent index of the degree to which investments are concentrated in a few sectors. As Table 8.2 illustrates, both measures suggest that variation in venture capital investing grew significantly between 1980 and 1994. The coefficient of variation in investment size (representing the range of capital requirements funded by the industry) increased 45%, while concentration decreased by 28%. A wider range of investments was supported, and capital was allocated more broadly across a number of sectors.

Hypothesis 1 suggests that such an increase in the variation of venture capital investments stems in part from an increase in the heterogeneity of the industry. As expected, the coefficient of variation in fund sizes has trended upward (see column A of Table 8.2). The 1994 value exceeded the 1980 value by 43%; over time, the standard deviation of fund sizes has increased significantly relative to the average. This has occurred largely because the most successful funds became more and more able to raise large funds, relative to the industry average. As the difference between the size of the largest

and smallest funds grew, the industry funded a broader range of investment sizes and sectors.

Hypothesis 2 predicts that an increase in the variation of venture capital investments is also partially driven by more diversity in the minimum investment that various venture capital firms make in a given year. The data reported in column B of Table 8.2 are consistent with this expectation. The coefficient of variation of the smallest investment that each venture capital firm makes in a given year went up 50% between 1980 and 1994. In the early 1980s, many funds participated in at least one seed round of financing, typically investing $100,000-$250,000 in these deals. By 1994, many of the most successful funds had grown so large that they chose to forgo such small investments. Some have withdrawn from seed financing altogether, focusing solely on larger investments in later rounds of capital raising. Others have remained active in early-stage financing but have increased their minimum investment threshold.

In the early 1980s, an entrepreneur looking for a small amount of first-round financing could, in principle, approach nearly any venture capital firm. Venture capitalists usually target returns of 10-20 times their investment in a portfolio company, and when funds were in the $25-$40 million range, a $100,000 commitment that produced a total return of $2 million was worthwhile. As firms began raising funds in excess of $100 million, they started to bypass such opportunities. In theory, a $100 million venture capital fund could earn its target rate of return by making 1,000 investments of $100,000 each, but in practice, no fund has enough highly trained people to make so many deals, much less monitor such a large number of portfolio companies. Because the industry relies on judgment and experience that take years to develop, venture capital firms have been unable to scale up the number of deals they can manage the way they have scaled up the amount of capital they can raise from limited partners. Consequently, the bigger a fund has gotten, the larger its minimum deal has tended to become. The manager of a $100 million fund tends to look for opportunities to turn a $2 million investment into a company worth at least $20-$40 million, not for opportunities to turn $250,000 into $2-$5 million. As Campbell's ideas

TABLE 8.2 Time Series of Variables Explored in This Study

	(A) CV* of Fund Size	(B) CV* of Minimum Investment	(C) CV* of VC Firm Age	(D) Specialist/Generalist Firms	(E) Specialist/Generalist Funds Raised	(F) CV* of Investments	(G) Sector Concentration in Investments
1980	0.55	1.18	0.77	1.36	0.79	1.92	0.63
1981	0.59	1.23	0.79	1.53	0.86	2.00	0.61
1982	0.64	1.43	0.82	1.30	0.79	2.04	0.61
1983	0.61	1.34	0.86	1.69	0.88	2.08	0.61
1984	0.64	1.21	0.81	1.42	0.75	2.17	0.61
1985	0.64	1.53	0.84	1.65	0.79	2.22	0.59
1986	0.64	1.29	0.86	1.56	0.81	2.22	0.57
1987	0.70	1.40	0.90	1.86	0.89	2.27	0.56
1988	0.72	1.41	0.92	2.03	1.08	2.33	0.54
1989	0.70	1.52	0.93	2.21	1.11	2.44	0.54
1990	0.68	1.63	0.96	2.23	0.99	2.44	0.52
1991	0.74	1.74	1.00	2.45	1.15	2.56	0.51
1992	0.76	1.59	0.98	2.57	1.24	2.70	0.50
1993	0.81	1.60	1.00	2.85	1.30	2.70	0.49
1994	0.79	1.77	1.01	2.85	1.26	2.78	0.49

*CV is coefficient of variation, the standard deviation/mean.

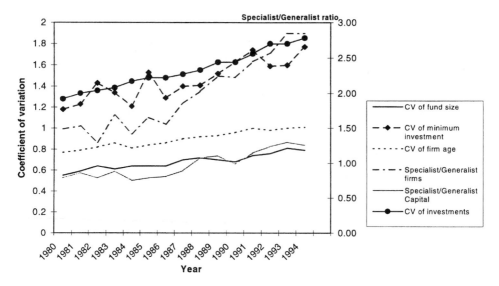

Figure 8.6. Variation in Investment Size

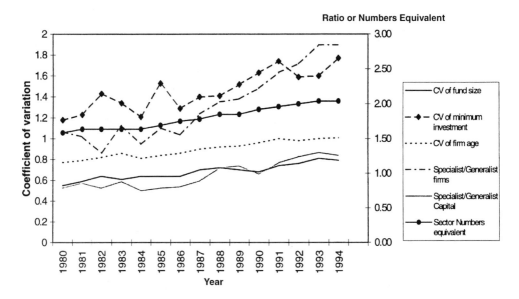

Figure 8.7. Variation in Sector Concentration

about downward causation suggest, changes in the distribution of characteristics in the venture capital industry, such as an increased dispersion in minimum investment sizes, have gone hand in hand with changes in the range of entrepreneurial opportunities funded by venture capital.

Hypothesis 3 argues that an increase in the dispersion of venture capital fund ages would be associated with an increase in the variation of venture capital investments. Column C of Table 8.2 demonstrates that the coefficient of variation in venture capital firm age increased by 31% between

1980 and 1994, which is what we would expect, given the increase in the variation of investments over the period. This has occurred because some of the oldest firms have survived for decades, others have exited after raising one or two funds, and many new entrants have attracted capital from limited partners.

In the early 1980s, when most venture capital firms were relatively young, and hence close to one another in age, the range of investments made by the industry was narrower. By the mid-1990s, a number of older firms had developed very long-standing ties with limited partners, other venture capital firms, prospective entrepreneurs, lawyers, investment banks, and other key actors. Such ties may have foreclosed certain types of investments, so newer funds find it more rewarding to seek new kinds of opportunities. Furthermore, between 1980 and 1994, a number of new industries fueled by venture capital investments sprung up. In many cases, these were pioneered by newer venture capitalists, not the veterans of the 1970s, most of whom built their reputations on investments in semiconductor and personal computer firms. As the range of firm ages increased, it appears that newer firms had both the incentive and the opportunity to create deals in arenas that were relatively neglected by more established sources of venture finance.

Hypotheses 4 and 5 link the rise of specialism in venture capital to increasing variation in venture capital investing. As columns D and E of Table 8.2 show, the ratio of specialists to generalists doubled between 1980 and 1994, while the ratio of capital controlled by specialists relative to that controlled by generalists increased by 60%. Although generalists began to raise much larger funds than ever before, a high rate of entry into venture capital by specialists has changed the overall demography of the industry. These specialists are quite focused on one sector, geographic region, or investment stage, and in the aggregate, they fund a more diverse range of portfolio company sizes and sectors. Consonant with resource-partitioning theory, generalists (especially large ones) tend to resemble one another, whereas specialists differentiate themselves. Venture capitalists have suggested to me that this stems from selection pressures exerted by prospective limited partners on those who would raise venture capital funds. On one hand, limited partners prefer established venture investors who have strong historical track records. On the other hand, limited partners strive to diversify their investment portfolios. Consequently, specialist venture capital firms can attract capital to the extent that they help limited partners diversify and are perceived as less attractive to the extent that they duplicate investments made by veteran generalist rivals. In fact, venture capitalists suggest, specialists and generalists have developed a more symbiotic than competitive relationship. Specialists make investments that fall outside the scope or below the capital threshold of generalists. Specialists enhance the values of their investments by syndicating later rounds of financing, bringing in generalists whose experience and social capital increase the likelihood of a successful initial public offering or acquisition.

Discussion

Since World War II, capitalist societies, particularly the United States, have evolved remarkable and unprecedented vicarious selection systems that channel capital to opportunity. For generations, entrepreneurs typically capitalized businesses because they either were personally wealthy or were personally acquainted with wealthy backers. Although this is still perhaps the predominant way new businesses are financed (by "angel" investors), thousands of businesses, particularly in high technology, are backed by a chain of intermediation that pools risk capital and allocates it from one set of strangers to another. Bank lending has always channeled funds from savers to borrowers not personally connected to them, but new businesses seldom are financed in this way. The emergence of venture capital as an institution and a profession has profoundly altered the evolutionary environment, at least for some kinds of organizations (particularly technologically innovative ones).

We can easily imagine a world in which the institutions of venture capital funded a very narrow range of highly similar enterprises. Were this so, venture capital would tend to reduce the degree of variation among organizations. Instead, it has turned out that venture capital funded an increasingly diverse portfolio of investments between 1980 and 1994. In terms of both investment size and industry sector, a trend toward increasing variation is unmistakable.

I have argued that the dynamics of the industry have led to increasing diversity among venture capital firms, which may help explain why venture capital has funded more rather than less variety over the years. Prosperous venture capital enterprises tend to undermine the business models that led to their initial success. Their track record allows them to raise one fund after another, always increasing in size (and hence in management fees). They are unable to scale up their activities proportionate to the amount of capital they can attract, because venture capitalists become competent through a long, slow development process. Consequently, they crowd out certain geographic and industry sectors where their social capital gives them great advantages, forcing newer, smaller venture capital firms to focus on different sectors and smaller enterprises.

Our understanding of entrepreneurial variation would be incomplete if we focused only on the direct selection environment for entrepreneurs. Venture capital is one of several vicarious selection systems that influence the degree of variety among new enterprises. Such systems help capitalist societies adapt rapidly to new technologies and markets by lowering the costs of experimentation. Entrepreneurs undergo vicarious selection before they ever book their first dollar of revenue; when they fail to win backing for their business plans, their efforts are redirected before they have to face the test of the marketplace.

Donald Campbell argued that to understand fully why a particular distribution of characteristics prevails at a given level of social analysis, we need to investigate both upward causation and downward causation. We cannot focus solely on upward causation, the microfoundations of adaptive advantage. If we treated venture capitalists simply as decision makers who allocate risk financing rationally, we could abstract them away when we seek to understand why there is more or less variation in entrepreneurial firms. The dynamics of the venture capital industry would be irrelevant. By examining downward causation, we come to understand how the changing distribution of characteristics in venture capital influences the range of entrepreneurial opportunities that are financed by these firms.

A fuller analysis of entrepreneurial variation would take into account other vicarious selection processes that winnow out prospective entrepreneurs. For example, to succeed, entrepreneurs usually must acquire not only capital but also talented people, distribution channels, and legitimacy. It would also look at the changing demography of other capital sources, such as angel investors, and indeed it might uncover interesting interrelationships. For example, several publications have reported that a number of successful entrepreneurs, particularly those who became rich in high-technology industries, have left active company management and are devoting themselves to investing in and nurturing start-ups. These "angel investors" compete with venture capitalists, particularly smaller specialists, because angels tend to focus on seed funding innovative firms with first-round investments. If the population of angel investors increases, the proportion of specialists in venture capital may decline, with implications for the distribution of venture capital investment. Paradoxically, venture capitalists who seed highly successful start-ups may be breeding a generation of potential competitors.

What are the implications of this chapter for the study of entrepreneurship within organization theory? Most important, the empirical exploration in this chapter points to a need for understanding how the venture capital industry coevolves with other members of the community that supports entrepreneurship in sectors where venture financing is significant. I have argued that the changing distribution of characters in venture capital influences the distribution of characteristics among entrepreneurs; the reverse certainly is true. Suppose, for example, that the population of newly founded firms producing tools for electronic commerce via the Internet is considerably larger, requires less capital, and has higher failure rates than other populations funded by venture capital. If this population became an important focus of venture financing, a different type of venture firm from those predominant today might prosper, attract capital, and increase in numbers.

Similarly, the venture capital industry in the future will coevolve with other members of the community that has grown up around servicing entrepreneurs. For example, the rise of small, specialist venture capital enterprises may create niches for new types of law firms, trade publications, technology incubators, regional economic development associations, and university institutes for studying entrepreneurship. An explosion of variety in the community might well alter the number and type of niches that venture capital firms occupy, and the nature of mutualistic or competitive relationships across niches.

Turning away from the specific setting of this chapter, I have attempted to illustrate an approach toward understanding organizations that I think has considerable promise: studying downward causation in a chain of systems that are related because higher levels are vicarious selection systems for lower levels. More and more scholars are studying the coevolution of hierarchically related systems; for example, see the chapters in this volume by Baum, Van de Ven and Grazman, and Madsen, Mosakowski, and Zaheer. What should the research agenda for such studies be?

Baum's chapter in this volume looks at a particular type of hierarchical relationship: the coevolution of wholes, downward with their parts and upward with larger systems of which they are in turn parts. These are nested whole-part hierarchies; the hierarchy I examine in this chapter is not. A venture capital firm is not composed of a set of portfolio companies. In the domain of entrepreneurship, corporate ventures (entrepreneurial ventures founded within existing firms) are an example of a system characterized by such a whole-part relationship.

The hierarchical system I study in this chapter is reciprocally causal, like whole-part systems; the evolving distribution of characteristics in entrepreneurial firms is influenced by the distribution of characters in venture capital firms, and vice versa. Reciprocal influence, however, is not the same as perfect symmetry. The higher levels in this system vicariously select the lower levels, but not vice versa. Limited partners select some subset of would-be venture capitalists, and venture capitalists in turn fund some subset of would-be entrepreneurs. Such systems are common in organization theory: Examples include regulatory agencies and the firms they regulate, banks and the firms to which they lend, or exclusive dealers and the vendors they represent.

I suggest that the research agenda for such hierarchies of vicarious selection should initially focus on three interrelationships. The first is the linkage between (a) the evolution of a vicarious selection system, (b) changes in what that evolving system selects, and (c) subsequent evolutionary changes in the population subject to indirect selection. For example, this study linked changes in venture capital firms to changes in the variation of selection choices made by those firms. A further step would be to gather more data on the individual portfolio companies, to see how the distribution of characteristics among them was influenced by the increasing variation of investments in them.

A second key interrelationship links a system with more than one superordinate system that acts on it as a vicarious selector. In studying the coevolution of vicarious selection hierarchies, it is particularly difficult to relate the evolution of one population (conceived as a change in the distribution of characteristics that interest the observer) to another, because most populations are subject to more than one vicarious selection system. For example, it can be quite difficult to relate changes in the population of bank lenders to changes in the population of firms to which they lend, because the population of borrowers is embedded in a larger community that exerts many influences on it. As a step toward generating middle-range theory (Merton, 1968), scholars should explore the interaction between a system and the vicarious selection systems that act on it. To continue the example, an interesting study might explore how a population of borrowers evolves as it is influenced by vicarious selection from lenders and concurrently by vicarious selection from regulatory agencies. What happens to such populations when selection pressures exerted by these two superordinate systems are incompatible?

A third key interrelationship is between three or more links in a hierarchy of vicarious selectors. For example, changes in the pool of limited partners may influence the pool of venture capital firms, in turn altering the distribution of characteristics among venture capital-funded portfolio companies. If we examine only the dyadic relationships in this chain, we may miss important properties of the chain as a whole. For example, an interesting study might examine whether the entry of new limited partners who allocate assets to venture capital for the first time ultimately results in increased variation among venture capital-financed portfolio companies.

Conclusion

Organization theory has seen an explosion in studies that examine entrepreneurial variations, the theme of this book section, using the concepts and analytical tools of organizational ecology. Frequently, their focus has been explaining why the entry rate into an industry is higher or lower at a given time or in a given environment. This is extraordinarily useful work, but it must be supplemented if we are to understand evolution within and among organizations. We have to understand not only how many firms will join a population under specified circumstances, but also how they change the composition of the population. The entry of a relatively large fraction of unusual organizations into a population has very different evolutionary implications from the entry of a cohort that reinforces the existing distribution of characteristics across firms.

To understand why we observe more or less entrepreneurial variation in a particular setting, we must examine why entrepreneurs conform to or deviate from available templates, a problem addressed by other chapters in this section. This is the problem of upward causation: Why do entrepreneurs benefit from being reproducers or innovators, and why would they face difficulties in copying apparently successful practices from other firms? In addition, we must examine why a greater or lesser range of business models is selected by indirect selective systems that have evolved to lower the cost of exploration and mutation. This is the problem of downward causation. Taking both

problems seriously will further Campbellian evolutionary perspectives aimed at understanding entrepreneurship as a source of variation in the organizational mosaic of society.

Notes

1. As Campbell notes, they may persist long after the environment has changed and they no longer succeed. Campbell identifies bureaucratic inertia with the detachment of indirect selection mechanisms from the ultimate external consequences of their operation.

2. I resist identifying all organization founders as entrepreneurs because it is possible to found an organization that offers little that is new. If entrepreneurship is a continuum, then the founder of a new business that strongly resembles existing organizations would appear to rate low in entrepreneurial behavior. Aldrich and Kenworthy's chapter in this volume presents an interesting continuum suggesting that entrepreneurs fall on a continuum from reproducer to innovator.

3. They also can distribute ownership shares in firms that remain privately held and independent, but this is unusual because their investors do not want to hold such positions. The investors contracted with venture capitalists to manage their private equity placements precisely because they have neither the time nor the expertise to monitor privately held firms.

4. Figures 8.1-8.5 show aggregate data through 1997, provided by Venture Economics Information Services. The hypotheses were explored with data through 1994 only because data on individual funds were available only through that year.

References

Adelman, S. (1969). Comment on the H concentration measure as a numbers equivalent. *Review of Economics and Statistics, 51,* 99-101.

Aldrich, H., & Fiol, M. (1994). Fools rush in? The institutional context of industry creation. *Academy of Management Review, 19,* 645-670.

Astley, G. (1985). The two ecologies: Population and community perspectives on organizational evolution. *Administrative Science Quarterly, 30,* 224-241.

Baum, J.A.C. (1996). Organizational ecology. In S. R. Clegg, C. Hardy, & W. R. Nord (Eds.), *Handbook of organization studies* (pp. 77-114). Thousand Oaks, CA: Sage.

Campbell, D. T. (1965). Variation and selective retention in socio-cultural evolution. In H. R. Barringer, G. I. Blanksten, & R. W. Mack (Eds.), *Social change in developing areas: A reinterpretation of evolutionary theory* (pp. 19-49). Cambridge, MA: Schenkman.

Campbell, D. T. (1974a). "Downward causation" in hierarchical systems. In F. J. Ayala & T. Dobzhansky (Eds.), *Studies in the philosophy of biology* (pp. 179-186). London: Macmillan.

Campbell, D. T. (1974b). Evolutionary epistemology. In P. A. Schilpp (Ed.), *The philosophy of Karl Popper* (pp. 413-463). La Salle, IL: Open Court.

Campbell, D. T. (1975). On the conflicts between biological and social evolution and between psychology and moral tradition. *American Psychologist, 30,* 1103-1126.

Carroll, G. R. (1985). Concentration and specialization: Dynamics of niche width in populations of organizations. *American Journal of Sociology, 90,* 1262-1283.

Coleman, J. (1988). Social capital in the creation of human capital. *American Journal of Sociology, 94,* S95-S120.

Hannan, M. T., & Freeman, J. H. (1989). *Organizational ecology.* Cambridge, MA: Harvard University Press.

Henderson, Y. K. (1989, July-August). The emergence of the venture capital industry. *New England Economic Review,* pp. 64-79.

Hirschman, A. O. (1964). The paternity of an index. *American Economic Review, 54,* 761.

Janeway, W. H. (1986). Doing capitalism: Notes on the practice of venture capitalism. *Journal of Economic Issues, 20,* 431-441.

Mayr, E. (1982). *The growth of biological thought: Diversity, evolution and inheritance.* Cambridge, MA: Harvard University Press.

Merton, R. (1968). *Social theory and social structure.* New York: Free Press.

Miner, A. S., & Haunschild, P. R. (1995). Population level learning. In B. Staw & L. Cummings (Eds.) *Research in Organizational Behavior* (Vol. 17, pp. 115-166). Greenwich, CT: JAI.

Popper, K. R. (1966). *Of clouds and clocks: An approach to the problem of rationality and the freedom of man.* St. Louis: Washington University Press.

Schoonhoven, C. B., Eisenhardt, K. M., & Lyman, K. (1990). Speeding products to market: Waiting time to first product introduction in new firms. *Administrative Science Quarterly, 35,* 177-207.

Schumpeter, J. A. (1934). *The theory of economic development.* Cambridge, MA: Harvard University Press.

Chapter 9

Suborganizational Evolution in the U.S. Pharmaceutical Industry

PAUL INGRAM
PETER W. ROBERTS

Much of the organizational research in the social-evolution tradition explicitly adopts an organization-level perspective, explaining population-level change as the accumulation of foundings and failures of relatively inert organizations (Baum, 1996). This perspective has been criticized by management theorists who argue that significant change also occurs within organizations (e.g., Barnett & Burgelman, 1996). Organization-level selection is also implicitly challenged by evolutionary theorists who identify the difficulty of applying selection arguments to groups of autonomous agents (Campbell, 1994). Partly in response to these challenges, researchers have begun to move their analyses inside the organization to examine suborganizational evolution (Baum & Singh, 1994; Haveman & Cohen, 1994; Ingram & Baum, 1997; Miner, 1987; Winter, 1990). This chapter joins several other chapters in this volume (see especially Madsen, Mosakowski, & Zaheer; Rosenkopf & Nerkar; and Van de Ven & Grazman) in extending this latter stream of research by examining evolutionary processes at a suborganizational (in our case, product) level of analysis.

The fundamental justification for examining evolution at a suborganizational level of analysis is that identifiable components of organizations may experience evolution independently of the organization as a whole. Consider the various types of multiunit organizations that are becoming increasingly common (Davis, 1996). Large conglomerate firms add and drop companies frequently through processes of acquisition and divestiture. International consumer-goods producers create national divisions that may then be dissolved or spun off. Large retail chains create or acquire, and then sell or close, stores or even whole divisions. As Madsen, Mosakowski, and Zaheer (this volume) show, foreign exchange firms open and close trading rooms. Even vertically integrated organizations (e.g., automobile manufacturers) close or divest components that may then operate independently or become parts of other organizations. The effects of these intraorganizational changes extend beyond the organization in question and are manifested quite dramatically at the population or industry level. The selection forces that operate on suborganizational components thus play a significant role in the evolution of whole industries.

Before proceeding with our arguments and analysis, a pair of examples of suborganizational evolution illustrates our motivation. In July, 1997, the Woolworth Corporation announced that it would close its remaining 400 F. W. Woolworth general merchandise stores. This chain grew from a single "five and dime" store located in Lancaster, Pennsylvania, in 1879, to include almost 1,500 stores in the early 1990s. The processes that seem to account for the rise and fall of F. W. Woolworth are familiar to students of organizational evolution. The chain originally offered an attractive mix of products in convenient downtown locations, which enabled it not only to flourish and grow, but even to earn an important position in American social history. More recently, changing shopping habits and the rise of competitive organizational forms (e.g., large discount and drug stores) caused a decline in the fortunes of the chain. What is perhaps surprising from the perspective of past research on organizational evolution, however, is that the significant organizational change associated with the rise and fall of the F. W. Woolworth stores occurred without a single organizational founding or failure. The thousands of individual stores that came and went were not individual organizations but components of the larger chain organization. Even now that all the general merchandise stores have disappeared, the Woolworth organization persists, because it has developed a number of other retail chains (e.g., Foot Locker) that are now major divisions of the organization. The history of Woolworth illustrates significant change in organizational and economic activity that appears to be consistent with evolutionary explanations but does not involve the founding and failure of whole organizations. Rather, the evolution occurred at the suborganizational level.

A second example is the empirical context of this chapter: the U.S. pharmaceutical industry. Grabowski (1989) has noted that roughly 1,200 novel drugs were introduced to the market between 1946 and 1991. Each of these innovations attracted a large number of imitative offerings, making the total number of new products over this period a considerably higher number. There is little doubt that the evolution of drug products produced within this industry is a reasonable metric for the state of economic activity in the industry. Schwartzman (1976) stresses that the evolving portfolio of products determines the profitability of a pharmaceutical firm, with high profits associated with newer and more innovative drugs. Moreover, the specific cadre of drugs being offered at any point in time influences the efficacy and cost effectiveness of state-of-the-art medical treatment. With this practical interest in the evolution of products within this industry, the question becomes the extent to which the pattern of evolution would be captured by an analysis focusing on organizational foundings and failures.

Table 9.1 indicates the separability of product-level critical events (i.e., introductions and removals) from the corresponding critical events at the organization level (i.e., foundings and failures). It breaks the product-level events into those that are dependent versus independent of organization-level events. Of 2,020 new products introduced in the United States between 1977 and 1993, new organizations (i.e., those founded in the same year the product appeared) accounted for only 124 (6%). The remaining 1,896 new products came from organizations that existed prior to the time of introduction. Of 900 products removed between 1977 and 1993, only 147 (16%) co-occurred with the cessation of their organizations. In 710 other removals, the organization that had offered the product continued to exist after its removal.[1] In total, of 2,920 product-level critical events between 1977 and 1993, only 271 (9%) co-occurred with organization-level critical events. These data show that, at least within the pharmaceutical industry, the large majority of product-level change is independent of organization-level change.

These two examples indicate the extent to which significant change at the industry level is missed by analysis that focuses on organizational critical events. This chapter builds from the above pharmaceutical example and examines suborganizational selection within the pharmaceutical industry. Although the empirical focus is on product-level selection, we first outline a theoretical framework

TABLE 9.1 Organizational Origins of Product Introductions and Deletions in the U.S. Pharmaceutical Industry, 1977-1993

	Products, 1977	*Introductions, 1977-1993*	*Removals, 1977-1993*	*Products, 1993*
Existing products	2,894			
Product introductions by organizations that previously existed		1,896 (94%)		
Product introductions by new organizations		124 (6%)		
Product removals by organizations that continued to exist			710 (79%)	
Product removals by organizations that ceased to exist			147 (16%)	
Product removals by organizations, fate unknown			43 (5%)	
Totals	2,894	2,020	900	4,014

SOURCE: Data are from IMS America.

that emphasizes the introduction and selection of organizational capabilities (Winter, 1990). The link between this framework and the empirical analysis is made by assuming that specific products are observable indicators of the presence of specific productive capabilities (comprising production, marketing, and distribution subroutines).

The balance of the chapter is structured as follows. The next section outlines issues that are particularly important for studying suborganizational evolution. First, we describe the role of routines as an elemental unit in firm performance and evolution. We justify the use of the product as the unit of analysis by showing that in our context, there is a stable relationship between routines and products. Second, we describe the need to consider two interrelated selection environments, one external and the other organizational. In the third section of the chapter, we describe some expectations for internal and external selection dynamics. The for-

mer set of hypotheses is derived from a strategic model of the firm wherein organizational routines are combined to develop an evolving set of productive capabilities. The latter set of hypotheses is developed by translating previous arguments about organizations in environments to the level of products in product markets. The penultimate section of the chapter illustrates the application of our ideas to an empirical context with an analysis of the founding rates of drug products in the U.S. pharmaceutical industry. Finally, we discuss outstanding issues and ideas relevant to future research on suborganizational evolution.

Routines, Capabilities, and Suborganizational Selection

Recognizing the need to move evolutionary analysis inside the organization leaves open the question of what unit of selection to emphasize. Whereas past research tended to examine whole organizations, other prospective candidates include divisions or local units, product or service offerings, work groups, employees, or any other elemental unit of organized activity. Winter (1990) suggests that because organizations may be modeled as collections of routines, researchers may study the adoption and abandonment of organizational routines as determinants of evolution at the industry level. With the routine as the unit of selection, one may develop an account of evolutionary change that does not rely on an organizational inertia assumption, as routines may come and go independently of organizational foundings and failures.

A routine (defined as a pattern of interactions that represents a successful solution to a particular problem), however, is an ambiguous construct (Cohen et al., 1996). On one hand, routines are comprised of subroutines, which are themselves combinations of microbehaviors on the part of participating individuals, as well as other inputs (Nelson & Winter, 1982). At the same time, one must clearly distinguish between static and dynamic routines. Given the complexity bound up in the routine construct, the following paragraphs outline a strategic view of the firm within which organizational routines play an important role. This formalizes a framework for suborganizational evolution that is driven by the introduction and abandonment of productive capabilities, which are distinct combinations of routines linked to the provision of specific products or services. The former characteristic ensures that the proposed framework is consistent with ongoing research in the evolutionary tradition, while the latter supports the following empirical analysis of new product introduction.

Within the strategic management literature, firms are modeled as bundles of productive capabilities. A capability refers to "a firm's capacity to deploy resources, usually in combination, using organizational processes, to effect a desired end" (Amit & Schoemaker, 1993, p. 35; see also Grant, 1991). In other words, a capability exists when a selection of inputs is combined effectively to achieve a specific end. Although the inputs in the

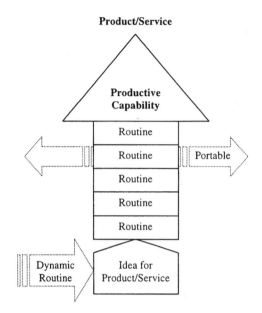

Figure 9.1. Productive Capabilities

above passage are resources, Winter (1995) alludes to considerable overlap between organizational resources and routines. In respect to this, Teece, Pisano, and Shuen (1997) suggest that capabilities comprise specific organizational routines (see Figure 9.1).

The second property of a productive capability is that it is honed to a particular product or service offering. These two properties suggest that a new capability emerges when a novel combination of routines is employed to provide an existing product or service. New capabilities also emerge when organizational routines are redeployed to provide new products or services. These possibilities for change over time force the consideration of a firm's dynamic routines alongside its static routines. Whereas static organizational routines are the building blocks of productive capabilities, dynamic routines are directed at learning and new product-process development (Teece et al., 1997). In other words, dynamic routines guide organizational learning processes that generate ideas for new offerings and/or novel combinations of routines, which in turn improve a firm's ability to deliver existing offerings. Without dynamic routines, one would not observe the emergence of novel productive capabilities, which is different from the incremental routine-specific learning that explains how productive capabilities are improved over time.

The final task for this section is to link the above framework to an empirical analysis of new product introductions within the pharmaceutical industry. Operationally, each product is traceable to a productive capability in the same way that Porter (1980) would draw a value chain for each. This does not suggest that products *are* productive capabilities; rather, the observation of a firm producing a specific product and selling it into a specific market is a tangible manifestation of a productive capability comprising a set of production-related routines, as well as marketing and distribution routines. In turn, each of these routines depends on the skill sets of firm employees, as well as a host of tangible and intangible assets including reputation and know-how assets.

Each firm may experience improvements in its routines and therefore become better in the design and execution of a particular productive capability. The drug approval process in the United States, however, mandates that each drug has strictly specified physical properties and is sold for strictly specified medicinal purposes. This suggests that changes in an organization's routines cannot qualitatively alter the physical properties of a product offering or the prescribed medical conditions for which the drug may be sold. Rather, changes in either of these two factors would lead to the emergence of a new product and therefore a new productive capability. This qualification makes it possible to study the evolution of productive capabilities within the pharmaceutical industry by studying the rates of new product introductions (and perhaps withdrawals).[2]

Dual Selection Environments

The decision to study suborganizational selection (in this case the selection of productive capabilities) forces us to explicitly recognize two selection environments. On one hand, products face selection pressures from the external environment. Modest theoretical translation is required to apply current thinking on competition and legitimation, for example, to the product level of analysis. Similarly, the bandwagon effects that underpin thinking on the effect of prior period introductions also apply at the product level. The same holds for carrying capacity arguments, which suggest a relationship between market size and critical events. On the other hand, interest in suborganizational selection requires consideration of an organizational selection environment.

One rationale for considering the effects of organizational selection environments is the observation of systematic differences across firms operating within the same competitive context (Rumelt, 1991). Whereas early economic treatments of the firm assumed that firms were identical in all dimensions except for size, current strategic management research points to systematic heterogeneity across firms in a number of critical respects. If current differences have no effect on the evolution of productive capabilities over time, one should expect new products (of different types) to emerge randomly across firms. It is likely, however, that differences in organizational environments do affect subsequent new product offerings, and explicit attention to such effects may begin to explain the evolution of firm heterogeneity within specific industrial contexts.

The Internal Selection Environment

Although a broad array of organizational features may affect the rate at which new products are introduced, the following analysis incorporates the effects of corporate coherence, dynamic capabilities, product-market diversification, and organizational size.

Coherence

Firms wanting to introduce new products must first access and then combine all the organizational routines that compose the associated productive capability (see Figure 9.1). This problem is considerably more tractable if the firm already possesses one or more of the component routines. In Penrose's (1959) theory of firm growth, opportunities for profitable expansion typically are found in a firm's underutilized productive routines. Assuming that some of these routines are portable across different productive capabilities, an incentive exists to exploit excess capacity in existing routines in the development of new productive capabilities. The prospect of economies of scope in the application of routines across different productive capabilities explains how firms generate increasingly diverse (but not incoherent) sets of productive capabilities over time. Teece and colleagues (1997) observe that despite the considerable diversity within the modern corporation, there is a strong tendency toward coherence, or relatedness, within each portfolio of activities. The authors suggest that the advantages of having access to valuable complementary assets (or routines) makes it likely that future opportunities will be exploited in areas that are close to a firm's current activities.

In the pharmaceutical industry, routines such as those associated with marketing drugs probably favor new product introductions in the near neighborhood of current product offerings. For example, a drug company that offers anti-hypertensive medications may have an easier time introducing a vasodilator because it already markets to a network of cardiovascular specialists, even though the underlying pharmacology of the two products may be quite different. This prospect of economies of scope in the application of established routines across related activities supports the following hypothesis:

Hypothesis 1: The rate of product introduction in a market will be higher if the organization already offers products in related markets.

One resource that may be employed in the development and introduction of new productive capabilities is market-specific legitimacy. Although a given product (or product type) may be highly legitimated in the eyes of a broader constituency, it is not necessarily legitimate in association with a specific organization. This lack of legitimacy may result even if the organization in question is highly legitimate in some other way.[3] In the light of this, as the number of products offered within a market increases, an organization will become a familiar and legitimate participant in that market. This familiarity and legitimacy should contribute to the acceptance of new products by that organization, and therefore have a positive effect on the rate of new product introduction. More generally, to the extent that efficiency and effectiveness in a given endeavor are a function of cumulated experience (e.g., Ghemawat, 1991), multiple products within a market may coincide with the development of complementary routines that are necessary to service that market (e.g., Dierickx & Cool, 1989). The prospect that certain complementary assets develop as a function of cumulative market-specific experience generates the following hypothesis:

Hypothesis 2: The rate at which products are introduced into a market will increase with the number of active products the organization offers in that market.

Dynamic Routines

Switching focus to a firm's dynamic routines, we expect that the likelihood of a firm introducing a new product into a given market will be conditioned on whether it possesses effective dynamic learning routines within that problem space. Recall from above that the knowledge recombinations that must precede the introduction of a new product are driven by a firm's learning routines. Even if a firm possesses a stock of underutilized routines, these will not manifest themselves in new productive capabilities unless the firm is able to develop effectively the new knowledge that supports novel capabilities. In prefacing her main arguments, Penrose (1959) is emphatic that alertness to new opportunities is a necessary precondition for the subsequent exploitation of underutilized resources: "The decision to search for opportunities is an enterprising decision requiring entrepreneurial intuition and imagination and must precede the 'economic' decision to go ahead with the examination of opportunities for expansion" (p. 34). Although it would be difficult to observe a firm's dynamic routines in the current empirical context, we may infer its ability to generate valuable new ideas within a particular market by whether it has recently introduced new products. Given these considerations, we hypothesize that

Hypothesis 3: The rate at which products are introduced into a market will increase with the number of products introduced by the organization into that market in the prior year.

Diversification

The coherence argument relates the likelihood of a firm introducing a new product into a particular market to its possession of routines that are tailored closely to that market. This section considers whether the extent of firm diversification may also have an impact on the rate of new product introductions. It was suggested above that competence and legitimacy may develop in the context of accumulated market-specific experience, and that firms may leverage these critical inputs by introducing new products into related product markets. The strategic framework depicted in Figure 9.1, however, does not restrict such leverage to highly proximate product markets. Although common wisdom would now counsel firms to "stick to their knitting," some do achieve high degrees of success competing with highly diverse portfolios of activities. Relating this observation back to Figure 9.1, we suggest that some firms are able to identify and exploit synergies across (seemingly) unrelated markets, especially because relatedness need not correspond perfectly to the degree of product-market overlap (Prahalad & Bettis, 1986).

It is therefore not inconceivable that a firm may stretch its existing competence by applying established routines in less proximate product markets. If this "stretch capability" is viewed as a higher-order organizational routine, we should expect firms with more diversification experience (i.e., those with more diverse portfolios of products) to be introducing more products into seemingly unrelated product markets. One indicator of routines for diversity is the current diversity of the organization's product offerings. To reach a state of diversity, an organization must have been successful in the past at introducing and maintaining diverse products. In other words, we expect that organizations will vary in the extent to which their new product introductions cohere to their old, and that some will simply be better at conceiving, introducing, and managing products of diverse types.

A second logic for expecting diversification to affect new product introduction rates is found by re-examining a firm's dynamic routines. Henderson and Cockburn (1994, 1996) studied the causes of relatively high innovative propensity among U.S. pharmaceutical firms. The factors they looked at include a firm's size, its scope of operations, its component competence (i.e., unique disciplinary expertise), and its architectural competence (the ability to access and integrate various types of expertise). Expectation of a component competence effect is based on logic similar to that which underpins our coherence hypothesis; however, expectation of an effect of economies of scope in research and development is based on the belief that there may be "internal spillovers of knowledge between programs that enhance each other's [innovative] productivities" (Henderson & Cockburn, 1996, p. 35).

Both the argument that diversification indicates a dynamic "stretch capability" and the argument that economies of scope contribute to innovation suggest that diversification will increase the rate of new product introduction. Both arguments, however, imply advantages only in markets that are unrelated to those the firm currently serves:

Hypothesis 4: The rate at which products are introduced into markets that are unrelated to an organization's current products will be higher when the diversity of current products is higher.

Firm Size

Finally, a large volume of research has addressed the Schumpeterian hypothesis that large firms should be responsible for a disproportionately large share of innovative output (e.g., Cohen & Levin, 1989; Kamien & Schwartz, 1982; Schwartzman, 1976). This conjecture is based on the belief that there may be economies of scale in the modern R&D facility (Henderson & Cockburn, 1996). These benefits of economies of scale may be offset at very large sizes, however, by the inertia and rigidity associated with the organizational structures that are required to manage the very large firm (Haveman, 1993). These offsetting effects support the following hypothesis:

Hypothesis 5: The rate at which products are introduced into the market will first decrease, then increase with the total sales of the organization.

The External Selection Environment

Although research in organizational ecology tends to focus on change at the organizational level, parts of the theory may be useful for explaining change at the suborganizational level. For example, selected arguments from organizational ecology address the effects of organizational demographics on market response to, and competition surrounding, economic activities. Market response and competition are important to new product introduction, so we derive expectations for rates of new product introductions from the organizational ecology arguments regarding density dependence and rate dependence.

Density

Increases in density are argued to affect both the legitimacy of and level of competition faced by organizations within a population (Carroll & Hannan, 1989). Legitimacy, which refers to the cognitive taken-for-grantedness of a form of organization, is thought to increase with density, but at a decreasing rate. Competition is argued to increase at an increasing rate with the number of organizations of a form. Competition makes it less likely that organizations of a form will be founded. The combined positive effect of legitimacy and negative effect of competition result in the prediction that foundings will depend nonmonotonically on the number of organizations of a form. The founding rate will first increase, then decrease as the number of organizations of a form increases. This prediction has been supported by empirical studies on a diverse set of organizational forms including labor unions, brewers, newspapers, life insurance companies, banks, day care centers, trade associations, and automobile producers (Baum, 1996).

The sources and effects of legitimacy on products should be as they are argued to be for organizations. As the number of products of a type increase, customers come to take it for granted and

are more willing to use it, and other organizations are more likely to produce synergistic products. Competition is also a concept that applies well to products. Research on localized competition shows that the intensity of competition between organizations depends on their similarity (Baum & Mezias, 1992), which suggests that the degree of competition between organizations of the same general form may really depend on the degree to which they offer the same products. Competition should increase at an increasing rate with the number of products of a type, and it should decrease the likelihood of introducing products of the type.

The above arguments result in a prediction that product introductions will first increase with the number of products as legitimacy increases, then decrease as competition overwhelms legitimacy advantages.

Hypothesis 6: The rate at which drug products are introduced to the market will first increase, then decrease with the number of active products in the market.

Prior Introductions

Delacroix and Carroll (1983) argue that rates of organizational founding also may depend on foundings in the prior year. Like density, previous foundings are argued to have a nonmonotonic effect: "Initially, prior foundings signal a fertile market to potential entrepreneurs, encouraging foundings. But as foundings increase further, competition for resources increases, discouraging foundings" (Baum, 1996, p. 84). The signaling of opportunity and competition provided by prior events should also apply to products. Introducing a product into an attractive market alerts other potential entrants to the existence of that market and informs them that another organization views the market as attractive. Of course, if a large number of new products are introduced in a period, potential entrants will wonder if the promise of the market has been completely absorbed by recent entrants.

Hypothesis 7: The rate at which drug products are introduced to the market will first increase, then decrease with the number of products introduced in the market in the prior year.

Finally, the competition portion of the density-dependence hypotheses posits that as the number of products increases, competition for scarce resources also increases. As an important control in this relationship, the carrying capacity of the focal market must be accounted for. Larger markets should support more introductions. This hypothesis is consistent with current thinking about pharmaceutical market competition. The pharmaceutical economics literature has long emphasized the massive financial outlays associated with bringing innovative new drugs to the market (e.g., Grabowski & Vernon, 1990; Schwartzman, 1976). As a corollary to this, one would expect that larger markets would serve as more attractive environments in which to recoup the high research and development costs. This expectation is validated by recent U.S. policy (the Orphan Drug Act), which offered tax breaks to encourage pharmaceutical organizations to conduct R&D in low-volume markets.

Hypothesis 8: The rate at which drug products are introduced to the market will increase with total market sales.

Control Variables

Pharmaceutical industry researchers have debated whether the changing structure of the pharmaceutical industry is making it increasingly difficult for firms to develop and capitalize on valuable drug innovations. Development is slowed by, among other things, more stringent regulation. At the same time, concern about a firm's ability to capitalize on its innovations is captured by Grabowski and Vernon (1990):

There is some evidence that product lifetimes are becoming shorter. A more rapid introduction of close substitutes to the pioneer drug compound in various therapeutic groupings is taking place . . . [and there is] much greater generic competition experienced in the post-patent period. (p. 805)

These concerns seem to predict a declining rate of innovative product introductions and an increasing rate of imitative product introductions. Whatever the net effect of these forces, these trends in the pharmaceutical industry require that we control for calendar time.

Pharmaceutical industry researchers have also paid considerable attention to regulatory changes, addressing how these changes affect pharmaceutical firm actions and pharmaceutical industry outcomes (Comanor, 1986). Although several prominent regulatory changes fall outside of our 1978-1993 sample period (e.g., the 1962 Kefauver amendments), the 1984 Watchman-Hatch Act "eliminated the requirement of . . . duplicative testing by generic entrants and granted drug innovators some restoration of the effective lives of their patents" (Caves, Whinston, & Hurwitz, 1991, p. 10). This latter enhancement in effective patent protection was intended to enhance incentives for innovation. At the same time, easing entry requirements by lowering the effective cost of imitation should have a similar effect on the rate of imitative product introduction.

Analysis

Intercontinental Medical Statistics America (IMS) has compiled pharmaceutical product sales data in the United States for at least the last 25 years; 15 years (1978 to 1993) of this data set are used in the following analysis. For every drug offering, IMS provides information on annual product sales, the product's therapeutic class and subclass membership, and year of introduction. IMS also provides annual data on total therapeutic class and subclass sales.[4] Note that we refer to the therapeutic subclasses, which categorize similar drugs, as product markets. In any year, a pharmaceutical firm may sell upwards of 100 different products. Moreover, the firms' portfolios of products change from one year to the next. To keep the project manageable, it was necessary to extract a subset of the products to be included in the analysis. It was decided that only those products that achieved at least $1 million in sales in some year during the sample period (i.e., all significant product offerings) would be included. A total of 1,262 products met this sampling criterion and were introduced by an organization whose identity was recorded by IMS (for 758 products that met the sampling criterion, no organizational identity was recorded). Although a large number of products are not included, the sampled products do account for approximately 90% of total U.S. pharmaceutical sales in any one year.

The dependent variable in the following analysis is the number of products introduced into a market by an organization in a year. The data matrix consists of the number of active markets times the number of organizations that were recorded as offering drug products in each year during the period under study. There were 71 organizations recorded in the data and 467 markets active at some point during the period of study. After dropping observations with missing data, we were left with 326,260 observations. Dependent variables such as ours are analyzed using event-count models, which analyze the number of occurrences of an event within a discrete period, in this case, the number of product introductions in a market by a firm in a year. We initially explored modeling product introductions using Poisson regression but found that the assumption that the conditional mean and variance of the dependent variable are equal was violated. In this case, the variance exceeded the conditional mean, a situation referred to as overdispersion. Overdispersion has an effect similar to heteroscedasticity in the linear regression model, allowing for consistent estimations of parameters but inconsistent estimates for standard errors, invalidating hypothesis testing. A negative binomial model responds to this problem by adding a parameter to model overdispersion. The overdispersion found in this case was of a variance-mean ratio that is linear in the mean: $var(y_i) = m_i + axm_i^2$. We used Cameron and Trivedi's (1986) second negative binomial model (Negbin II) for this form of overdispersion and estimated negative binomial models using the statistical package LIMDEP (Greene, 1992). The independent variables were all lagged one year in the models (variable definitions are found in the second column of Table 9.2).

The third column of Table 9.2 reports the results. Overall, the model is a significant improvement over the restricted-slopes model, with a χ^2 value of 3,189 with 15 degrees of freedom. As predicted by Hypothesis 1, an organization is more likely to introduce a product into a market when it already participates in related markets. This finding corroborates the expectation of coherence in the introduction of new drug products. Related to coherence, the results also suggest that organizations are significantly more likely to introduce a new product into a market the more products they already sell into that market. This supports Hypothesis 2 by suggesting that possession of experience-based assets such as legitimacy (or competence more generally) positively affects firm's decisions to introduce new products. Turning to dynamic capabilities, firms also are significantly more likely to introduce new products the more products they introduced to the market in the previous year (supporting Hypothesis 3). With respect to diversification, we find that high levels of product-market diversification increased the rate of product introduction. This positive effect of diversification is wholly offset by the negative coefficient of the interaction between the dichotomous variable that has a value of one if the firm has a product in a related market and product-market diversification. This indicates that a higher rate of new product introduction as a function of diversification occurs in markets where the organization does not have related products (and not in markets where it does have related products), as predicted by Hypothesis 4. Finally, Hypothesis 5, which predicts an inverted U shaped effect of organization size on the rate of introductions, is not supported.[5] Our models indicate no effect of organization size on the rate of new product introductions.

Turning to the external environment, Hypothesis 6, which predicts an inverted U shaped impact of total number of products in the market, is supported by the positive first-order and negative second-order effects of that variable. Likewise, the total number introductions to the market in the prior year has an inverted U shaped relationship, as predicted by Hypothesis 7. Hypothesis 8, which predicts more introductions in larger markets, is supported by the positive coefficient of market size. Finally, the control variables indicate that the rate of introduction falls as a function of historical

TABLE 9.2 New Product Introductions in the U.S. Pharmaceutical Industry

Variable	Operationalization	Result
Intercept		-8.0146**
		(0.1714)
(H1) Product in related markets	One for markets in a class if the firm offers any products in that class	2.3282**
		(0.1892)
(H2) Products in market, organization	Organization's products in market	0.5715**
		(0.0275)
(H3) Prior introductions, organization	Organization's introductions into market (previous year)	1.0163**
		(0.1386)
(H4) Product-market diversification	Entropy measure of diversification	0.6464**
		(0.0716)
Product in related markets × diversification		-0.6245**
		(0.0871)
(H5) Organization size	Pharmaceutical sales (billions of $)	0.12070
		(0.1610)
(Organization size)^2		-0.0383
		(0.0696)
(H6) Products in market	Total products in market	0.1077**
		(0.0080)
(Products in market)^2		-0.0018**
		(0.0002)
(H7) Prior introductions	Introductions into market (previous year)	0.1134**
		(0.0360)
(Prior introductions)^2		-0.0085**
		(0.0026)
(H8) Market size	Market sales (billions of $)	1.3743**
		(0.1283)
Year		-0.0877**
		(0.0158)
Post-1984		0.2982*
		(.1191)
Overdispersion parameter		5.9458**
		(0.6370)
Observations		326,360
Product introductions		1,262
Log-likelihood		-6,736.19

*$p < 0.01$; **$p < 0.001$.

time but is bumped up by the passage of legislation in 1984.

Discussion and Conclusion

The main thrust of this chapter has been to continue the recent advances by evolutionary researchers in the direction of suborganization research. In doing so, we highlight a number of issues that relate to the appropriate level of analysis and to the significance of recognizing the additional organizational selection environment that must be considered by researchers interested in suborganizational evolution. Our empirical analysis situated within the U.S. pharmaceutical industry over the 1978-1993 period begins to delve deeper into these two issues by first suggesting that products (as manifestations of organizational productive routines) are meaningful units of analysis. Given that the regulatory environment strictly prescribes the physical properties of an approved drug product as well as the prescribed uses for that drug, it is feasible to consider each product as a relatively inert organizational artifact. As such, the specific production, marketing, and distribution efforts associated with each product entail an overall productive capability that is meaningful for researchers interested in industrial evolution.

We also demonstrate that several attributes of the organizational selection environment have predictable effects on the founding of these new organizational productive capabilities. Note how this finding differs from, but complements, insights delivered by Madsen, Mosakowski, and Zaheer (this volume), who provide evidence that internal selection dynamics influence organizational outcomes. Our findings suggest a reciprocal relationship between internal selection and organizational outcomes, with outcomes such as coherence, expertise, and legitimacy in product markets feeding back into the selection process. Moreover, these effects are incremental to those exerted by the external selection environment.

These findings are particularly compelling in the light of the recent attention to dynamic features of organizations as sources of competitive advantage (Teece et al., 1997). Teece and colleagues indicate that the internal selection environment of an organization may be a key to understanding how organizational capabilities develop over time. In addition to the basic features of the internal selection environment studied herein, future work should examine the strategic dimensions of this internal selection environment. Managers are able to control dimensions of internal selection (e.g., by setting the rate of return required for proposed products) to make the introduction of new products and the persistence of old products more or less likely. The strategic dimensions of the internal selection environment may be one of the most significant dynamic capabilities available to organizations.

Substantively, the analysis indicates compelling results at the organizational and market levels of selection. At the organizational level, there is strong evidence for coherence and for experience-related assets. At the same time, there is evidence that diversified firms are more likely to introduce

new products. This latter effect, however, is exclusive to unrelated markets. We also find evidence of dynamic capabilities in the form of a tendency for current rates of introduction to reflect past rates. At the market level, our findings regarding product introductions mirror others on organizational foundings. The rate of product introductions has an inverted U-shaped relationship to the number of products in the market and the number of products introduced to the market in the previous year. This supports, at the product-market level, ecological arguments about competition, legitimacy, and information. The founding rate is higher in larger markets, indicating that product introductions respond to the carrying capacity of a niche, just as organizational foundings do.

Of course, several issues did not receive sufficient attention in this chapter. First, the choice of the appropriate level of analysis is likely to be context specific. In the context of the pharmaceutical industry, it makes sense to look at the introduction and withdrawal of specific products; however, in other contexts, researchers may justifiably look at different units of selection at either a super- or a subordinate level of analysis. Concomitantly, researchers may need to look at the effects of (and indeed the interactions among) a diverse range of selection environments and levels (micro-activities, subroutines, productive routines, organizations). Questions that may emerge in future research relate to the conditions under which we might expect to see complex interrelationships across these various levels of selection. Other questions, revisiting the embeddedness of organizations, routines, subroutines, and microbehaviors, might concern when to expect selection at one level to imply nontrivial change at a higher level.

Notes

1. For 43 removals, the fate of the organization could not be determined.

2. It also suggests qualifications to the possible replication of this research in other empirical contexts.

3. For example, Freeman and Boeker (1984) note that "a bank selling hamburgers at some of its teller windows would be viewed by all as inconsistent" (p. 71).

4. The IMS drug products are organized hierarchically. Example of the major class categories used by IMS include analgesics; antacids and antiflatulents; antiarthritics; anti-infectives, systemic; antispasmodic/antisecretory; biologicals; respiratory therapy; cancer/transplant therapy; cardiovascular therapy; contraceptives; cough/cold preparations, RX; cough/cold preparations, OTC; dermatologicals; dermatologicals, proprietary; diabetes therapy; diagnostic aids; diuretics; hormones; hospital solutions; nutrients and supplements; ophthalmic preparations; psychotherapeutic drugs; vitamins; and miscellaneous ethical. The following list shows that products are organized into a hierarchical structure that is similar to the Standard Industrial Classification (SIC) system that is commonly used to organize firms into industries:

```
30000 Cancer/Transplant Therapy
    30100 . . .
    30200 . . .
31000 Cardiovascular Therapy
    31100 Antihypertensive Drugs
        31110 . . .
        31140 Ace Inhibitors
            31141 Ace Inhibitors, Alone
```

5. In supplementary analysis (not shown), we looked for a monotonic effect of organization size on the introduction rate and found none.

References

Amit, R., & Schoemaker, P. (1993). Strategic assets and organizational rent. *Strategic Management Journal, 14*, 33-46.

Barnett, W., & Burgelman, R. (1996). Evolutionary perspectives on strategy. *Strategic Management Journal, 17*, 5-19.

Baum, J.A.C. (1996). Organizational ecology. In S. R. Clegg, C. Hardy, & W. R. Nord (Eds.), *Handbook of organizational studies* (pp. 77-114). Thousand Oaks, CA: Sage.

Baum, J.A.C., & Mezias, S. (1992). Localized competition and organizational failure in the Manhattan hotel industry, 1898-1990. *Administrative Science Quarterly, 37*, 580-604.

Baum, J.A.C., & Singh, J. V. (1994). Organizational hierarchies and evolutionary processes: Some reflections on a theory of organizational evolution. In J.A.C. Baum & J. V. Singh (Eds.), *Evolutionary dynamics of organizations* (pp. 379-402). New York: Oxford University Press.

Cameron, A. C., & Trivedi, P. K. (1986). Econometric models based on count data: Comparisons and applications of some estimators and tests. *Journal of Applied Econometrics, 46*, 347-364.

Campbell, D. (1994). How individual and face-to-face-group selection undermine firm selection in organizational evolution. In J.A.C. Baum & J. V. Singh (Eds.), *Evolutionary dynamics of organizations* (pp. 23-38). New York: Oxford University Press.

Carroll, G., & Hannan, M. (1989). Density dependence in the evolution of populations of newspaper organizations. *Administrative Science Quarterly, 54*, 524-541.

Caves, R., Whinston, M., & Hurwitz, M. (1991). *Patent expiration, entry, and competition in the U.S. pharmaceutical industry* (Brookings Papers on Economic Activity). Washington, DC: Brookings Institute.

Cohen, M. D., Burkhart, R., Dosi, G., Egidi, M., Marengo, L., Warglien, M., & Winter, S. (1996). Routines and other recurring action patterns of organizations: Contemporary research issues. *Industrial and Corporate Change, 5*, 653-698.

Cohen, W., & Levin, R. (1989). Empirical studies of innovation and market structure. In R. Schmalansee & R. Willig (Eds.), *Handbook of industrial organization* (Vol. 2, pp. 1059-1107). New York: Elsevier Science.

Comanor, W. (1986). The political economy of the pharmaceutical industry. *Journal of Economic Literature, 24*, 1178-1217.

Davis, G. (1996). [Review of *Evolutionary dynamics of organizations.*] *Administrative Science Quarterly, 41*, 538-540.

Delacroix, J., & Carroll, G. (1983). Organizational foundings: An ecological study of the newspaper industries of Argentina and Ireland. *Administrative Science Quarterly, 28*, 274-291.

Dierickx, I., & Cool, K. (1989). Asset stock accumulation and sustainability of competitive advantage. *Management Science, 35*, 1504-1511.

Freeman, J. H., & Boeker, W. (1984, Spring). The ecological analysis of business strategy. *California Management Review*, pp. 73-86.

Ghemawat, P. (1991, March-April). Building strategy on the experience curve. *Harvard Business Review*, pp. 143-149.

Grabowski, H. (1989). An analysis of U.S. international competitiveness in pharmaceuticals. *Managerial and Decision Economics* (Special issue), 27-33.

Grabowski, H., & Vernon, J. (1990). A new look at the returns and risks to pharmaceutical R&D. *Management Science, 36*, 804-823.

Grant, R. (1991, Spring). The resource-based theory of competitive advantage: Implications for strategy formulation. *California Management Review*, pp. 114-135.

Greene, W. H. (1992). *LIMDEP: User's manual and reference guide. Version 6.0.* Bellport, NY: Econometric Software, Inc.

Haveman, H. A. (1993). Organizational size and change: Diversification in the savings and loan industry after deregulation. *Administrative Science Quarterly, 38*, 20-50.

Haveman, H. A., & Cohen, L. E. (1994). The ecological dynamics of careers: The impact of organizational founding, dissolution and merger on job mobility. *American Journal of Sociology, 100*, 104-152.

Henderson, R., & Cockburn, I. (1994). Measuring competence? Exploring firm effects in pharamceutical research. *Strategic Management Journal, 15*, 63-84.

Henderson, R., & Cockburn, I. (1996). Scale, scope and spillovers: The determinants of research productivity in drug discovery. *RAND Journal of Economics, 27*, 32-59.

Ingram, P., & Baum, J.A.C. (1997). Chain affiliation and the failure of Manhattan hotels, 1898-1980. *Administrative Science Quarterly, 42,* 68-102.

Kamien, M., & Schwartz, N. (1982). *Market structure and innovation.* Cambridge, UK: Cambridge University Press.

Miner, A. S. (1987). Idiosyncratic jobs in formalized organizations. *Administrative Science Quarterly, 32,* 327-332.

Nelson, R. R., & Winter, S. G. (1982). *An evolutionary theory of economic change.* Cambridge, MA: Harvard University Press.

Penrose, E. (1959). *The theory of the growth of the firm.* New York: John Wiley.

Porter, M. E. (1980). *Competitive strategy.* New York: Free Press.

Prahalad, C. K., & Bettis, R. (1986). The dominant logic: A new linkage between diversity and performance. *Strategic Management Journal, 7,* 485-501.

Rumelt, R. P. (1991). How much does industry matter? *Strategic Management Journal, 12,* 167-185.

Schwartzman, D. (1976). *Innovation in the pharmaceutical industry.* Baltimore: Johns Hopkins University Press.

Teece, D. J., Pisano, G., & Shuen, A. (1997). Dynamics capabilities and strategic management. *Strategic Management Journal, 18,* 509-534.

Winter, S. G. (1990). Survival, selection and inheritance in evolutionary theories of organization. In J. V. Singh (Ed.), *Organizational evolution: New directions* (pp. 269-297). Newbury Park, CA: Sage.

Winter, S. (1995). Four Rs of profitability: Rents, resources, routines and replication. In C. Montgomery (Ed.), *Resource-based and evolutionary theories of the firm* (pp. 147-178). Boston: Kluwer Academic.

Chapter 10

On the Complexity of Technological Evolution

Exploring Coevolution Within and Across Hierarchical Levels in Optical Disc Technology

LORI ROSENKOPF
ATUL NERKAR

Despite the best intentions of researchers, studies of technological evolution remain idiosyncratic and atheoretical. Much of this problem can be attributed to the complex, often hierarchical relationships among products and technologies. Most studies of technological evolution rely on data about a particular component of a product or larger system without regard for the interdependence between multiple components. Concepts and conclusions drawn from particular components may or may not translate to other components or the full system. For example, Tushman and Murmann (1998) argue that the concept of "dominant design," originally conceived at the product level, is instead relevant at a subproduct level or in a "nested hierarchy of subsystems." Debates over whether technology evolves incrementally or in a punctuated fashion are fueled by researchers who tend to focus only on particular components of a product or only on system-level attributes.

Given the emphasis on the evolution of hierarchies in the biological and sociocultural evolution literature, our aim in this chapter is to use these hierarchical ideas to suggest a framework that helps us observe and organize the complexity of technological evolution. We view the evolution of product hierarchies as the result of variation, selection, and retention processes (Campbell, 1965) enacted by organizational entities on underlying technological know-how. Coevolution promotes complexity in two ways. First, interdependent technological entities coevolve *within* each level of

AUTHORS' NOTE: We appreciate financial support from both the Huntsman Center for Global Competition and Innovation at the Wharton School and the Wharton Entrepreneurial Center. Joel Baum and Bill McKelvey offered many helpful comments, and Anjana Pandey provided research assistance.

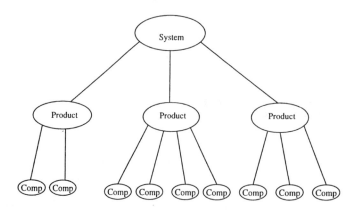

Figure 10.1. The Product Hierarchy

the hierarchy. Second, evolution at any level of the hierarchy causes evolution *across* other levels of the hierarchy (Campbell, 1974, 1990, 1994). We illustrate our ideas using patent, product, and standards data from the optical disc industry, as well as a host of examples culled from other industries. We show that simultaneous consideration of evolutionary processes within and across levels of the product hierarchy helps us to understand technological evolution as consisting of both incremental and punctuated evolutionary processes.

We begin the chapter with a description of the product hierarchy and the communities that influence the evolution of each level of the hierarchy. We then turn to the biological and sociocultural evolution literature for coevolutionary concepts that illuminate the evolution of product hierarchies. With these tools in hand, we reexamine debates about the nature of technological evolution.

Product Hierarchies

Several scholars have written about the hierarchical nature of complex products (Clark, 1985; Simon, 1969). To understand technological evolution, it is fruitful to view products as systems (Tushman & Rosenkopf, 1992). In such a framework, products are composed of interdependent components and are coordinated into systems of use, as depicted in Figure 10.1. In this section, we describe each level of this system-based hierarchy

and identify the organizational entities that enact innovation at each level.

Components

Most products, as well as processes, are composed of identifiable components. Thus, photolithographic aligners contain a light source, a lens for focusing, an alignment system, and a mechanical system to hold the mask and wafer in place (Henderson & Clark, 1990). Flight simulators include software/mathematical models, visual systems, motion systems, computing hardware, and avionics (Rosenkopf & Tushman, 1998). In both these examples, evolutionary trajectories may be identified for each of the components.

For each component technology, a broad community of organizational actors produces variations. The biotechnology community, for example, is far more diffuse than the dedicated biotechnology firms alone. Other actors contributing to the development of the technology include universities, research labs, and pharmaceutical firms linked together in "networks of learning" (Powell, Koput, & Smith-Doerr, 1996). Likewise, the community of actors involved in the development of laser technology is not limited to manufacturers, universities, and research labs, but also includes governmental and military bodies. We can observe that patents in the optical disc arena are held by a diverse set of actors—although companies such as Sony, Philips, and Matsushita are key players, research laboratories such as Battelle and government military organizations also hold patents in the area. Because the underlying technology for optical disc components is useful in many different types of products, the manufacturers are not merely optical disc firms but also come from the health care and semiconductor industries. An even less broadly applicable set of technologies, those applied to cochlear implants, were generated by an extended community (Van de Ven & Garud, 1993).

For a given product, then, multiple communities are involved in the technological evolution of the product because products are composed of multiple components. Some actors will be involved in many of these communities, particularly the product manufacturers, while other actors may be involved in only one community because their central focus is a particular component rather than the overall product. To maintain some consistency of terms across our hierarchy, we will call the communities shaping the development of components "component-specific communities," because we will encounter communities at other levels of the hierarchy as well.

Products

Because components are bundled into products, interdependence between components strongly affects the evolution of products. Several studies of technological evolution of products have focused on the development of one major component of that product, such as the central processing unit of a microcomputer (Anderson & Tushman, 1990; Tushman & Anderson, 1986). More recent studies have acknowledged the complex relationships among evolving components (Henderson & Clark, 1990; Iansiti & Khanna, 1995; Tushman & Murmann, 1998).

Unlike component-level evolution that results from diffuse community activity, the locus of product-level evolution rests squarely at the level of the firm. Product manufacturers select the appropriate component technologies and designs and bundle them into products that provide the functionality that the firm deems appropriate. Thus, two manufacturers might develop very different products that perform the same function, such as Bulova's

tuning fork watches and the Swiss-made mechanical watches. Likewise, whereas Sony and Philips utilized an optical pickup for their CD players, early digital systems made by JVC and Matsushita utilized a diamond-tipped stylus. This firm-level selection and bundling of component-level technologies provides variation at the product level, and this variation is maintained because of path-dependent processes of exploration and exploitation (Cohen & Levinthal, 1990; Helfat, 1994; March, 1991; Nelson & Winter, 1982).

Systems

At the next level, products are coordinated into systems of use. Thus, a radio transmitter is not useful unless paired with receivers that understand the same signals (Rosenkopf & Tushman, 1994). Standards are the most evident markers of system-level evolution and are particularly prominent for communications-oriented products, yet even simple products like contact lenses will not function unless they are accompanied by a set of compatible solutions and ancillary products. In the case of optical disc technology, the recent format war between two groups illustrates this phenomenon. Philips and Sony, the original developers of the CD system, proposed a new system called MMCD (multimedia compact disc) to replace CD in 1996. At the same time, Toshiba and Matsushita developed a competing format called SD (super density). The product war was avoided through negotiations resulting in a new hybrid format called DVD (digital versatile disk). Similar dynamics can be observed in the definition of HDTV standards and digital cellular technology.

As for components, system selection is accomplished through the coordinated activity of a broad community of actors, which we will call a "system-level community." The coordination of products into systems engenders mutualism among the members of a community (Barnett, 1990). Each of these actors will determine their preferences on varied dimensions of merit, so consensus-building becomes paramount. Ultimate convergence on a standard, or dominant design, takes time; once it occurs, system-level evolution tends to elaborate incrementally on this agreed-upon paradigm.

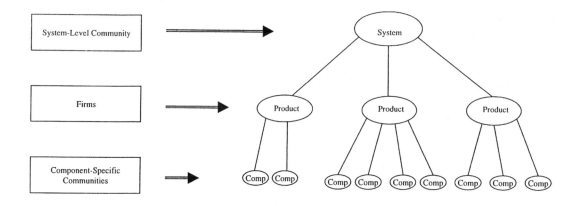

Figure 10.2. Selection Entities and the Product Hierarchy

Thus, system-level evolution tends to be observed as a process of punctuated equilibrium. Once a punctuation occurs, we frequently observe processes of Darwinian selection among product manufacturers, as shakeouts occur (Baum, Korn, & Kotha, 1995; Suarez & Utterback, 1995).

Summary

A systems perspective on products allows us to consider three levels of complexity, ranging from the lower-level components of products to the higher-level coordination of products into systems. Simultaneous processes of variation, selection, and retention, also called Darwin machines (McKelvey, 1997), operate and interact at each of these three levels. We display the selection entities—a system-level community, firms at the product level, and component-specific communities—in conjunction with the product hierarchy in Figure 10.2. As we examine various facets of technological evolution, we will use Figure 10.2 as a base from which we can illustrate different interactions.

Insights From Biological and Sociocultural Hierarchies

As studies of biological and sociocultural evolution indicate, a thorough understanding of tech-

nological evolution requires simultaneous consideration of coevolutionary effects both within hierarchical levels and across hierarchical levels. We address both types of coevolution in this section.

Within-Level Coevolution

Bundling and coordination of components into products means that technological developments in certain components will spur developments in other components. Likewise, innovations at the product level will spur innovations in other products that are bundled into systems. These "leading" components or products have been called "core subsystems" (Tushman & Murmann, 1998; Tushman & Rosenkopf, 1992). In watches, for example, the substitution of batteries for springs as the power source led to a host of interdependent innovations. For example, in the oscillation component, the escapement could now be replaced by the more accurate battery-powered tuning forks or quartz crystals.

A *reverse salient* (Hughes, 1983) is a component that lags the development of other components in the product. Hughes's analogy is a military one—in the military, a reverse salient refers to a flank of the regiment that has fallen behind the rest of the regiment, and for the rest of the regiment to realize its progress, the reverse salient must catch up to the regiment to solidify the advance. Likewise, potential technological improvements in many components of a product will not be realized if any particular component has not advanced enough to capitalize on these potential gains. Examples of reverse salients abound. In flight simulators, advances in the mathematical modeling of motion and visual capabilities had occurred but could not be achieved in actual simulators until the speed of computing hardware could accommodate these calculations in real time. Likewise, in the automobile industry, car designers recognized the advantages of aerodynamically shaped bodies in the 1950s but could not produce these models until the advent of more sophisticated press tools in the 1970s. Thus, in a product (or system), the more advanced components (or products) create the reverse salient, which is a specific problem in a bottleneck component. Firms direct their efforts into correcting this reverse salient. Thus, evolution in other components creates the impetus for evolution in the reverse salient component.

A limitation of the 1982 CD technology was its inability to store enough data for a full 3-hour movie. This limitation arose because storage technology restricted the amount of material that could be placed on the disc, and the laser wavelength used in the optical pickup was appropriate for that density and not beyond. The desire to improve CD technology so that it could store full-length movies spurred firms to improve both the storage and pickup components, and these improvements became critical features of DVD technology. Likewise, the original CD players could not reproduce sound with high quality until error correction mechanisms were improved. Sony was able to use error correction coding that had been developed for other purposes.

Analysis of optical disc patent classifications reveals interdependence between the optical pickup, the digital-analog converter, and the storage components (see the appendix to this chapter). A substantial number of the patents for these three components are "cross-classified," meaning that the patent represents simultaneous innovation in more than one of these components. What is it about the underlying technology that suggests this strong interdependence between certain components? Storage and conversion would have co-

evolved directly with optical pickups for two reasons. First, the digital to analog conversion is not required unless there is a digital input that is provided by the optical pickup. Second, the optical pickup is relevant only for information stored digitally; it would not be useful for a gramophone record. Thus, the development of optical pickups occurred jointly with development in digital storage and digital-analog converters.

Yet another example of within-level evolution is Henderson and Clark's (1990) "architectural innovation." In contrast to component-specific innovations, which they term "modular innovations," architectural innovations transform the relationships between components. For photolithographic aligner technology, the introductions of proximity aligners, scanning projection aligners, and both first- and second-generation steppers served as architectural innovations.

Cross-Level Coevolution

Two interrelated concepts about the evolution of hierarchies may be used to generate insights about technological evolution. These include Campbell's (1974, 1990) notion of "downward causation" and Campbell's (1994) acknowledgment of the conflicts between evolutionary outcomes at multiple levels, which has been termed "whole-part coevolutionary competition."

Downward Causation

Campbell (1990) offers the following description of "downward causation":

Where natural selection operates through life and death at a higher level of organization, the laws of the higher level selective system determine in part the distribution of lower level events and substances. Description of an intermediate-level phenomenon is not complete by describing its possibility and implementation in lower level terms. Its presence, prevalence, or distribution (all needed for the complete explanation of biological phenomena) will often require reference to laws at a higher level of organization as well. . . . For biology, all processes at the lower levels of a hierarchy are restrained by, and act in conformity to, the laws of the higher levels. (p. 4)

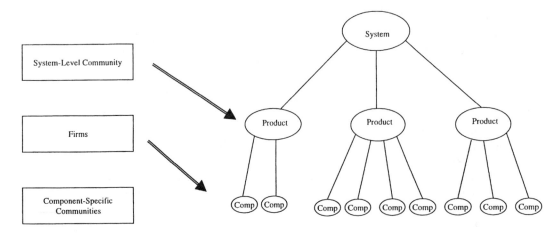

Figure 10.3. Downward Causation

Downward causation, then, is one important facet of technological evolution.[1] The vast range of technological innovations that are developed at the component level within organizational communities all conform to some underlying microlevel laws that enable their demonstration and operation, yet any bundling of multiple interdependent components into products rests on the coordination of these interdependencies and rules out many combinatorial options. Furthermore, the "laws" operating at the product level are not solely grounded in technological capabilities but also rest on many principles of firm competition and market satisfaction. Thus, it is not sufficient, when explaining technological evolution, to demonstrate component-level trajectories and expect their necessary incorporation into product-level trajectories. Similar outcomes can be imagined for the coordination of products into systems. Figure 10.3 displays downward causation in the product hierarchy, with higher-level selection entities determining which product or component variations will be retained.

The optical disc industry offers an example of the system-level community shaping product outcomes. A long history of developments in the process of digitizing information culminated in the introduction of three competing optical disc systems at the 1977 Audio Fair in Tokyo. Different coalitions of firms supported each of these systems (Philips and Sony for CD, Matsushita and JVC for

AHD, and Telefunken and Decca for MD). Although all three approaches constituted workable alternatives, CD technology became the de facto standard. Although some arguments can be made for the technological superiority of CD over the other two approaches (more digitalization and less physical contact led to less deterioration over time, better error correction codes), much of the CD dominance must be attributed to the strong ties that Philips and Sony had with the music industry, particularly in Europe. As the entertainment industry looked to increase sales through the introduction of a new format (replacing LPs), the CD system was the obvious approach.

Whole-Part Coevolutionary Competition

Campbell (1994) recognized that evolutionary outcomes at different levels may undermine rather than complement each other. He claims that "this mixture of cultural-level of group selection and biological individual selection means that firm-level adaptations will be under continual undermining pressures from individual and face-to-face group preferences" (p. 38). At the different levels, survival of the relevant organizational entities is governed by different selection mechanisms, which are subject to many discrepancies.[2] Figure 10.4 displays whole-part coevolutionary competition in the product hierarchy—selection among

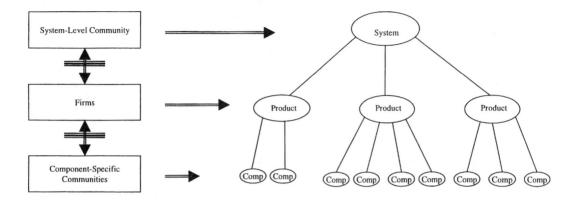

Figure 10.4. Whole-Part Coevolutionary Competition

variants at one level conflicts with selection at other levels.

This conflict between selection processes at different levels is aptly demonstrated in the optical disc industry. To adjudicate the competition between the CD, AHD, and MD approaches, the industry created a Digital Audio Disc Council (DADC) in 1979. The DADC contained 47 members from the industry, and its primary objective was to determine a standard industry format for the technology soon to be commercialized. Such a standard obviously would increase the technology's growth potential, because users would not be faced with a proliferation of incompatible devices and media. The DADC could not agree on a standard, because each approach was supported by a coalition interested only in promoting its own well-being. Ultimately, the committee merely issued a report describing the merits and problems with each system, thereby providing no solution to the problem. The system-level problem of converging on a particular standard thus was left unresolved because of the necessarily selfish actions of smaller coalitions of firms seeking to promote their own technologies, and hence their own well-being.

Another important facet of technological evolution is that the selection of higher-level outcomes frequently shapes, and even redirects, subsequent lower-level evolutionary activities by firms and other entities. Thus, subsequent lower-level vari-

ations are not random, as they would be in Darwinian evolution. Instead, firm-level path-dependent processes, like learning, dramatically narrow the path of stochastic variation at lower levels, resulting in Lamarckian evolution (Baum & Singh, 1994; Nelson & Winter, 1982).

This notion is analogous to Kuhn's (1970) concept of "normal science," where convergence on a particular new scientific paradigm indicates anomalies that arise through application of this paradigm. The search for scientific knowledge, then, becomes focused on "puzzle solving"—activities that can erase these anomalies within the context of the new paradigm. Tushman and colleagues (Anderson & Tushman, 1990; Rosenkopf & Tushman, 1994, 1998; Tushman & Anderson, 1986; Tushman & Rosenkopf, 1992) have used the term "normal technology" to reflect a similar redirection of innovative activity to elaborate dominant designs. Because dominant designs may be identified at multiple levels of analysis (Tushman & Murmann, 1998), this redirection can occur at multiple levels of the product hierarchy.[3]

Technological Evolution: Incremental or Punctuated?

Simultaneous consideration of within-level and cross-level coevolution, as described above, generates a richer understanding of technological evolution. This approach helps us avoid the trap of overgeneralizing results gleaned from a narrow focus on restricted parts of the hierarchy. Such foci, we believe, are the sources of the debate about whether technological evolution should be characterized by incremental or punctuated equilibrium models. We argue that technological evolution simultaneously comprises incremental and punctuated trajectories throughout the product hierarchy, and we illustrate these trends using our optical disc example.

Incremental and Punctuated Views of Evolution

Some authors focus on dramatic "technological discontinuities" that demark technological evolution through order-of-magnitude improvement in the technical performance of products or processes (e.g., Tushman & Anderson, 1986). In contrast, others argue that technological evolution is not punctuated but in fact incremental (e.g., Brown & Eisenhardt, 1997). Still others argue for something of a hybrid approach: Dramatic change results not from the spontaneous generation of dramatically different technologies but rather from "speciation," the application of existing technologies in new domains (Levinthal, 1998). These types of debates are echoed by the biological evolution literature.

McKelvey (1997) points out that evolutionists who observe microlevel processes of biological evolution generate incremental models based on replication of genes, whereas "macroevolutionists" generate punctuated equilibrium models of biological evolution rooted in context and interaction. Our reading of the technological literature observes this same difference: Technological incrementalists focus more on lower levels of the product hierarchy, while punctuationists focus more on higher levels of the product hierarchy.

One camp of authors demonstrates the incremental nature of technological change by focusing on component-level and/or product-level evolution. Dosi (1984) offers the notion that technology follows predictable trajectories, building on Nelson and Winter's (1982) characterization of local search by firms. More recently, Helfat (1994) has demonstrated that firm tendencies to invest in specific R&D areas are inertial. Rosenbloom and Cusumano (1987) demonstrate that the development of the videocassette recorder industry was the culmination of more than 20 years of technological development. Focusing on the cochlear implant industry, Van de Ven and Garud (1993) suggest an accumulation perspective, where technology evolves incrementally as a result of an accumulation of institutional arrangements, resource endowments, and technical economic activities. Podolny and Stuart (1995) demonstrate evolutionary trajectories by using semiconductor patents to identify "technological niches" that spur continued patenting activity. Studies of this type tend to focus on more microlevel events, projects, or innovations to highlight the building blocks of technology, knowledge, and organization.

In contrast, at the highest level of the product hierarchy, numerous studies have detailed the complex set of social, political, organizational, and institutional forces that bear on the outcomes of technological evolution. Hughes (1983) shows how the electrical supply systems of Britain, Germany, and the United States utilize different technologies and attributes these differences to varying political and institutional environments in the three countries. Likewise, the rise of pilot training and certification systems based on "full flight simulators" in the 1980s was not the result of some inherent technological advantage of these systems over their competitors but rather resulted from the coordinated activity among full flight simulator supporters such as aircraft manufacturers, simulator manufacturers, airlines, and regulators (Rosenkopf & Tushman, 1998).

Observing Multiple, Simultaneous Evolutionary Processes for Optical Disc Technology

In other work, we have observed incremental evolution of components by examining patenting activity for each of the eight components (Nerkar & Rosenkopf, 1997). In short, the number of patents for any component in a given year is a very strong predictor of the number of patents in the subsequent year. Thus, the level of development activity for each component evolves only incrementally. Additional citation analysis (detailed in the appendix to this chapter) demonstrates several themes. First, for each component, the largest percentage of citations to other optical disc patents is to those of the same component, suggesting incremental patterns of knowledge building. Second, citations to other components are numerous, however, demonstrating within-level coevolutionary patterns. Third, a significant proportion of citations is drawn from non–optical disc technologies. This application of other technologies to the optical disc domain suggests that speciation may indeed occur.

At the product level, examination of trademarks registered for gramophone, CD, and DVD products (detailed in the appendix to this chapter) demonstrates additional evolutionary trends. Although the number of products of each of these types, like components, evolves incrementally, the more dramatic transition between gramophone and CD systems derives from the cumulation of products over several years. The latest rise of DVD products may herald the arrival of a DVD system-level discontinuity as well.

Conclusions

Our discussion of technological evolution at multiple levels of the product hierarchy highlights the complexity of evolutionary processes as well as Campbell's contributions to these themes. Technological evolution is best characterized as variation, selection, and retention processes (Campbell, 1965) operating both within and between hierarchical levels; models focusing on only one level will be incomplete. Any model of technological evolution must consider not only the hierarchical nature of components, products, and systems but also the organizational hierarchy of multiple component-specific communities, firms, and the system-level community that generates selection pressures. We hope that this discussion stimulates research that focuses squarely on organizational evolution to consider the impact of product-level decisions in the context of firm capabilities, such as that by Ingram and Roberts (this volume).

Coevolutionary effects occur both within and across levels of the product hierarchy. Within levels, technological developments in certain components spur developments in other related components, just as technological developments in certain products spur developments in related products. This evolution takes place in the context of a multilevel selection environment, so we observe downward causation (Campbell, 1974, 1990). Product and system outcomes result from interaction between lower-level variation processes and higher-level selection processes. In optical disc technology, we observed how manufacturers selected among underlying variations in component technologies as they bundled these components into products such as the CD, MD, AHD, and VHD players we describe. At the same time, these four approaches represent variation at the product level, which were then selected on by broader organizational communities as systems were generated.

As we know from simulations of multiple, interdependent components (Baum, this volume; Kauffman, 1993; Levinthal, 1997), it is difficult to predict specific higher-level outcomes even though there are underlying, understandable processes at microlevels. In addition, whole-part coevolutionary competition (Campbell, 1994) arises because of the hierarchical nature of technological systems and their associated communities. Despite these dilemmas of prediction and competition, firms need to recognize these processes and attempt to influence all relevant selection entities.

By focusing on multiple levels of product evolution, our discussion sheds light on the ongoing debate between incremental and punctuated models of technological change. Our patent, product, and standards data from the optical disc arena demonstrate that by simultaneously considering multiple levels of the product hierarchy, we can simultaneously observe more incremental evolution of the underlying technologies and more punctuated evolution of the overall product systems. Using multiple methodological approaches at the various levels, then, helps reconcile incremental and punctuated views of technological evolution. Our perspective is that it is not an either/or question, but rather that technological evolution, because of its hierarchical nature, consists of simultaneous incremental and punctuated processes. Interestingly, this is a perspective that is similar to Van de Ven and Grazman's (this volume) perspective on the evolution of organizational forms— joining and crossing of different routines in the context of multilevel selection pressures.

Finally, our chapter highlights the value of patent data as empirical indicators of variation, selection, and retention processes. Unlike case histories or simulations, patent data offer a systematic record of actual variation, selection, and retention through their system of generation, classification, and citation. Future research can do much more to untangle these effects, not only for technology but also in tying in the role of the patenting organizations as well as the commercializable outputs of these patents.

Appendix:
Optical Disc Technology

D ata on optical disc technologies were drawn from multiple sources. Patent data were used to represent knowledge increments, and anecdotal reports of the evolution of products and standards were culled from books, trade journals, and popular press articles. In this section, we describe the structure of an "optical disc hierarchy," specify the construction of the data set, and report some brief empirical results.

Product Hierarchy

Optical disc systems, most simply, are composed of two products: a disc for storage and a player for retrieval and output. Eight components of these products were identified by consulting technical sources (Nakajima & Ogawa, 1992; Pohlmann, 1989). Each of the components is briefly described in Table 10.A1, and a cursory overview of the composition of an optical disc system can be gleaned from the schematic diagram displayed in Figure 10.A1.

Sound, video, or data information is stored on a polycarbonate *disc* (component 7) in the form of "pits." The arrangement, or density, of the pits governs the storage capacity of the disc (component 5). During storage, or recording, pits are generated by a laser beam (component 2) whenever the digital signal is 1. This stored digital information can later be retrieved with an optical disc *player*. The player's optical pickup employs a laser beam (component 4) and directs the digital signals to a processor (component 3), which decodes the signal and converts it into analog output that is either sound, video, or data. The transducer linear guide ensures that the signals are picked up properly by the optical pickup (component 6). The servo system (component 1) controls the motor and spindle on which the disc rotates and also helps focus the laser beam on the pits. The entire system is controlled via a microprocessor-based central processing unit.

The only component not shown in Figure 10.A1 is the measurement of electricity signals, which is essential to all parts of the system. We designate this technology as component 8. The dotted lines in Figure 10.A1 indicate that the CPU is not being considered as part of the evolution of the general evolution of the optical disc system. The lines with arrows in both directions indicate a feedback mechanism that allows for error correction.

TABLE 10.A1 Components of an Optical Disc System

Component	Name	Function	Patent Subclasses
1	Optical servo system	Control motor, spindle, and focusing of optical pickup	369#44-46
2	Optical storage	Construct pits via laser beam	369#13
3	Control of information signal	Convert digital signal into analog output	369#48
4	Laser beam technology	Store and reproduce digital information using laser pickups	369#100-125
5	Optical track structure	Format pits (via specification of density)	369#275
6	Transducer assembly linear guide	Read digital signal and correct errors	369#249
7	Material	Physical medium of disc	346#135.1
8	Measuring electricity signals	Transmission of information throughout optical disc system	324#244,96

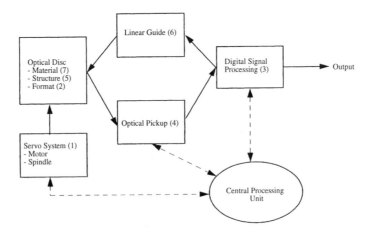

Figure 10.A1. Schematic Diagram of an Optical Disc System

Data

Given these eight components, the patent system manual of classification was searched to ascertain the technical subclasses that should correspond to each component. This set of technical subclasses was compared to those designated by Miyazaki (1995) in her extensive analysis of the patent classification system, which led us to add two additional subclasses to our set. The complete set of subclasses corresponding to each component is displayed in Table 10.A1. A total of approximately 3,600 patents was granted in these areas between 1971 and 1995. These patents were downloaded from the U.S. Patent and Trade Examiners Database. The yearly numbers of trademarks registered for gramophone, CD, and DVD products also were collected from this database.

Component-Component Citations

Citations represent a mechanism of selection—certain patents continue to influence subsequent developments in optical disc technology, and citation indicates replication and extension of previously developed technology. Table 10.A2 displays the distribution of patent citations between optical disc components. In each row of the table, we can observe the percentage distribution of citations from that component to any of the eight components, as well as to subclasses that are outside optical disc technology ("other"). The overall patterns of citation suggest the influence of any component on another. Two trends are evident. First, more than half of all citations from optical disc patents are to patents outside our optical disc boundary, creating ample fodder for importation of

TABLE 10.A2   Component-Component Citations

Component	1	2	3	4	5	6	7	8	Other	Total
1	28.1	2.1	2.1	17.7	1.0	0.0	1.0	0.0	47.9	96
2	5.6	24.9	1.6	23.3	1.8	0.0	1.8	0.0	41.0	502
3	4.1	4.1	21.8	17.3	3.6	0.0	0.5	0.0	48.6	220
4	11.2	4.2	2.5	27.9	2.8	0.0	1.5	0.0	49.7	3,627
5	5.9	0.0	0.0	17.6	11.8	0.0	5.9	0.0	58.8	17
6	4.3	0.0	0.0	3.2	1.1	13.8	4.3	0.0	73.4	94
7	0.3	0.7	0.0	3.8	3.3	0.3	17.4	0.1	74.1	1,437
8	0.0	0.0	0.0	0.0	1.5	0.0	0.0	47.8	50.7	67
Total	482	300	147	1,245	171	19	322	33	3,341	6,060

NOTE: Matrix entry (i, j) = percentage of component i's patent citations to component j. Entries in the Total row and column represent numbers of citations; row i totals represent the total number of citations made by patents for component i, and column j totals represent the total number of citations received by patents for component j.

preexisting technology into a new domain. For example, Sony's error correction techniques drew on coding techniques found in a separate patent class. Second, among the citations that remain within the optical disc boundary, the greatest percentages of these are within-component citations, suggesting incremental evolutionary trajectories at the component level.

Cross-Classification of Patents

The classification system for patents allows us to measure the extent to which any two components are directly related. Because patents may be assigned to more than one technological class, we can ascertain how many patents for a given component are closely related to other components. In optical disc technology, 2,012 patents were assigned to component 4 (optical pickup–laser), which is our most highly populated component. Of these 2,012 patents, 448 were cross-classified in other components. The breakdown of these 448 cross-classifications across the other seven components is displayed in Table 10.A3. Although a naïve hypothesis might suggest that the number of cross-classifications should be roughly proportional to the overall number of patents classified in the other component, a quick glance at the percentages in Table 10.A3 demonstrates that certain components (namely, components 2 and 3) are disproportionately cross-classified with component 4. This indi-

TABLE 10.A3   Cross-Classification of Patents

Component	1	2	3	5	6	7	8
Cross-classified w/component 4	55	197	101	9	4	82	0
Total number of patents	805	243	111	682	74	1,104	178
% cross-classified patents	7	81	91	1	5	7	0

NOTE: Total number of component 4 patents = 2,012, total number of component 4 cross-classified patents = 448, and proportion of Class 4 cross-classified patents = 22%.

cates a strong relationship between technological developments in each of these areas.

Trademarks Registered

Figure 10.A2 graphs the number of trademarks registered for gramophone, CD, and DVD products. Again, we observe that the number of products evolves only incrementally, and it is only through the cumulation of products of multiple years that we can observe transitions between system-level regimes. Thus, we see how CD products overtook gramophone products in the 1980s. During this time, Sony and Philips continued to play the major role in the development of CD technologies with their introductions of CD-ROM, CD-I, and CD-V variants. All these CD variants were

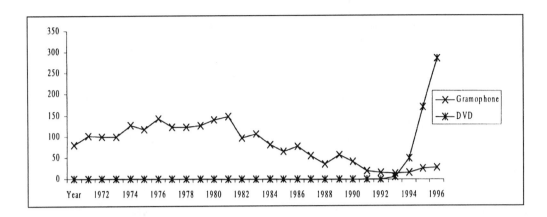

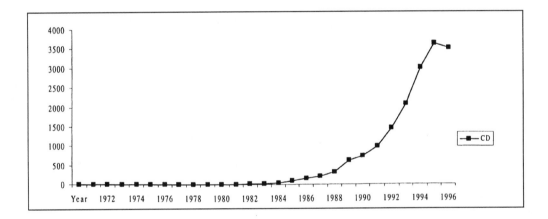

Figure 10.A2. Product-Level Evolution Measured by Number of Trademarks Registered

limited in their storage capacity, and approaches that dealt with the capacity constraint (Sony's DAT and Philips/Matsushita's DCC) were plagued by piracy concerns.

Similar dynamics recently have occurred with the rise of DVD products. The storage and piracy concerns were addressed through the application of improved technologies in the storage and pickup components. A Toshiba-led coalition developed the super density (SD) format, while Sony and Philips jointly developed MMCD. With the memory of the Beta/VHS wars and the ineffectiveness of the Digital Audio Disc Council still in the minds of these industry players, both groups joined to-gether to form a 10-company coalition that un-veiled the DVD standard.

Notes

1. Contextualist approaches such as downward causation are hotly debated in the evolutionary literature. Although we argue that downward causation is an important facet of techno-logical evolution, we recognize that the competing reductionist approaches also apply, and we discuss them later in this section.

2. Baum (this volume) attacks this problem and derives insights for managing it through an application of Kauffman's *NK[C]* model.

3. Kuhn's reductionist approach has been challenged as well, and current evolutionary thinking recognizes that both contextualist and reductionist approaches may operate simultaneously, as we argue in the technological arena.

References

Anderson, P., & Tushman, M. L. (1990). Technological discontinuities and dominant designs: A cyclical model of technological change. *Administrative Science Quarterly*, *35*(4), 604-633.

Barnett, W. P. (1990). The organizational ecology of a technological system. *Administrative Science Quarterly*, *35*(1), 31-60.

Baum, J., Korn, H., & Kotha, S. (1995). Dominant designs and population dynamics in telecommunications services: Founding and failure of facsimile transmission service organization, 1965-1992. *Social Science Research*, *24*, 97-135.

Baum, J.A.C., & Singh, J. V. (1994). Organizational hierarchies and evolutionary processes: Some reflections on a theory of organizational evolution. In J.A.C. Baum & J. V. Singh (Eds.), *Evolutionary dynamics of organizations* (pp. 3-20). New York: Oxford University Press.

Brown, S. L., & Eisenhardt, K. M. (1997). The art of continuous change: Linking complexity theory and time-paced evolution in relentlessly shifting organizations. *Administrative Science Quarterly*, *42*, 1-34.

Campbell, D. T. (1965). Variation and selective retention in socio-cultural evolution. In H. R. Barringer, G. I. Blanksten, & R. W. Mack (Eds.), *Social change in developing areas: A reinterpretation of evolutionary theory* (pp. 19-48). Cambridge, MA: Schenkman.

Campbell, D. T. (1974). "Downward causation" in hierarchically organized biological systems. In F. J. Ayala & T. Dobzhansky (Eds.), *Studies in the philosophy of biology* (pp. 179-186). London: Macmillan.

Campbell, D. T. (1990). Levels of organization, downward causation, and the selection-theory approach to evolutionary epistemology. In G. Greenberg & E. Tobach (Eds.), *Theories of the evolution of knowing* (pp. 1-17). Hillsdale, NJ: Lawrence Erlbaum.

Campbell, D. T. (1994). How individual and face-to-face-group selection undermine firm selection in organizational evolution. In J.A.C. Baum & J. V. Singh (Eds.), *Evolutionary dynamics of organizations* (pp. 23-38). New York: Oxford University Press.

Clark, K. B. (1985). The interaction of design hierarchies and market concepts in technological evolution. *Research Policy*, *14*(5), 235-251.

Cohen, W. M., & Levinthal, D. A. (1990). Absorptive capacity: A new perspective on learning and innovation. *Administrative Science Quarterly*, *35*(1), 128-152.

Dosi, G. (1984). *Technical change and industrial transformation*. New York: St. Martin's.

Helfat, C. E. (1994). Firm-specificity in corporate applied R&D. *Organization Science*, *5*(2), 173-184.

Henderson, R. M., & Clark, K. B. (1990). Architectural innovation: The reconfiguration of existing product technologies and the failure of established firms. *Administrative Science Quarterly*, *35*(1), 9-30.

Hughes, T. (1983). *Networks of power.* Baltimore: Johns Hopkins University Press.

Iansiti, M., & Khanna, T. (1995). Technological evolution, systm architecture and the obsolescence of firm capabilities. *Industrial and Corporate Change*, *4*, 333-361.

Kauffman, S. (1993). *The origins of order: Self-organization and selection in evolution.* New York: Oxford University Press.

Kuhn, T. (1970). *The structure of scientific revolutions.* Chicago, University of Chicago Press.

Levinthal, D. A. (1997). Adaptation on rugged landscapes. *Management Science*, *43*(7), 934-950.

Levinthal, D. (1998). The slow pace of rapid technological change: Gradualism and punctuation in technological change. *Industrial and Corporate Change*, *7*, 217-248.

March, J. (1991). Exploration and exploitation in organizational learning. *Organization Science*, *2*, 71-87.

McKelvey, B. (1997). Quasi-natural organization science. *Organization Science*, *8*, 352-380.

Miyazaki, K. (1995). *Building competencies in the firm: Lessons from Japanese and European optoelectronic firms.* New York: St. Martin's.

Nakajima, H., & Ogawa, H. (1992). *Compact disc technology..* Burke, VA: IOS Press.

Nelson, R. R., & Winter, S. G. (1982). *An evolutionary theory of economic change.* Cambridge, MA: Harvard University Press.

Nerkar, A., & Rosenkopf, L. (1997). *In the eye of the beholder: Reconciling incremental and punctuated equilibrium views on technological evolution.* Unpublished manuscript, University of Pennsylvania.

Podolny, J., & Stuart, T. (1995). A role-based ecology of technological change. *American Journal of Sociology*, *100*, 1224-1260.

Pohlmann, K. C. (1989). *The compact disc: A handbook of theory and use.* Madison, WI: A-R Editions.

Powell, W., Koput, K., & Smith-Doerr, L. (1996). Interorganizational collaboration and the locus of innovation: Networks of learning in biotechnology. *Administrative Science Quarterly*, *41*, 116-145.

Rosenbloom, R. S., & Cusumano, M. A. (1987). Technological pioneering and competitive advantage: The birth of the VCR industry. *California Management Review*, *29*(4), 51-76.

Rosenkopf, L., & Tushman, M. (1994). The co-evolution of technology and organizations. In J.A.C. Baum & J. V. Singh (Eds.), *Evolutionary dynamics of organizations* (pp. 403-424). New York: Oxford University Press.

Rosenkopf, L., & Tushman, M. (1998). The coevolution of community networks and technology: Lessons from the flight simulation industry. *Industrial and Corporate Change*, *7*, 311-346.

Simon, H. A. (1969). *The science of the artificial.* Cambridge, MA: MIT Press.

Suarez, F. F., & Utterback, J. M. (1995). Dominant designs and the survival of firms. *Strategic Management Journal, 16*(6), 415-430.

Tushman, M. L., & Anderson, P. (1986). Technological discontinuities and organizational environments. *Administrative Science Quarterly, 31*(3), 439-465.

Tushman, M. L., & Murmann, J. (1998). Dominant designs, technology cycles, and organizational outcomes. *Research in Organizational Behavior, 20,* 231-266.

Tushman, M., & Rosenkopf, L. (1992). On the organizational determinants of technological change: Toward a sociology of technological evolution. In B. Staw & L. Cummings (Eds.), *Research in organizational behavior* (pp. 311-347). Greenwich, CT: JAI.

Van de Ven, A. H., & Garud, R. (1993). Innovation and industry development: The case of cochlear implants. In R. Burgelman & R. Garud (Eds.), *Research on technological innovation and management policy* (pp. 1-46). Greenwich, CT: JAI.

Chapter 11

Evolution in a Nested Hierarchy

A Genealogy of Twin Cities Health Care Organizations, 1853-1995

ANDREW H. VAN DE VEN
DAVID N. GRAZMAN

> The tree of life has been a universal and persistent metaphor since the beginning of human culture—for good reason. Life, whether represented in terms of genealogy or phylogeny, is a branching process, and the unity of living things is best expressed in terms of its hierarchy.
>
> —*Arnold and Fristrup (1982, p. 113)*

How and why did the organizational arrangements we see today in an industry emerge and change into their present forms? This question is central to understanding how new forms of organizations emerged and evolved from lineages of ancestral forms that existed in earlier social, economic, and political conditions. Answers to this question are pragmatically useful in guiding managers, based on what was learned in the past, to respond to changing organizational and environmental conditions.

Unfortunately, as Kimberly and Bouchikhi (1995, p. 9) lament, few speak to the question of how an organization's past shapes its present and may constrain its future. They go on to argue that "without an appreciation for past experience, present behavior and future action cannot be fully understood" (p. 10). Hannan and Freeman (1989)

AUTHORS' NOTE: We greatly appreciate useful comments on earlier drafts of this chapter from Bill Barnett, Joel Baum, Erhard Bruderer, Robert Burgelman, Joe Galaskiewicz, Heather Haveman, John Kimberly, Bill McKelvey, Dick Scott, Steve Shortell, Jitendra Singh, Pamela Tolbert, and Mike Tushman. We also thank James Fogerty and Mark Greene of the Minnesota Historical Society for their training and assistance in archival research.

state that "the ability of a society as a whole to respond to changing conditions depends on the responsiveness of its constituent organizations and on the diversity of its organizational populations" (p. 3). Diverse organizational forms constitute a repository of solutions to the problem of organizing, which increase the flexibility and innovation capacity of an industry or population of organizations (Carroll & Hannan, 1995, p. 8). Although these solutions exist in diverse organizational arrangements, their rationale is rooted in ancestral forms and practices.

There is no one comprehensive theory of organizational change able to explain how and why organizations grow and develop over time as they do. Although alternative theories are available (Van de Ven & Poole, 1995), interest in biological analogies of evolution throughout the social sciences has led many scholars in the 1980s and 1990s to explain the dynamics that govern organizational change as a sociocultural evolutionary process. As a pioneer of this perspective, Campbell (1969) introduced a recurrent, probabilistic model of variation, selection, and retention to explain this evolutionary process.

Two key problems have limited application of this evolutionary model to studying organizational change. First, whereas the lineage of biological entities is based on the sexual propagation of genes and DNA, social organizations lack a functional equivalent addressing how organizational traits or competencies are inherited or transmitted across generations (McKelvey, 1982). Second, as in the biological model, is the fundamental need to consider social organizations within a nested hierarchical structure, such as individuals within organizations within industries or populations, and how evolutionary processes work within and between nested hierarchical levels. For 20 years, social and biological evolutionary theorists have proposed alternative ways of addressing these problems, with varying degrees of success.

In this chapter, we build on the work of Campbell (1974, 1990) and others to suggest a way of addressing these long-standing obstacles to a more complete evolutionary theory of organizations. This chapter comprises five parts. Part I reviews some approaches that evolutionary scholars have

developed for dealing with inheritance and hierarchy, and it sketches out our framework for studying organizational evolution in a nested hierarchy. Part II empirically grounds the proposed framework by describing methods we used to historically trace the evolution of the Twin Cities' (Minneapolis and St. Paul, Minnesota) health care systems. Part III presents the constructed genealogies, or historical lineages, of change events in management, organization, and industry arrangements for these organizations, the major providers of local health care services. Part IV presents a set of propositions, derived from the genealogies, concerning how adaptation and selection processes interact under different conditions to influence the branching and persistence of organizational forms over time, and Part V offers conclusions.

Part I: Conceptual Overview

The Problem of Inheritance

Alternative theories of social evolution can be distinguished in terms of how traits are inherited and the unit of analysis.[1] Organizational scholars who adopt a Darwinian view of evolution (e.g., Hannan & Freeman, 1977, 1989; McKelvey, 1982) argue that traits are inherited through intergenerational processes, whereas most organizational scholars who follow a Lamarckian view (e.g., Boyd & Richerson, 1985; Burgelman, 1991; Nelson & Winter, 1982; Singh & Lumsden, 1990) argue that traits also can be acquired within a generation through learning and imitation. As McKelvey (1982) points out, the problem is that, to date, no adequate way has been found to operationally identify an organizational generation or a vehicle for transmitting or inheriting traits from one generation to the next. Thus, the Lamarckian view sidesteps (but does not solve) a central impediment to research on organizational evolution.[2]

Failing an adequate solution to this problem, population ecologists have used organizational birth and death rates as proxy measures of an organizational generation and have examined the proposition that organizational death rates should decline monotonically with age after a brief period of growth in organizational density. (See reviews by Barnett and Carroll [1995], Baum [1996], and Hannan, Carroll, Dundon, and Torres [1995]). Organizational births, often measured as the entrance of new firms into a population, are assumed to be the carriers of either retained ancestral forms or newly selected organizational variations. Organizational deaths, often measured by firm dissolutions—including mergers, acquisitions, or name changes—are assumed to be the carriers of organizational forms selected out by the environment and becoming extinct.

Rates of organizational births and deaths provide useful information about the diffusion of an organizational form but do not capture *how* an organizational form evolves across generations. Novel organizational forms that develop are neither imprinted nor necessarily determined at organizational birth; rather, these new forms emerge and change at different times throughout an organization's life span. Conversely, mergers, acquisitions, strategic affiliations, and name changes, which commonly have been used as indicators of organizational death or mortality, are instead important markers of the union and ascent of new generations of organizational forms. New forms of organizations are often the hybrid products of diverse ancestral forms of organizational arrangements.

As an alternative to organizational births and deaths, we propose that *novel change events in the lineage of an organizational entity* be used as markers of a new generation of organizational forms. In the literature on organizational innovation, novelty typically is defined as the recombination of old forms, schemes, or ideas in ways that are new and unique to the organization's experience (Rogers, 1983; Van de Ven, 1986; Zaltman, Duncan, & Holbek, 1973). As this definition suggests, new generations of organizational forms are often (but not always) produced by events that couple or recombine preexisting organizational resources, competencies, and arrangements to either create a new organizational form or to extend an ancestral form.

Ancestral resources that are recombined to create these new generations can exist either within or outside the subject organization. Internal organiza-

tional growth occurs when ancestral forms are situated within organizations, such as with internal investments or recombinations of existing units, resources, or competencies that create or renovate an organizational program, product, service, or routine. External organizational growth occurs when resources and components of different organizations are combined, as evidenced in the significant rise of mergers, acquisitions, strategic affiliations, and joint ventures. Moreover, because ancestral forms crossed to produce new forms often are nested in complex networks of interdependent hierarchies within and between organizations, their recombinations often generate new hybrid forms of organization.

These alternative ways to recombine ancestral organizational forms to create new ones are not captured by examining organizational birth and death rates in a population. Instead, we argue that a genealogical study may better capture how organizational forms are created, modified, and reproduced through the recombination or interaction of their progenitors. A *genealogy* is a record of descent or lineage of a group from its ancestors until the present day.

The concepts of branching and persistence are useful in historically tracing the lineage of organizational forms. *Branching* is the emergence of novel forms of structure (i.e., variations), and *persistence* is the temporal duration (i.e., retention) of each structural form in the genealogy of an organization.[3] As applied to a focal organization, a *branch* is defined as a unique form of structure that an organization exhibits for a period of time in its life span.

Hannan and Freeman (1984) and Tushman and Romanelli (1985) argue that the core dimensions of an organizational form (or branch) include its mission, authority structure, technology, and product market. Figure 11.1 depicts three branches in the genealogy of a fictitious health care organization. Initially founded as a hospital (branch A) and differentiated into a primary care referral clinic (branch B), the organization subsequently evolved into a multispecialty clinic (branch C). Within each branch, numerous adaptation events occurred that replicated that particular form and extended its persistence. For example, the hospital branch (A)

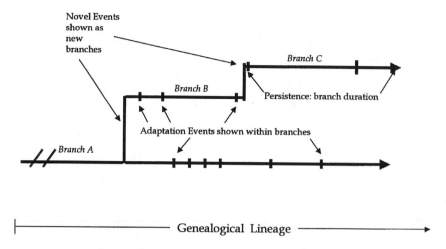

Figure 11.1. Core Concepts: Branching and Persistence

has persisted since the organization's founding through a series of adaptation events that replicated and extended its form by remodeling and adding to the initial hospital, opening new hospital sites, or acquiring formerly independent hospitals. As this example suggests, substantive features of branches are historically unique to specific organizations.[4]

Our definitions of branching and persistence are similar to Tushman and Romanelli's (1985, p. 179) organizational reorientations (when simultaneous and discontinuous changes occur in core organizational features) and convergence (when incremental and adaptive changes occur that reproduce and extend the temporal duration of an existing organizational form). Branching events represent what Watzlawik, Weakland, and Fisch (1974) and Meyer, Brooks, and Goes (1990) call "second-order" changes, which create novel forms that are unprecedented departures from ancestral structural arrangements in an organization's lineage. The persistence of a branch is produced by "first-order" change events that replicate and extend the longevity of a structural form relative to other forms in an organization's genealogy.

March's (1991) discussion of the trade-offs between exploration and exploitation behaviors also apply to branching and persistence. Maintaining an appropriate balance between exploration (branching-oriented) behaviors and exploitation (persisting with a branch) are essential for organizational learning and survival. March develops a model implying that periods when exploitation and persistence of a given branch overwhelm exploration and branching tend to increase short-run effectiveness (fitness) but decrease the long-run adaptability and survival capability of the organization.

Focusing on the emergence and persistence of branches provides a way to examine where variations come from and how they are passed on through an organizational lineage. As Romanelli's chapter in this volume states, the origins of variations (i.e., branching) have yet to be explained; they have been assumed to be rare, discrete occurrences produced by random or "blind" chance (Campbell, 1974; McKelvey, 1982), individual genius (Anderson and Tushman, 1990, p. 605), or "whatever reason. . . . They just happen. . . . [Natural selection] is indifferent to the ultimate source of variation. . . . Variations are the raw material from which the selection process culls those structures or behaviors that are most suitable, given the selection criterion" (Aldrich, 1979, pp. 28, 34).

To say that organizational variations can not be predicted ex ante does not necessarily lead to the conclusion that branches in an organizational lineage are random. Campbell (1974) emphasized that they may be "blind" but conditioned by other unobserved factors. Branching events also can be triggered or constrained by events at other levels in a nested hierarchy of organizational entities. Specifically, we conjecture that seemingly random causes of novel branching events in an organizational lineage are more likely to be triggered by events occurring at different ecological levels than by events occurring at the same level. Conversely, because of path-dependent learning and inertial forces, adaptation events that extend the persistence of branches in a lineage are more likely to be triggered by preceding adaptation events occurring at the same level than by events occurring at other ecological levels. Elaboration of these conjectures requires a hierarchical perspective of evolutionary dynamics.

The Problem of Nested Hierarchy

Most applications of evolutionary theory in the study of organizational change have been conducted at the population level of analysis (e.g., Carroll & Hannan, 1989; Hannan & Freeman, 1977, 1989); however, Burgelman (1991) and Singh and Lumsden (1990) have adopted the evolutionary model to explain strategy making within organizations, and Weick (1979) and Gersick (1991) applied parts of evolutionary theory at a microlevel to explain the social-psychological processes of organizing. Burgelman (1991), for example, examined strategy making as an intraorganizational evolutionary process of variation, selection, and retention. He viewed variations as deriving from managers' initiatives to compete for scarce resources, selection processes being exerted through corporate resource allocation mechanisms, and retention taking the form of corporate strategy that defines the areas in which the firm has learned it can operate successfully.

Thus, although the evolutionary model has been used to study processes of variation, selection, and retention at different organizational levels, seldom has it been used to study change across levels. Although a hierarchically based model has been acknowledged as useful in *describing* organizational life, it has yet to be incorporated into *explanations* of organizational evolution.[5] As a result, we know little about how or why evolutionary processes in one level facilitate or constrain evolution at other levels of a nested ecological hierarchy.

Meyer and colleagues (1990) provide an insightful account of how their research design, reflecting good contemporary theory, was unable to adequately measure or explain the hyperturbulent changes experienced by hospitals and the health care industry during the 1980s in the San Francisco Bay area. They concluded that "the most pressing need was to develop a broader framework for thinking about organizational change . . . [one that examines] the *mode* of change (continuous or discontinuous) [our persistence and branching] and the *level* at which it occurs (organization or industry)" (Meyer et al., p. 71). Following Campbell (1974), Baum and Singh (1994) and Miner (1994) also called for an expansion of evolutionary theory to include study of the processes of variation, selection, and retention *between* different levels of organizational entities.

The nested hierarchical structure of individuals within organizations within populations or industries is fundamental to understanding organizational life. The organization itself represents but a single level of analysis, both encompassing and being encompassed by other levels. Organizations are viewed as evolving systems nested in other coevolving systems at higher (e.g., industry or population) and lower (e.g., work groups or individual managers) levels of analysis. At an even higher community level of analysis, Astley (1985) described how multiple populations of organizations also go through their own variation, selection, and retention processes as they coevolve with lower-level organizational and management changes, as well as more macro technological and social developments, as illustrated in Schumpeterian cycles of creative destruction.

Figure 11.2 illustrates this view of studying evolution in a nested ecological hierarchy encompassing three levels: individual managers within organizations within a community or industry. These three levels are not exhaustive, as each can be decomposed into sublevels depending on how the overall system is conceptualized. Entities at each level evolve their own historical lineages in terms of a set of unique properties that cannot be expressed as simple aggregations or disaggregations of lower- or higher-level units. As explained in the next section, the horizontal axis (time) traces the

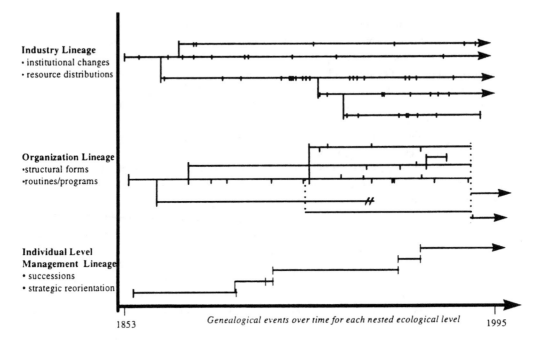

Figure 11.2. Design for Studying Lineages in Nested Hierarchy

lineages at each ecological level in terms of change events occurring in a few key dimensions.

For example, at the managerial level, the genealogy is based on changes in the succession of top managers and their strategic orientations. At the organizational level, a genealogy traces the changes over time in an organization's structures, forms, or routines, while the industry or community-level genealogy reflects a host of macro issues, such as demographic shifts, changes in resource levels, and changes of institutional, professional, or regulatory rules and norms. Figure 11.2 shows patterns of branching and persistence in the lineages of entities at each level, based on whether the change events represent novel variations (branching) or adaptations that extended the persistence of a given branch (as was illustrated in Figure 11.1).

There are several important theoretical implications of a nested hierarchical perspective of organizational evolution. First, *selection and adaptation processes can work simultaneously and differently at each level in a nested hierarchy.* Arnold and Fristrup (1982) and Gould (1989) point out that classical Darwinism locates the sorting of evolutionary change at the level of the unitary organism. This sorting is natural selection operating through the differential births and deaths of individual organisms, as exemplified by many population ecology studies of organizational birth and death rates. Gould's punctuated equilibrium model adds a hierarchical dimension to evolutionary theory by distinguishing sorting (the growth or decline of organisms of a given species) from speciation (the process by which new species or groups are formed).

This hierarchical view of evolution is important for understanding how selection and adaptation might occur at multiple levels. At any focal level, *selection* focuses on the evolutionary process of choosing or shifting between new branches (i.e., variations or speciations), while *adaptation* is the class of heritable characters that have a positive influence on the fitness of an entity within a constraining situation; that is, on extending the persistence of a particular branch. Selection therefore assumes branching in a lineage, while adaptation assumes fitting or adjusting within a selected branch. Arnold and Fristrup (1982) go on to argue that branching and persistence are the essential components of fitness at all levels. Branching indicates variation or speciation rates, whereas persistence indicates the fitness (or extinction rates) of entities in selected branches.

A second implication of this hierarchical view is that *relationships between levels may be both positive and negative.* Arnold and Fristrup (1982, p. 127) note that although the Darwinian view of selection draws attention to the harmony of form and function in organisms, we cannot expect all characteristics to be adaptive at all levels in the hierarchy. As Baum points out in his chapter in this volume, evolution takes place simultaneously at each level in the nested hierarchy. Entities at all these levels (individual, organization, community/industry) try to optimize fitness. What is best for an entity at one level, however, generally will not be the best for entities at other levels. Thus, entities at different levels compete to direct activities and resources that favor their own survival.

For example, a selfish or opportunistic top manager may select strategies and clone successors that extend the persistence of his or her leadership regime, at the expense of decreasing the adaptiveness or fitness of the structural form of the encompassing organization. Overspecialization of organizational forms, produced by exploiting the persistence of selected branches at the expense of exploring alternative branches, increases short-term advantages for an organization, but at the industry disadvantage of limiting variations for population-level selection processes.

Given individual self-interest norms, why should these suboptimal behaviors of selfishness and overspecialization by microlevel entities ever stop? Agency theory addresses the moral hazard problem of selfishness by aligning the incentives of managerial agents with those of the organizational principals at the individual level (Barney & Ouchi, 1986). Other researchers have viewed the problem of overspecialization as evidence of organizational momentum or inertia produced by path-dependent processes that direct an organization to exploit and build competencies in its existing core branch with time (Arthur, 1989; Lant & Mezias, 1992).

A hierarchical perspective takes a different approach to these problems, which represent cases of negative interaction between lower-level advantage and higher-level disadvantage. Higher-level entities eventually will "notice" the selfish individual agent or the overspecialized organization when the cost of persisting with these lower-level branches becomes high enough to entail negative selection at the next higher level. If no negative selection from a higher level suppresses an advantageous lower-level phenomenon, then it might sweep through a population (as in the case of the U.S. automobile industry in the 1960s) and make the niche vulnerable to negative selection from an even higher or broader level in the hierarchy (e.g., foreign automobile manufacturers). As Gould (1982a, p. 385) proposes, negative interaction between levels may be an important principle in maintaining stability or holding rates of change within reasonable bounds. Here, stability represents a balance between positive selection at one level and the negative selection it eventually elicits at another level in a nested ecological hierarchy.

A third implication is that *the relative dominance of evolutionary processes at macro- and microlevels is a matter of time scale and spatial variation.* As evolution takes place in a nested hierarchy, we would expect to see a greater number of variations at lower levels because of a shorter time scale, although the magnitude of these variations is likely to be smaller because of their lower level of complexity. Because time scales associated with branching and persistence are far shorter for individual selection than for group selection, on average, the rate of evolution at microlevels should generally exceed that at macrolevels (Arnold & Fristrup, 1982).

In terms of ecological space, the number of entities at lower levels by definition exceeds the number at higher levels; that is, a single industry may contain 100 organizations with 100,000 employees within them. Microlevel selection should predominate at the macrolevel because there are more variations available for selection. The scale of variations at higher-level groups, however, are almost always greater than those between lower-level individuals. Larger differences between higher-level groups tend to be maintained by less frequent interaction patterns between groups than within groups. These interaction patterns reduce differences within groups and maintain heterogeneity between groups. As a consequence, even though higher-level selection may occur less frequently, when macrolevel selection events occur, they tend to produce more dramatic changes than when microlevel selection events occur.

Finally, *selection at a given level in the hierarchy requires competition for scarce resources among entities competing at that level*. Macrolevel resource scarcity constrains (but does not direct) selection and adaptation paths by setting boundary conditions and influencing the availability of the raw material for lower-level evolution. Benign or abundant periods at the macrolevel tend to relax boundaries for experimentation and branching by lower-level entities. These observations provide one way to reconcile the ongoing debate between strategic choice and population ecology theories of organizational change (see Astley and Van de Ven, 1983). During benign or abundant environmental periods, or when organizations have managed to efficiently stockpile slack resources, choices and actions by individual managers potentially can have their greatest effects on changes in organizational form. During periods of increasing industry scarcity and competitiveness, however, particularly when organizational coffers are low, macrolevel selection tends to exert greater influence than microlevel selection events on changes in a focal organization (Grazman & Van de Ven, 1995).

Our basic proposition of evolution within a nested hierarchy is that *the emergence and persistence of branches in the lineage of any focal level are reciprocally influenced by changes in their own lineages as well as the lineages of other levels*. To keep this exploratory study manageable, we examine this proposition by focusing on the organization as the key level to be explained in a nested hierarchy of the Twin Cities' health care managers, organizations, and industry. Here, we propose that the branching and persistence of the organization's structural forms are directed and constrained by (a) the organization's ancestral structural forms, (b) changes in the lineage of top management succession and strategies at a lower individual level,

and (c) changes in the lineage of demographic and institutional arrangements at a higher industry level. Although this proposition reflects the complexity of evolutionary dynamics, it also underscores the essential unity of its theoretical structure. No single level can be understood fully except in the context of its position in the evolutionary hierarchy. Moreover, the diverse mechanisms that operate at each level may have either positive or negative relationships on patterns of branching and persistence at other levels.

Part II: Research Design

Adopting the design in Figure 11.2, we constructed genealogies of the historical lineages of change events in top management succession, organizational structure, and industry conditions for four major health care providers: the Allina Health System, HealthPartners, HealthSystem Minnesota, and Fairview Health System. Each of these qualifies, under 1993 MinnesotaCare legislation, as an "integrated service network" or ISN. As of 1995, this oligopoly had grown to control nearly 70% of the area's health care provider market, as measured in lives covered, patients served, and licensed hospital beds. Ranging in asset size from approximately $352 million to $922 million in 1993, each provides a broad array of health services, ranging from home health to acute hospital inpatient services. In addition, each is involved in and competes with other health maintenance organizations, health plans, and provider networks.

To construct the genealogies, historical data were collected through an intensive search of publicly available records and by conducting interviews with top managers and other knowledgeable informants. Archival records were retrieved from the Minnesota Historical Society, the Minnesota Hospital Association, other health care associations, and public libraries, as well as from broad searches of local newspapers and magazines. We found the histories of the four organizations to be fairly well documented considering the 140-year time span. Our research was aided by the fact that historians and journalists have recognized the central role of health care in society over the last century and have documented it accordingly (Starr, 1982).

Events representing changes were identified, recorded, and compiled into lineages at three levels (management, organization, industry) for each organization, and date back to changes in their earliest recognizable "ancestors." The following definitions were used to identify events at each level:

- *Managerial events* were defined as changes in the tenure or appointments of top managers, including chief administrators and physicians, and changes in organizational strategies that were directly attributable to senior managers. Managers were identified as individual leaders of one of the four organizations or their predecessors.
- *Organizational events* were defined as changes in structures and routines, as indicated by foundings and openings or closings of organizational units or programs, as well as joint ventures, mergers, and affiliations with other organizations. We differentiated internal and external forms of growth depending on the source of resources involved in the event.
- *Industry events* included changes in environmental resources or industrywide institutions, including changes in regulatory, professional, or economic policies affecting the Twin Cities' health care organizations.

Following Van de Ven and Poole (1990), events were recorded in chronological order and coded according to detailed decision rules. Ideally, each event included the name of the actor, the action taken or change made, the date the action took place, the outcome of the action (if known), and an explanation of why the action took place. Where particular event detail was sparse or missing, other event details were still recorded. Overall, the data set contains 556 events, each coded by organization affiliation, event type, and ecological level.

To determine coding reliability, two individuals unfamiliar with this research coded a random sample of 20% of the events. Agreement between the authors and the coders on event codes exceeded 94% with most discrepancies resolved by brief discussion and clarification. Prior to these discussions, however, we examined for systematic bias and found none. That is, no particular decision rule or code resulted in unreliable miscoding, leading us to conclude that coding procedures were applied consistently to all events.

Once events were entered and coded into a database, event chronologies and organizational history diagrams were prepared and distributed to informants to verify accuracy and to help identify existing gaps in the genealogies. Informants ranged from officials of industrywide organizations, such as the Minnesota Hospital Association, to retired secretaries whose careers spanned almost as many years as some of the organizations. Their perspectives provided useful information for clarifying events and identifying missing events. They provided many anecdotes and observations simply not available from any conventional source and were very helpful to us in understanding, qualitatively, how events at different levels interrelated.

Finally, we examined the substance of events to identify distinct branches in the lineages within levels. Identifying branches required making qualitative judgments, based on novel events, as to when unique forms emerged. These judgments are discussed below as we describe the identified branches in each lineage. *Novel events* suggested new branches in a lineage when they resulted in a new form or scheme that was unprecedented. *Adaptation or persistence events* can be thought of as replications or revisions that extended the duration of branches already in existence. Although, at best, our events capture only a sample of the historical past, they help point to when new branches emerged and how long they persisted.

Part III: Descriptive Findings

We present our results by first outlining the changes that took place within the multiple genealogies of each of the four major Twin Cities health systems. Although the full data set includes much greater detail than what is presented here, these abbreviated descriptions address our research question of how the organizational arrangements that we see today in the Twin Cities' health care industry evolved into their present forms. Following these descriptions, we offer our interpretations as to why these arrangements evolved as they did by analyzing temporal relationships within and

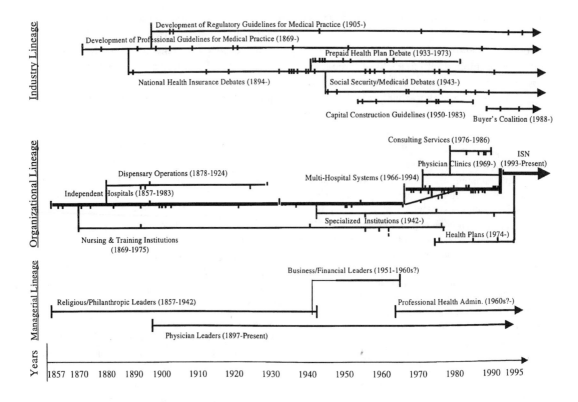

Figure 11.3. Allina's Lineages

between different lineages, and within and across the nested hierarchical levels.

Industry Institutional Lineage

At the industry level, the development of public policies and institutional arrangements affecting health care in the Twin Cities coincided with those emerging throughout the nation, though some policies influenced Minnesota in different ways because of the state's unique characteristics. Depicted in the top level of Figures 11.3-11.6, the industry lineages for the four organizations are identical (except for a different starting point) as each evolved within the same environment. The branches we identify here are subjective interpretations of the event data collected.

Seven distinct branches (indicated by 69 events) were identified as reflecting the lineages in the evolution of industry-level institutions. Broadly

defined, the branches reflect major policy shifts and discussions relating to the institutionalization of physicians and medical practice, health regulation, national health insurance, prepaid health plans, Medicare and Medicaid legislation, regional health planning, and purchasing cooperatives.

The earliest industry branch, the institutionalization of medical practice guidelines, reflects the medical profession regulating and controlling the behaviors of its own practitioners. During the late 19th and early 20th centuries, when medicine was unregulated, physicians were largely mistrusted, hospitals were feared, and most citizens only reluctantly sought treatment. With the formation of the Minnesota State Medical Society in 1869, the issue of self-regulated practice emerged as a branch within the industry lineage, representing a novel introduction with a series of subsequent events reflecting persistence within the branch. Some of these events included the formation of the Associa-

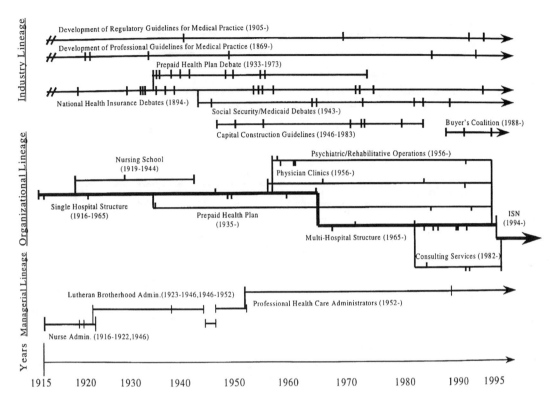

Figure 11.4. Fairview's Lineages

tion of American Medical Colleges in 1890 and the establishment of the Council on Medical Education in 1904, all the way up to the current day as the American Medical Association continues to draft and enforce numerous professional standards.

With increased centralization of power by the medical profession itself, government regulation coevolved as a counterforce to the corruption and other abuses many believed would develop. Federal and state governments began to take a more active role in regulating the industry at the turn of the century and clearly in this role. The regulatory branch identified contains significant events such as establishment of the Food and Drug Administration (1906), the setting of price ceilings by the Department of Health, Education and Welfare (1969), and Minnesota's own reform efforts embodied in the MinnesotaCare legislation (1992).

As presented in Figures 11.3 through 11.6, several other branches emerged and have continued, with one exception, to characterize the set of issues relevant to today's health care policymakers and organizational managers. The debate over government-mandated health insurance, at both the state and federal levels, began in 1894, with a rallying of support during Teddy Roosevelt's second presidential campaign. As public support for state-run insurance waxes and wanes, various politicians have taken up the cause, including Presidents Kennedy and Clinton. Although never implemented, national health insurance efforts, and their repeated resurrections, continue to influence the national health care debate. Related to this branch, but emerging as a novel variation, was the prepaid health plan. Emerging from the Depression and the economic uncertainties it created, prepaid plans were developed to minimize financial risks to both patients and providers. Their development was quite controversial, however, and even was prohibited in many states, including Minnesota, until

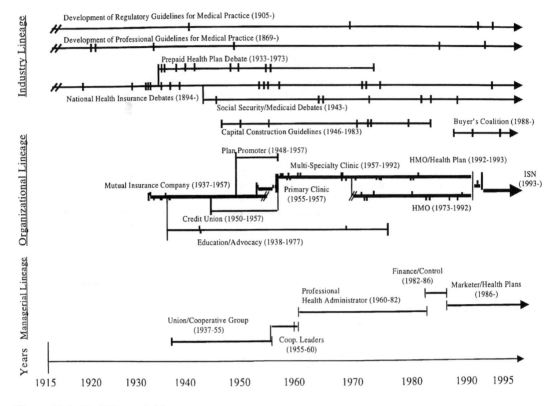

Figure 11.5. HealthPartner's Lineages

1955. The fights surrounding their establishment were quite heated. At the federal level, the passage of the HMO Act of 1973 represented an end, of sorts, to these debates as prepaid health plans found formal legitimacy in the body politic. Today, managed care and capitation are direct beneficiaries of this industry branch.

Another novel approach to health insurance resulted in elements of the Social Security program, beginning during Franklin Roosevelt's presidency, and the establishment of Medicare/Medicaid during the Kennedy and Johnson administrations. These two programs have defined the government's role as a major payer in the health care system, at federal and state levels, and the issues they have raised, such as eligibility, welfare reform, and benefit structures, collectively shape this industry branch.

Although the branches mentioned above affected Minnesota as well as the rest of the nation,

the two other industry branches we identified are more specific to the Minnesota experience. These branches represent institutional responses to controlling an overcapacity of building in the system and attempts to curb the escalating costs of health care. Both branches exemplify how selection processes at an industry level can suppress advantageous lower-level organizational adaptation processes. Prior to and immediately following World War II, many new hospitals were built in the Twin Cities area as organizations and municipalities alike experienced unprecedented growth. Because resources were readily available, few organizations paid attention to the overcapacity they were creating as the number of hospitals and clinics in the region continued to grow (Halvorson, 1993). The issue of an overcapacity of construction first emerged and was formally addressed by the Minneapolis Hospital Research Council in 1950 when it underwrote a study of conditions in the local

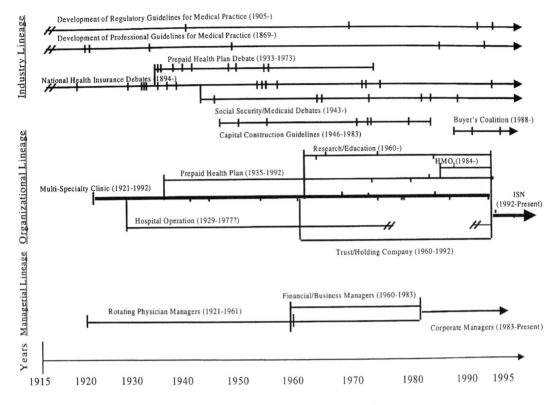

Figure 11.6. HealthSystem Minnesota's Lineages

industry, recommending either closure of hospitals or some form of consolidation. Until 1983, when the Metropolitan Health Board, an appointed oversight committee charged with managing the rate of growth in the industry, disbanded, efforts to limit growth and expansion were an important industry branch.

The last branch we identified began in 1988 as health care purchasers joined forces to curb escalating health care costs and formed the Business Health Care Action Group (BHCAG), a purchasing coalition of 23 large employers. Although prior cost control efforts generally had failed, the BHCAG has wielded significant strength and had unexpected success in driving consolidation in the Twin Cities' health care industry. In fact, the BHCAG executive director repeatedly noted his surprise at how influential the coalition had become. His observation was affirmed in our discussions with organizational CEOs, all of whom stressed efforts their organizations were undertaking to respond to the major market shifts represented in increased consumer purchasing power. As the coalition matures, further purchaser integration efforts continue to shape organizational forms, practices, and industry institutions.

Organizational and Managerial Lineages

As the Minnesota industry evolved, so too did the organizational and managerial lineages composing the four systems we chose to study. Shown in Figures 11.3 through 11.6, these lineages and the series of events that define them provide numerous examples of selection and adaptation processes acting concurrently within and across the levels of the nested hierarchy.[6] As with the industry lineages, we present here only a very general narrative of our findings.

Allina's Lineages

Figure 11.3 depicts the lineages of Allina, the largest and most vertically integrated of the systems, which emerged through affiliations and mergers of many hospitals and facilities over a period of more than 100 years. Allina's organizational lineage has been dominated by a hospital-based structure since the founding of its first hospital in 1857, with subbranches capturing ancillary organizations that formed, such as nursing schools and dispensaries for the medically indigent. Initially, most hospitals belonging to Allina (and those that subsequently folded into Allina) were independent and affiliated with religious denominations or physician groups. Beginning in the mid-1920s, these hospitals contemplated alliances and joint ventures to achieve greater efficiencies, leverage religious affiliations, or expand geographically. Hospital mergers began, in earnest, in the years surrounding World War II.

By 1966, hospital mergers were less prevalent, and the multihospital system grew in importance as a dominant organizational form. These larger systems began to purchase and acquire physician clinics around 1969 to ensure a steady stream of inpatient referrals. For the next two decades, the multihospital systems grew in size and scope through more mergers and affiliations. Although other organizational branches can be identified (e.g., specialized institutions, consulting services, health plans), the core branch of Allina was dominated by multihospital systems.

In 1993, HealthSpan, the product of two multihospital systems merging in 1992, joined with Medica, a financing organization, to become Allina, a fully integrated service organization made up of hospitals, physician practices, and a health plan, all under a unified governance structure. Although its leaders had stated that the merger took place in response to the BHCAG's request for proposals for an integrated system, Allina was not chosen for the contract. Nevertheless, Allina, with its 19,600 employees, reported a successful first year (1994) with revenues of $2.2 billion.

Allina's managerial lineage reflects its strong tradition of independent hospitals and the visionaries behind them. Although many managers and leaders contributed to Allina's precursor hospitals, we identified four general branches within this lineage. The first branch, which began prior to the Civil War, was a reflection of health care during this period: religious institutions and poorhouses. Until World War II, most managers were religious leaders or philanthropists with a strong moral commitment to serving the community. Individuals like Sarah Knight, Sister Elizabeth Kenny, and Dr. Amos Abbott strongly influenced how Allina's organizations functioned in the past, as well as today. With more mergers, requirements for more complex managerial skills increased. Business administrators were brought into the hospitals and systems beginning in the 1950s and 1960s. By the mid-1960s, almost all chief executives of the hospital were trained in health care administration. Only since the early 1990s have we seen the emergence of a new branch as physicians seek and hold administrative positions throughout Allina.

Fairview's Lineages

We identified seven branches in the organizational lineage of the Fairview Health System, presented in Figure 11.4. Like Allina, Fairview's core branch since its founding has been a hospital-based structure; however, Fairview's core hospital branch evolved through internal growth almost exclusively, unlike Allina's reliance on external mergers and acquisitions. Beginning with a single hospital in 1916 and persisting until the second hospital opened in 1965 (representing one of the first multihospital systems in the United States), Fairview has remained fairly consistent in its approach to growth, with less important branches, such as specialized hospitals and consulting services, also contributing to the organization's lineage.

Although Fairview began quietly to purchase physician practices in the mid-1950s, this effort increased as other organizations merged and consolidated in the 1980s and 1990s. Fairview announced a novel partnership with Blue Cross/Blue Shield of Minnesota in 1994, catapulting it forward as an integrated organization with affiliated hospitals, physicians, and an insurer/health plan.

Fairview's managerial lineage can be classified into three major branches. Fairview, with deep historical roots in the Lutheran church, was first led by church lay leaders driven by their spiritual belief of caring for others. This branch shaped Fairview's development exclusively until 1946, when a few Lutheran businessmen were seated on the board. In 1952, Carl Platou, with professional health administration training, assumed the administrator role, which he held until 1989. This branch has continued to persist under the current regime of Chief Executive Richard Norling.

HealthPartners' Lineages

HealthPartners has a colorful genealogy, presented in Figure 11.5, that originated with the cooperative movement at the periphery of legitimate health care. Founded in 1937 as a mutual insurance company because cooperative practice was prohibited by Minnesota law, Group Health (HealthPartners' key predecessor) and its founders initially operated various "interim" organizations, such as a credit union and an advocacy group. When cooperative medicine became legal in 1955, Group Health organized first as a primary care health clinic (lasting less than 2 years) and then as a multispecialty clinic. Although legal, the clinic and its philosophy were fiercely rejected by the medical establishment, and Group Health found it necessary to continue its advocacy role to acquire acceptance from physicians, hospitals, and the public.

Once established, Group Health focused on internal growth by expanding its multispecialty clinics until 1993. Throughout the 1970s and 1980s, Group Health grew geographically by opening suburban clinics offering the same services as its main St. Paul clinic. With its expertise as an early health maintenance organization, Group Health became heavily involved with HMOs as a provider and consultant after passage of the HMO Act of 1973 and Minnesota's earlier similar legislation. Group Health branched into an integrated service network (ISN) in 1993 when it consolidated its clinics and health plans, merged with Ramsey Hospital in St. Paul, and changed its name to Health-Partners.

HealthPartners' managerial lineage mirrors its organizational lineage. With roots deep in the co-operative movement, Group Health's first leaders were cooperative and union activists and ideologues. As Group Health grew, disagreements among colleagues created tensions that led to the hiring of a new executive from New York, experienced in running a large insurance plan there. After his 22-year tenure, Group Health brought in leaders with tough financial and budgeting controls to pull the organization out of fiscal crisis. Although lasting only 4 years, this branch returned Group Health to financial health and set the stage for more market-oriented leadership. George Halvorson, with strong credentials in marketing, assumed the CEO role in 1986 and transformed Group Health into an integrated organization in the 1990s. Halvorson was selected and featured as the "CEO of the Year" by *Minnesota Business Monthly* in 1994.

HealthSystem Minnesota's Lineages

HealthSystem Minnesota's organizational lineage, shown in Figure 11.6, tracks two similar multispecialty physician clinics. HealthSystem Minnesota's two clinics were created and managed by their physicians. The Nicollet Clinic was founded in 1921 as a multispecialty clinic and merged in 1983 with the St. Louis Park Medical Center, founded in 1951. Both clinics initially focused on providing care in a clinical setting, though they had different arrangements with hospital and prepaid health plans prior to their merger. In 1960, legal issues created the need to change the St. Louis Park Medical Center's governance structure from a partnership to a trust/holding company structure. As part of this new organization, an important research and education foundation was established. Bastien (1989) studied the 1983 merger and reported that it was a particularly difficult and painful endeavor for both clinics, as they had numerous duplicate, rather than complementary, services and both targeted Minneapolis' western suburbs. HealthSystem Minnesota was created in 1992 with the announcement of a merger between the Park-Nicollet Medical Center and Methodist Hospital.[7] Because the multispecialty clinic and hospital have limited redundant services, the merger is reported to have progressed with less difficulties than the original merger of the two clinics.

Both the Nicollet Clinic and the St. Louis Park Medical Center were founded by physicians as partnerships and were operated as such until the 1960s. As best we can determine, administrative authority rotated among physicians, and major decisions were subject to partners' approval. In 1960, a trust structure was set up that mandated tighter controls and a more businesslike manager to oversee the clinics' operations. As competition continued to erode operating margins, the Nicollet/St. Louis Park merger in 1983 resulted in a clear move toward empowering trained health care administrators as organizational managers. HealthSystem Minnesota's current CEO, Dr. James Reinertsen, represents the emergence of a new managerial branch defined by the physician-manager.

Part IV: Analysis of the Genealogies

Several evolutionary patterns emerge from the descriptions of how organizational and managerial lineages evolved, leading us to the following inductive propositions about evolution within a nested hierarchy. We emphasize again, however, that these propositions represent inductions based on the genealogies of four Twin Cities health care organizations and are *not* empirically tested here; they remain to be tested elsewhere. Nevertheless, they illustrate some new insights and implications generated by examining organizational evolution within a nested hierarchy.

1. Several equally viable paths of evolution are possible for organizations facing the same population environment. Thus, there is equifinality in evolution.
2. The longer organizational branches persist, the more they change. Branch persistence increases with adaptations (anagenesis) and decreases with inertia.
3. Resource scarcity tightens the relationships between levels and increases the explanatory power of the nested evolutionary model.
4. Branching in organizational forms (cladogenesis) occurs through two interacting cycles: (a) a hierarchical cycle of positive and negative feedback

loops between levels, and (b) a temporal cycle of divergent and convergent branching within lineages.

1. Equally Viable Paths of Organizational Evolution

Although founded at different times and with different structural foundations, each of the four organizations evolved into an ISN (integrated service network) organization, consisting of hospitals, physician practices, health care financing, and allied health services. The four organizational lineages show quite different progressions in which the basic ISN components were developed or acquired.

- Allina began as both religious and philanthropic hospitals, then changed into a multihospital system by affiliating and acquiring hospitals and systems, which, in turn, acquired physician practices to obtain steady referrals, finally merging with an insurance plan to become an ISN.
- Fairview began as a Lutheran hospital and internally developed a multihospital system by building hospitals at satellite sites, while managing them together. With other systems and clinics, Fairview established a prepaid plan, eventually assuming full ownership of it. Finally, it affiliated with independent clinics to secure patient referrals and became an ISN.
- HealthPartners was based in a cooperative ideology. It was founded as a mutual insurance company, branched out as a cooperative group practice when state law changed to permit cooperative medicine, and operated as a multispecialty clinic and HMO until it acquired a major hospital and consolidated all its branches into an ISN.
- HealthSystem Minnesota's lineage traces the merger of two multispecialty clinics, one of which operated a hospital and both of which had prepaid health plans, also merged. Prior to and following the merger, the organization operated similarly, opening clinics throughout Minneapolis's growing western suburbs and extensively referring patients to a large nearby hospital, which eventually was acquired, forming an ISN.

If we adopt the common evolutionary view that persistent survival is a measure of fitness, then all four lineages approximate the same level of fitness because each has survived under an almost identical set of changing environmental conditions, suggesting equifinality. *Equifinality* means that there are several equally plausible paths of organizational evolution under the same environmental conditions, leading us to the first inductive proposition.

> *Proposition 1:* There are multiple equally successful paths of evolution for organizations facing the same community environment.

It is important to distinguish *path* from *outcome* of an evolutionary process. The literature to date has focused on outcomes and the proposition that organizations exposed to similar environmental pressures and conditions must adopt similar structural forms if they are to survive in the long run (Carroll & Hannan, 1995; Hannan & Freeman, 1989). This proposition focuses on the evolutionary path. The outcome prediction is based on an assumption that the environment strongly influences the course of evolution. By tracing an organizational genealogy, however, this study shows that evolutionary paths of the four organizations were substantially different. Thus, although the evolutionary outcomes (the ISNs) were identical, the paths were quite different, even though the environment was the same. At a general level, we saw variations in types of systems (hospital based vs. clinic based) and predominant mode of growth (internal vs. external). Clearly, the four organizations evolved in significantly different ways.

Although identical environmental forces may explain why the four organizations evolved into a particular form, they do not explain why the organizations followed such different evolutionary paths. We propose that forces at other levels of the nested hierarchy may explain these differences. One plausible explanation may be the persistence of imprinting effects at organizational founding. Another explanation may be the influence of managerial interventions at the microlevel of the nested hierarchy. These alternative explanations (examined below) are consistent with the assumption that selection and adaptation processes can work simultaneously and differently between levels in a nested hierarchy.

2. Persistence and Adaptation of Founding Organizational Branches

The darker lines, one in each of Figures 11.3 through 11.6, indicate that each organization, at its founding, was imprinted with a unique form reflecting its founders' strategies and values. Without exception, the core branch persisted despite numerous adaptations that merely extended duration (fitness) of the form. Adaptations often included internal growth, such as expansions, as well as external growth, as in the case of affiliations, mergers, and acquisitions.[8] The remarkable persistence of these core organizational branches provides evidence both for imprinting effects of organizational founders *and* for *anagenesis*, defined as adaptive changes within branches over time (McKelvey, 1982).

As an example, the hospital of 1859 bears little resemblance to the hospital of 1995, yet most would recognize both as hospitals. The hospital form of organization has evolved through numerous adaptive changes, accumulating over time to produce unforeseen metamorphic changes. The institution, however, has remained relatively intact. Sarah Knight, a devout Methodist and founder of Asbury Hospital in 1892, never could have foreseen how her hospital founded "to serve the poverty stricken" would transform into a world-class tertiary hospital, renamed Methodist Hospital, added into a multihospital system in 1983, only to be acquired in 1993 as part of HealthSystem Minnesota. Sarah Knight probably would roll in her grave at what has happened to her hospital (she died in 1928). Such observations suggest the following proposition:

> *Proposition 2:* The longer organizational branches persist, the more adaptive they are, and the more they change from their original forms.

This proposition calls into question the assumption that persistence is an indicator of organizational inertia; it may be better viewed as an indicator of adaptive survival. At issue here is the question of whether a founding form is imprinted at birth, remaining relatively unchanged over time because of inertial forces (as population ecology posits), or whether it adapts and becomes isomorphic with changing institutional norms (as institutional and adaptation theories posit).

In his seminal analysis of organizational foundings, Stinchcombe (1965) suggested that new organizational forms emerge from new branches, and that branches, once formed, tend to persist relatively unchanged. Aldrich (1979) built on this by arguing that natural selection operates freely while various institutionalized traditions, vested interests, and competencies serve as powerful inertial forces that prevent change and permanently imprint the founding form onto the organization. If this is true, then the variety of organizational branches observed at any given time reflects variations in founding conditions, with some branches endowed with survival advantages (Brittain & Freeman, 1980).

Organizational adaptation theorists assume that organizations are malleable institutions with strategic directions set and changed by managers, arguing that organizational survival or effectiveness requires that structural forms match environmental demands (Lawrence & Lorsch, 1967; Thompson, 1967). Institutional theorists relaxed the strategic intention component of this argument by recognizing society's convergent institutional forces that compel organizations to become more isomorphic (i.e., similar) if they are to be considered legitimate by key stakeholders, such as employees, customers, creditors, and regulators (Barley & Tolbert, 1995; Scott, 1995). If this view is true, then the organizational branches that one observes at any given time will be those that have survived the fitness criteria of an economic and institutional environment.

The persistence of founding branches in the lineages of our organizations suggests that both perspectives are partly right and partly wrong. Figures 11.3 through 11.6 show that core founding branches have persisted in some commonly recognized form over many years. We argue here, however, that persistence does not indicate inertia. On the contrary, branch persistence was possible only with numerous adaptation events that changed the branch's form and allowed it to coevolve with other branches and lineages in the nested hierarchy. The data provide ample evidence that adaptation and

change by anagenesis is a major part of the explanation of how and why these organizations evolved as they did. Adaptation theorists have largely ignored the founding forms of organizational branches because the theory generally treats history as immaterial to effectiveness. History clearly matters, however, if one is to know what kinds of past investments, practices, and experiences facilitate and inhibit an organization's particular abilities to acquire necessary competencies and technologies for future competitive advantage.

3. The Moderating Influence of Environmental Resource Scarcity

The Twin Cites' health care industry evolved over a 140-year period, the first century of which can be characterized as a benign environment with an abundant and growing demand for health services and almost no competition among providers. That situation changed dramatically around the early 1960s, as decreases in urban population, escalating health care costs, and an increasing number of legislative efforts at health care reform all signaled tighter competition for available health resources in the Twin Cities. These historical conditions provided the opportunity to look for different statistical relationships among the three lineages in the nested hierarchy (management, organization, and industry) during the abundant and scarce resource periods.

Table 11.1 shows concurrent and lagged correlations between yearly aggregations of events in industry, management, organizational branching, and adaptation for the periods of resource abundance (1859-1962) and resource scarcity (1963-1994). The break point, 1963, was selected based on qualitative analysis of industry and demographic conditions, as is reported in more detail in Grazman and Van de Ven (1995). Concurrent correlations between events at the industry level and both managerial and organizational level events are larger during the scarce period than they are during the benign period, though they lack statistical significance. Specifically, when comparing the abundant and scarce periods, industry events correlate more strongly with managerial events ($r = .11$ vs. $r = .25$), organizational branching events ($r = .16$

TABLE 11.1 Concurrent and Lagged Correlations Among Events at Nested Levels During Abundant Period (1859-1962) and Resource Scarce Period (1963-1995)

	Industry/Community Events (t)		Management Events (t)		Organizational Branching Events (t)		Organizational Adaptation Events (t)	
	Abundant Period	Scarce Period	Abundant Period	Scarce Period	Abundant Period	Scarce Period	Abundant Period	Scarce Period
Concurrent correlations								
Industry/community (*t*)	1.00	1.00						
Management (*t*)	.11	.25	1.00	1.00				
Organizational branching (*t*)	.16	.59**	.14	.18	1.00	1.00		
Organizational adaptation (*t*)	.00	.21	.43**	.37*	.21*	.20	1.00	1.00
Lagged correlations								
Industry/community (*t* – 1)	.14	.08	.14	–.16	.14	.29	.12	–.30*
Management (*t* – 1)	.00	.04	.32**	–.15	.13	.37*	.20*	.18
Organizational branching (*t* – 1)	–.11	.03	.10	–.01	.31**	.34*	.28**	.01
Organizational adaptation (*t* – 1)	–.01	.04	.14	–.19	.25**	–.06	.06	.19

*p < .05; **p < .01 (two-tailed significant correlations).

vs. $r = .59$), and organizational adaptation events ($r = .00$ vs. $r = .21$). Only slight changes were observed for correlations between managerial and organizational branching and adaptation events in the two resource periods. These initial patterns suggest to us that industry level events become more tightly related to or coupled with managerial and organizational events under conditions of environmental resource scarcity.

Table 11.1 also shows that significant positive lagged correlations between organizational branching and adaptation events during the abundant period ($r = .25$ and .28, respectively) disappear entirely during the scarce period ($r = -.06$ and .01). During the scarce resource period, lagged management events become significant and positively correlated with subsequent organizational branching events ($r = .37$, $p < .05$), whereas their relation during the benign period ($r = .13$) was insignificant. Lagged industry events switch sign (from $r = +.12$ to $r = -.30$) and become strongly negatively correlated with organizational adaptation events in the next year. Finally, although not statistically significant, during the abundant period, prior industry-level events were positively correlated with subsequent managerial events ($r = +.14$), but during the resource-scarce period, this

relationship reversed direction ($r = -.16$). Although not conclusive, these correlations do suggest that organizational branching and adaptation events were most strongly associated with prior similar events under abundant conditions, and these endogenous relationships dwindled as industry and managerial relationships emerged to exert both positive and negative effects on branching and adaptation under scarce resource conditions.

To explore these correlations further, we conducted two time-series regression analyses, separating the abundant and scarce periods. We kept this exploratory analysis as simple as possible by examining two equations that predict branching or adaptation events as a function of (a) prior changes in institutional industry arrangements, (b) changes in top management succession and strategies in the previous year, and (c) prior branching and adaptation events.

Results of these regression analyses[9] appear in Table 11.2. For each dependent variable, the table shows the regression coefficient and its significance for each lagged independent variable in the rows, as well as the adjusted R^2 for the overall equation. Statistically significant results ($p < .05$) are presented in Figure 11.7. As the diagrams in Figure 11.7 vividly portray, the only significant

TABLE 11.2 Beta Estimates From Time Series Regressions (AR1) on Branching and Adaptation Events in Organizational Lineages During Abundant and Scarce Environmental Periods

| Independent Variables | Abundant Period (1859-1962) | | Scarce Period (1963-1995) | |
	Organizational Adaptation	Organizational Branching	Organizational Adaptation	Organizational Branching
Constant	.14*	.06	1.82**	1.58*
Top management events $(t-1)$	.11	−.02	.87	1.82**
Industry events $(t-1)$	.08	.16	−.62**	−.05
Organizational adaptation events $(t-1)$	.29**	.51**	.27	.17
Organizational branching events $(t-1)$	.33**	.19*	.05	−.24
Rho	−.47**	−.33*	.30	.28
Adjusted R^2	.13	.13	.18	.14
N (number of years)	104	104	31	31

*$p < .05$; **$p < .01$.

Illustration of Results During Abundant Environmental Period (1859-1962)　　　Illustration of Results During Scarce Environmental Period (1963-1995)

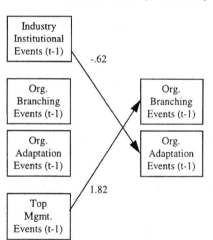

Figure 11.7. Beta Estimates From Time Series Regressions

predictors of branching and adaptation during the benign environmental period are prior branching and adaptation events occurring at the same level. Neither industry or top management events appear to statistically influence organizational changes during this period. When conditions shift to resource scarcity, however, the diagrams show that the previously significant path-dependent relationships among branching and adaptation events vanish, as industry events become a significant negative predictor of subsequent adaptation events and as top management events become the only significant positive predictor of subsequent branching events.

Overall, these exploratory findings indicate that interlevel evolutionary processes in a nested hierarchy require some element of resource scarcity to operate. Specifically, these findings suggest two propositions on the moderating effects of resource scarcity on branching and adaptation.

Proposition 3: The strength of relationships between management, organization, and industry/ community levels in a nested hierarchy increases under conditions of resource scarcity.

Proposition 4: Positive and negative feedback loops between levels, triggered by shifts in resource scarcity, can both promote and constrain branching and adaptation events in organizational lineages.

Examination of the genealogies themselves provides some further insights into these propositions. We found numerous instances where events taking place at one level had an immediate and direct effect on those taking place at other levels, particularly during the period of resource scarcity. For example, the passage of MinnesotaCare legislation in the early 1990s was itself a product of intralevel evolution as it reflected outcomes of numerous prior industry and institutional events aimed at reforming Minnesota's health system. When resources grew tighter, higher-level selection led to adjustments by lower-level entities (i.e., provider organizations) to preserve their own fitness. Organizations were forced to innovate to balance patient needs with newly imposed regulations.

The convergence of different lineages into an almost identical form shaped by higher-level constraints is another indicator of tighter interlevel connectedness under scarce conditions. In the case of managerial lineages, we currently find almost identical branches dominating the four organizations today: professional health administrators with some movement toward physician-administrators. Although each organization was led initially by *very* different types of managers (cooperativists, physicians, philanthropists, religious leaders), these branches persisted, relatively unchanged, throughout most of the benign period. Coinciding with increased competition for resources during the early 1960's, however, previously distinct managerial lineages converged and became more homogenous as the skills that health administrators (and increasingly, physician-managers) possessed grew to be the minimum skills leaders needed to operate effectively in the industry.

Lower-level arrangements may also constrain higher-level speciation processes in a nested hierarchy. As one Minnesota legislator described, health reform choices were directly limited by existing organizational arrangements in the state. Instead of considering all options, legislators were bound by organizational interests already in place if they wanted to control health care costs and increase access. Intentionally designed or not, industry-level evolution was constrained by lower-level organizational arrangements.

Resource scarcity also appears to increase coevolution among competing organizations. As George Halvorson, HealthPartners' CEO, commented at a 1995 American Hospital Association conference, HealthPartners' strategy of building informal alliances with physician groups was severely constrained by the lack of available independent groups caused by Allina's aggressive strategy of purchasing them first. The interconnectedness of the Allina and HealthPartners strategies, as one example, has tightened significantly as resources decrease and competition increases. Qualitative analysis of all four organizations' strategies over the last two decades shows numerous cases of coevolution as each organization is required to shape and reshape its strategy in relation to its closest competitors. The foregoing evidence suggests that resource scarcity tightens relationships between levels and can trigger both positive and negative interactions between levels. According to Gould (1982a), these interactions may serve to regulate the rates of change within each level of the nested hierarchy to reasonable bounds.

4. Cycles of Divergent and Convergent Organizational Branching

In addition to positive and negative interactions between levels, we also observed cycles of divergent and convergent branches in the lineages of the four organizations. Figures 11.3 through 11.6

showed that while changes in organization oc- curred incrementally, a majority of the major branching events occurred in two major waves, one in the 1960s and one in the 1990s. We already have argued that the early 1960s marked a transition point where resources became relatively scarce. There is some evidence that the 1990s are marking the beginning of a new phase, as health care orga- nizations report record levels of operating sur- pluses. If this assumption is correct, and we are moving into a new industry phase (as many be- lieve), this temporal coincidence suggests that shifting resource conditions may be influencing this branching cycle, although other factors, such as technological innovations and institutional re- forms, could be triggering the cycle as well.

Structural diversification appears to be the strat- egy that top managers adopted when initial condi- tions of resource scarcity and competition emerged in the 1960s. Figures 11.3 through 11.6 show that near the 1960s, the organizational lineages become more complex as branches diverged to reflect mul- tispecialty clinics, multihospital systems, and more prepaid health plans. For example, multihospital systems appeared in Allina and Fairview within 1 year of another (1965). Most of these multiple parallel branches remained intact until the 1990s.

Structural consolidation, on the other hand, ap- pears to be the dominant 1990s strategy as a way to protect organizations from competitive forces in the Twin Cities' health care industry. Figures 11.3- 11.6 show that during the 1990s, the multiple par- allel branches in the lineages of the organizations converge toward a common ISN form of structure. Convergence is occurring through vertical hierar- chical integration (as emphasized by Allina and HealthSystem Minnesota), as well as by estab- lishing long-term relational contracts between hos- pitals, clinics, and health plans (as in the cases of Fairview and HealthPartners).

Going farther back in time, we see a similar (though less dramatic) transition period in the 1930s coinciding with the Great Depression. As physicians and hospitals experienced financial dif- ficulties because many Americans were unable to obtain health care or pay their bills, nonphysician providers formed a variety of prepaid health plans and undertook lobbying efforts in 1935 to allow for

cooperative medicine and increased diffusion of the prepaid health plans. The opposing lobbying efforts of medical societies fueled a 20-year debate and constrained passage of state law until 1955, with terms and options that constrained health providers and insurers. These institutional con- straints, in turn, led to consolidations and elimina- tion of some existing health plans; that is, another historical example of divergent and convergent evolution of organizational lineages.

These historical examples of cycles of conver- gent and divergent branching in organizational lineages generalize into the following inductive proposition:

> *Proposition 5:* Periods of environmental scarcity promote temporal cycles of divergent and conver- gent branching in organizational forms.

As environmental resources decline, organiza- tions left with slack internal resources are moti- vated to respond to changing conditions by devel- oping and experimenting with alternative organizational arrangements, leading to divergent branching. As organizational slack depletes over time, depending on the degree and duration of environmental scarcity, there is another shift to- ward convergence in the branching of organiza- tional forms as each is forced, once again, to look outward for alternative sources of environmental resources.

Part V: Conclusion

This study explored how new organizational structures emerge and evolve in a lineage from ancestral forms by the crossing and joining of existing organizational units, resources, and com- petencies to create new generations of organiza- tional forms for the case of the Twin Cities' health care community. We adopted a framework that views organizations as evolving systems nested in other evolving systems at higher (industry or com- munity) and lower (individual top managers) levels of analysis. The framework focuses on how pro- cesses of adaptation and selection operate to direct and constrain evolution in this nested hierarchy of managers within organizations within an industry.

Adopting a Mendelian genetics approach to evolution, we introduced a new methodology for examining the lineage of organizational forms across generations and focused on the origins and ascent of these forms through the recombination of earlier forms. We empirically grounded the framework by constructing genealogies from historical change events in management, organization, and industry arrangements for four major health care delivery organizations that cooperate and compete in the Minneapolis-St. Paul metropolitan areas. Our analysis of evolution within a nested hierarchy found an innovative and systematic way to study how and why organizations within an industry emerged and changed into their present forms.

Our findings motivate new insights on management adaptation and environmental selection perspectives for explaining how and why organizations evolve over their histories, including the inductive propositions that

1. There are equally viable paths of evolution for organizations facing the same environment,
2. The longer organizational forms persist, the more they change,
3. Environmental resource scarcity tightens relationships between levels and increases the relevance of a nested evolutionary model, and
4. Evolutionary change may be explained through a hierarchical cycle of positive and negative feedback loops between levels and a temporal cycle of divergent and convergent branching within organizational lineages over time.

Without question, these inductive inferences require much further research and testing because they are limited to this particular genealogical study and provided only mixed results. If future research substantiates our findings elsewhere, however, it could suggest some new practical roles for organizational managers. We found that organizational evolutionary paths are influenced by imprinting founding effects *and* by strategic managerial actions. Analogous to the Mendelian task performed by plant and animal breeders, the manager's central role might become one of creating

synergy or positive heterosis in the organization's pedigree of structural forms by selecting and recombining existing units and resources in novel ways to produce new generations of organizational forms with desired traits. Fitness, measured by branch persistence, uses survival as a minimal satisficing criterion of performance. More discriminating measures of evolutionary performance are necessary to study and differentiate superior and inferior organizational lineages. Meyer and Zucker's (1989) set of "permanently failing organizations" represents inferior lineages of organizational forms that continue to survive and reproduce.

In addition to "organizational genetic engineering," this research emphasizes the importance of managerial stewardship. Stewardship requires understanding the pedigree of an organization's culture, structure, and competencies in making and implementing subsequent changes in organizational designs. The good steward optimizes and advances the organization's inheritance; the bad steward does not understand this genealogy and fritters it away through deleterious recombinations and mergers of organizational units. Understanding the roles of organizational breeding and stewardship requires much greater historical knowledge of an organization's lineage and of its evolutionary trajectory than is reflected in strategic management theory and practice. It also emphasizes the role of environment and management practices in achieving the potential performance in a given generation of organizational forms.

Notes

1. Van de Ven and Poole (1995) point out that another distinction often made between social evolutionary theories is whether change proceeds gradually and incrementally or rapidly and abruptly. Social Darwinian theorists emphasize a continuous and gradual process of evolution. In *The Origin of Species*, Darwin (1936) wrote, "as natural selection acts solely by accumulating slight, successive, favourable variations, it can produce no great or sudden modifications; it can act only by short and slow steps" (p. 361). Other evolutionists posit a saltational theory of evolution, such as punctuated equilibrium (Arnold & Fristrup, 1982; Gould & Eldredge, 1977), which Tushman and Romanelli (1985) and Gersick (1991) introduced to the management literature. As we discuss in Part IV, whether

evolutionary change proceeds at gradual versus saltational rates is an empirical matter, for the rate of change does not fundamentally alter the theory of evolution—at least as it has been adopted by organization and management scholars.

2. Traditionally, evolution focused on intergenerational processes of inheritance, whereas development dealt with intragenerational processes of growth and change within the life span of an entity. The Lamarckian view that heritable traits can be acquired within generations collapses this distinction between evolution and development. Although this shifts the problem from intergenerational inheritance to intragenerational development, it does not eliminate the problem of understanding how organizational traits or competencies are developmentally acquired within a generation or are transmitted and ascend from one generation to the next.

3. McKelvey (1982) applies the concepts of branching and persistence for studying evolution in organizational lineages. In chapter 9, he points out that in biology the branching kind of evolution is called *cladogenesis*, whereas persistent adaptation and change in a lineage with no branching is known as *anagenesis*.

4. We do not make the claim that these core features of an organizational form constitute an analogue to genes or DNA material that are transmitted from generation to generation in biological evolution. The vehicle for transmitting or inheriting traits from one organizational branch or generation to the next remains unknown, although Baum and Singh (1994) have made constructive advances in defining the core elements of a genealogical hierarchy. Instead, we only claim that changes in these observable core features represent indicators of the emergence of a new organizational form or branch.

5. The development of an explanatory role for hierarchical structure in evolutionary theory represents a vibrant vein of research in evolutionary biology. See, for example, Arnold and Fristrup (1982), Buss (1987), Gould (1982a, 1982b), and Gould and Eldredge (1977).

6. We use two conventions in these diagrams to display qualitative information about organization-level events. First, novel events representing new subbranches are noted by markings above the branch line, whereas adaptation events appear below the branch line. Thus, we can more easily interpret patterns within and across systems. Second, we identified core branches, marked by a slightly heavier line, as the branch most directly reflecting organizational heritage and most central to its historical character.

7. Methodist Hospital had been affiliated with the HealthOne system but ceded from it when it merged with HealthSpan, Allina's predecessor. The historical record includes several other examples of migrations in ownership or affiliations of entities between predecessors of the four major systems.

8. Although population ecologists count mergers or acquisitions as incidences of organizational death, our genealogies show that these acts often were rooted in a desire to either adapt and extend a branch or to create a novel branch.

9. Independent variables were lagged one year $(t-1)$ to predict the dependent variable in year t. The lagged dependent variable is used as an independent variable in each equation to capture path-dependent effects. Event data was aggregated into fixed yearly intervals, because we assumed that interval to be most meaningful for historical data. To correct for serial correlation, we used an AR1 (autoregressive, lagged one time period) procedure.

References

Aldrich, H. (1979). *Organizations and environments.* Englewood Cliffs, NJ: Prentice Hall.

Anderson, P., & Tushman, M. L. (1990). Technological discontinuities and dominant designs: A cyclical model of technological change. *Administrative Science Quarterly, 35*(4), 604-633.

Arnold, A. J., & Fristrup, K. (1982). The theory of evolution by natural selection: A hierarchical expansion. *Paleobiology, 8*(2), 113-129.

Arthur, W. B. (1989). Competing technologies, increasing returns, and lock-in by historical events. *The Economic Journal, 99*, 116-131.

Astley, W. G. (1985). The two ecologies: Population and community perspectives on organizational evolution. *Administrative Science Quarterly, 30*, 224-241.

Astley, W. G., & Van de Ven, A. H. (1983). Central perspectives and debates in organization theory. *Administrative Science Quarterly, 28*, 245-273.

Barley, S. R., & Tolbert, P. S. (1995). *Institutionalization and structuration: Studying the links between institutions and actions.* Unpublished manuscript, Stanford University and Cornell University.

Barnett, W. P., & Carroll, G. R. (1995). Modeling internal organizational change. *Annual Review of Sociology, 21*, 217-236.

Barney, J. B., & Ouchi, W. B. (Eds.). (1986). *Organizational economics.* San Francisco: Jossey-Bass.

Bastien, D. T. (1989). Communication, conflict and learning in mergers and acquisitions. In A. H. Van de Ven, H. L. Angle, & M. S. Poole (Eds.), *Research on the management of innovation: The Minnesota studies* (pp. 367-396). New York: Ballinger/Harper & Row.

Baum, J.A.C. (1996). Organizational ecology. In S. R. Clegg, C. Hardy, & W. Nord (Eds.), *Handbook of organization studies* (pp. 77-114). Thousand Oaks, CA: Sage.

Baum, J.A.C, & Singh, J. V. (1994). Organizational hierarchies and evolutionary processes: Some reflections on a theory of organizational evolution. In J.A.C. Baum & J. V. Singh (Eds.), *Evolutionary dynamics of organizations* (pp. 3-20). New York: Oxford University Press.

Boyd, R., & Richerson, P. J. (1985). *Culture and the evolutionary process.* Chicago: University of Chicago Press.

Brittain, J. W., & Freeman, J. H. (1980). Organizational proliferation and density dependent selection. In J. R. Kimberly & R. H. Miles (Eds.), *The organizational life cycle* (pp. 291-338). San Francisco: Jossey-Bass.

Burgelman, R. A. (1991). Intraorganizational ecology of strategy making and organizational adaptation: Theory and field research. *Organization Science, 2*(3), 239-262.

Buss, L. W. (1987). *The evolution of individuality.* Princeton, NJ: Princeton University Press.

Campbell, D. T. (1969). Variation and selective retention in socio-cultural evolution. *General Systems, 16,* 69-85.

Campbell, D. T. (1974). Evolutionary epistemology. In P. A. Schilpp (Ed.), *The philosophy of Karl Popper* (pp. 413-463). La Salle, IL: Open Court.

Campbell, D. T. (1990). Levels of organization, downward causation and the selection-theory approach to evolutionary epistemology. In G. Greenberg & E. Tobach (Eds.), *Theories of the evolution of knowing* (pp. 1-17). Hillsdale, NJ: Lawrence Erlbaum.

Carroll, G. R., & Hannan, M. T. (1989). Density dependence in the evolution of populations of newspaper organizations. *American Sociological Review, 54,* 524-541.

Carroll, G. R., & Hannan, M. T. (Eds.). (1995). *Organizations in industry: Strategy, structure and solution.* New York: Oxford University Press.

Darwin, C. A. (1936). *The origin of species.* New York: Modern Library.

Gersick, C. J. (1991). Revolutionary change theories: A multilevel exploration of the punctuated equilibrium paradigm. *The Academy of Management Review, 16*(1), 10-36.

Gould, S. J. (1982a). Darwinism and the expansion of evolutionary theory. *Science, 216,* 380-387.

Gould, S. J. (1982b, April 15). Punctuated equilibrium—A different way of seeing. *New Scientist,* pp. 137-141.

Gould, S. J. (1989). Punctuated equilibrium in fact and theory. *Journal of Social and Biological Structures, 12,* 117-136.

Gould, S. J., & Eldredge, N. (1977). Punctuated equilibria: The tempo and model of evolution reconsidered. *Paleobiology, 3,* 115-151.

Grazman, D. N., & Van de Ven, A. H. (1995). *Different times and different places: The role of scarcity in organizational selection and adaptation.* Unpublished manuscript, Strategic Management Research Center, University of Minnesota, Minneapolis.

Halvorson, G. C. (1993). *Strong medicine.* New York: Random House.

Hannan, M. T., Carroll, G. R., Dundon, E. A., & Torres, J. C. (1995). Organizational evolution in a multinational context: Entries of automobile manufacturers in Belgium, Britain, France, Germany, and Italy. *American Sociological Review, 60*(4), 509-528.

Hannan, M. T., & Freeman, J. (1977). The population ecology of organizations. *American Journal of Sociology, 82,* 929-964.

Hannan, M. T., & Freeman, J. (1984). Structural inertia and organizational change. *American Sociological Review, 49,* 149-164.

Hannan, M. T., & Freeman, J. (1989). *Organizational ecology.* Cambridge, MA: Harvard University Press.

Kimberly, J. R., & Bouchikhi, H. (1995). The dynamics of organizational development and change: How the past shapes the present and constrains the future. *Organization Science, 6*(1), 9-18.

Lant, T. K., & Mezias, S. J. (1992). An organizational learning model of convergence and reorientation. *Organization Science, 3,* 47-71.

Lawrence, P. R., & Lorsch, J. W. (1967). Differentiation and integration in complex organizations. *Administrative Science Quarterly, 12*(1), 1-47.

March, J. G. (1991). Exploration and exploitation in organizational learning. *Organization Science, 2*(1), 71-87.

McKelvey, B. (1982). *Organizational systematics: Taxonomy, evolution, classification.* Berkeley: University of California Press.

Meyer, A. D., Brooks, G. R., & Goes, J. B. (1990). Environmental jolts and industry revolutions: Organizational responses to discontinuous change. *Strategic Management Journal, 11*(Summer), 93-110.

Meyer, M. W., & Zucker, L. G. (1989). *Permanently failing organizations.* Newbury Park, CA: Sage.

Miner, A. S. (1994). Seeking adaptive advantage: Evolutionary theory and managerial action. In J.A.C. Baum & J. V. Singh (Eds.), *Evolutionary dynamics of organizations* (pp. 76-89). New York: Oxford University Press.

Nelson, R. R., & Winter, S. G. (1982). *An evolutionary theory of economic change.* Cambridge, MA: Harvard University Press.

Rogers, E. (1983). *Diffusion of innovations* (3rd ed.). New York: Free Press.

Scott, W. R. (1995). *Institutions and organizations.* Thousand Oaks, CA: Sage.

Singh, J. V., & Lumsden, C. J. (1990). Theory and research in organizational ecology. *Annual Review of Sociology, 16,* 161-195.

Starr, P. (1982). *The social transformation of American medicine: The rise of a sovereign profession and the making of a vast industry.* Cambridge, MA: Basic Books.

Stinchcombe, A. L. (1965). Social structure and organizations. In J. G. March (Ed.), *Handbook of organizations* (pp. 142-193). Chicago: Rand McNally.

Thompson, J. D. (1967). *Organizations in action.* New York: McGraw-Hill.

Tushman, M. E., & Romanelli, E. (1985). Organizational evolution: A metamorphosis model of convergence and reorientation. In B. Staw & L. Cummings (Eds.), *Research in organizational behavior* (Vol. 7, pp. 171-222). Greenwich, CT: JAI.

Van de Ven, A. H. (1986). Central problems in the management of innovation. *Management Science, 32*(5), 590-607.

Van de Ven, A. H., & Poole, M. S. (1990). Methods for studying innovation development in the Minnesota Innovation Research Program. *Organization Science, 1,* 313-335.

Van de Ven, A. H., & Poole, M. S. (1995). Explaining development and change in organizations. *Academy of Management Review, 20*(3), 510-540.

Watzlawik, P., Weakland, J. H., & Fisch, R. (1974). *Change: Principles of problem formulation and problem resolution.* New York: Norton.

Weick, K. E. (1979). *The social psychology of organizing* (2nd ed.). Reading, MA: Addison-Wesley.

Zaltman, G., Duncan, R., & Holbek, J. (1973). *Innovations and organizations.* New York: Wiley.

Part III

Process-Level Analysis and Modeling

Chapter 12

Static & Dynamic Variation and Firm Outcomes

TAMMY L. MADSEN
ELAINE MOSAKOWSKI
SRILATA ZAHEER

A number of authors debate whether differences in firm behavior are driven by macro-evolutionary processes such as the interaction between firms and their external environments (Aldrich & Pfeffer, 1976; Carroll & Hannan, 1989; Hannan & Freeman, 1977, 1984, 1989), or micro-evolutionary processes such as intrafirm evolutionary processes or organizational adaptation (Andrews, 1980; Burgelman, 1991, 1994; Cyert & March, 1963; Lawrence & Lorsch, 1967; Miner, 1994; Pfeffer & Salancik, 1978; Thompson, 1967). Recent research shifts attention away from the micro versus macro debate and focuses instead on the reciprocal interactions across levels of analysis that shape firm strategy and performance (e.g., Henderson & Mitchell, 1997). We extend the existing research by exploring the interaction between firm performance and subsequent variation behavior. Empirical studies rarely make this link, choosing instead to focus on population-level or

macro forces influencing firm change activities and firm evolution.

A central step in understanding firm evolution and the drivers of firm differences involves identifying the foundations upon which distinctive and difficult-to-replicate advantages can be built (Teece & Pisano, 1995). Adopting a hierarchical approach to the study of firm evolution, we view a firm's ability to create (variation), select, and retain knowledge and competencies as crucial components of a firm's dynamic capability and potentially important drivers of firm heterogeneity. Although strategy research has examined firm integration capabilities (retention) (Henderson, 1995; Iansiti & Clark, 1994) and organizational evolution research has investigated firm change behavior (variation) (e.g., Amburgey, Kelly, & Barnett, 1993; Baum, 1990; Delacroix & Swaminathan, 1991; Ginsberg & Baum, 1994; Haveman, 1994; Mitchell, 1989; Singh, House, & Tucker, 1986),

AUTHORS' NOTE: The authors thank Howard Aldrich, Joel Baum, Amy Kenworthy, Bill McKelvey, Peter Roberts, and other participants at the Toronto conference for comments on this research. We also thank Jose De La Torre and the Center for International Business Education and Research, UCLA, for providing funding for a portion of this research. All errors are the responsibility of the authors.

few studies have empirically tested the inter-relationships among intrafirm variation and retention activities and the effects of firm performance on future variation behavior.

Although research suggests that variation, selection, and retention (VSR) linked together in a balanced relationship underlie a firm's adaptive capacity (Burgelman, 1994; Campbell, 1969, 1994; Madsen & McKelvey, 1996), intrafirm VSR activities may not always occur in combination or in a productive combination. Firms differentially invest in the amount of variation, selection, or retention activity they conduct, which results in varied patterns of change behavior. Although each variation or change adopted by the firm might enhance performance, the amount of VSR activity the firm undertakes is what distinguishes the firm from its competitors. For instance, when a variation selected and retained by a firm does not match environmental needs, the firm's likelihood of survival decreases. This does not necessarily mean that the firm will fail, but it does mean that the firm's adaptive capacity becomes crucial for survival. Consequently, how proficiently each component of the VSR process is managed and how effectively links among the VSR processes are managed influence a firm's ability to generate rents (Campbell, 1969, 1994) and sustain firm heterogeneity. Thus, rather than examine the benefits firms accrue from specific variations or the conditions under which intrafirm VSR processes will generate rents for the firm, we explore the drivers of a firm's adaptive capacity.

Organizational evolution research emphasizes that the intrafirm evolutionary process will be effective only when firms engage in a high amount of variation activity and a diverse set of variations (Campbell, 1969, 1991, 1994; McKelvey & Aldrich, 1983). This research directs attention to two conditions necessary for the development of an adaptive capability and two types of variation behavior, *static variation* and *dynamic variation*. Static variation captures the breadth, or amount of heterogeneity, in a particular firm behavior across units of a firm in a cross section of time. Dynamic variation represents the amount of firm change behavior over time. Prior research empirically examines the relationship between dynamic variation

and firm survival (Madsen, Mosakowski, & Zaheer, 1997). This exploratory study flips the focus of attention to the role of static variation in firm evolution and the effects of performance on subsequent static and dynamic variation activity.

We test the coevolution of intrafirm variation and firm outcomes by examining the interaction of firm performance and subsequent static and dynamic variation activity in a longitudinal study of the Foreign Exchange Trading (FX) industry from 1973 to 1993. Examining intrafirm evolutionary activities in the FX industry should provide a robust test of the role of variation in firm evolution because we expect VSR effects to be more prominent in such high-velocity environments. A detailed industry description is included in Appendix A of this chapter.

The results should inform strategy research with a depiction of the interaction between firm change capabilities and prior firm performance, and the interrelationships among firm change and diffusion capabilities. They will also inform organizational evolution research by specifying links between micro and macro processes, such as the interaction between variation at the intrafirm level (e.g., in a unit of the firm) and retention at the firm level. Subsequent sections discuss the coevolution of VSR processes across levels of analysis, explore the role of intrafirm variation in firm evolution, and present hypotheses. We conclude with a discussion of the results and implications of this research for the study of organizational evolution and strategy.

The Coevolution of VSR Processes

Evolutionary processes span multiple levels of analysis (intrafirm, firm, industry population, and community) nested in a hierarchy (Aldrich, 1979; Baum, this volume; Baum & Singh, 1994; Campbell, 1974, 1991, 1994). Traditionally, evolutionary research adopts a firm or population level of analysis, focusing on the death and replacement of firms with regard to the competitive environment. While population selection occurs, its "effects are undermined by organizational selection processes" (Campbell, 1994, p. 24); that is, evolution is driven primarily by the coevolution of multilevel micro and macro VSR processes (Baum & Singh, 1994; McKelvey, 1997). At each level of analysis, variation, selection, and retention activities, coupled together, represent a locomotive for knowledge development or a *Darwin machine* (Plotkin, 1994).[1] These *Darwin machines* operate to optimize firm behavior relative to the competitive context. For instance, to sustain performance in a turbulent environment, firms may change their experience-based knowledge by adopting variations in their blueprints (Hannan & Freeman, 1977), competencies (McKelvey, 1982), or routines (Nelson & Winter, 1982) and diffusing (via retention) these variations across the firm.

Several authors advocate an exploration of the nested evolutionary hierarchy for the study of the drivers of a firm's pattern of behavior or the "natural order" in organizations (Baum & Singh, 1994; Campbell, 1974, 1982, 1994; Lomi & Larsen, this volume; McKelvey, 1997, p. 358). Two critical components of these perspectives include the coevolution of VSR processes within and across levels of analysis, and the link between VSR processes and the context in which they operate. Building on this work, we argue that firm idiosyncrasies stem from the coevolution of VSR processes. How does VSR at one level of analysis, such as the intrafirm level, coevolve or interact with the next higher level in the hierarchy? Variations are segregated out at two levels: (a) intrafirm level—firms develop *variations* from which *managers select*, and (b) firm level—*external forces select* some firms over others based on the variations retained by the firms. Two levels of retention also exist: (a) intrafirm level—variations selected by managers and retained by the firm are *diffused throughout the firm*, and (b) firm level—variations, retained by a firm that is favored by external selection agents, *are diffused throughout the population*. The coevolution of VSR processes illuminates two sets of learning or knowledge-building processes: (a) *intrafirm level:* firms learn from experimentation and the performance of selected variations—trial and error learning and diffusion of experience-based knowledge, and (b) *firm level:* firms learn from other firms operating in the population—diffusion, imitation, or copying of industry best practices or experiences—population learning (Miner & Haun-

schild, 1995). Thus, VSR processes form evolutionary, knowledge-building machines (Campbell, 1969; Plotkin, 1994; Weick, 1979) that interact (intrafirm selection processes are influenced by external selection processes and vice versa), influence change processes, underlie organizational and population-level learning, and shape firm differences. We begin by exploring the role of intrafirm variation in firm evolution.

Intrafirm Variation and Firm Evolution

Variation constitutes an alteration in state, form, or function of the firm. Variations are trial-and-error learning events (Alchian, 1950) that are "blind" as to their adaptive efficacy (Aldrich, 1979; Campbell, 1969, p. 70; Weick, 1979). These events provide the raw material for the trial-and-error process and form the basis for firm learning opportunities (Campbell, 1982). In an uncertain or changing environment, managers do not necessarily know which variations will contribute to long-term firm survival.[2] A critical managerial decision involves determining how much variation activity is necessary to sustain a firm's competitive position in a dynamic environment. Variation activity is driven primarily by firm experimentation and innovation activities (Burgelman, 1991; Miner, 1994); thus, it plays a central role in knowledge creation (Campbell, 1994; Leonard-Barton, 1995; Nonaka & Takeuchi, 1995) and organizational learning (Argyris & Schön, 1978; Nonaka, 1994; Senge, 1990).

Traditionally, empirical studies of intrafirm variation focus on the benefits or hazards of changes in various firm characteristics relative to population evolution, the effects of cumulative change on population dynamics, or the factors influencing firm rates of change (Amburgey et al., 1993; Baum, 1990; Delacroix & Swaminathan, 1991; Ginsberg & Baum, 1994; Haveman, 1994; Mitchell, 1989; Singh et al., 1986). Because of data limitations, longitudinal research often captures only whether or not a change event occurs rather than the amount of firm change behavior pursued (an exception is Madsen et al., 1997). Several qualitative studies of VSR enhance our understanding the role of intrafirm variation in firm evolution (Burgelman, 1991, 1994; Galunic & Eisenhardt, 1996), but few examine the reciprocal relationship between intrafirm variation and firm outcomes.

Furthermore, intrafirm variation activity may occur in various amounts or forms, which present different benefits or hazards for the firm. For example, prior research suggests that high and low amounts of intrafirm *dynamic variation* activity (the amount of change in firm behaviors over time) might be dysfunctional for the firm (Levinthal, 1991; Madsen et al., 1997; March, 1991). Research also often considers different forms of change, such as revolutionary or incremental change (Miller & Friesen, 1980, 1982; Tushman & Romanelli, 1985), but less emphasis is placed on the trade-offs between engaging in multiple heterogeneous experiments simultaneously (static variation in multiple dimensions) versus a set of experiments over time (dynamic variation).

Exploring the Role of Static Variation in Firm Evolution

Static variation provides an indicator of the amount of heterogeneity in a particular firm behavior across the firm at a point in time. Two competing views underscore the importance of static variation in firm evolution. First, the VSR framework implies that the more variable the trials, the greater chance that an advantageous trial will be found (Aldrich & Kenworthy, this volume; Campbell, 1960, 1969, 1991). Thus, increasing the variability or breadth of trials investigated enhances the effectiveness of the VSR process (Campbell, 1960, 1969, 1982) and, in turn, the rate at which firms adjust to the competitive environment. Variability or breadth refers to the different types of variations or trials a firm undertakes in a particular firm behavior or activity. For example, consider two firms searching for an optimal logistics system. Firm A pilot tests multiple variants of the logistic system simultaneously (i.e., static variation in one firm behavior). In contrast, firm B investigates the performance of only one logistics system. According to Campbell's logic, firm A's investment in multiple simultaneous trials or static variation activity will improve the firm's rate of identifying an

optimal solution as well as the firm's chance of finding the best alternative. The alternative view argues that static variation beyond a certain threshold may have adverse implications for firm performance and survival.

Adaptive Static Variation Activity

Static variation may enhance firm performance and survival chances in numerous ways. Research argues that firms competing in turbulent environments may be better off when they engage in multiple changes simultaneously (Brown & Eisenhardt, 1997; D'Aveni, 1994). These multiple simultaneous variations may be necessary for the firm to break out of competency traps or respond rapidly to the environment. For example, static variation may enhance firm survival chances in high-velocity environments such as the FX industry, where firms may experience a limited window of opportunity for adaptation (Tyre & Orlikowski, 1994) and where timing relative to the environment is critical.

Multiple changes might also be more adaptive than partial organizational adjustments due to organizational complexity. To the extent that complementarities exist across the firm, or that the firm is tightly coupled, adopting one trial or partially adjusting to the environment may reduce complementarities across the firm, at least initially (Athey & Stern, 1997; Milgrom & Roberts, 1990, 1995). Barnett and Freeman (1997) suggest that these lost complementarities result in increased costs for the firm in the form of coordination uncertainty. As a result, tightly coupled organizations may be better off when they investigate and adopt multiple changes simultaneously, resulting in an entirely new set of complementarities or a new organizational configuration (Barnett & Freeman, 1997; Henderson & Clark, 1990; Miller & Friesen, 1980, 1982; Tushman & Romanelli, 1985). Increases in static variation might signal a firm's attempt to engage in multiple changes simultaneously so as to adopt a new organizational configuration. Similarly, increases in static variation in multiple behaviors, such as organizational structure and strategy, might illustrate a firm's attempt to engage in multiple heterogeneous changes simultaneously to further promote a new set of complementarities.

High complementarity among the firm's units might also increase the "strength of inertia" within the firm (Hannan & Freeman, 1984). In a dynamic environment, increases in static variation activity may assist tightly coupled firms in breaking from core rigidities and overcoming inertia. Thus, firms may engage in static variation in one or more dimensions of behavior in order to enhance the efficiency of the variation process, respond rapidly to turbulent environmental conditions, adopt a new organizational configuration, or overcome inertia. Increasing static variation might, in turn, increase the firm's rate of adjustment to the environment.

Dysfunctional Static Variation Activity

Although Campbell (1960) emphasizes that a diverse variation portfolio plays a critical role in knowledge generation, a threshold may exist beyond which additional variation diversity is dysfunctional. For example, engaging in multiple experiments simultaneously may increase the complexity of the intrafirm selection process and, in turn, compromise the usefulness of the learning process (Lounamaa & March, 1987). If we consider each variation as a potential learning frontier, then too much static variation, or static variation beyond a certain threshold, may overload the firm's ability to comprehend, interpret, and evaluate all the variations undertaken. Consequently, managers may select variations that satisfice rather than optimize behavior, or select variations that do not match environmental demands. As a result, firms increasing static variation may realize the costs of experimentation without the benefits. Furthermore, learning might be complicated by simultaneous variation activity. Exploring multiple variations simultaneously in order to speed up the learning process may not necessarily culminate in an optimal outcome (Levitt & March, 1988). Rapid change may result in random drift rather than performance enhancement when firms adopt a diverse set of variations prior to fully understanding the environment (Lounamaa & March, 1987). In an uncertain and volatile environment, slow learning may produce more functional results (March, 1991). For instance, a slow learning approach

might allow the firm to achieve variation breadth over a longer period of time and may reduce the complexity of the selection process.

In addition, exploring multiple variations simultaneously at the expense of building on existing know-how may culminate in a resetting of a firm's liability of newness clock, thus exposing firms to the risks associated with young firms (Freeman, Carroll, & Hannan, 1983; Stinchcombe, 1965). Hannan and Freeman (1984) argue that inertia provides an external selection benefit to firms and that increases in organizational variation will decrease firm survival chances. Following structural inertia theory, increasing the breadth of trials in one firm behavior might adversely affect the accountability and reliability of the existing organization and, in turn, increase the likelihood of organizational failure. In a study of the hotel industry, Ingram (1996)[3] examines the extent of heterogeneity among a hotel chain's units within a given year and finds that too much heterogeneity among units of the firm increases firm exit rates. Last, consistency or low variability in behaviors may contribute to higher performance. For instance, additional search and experimentation might be wasteful when several almost optimal variations exist (Bowman, 1963; Makadok & Walker, 1996).

The preceding arguments and findings emphasize that one set of firm capabilities, static variation, plays a prominent role in firm evolution, thus motivating further exploration of the relationship between firm performance and variation activity. Traditionally, research examines the drivers of firm performance, but what induces a firm to increase or decrease intrafirm variation behavior? In the following section, we shift the focus of attention to the interaction between firm performance and subsequent variation behavior in order to enhance our understanding of the coevolution of VSR processes across levels of analysis and across time. We focus on similarities in the relationships between performance and subsequent static and dynamic variation activity. In the spirit of exploratory analysis, we pose two competing hypotheses. One view contends that past success will contribute to a decrease in static and dynamic variation activity. The opposing perspective argues that static and dynamic variation activity increases with past success.

Variation and Firm Performance

Intrafirm VSR constitutes a continuous trial-and-error learning process (Campbell, 1969; Weick, 1979) in which past performance conditions future VSR behavior and the balance achieved in the VSR process. Positive feedback on previously selected variations might result in a decrease in variation behavior and an increase in retention behavior so as to promote firm accountability and reliability (Hannan & Freeman, 1984). Similarly, a number of authors suggest that success may decrease firm incentives for scanning and experimentation (Cyert & March, 1963; March, 1991; Miller, 1994; Miller & Chen, 1994; Milliken & Lant, 1991). Firms will tend to replicate efficient routines or adopt routines that are correlated with past success (Levitt & March, 1988; March, 1991; Miller, 1994; Rumelt, 1984). This replication process operates as a cycle in which the reinforcement of each routine assists in refining the competency, which increases the likelihood of a firm repeating the behavior in the future (Nelson & Winter, 1982). Consequently, past success may drive firms to adjust the balance in the VSR process in favor of building on past experience (retention) versus exploring new alternatives (variation).

Hypothesis 1: Increases in performance will be associated with a subsequent decrease in intrafirm variation activity.

Alternatively, building on past experience by imitating successful outcomes may not always culminate in homogeneity across the units of a firm. Miner and Raghavan (this volume) suggest that *inter*organizational outcome imitation, or "copying practices that have appeared to have good consequences for others," might increase or decrease heterogeneity across a population of firms. Applying this concept at the *intra*organizational level, a bank might identify a successful behavior in one of its trading rooms and copy this behavior across other trading rooms it operates. Several endogenous factors, however, may impede a bank's convergence to a common set of behaviors for its trading rooms. For example, similar to processes at

the interorganizational level, the rules a bank uses in replicating a behavior or practice across its trading rooms may vary, giving rise to different patterns of behavior in each room rather than continuity across rooms. In addition, when causal ambiguity exists as to the effects of a change in behavior on firm outcomes, outcome imitation may result in heterogeneity rather than homogeneity across the units of the firm. It follows that firms that attempt to replicate successful intraorganizational behaviors may foster further heterogeneity across units of the firm. Consequently, static and dynamic variation may increase with past success.

Research also argues that increases in past performance may provide the firm with additional resources to explore new markets and enhance chances of continued success (Mueller, 1977). For example, successful firms may accrue slack resources that can be utilized in a variety of ways (Cyert & March, 1963; Pfeffer & Salancik, 1978; Singh, 1986), such as for innovation or experimentation. Such innovation or experimentation behavior may occur all at once (static variation) or over a period of time (dynamic variation). Although research suggests that experimentation resulting from slack resources may not culminate in a firm abandoning the behaviors that gave rise to the slack initially (Greve, 1998), dynamic environmental conditions might motivate a firm to modify and/or discard its previous behaviors in pursuit of sustaining its competitive position. For example, Greve (1998) finds that changes in market conditions facilitate organizational change activity. Furthermore, Miller (1994) shows that performance is associated with firm search and experimentation behavior and, thus, adaptation and firm evolution.[4] Audretsch (1995) also identifies a positive relationship between performance and subsequent innovation activity for firms operating in turbulent environments. Building on these characterizations, we argue that increases in performance might culminate in an increase in intrafirm static and dynamic variation behavior.

Hypothesis 1A: Increases in performance will be associated with a subsequent increase in intrafirm variation activity.

Data and Research Design

The data were collected from annual publications of the *Foreign Exchange and Bullion Dealers Directory* (Hambros Bank, 1973-1993) and occurred in two phases. Phase 1 involved the documentation of all the market-making trading rooms operating in the FX industry (approximately 26,763 rooms held by more than 1,564 parent banks worldwide) from 1973 to 1993, their parent bank affiliation, the number of traders in each room, the number of hierarchical levels in a room, the trading room location (city and country), and room exit events. The trading rooms were located in 47 countries by 1993, and the parent banks were headquartered in 65 different countries worldwide. Phase 2 data include all the names and positions of the traders operating in the industry during the 21-year period (approximately 150,000 names). The number of names documented per directory year ranges from 2,965 in 1973 to 11,522 in 1993. An algorithm was developed that defines the amount of cumulative experience each trader has in any given year using the Phase 2 data.

Telephone interviews were also conducted with traders in the United States to supplement the archival data. The purpose of the interviews was to understand which features might be critical to trading room operations and performance. All interviews were semistructured, and respondents were asked the same set of questions. Of the 25 interviews conducted, all traders indicated that two dimensions were critical to performance: (a) the experience of traders operating in the trading room and (b) how the room was organized.

The data are left censored: Many rooms existed prior to 1973. We acknowledge that by beginning the observation period in 1973, the risk of introducing errors resulting from left censoring is present (Hannan & Carroll, 1992; Tuma & Hannan, 1984, pp. 128-135). Although data are available prior to 1973, the industry operated under the Bretton Woods Agreement and was drastically different from the industry that emerged following the breakdown of Bretton Woods. Thus, it is believed that 1973 provides an appropriate demarcation in the industry time line to start this analysis.

The sample used in this analysis represents all banks with multiple trading rooms participating in the interbank currency market. In the FX industry, 432 multiunit banks existed from 1973 to 1993. We focus on banks operating multiple trading rooms in order to define the *amount* of variation and retention firms pursue concurrently, and to capture intrafirm diffusion activities.

VSR Variables: Dynamic Variation, Static Variation, and Retention

The central variables in this study derive from the outcomes of intrafirm selection activity. To define the dynamic variation and retention constructs, we classify a room's behavior into three event categories: dynamic variation (DV), retention (RET), or no change (NC). Although the NC construct is not included in the analysis, its incorporation in the research design serves two critical purposes: (a) to capture cases where a dynamic variation event (change) or retention event (diffusion and replication) does not occur, and (b) to provide for three mutually exclusive events. With this design, dynamic variation and retention are not simply opposite constructs, and the operational measures align more sharply with the theoretical definitions.

Based on the trader interviews, this study examines the extent of static variation, dynamic variation, and retention of two key trading room characteristics: (a) the level of hierarchy in the trading room and (b) the total amount of trader experience represented in each room. The following sections define why these characteristics influence room performance and how each room characteristic is measured. Subsequent sections operationalize the bank-level dynamic variation, static variation, and retention measures using these two characteristics.

Room Characteristics

Level of Hierarchy. The level of hierarchy in a trading room equals a count of the number of levels of management within each room and varies from one to six across trading rooms in the sample. The level of hierarchy in a room may directly influence trader profitability and trading room performance. The level of hierarchy constitutes a component of organizational design determining the structure and authority relationships within the trading room. Too many levels of hierarchy might result in high bureaucratic costs (such as costs of coordination) and bureaucratic rigidities (Crozier, 1964; Merton, 1957), in turn directly influencing firm profits. In the FX industry, traders are required to make rapid decisions based on their expertise and "instinctive dealing" sense (Tygier, 1988). Consequently, effective trading requires freedom from constraints. Traders need to be able to make decisions in seconds and have the authority to execute large trades immediately as and when opportunities arise. Multiple levels of hierarchy in a trading room may hinder their ability to do so. Furthermore, although traders have to be subject to oversight, it is particularly important for senior managers to maintain a good sense of what occurs on the trading floor (S. Zaheer, 1992, 1995a, 1995b). Again, multiple levels of hierarchy between senior managers and the traders on the floor can lead to senior managers being too far removed from the floor and consequent lacking in the deep personal knowledge of what goes on at each trading desk that is necessary for effective control. As a result, there is no obvious solution to the problem of how much control and how many levels of hierarchy are appropriate in a trading room. Thus, banks will adopt changes in the room level of hierarchy in order to learn what level of hierarchy best facilitates trader performance and, in turn, room profitability. Once identified, these best practices or typical characteristics will then be transferred across rooms operated by the bank.

The level of hierarchy within a trading room may change based on the number of traders in each room; therefore, we control for room size (defined as the number of traders) when examining changes in room hierarchy levels. For each room in every year, we define an administrative ratio (AR) which is equal to the number of levels of hierarchy divided by room size (the number of traders operating in each room). The administrative ratios are then standardized relative to the previous year using the Z statistic (Loether & McTavish, 1988). This step is taken to avoid the claim that shifts in

the value of the administrative ratio at time t relative to time $t - 1$ are attributed to changes in the distribution in the industry (i.e., we standardize the distributions to control for potential confound from population drift). This approach permits a robust comparison of room characteristics across years. The Z statistic is specified as

$$Z(AR)_t = \frac{AR_t - u_{t-1}}{s_{t-1}},$$

where AR_t is the administrative ratio at time t, u_{t-1} is the population mean at time $t - 1$, s_{t-1} is the population standard deviation at time $t - 1$, and $Z(AR)_t$ is the Z statistic for the room at time t. We expect bank downsizing rates to increase with increases in the bank's mean room administrative ratio.

Trader Experience. Given the speculative nature of the FX industry, trader experience plays a large role in a firm's ability to achieve success. Traders within a room often work together to accomplish trades or pull the room out of a weak position. In this way, rookie traders benefit from the expertise of more experienced traders. The skills required for success in this industry are driven largely by practical experience built on a base of theoretical expertise (Tygier, 1988). An important quality that stems from industry experience is "instinctive dealing," which Tygier (1988) defines as the ability to sense the trends in the market. Theoretical knowledge of macro-environmental forces acting on countries whose currencies are traded, along with an awareness of their influence on the market, is also an important part of the job, but not a substitute for practical experience. Experience in trading, however, is not without its downside. The task of trading requires intense concentration and energy, favoring youth over experience. Burnout among older traders is common (S. Zaheer, 1992, 1995a). Thus, more experience is not always better than less experience, and, as is the case with the appropriate hierarchical levels in a trading room, it is not obvious what the appropriate level of experience should be in a trading room. Hence, trading rooms will also have to experiment with what level of experience leads to the best trader performance. Trader profitability ultimately influences room profitability and, in turn, bank profitability. Thus, we consider trader experience as an important driver of room and bank performance.

The total amount of trader experience in each trading room (EXP) is the sum of the experience of the traders operating in that room. An algorithm was developed to calculate the cumulative amount of trader experience (number of years the trader has worked in the industry) from 1973 to 1993 for each trader. The algorithm compares a trader's last name, first initial, and second initial across years. When a match occurs (all three parts at time t match all three parts at time $t - 1$), the trader's experience count is incremented. Whenever possible, the experience measures were constructed independent of trader location (i.e., room and bank location). Only in cases where a match is ambiguous because of missing data on middle initials are data on the bank and country assignments used. The algorithm was designed to measure cumulative trader experience; thus, the experience counter is not reset to zero when a trader moves to a new location or works for a different bank. For example, consider a trader who works for Citibank for 3 years and then works for Fuji Bank for 2 years. Based on the matching algorithm, the trader's total experience is equal to 5 years.

Similar to the level of hierarchy in a trading room, the total amount of trading room experience might vary if the number of traders operating in the room changes. For each room in every year, an experience ratio (ER) is defined that is equal to the total amount of experience represented by the traders operating in the room divided by the number of traders operating in each room. The room experience ratios are then standardized relative to the previous year's distribution using the Z statistic, as follows:

$$Z(\text{ER})_t = \frac{\text{ER}_t - u_{t-1}}{s_{t-1}},$$

where ER_t is the experience ratio at time t, u_{t-1} is the population mean at time $t - 1$, s_{t-1} is the population standard deviation at time $t - 1$, and $Z(\text{ER})_t$ is the Z statistic for the room at time t. We expect bank downsizing rates to decrease with increases in the bank's mean room experience ratio.

VSR in Room Characteristics

In this section, we discuss the transformation of the room characteristic variables (AR and ER) into measures of no change, dynamic variation, static variation, and retention. We calculate the existence of dynamic variation, retention, and no change with respect to the prior year at the room level, then sum the dynamic variation and retention event counts across the bank for each year. These bank-level variables are then standardized for the number of rooms a bank is operating, because the total dynamic variation and retention amounts will vary relative to bank size (number of rooms). All variables are time varying. Appendix B to this chapter provides a detailed technical description of the operationalization of the no change, dynamic variation, and retention variables.

No Change Events. A no change event is defined as the room maintaining the same practices from year to year. First, we examine cases where the room administrative ratio (AR) at time $t - 1$ equals the room administrative ratio at time t. When the room administrative ratios are equal from t to $t - 1$, we calculate a change in the room's Z score from $t - 1$ to t. Next, we define the minimum and maximum change in room Z scores for the population for each year. The maximum and minimum change in Z score values are used to define a window around the room's Z score. (This is performed only for cases where $\text{AR}_t = \text{AR}_{t-1}$.) If the room's Z score at t fits within this window, then a no change event has occurred—the bank has maintained the same practice in the room relative to the previous year.

The no change estimation for experience ratio (ER) is constructed in a similar fashion, except for an adjustment for the fact that trader experience increases over time. When the number of traders remains the same at time $t - 1$ and time t, and the total room experience at time t is equal to the room experience at time $t - 1$ (plus the number of traders —τ), then we estimate the difference in the room Z scores across years. Thus, in operationalizing no change events in room experience ratios, we adjust for the effect that total room experience evolves with cumulative trader experience. Once the difference in Z scores is estimated, we follow the same logic as for the administrative ratio. We estimate a window around the Z score. If the room's Z score at time t fits within the window, then a no change event has occurred.

Dynamic Variation. Dynamic variation is measured by meaningful changes in each bank's trading room characteristics over time. Because only the variations selected and retained by the firm are subject to external selection agents (Alchian, 1950; Nelson & Winter, 1982), we focus on the actual variations in room practices that a bank pursues. The operational design defines variations as those room practices that are (a) different from the room's practices in the previous year and (b) different from the bank's typical characteristics or practices in the previous year. Thus, a variation is not simply any type of change, but a change that substantially differs from the bank's previous room behavior—a novel change. In this context, a bank's typical characteristic or practice refers to a routine use or behavior. We argue that a typical characteristic or practice represents an important behavior within the firm for which an indication of superiority exists with respect to alternative intrafirm practices. As the number of a bank's trading rooms adopting a similar organizational practice increases, that organizational practice becomes institutionalized (Tolbert & Zucker, 1983). We argue that this legitimization process provides an indicator of the effectiveness of the practice. In defining a bank's previous state, we identify the mean for a particular characteristic (administrative ratio and experience ratio) across the rooms operating for the bank in the previous year. A bank's previous state is estimated for every year. A dynamic variation event occurs when (a) a bank's incumbent trading room's characteristics or practices at time t differ from behavior in the previous year $(t-1)$ and differ from the bank's typical characteristics or practice in the previous year $(t-1)$ (i.e., its previous state), or (b) a bank's new trading room's characteristics or practices differ from the bank's previous state or typical characteristics at time $t-1$.

Static Variation. Static variation measures the amount of variation heterogeneity activity in a cross section of time. To operationalize static variation, we define a bank's mean administrative ratio and mean experience ratio based on all the rooms the bank is operating each year. We then calculate the standard deviation from the mean for the administrative ratio and the experience ratio. We use the standard deviation as an indicator of the amount of variability in organizational practices the bank is engaging in, across its rooms, within a cross section of time.

Retention. Retention involves the managerial choice to diffuse and replicate previously adopted variations or practices throughout the bank. A retention action is defined as a room adopting a practice that differs from that room's behavior in the previous year but is the same as the bank's previous state. A retention event occurs when (a) a bank's incumbent trading room at time t displays characteristics that differ from the room's behavior in the previous year $(t-1)$ but match the bank's previous state (time $t-1$), or (b) a room opens with characteristics that match the bank's previous state.

Control Variables

The FX industry constitutes a turbulent and volatile environment. In such a context, where the competitive pressures facing firms are high, firms may increase experimentation or variation behavior in order to maintain and/or enhance their position. We use industry size, operationalized as the number of trading rooms operating in the industry in a given year, to control for the competitive pressures facing firms in their environment. We also control for firm size effects because large firms might be more susceptible to inertial effects that constrain variation activity. Firm size is defined as the number of trading rooms a bank is operating in a given year. We include controls for a firm's experience with static and dynamic variation activity using cumulative static variation and cumulative dynamic variation measures. The cumulative static variation measure represents the sum of a firm's static variation activity from the firm's founding year to the year prior to the current year, or time $t - 1$ (i.e., the cumulative measure does not include the amount of static variation in the current year). The cumulative dynamic variation measure is constructed in a similar fashion. Each model controls for cross effects by including variables for the two variation and retention components not represented by the dependent variable. For example, when the dependent variable is static variation, we include control variables for dynamic variation and retention. To control for period effects, we include a set of dummy variables for each year of study. All variables are time-varying.

Model Specification and Estimation: Firm Performance and Subsequent Variation

To explore the question of what motivates intrafirm variation activity, we use pooled time-series regression analyses. The models estimated are as follows:

$$\text{Static Variation}_t = a_1 + \beta_1 \text{Performance}_{t-1} + \delta X_t + \varepsilon \qquad (1)$$

$$\text{Dynamic Variation}_t = a_1 + \beta_1 \text{Performance}_{t-1} + \delta X_t + \varepsilon. \qquad (2)$$

We examine the preceding models twice (for variation in two different trading room behaviors). The X represents a vector of control variables, and δ represents the corresponding vector of coefficients estimating the covariates' effects on the dependent variable. The β_1 is the coefficient estimating the independent variable's effects on the dependent variable, and ε captures the error term. We use a parent bank's industry ranking (*Financial Times*, 1973 to 1993) in the prior year $(t - 1)$, referenced as Performance$_{t-1}$, as a proxy measure of past firm performance. The independent and dependent variables are firm mean centered to remove unobservable firm-level effects. We also use a proportionality variable to correct for heteroskedasticity effects. This approach is appropriate when the error variance is proportional to one of the independent variables (Greene, 1993). In our framework, the error variance is proportional to firm size; thus, we divide each variable in the regression equations by

the square root of firm size. In addition, we use an AR1 model (autoregressive with one period lag) to correct for potential first-order serial autocorrelation. This method provides consistent and efficient estimates of the regression parameters (Greene, 1993).

Results

Table 12.1 displays the path-dependent links between firm performance and subsequent VSR behavior.[5] We first examine the relationship between prior performance and static variation (AR) in Model 1. Model 2 presents the results for the effects of prior performance on firm dynamic variation (AR). Models 3 and 4 repeat the analyses using static variation (ER) and dynamic variation (ER).

Models 1 and 3 show a negative relationship between firm performance (Performance$_{t-1}$) and subsequent static variation (SV(AR) and SV(ER)), but the coefficients are not significant. These results suggest that increases in prior firm performance contribute to a decrease in intrafirm static variation, but a lack of support exists for the hypotheses. Findings also indicate that experience with static variation (Cumulative SV(ER)) tends to increase future static variation activity, but experience with static variation (AR) decreases future static variation behavior. Thus, experience with changing the mix of traders across rooms will tend to promote future firm heterogeneity, whereas experience with changes in the administrative structure of rooms is less likely to result in similar changes in the future. These findings also suggest that banks may change trading room administrative structures less frequently or that banks may converge toward a standard administrative structure more quickly than a standard experience mix. As expected, dynamic variation (DV(AR) and DV(ER)) is significant and positively associated with static variation (AR and ER). The coefficients for retention (RET(AR) and RET(ER)) are also significant but negatively associated with static variation (AR and ER). The coefficient for firm size is positive for both models but significant only in Model 1. Industry size is positive and significant

TABLE 12.1 The Effects of Firm Performance$_{(t-1)}$ on Intrafirm Variation Activity

	SV(AR) 1	DV(AR) 2	SV(ER) 3	DV(ER) 4
Constant	−.11****	−.08	.08	−.03*
	(.03)	(.06)	(.26)	(.04)
Industry size	.00003*****	.00002	−.000006	−.000004
	(.000007)	(.00004)	(.00007)	(.00001)
Firm size	.03***	−.005	.07	−.006
	(.01)	(.02)	(.11)	(.01)
Performance $_{(t-1)}$	−.00007	−.00008	−.0005	.0001**
	(.0004)	(.00008)	(.0004)	(.00008)
SV(AR)		.81*****		
		(.04)		
Cumulative SV(AR)	−.006***			
	(.002)			
Cumulative DV(AR)		−.02*****		
		(.003)		
DV(AR)	.16*****			
	(.009)			
RET(AR)	−.07*****	−.32*****		
	(.008)	(.01)		
SV(ER)				.04*****
				(.004)
Cumulative SV(ER)			.02*****	
			(.003)	
Cumulative DV(ER)				−.008**
				(.003)
DV(ER)			1.50*****	
			(.13)	
RET(ER)			−.38***	−.59*****
			(.11)	(.01)
Rho	−.3*****	.01	−.08***	−.002
	(.02)	(.02)	(.02)	(.02)
R^2	.32	.41	.25	.58
Number of firms	432	432	432	432

NOTE: Standard errors are in parentheses. The dependent variables associated with each model are listed in the first row of the table. SV = static variation, DV = dynamic variation, RET = retention, AR = administrative ratio, ER = experience ratio.
*$p < .1$; **$p < .05$; ***$p < .01$; ****$p < .001$; *****$p < .0001$.

for Model 1, indicating that static variation (AR) activity may increase in response to the competitive environment.

Consistent with Model 1, the coefficient for prior firm performance relative to dynamic variation (AR) (Model 2) is negative, but it is not significant. In contrast, prior firm performance is positive and significantly related to dynamic variation (ER). Thus, findings partially support Hypothesis 1A and suggest that dynamic variation

(ER) increases with increases in past performance. The coefficients for the cumulative dynamic variation variables (AR and ER) are negative and significant. These results emphasize that experience with dynamic variation activity plays a crucial role in future dynamic variation behavior. Consistent with Models 1 and 3, the coefficient for retention is negative and significant for Models 2 and 4. Thus, firm dynamic variation decreases with increases in firm retention behavior. The effects of industry size and firm size are not significant. The rho terms (serially correlated AR1 terms) are significant for Models 1 and 3.

The results suggest partial support for the path-dependent relationship between firm performance and variation activity. Past success increases dynamic variation (ER) but, in general, is not significant relative to static variation behavior and dynamic variation (AR). Subsequent sections present the limitations of this study, discuss the results in greater detail, and define the contributions of this research to the study of organizational evolution and strategy.

Discussion and Conclusions

To explore the path-dependent relationships between firm performance and intrafirm change behavior, we pose a set of alternative hypotheses. Overall, past performance did not seem to affect the level of firm static variation but did show some positive effects on the amount of firm dynamic variation. Although the results are mixed, the findings suggest that firms in the FX industry tend to increase dynamic variation in experience following positive performance. Notably, experience with dynamic variation tends to reduce future dynamic variation activity, but experience with static variation in the room's trader experience mix tends to increase heterogeneity in the experience mix across the rooms of a bank. Findings illustrate that examining different types of variation behavior in conjunction with firm retention activity will enhance our understanding of the role of variation and retention in firm outcomes and vice versa. Prior to expanding on the results, we discuss the limitations of this research.

An essential component of the intrafirm evolutionary process involves consistent selection criteria (Campbell, 1960). We focus on the outcomes of intrafirm selection activity, and a central assumption of this research is that the firms utilize consistent selection criteria. We recognize that firm selection criteria may change over time with changes in bank management or changes in the overall strategy for the bank. Differences in selection criteria might affect the amount of variation activity the

firm engages in as well as what type of variation activity the firm pursues (e.g., static vs. dynamic or both). Furthermore, at a lower level of analysis, VSR entails a sequential process of events. Numerous VSR sequences might occur at any one point in time and contribute differentially to firm outcomes. We suggest that VSR sequence performance is affected by the total amount of intrafirm VSR behavior and thus examine the relationships between firm outcomes and the amount of intrafirm variation activity. An alternative research approach entails examining multiple individual VSR sequences (see Ginsberg & Baum, 1994) and their link to firm performance. Although this alternative approach might identify links between prior firm performance and a particular variation action, understanding the relationship between performance enhancements and specific VSR sequences, and vice versa, may be confounded by causal ambiguity. Thus, we focus on investigating the systematic effect of performance on subsequent variation behavior.

Campbell (1960) and Weick (1979) argue that all three VSR mechanisms are necessary for learning to occur within organizations. Results identify particular variation behaviors that contribute to organizational learning and highlight variation and retention behaviors that might constrain the trial-and-error learning process. We also recognize that different sources of variation might exist that influence organizational learning. For example, banks and rooms may learn through communities of practice (Brown & Duguid, 1991) or from collective population-level variation activities (Miner & Haunschild, 1995). Future research might examine how different sources of variation activity influence firm survival chances.

We examine static variation in two trading room characteristics, trader experience and level of hierarchy in a trading room. Although these two dimensions are critical to trading room effectiveness, firm success may induce experimentation in other dimensions of behavior. Our analysis uses archival data that offer several advantages such as a dynamic exploration of firm behavior across multiple levels of analysis. In pursuit of large sample longitudinal analysis, we trade off capturing the type of data often generated via case studies or in-depth qualitative analysis. Thus, the benefits provided by an archival approach also may be viewed as limitations (e.g., less in-depth data on FX bank and trading room experimentation activities). Despite these varied limitations, significant results still emerge from the analyses. Given these conditions, the findings may command more exploratory significance.

Our measure of bank dynamic variation captures changes that increase or decrease the amount of experience in a trading room. We focus on the amount of dynamic variation activity that a bank engages in rather than differences in the direction of change in each trading room. Differences in past performance, however, might influence whether a bank increases or decreases the experience mix in a trading room. For example, poor performance may drive a bank to increase the experience mix in a room. This study provides a first step in explicating different forms of variation behavior (i.e., static and dynamic). Future research might further disaggregate dynamic variation into two components: dynamic variation activity associated with a bank increasing the experience in its trading rooms and dynamic variation associated with a bank decreasing the experience in its trading rooms. Linking these two dynamic variation forms to prior performance will clarify the relationship between firm success or failure and future variation activity.

Last, this exploratory study focuses on identifying the coevolution between prior firm performance and variation activity. To test the hypotheses, we use parent bank industry rank as a proxy measure for firm performance. Although we recognize that an alternative performance measure might increase the robustness of the empirical analysis, in the FX industry, standard firm performance measures are difficult to capture and in most cases are not available because of different requirements across countries. Consequently, we use parent bank rank based on data from an industry ranking.

This study illustrates the hierarchical nature of the evolutionary process and points to the critical interactions between levels of analysis. Path dependence, acquired characteristics, and inertia influence a firm's current stock of variation activity. Prior performance and experience with variation and retention also condition investment in the current stock of variation capabilities. Past success tends to increase the amount of change in experience mix that firms adopt over time, but not necessarily the heterogeneity in behaviors across firm subunits in a cross section of time. Firms in the FX industry may adopt a slow learning strategy by introducing a small number of changes over time rather than a diverse set of changes simultaneously. Thus, firms may try to ride the wave of success rather than introduce a lot of changes at once and potentially disrupt performance. Future research considering differences in firm learning strategies might further distinguish the relationship between performance outcomes and static and dynamic variation activity. For example, a substantial drop in performance might generate a flurry of static variation activity, rather than dynamic variation activity, as a firm attempts to speed up the learning process in pursuit of a rapid recovery.

Furthermore, if we consider each variation as a potential learning opportunity (Campbell, 1982), past success may enhance future learning opportunities and a firm's ability to maintain an adaptive capacity. Although the firm's cumulative stock of static and dynamic variation and retention experience may buffer the firm from immediate hazards, the experience that a firm accumulates with variation behavior reduces a firm's investment in future variation activity in at least three of the models examined (the exception being static variation [ER]). Rather than provide momentum for increasing change activity, past experience gives rise to an inertia effect. This finding is consistent with the competency traps concept (Levitt & March, 1988) or the idea that firm strengths and successes often sow the seeds for failure (Miller, 1990).

One contribution of this research has been to capture the magnitude of firm variation and retention activity in two dimensions of firm practices as well as to identify two types of variation behavior. By identifying the quantity of static variation, dynamic variation, and retention activity that each firm is pursuing, we direct attention to the relationship between firm outcomes and investments in activities that underlie firm dynamic capabilities. In addition, examining components of the intrafirm variation process sheds light on different mechanisms influencing a firm's adaptive capacity. These results illustrate the need for further investigation of the characteristics of intrafirm change processes relative to firm evolution.

We also draw links to strategy research in two ways. First, the strategy literature increasingly directs attention to the foundations upon which persistent firm heterogeneity can be built (Teece & Pisano, 1995). For example, evidence of firm heterogeneity must exist for the resource-based view to hold (e.g., Barney, 1991; Dierickx & Cool, 1989; McGahan & Porter, 1997; Peteraf, 1993; Rumelt, 1991; Wernerfelt, 1984). We view a firm's ability to experiment, over time (dynamic variation), in a cross section of time (static variation), and across multiple behavioral dimensions simultaneously as central to the development of a dynamic capability and persistent firm heterogeneity. Second, our study provides a longitudinal empirical assessment of the interrelationships among components of a

dynamic capability and the effects of performance on subsequent firm differences in change behavior. Although strategy research recognizes the reciprocal interactions between firm outcomes and firm capabilities as critical (Henderson & Mitchell, 1997), few longitudinal empirical studies test how performance shapes multiple forms of firm change behavior.[6]

The VSR framework provides an opportunity to explicate the activities of the firm that play a critical role in learning and survival. This research identifies the complexity of VSR capabilities, their interdependencies, and the drivers of firm differences. Exploring the core activities underlying VSR and their relationship to past success illuminates the interactive nature of evolutionary processes and the foundations for intrafirm, firm, and population coevolution.

Appendix A:
The Foreign Exchange Trading Industry

The Industry Level: Industry Background

The foreign exchange (FX) market is a global network of buyers and sellers of currencies linked through a web of telephone and electronic communication (A. Zaheer & S. Zaheer, 1997; S. Zaheer, 1992; S. Zaheer & A. Zaheer, 1997). In this industry, players do not meet face to face to complete transactions, nor is there a central meeting location for such transactions. Foreign exchange traders are dispersed worldwide in offices of major commercial banks and use various telecommunications mechanisms to facilitate currency exchange. Three main centers handle approximately 60% of the market: London, New York, and Tokyo. In 1995, interbank currency trading worldwide had a net turnover of $1.23 trillion per day (Bank for International Settlements, 1996).

The FX trade industry is extremely dynamic. The scramble by traders and banks following the recent London-based Barings PLC bank collapse illustrates the type of market dynamics prevalent in the industry (*Wall Street Journal*, February 28, 1995, p. A1). Industry turbulence is manifested in a high enough degree of market share mobility to sustain uncertainty regarding rival firms' actions. Thus, we expect the competitors to exhibit continuous evolution coupled with entry and exit.

The Firm Level: Parent Banks

The FX market has evolved from a market designed to serve primarily customers (importers and exporters) who need to purchase currencies to an interbank market. The interbank market constitutes the core of the FX market and is composed of commercial banks (the parent banks) that continuously buy and sell currencies to each other (Tygier, 1988). Parent banks differ with regard to whether they operate multiple FX trading rooms in multiple locations or a single trading room. On average, parent banks operate only one FX trading room in a city and, with a few exceptions, one FX trading room in a country.

Because banks are fairly closely regulated in most of the world (although their currency trading operations are not), their operations in different countries tend to be incorporated as separate and legal accounting entities (S. Zaheer & Mosakowski, 1997). A parent bank's trading rooms operating in different countries typically are independent of one another but are coupled together by the fact that they are owned by the same parent bank and share in the benefits and costs of being part of the parent bank's network. For example, a bank's trading rooms might share information or practices with one another, but they typically do not trade with one another.

More than 85% of trading in this market is dominated by speculative transactions based on short-term trends in currencies (Bank for Institutional Settlements, 1996; Douch, 1989; Ohmae, 1990; S. Zaheer, 1995a). This represents a dramatic shift from pre-1972 market conditions. Prior to 1972, exchange rates were fixed under the Bretton Woods Agreement and trading was a customer driven business with speculation limited to a trader's "best guess" at when a government might devalue its currency (Tygier, 1988; S. Zaheer, 1995a). The Bretton Woods Agreement was dissolved in December, 1971, and by 1973 free-floating exchange rates had replaced fixed parities (Loosigian, 1981; Tygier, 1988). As a result, banks engaged in FX trading were confronted with additional uncertainties and risks and were forced to change their strategies and practices to deal with market fluctuations. In addition, traders had to adapt their behaviors to new market conditions characterized by rapid change where reaction and execution speed was critical. Furthermore, trader experience accumulated in previous years did not necessarily represent an advantage under the new market conditions.

The Intrafirm Level:
The FX Trading Room

A group of active interbank currency trading rooms, identified as market makers in the industry, constitutes a central niche within the foreign exchange market. Market makers are those trading rooms that both buy (bid) and sell (offer) the same currency (S. Zaheer, 1995a; S. Zaheer & Mosakowski, 1997). In this way, market makers provide for the immediate execution of orders from foreign exchange buyers and sellers (Grabbe, 1991). Market makers deal primarily with one another, thus maintaining liquidity in the market (Grabbe, 1991). Approximately 1,564 trading rooms operating worldwide identified themselves as market makers in 1993, associated with about half that number of parent banks in 1993 (Hambros Bank, 1993). Two thirds of these rooms account for 80% of transactions worldwide (A. Zaheer & S. Zaheer, 1997). Market makers engage in both speculative trades and trades for customer accounts, with the latter constituting less than 15% of transactions (Goedhuys, 1985; Grabbe, 1991).

Several advantages accrue to rooms operating as market makers. These include an increase in the amount of information flowing into the trading room from other banks. The volume of "incoming calls" increases the probability that the market maker will be able to trade at prices it quotes versus prices quoted by the other party (A. Zaheer & S. Zaheer, 1997). Given the speculative nature of the market, information flows are essential to sustaining competitive advantage. Market making also has its costs. For example, in periods characterized by extremely volatile prices, a market maker's commitment to always be prepared to buy or sell with a fairly narrow spread increases its risk of losing money relative to other types of trading operations.

Entry and exit barriers are relatively low in this industry. Although exchange control regulation may preclude entry in any one country, few market restrictions exist (Douch, 1989; S. Zaheer, 1995a) and entry costs are low. Establishing a market maker trading operation requires, at a minimum, a Reuters monitor, phone lines, and some back office support to confirm and account for deals (S. Zaheer, 1995a). To compete in the market maker niche, a trading room also must establish credit lines with a large number of banks and begin quoting bid and offer prices with reasonably narrow spreads. It must also publicize its capability to provide bid and offer quotes, by word of mouth and by requesting a listing in an established market maker's directory such as the *Foreign-Exchange and Bullion Dealers Directory* (Hambros Bank, 1973-1993).

The Individual Level: The FX Trader

Given the speculative nature of the industry, trader experience plays a large role in a firm's ability to achieve success. Traders in each room often work together as a team to accomplish trades or pull the room out of a weak position prior to the market closing for the day. Teams often are composed of traders with different levels of expertise so that the rookie traders have the opportunity to learn from the more experienced traders. Furthermore, no standard answers exist for what makes an effective trader. The skills required for success are driven largely by practical rather than theoretical expertise (Tygier, 1988). Successful dealers must have a solid understanding of the dynamic nature of the market and can not afford to be myopic. One important quality that results from experience in the industry is "instinctive dealing," which Tygier

(1988) defines as the ability to sense the trends in the market (i.e., sensitivity to rate movements and market liquidity, and the ability to be flexible). A. Zaheer and S. Zaheer (1997) also identify "alertness" and "responsiveness" to information as capabilities that contribute to success in these markets. Although they identify alertness and responsiveness as organizational capabilities, the experience and abilities of the traders in the firm are likely to influence these organizational capabilities. Theoretical knowledge of macro-environmental

forces acting on countries whose currencies are traded, along with an awareness of their influence on the market, is also an important part of the job, but not a substitute for practical experience. Last, success is largely a function of the dealer's profitability (Tygier, 1988). Dealer profitability ultimately influences room profitability and, in turn, the bank's profitability. That is, the individual level influences intrafirm-level outcomes, which influence firm-level outcomes and, in turn, competitive dynamics.

Appendix B:
Variable Operationalization—Technical Description

No Change Event Operationalization

The following illustrates the operationalization of a no change event when examining administrative ratios (AR) for each room across years. If

$$AR_t = AR_{t-1}, \text{ then}$$

$$\Delta Z(AR)_t = Z(AR)_t - Z(AR)_{t-1},$$

where the room $\Delta Z(AR)_t$ is the difference between the room's Z scores for room AR_t and room AR_{t-1} values. The next step involves defining the sample minimum and maximum $\Delta Z(AR)$ values for each year ($\Delta Z(AR)$min and $\Delta Z(AR)$max) and the mean Z score for each bank in every year. To define whether a room experiences a no change event for scenarios where rooms have similar administrative

ratios but different Z scores (because of the Z score transformation), we perform the following steps:

If $\Delta Z(AR)$min$_t > 0$ then $X(AR)$min$_t =$
$Z(AR)_{t-1} - \Delta Z(AR)min_t$.

If $\Delta Z(AR)$min$_t < 0$ then $X(AR)$min$_t =$
$Z(AR)_{t-1} + \Delta Z(AR)min_t$.

If $\Delta Z(AR)$max$_t > 0$ then $X(AR)$max$_t =$
$Z(AR)_{t-1} + \Delta Z(AR)max_t$.

If $\Delta Z(AR)$max$_t < 0$ then $X(AR)$max$_t =$
$Z(AR)_{t-1} - \Delta Z(AR)max_t$.

The $X(AR)$min and $X(AR)$max values are used to define a window around the Z score at time t. If the room $AR_t =$ the room AR_{t-1}, *and* the room $Z(AR)_t <$

$X(AR)max_t$, *and* the room $Z(AR)_t > X(AR)min_t$ then a no change event occurred—the bank maintained the same practice in the room relative to the previous year. The no change estimation for the room experience dimension is constructed in a similar fashion. The following illustrates the operationalization of a no change event for room experience ratios across years. If:

$$\tau_{t-1} = \tau_t = \tau \text{ and}$$

$$EXP_{t-1} = EXP_t + \tau, \text{ then}$$

$$\Delta Z(ER)_t = Z(ER)_t - Z(ER)_{t-1},$$

where τ_{t-1} and τ_t equal the number of traders operating in a room at time $t-1$ and time t, respectively; EXP_{t-1} is the total amount of room experience at time $t-1$; EXP_t is the total amount of room experience at time t; and $\Delta Z(ER)_t$ is the difference between the room Z scores for the room experience ratio at times t and $t-1$. When the number of traders remains the same at time $t-1$ and time t, and the total room experience at time t is equal to the room experience at time $t-1$ plus the number of traders, then we estimate the difference in the Z scores across years. To determine whether room experience remains the same or differs over time, we must consider whether the number of traders in the room remains the same at time $t-1$ and time t. A change in the number of traders operating in a room might result in a different mix of trading room experience. Assuming that the same traders are working in the room, if the number of traders remains identical, then total room experience at time t will equal the room experience at time $t-1$ plus the number of traders (τ) (experience is represented by person-years, and trader experience is incremented each year). Thus, in operationalizing room no change events, we adjust for the effect that total room experience evolves with cumulative trader experience.

The next step in estimating room no change events involves calculating the sample's minimum and maximum ΔZ values for each year ($\Delta Z(ER)min$ and $\Delta Z(ER)max$) and the mean room Z score for each bank in every year. To further evaluate whether a room experiences a no change event for cases where rooms satisfy conditions (1) and (2) above but have different Z scores (because of the Z score transformation), we perform the following steps:

$$\text{If } \Delta Z(ER)min_t > 0 \text{ then } X(ER)min_t = Z(ER)_{t-1} - \Delta Z(ER)min_t.$$

$$\text{If } \Delta Z(ER)min_t < 0 \text{ then } X(ER)min_t = Z(ER)_{t-1} + \Delta Z(ER)min_t.$$

$$\text{If } \Delta Z(ER)max_t > 0 \text{ then } X(ER)max_t = Z(ER)_{t-1} + \Delta Z(ER)max_t.$$

$$\text{If } \Delta Z(ER)max_t < 0 \text{ then } X(ER)max_t = Z(ER)_{t-1} - \Delta Z(ER)max_t.$$

The $X(ER)min$ and $X(ER)max$ values are used to define a window around the Z score. If conditions (1) and (2) hold, *and* the room $Z(ER)_t < X(ER)max_t$, *and* the room $Z(ER)_t > X(ER)min_t$, then a room no change event occurred—the bank maintained the same practice in the room relative to the previous year.

Dynamic Variation Event

Variation is an alteration in state, form, or function of the firm. Because only the variations selected and retained by the firm are subject to external selection agents (Alchian, 1950; Nelson & Winter, 1982), we focus on the actual variations in room practices that the bank pursues. Variation is measured by changes in each bank's trading room practices over time. The operational design defines variations as those room practices that are (a) different from the room's practices in the previous year and (b) different from the bank's typical or baseline practices in the previous year. In defining a bank's baseline or typical practice (its "previous state"), we identify the bank's mean behavior for a particular practice (administrative ratio and experience ratio) across the rooms operating for the bank. The typical practice of a bank in any given year is defined by the mean room Z score for each bank. The mean room Z score for the administrative ratio is specified as

$$(u_{ar})_{t-1} = (\sum_{i=1}^{n} Z(AR)_{t-1})/(n),$$

where n is the number of rooms a bank is operating at time $t-1$, $Z(AR)_{t-1}$ is the room Z score based on the administrative ratio for each room, and $(u_{ar})_{t-1}$ is the mean Z score for the bank (bank level). The mean Z score for the room experience ratio is defined as

$$(u_{er})_{t-1} = (\sum_{i=1}^{n} Z(ER)_{t-1})/(n),$$

where n is the number of rooms a bank is operating at time $t-1$, $Z(ER)_{t-1}$ is the room Z score based on the total experience in each room at time $t-1$, and $(u_{er})t-1$ is the mean Z score for the bank (bank level). A bank's baseline practice is estimated for every year. A variation event occurs when (a) a bank's existing trading room(s) adopts a practice that is different from the room's behavior in the previous year and different from the bank's typical practice in the previous year, and (b) when a bank's new trading room(s) (entry) does not match the bank's baseline practice in the previous year. The following details the construct design specifics.

For existing rooms, a room variation event in AR occurs when

1. The room AR_t is not equal to the room AR_{t-1} and the room $Z(AR)_t$ is not equal to the room $Z(AR)_{t-1}$, and

2. The room $Z(AR)_t > ((u_{ar})_{t-1} + 1)$ or the room $Z(AR)_t < ((u_{ar})_{t-1} - 1)$.

For new trading rooms (entry), a room variation event in AR occurs when

1. The room $Z(AR)_t > ((u_{ar})_{t-1} + 1)$ or the room $Z(AR)_t < ((u_{ar})_{t-1} - 1)$

(for entrants, $Z(AR)_t$ is the room's Z score the first year it existed—in the above example this is referenced as t).

For existing rooms, a room variation event in ER is defined as

1. The room ER_t is not equal to the room ER_{t-1} and the room $Z(ER)_t$ is not equal to the room $Z(ER)_{t-1}$, and

2. The room $Z(ER)_t > ((u_{er})_{t-1} + 1)$ or the room $Z(ER)_t < ((u_{er})_{t-1} - 1)$.

For new trading rooms (entry), a room variation in ER is defined as

1. The room $Z(ER)_t > ((u_{er})_{t-1} + 1)$ or the room $Z(ER)_t < ((u_{er})_{t-1} - 1)$.

The range around the mean practice is defined by plus or minus the population standard deviation of the Z score. Sensitivity analysis was performed to define the appropriate window around the bank's mean to constitute a change from or toward the baseline practice. The analysis supports the use of plus or minus the population's standard deviation of the Z score.

Retention Event

Retention involves the managerial choice to diffuse and replicate previously adopted practices throughout the bank. A retention action is defined as the room adopting a practice that differs from that room's practice in the previous year but is the same as the bank's baseline practice in the previous year. Retention events occur when (a) the bank's existing trading room(s) in a year adopt the baseline practice from the previous year, and (b) a room opens with characteristics that match the baseline practice from the previous year. Specifics of the operational design follow.

For existing rooms, a room retention event in AR occurs when

1. The room AR_t is not equal to the room AR_{t-1} and the room $Z(AR)_t$ is not equal to the room $Z(AR)_{t-1}$, and

2. $((u_{ar})_{t-1} - 1) < \text{room } Z(AR)_t < ((u_{ar})_{t-1} + 1)$.

For new trading rooms (entry), a room retention event in AR occurs when

1. $((u_{ar})_{t-1} - 1) < \text{room } Z(AR)_t < ((u_{ar})_{t-1} + 1)$

(for entrants, $Z(AR)_t$ is the room's Z score the first year it existed—in the above example this is referenced as t).

For existing rooms, a room retention event in ER is defined as

1. The room ER_t is not equal to the room ER_{t-1} and the room $Z(ER)_t$ is not equal to the room $Z(ER)_{t-1}$, and

2. $((u_{er})_{t-1} - 1) < \text{room } Z(ER)_t < ((u_{er})_{t-1} + 1)$.

For new trading rooms (entry), a room retention event in ER is defined as

1. $((u_{er})_{t-1} - 1) < \text{room } Z(ER)_t < ((u_{er})_{t-1} + 1)$.

The dynamic variation and retention counts for each room are summed across the bank (aggregated to the bank level) and represent the total amount of dynamic variation and retention each bank is pursuing in any given year (bank level, time-varying variables). These values are standardized for the number of rooms a bank is operating because the total dynamic variation and retention amounts will vary relative to bank size.

Notes

1. Plotkin credits William Calvin, an American neurobiologist, for the term "Darwin machines."

2. Variations occur in numerous ways: (a) purposeful variation in response to environmental pressures (Winter, 1971), (b) planned variation (Campbell, 1969; McKelvey, 1994), (c) stochastic variation (Campbell, 1969; McKelvey, 1994),

and (d) recombinations of old and new routines not currently acknowledged as distinct for the firm (Nelson & Winter, 1982).

3. Ingram (1996) uses firm heterogeneity as a control variable in his study (measured by the standard deviation of the sizes of a hotel chain's units).

4. We recognize that several authors adopt a more calculative or rational approach to argue the opposite—that failure increases subsequent search and experimentation (Cyert & March, 1963; March & Shapira, 1992; March & Simon, 1958; Mosakowski, 1996).

5. To streamline the reporting of results, Table 12.1 does not include the results of the year dummy variables.

6. Haveman (1993) investigates the effect of organizational size on rates of change (change in diversification strategies), controlling for firm financial performance.

References

Alchian, A. (1950). Uncertainty, evolution and economic theory. *Journal of Political Economy, 58,* 211-221.

Aldrich, H. E. (1979). *Organizations and environments.* Englewood Cliffs, NJ: Prentice Hall.

Aldrich, H. E., & Pfeffer, J. (1976). Environments of organizations. *Annual Review of Sociology, 2,* 79-105.

Amburgey, T. L., Kelly, D., & Barnett, W. P. (1993). Resetting the clock: The dynamics of organizational change and failure. *Administrative Science Quarterly, 38,* 51-73.

Andrews, K. R. (1980). *The concept of corporate strategy.* Homewood, IL: Irwin.

Argyris, C., & Schön, D. (1978). *Organizational learning.* Reading, MA: Addison-Wesley.

Athey, S., & Stern, S. (1997, October). *An empirical framework for testing theories about complementarity in organizational design.* Paper presented at the INFORMS Conference (Organization Science Track), Dallas.

Audretsch, D. B. (1995). Firm profitability, growth and innovation. *Review of Industrial Organization, 10,* 579-588.

Bank for International Settlements. (1996). *Central bank survey of foreign exchange and derivatives market activity 1995.* Basil: Author.

Barnett, W. P., & Freeman, J. (1997, August). *Too much of a good thing?: Product proliferation and organizational failure.* Paper presented at the Academy of Management Meetings, Boston.

Barney, J. B. (1991). Firm resources and sustained competitive advantage. *Journal of Management, 17,* 99-120.

Baum, J.A.C. (1990). Inertial and adaptive patterns in organizational change. In *Academy of Management Best Papers Proceedings* (pp. 165-169). Madison, WI: OMNIPRESS.

Baum, J.A.C., & Singh, J. V. (1994). *Evolutionary dynamics of organizations.* New York: Oxford University Press.

Bowman, E. H. (1963). Consistency and optimality in managerial decision making. *Management Science, 9*(2), 310-321.

Brown, J. S., & Duguid, P. (1991). Organizational learning and communities-of-practice: Toward a unified view of working, learning, and innovation. *Organization Science, 2*, 40-57.

Brown, S. L., & Eisenhardt, K. M. (1997). The art of continuous change: Linking complexity theory and time-paced evolution in relentlessly shifting organizations. *Administrative Science Quarterly, 42*, 1-34.

Burgelman, R. A. (1991). Intraorganizational ecology of strategy-making and organizational adaptation: Theory and field research. *Organization Science, 2*, 239-262.

Burgelman, R. A. (1994). Fading memories: A process theory of strategic business exit in dynamic environments. *Administrative Science Quarterly, 39*, 24-56.

Campbell, D. T. (1960). Blind variation and selective retention in creative thought as in other knowledge processes. *Psychological Review, 67*, 380-400.

Campbell, D. T. (1969). Variation and selective retention in socio-cultural evolution. *General Systems, 16*, 69-85.

Campbell, D. T. (1974). Evolutionary epistemology. In P. A. Schilpp (Ed.), *The philosophy of Karl R. Popper* (Vol. 14, pp. 413-463). La Salle, IL: Open Court.

Campbell, D. T. (1982). The "blind-variation-and-selective-retention" theme. In J. M. Broughton & D. J. Freeman-Moir (Eds.), *The cognitive-developmental psychology of James Mark Baldwin: Current theory and research in genetic epistemology* (pp. 87-97). Norwood, NJ: Ablex.

Campbell, D. T. (1991). Methods for the experimenting society. *Evaluation Practice, 12*(3), 223-260.

Campbell, D. T. (1994). How individual and face-to-face-group selection undermine firm selection in organizational evolution. In J.A.C. Baum & J. V. Singh (Eds.), *Evolutionary dynamics of organizations* (pp. 23-38). New York: Oxford University Press.

Carroll, G. R., & Hannan, M. T. (1989). Density delay in the evolution of organizational populations: A model and five empirical tests. *Administrative Science Quarterly, 34*, 411-430.

Crozier, M. (1964). *The bureaucratic phenomenon.* Chicago: University of Chicago Press.

Cyert, R. M., & March, J. G. (1963). *A behavioral theory of the firm.* Englewood Cliffs, NJ: Prentice Hall.

D'Aveni, R. A. (1994). *Hypercompetition: Managing the dynamics of strategic maneuvering.* New York: Free Press.

Delacroix, J., & Swaminathan, A. (1991). Cosmetic, speculative, and adaptive organizational change in the wine industry: A longitudinal study. *Administrative Science Quarterly, 36*, 631-661.

Dierickx, I., & Cool, K. (1989). Asset stock accumulation and sustainability of competitive advantage. *Management Science, 35*, 1504-1511.

Douch, N. (1989). *The economics of foreign exchange.* Westport, CT: Quorum.

Freeman, J., Carroll, G. R., & Hannan, M. T. (1983). The liability of newness: Age dependence in organizational death rates. *American Sociological Review, 48*, 692-710.

Galunic, D. C., & Eisenhardt, K. M. (1996). The evolution of intracorporate domains: Divisional charter losses in high-

technology, multidivisional corporations. *Organization Science, 7*, 255-282.

Ginsberg, A., & Baum, J.A.C. (1994). Evolutionary processes and patterns of core business change. In J.A.C. Baum & J. V. Singh (Eds.), *Evolutionary dynamics of organizations* (pp. 127-151). New York: Oxford University Press.

Goedhuys, D. (Ed.). (1985). *The foreign exchange market in the 1980s.* New York: Group of Thirty.

Grabbe, J. O. (1991). *International financial markets* (2nd ed.). New York: Elsevier.

Greene, W. H. (1993). *Econometric analysis.* New York: Macmillan.

Greve, H. R. (1998). Performance, aspirations, and risky organizational change. *Administrative Science Quarterly, 43*, 58-86.

Hambros Bank. (1973-1993). *Foreign exchange and bullion dealers directory.* London: Author.

Hannan, M. T., & Carroll, G. R. (1992). *Dynamics of organizational populations.* New York: Oxford University Press.

Hannan, M. T., & Freeman, J. (1977). The population ecology of organizations. *American Journal of Sociology, 83*, 929-984.

Hannan, M. T., & Freeman, J. (1984). Structural inertia and organizational change. *American Sociological Review, 49*, 149-164.

Hannan, M. T., & Freeman, J. (1989). *Organizational ecology.* Cambridge, MA: Harvard University Press.

Haveman, H. (1993). Organizational size and change: Diversification in the savings and loan industry after deregulation. *Administrative Science Quarterly, 38*, 20-50.

Haveman, H. (1994). The ecological dynamics of organizational change: Density and mass dependence in rates of entry into new markets. In J.A.C. Baum & J. V. Singh (Eds.), *Evolutionary dynamics of organizations* (pp. 152-166). New York: Oxford University Press.

Henderson, R. (1995). The evolution of integrative capability: Innovation in cardiovascular drug discovery. *Industrial and Corporate Change, 3*(3), 607-629.

Henderson, R., & Clark, K. B. (1990). Architectural innovation: The reconfiguration of existing product technologies and the failure of established firms. *Administrative Science Quarterly, 35*, 9-30.

Henderson, R., & Mitchell, W. (1997). The interactions of organizational and competitive influences on strategy and performance. *Strategic Management Journal, 18*(Special issue), 5-14.

Iansiti, M., & Clark, K. B. (1994). Integration and dynamic capability: Evidence from product development in automobiles and mainframe computers. *Industrial and Corporate Change, 3*, 557-605.

Ingram, P. (1996). Organizational form as a solution to the problem of credible commitment: The evolution of naming strategies among U.S. hotel chains, 1896-1980. *Strategic Management Journal, 17*, 85-98.

Lawrence, P. R., & Lorsch, J. W. (1967). *Organization and environment: Managing differentiation and integration.*

Boston: Harvard University, Graduate School of Business Administration.

Leonard-Barton, D. (1995). *Wellsprings of knowledge: Building and sustaining the sources of innovation.* Cambridge, MA: Harvard Business School Press.

Levinthal, D. A. (1991). Organizational adaptation and environmental selection—interrelated processes of change. *Organization Science, 2,* 140-145.

Levitt, B., & March, J. (1988). Organizational learning. *Annual Review of Sociology, 14,* 319-400.

Loether, H. J., & McTavish, D. C. (1988). *Descriptive and inferential statistics* (3rd ed.). Boston: Allyn & Bacon.

Loosigian, A. M. (1981). *Foreign exchange futures: A guide to international currency trading.* Homewood, IL: Irwin.

Lounamaa, P., & March, J. G. (1987). Adaptive coordination of a learning team. *Management Science, 33,* 107-123.

Madsen, T. L., & McKelvey, B. (1996). Darwinian dynamic capability: Performance effects of balanced intrafirm selection processes. *Academy of Management Best Papers Proceedings* (pp. 26-30). Madison, WI: OMNIPRESS.

Madsen, T. L., Mosakowski, E., & Zaheer, S. (1997, August). *Intrafirm evolutionary processes and competitive advantage: A study of global financial services.* Paper presented at the Academy of Management Meetings, Boston.

Makadok, R., & Walker, G. (1996). Search and selection in the money market fund industry. *Strategic Management Journal, 17,* 39-54.

March, J. G. (1991). Exploration and exploitation in organizational learning. *Organization Science, 2,* 71-87.

March, J. G., & Shapira, Z. (1992). Variable risk preferences and the focus of attention. *Psychological Review, 99,* 172-183.

March, J. G., & Simon, H. A. (1958). *Organizations.* New York: Wiley.

McGahan, A. M., & Porter, M. E. (1997). How much does industry matter, really? *Strategic Management Journal, 18,* 15-30.

McKelvey, B. (1982). *Organizational systematics: Taxonomy, evolution and classification.* Berkeley: University of California Press.

McKelvey, B. (1994). Evolution and organization science. In J.A.C. Baum & J. V. Singh (Eds.), *Evolutionary dynamics of organizations* (pp. 314-326). New York: Oxford University Press.

McKelvey, B. (1997). Quasi-natural organization science. *Organization Science, 8,* 352-380.

McKelvey, B., & Aldrich, H. E. (1983). Populations, natural selection and applied organizational science. *Administrative Science Quarterly, 28,* 101-128.

Merton, R. K. (1957). *Social theory and social structure.* New York: Free Press.

Milgrom, P., & Roberts, J. (1990). The economics of manufacturing: Technology, strategy, and organization. *American Economic Review, 80,* 511-528.

Milgrom, P., & Roberts, J. (1995). Continuous adjustment and fundamental change in business strategy and organization.

In H. Siebert (Ed.), *Trends in business organization* (pp. 231-258). Tubingen: J.C.B. Mohr.

Miller, D. (1990). The Icarus paradox: How exceptional companies bring about their own downfall. New York: Harper-Collins.

Miller, D. (1994). What happens after success: The perils of excellence. *Journal of Management, 31,* 324-358.

Miller, D., & Chen, M. J. (1994). Sources and consequences of competitive inertia. *Administrative Science Quarterly, 39,* 1-23.

Miller, D., & Friesen, P. H. (1980). Momentum and revolution in organizational adaptation. *Academy of Management Journal, 23,* 591-614.

Miller, D., & Friesen, P. H. (1982). A quantum view of evolution and revolution: Structural change in organizations. *Journal of Management Studies, 19,* 131-151.

Milliken, F. J., & Lant, T. K. (1991). The effects of an organization's recent performance history on strategic persistence and change. *Advances in Strategic Management, 7,* 129-156.

Miner, A. S. (1994). Seeking adaptive advantage: Evolutionary theory and managerial action. In J.A.C. Baum & J. V. Singh (Eds.), *Evolutionary dynamics of organizations* (pp. 76-89). New York: Oxford University Press.

Miner, A. S., & Haunschild, P. R. (1995). Population level learning. *Research in Organizational Behavior, 17,* 115-166.

Mitchell, W. (1989). Whether and when? Probability and timing of incumbents' entry into emerging industrial submarkets. *Administrative Science Quarterly, 34,* 208-230.

Mosakowski, E. (1996). *Managerial prescriptions under the resource-based view of strategy: The example of motivational techniques.* Unpublished manuscript, University of California, Los Angeles.

Mueller, D. (1977). The persistence of profits above the norm. *Econometrica, 44,* 369-380.

Nelson, R. R., & Winter, S. G. (1982). *An evolutionary theory of economic change.* Cambridge, MA: Belknap Press.

Nonaka, I. (1994). A dynamic theory of organizational knowledge creation. *Organization Science, 5*(1), 14-37.

Nonaka, I., & Takeuchi, H. (1995). *The knowledge-creating company.* Oxford, UK: Oxford University Press.

Ohmae, K. (1990). *The borderless world.* New York: Harper Business.

Peteraf, M. (1993). The cornerstones of competitive advantage: A resource-based view. *Strategic Management Journal, 14,* 179-191.

Pfeffer, J., & Salancik, G. R. (1978). *The external control of organizations.* New York: Harper & Row.

Plotkin, H. (1994). *Darwin machines and the nature of knowledge.* Cambridge, MA: Harvard University Press.

Rumelt, R. P. (1984). Towards a strategic theory of the firm. In R. B. Lamb (Ed.), *Competitive strategic management* (pp. 556-570). Englewood Cliffs, NJ: Prentice Hall.

Rumelt, R. P. (1991). How much does industry matter? *Strategic Management Journal, 12,* 167-186.

Senge, P. M. (1990). *The fifth discipline: The age and practice of the learning organization.* London: Century Business.

Singh, J. V. (1986). Performance, slack and risk-taking in organizational decision-making. *Academy of Management Journal, 29*(3), 562-585.

Singh, J. V., House, R. J., & Tucker, D. J. (1986). Organizational change and organizational mortality. *Administrative Science Quarterly, 31,* 171-193.

Stinchcombe, A. L. (1965). Social structure and organizations. In J. G. March (Ed.), *Handbook of organizations* (pp. 153-193). Chicago: Rand McNally.

Teece, D. J., & Pisano, G. (1995). The dynamic capabilities of firms: An introduction. *Industrial and Corporate Change, 3,* 537-556.

Thompson, J. D. (1967). *Organizations in action.* New York: McGraw-Hill.

Tolbert, P. S., & Zucker, L. G. (1983). Institutional sources of change in the formal structure of organizations: The diffusion of civil service reform. *Administrative Science Quarterly, 28,* 22-39.

Tuma, N. B., & Hannan, M. T. (1984). *Social dynamics: Models and methods.* New York: Academic Press.

Tushman, M. L., & Romanelli, E. (1985). Organizational evolution: A metamorphosis model of convergence and reorientation. In L. L. Cummings & B. M. Staw (Eds.), *Research in organizational behavior* (Vol. 7, pp. 171-222). Greenwich, CT: JAI.

Tygier, C. (1988). *Basic handbook of foreign exchange: A guide to foreign exchange dealing* (2nd ed.). London: Euromoney Publications.

Tyre, M. J., & Orlikowski, W. J. (1994). Windows of opportunity: Temporal patterns of technological adaptation in organizations. *Organization Science, 5,* 98-118.

Weick, K. (1979). *The social psychology of organizing.* Reading, MA: Addison-Wesley.

Wernerfelt, B. (1984). A resource-based view of the firm. *Strategic Management Journal, 5,* 171-180.

Winter, S. G. (1971). Satisficing, selection and the innovating remnant. *Quarterly Journal of Economics, 85,* 237-261.

Zaheer, A., & Zaheer, S. (1997). Catching the wave: Alertness, responsiveness and market influence in global electronic networks. *Management Science, 43,* 1493-1536.

Zaheer, S. (1992). *Organizational context and risk-taking in a global environment: A study of foreign exchange trading rooms in the US and Japan.* Unpublished doctoral dissertation, MIT.

Zaheer, S. (1995a). Circadian rhythms: The effects of global market integration in the currency trading industry. *Journal of International Business Studies, 25*(4), 699-728.

Zaheer, S. (1995b). Overcoming the liability of foreignness. *Academy of Management Journal, 38,* 341-363.

Zaheer, S., & Mosakowski, E. (1997). The dynamics of the liability of foreignness: A study of global survival in financial services. *Strategic Management Journal, 18*(6), 439-463.

Zaheer, S., & Zaheer, A. (1997). Country effects on information seeking in global electronic networks. *Journal of International Business Studies, 27*(1), 77-100.

Chapter 13

Organizations as Networks of Action

BRIAN T. PENTLAND

In standard theories of organization, structure is in the foreground and action is in the background. We tend to see organizations as collections of individuals or subunits, and to measure the variable properties of those individuals or subunits. But if we reversed figure and ground, and viewed organizations as patterns of action, what could we see? Patterns of action, conceptualized as organizational routines, are a central aspect of organization theory (Hannan & Freeman, 1983; March & Simon, 1958; Nelson & Winter, 1982). Some even have argued that organizations are *essentially* repetitive patterns of action (Geser, 1992). Much of the work on agent-based modeling of organizations (e.g., Masuch & LaPotin, 1989) explores the connection between organization-level phenomena and microlevel patterns of action. McKelvey (1997, p. 358) argues that although microlevel processes are stochastic, in the sense that they may vary idiosyncratically from time to time, they embody "patterned regularities" that provide a basis for rigorous theorizing about an organization as a whole.

It is ironic, then, that the major modes of explanation or analysis used in the organizational sciences do not generally focus on actions or their sequence. Most of our research focuses on the variable properties of entities at various levels of analysis, such as individuals, groups, task units, establishments, or organizations. Even network analysis, which emphasizes patterns of relations, generally focuses on the relations among static entities. Thus, our major methodological frameworks leave out an obvious and perhaps essential feature of organization: patterns of action. Although there has been increased interest in the analysis of sequences of action (e.g., Abbott, 1990; Abell, 1987), these techniques have just begun to be applied to empirical research in the organizational sciences (e.g., Pentland & Reuter, 1994; Sabherwal & Robey, 1993).

Part of the problem, of course, is that one cannot "see" patterns of action or processes. They typically are distributed in time and space, making it difficult to observe a coherent sequence in its entirety. Many significant processes are distributed between organizational subunits as well, making it difficult even for participants to explain what happens. Consequently, if we are to conduct empirical work in the domain of action, we need techniques for summarization and comparison that allow us to capture significant aspects of a process as a whole. Although variable properties, such as cycle time, quality, or cost, have practical value in benchmarking, they provide little insight into the underlying phenomena. This potentially rich area of theorizing is limited by our inability to operationalize the central construct—patterns of action—in a valid and reliable way.

The purpose of this chapter is to introduce a formal approach to organizational analysis that puts patterns of action directly in the foreground. By coding sequences of actions in an organization, one can generate a matrix that summarizes the actions and the relations among them. This matrix represents a "network of actions" that can be analyzed using the same graph-theoretic techniques that have been applied to networks of people and other entities. The contribution here is not to introduce new mathematical tools for the analysis of action but to apply existing tools to a new kind of data. The advantage of network models is the availability of well-known quantitative measures, such as centrality and density. When applied to networks of action, these measures provide an interesting basis for theorizing about a range of significant organizational phenomena.

Representing routines as networks of action also facilitates the application of Campbell's (1969) concept of blind-variation-and-selective-retention. Routines are like ruts in the road: There are commonly followed paths, but there are always variations (Pentland & Reuter, 1994). Over time, some variations may become new ruts. An appropriately constructed network provides a formal representation of this metaphor, to detect variations and map them over time. In the domain of action, "blind variation" is commonplace, as exceptional circumstances force us out of our ruts. So is selective retention: When a course of action succeeds, we try to repeat it. Several of the chapters in this volume (e.g., Madsen, Mosakowski, & Zaheer; Ingram & Roberts) address VSR concepts in considerable detail. Although I will not concentrate on this particular application in this chapter, it provides an implicit backdrop for everything that follows.

After discussing some related literature, I introduce a technique for generating a network of actions and illustrate it with some previously unpublished data on software support hot lines. The body of the chapter explores the interpretation of familiar concepts such as density, centrality, and cliques when applied to the patterns of action in an organization and then discusses some possibilities for applying these concepts in familiar areas such as institutional theory, organizational ecology, and organizational learning. Although a full exposition of any one of these applications would require an entire paper, they are included here to illustrate the potential power of this approach.

Why Networks of Action?

Although representing organizations as networks of action is a significant departure from mainstream organizational theory, it is not without precedent. A variety of related ideas in the organizational literature provide some suggestive guidance on what might be possible if this approach could be developed more fully.

Comparison With Traditional Social Networks

As a starting point, it may be instructive to compare the method described here with the general steps one might use to construct a traditional social network of ties between individuals. To measure a social network, a list of all relevant individuals who may be members of the network usually is prepared. This might be all the employees in a department or all the members of a social club. Guided by one's theoretical interest, one then identifies the kinds of relations (or ties) that one wishes to map. The relations often are operationalized using a survey instrument that is given to each member of the network. To map an advice network, for example, the survey might ask, "Who do you ask for advice about work-related problems?" The data collected in this way can be used to identify the sources and targets of advice-seeking relationships throughout the network. This approach takes a single event category (advice seeking) and asks members of the organization to identify all instances of it (as primed or instructed by the survey instrument). We have no data about why advice was sought or what happened as a result. The precursors and antecedents of this event are excluded.

By contrast, the method described here would attempt to locate advice seeking, rather than advice seekers, in a larger network of actions for problem solving. To do so, one would gather data that covered whole sequences of events where advice was sought or problems were being solved. These stories would include a lexicon of other kinds of actions relevant to problem solving, such as problem identification, alternative generation, and so on. One would use this lexicon of actions to code the problem-solving episodes among employees of a department, or members of a social club, or whatever. The coding process would generate sequences of events that describe problem-solving episodes and could be converted into a network with formal properties analogous to a traditional social network. Because the network explicitly encodes the antecedents and consequences of each action in the lexicon, including advice seeking, it preserves information about the relations between actions that are lost in other methods. The question is how to put this data to use.

Institutions as Patterns of Action

The most immediate and obvious area of application would be in institutional theory. I will return to this topic later, but for the time being, consider this definition from Jepperson (1991): *"Institution* represents a social order or pattern that has attained a certain state or property; *institutionalization* denotes the process of such attainment. By *order* or *pattern,* I refer, as is conventional, to standardized interaction sequences" (p. 145). Like Geser (1992), Jepperson (1991) places patterns of action at the center of the phenomenon. The interaction sequences that are associated with any particular institution may vary in degree of "taken for grantedness," formalization, and so on. They also may come bundled with an elaborate package of social, technological, and structural arrangements that en-

able and constrain them. Consequently, it would be an error to completely identify institutions with the patterns of action per se. Still, we recognize and define institutions by the "standardized interaction sequences" that they produce and reproduce.

Process Grammars and Networks of Action

Although the explicit analysis of these institutionalized interaction sequences is at an early stage of development in the organizational literature, there have been attempts to create formal network models. Abell (1987) explores the epistemological foundations of modeling social actions using network representations, such as directed graphs. He provides formal models of social processes in which each node represents an action or event. These models can be summarized in matrix form or displayed as a directed graph. Network models, in the form of Markov transition matrices, also have been used to represent interaction processes (e.g., Gottman & Roy, 1990). These kinds of directed graphs can be interpreted as finite state grammars (Chomsky, 1956). Each node in the graph can be used to represent a symbol in the "language," and the transitions between nodes define the possible "sentences" in that language.

The use of finite state grammars in the representation of natural language is somewhat limited, but they are an excellent tool for modeling a wide variety of computational and organizational processes. The familiar flowchart, for example, is a special kind of directed graph. A flowchart can be seen as a finite state grammar that defines the valid ways in which a process may be performed. In this respect, the framework discussed here represents an extension of previous grammatical models of organizational processes (Pentland & Reuter, 1994). Although phrase structure grammars have superior expressive power, directed graphs have the advantage of being induced easily from observational data.

Cause Maps and Dynamic Systems

Two widely used methods for mapping real or perceived relations among activities or events are cause maps and system dynamics. In a sense, these techniques are specialized versions of the idea I am describing here because they focus on particular kinds of relations. For example, "cause maps" (Bougon, Weick, & Binkhorst, 1977) represent causality between events as perceived by research subjects. The lexicon of actions is open ended, and the relation being graphed is causality. As Nelson and Mathews (1991) note, cause maps can be seen as matrix (or network) representations of processes. The events or actions in the map are the nodes, and the causal relations are the links.

System dynamic models (Forrester, 1968) also embody networks of causal relationships between events or activities. Although some applications of system dynamics center on the construction of the causal map at a qualitative level (e.g., identifying positive and negative feedback loops), much of the work in this literature depends on identifying specific, quantifiable relations. For example, if production increases but sales do not, inventory increases by a specific amount. This makes it possible to create formal computational representations that can be used to simulate the dynamics of the system. Computational accuracy sets a very high standard of rigor for the description of a process. In addition to merely identifying relationships, one must estimate the magnitude of the parameters that govern those relationships. As we shall see, the approach I am describing here could be used to derive causal models such as these, but probably not for purposes of simulation. Also, there is no need to limit oneself to causal relations when constructing a network of actions.

The Process Handbook

An example of action networks that do not rely on causal relations is *The Process Handbook* (Malone et al., in press). The handbook is an electronic database of process descriptions, each of which can be interpreted as a network of action. Each process description consists of a set of activities and, if so desired, the relationships between those activities. The representation emphasizes a coordination theory perspective (Malone & Crowston, 1994), so the relationships among actions include various kinds of dependencies, such as

flow, fit, and sharing. The database currently contains more than 3,000 process descriptions, not all of which have information about dependencies. In other words, many of the process descriptions include only decompositions of the process steps without the data necessary to construct a network of relations among those steps. As more process descriptions are collected, it is anticipated that more complete process descriptions—including dependencies—will be included. So far, the primary applications of the handbook have been oriented toward process improvement and organizational design (Malone et al., in press). By making a library of process descriptions accessible in a structured way, with a sophisticated interface, the handbook provides designers with a novel tool for inventing new processes. At the same time, the database itself eventually may provide organization theorists with a rich set of empirical materials with which to work.

Narrative Analysis

Abbott (1992) has argued that we should treat narrative as the fundamental building block of social analysis (see also Abell, 1987). As we shall see, the general approach described here also has some parallels to the analysis of narrative structure (Bal, 1985; Propp, 1928/1977; Todorov, 1981). Each entry in *The Process Handbook*, for example, can be seen as a stylized story about an organizational process. Readers familiar with postmodern (sometimes known as "poststructuralist") analysis will realize that this approach treats narrative as objectively given and analyzable independent of context. That is an important limitation that is worth mentioning because stories and the actions they describe depend on context for meaning. The data are narrative, but the epistemology is positivist, in the sense that the events described in the stories are taken at face value. This results in what Abbott (1992) calls "narrative positivism." The general approach hinges on our ability to code narrative data objectively, thereby rendering it available for more formal methods of analysis. In practice, of course, the significance and interpretation of any action, no matter how objective it may seem, is never completely fixed. In this regard, the method discussed here depends on taking a particular perspective and achieving reliability within that perspective through the use of multiple coders or standard coding techniques. In this respect, it is no more difficult or unusual than any other method for sequential data analysis.

Mapping a Network of Actions

To analyze patterns of action, we must collect sequential data. By "sequential," I mean temporally ordered events (Abbott, 1990). This is not the same as time-series data, which consist of temporally ordered values for one or more variables (e.g., quarterly reports of productivity or employment). Depending on the phenomenon under investigation, sequential data may include many different kinds of events. For example, Corsaro and Heise (1990) investigate routine interactions among children on a playground, which comprise events such as chasing, fleeing, displaying fear, and so on. Pentland and Reuter (1994) investigated technical support hot lines, which include events such as opening, transferring, escalating, and closing a problem report. As in variance-based research (Mohr, 1982), in which the choice of variables is guided by theory, the choice of relevant events also is theoretically driven (Abbott, 1990; Corsaro & Heise, 1990). For organizational decision-making processes, for example, one might include events that represent generation of alternatives, establishing criteria, and so on (Olson, Herbsleb, & Reuter, 1994).

Networks of actions are most appropriate as models of routines: organizational processes that are reasonably well defined and repetitive. With the increasing prevalence of electronic communications, databases, and workflow support systems, some kinds of sequential data are becoming more readily available. Still, getting useful accounts of what goes on inside organizations can be difficult and time-consuming. The problem is similar to that faced by anyone who engages in process mapping—how to get a reasonable picture of events and their interrelationships. Broadly speaking, the three main choices are the same as they ever were: interview, observation, and archive. Survey methods probably are inappropriate because of the complexity of the material being collected.

Coding Sequential Data

Interview, observation, and archival methods all can produce textual data that describe sequences of events or actions: what happened first, what came next, and so on. To generate a network, the text needs to be coded, and any approach that will produce coded sequences can be used. There are two essential aspects to consider: (a) a definition of the events to be coded and (b) a definition of the relations between these events (Abbott, 1990; Corsaro & Heise, 1990). This is analogous to the problem of identifying individuals in a traditional social network and the relations among them.

As with any such reduction of narrative to its structural elements, a variety of issues must be considered. First, one must consider the perspective from which the codes are created. One major distinction is between etic coding, which uses a priori theoretical categories, and emic coding, which uses culturally grounded native categories. Pentland (1992), for example, develops an emic category scheme for software support and hypothesizes that those categories might be more generally applicable. To facilitate comparability across organizations, of course, a common coding scheme needs to be used. A variety of different a priori frameworks have been developed to facilitate comparison of work processes, many of which are used for job analysis (Fleishman & Quaintance, 1984). The particular choice of coding scheme has to be driven, ultimately, by the theoretical categories relevant to the research question. Note that this is quite different from constructing a traditional social network, where one may choose to include or exclude certain individuals, but the identities of the individuals included basically are given. In constructing a network of actions, the "identities" of the nodes are defined and constructed as part of the research process.

Second, one must consider the granularity (or level of detail) at which coding should take place. Abell (1987) does an excellent job of exploring the roots of this problem and provides some guidance on how to deal with it. Unlike a traditional social network, in which individuals are irreducible, one can always subdivide actions into increasingly minute constituents. As Abell (1987) points out, the sociological insights that one might gain from this kind of reductionism are quickly exhausted. The goal is to choose a level of granularity that corresponds to the problem at hand. As in a traditional sociogram, one can aggregate constituents into larger units, if that proves useful.

Relations Between Actions

Once the core set of events or actions that constitute the nodes of the network have been identified, one must identify the relations between them. Identifying relationships between nodes is fundamental to the idea of a network. Network data express relationships between the elements, or nodes, in the network. In traditional social networks, relationships may reflect attitudes, interaction, familial relationships, and so on (Wasserman & Faust, 1994). In the domain of events or actions, however, the kinds of relations are quite different.

The simplest kind of relation between actions is sequential adjacency (action B follows action A). Sequential adjacency seems closest to our intuitive sense of a "pattern" of action because it defines what actions follow others. It is the most easily observed and probably the most reliably measured. Given a coded sequence of action—A, B, C— sequential adjacency of the actions is self-evident. These relations also can be quantified by counting the number of times one action follows another. If these frequencies are normalized appropriately, then the matrix represents a Markov process (Wasserman & Faust, 1994). Unfortunately, actions that follow in sequence may do so for a variety of reasons that may or may not reflect any underlying causal process. This is the conceptual equivalent of the familiar distinction between correlation and causation in variance-based analysis. For example, coffee and dessert usually are served at the end of a meal, but that sequential relationship is imposed, if at all, by cultural norms. This limitation does not invalidate the data, of course; it merely suggests caution while interpreting it.

One can also graph causal relations between events, including whether one event is necessary, sufficient, or both, in causing another event. Causal relations are used to create cause maps (Bougon et al., 1977) as well as process theories of various kinds (Mohr, 1982). They state the necessary and/or sufficient conditions for various events to occur. Corsaro and Heise (1990) describe the use of ethnographic data to create "event structure" models that map the "prerequisite" relation between events; they identify the necessary (but not sufficient) conditions for action to proceed. Although identifying such relations is considerably more time-consuming and difficult than merely identifying sequential adjacency, they can be summarized in a directed graph and analyzed in the manner described here.

Other kinds of relations between actions may be of interest. As I will discuss later, Weick and Roberts (1993) identify "heedfulness" as the central relation in their theory of collective mind. Malone and colleagues (in press) have identified several other kinds of relations that can exist between activities, such as sharing the same resources or contributing to the same output. In these cases, the relationship between the two activities or events is nondirectional, and there may be no causal or even sequential relationship. Clearly, however, sharing resources (such as budget, personnel, space, or raw materials) is critical as a relationship, both in theory and in practice.

Extracting Network Data From Coded Sequences

To create a network that represents sequential adjacency, the basic procedure for converting coded narrative into matrix form is purely mechanical and could be automated with a simple computer program. This is because the difficult interpretative work of identifying events and their boundaries has been done in the coding process. Once the data have been reduced to strings of coded symbols, they can be manipulated algorithmically. If the relations of interest are causal, or reflect other kinds of interdependence between the events, then constructing the network is considerably more difficult (Corsaro & Heise, 1990). For such relations, one needs to test a hypothesis of the form "event A causes event B" for each pair of events in the lexicon. Establishing this kind of relationship obviously is a lot of work. To represent sequences of events, however, the task is much simpler. One simply looks for sequentially adjacent events or actions in the coded narrative. In this procedure, one asks, "What happened next?" and records the answers in a single mode matrix of actions. Note that this procedure works only when the coded data are arranged in sequential order.

Example: Software Support at Advanced Publishers

This example comes from a study of software support hot lines that I have described elsewhere (Pentland, 1992; Pentland & Reuter, 1994). I call the organization "Advanced Publishers" because the product it sells and supports is a sophisticated text and graphics package for publishing technical documentation and other complex documents. At the time of the study, the software was available only on high-end Unix workstations from vendors such as Sun, Apollo, Digital and Hewlett-Packard—it was not "consumer" software. Typical users included writers and graphic designers, and the product required a high level of support. The data analyzed here describe the process used to provide technical support to Advanced Publishers' customers. The data are archival records from a database that support specialists use to keep track of information on customer problems as they are being solved.[1] The records are reasonably accurate because the people keeping them depend on them to get their work done. In addition, support specialists are evaluated, in part, on how well they keep track of their calls in this database. Nevertheless, to the extent that their needs and objectives are different from mine, one has to exercise some caution in interpreting any findings based on this kind of data.

The raw data consist of printouts of all the steps taken to answer or solve a particular question. In all, 130 sequences were coded using archival re-

cords from the software support database. The lexicon of actions used to code these sequences includes basic steps such as opening the call, assigning it to a support person, requesting more information (from the customer), running tests, looking up information, and asking for help, as well as the "organizing moves" that delineate the structure of the software support organization, such as transferring, escalating, and referring (Pentland, 1992).

The coded sequences can be used to create a directed graph, as shown in Figure 13.1. The arrows in this graph represent sequential adjacency in the coded call sequences. In this representation, ties with only a single occurrence in the data set have been suppressed. Ties that occur 10 or more times have been displayed in bold, to indicate their greater frequency. The actual transition frequencies are displayed in Table 13.1. Note that a few of the ties are shown as bidirectional to minimize the number of separate lines; these events followed each other. Also, note that "run tests" followed itself in at least some of the sequences. Unlike a network of people, actions can be reflexively related, following themselves in the sequence.

In this figure, there are some definite "ruts in the road" that suggest a very simple process. Calls are opened and assigned to a support specialist. Once assigned, the support specialist either begins to diagnose immediately (based on information provided) or requests additional information. In either case, the next step is to make a diagnosis and then close the call. In some cases, it is necessary to run tests to confirm the problem or the solution. After tests are run, there is a diagnosis, and the call is closed. These patterns represent the most typical scenario and, in a sense, the most routine scenario. At the same time, there are several less frequently traveled paths that add variety to the routine. For example, it is sometimes necessary to request more information (after trying to make a diagnosis), or to look up information (in documentation or online). In other cases, when a problem cannot be resolved by the specialist to whom it was originally assigned, it is necessary to transfer the call to another specialist or escalate the call to management.

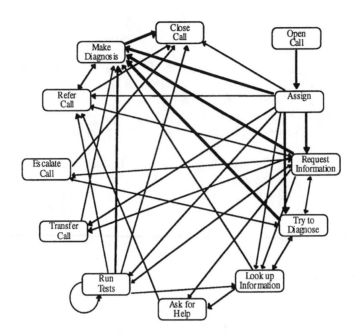

Figure 13.1. Directed Graph of the AP Software Support Process

TABLE 13.1 Transition Matrix for Software Support Process

						To						
From	*1*	*2*	*3*	*4*	*5*	*6*	*7*	*8*	*9*	*10*	*11*	*12*
1. Open call		130										
2. Assign	30	24	8			9	5	1	6	51	6	
3. Request information				7	3	2	5	3	3	3	11	1
4. Try to diagnose		3			1		13			1	12	1
5. Look up information		1	2			2	1	1		1	6	
6. Ask for help		1					1			2		
7. Run tests		2	1		2		2	1		8	13	3
8. Transfer call		1	1								7	1
9. Escalate call		1	1								1	2
10. Refer call		1	2						1		11	10
11. Make diagnosis										4		106
12. Close call												

NOTE: $N = 130$ calls. For visual clarity, cells with zeros have been suppressed.

Some Methodological Issues

As with any method, there are a variety of limitations and considerations concerning the ways data can be collected and interpreted. Many of these considerations are similar to those one encounters when attempting to collect traditional social network data. A great deal more could be said, of course, but it is worth at least mentioning these issues here.

One central issue is that the units of observation—the lexicon of actions—are constructed through the research process, not objectively given. By varying the level of granularity (or detail) at which data are collected and represented, a very different picture would emerge. Thus, it is important to recognize that there could be many different pictures that equally well represent the same process.

In addition, the notion of sequence is not necessarily as well defined as we might like. We know from formal analysis of narrative (Bal, 1985) that many different narratives can be used to convey the same underlying *fabula*, or story structure. Sequence can be manipulated for dramatic effect, for example, without changing the underlying story being told. Mystery buffs no doubt will have noticed that even though the victim may have grown cold by the end of the first chapter, the murderer usually is not revealed until the last. These kinds of structural transformations work wonders for literature, but they introduce noise into the method described here. To solve this problem, narrative data would need to be arranged chronologically before analysis. This issue was resolved automatically in the Advanced Publishers example because the call tracking database time-stamps each record and displays them in chronological order.

The boundary of the network is also an artifact of the research process. Because everything is connected to everything else, where does one draw the line? In the Advanced Publishers example, the boundary seems clear because each call to the software support hot line has a clear beginning and end. These interactions, however, occur in the context of at least three other processes that one could equally well want to include: (a) the customer's own work process, (b) the software quality control process (i.e., bug fixing and the "maintenance" release cycle), and (c) the overall sales process between the vendor and the customer. In the context of the customer's work process, calls to software support could be aberrations or a part of the daily routine, and calls could have very different consequences for the customer's work. There is no way to tell from the data reported here. In the context of the overall maintenance and bug fixing process, customer problems and bug reports are one important input, but the actual "release cycle," as it is called, involves many other steps. Individual bugs are fixed; new features, if any, are added; unit testing is conducted, where parts of the software are tested to make sure that problems have been fixed without introducing new ones; and various levels of system testing also are performed (see Crowston, 1997, for a discussion of this process). In the context of that network, responding to individual customer calls is a minor subroutine. Finally, in the context of the overall relationship between the vendor and the customer, answering a particular question may be a relatively minor event or a huge one, depending on the question. As anyone dealing with complex software well knows, the devil is in the details; if there is a particular function or feature that is failing to perform adequately, it could undermine the entire relationship between the two organizations.

One guide to the boundary question may arise from a narrow, structuralist definition of narrative (Bal, 1985) that consists of a temporally ordered sequence of events with a clear beginning, middle, and end. The structure of the "story" depends on what White (1981) refers to as the moral or authoritative context. In other words, one recognizes the beginning and end of a story because, at the beginning, there typically is some challenge to the existing order, and at the end is some resolution with respect to that order. In fairy tales, when evil descends upon the empire, the hero sets out to put things right. Less dramatically, a customer calls with a problem, and the software support specialist tries to fix it. Within organizations, moral context could be framed more simply in terms of goals or objectives. In other words, one might draw the boundaries of the network around that set of events which relates to a particular goal or set of goals. I think there is no easy answer to this problem; as in a traditional network, boundaries must be somewhat arbitrary. As long as one is aware of the constructed nature of such boundaries (both by participants and researchers), and the authoritative contexts that inform them, one can make informed decisions about how they should be drawn.

Interpreting Networks of Action

Representing the actions occurring in an organization as a network makes it possible to apply conventional tools of network analysis. The difficulty, of course, is that the familiar mathematical formalisms such as centrality, density, clusters, and so on have very different interpretations when computed in the domain of actions rather than in the domain of individuals. In this section, I will explore some ways that the network of actions can be interpreted. As in traditional social networks, the specific relations and the characteristics of the nodes in the network are crucial to the story one tells. For example, if one is examining the pattern of ties between Florentine families in the 15th century (Padgett & Ansell, 1993), it matters that one of those families was the Medici. The significance of the identity of particular nodes may be just as high in the kinds of networks described here. For example, if one of the events in the network is particularly important (for example, closing a sale), then the significance of the network as a whole would likely depend on that particular node. Like any process representation, it seems likely that just having the network map (or going through the exercise of creating it) could have considerable practical value.

The theoretical value, however, remains to be developed. Networks of action could be applied to organization theory in a variety of different ways. The value hinges on the idea that network measures, such as density, have theoretically relevant and interesting interpretations when applied to networks of action. Abbott (1990) notes that in general, when one is studying patterns of action, one can explore their antecedents, their consequences, or the patterns themselves. Thus, one could ask what leads some networks to be more or less dense than others, or what the consequences of increasing network density may be, and so on. Before advancing specific propositions, let's explore how some familiar network measures can be interpreted in this domain.

Clusters and Cliques

Wasserman and Faust (1994) define many different techniques for computing cohesive sub-graphs of a network. These include cliques, n-cliques, k-plexes, k-cores, and lambda sets. These represent different formal algorithms for extracting sets of nodes that are more tightly interconnected than their neighbors. In a traditional network, these clusters of individuals represent social groups of various kinds; in the domain of action, I would argue that these clusters of actions represent organizational routines—sequences of action that are tightly connected and yet distinct from other sequences in the organization. Routines are cohesive, integrated chunks of action.

If one imagines a network of actions that includes a wide range of different actions or activities, routines would naturally emerge as the actions that cluster together. Even a purely descriptive study of "membership" in such cliques could be quite interesting, if applied to the right kinds of processes. For example, one might study the comparative structure of strategy formation or new product design. To the extent that important clusters of actions can be viewed as representing "core competencies," this method provides a way of operationalizing this elusive construct very concretely. Gathering the data would be expensive, but with adequate resources, one could begin to study the antecedents and consequences of these clusters as well.

If one can identify clusters in this way, one can also identify connections between clusters. Exploring linkages between routines creates some interesting possibilities. From a practical point of view, one might want to know how the budgeting process interacts with the hiring process. On a more theoretical level, an action-based perspective presents an alternative view of the concept of "boundary spanning." Rather than looking for individuals who create linkages between formal (or informal) groups, one could look for events that create linkages between routines. Boundary spanning events could be an interesting topic of research in and of themselves.

Reachability and Distance

Measures of "reachability" or distance are a basic tool in the analysis of networks. In traditional social networks, the famous "small world" experiments provide a vivid reminder of the combinatorial power of network ties. In the domain of actions, distance would have a rather different interpretation: How many steps away is the event of interest? This kind of metric could have practical interest as a benchmarking tool (e.g., how many steps between order and fulfillment?) A simple theoretical application of this concept concerns the existence of isolates—unreachable nodes—in a network. Imagine that one has started with a lexicon that covers a wide variety of possible processes in a given domain—such as decision making or problem solving. If "voting" or "advice seeking" emerges as an isolate, it means that these actions never occur in that network: They do not appear in any of the sequences. Alternatively, if certain nodes in a directed graph have only inbound links or outbound links, it means that such events begin or terminate the processes in which they occur. In the Advanced Publishers data, "open call" and "close call" are examples of such nodes. One could certainly arrive at these conclusions without all the analytical overhead of creating a network, but it is reassuring to know that concepts such as distance have straightforward, meaningful interpretations, because other network measures (such as centrality) depend on them.

Centrality

There also are many different ways to measure centrality in a network (Wasserman & Faust, 1994). These measures generally indicate that a node is on the path between many other nodes in the network. In a network of action, actions that are "on the path" of many different routines are likely to be potential "bottlenecks"—points of vulnerability or opportunity, depending on one's point of view. From a practical standpoint, this is obviously valuable information. More theoretically, one might compare the centrality of certain kinds of actions in different networks. For example, one might measure the centrality of voting as a part of a network that represents organizational decision making. Bougon and colleagues (1977) use the related concepts of in-degree (number of inward links in a directed graph) and out-degree (number of outward links) to analyze cause maps. In a cause map, events or actions that have a high out-degree

are like "root causes"—they lead to a large number of other events.

Density

Network density can be measured in many different ways as well (Wasserman & Faust, 1994). One simple measure of density in a social network is the average number of ties per node, normalized by the total number of possible ties. Intuitively, density provides a measure of the connectedness of the individuals in the network. Figure 13.2 shows how one might interpret network density for two different kinds of relations.

A low-density graph of sequential adjacency depicts a situation in which one event follows another in an order flow. In the limiting case (shown in Figure 13.2), the sequence is perfectly linear. As density increases, it means that many different events were observed to follow any given event. Intuitively, it would be very difficult to discern a pattern in this situation. In the limiting case (all ties, density = 1.0), any event could follow any other event.

If the relationship being graphed is causality (necessary and sufficient), the same basic intuitions apply, but the implications are much stronger. A low-density causal chain is easy to understand, and it would be easy to predict its behavior. A high-density causal chain is like a bomb waiting to go off. If one event is triggered, many others will follow. Unless there is negative feedback in the system to limit the self-reinforcing loops, the action would quickly go out of control. This observation leads to the intuitive expectation that dense networks may be quite rare in real organizations. One thing leads to another—but probably not to five others, at least not directly. This intuitive assertion begins to get us into the realm of organization theory, the subject to which we turn next.

Using Networks of Action in Organizational Theory

One might use networks of action in a variety of ways in traditional organizational theory. As mentioned in the introduction, each of these topics potentially could require an entire manuscript. This

	Sequential Adjacency	Causality
Low Density	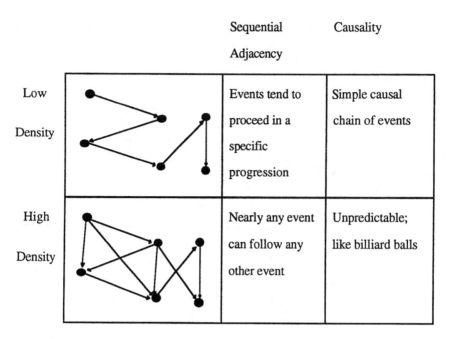	Events tend to proceed in a specific progression	Simple causal chain of events
High Density		Nearly any event can follow any other event	Unpredictable; like billiard balls

Figure 13.2. Interpretations of Network Density

discussion is sketchy, at best, and is meant to be illustrative and perhaps a little provocative. My purpose is to suggest possible connections between the properties of these networks and more familiar concepts from organization theory. I hope that the reader may think of other, better ways that these analytical tools might be applied. The core argument is simple: Routines are a central, if implicit, part of organization theory, and networks of action provide a novel way of operationalizing and measuring this central construct. So, assuming we could somehow get the data, how could we put these measures to use?

Institutional Theory

As mentioned earlier, institutional theory is a natural place to apply networks of action. In this volume, for example, Miner and Raghavan discuss various ways in which routines are copied or imitated. Romanelli (this volume) also explores the issue of copying of routines in variation and selective retention. If we conceptualize a routine as a network of actions, it could help clarify what we mean when we say that a routine has been "cop-

ied." For example, the proliferation of a particular technical artifact may or may not entail copying a particular pattern of action. For example, certain software products, such as Lotus Notes®, can be adopted to support a wide range of different internal processes. Other products may support only a particular process. In this way, networks of action would allow us to explore the extent to which the diffusion of technology promotes the diffusion of organizational forms. More generally, one could investigate the extent to which a population of organizations has really copied a routine, rather than just adopting legitimating surface features.

On a deeper level, networks of action may offer a way to operationalize the concept of institutionalization itself. Institutionalized processes are based on reciprocal expectations of predictability, so they should be more predictable, with fewer deviations than processes that are not institutionalized. Without going any farther, one might hypothesize a relationship between the perceived legitimacy of a process and the density of the network of action that represents it. An excessively dense network tends to be unpredictable: Too many possibilities exist at each step compared to a relatively sparse network. This line of argument suggests that increased legitimacy could be associated with decreased network density. In other words, as a process becomes more institutionalized, its density may decline.

Whether true or not, these propositions suggest the kinds of relationships one might want to investigate using networks of action. In this case, an empirical test seems justified because one could make the counterargument that increasing legitimacy and institutionalization may be accompanied by a larger repertoire of exceptions and variations. That is, expectations become elaborated, not narrowed, so the range of possible sequences should increase. Alternatively, one could argue that over time, as a process becomes more institutionalized, additional constraints and affordances grow up around it. In effect, the ruts in the road grow deeper, and one should observe fewer deviations from the straight and narrow. It is quite possible, of course, that both are true—that networks become more or less dense over time for a variety of reasons. Either way, networks of action could help identify those reasons and their consequences, if any, for organizations.

Ecological Theory

It is difficult to imagine actually applying the method described here in the domain of organizational ecology. How could one collect time-series network data, since founding, for every member of a population? If we allow ourselves the luxury of temporary omniscience, it is interesting to speculate about the relevance of these ideas for organizational ecology. The point of connection, of course, is the lowly routine—the "genetic material" for organizations (Nelson & Winter, 1982).

The concept might be applied in two ways. The first was suggested by Salancik and Leblebici (1988), who used grammatical models to generate alternative organizational forms. These "forms" were representations of canonical sequences of events that one might encounter in a food service transaction (i.e., a restaurant). If one takes this view seriously, then the appropriate unit of analysis for vital rates (founding, transformation, and mortality) should be the patterns themselves, not firms or establishments. This is in line with the argument that Ingram and Roberts (this volume) and McKelvey (1982) make concerning evolution in organizations, and that characterizes the mainstream view of evolution in biological species: It is the relative frequency of genes in the gene pool that matters, not the fitness of particular individuals or the number of individuals (Kaufman, 1993). Of course, once our temporary omniscience wears off, none of us is likely to attempt measuring these vital rates anytime soon. But from this point of view, organizational ecology is less about environmental selection of *firms* than it is about environmental selection of *processes*. The fact that processes are embedded in firms that have an independent economic and legal existence is an unfortunate source of complication and noise.

The second, more realistic, application would be as a measure of inertia. Recall that inertia is a property of organizations that makes them vulnerable to selection, and that it is most acute in the core of an organization. That is, although an organization may undergo considerable adaptation in many of its functions, its core usually will be highly resistant to change. Hannan and Carroll (1995) suggest that the "core" of a firm can be operationalized using four indicators: the basic mission of the organization, the form of authority, the basic technology, and the marketing strategy. Although these indicators clearly are important, it strikes me that their choice probably was influenced to some extent by the practical necessity of getting several decades of time-series data on hundreds of establishments. They are not bad indicators, but they are somewhat distant indicators of the underlying construct.

How can networks of action help us do better? If routines really are the genetic material (Nelson & Winter, 1982), and the patterns of action in an organization really do express its productive competence, then a network of actions might be a more valid way to operationalize the "core" of an organization. If so, then one might begin to explore the extent to which these networks (routines, genes) actually demonstrate the kind of inertia ascribed to them. There is good reason to expect that they do, of course. In particular, one might hypothesize a relationship between inertia and the structure of the underlying network of actions. Recall that routines are represented as cliques: tightly clustered bundles of activity. If we take the genetic metaphor seriously for a moment and assume that the routines themselves are largely inertial (because they are so tightly linked to the technology, or the marketing strategy, or the other "core" indicators), then an organization with more "genetic material" should have a harder time changing. It is nailed down in more places, so to speak.

Inertia also should tend to increase if the linkages between these routines (the boundary spanning events) are too few in number. This connects to the previous argument concerning legitimacy and suggests that increasing legitimacy may go with increased inertia. The intuition is that if there are few paths between routines, there is less flexibility—less likelihood that the organization can selectively deploy the routines. Rather, they will tend to follow in lockstep, as they always have, in spite of changing environmental conditions. Again, the point here is not to defend the particular argument but to demonstrate that networks of action provide a whole new vocabulary in which to cast such debates.

Collective Mind and Organizational Learning

In the domain of organizational learning, networks of action offer a way to operationalize the concept of "organization mind" (Sandelands & Stablien, 1987) or "collective mind" (Weick & Roberts, 1993). To the extent that it is possible to operationalize these concepts more concretely, that would provide additional tools for research in areas such as organizational learning or high-reliability organizations. Weick and Roberts (1993) define collective mind as "a pattern of heedful interrelations of actions in a social system" (p. 357). Sandelands and Stablien (1987) also suggest that "organization mind" exists in the connections between behaviors, rather than the connections between people. They argue that at the organizational level, knowledge is located in patterns of behavior. Weick and Roberts (1993) also focus on mind as "activity" rather than as "entity," a distinction that mirrors Weick's (1979) emphasis on "organizing"

rather than "organization." In their theory of collective mind, the key relation between activities is "heedfulness," which is composed of contributing, representing, and subordinating, as well as a variety of more specific behaviors. In simple terms, it means acting in ways that take into account the actions of others.

Weick and Roberts (1993) offer a detailed and highly nuanced description of this phenomenon, illustrated with examples from aircraft carrier operations. Although the result is compelling, the concept of collective mind seems quite difficult to operationalize in a valid or reliable way. It is a hard problem, and they offer an admittedly rough approach, which is worth quoting at some length:

> A crude way to represent the development of a collective mind is by means of a matrix in which the rows are people and the columns are either the larger activities of contributing, representing, and subordinating, or their component behaviors (e.g., converging with, assisting, or supplementing). Initially, the cell entries can be a simple "yes" or "no." "Yes" means a person performs that action heedfully; "no" means the action is done heedlessly. The more "yeses" in the matrix, the more developed the collective mind. (Weick & Roberts, 1993, p. 365)

It is interesting to note that whereas collective mind is described as emerging from a pattern of interrelations among actions, the matrix they describe is focused on people. This reflects a consistent tension that underlies their exposition—*people* are interrelating, but *actions* are interrelated. As a result, the proposed matrix would describe the way people are behaving (heedfully or not), but it would not describe what they are actually doing. The matrix they describe would be unable to differentiate a flight crew from a jazz ensemble, because it makes no reference to the content of the work.

If one were to apply the method proposed here to the concept of collective mind as described by Weick and Roberts (1993), it would push the actions squarely into the foreground. Both dimensions of the matrix would be actions; the people would be implicit. The relation between actions could be a summary measure of heedfulness, or one could create separate networks to capture the extent of contribution, representation, subordination, and so on. By explicitly representing the relation of heedfulness between actions, such a matrix would be a much better model of the concept of collective mind. Of course, as Weick and Roberts (1993) point out, collective mind is built continuously by people interacting, old-timers coaching newcomers, and so on. Any representation of such a mind would necessarily be a snapshot—restricted to the moment or moments in time when data were collected.

Such a model nevertheless would have several interesting features. First, it would retain the ability to express an overall level of heedfulness (as represented by average tie strength, or one of the measures of network density). More heedful networks would be stronger and more dense. Second, it would explicitly represent the kind of work being done. If there were potential weaknesses, they could be located in terms of the specific activities being performed (using measures of centrality, for example). Third, this kind of network would express the structure of information processing in the organization. By mapping the degree of heedfulness in relation to "boundary spanning" events (those that trigger internal activity based on external events), a network of actions could provide a very detailed picture of how an organization reacts (or fails to react) to information. Fourth, and perhaps most important, because the nodes being connected are actions (or behaviors or events), they can be seen as binary: At any point in time, they are either occurring or not. In this representation, the degree of heedfulness is separated from the activity itself, which may be quite heedful of certain considerations and, at the same time, quite heedless of others. That kind of selective interconnection—the pattern of heedfulness—is easily captured in a network.

Again, a full exposition of this issue deserves a separate paper, but such models are basically connectionist networks (Davis, 1992). In particular, the kind of network I have outlined here (connections between binary nodes that change state selectively based on the state of the other nodes) embodies Kaufman's (1993) approach to modeling

complex dynamic systems. In this framework, "organization mind" could be simulated and allowed to evolve through a process of blind-variation-and-selective-retention, if one chose to do so. Regardless of how one feels about computational modeling and simulation, the possibility of doing so profoundly reinforces Weick and Roberts's (1993) basic insight: Collective mind is an inherent property of all organizations. More specifically, it is an inherent property of all organized pattern's of action. Ironically, Weick and Roberts (1993) argue that the application of connectionist models to organizations is problematic for a variety of reasons, but mainly because they view organizations as networks of interacting *people*. If we reversed figure and ground and focused on actions rather than actors, as the concept of collective mind seems to require, we surely would lose much of the social nuance in Weick and Roberts (1993). What we might gain remains to be seen.

Conclusion

Whether you can see yourself using these methods in your own research or not, it is interesting to speculate about what we might learn by putting actions into the foreground. Potentially large costs of data collection make it difficult to imagine that this will become the method of choice for organizational research anytime soon. Still, some of the central ideas in organization theory can be recast in these terms. We implicitly rely on concepts such as routines, inertia, and information processing all the time; networks of action provide a formal way of operationalizing these constructs. By reflecting on what might be involved in creating valid, reliable measures of these networks, and speculating about their possible application to organization theory, I hope I have provoked some thought.

Note

1. I analyzed data from a similar database in Pentland and Reuter (1994) to create a grammatical, phrase structure model

of the work process, but the archival data from Advanced Publishers have never been analyzed for publication.

References

Abbott, A. (1990). A primer on sequence methods. *Organization Science, 1,* 375-392.

Abbott, A. (1992). From causes to events: Notes on narrative positivism. *Sociological Methods and Research, 20,* 428-455.

Abell, P. (1987). *The syntax of social life: The theory and method of comparative narratives.* New York: Clarendon.

Bal, M. (1985). *Narratology: Introduction to the theory of narrative.* Toronto: University of Toronto Press.

Bougon, M., Weick, K. E., & Binkhorst, D. (1977). Cognition in organizations: An analysis of the Utrecht Jazz Orchestra. *Administrative Science Quarterly, 22*(4), 606-639.

Campbell, D. T. (1969). Variation and selective retention in socio-cultural evolution. *General Systems, 16,* 69-85.

Chomsky, N. (1956). Three models for the description of language. *IRE Transactions on Information Theory, 2,* 113-124.

Corsaro, W. A., & Heise, D. R. (1990). Event structure models from ethnographic data. In C. C. Clogg (Ed.), *Sociological methodology: 1990* (pp. 1-57). Oxford, UK: Basil Blackwell.

Crowston, K. G. (1997). A coordination theory approach to organizational process design. *Organization Science, 8,* 157-175.

Davis, S. (1992). *Connectionism: Theory and practice.* New York: Oxford University Press.

Fleishman, E. A., & Quaintance, M. K. (1984). *Taxonomies of human performance.* New York: Academic Press.

Forrester, J. W. (1968). *Principles of systems.* Cambridge, MA: MIT Press.

Geser, H. (1992). Towards an interaction theory of organizational actors. *Organization Studies, 13*(3), 429-451.

Gottman, J. M., & Roy, A. K. (1990). *Sequential analysis: A guide for behavioral researchers.* Cambridge, UK: Cambridge University Press.

Hannan, M. T., & Carroll, G. R. (1995). An introduction to organizational Ecology. In G. R. Carroll & M. T. Hannan (Eds.), *Organizations in industry: Strategy, structure and selection* (pp. 17-31). New York: Oxford University Press.

Hannan, M. T., & Freeman, J. R. (1983). Structural inertia and organizational change. *American Sociological Review, 29,* 149-164.

Jepperson, R. L. (1991). Institutions, institutional effects, and institutionalism. In W. W. Powell & P. J. DiMaggio (Eds.), *The new institutionalism in organizational analysis* (pp. 143-163). Chicago: University of Chicago Press.

Kaufman, S. A. (1993). *Origins of order: Self organization and selection in evolution.* New York: Oxford University Press.

Malone, T. W., & Crowston, K. G. (1994). The interdisciplinary study of coordination. *Computing Surveys, 26,* 87-119.

Malone, T. W., Crowston, K., Lee, J., Pentland, B. T., Dellarocas, C., Wyner, G., Quimby, J., Osborne, C., Bernstein, A., Herman, G., Klein, M., & O'Donnell, E. (in press). Tools for inventing organizations: Toward a handbook of organizational processes. *Management Science.*

March, J. G., & Simon, H. A. (1958). *Organizations.* New York: John Wiley and Sons.

Masuch, M., & LaPotin, P. (1989). Beyond garbage cans: An AI model of organizational choice. *Administrative Science Quarterly, 34*(1), 38-67.

McKelvey, B. (1982). *Organizational systematics: Taxonomy, evolution, classification.* Berkeley: University of California Press.

McKelvey, B. (1997). Quasi-natural organization science. *Organization Science, 8*(4), 351-380.

Mohr, L. (1982). *Explaining organizational behavior.* San Francisco: Jossey-Bass.

Nelson, R. E., & Mathews, K. M. (1991). Cause maps and social network analysis in organizational diagnosis. *Journal of Applied Behavioral Science, 27*(3), 379-398.

Nelson, S. G., & Winter, R. R. (1982). *An evolutionary theory of economic change.* Cambridge, MA: Harvard University Press.

Olson, G. M., Herbsleb, J. D., & Reuter, H. H. (1994). Characterizing the sequential structure of interactive behaviors through statistical and grammatical techniques. *Human Computer Interaction, 9,* 427-472.

Padgett, J. F., & Ansell, C. K. (1993). Robust action and the rise of the Medici, 1400-1434. *American Journal of Sociology, 98,* 1259-1319.

Pentland, B. T. (1992). Organizing moves in software support hot lines. *Administrative Science Quarterly, 37,* 527-548.

Pentland, B. T., & Reuter, H. H. (1994). Organizational routines as grammars of action. *Administrative Science Quarterly, 39*(3), 484-510.

Propp, V. (1977). *Morphology of the Russian folktale.* Austin: University of Texas. (Original work published 1928)

Sabherwal, R., & Robey, D. (1993). An empirical taxonomy of implementation processes based on sequences of events in information system development. *Organization Science, 4*(4), 548-576.

Salancik, G. R., & Leblebici, H. (1988). Variety and form in organizing transactions: A generative grammar of organization. In N. DiTomaso & S. B. Bacharach (Eds.), *Research in the sociology of organizations* (Vol. 6, pp. 1-32). Greenwich, CT: JAI.

Sandelands, L. E., & Stablien, R. E. (1987). The concept of organization mind. In S. Bacharach & N. DiTomaso (Eds.), *Research in the sociology of organizations* (Vol. 5, pp. 135-161). Greenwich, CT: JAI.

Todorov, T. (1981). *Introduction to poetics.* Minneapolis: University of Minnesota Press.

Wasserman, S., & Faust, K. (1994). *Social network analysis: Methods and applications.* New York: Cambridge University Press.

Weick, K. E. (1979). *The social psychology of organizing* (2nd ed.). New York: Random House.

Weick, K. E., & Roberts, K. H. (1993). Collective mind in organizations: Heedful interrelating on flight decks. *Administrative Science Quarterly, 38*(3), 357-381.

White, H. (1981). The value of narrativity in the representation of reality. In W.J.T. Mitchell (Ed.), *On narrative* (pp. 1-24). Chicago: University of Chicago Press.

Chapter 14

Evolutionary Models of Local Interaction

A Computational Perspective

ALESSANDRO LOMI
ERIK R. LARSEN

The problem of how the actions of self-interested—but boundedly rational—individuals produce and reproduce the regularities that are observable at more aggregate levels of analysis is at the core of current debates in organization science. This problem—generally known in the social sciences as the "micro-to-macro" or "aggregation" problem—presents itself across various levels of organizational analysis and is related in a fundamental way to the question of reversibility of social systems, that is, to the uniqueness of the link between the sequence of states occupied by individual units over time, and system-level configurations (Hannan, 1997; March, 1994). For its importance and elusiveness, the solution of this problem is seen by some as the Holy Grail of social theories (DiMaggio, 1991). Alexander and Giesen (1987) trace the modern philosophical roots of the micro-macro chasm back to the early divide between J. S. Mill's liberalist doctrine and the holistic orientations of Hegel and Rousseau.

The main theoretical issues in the background of this chapter—how evolutionary processes simultaneously induce *and* transcend spatial, social, and cultural boundaries—was a recurrent theme in the work of Donald T. Campbell (1958, 1974, 1990, 1994) and recently has been rediscovered as one of the most central issues in contemporary organizational theory and empirical research (Baum & Haveman, 1997; Baum & Mezias, 1992; Baum & Singh, 1994; Burt, 1988; Hannan, 1997; Hannan, Carroll, Dundon, & Torres, 1995; Hannan & Freeman, 1986; Lomi, 1995; Singh, 1993). As we hope to be able to clarify in the course of this chapter, we see the problem of how organizations evolve in subsystems of larger systems as related in a fundamental way to issues of reversibility of social systems.

Following Gutowitz (1991), it is useful to distinguish between two aspects of the problem of reversibility. The first, which can be called the "forward problem," is this: Given a set of decision rules that characterize the local behavior of micro social units (e.g., maximization of expected utility or minimization of transaction costs), can we predict the global properties of the system generated by the interaction among these units (e.g., differentiation in an organization or efficiency in a market)? The second, which can be called the "backward problem," is this: Given the properties of a social system (e.g., asymmetric mutualism within an organizational community), can we find a local rule (or set of rules) that—if adopted by all the elementary units in the system—would induce and sustain these properties?

To illuminate selected aspects of these problems, in this chapter we present and discuss a class of evolutionary models based on the theory of cellular automata (Gutowitz, 1991; Packard & Wolfram, 1985; Wolfram, 1983, 1984). The central feature of this analytical framework is that although interaction rules and—ultimately—individual choice mechanisms are defined strictly at the local level, over time they induce highly regular system-level consequences. The class of models for organizational processes that we propose is grounded in the theoretical belief that one of the unique characteristics of the evolution of social systems is their "ability to reproduce the elements of which they consist by using the elements of which they consist" (Luhman, 1987, p. 113), and on the assumption that this process of reproduction is made possible by the recursive application of local rules of interaction ("routines") among elementary (i.e., "nondecomposable") units (Drazin & Sandelands, 1992). In keeping with current theories of organizations and markets (Hannan & Freeman, 1984; Leifer & White, 1987; Nelson & Winter, 1982), processes of reproducibility and recursive decision making are at the core of our modeling efforts.

We organize the chapter as follows. In the next section, we briefly discuss some of the implications of the micro-macro problem for theories of organizations, and we introduce a modeling framework that we believe speaks directly to issues of aggregation and disaggregation in the study of multilevel hierarchical systems. To exemplify the value of the modeling framework that we propose, in the third section we present two simulation-supported case studies centered on well-known prob-

lems in the study of collective action. Finally, in the fourth section we conclude the chapter by discussing some of the problems and promises of this class of computational models for the progress of evolutionary theories of organizations.

Dynamic Models of Local Interaction

Action and Structure in Multilevel Systems

To paraphrase the words of Coleman and Fararo (1992), no completely satisfactory theory of organization exists because no theory is available that simultaneously (a) explains the behavior of organizational systems, rather than the behavior of the individuals; (b) provides a psychological theory or model of individual motivation; and (c) establishes clear rules of transition between the level of behavior of individual actors and the level of organizational system behavior. In other words, no theory is available that helps students of organizations to reconstruct a nonfunctionalist link between structure and agency (Alexander & Giesen, 1987; Hannan, 1991).

For example, contemporary ecological theories of organizations typically (even if not exclusively) concentrate on the dynamics of composite actors called "organizational populations" but usually are silent about the role, if any, of individual action (Hannan & Carroll, 1992; Hannan & Freeman, 1989). According to this macro perspective, organizational evolution is driven by competitive and institutional forces outside the control of any one individual actor. As a consequence, this way of thinking about organizations is seen by some as "a little bit like a murder mystery in which the victim is killed for no reason at all. That is one does not get any sense of the reasons of individual motives that account for a particular organization and the characteristics it has" (Olson, 1986, pp. 178-179).

Building on the notion of bounded rationality introduced by Simon (1951, 1957) and March and Simon (1958), theories based on the psychology and economics of individual choice have taken the opposite route to understand organizational phenomena, and have started from the microfoundations of purposive action to try to reduce organizational structures and routines to cognitive limits in the information processing capacities of individual agents. Critics of this way of thinking about organizations question the value of this research strategy and wonder "whether there is a tight coupling between motives of participants and the collective action of organizations [given] the frequency with which unanticipated consequences of organizational action dominated the intended consequences" (Hannan, 1986, p. 179).

This distinction between micro- and macrolevels of analysis is the source of one of the most vexing problems in organization science because organizations evolve as multilevel hierarchical systems and units of observation rarely match units of analysis (Freeman, 1978; March, 1994; Simon, 1962; Singh, 1993). As a consequence, Galtung's "fallacy of the wrong level"—making direct translation of properties or relations from one level to another—is a common feature of organization studies regardless of the level at which action is analyzed.

Selected examples of current research topics in which an explicit connection between micro- and macrolevels is both needed and hard to specify *uniquely* include the relationship between economic rivalry and ecological competition (Barnett, 1997; Barnett & Carroll, 1987; Lomi & Larsen, 1997); between processes of individual variation and population-level retention (Aldrich, 1979; Campbell, 1969); between search routines, selection, and the diffusion of innovation (Nelson & Winter, 1982); between cultural transmission, cultural persistence, and institutionalization (Harrison & Carroll, 1991; Zucker, 1977); between the effects of density-dependent legitimation across different levels of spatial aggregation (Hannan et al., 1995); between individual decision-making rules and the aggregate flow of people, problems, and solutions through organizations (Cohen, March, & Olsen, 1972); between motivation and turnover (Krackhardt & Porter, 1985); between individual knowledge and group stability (Carley, 1991); between mobility and control (Padgett, 1990); between individual production decisions and market structures (Leifer & White, 1987); between the sense of confusion and ambiguity experienced by

individuals at work, and the fact that organizations most of the time do get things done in a predictable and cyclical way (Cohen & March, 1974); and—finally—the relationship between programs of quality improvement of specific production processes and overall organizational performance (Sterman, Repenning, & Kofman, 1997).

At a surface level, it is not at all clear that these very different organizational problems—and the correspondingly different methods and theoretical frameworks that have been adopted to address them—have anything in common apart from being members of our arbitrary list. At a deeper level, however, the various examples of organizational research that we mentioned share a surprisingly similar set of problems related to the specification of how aggregate outcomes emerge from the interaction of individual units (however defined) because—as White, Boorman, and Breiger (1974) put it, 'All sociologists' discourse rests on primitive terms . . . which *require* an aggregation principle in that their referents are aggregates of persons, collectivities, interrelated positions, or generalized actors" (p. 733). Note that this problem is independent of the starting point. Macro theorists face issues of sensitivity of their models to alternative assumptions about micro behavior, and hence of stability of their "generalized" actors (DiMaggio, 1994). Conversely, micro theorists carry the burden of specifying how their assumptions about individual behavior translate into more or less permanent aggregates (e.g., groups, organizations, or markets).

How might we integrate these abstract considerations into a coherent modeling framework? Building on our recent research efforts (Lomi & Larsen, 1995, 1996, 1997, 1998), in the following section we present a qualitative description of the internal structure of one- and two-dimensional cellular automata models. We introduce this class of models as one of the simplest ways in which connectivity among a set of social objects can be represented and illustrate the value of this modeling framework through concrete applications to generic types of problems frequently encountered in the study of decentralized organizational systems. In our discussion, we avoid as much as possible technical details that can be found elsewhere

(Wolfram, 1994) and concentrate on those features of the analytical approach that make it particularly useful to students of organizations.

Computational Models of Organizational Evolution

Under conditions of bounded rationality—which prevents individual agents from processing global information about the configuration reached by the system as a whole—and weak centralization—which increases the cost for individuals to form a shared understanding of what configurations of the system are desirable at given point in time—questions arise about the laws of composition according to which interdependent individual actions are transformed into some form of collective order. Obviously, a modeling framework is needed that can incorporate the local character of individual strategies while simultaneously accounting for the emergent regularities that become visible only at more aggregate levels of analysis.

Cellular automata are mathematical representations of social or physical systems in which many simple components interact according to local rules but produce complicated patterns of collective behavior. Cellular automata seem to capture essential features of economic and social organizations because—as Drazin and Sandelands (1992) put it, "organization can be explained by observation and categorization of interactions of independent actors whose behavior is governed by a system of recursively applied rules" (p. 236). But how—exactly—does the iteration of local rules that govern the behavior of independent actors produce and reproduce the aggregate regularities that we often associate with organizational structures?

Suppose that an organizational system (e.g., a "market") can be defined such that agents (elementary decision-making units) occupy cells (or "sites") on a d-dimensional lattice ($d \epsilon N$), and that the behavior of each unit can be completely characterized in terms of a variable S^i_t that defines the state of unit i at time t (where $i = 1, 2, .., N$; $t = 1, 2, \ldots, T$). Suppose further that the state occupied by each cell on the lattice at time $t + 1$ depends only on (a) its own state and (b) the state assumed by a finite number of neighbors at time t. Then an individual "choice" can be represented in terms of a transition function ϕ that maps $S^i_t \rightarrow S^i_t + 1$. In a one-dimensional lattice ($d = 1$), the transition function can be represented as

$$S^i_t = \phi(S^{i-k}_{t-1}, S^{i-k+1}_{t-1}, \ldots, S^i_{t-1}, S^{i+k}_{t-1}, \quad (1)$$

where S^i_t is the state occupied by cell i at time t, ϕ is a Boolean function that determines a mapping from one set of neighborhood states to a set of site states, and k defines the range of local interaction. This mapping is defined in terms of a set of local rules described by an 8-digit binary string. Because any 8-digit binary string identifies a specific cellular automata, there are 256 possible rules in a one-dimensional model with nearest-neighbor interaction. Figure 14.1 illustrates the internal mechanics of a one-dimensional model in which the state of the central cell i at time $t + 1$ ($= 0$) results from the application of the following rule: "Let any cell that is central in the local sequence [1, 0, 1] at time t *go to* [0] at time $t + 1$."

To set this apparently simple system in motion and simulate its dynamic behavior, we now need to define its (a) range of local interaction, (b) initial conditions, (c) boundary conditions, and (d) recursive updating mechanism. The range of the rule (k) defines the number of cells that affect (and are affected directly by) the central cell. The initial conditions needed to set the system in motion can be determined by a random allocation of cells to states, or by assignment of a nonzero value to a single cell. Boundary conditions can be set either by assigning fixed random values to cells at the boundary of the system (fixed boundary conditions) or by bending the one-dimensional system represented in Figure 14.1 and placing the cells on a ring so that the first and the last cells are adjacent (periodic boundary conditions). In cellular automata models, space and time are discrete, and cellular agents can take on only a finite (and usually small) number of discrete states. The sequence of states occupied by individual cells evolves synchronously in discrete steps according to the values of the cells in a neighborhood of radius k. The state of each cell on the lattice is updated homogene-

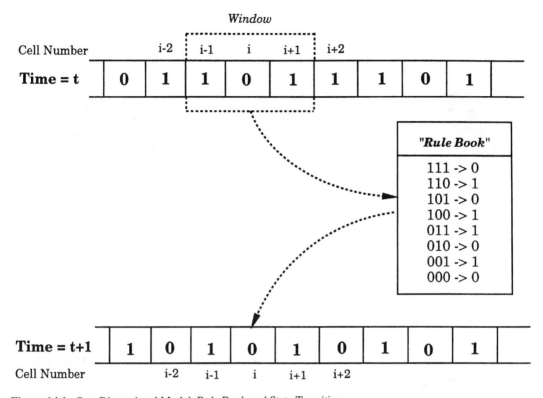

Figure 14.1. One-Dimensional Model: Rule Book and State Transition

ously (the evolution of every cell is regulated by the same local rule) and synchronously (the state of every cell is updated at the same time in discrete time steps). The reader interested in the mathematical details and the substantive implications of these alternative analytical choices is referred to Toffoli and Margolus (1987), Wolfram (1983), and Martin, Odlyzko, and Wolfram (1984).

One-dimensional cellular automata models have been adopted extensively in computer science (Nishio, 1981), physics (Wolfram, 1983, 1984), and chemistry (Canning & Droz, 1990). In the social sciences, selected areas of application of one-dimensional cellular automata models include economic cycles (Albin, 1987), decentralized market exchange (Albin & Foley, 1992), competition and collusion (Keenan & O'Brian, 1993), and voting behavior (Lomi & Larsen, 1995).

As a natural extension of the model just described, two-dimensional cellular automata models offer a more realistic (and interesting) representation of the connectivity among the many elementary components of a completely decentralized social system. Two-dimensional models allow for a wide variety of neighborhood structures; hence, they facilitate the exploration of alternative hypotheses about how micro-connectivity affects the aggregate dynamics of social systems. Figure 14.2 illustrates three possible neighborhood structures for two-dimensional cellular automata.

As before, each cell in the two-dimensional lattice represents an elementary computational unit that transforms input information about the states of its neighbors at time t into an action defined in terms of possible state transitions at time $t + 1$. A fixed rule is used to update the state of every cell in the lattice synchronously. As in the one-dimensional case, the extension of a neighborhood is determined by k, the parameter that regulates the range of local interaction. For example, when $k = 1$, the corresponding Moore neighborhood includes the eight cells that touch a given cell (plus

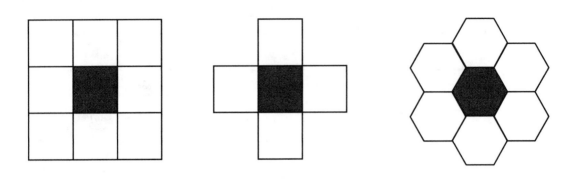

Figure 14.2. Possible Neighborhood Structures for Two-Dimensional Cellular Automata

the central cell itself), whereas when $k = 2$, each local neighborhood contains 24 cells (plus the central cell itself), and so on. The generic description of a two-dimensional automata is

$$S_{i,j}^t = \theta \left(\sum_{i=i-k}^{i=i+k} \sum_{j=j-k}^{j=j+k} S_{i,j}^{t-1} \right), \qquad (2)$$

where S_{ij}^t is the state of cell $a_{i,j}$ at time t and ϕ is the transition function. Despite the simplicity of their construction, cellular automata of this kind have been found able to produce extremely complicated behavior, and one often must resort to experimental methods (e.g., simulation) to elucidate their aggregate dynamical properties. The interested reader is referred to Packard and Wolfram (1985) for an introduction to two-dimensional cellular automata models. Here, we observe that—as in the one-dimensional model—decisions about initial conditions, boundary conditions, and the type of updating mechanism are needed before the aggregate behavior of this discrete dynamical system can be analyzed. In the examples that we present below, initial conditions are determined by a small cluster of nonzero sites in a background of zero sites. Boundary conditions are determined by assigning a fixed random value to the m cells that are nearest to the border of the lattice. Finally, Figure 14.3 illustrates how the updating mechanism operates in

a two-dimensional cellular automata model with nearest neighbor interaction.

Applications of two-dimensional cellular automata to problems in the natural and physical sciences (Packard & Wolfram, 1985), chemistry (Walgraef, 1995), biology (Blomberg & Cronhjort, 1995; Hogeweg, 1988), and ecology (Lindgren & Nordahl, 1996; Nowak & May, 1992) are becoming increasingly common. In the social sciences, selected areas of application of two-dimensional cellular automata models include the ecological dynamics of organizational populations (Lomi & Larsen, 1996, 1997), the formation of cultural patterns (Axelrod, 1995), the effect of elites on the stability of political systems (Brown & McBurnett, 1993), the evolution of strategy (Lomi & Larsen, 1997), and the effects of imitation on profit margins (Larsen & Markides, 1997).

Case Studies

To illustrate the value of the modeling framework that we propose, we now present two simulation-supported case studies designed to (a) reveal the computational structure of problems typically encountered in the study of collective action and (b) represent this structure as a model that can be simulated. In the first case study, we take as the starting point an example discussed by Jon Elster in his work on social order and social norms

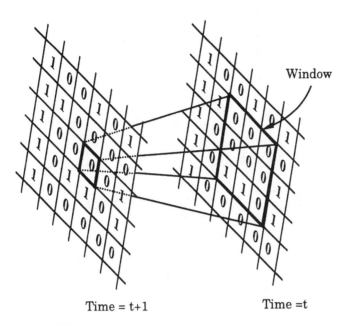

Time = t+1   Time =t

Figure 14.3. Two-Dimensional Model: Local Rules and State Transitions

(1989a, 1989b) and formalize it as a one-dimensional cellular automata to study possible connections between alternative micro-behavioral rules and their collective consequences. Among other things, we use this first example to illustrate the multiple connections existing between (unobservable) individual values and their (observable) system-level implications in the absence of any form of centralized authority, or coordination mechanism. In the second case study, we explore the dynamics of local interaction in the context of a stylized voting system in which individual agents vote following a strict majority rule defined over partially overlapping local neighborhoods. We use this second example to illustrate the relationship among norms, chance mutation, and system stability under conditions of direct and diffuse positional externalities.

The Evolutionary Dynamics of "Communities of Values"

> People are responding to an environment that consists of other people responding to *their* environment, which consists of people responding to an environment of people's responses. (Schelling, 1978, p. 14)

To illustrate the problem of cooperation and collective order in social systems, Jon Elster (1989a, 1989b) provides the following example that we now restate in a slightly modified form. Consider a community of farmers who own adjacent plots arranged around a lake, as depicted in Figure 14.4.

To expand the amount of cultivated land—and increase their revenues—farmers would like to fell trees on their respective properties, but farmers know that deforestation will bring erosion, which in turn will reduce the amount of land available for cultivation. Farmers are aware that that erosion will occur in any given plot if and only if trees are felled on that plot and the two adjacent ones. The situation is interesting because there is nothing that farmers can do individually to prevent erosion: They need to find some way to coordinate their actions. If each individual farmer pursues a utility-maximizing strategy (and utility is a function of expected revenue), then the aggregate outcome will be total deforestation. As a consequence, all land will be lost to the lake and everyone will be worse off—unless some form of "political" (i.e., nonlocal) solution is found. A second aggregate equilibrium outcome could be that no farmer will fell his or her trees. This might happen because the

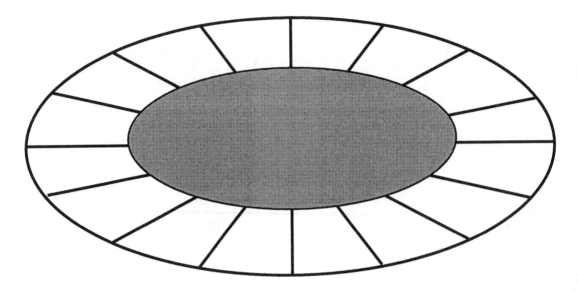

Figure 14.4. Elster's Farming Community

fear of erosion generates some form of "solidarity," or simply because farmers distrust one another. In this case, very different—in fact opposite— assumptions about micro motives ("solidarity" vs. "distrust") will generate the same macro outcome because in either case trees will be kept on all the plots.

Equilibrium situations that are intermediate between "none" and "all" also are possible. For example, trees could be kept in every third plot. This equilibrium solution is stable because owners of plots with trees have no "rational" incentive to cut, and owners of plots without trees have no incentive to plant. The question in this intermediate case is this: Who will bear the private cost of securing a collective benefit? In terms of the general question that we address in this chapter, we may ask, How can we link alternative assumptions about micro rules of behaviors and their aggregate system-level consequences?

To illustrate how the modeling framework that we introduced in the previous section can help to generate insight into these matters, we start by reframing Jon Elster's example as a one-dimensional cellular automaton. Let the plots of land containing trees be represented by "1s" and plots

without trees by "0s." These are the two (mutually exclusive) states that each individual unit can be in at any one time. Suppose now that there are two types of farmers: "Kantians" and "Utilitarians." The first type of farmer does not consider the cost to himself of cooperating. He refuses to act on the basis of principles that he would not want to see everyone else adopt. For this reason—and following Elster (1989a, chap. 5)—we call him the "Kantian" farmer. He will plant trees on his plot if he discovers that his neighbors have cut theirs. If he has trees on his plot but both his right and left neighbors do not, the Kantian farmer will keep his trees to avoid erosion in both his and his neighbors' properties. The micro rules that regulate the behavior of the Kantian farmer are described in Table 14.1, which enumerates the states assumed by all possible triples of adjacent plots (column 1, 2 and 3) at time $t - 1$, the state of the central plot at time t (column 4), and a verbal description of individual rules of behavior underlying the different state transitions.

In Table 14.1, column 4 contains the specific rule that we use to simulate the evolutionary dynamics of our artificial rural community in which all members are Kantian farmers. Figure 14.5 represents

TABLE 14.1 Kantian Farmer: Rules of Local Interaction

S^{i-1}_{t-1}	S^{i-1}_{t-1}	S^{i}_{t-1}	S^{i}_{t}	*Rules of Local Interaction*
1	1	1	0	I will cut my trees provided that there are trees in all adjacent plots.
1	1	0	1	I will keep my trees so that at least two out of three plots have trees.
1	0	0	1	I will plant trees because only one plot has trees.
1	0	1	0	I do not need to plant trees since both my neighbors have trees.
0	1	1	1	I will keep my trees so that at least two out of three plots have trees.
0	0	0	1	I will plant trees because none of my neighbors seem to have trees.
0	0	1	1	I will plant trees because only one plot has trees.
0	1	0	1	I keep my trees because I am the only one having trees.

the first 75 time periods in the evolution of the system with periodic boundary conditions initialized by randomly assigning three plots with trees to sites on a ring with 100 cells. Every time period, the system expands by one row, while by column it is possible to track the sequence of states occupied by each cell over time.

Figure 14.6 represents the same situation, but with a random initial allocation of states ("trees" = 1/black; "no trees" = 0/gray) to sites. As before, the system expands by one row every time period. Unlike the previous case, system behavior here is more differentiated. By column, it is possible to find individual farmers who will never have trees on their property (solid vertical gray stripes), farmers who will always keep trees on their property (solid vertical black stripes), and farmers who will switch periodically between states. Note how the same individual choice mechanism can generate and sustain very different patterns of behavior over time. No assumptions about the heterogeneity of individual preferences are needed for individual differences to emerge.

Figure 14.7 illustrates the aggregate number of plots with trees over time (obtained by counting and plotting the number of 1s or black cells in each row of Figure 14.6). At the aggregate level, a community of Kantian farmers will be characterized by a periodic oscillatory motion with fixed amplitude in which the same states will be visited infinitely many times, and without any tendency to converge to equilibrium.

We called the second type of farmer "Utilitarian" because she will not be the first in the neighborhood to plant trees in her plot (i.e., she refuses to contribute to public goods because she is sensitive to her own cost of cooperating). She will systematically try to free ride on her neighbors by cutting the trees on her plot and expanding cultivated land, if both her neighbors maintain trees on their plots. Finally, if her neighbors do not have trees on their plots, she would rather cut her trees than let others free ride on her (i.e., she is sensitive to her position *relative* to others and does not act on absolute "categorical imperatives," as the Kantian farmer would do). Table 14.2 summarizes the micro behavior of the Utilitarian farmer in terms of the corresponding cellular automata rule in column 4.

Figure 14.8 illustrates the behavior of a model that is initialized by placing a single nonzero (black) cell in an array of zero (gray) cells, and then simulating 75 time periods to observe the diffusion process implied by the local rule of interaction. As

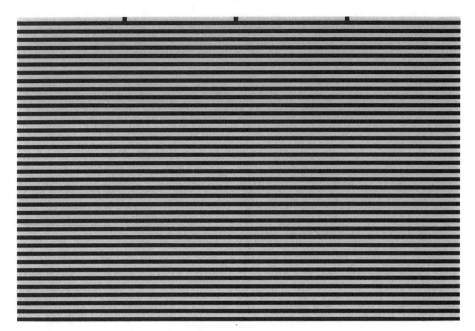

Figure 14.5. Kantian Farmer With Fixed Initial Conditions: Time From 1 to 75
NOTE: Black denotes plots with trees; gray denotes plots without trees.

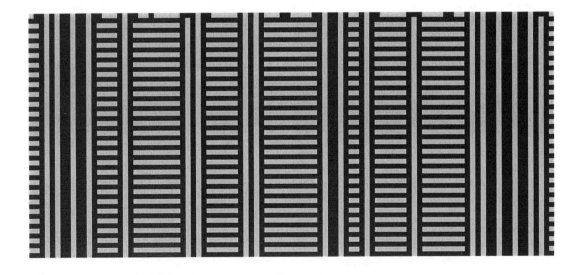

Figure 14.6. Kantian Farmer With Random Initial Conditions: Time From 1 to 50
NOTE: Black denotes plots with trees; gray denotes plots without trees.

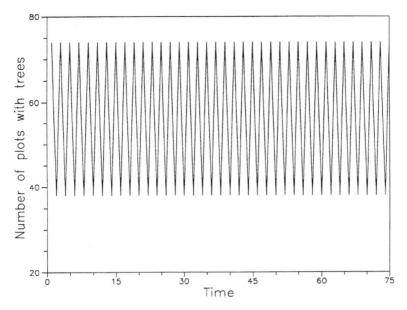

Figure 14.7. Number of Plots With Trees in the Community of the Kantian Farmers

TABLE 14.2 Utilitarian Farmer: Rules of Local Interaction

S^{i-1}_{t-1}	S^{i-1}_{t-1}	S^i_{t-1}	S^i_t	*Rules of Local Interaction*
1	1	1	0	I will cut my trees because there are trees in all adjacent plots.
1	1	0	1	Since at least one other plot has trees besides mine, I will do nothing.
1	0	0	1	I will plant trees because only one adjacent plot has trees.
1	0	1	0	I do not need to plant trees because both my neighbors have trees.
0	1	1	1	Since at least one other plot has trees besides mine, I will do nothing.
0	0	0	0	I will not be the first to plant trees.
0	0	1	1	I will plant trees because only one adjacent plot has trees.
0	1	0	0	I will not be keeping my trees to let others benefit.

before, configurations at successive time steps are shown as successive lines. The result is the presence of large areas without trees (light gray triangles) that have a tendency to contract and expand periodically. Another important feature of the aggregate structure of this system is its self-similarity: If expanded, a part will reproduce the whole. Note that at time 65, the aggregate number of trees (36) is close to the optimal (33, or 1 every 3 plots), although the distribution of trees is nonoptimal.

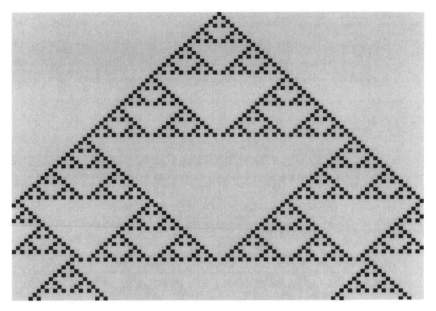

Figure 14.8. Utilitarian Farmer With Fixed Initial Conditions: Time From 1 to 75
NOTE: Black denotes plots with trees; gray denotes plots without trees.

Figure 14.9. Utilitarian Farmer With Random Initial Conditions: Time From 1 to 50
NOTE: Black denotes plots with trees; gray denotes plots without trees.

Figure 14.9 represents the same model initialized by random allocation of states to sites. In this case, the aggregate structure of the system is very fragmented. No adjacent three plots will stay without trees for longer than 5 periods, and no plots occupy the same state for longer than 10 consecu-

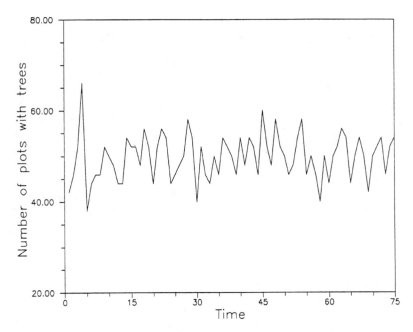

Figure 14.10. Number of Plots With Trees in the Community of Utilitarian Farmers

tive time periods. This outcome is quite different from the case of the Kantian community, in which we observe a more evident and permanent "division of labor."

Figure 14.10 illustrates the aggregate number of plots with trees over time (obtained by counting and plotting the number of 1s, or black cells, in each row of Figure 14.9). As before, at the aggregate level, a community of Utilitarian farmers will look very different from a community of Kantian farmers (compare Figure 14.10 with Figure 14.7). The number of plots with trees in the Utilitarian community fluctuates around a mean without detectable cycles, and without an obvious tendency to settle down to an equilibrium. The range of fluctuation, however, is reduced. It is also worth noticing that—as one would expect—the mean number of plots with trees is below that found in the community of Kantian farmers. In both cases, the mean aggregate number of trees is above the minimum required to sustain the community, but the distribution of plots differs significantly.

What if the two communities are not segregated by type of farmers, and Kantian and Utilitarian have to coexist in the *same* community? This type

of question can be addressed in our modeling framework by designing a system in which the different types of farmers are mixed in various proportions, then randomly assigned to sites. For example, in Figure 14.11a, Kantians and Utilitarians are mixed in equal proportions, whereas the frame represented in Figure 14.11d is generated by a system containing 90% Utilitarian farmers. Stable subcommunities of varying size are observable regardless of the mixing regime, indicating that competitive exclusion is not the norm in this kind of system. In panel 14.11b, four detectable (and partially segregated) Kantian communities survive in an environment dominated by Utilitarians.

Figure 14.12a contains the time series graph of the aggregate number of plots with trees under alternative mixing regimes. At the aggregate level, there is no significant difference in the number of plots with trees over time (because the time-series graphs overlap), although the spatial organization of the four systems is quite different (as clearly shown in Figures 14.11a, b, c, and d). Figures 14.12b-e illustrate the proportion of sites with trees (over the total number of sites) for the two types of farmers under alternative mixing regimes. The up-

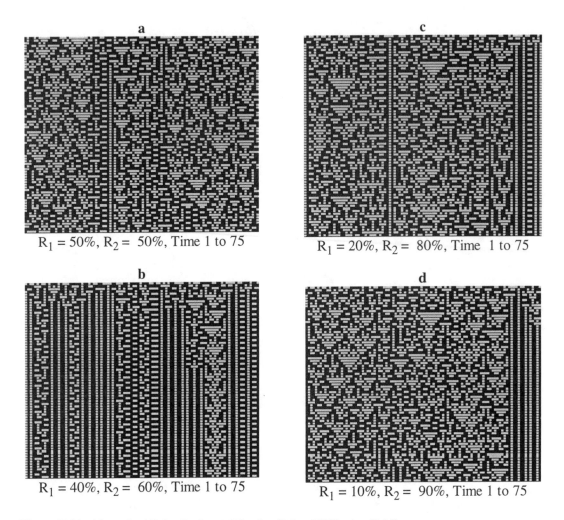

Figure 14.11. Alternative Mixing Regimes of Kantian (R_1) and Utilitarian (R_2) Farmers

per line in the graphs always represents the proportion of plots with trees owned by Kantian farmers. We note that a high proportion of Kantian farmers is associated with a lower proportion of plots with trees owned by Utilitarians (compare, for example, Figures 14.12b and 14.12e). This happens because of the Utilitarians' systematic tendency to free ride. Although the mean proportion of plots with trees owned by Kantian farmers is relatively stable, the volatility of the series increases as the proportion of Utilitarians in the community increases.

To facilitate the illustration of selected features of our modeling framework, we chose a suitably simple example. It is not difficult to modify the basic model to incorporate additional complications such as, for example, explicit competitive links between the two types of "species" and the definition of a payoff matrix associated with different strategies that they can play. This would make the model similar to that of Nowak and May (1993). Another possibility would be to modify the updating mechanism so that the sequence of states assumed by a cell on the lattice depends on the kind of cells that happen to be in its neighborhood. This would make the model similar to a spatial version of Axelrod's (1984) model. The evolutionary im-

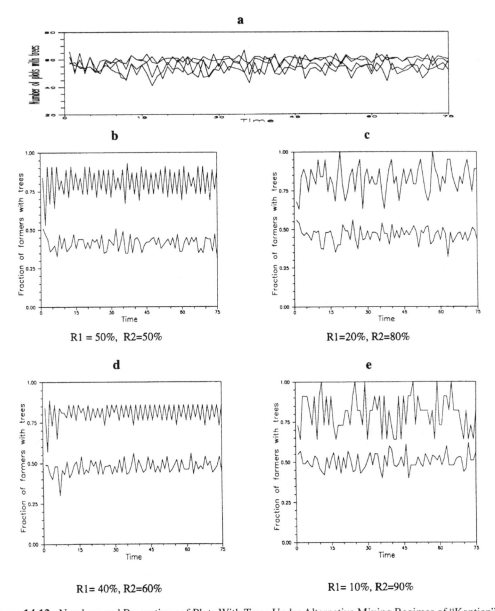

Figure 14.12. Numbers and Proportions of Plots With Trees Under Alternative Mixing Regimes of "Kantian" (R_1) and "Utilitarian" (R_2) Farmers

NOTE: Figure 14.12a shows the total number of plots with trees. Figures 14.12b-e show proportions of plots with trees for the two types of farmers; Kantian farmers (R_1) are the top line in each figure.

plications of alternative assumptions about memory structures could then be explored (Lindgren & Nordahl, 1996).

Of great analytical interest is the discovery of invariants in the evolution of systems similar to those discussed in this example. An example of possible invariant in the two-state, one-dimensional model that we presented is the ratio of cells in the system that occupy state "1" to those that occupy state "0," because in some cases this quantity has been shown to be insensitive to variations in local rules. In physics applications, this quantity typically is referred to as magnetization of the system (Canning & Droz, 1990).

Shifting Involvements and Majority Rule

> There are no societies, only individuals interacting with each other. Yet the structure of interaction allows us to identify clusters of individuals who interact more strongly with each other than with people in other clusters. (Elster, 1989a, p. 248)

In this second case study, we explore the surprisingly rich dynamic behavior of an artificial political system in which individual "citizens" behave according to a simple majority rule. Building on the basic model of Brown and McBurnett (1993), our goal here is to tell an interesting and credible aggregate story starting from assumptions on micro rules of interaction among individual objects in a large social system without any global coordination mechanism. In a voting system, the aggregation of individual preferences into some kind of "collective preference" is complicated by the apparently obvious fact that "A voter imitates other voters, but at the same time they imitate him" (Nelson, 1994, p. 92).

Possibly the most commonly discussed example of a micro rule of interaction among social units is the deterministic majority rule, according to which a given option is collectively preferred if enough individuals prefer it to alternative options that are equally available, where exactly how many individuals is "enough" is defined in terms of more or less arbitrary majority threshold. We concentrate on the majority rule because it is straightforward, because it is adopted in a wide range of real-life decision situations that require the aggregation of individual preferences, and because, as Schubik (1982) put it, "The simple majority rule plays a central role in the theory of group choice (voting) and the theory of group preference (utility aggregation)" (p. 109).

Suppose that members of a political system face a binary voting choice situation ("0" or "1"), and suppose that individual members are aware of—and are influenced by—the choice of only a limited number of alters that are proximate in their social

networks. Suppose further that individual voting choices at time $t + 1$ are made following a simple majority rule, according to which individuals will select the option chosen at time t by the majority of alters in their immediate social networks—defined as neighborhoods of range k in a regular two-dimensional lattice.

At time t, the number of individuals voting "1" in any k-neighborhood is

$$\alpha_{i,j}^t = \sum_{i=i-k}^{i=i+k} \sum_{j=j-k}^{j=j+k} S_{i,j}^{t-1} \tag{3}$$

where $S^{t-1}_{i,j}$ is the state occupied by each cell at time $t - 1$. The decision rule followed by each individual can be formalized as the following:

$$S_{i,j}^t = \begin{cases} \text{if } \alpha > \tau \ \textit{Then} \ S_{i,j}^t = 1 \\ \text{Otherwise } \ S_{i,j}^t = 0 \end{cases} \tag{4}$$

where τ is the majority threshold above which an individual will choose "1." The four space-time frames reported in Figure 14.13 illustrate the evolutionary dynamics of this stylized voting system initialized by random allocation of states to sites. The system displays a tendency toward self-organization, in the sense that after 25 periods, the disordered initial configuration has evolved into localized stable areas of "consensus" (or clique-like substructures) with no further tendency toward change.

The system is extremely sensitive to the threshold value t. When $k = 1$ (i.e., in the nearest neighbor model), any value of τ different from 5 will induce "instantaneous propagation," causing the system to converge rapidly to 0 (if $\tau < 5$) or 1 (if $\tau > 5$). Similar issues of sensitivity arise with respect to initial conditions. For example, Figure 14.14 shows how different initial random allocations of states to sites in the lattice produce different patterns of spatial organizations, even if the aggregate proportion of "1" votes does not differ significantly in the four cases—as should be expected. In this case, the same micro rule of behavior produces similar aggregate results, and this is consistent with intuition. Different intermediate structures (homogeneous clusters or "cliques"), however, will

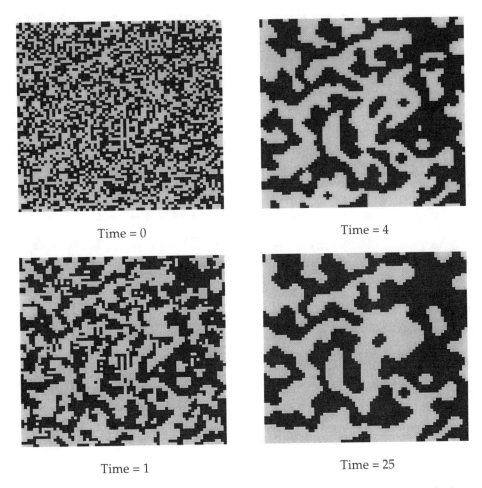

Time = 0   Time = 4

Time = 1   Time = 25

Figure 14.13. Space-Time Patterns in the Evolution of the System During 25 Successive Rounds in the Case of $k = 1$, $\tau = 5$

emerge as a specific path-dependent feature of the system.

Changes in the range of local interaction represent a third element to which the system is extremely sensitive. This is so because the size of local social networks determines the propagation features of the system. Figure 14.15 shows that as k increases from 1 to 3, the spatial organization of the system becomes coarser and segregation increases. When $k = 3$ (each local network includes 34 alters plus the central cell), the system is clearly partitioned into two homogeneous "factions." The spatial organization of the factions, their relative size, and the extent to which they are segregated is controlled by τ. When $k = 3$ and $\tau = 26$, the 0-faction will control more than 80% of the system.

When $\tau = 25$, the 1-faction will win approximately 75% of the total votes. Any $\tau > 26$ or $\tau < 25$ will result in the instantaneous propagation of 1-votes and 0-votes, respectively.

Even if the link between micro motives and macro behavior in the models that we simulated is at times hard to predict and—in general—not unique, the models themselves are purely deterministic. In a fundamental sense, this is exactly what makes them interesting. Although there are many ways of introducing random elements in cellular automata models of social processes (Lomi & Larsen, 1995), here we want narrow our focus on the role of variation—a central theme of this volume. Consider the setup of the two-dimensional voting model defined in Equations (3) and (4).

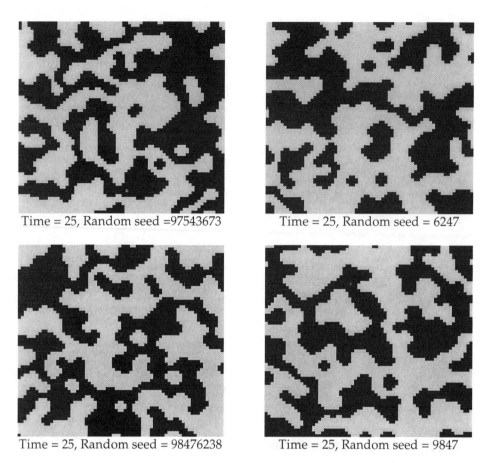

Time = 25, Random seed =97543673   Time = 25, Random seed = 6247

Time = 25, Random seed = 98476238   Time = 25, Random seed = 9847

Figure 14.14. The Effect of Initial Conditions on the Final Pattern of Votes in the Case of $k = 1$, $\tau = 5$

Now let each voter face a (small) probability of "mutation," defined as the probability that a voter might choose not to conform to the majority in their neighbors. There are several micro assumptions that can be invoked to justify mutation in this setting: Individuals may end up voting against the majority because they make mistakes, or because they are misinformed about what the others do, because they have a hidden agenda, or simply because they "do not want to belong to a group that accepts them as members" (Lomi & Larsen, 1994). Obviously, each of these assumptions implies a different meaning of "learning," and perhaps a different notion of "identity."

Figure 14.16 plots the aggregate number of "1" votes in situations defined in terms of different mutation rates. The time-series plots illustrate that the strength of path dependence increases as the mutation rate increases, although there is no easy way of predicting in which direction. For example, when the probability of voting against the majority is 0.03, "1" voters will establish their dominance early in the evolution of the system and gradually expand ever after. When the probability of voting against the majority is increased to 0.05, the number of "1" voters will decline exponentially during the first 1,500 time periods, then gradually stabilize at a permanently lower level. When we increase the probability of chance mutation to 0.10, the aggregate number of "1" voters increases rapidly during the first 800 time periods, then stabilizes at a constant level. The counterintuitive implication of these results is that—if the system is sensitive to initial conditions—early chance mutations may

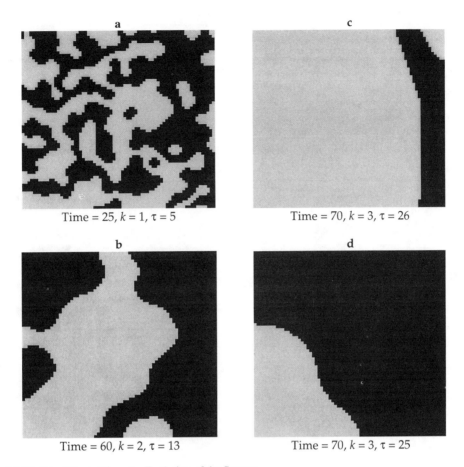

Time = 25, $k = 1$, $\tau = 5$

Time = 70, $k = 3$, $\tau = 26$

Time = 60, $k = 2$, $\tau = 13$

Time = 70, $k = 3$, $\tau = 25$

Figure 14.15. The Effect of k on the Evolution of the System

progressively increase the stability of the system by reinforcing the tendency toward a given solution (e.g., all 1s or all 0s). In other words, mutation at the individual level does not necessarily reflect itself in system-level diversity.

Obviously, we represented only the simplest possible situation, in which the probability of chance mutation does not vary over time. It would be straightforward to modify the model and make the mutation rate a (more or less arbitrary) function of time, provided—of course—that theoretical or empirically grounded reasons exist to believe that mutation rates vary predictably over the evolutionary history of a system. As we mentioned, theoretical suggestions in this sense are likely to be highly dependent on the specific meaning of "learning" that one finds useful in specific circumstances.

Discussion and Conclusion

Ways of thinking about the evolutionary dynamics of social and economic institutions differ in what are selected as the most interesting features of evolutionary processes. The computational models that we discussed in this chapter are based on what we consider to be three of the most salient characteristics of the evolutionary dynamics of organizations viewed as multilevel social systems in which "Units of adaptation are nested, so that some adapting units (e.g., individuals) are integral parts of other adapting units (e.g., organizations)" (March, 1994, p. 43).

The first is the unique ability of organizations to reproduce their structures by recombining their existing components into new formations over

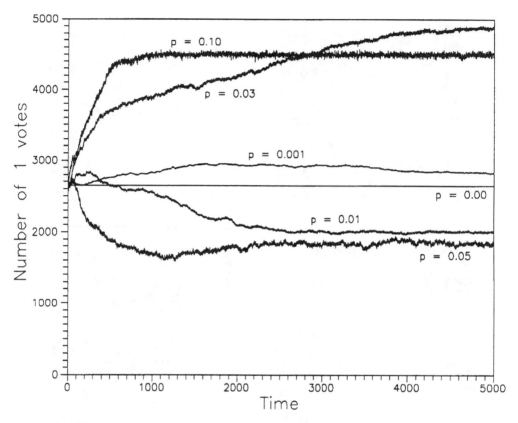

Figure 14.16. The Evolution of "1" Votes Over Time as a Function of the Probability *p* of Chance Mutation

relatively short periods of time. In the theoretical literature, this type of social reproduction has been variously defined as the "autopoietic" (Drazin & Sandelands, 1992), "self-referential" (Luhman, 1987), or "recombinant" (Stark, 1996) quality of organizational and social structures. The second is that interaction among elementary units is governed by recursive rules and routines that become the main "source of continuity in behavioral pattern of organizations" (Nelson & Winter, 1982, p. 96). The existence of routinized rules of interaction obviously is related to processes of reproduction because routinization facilitates reproducibility (Hannan & Freeman, 1984). The third property that we considered as central to the understanding of the evolutionary dynamics of organizational systems is that individual units respond only to considerations that are local in a physical, temporal, or cognitive sense; that is, elementary units

of social systems process only local information. This assumption is consistent with what we know about processes of adaptive learning within and between organizations because "most theories of learning and selection are theories of local adaptation. They assume a process in which the relevant factors are localized in time and space" (March, 1994, p. 42).

Building on these considerations, we proposed in this chapter a specific way in which these features can be incorporated in a coherent modeling framework inspired by the theory of cellular automata—mathematical idealizations of discrete dynamic systems that are of sufficiently simple construction but exhibit complex and varied dynamic behavior. We illustrated the value of this analytical framework by conducting two simulation experiments designed to address general problems of collective action. We showed how the basic framework can be modified to accommodate specific elements that characterize social—as opposed to physical—systems.

The short case studies that we reported represent particularly salient illustrations of the role of routines (recursive decision rules that regulate individual behavior) in population-level selection processes. As Miner and Raghavan discuss elsewhere in this volume, diffusion and imitation of decision rules are typically portrayed as variance-reducing processes. Although this view is clearly consistent with the neo-institutionalists' insistence on isomorphism in interorganizational fields, our simulation experiments show that—under plausible assumptions about rules of local interaction—population-level homogeneity does not follow directly (or necessarily) from processes of imitation and diffusion of individual behavior. As Miner and Raghavan (this volume) suggest, repeated imitation can induce and sustain a variety of system-level behaviors ranging from stable to oscillatory to periodical. The results of our simulation lend credibility to this conjecture and—in a sense—take it a step further. Although Miner and Raghavan (this volume) and Haunschild and Miner (1997) see the identity of imitating agents (Who are the agents?) and type of imitation strategy (What exactly do they imitate and how?) as the main elements behind population-level heterogeneity, in our model we show that—if individual agents have spatial extension—population-level heterogeneity will emerge even in the absence of any individual difference in identities or strategies. Our emphasis on the granularity and spatial extension of the organizational world implies a shift of the focus of attention away from the detailed characterization of individual differences and toward the micro connectivity of organizational agents; that is, toward the structure and dynamics of social networks. This conclusion speaks directly to some of the issues addressed by Madsen, Mosakowski, and Zaheer (this volume). Both our chapter and theirs imply that variation should not be studied independently of its propagation features, or its consequences at more aggregate levels. Seen from this perspective, the coupling between structural levels should be treated as a genuine empirical question.

In their current hypersimplified form, our representations are clearly far from being fully developed. The first basic limitation of the modeling framework is its synchronous updating mechanism. The state of every site on the lattice is updated at the same discrete time steps. Although this computational structure is generally considered a reasonable assumption in models of physical and chemical systems (Wolfram, 1986), its realism for modeling the mechanics of social and ecological processes can be questioned (Hogeweg, 1988). Asynchronous models are not difficult to build; however, Huberman and Glance (1993) argued that the behavior of the system is extremely sensitive to the assumption of synchronous updating.

The second limitation concerns the fact that the same rule is used to update the state of every cell in the lattice. By mixing agents who follow different local rules within the same system, in our first case study we showed one way in which this inherent limitation of cellular automata models can be removed to make the analytical framework more directly relevant to social scientists.

A third set of limitations concerns the specific tessellation structure chosen; that is, the structure of the lattice. The structure of the lattice raises crucial interpretation issues because—unlike models based on discrete neural or random networks—in cellular automata models, the structure of the lattice is fixed; that is, connectivity structures do not evolve over time. Within this modeling framework, it could be useful to explore the implications of alternative tessellation structures. Hexagonal and triangular arrays are less commonly used than square lattices, but they may be equally plausible in specific situations (Gutowitz & Victor, 1989). In principle, it could be possible to abandon a fixed integer lattice structure completely by placing cells at the vertices of a digraph so that both individual states of the cells and the structure of communication among cells can be made dependent on local rules. Only very recently has this direction been explored, and results available to date are mostly theoretical (Garzon, 1990).

Despite these varied limitations, we believe that our current work illustrates the great potential of computational models of organizations to further our understanding of the evolutionary dynamics of social systems by revealing the connection between organized collectivities and complex computational systems.

References

Albin, P. (1987). Microeconomic foundations of cyclical irregularities or "chaos." *Mathematical Social Sciences, 13*, 185-214.

Albin, P., & Foley, M. (1992). Decentralized, dispersed exchange without an auctioneer. A simulation study. *Journal of Economic Behavior and Organization, 18*, 27-51.

Aldrich, H. (1979). *Organizations and environments.* Englewood Cliffs, NJ: Prentice Hall.

Alexander, J. C., & Giesen, B. (1987). The long view on the micro-macro link. In J. C. Alexander, B. Giesen, R. Münch, & N. Smelser (Eds.), *The micro-macro link* (pp. 1-44). Berkeley: University of California Press.

Axelrod, R. (1984). *The evolution of cooperation.* New York: Basic Books.

Axelrod, R. (1995). *The convergence and stability of cultures: Local convergence and global polarization* (Working Paper 95-03-028). Santa Fe, NM: Santa Fe Institute.

Barnett, W. (1997). The dynamics of competitive intensity. *Administrative Science Quarterly, 42*(1), 128-160.

Barnett, W., & Carroll, G. (1987). Competition and mutualism among telephone companies. *Administrative Science Quarterly, 37*, 580-604.

Baum, J.A.C., & Haveman, H. A. (1997). Love thy neighbor? Differentiation and agglomeration in the Manhattan hotel industry, 1898-1990. *Administrative Science Quarterly, 42*, 304-338.

Baum, J.A.C., & Mezias, S. J. (1992) . Localized competition and organizational failure in the Manhattan hotel industry, 1898-1990. *Administrative Science Quarterly, 37*, 580-604.

Baum, J.A.C., & Singh, J. V. (1994). Organizational hierarchies and evolutionary processes: Some reflections on a theory of organizational evolution. In J.A.C Baum & J. V. Singh (Eds.), *Evolutionary dynamics of organizations* (pp. 3-22). New York: Oxford University Press.

Blomberg, C., & Cronhjort, M. (1995). Modeling errors and parasites in the evolution of primitive life: Possibilities of spatial self-structuring. In J. L. Casti & A. Karlquist (Eds.), *Cooperation and conflict in general evolutionary processes* (pp. 15-62). New York: Wiley.

Brown, T., & McBurnett, M. (1993, May). *The emergence of political elites.* Paper resented at the European Conference on Artificial Life, Brussels.

Burt, R. E. (1988). The stability of American markets. *American Journal of Sociology, 93*, 356-395.

Campbell, D. T. (1958). Common fate similarity and other indices of the status of aggregates of persons as social entities. *Behavioral Science, 3*, 14-25.

Campbell, D. T. (1969). Variation and selective retention in socio-cultural evolution. *General Systems, 16*, 69-85.

Campbell, D. T. (1974) . Downward causation in hierarchically organized biological systems. In F. Ayala & T. Dobzhansky (Eds.). *Studies in the philosophy of biology* (pp. 179-186). Berkeley: University of California Press.

Campbell, D. T. (1990). Levels of aggregation, downward causation and the selection theory approach to evolutionary epistemology. In G. Greenberg & E. Tobach (Eds.), *Theories of the evolution of knowing* (T. Schneirla Conference Series, Vol. 4, pp. 1-17). Hillsdale, NJ: Lawrence Erlbaum.

Campbell, D. T. (1994). How individual and face-to-face-group selection undermine firm selection in organizational evolution. In J.A.C. Baum & J. V. Singh (Eds.), *Evolutionary dynamics of organizations* (pp. 23-38). New York: Oxford University Press.

Canning, A., & Droz, M. (1990). A comparison of spin exchange and cellular automaton models for diffusion-controlled reactions. *Physica D, 45*, 285-292.

Carley, K. (1991). A theory of group stability. *American Sociological Review, 56*, 331-354.

Cohen, M. D., & March, J. (1974). *Leadership and ambiguity.* Cambridge, MA: Harvard Business School Press.

Cohen, M. D., March, J. G., & Olsen, P. (1972). A garbage can model of organizational choice. *Administrative Science Quarterly, 17*, 1-25.

Coleman, J. S., & Fararo, T. J. (1992). Introduction. In J. Coleman & T. Fararo (Eds.), *Rational choice theory: Advocacy and critique* (pp. ix-xxii). Newbury Park, CA: Sage.

DiMaggio, P. (1991). The micro-macro dilemma in organizational research: Implications of role-system theory. In J. Huber (Ed.), *Micro-macro linkages in sociology* (pp. 76-98). Newbury Park, CA: Sage.

DiMaggio, P. (1994). The challenge of community evolution. In J.A.C. Baum & J. V. Singh (Eds.), *Evolutionary dynamics of organizations* (pp. 444-450). New York: Oxford University Press.

Drazin, R., & Sandelands, L. (1992). Autogenesis: A perspective on the process of organizing. *Organization Science, 3*(2), 230-249.

Elster, J. (1989a). *The cement of society.* New York: Cambridge University Press.

Elster, J. (1989b). *Nuts and bolts for the social sciences.* New York: Cambridge University Press.

Freeman, J. (1978). The unit of analysis in organizational research. In M. Meyer (Ed.), *Environment and organizational structure* (pp. 335-351). San Francisco: Jossey-Bass.

Garzon, M. (1990). Cellular automata and discrete neural networks. *Physica D, 45*, 430-440.

Gutowitz, H. A. (Ed.). (1991). *Cellular automata: Theory and experiment.* Cambridge, MA: MIT Press.

Gutowitz, H. A., & Victor, J. D. (1989). Local structure theory: Calculations on hexagonal arrays. *Journal of Statistical Physics, 54*, 495-514.

Hannan, M. T. (1986). Ecological theory: General discussion. In S. Lindenberg, J. S. Coleman, & S. Nowak (Eds.), *Ap-*

proaches to social theory. New York: Russell Sage Foundation.

Hannan, M. T. (1991). *Aggregation and disaggregation in the social sciences.* Lexington, MA: Lexington Books.

Hannan, M. T. (1997). Inertia, density, and the structure of organizational populations: Entries in European automobile industries, 1886-1981. *Organization Studies, 18* 193-228.

Hannan, M., & Carroll, G. (1992). *Dynamics of organizational populations.* New York: Oxford University Press.

Hannan, M., Carroll, G., Dundon, E., & Torres, J. (1995). Organizational evolution in a multinational context: Entries of automobile manufacturers in Belgium, Britain, France, Germany, and Italy. *American Sociological Review, 60,* 509-528.

Hannan, M. T., & Freeman, J. (1984). Structural inertia and organizational change. *American Sociological Review, 49,* 149-164.

Hannan, M. T., & Freeman, J. (1986). Where do organizational forms come from? *Sociological Forum 1,* 50-72.

Hannan, M., & Freeman, J. (1989). *Organizational ecology.* Cambridge, MA: Harvard University Press.

Harrison, J. R., & Carroll, G. R. (1991). Keeping the faith: A model of cultural transmission in formal organizations. *Administrative Science Quarterly, 36*(4), 552-558.

Haunschild, P., & Miner, A. (1997). Modes of inter-organizational imitation: The effect of outcome salience and uncertainty. *Administrative Science Quarterly, 42*(3), 472-500.

Hogeweg, H. (1988). Cellular automata as a paradigm for ecological modeling. *Applied Mathematics and Computation, 27,* 81-100.

Huberman, B. A., & Glance, N. S. (1993). Evolutionary games and computer simulations. *Proceedings of The National Academy of Science, 90,* 7716-7718.

Keenan, D., & O'Brian, M. (1993). Competition, collusion and chaos. *Journal of Economic Dynamics and Control, 17,* 327-353.

Krackhardt, D., & Porter, L. (1985). When friends leave: A structural analysis of the relationship between turnover and stayer's attitude. *Administrative Science Quarterly, 30,* 242-261.

Larsen, E. R., & Markides, C. (1997). *Imitation and the sustainability of competitive advantage* (Working paper SLRP-28). London: London Business School.

Leifer, E., & White, H. (1987). A structural approach to markets. In M. Mizruchi & M. Schwartz (Eds.), *Intercorporate relations* (pp. 85-108). New York: Cambridge University Press.

Lindgren, K., & Nordahl, M. (1996). Cooperation and community structures in artificial ecosystems. In C. Langton (Ed.), *Artificial life* (pp. 15-37). Cambridge, MA: MIT Press.

Lomi, A. (1995). The population ecology of organizational founding: Location dependence and unobserved heterogeneity. *Administrative Science Quarterly, 40,* 111-144.

Lomi, A., & Larsen, E. (1994). *Would you belong to a club that accepted you as a member? A note on the macro-dynamics of micro-rules of social interaction* (Learning Centre Work-

ing Paper Series No. 94-12). London: London Business School.

Lomi, A., & Larsen, E. R. (1995). The emergence of organizational structure. In R. Burton & B. Obel (Eds.), *Design models for hierarchical organizations* (pp. 209-231). Boston: Kluwer Academic.

Lomi, A., & Larsen, E. R. (1996). Interacting locally and evolving globally: A computational approach to the dynamics of organizational populations. *Academy of Management Journal, 39*(4), 1287-1321.

Lomi, A., & Larsen, E. R. (1997). A computational approach to the evolution of competitive strategy. *Journal of Mathematical Sociology, 22*(2), 151-176.

Lomi, A., & Larsen, E. R. (1998). Density delay and organizational survival: Computational models and empirical comparisons. *Journal of Mathematical and Computational Organization Theory, 3*(4), 219-247.

Luhman, N. (1987). The evolutionary differentiation between society and interaction. In J. C. Alexander, B. Giesen, R. Münch, & N. Smelser (Eds.), *The micro-macro link* (pp. 112-134). Berkeley: University of California Press.

March, J. G. (1994). The evolution of evolution. In J.A.C. Baum & J. V. Singh (Eds.), *Evolutionary dynamics of organizations* (pp. 39-52). New York: Oxford University Press.

March, J. G., & Simon, H. A. (1958). *Organizations.* New York: Wiley.

Martin, O., Odlyzko, A. M., & Wolfram, S. (1984). Algebraic properties of cellular automata. *Communication in Mathematical Physics, 93,* 219-258.

Nelson, P. (1994). Voting and imitative behavior. *Economic Inquiry, 32,* 92-102.

Nelson, R. R., & Winter, S. G. (1982). *An evolutionary theory of economic change.* Cambridge, MA: Belknap Press.

Nishio, H. (1981). *Real time sorting of binary numbers by 1-dimensional cellular automata.* Unpublished manuscript, Kyoto University.

Nowak, M. A., & May, R. M. (1992). Evolutionary games and spatial chaos. *Nature, 359,* 826-829.

Nowak, M. A., & May, R. M. (1993). The spatial dilemmas of evolution. *International Journal of Bifurcation and Chaos, 3*(1), 35-78.

Olson, M. (1986). Ecological theory: General discussion. In S. Lindenberg, J. S. Coleman, & S. Nowak (Eds.), *Approaches to social theory.* New York: Russell Sage Foundation.

Packard, N. H., & Wolfram, S. (1985). Two dimensional cellular automata. *Journal of Statistical Physics, 38,* 901-946.

Padgett, J. (1990). Mobility as control: Congressmen through committees. In R. L. Breiger (Ed.), *Social mobility and social structure* (pp. 27-58). New York: Cambridge University Press.

Schelling, T. C. (1978). *Micromotives and macrobehavior.* New York: Norton.

Schubik, M. (1982). *Game theory and the social sciences: Concepts and solutions.* Boston: MIT Press.

Simon, H. A. (1951). A formal theory of the employment relation. *Econometrica, 19,* 293-305.

Simon, H. (1957). *Administrative behavior.* New York: Free Press.

Simon, H. (1962). The architecture of complexity. *Proceedings of the American Philosophical Society, 106,* 467-482.

Singh, J. (1993). Review essay: Density dependence theory: Current issues, future promise. *American Journal of Sociology, 99,* 464-473.

Stark, D. (1996). Recombinant property in East European capitalism. *American Journal of Sociology, 101*(4), 993-1027.

Sterman, J. D., Repenning, N. P., & Kofman, F. (1997). Unanticipated side effects of successful quality programs: Exploring a paradox of organizational improvement. *Management Science, 43*(4), 503-521.

Toffoli, T., & Margolus, N. (1987). *Cellular automata machines—A new environment for modeling.* Cambridge, MA: MIT Press.

Walgraef, D. (1995). Turing structures in chemical and materials instabilities. In P. E. Cladis (Ed.), *Spatio-temporal patterns in nonequilibrium complex systems* (pp. 425-436). Reading, MA: Addison-Wesley.

White, H., Boorman, S. A., & Breiger, R. L. (1974). Social structure from multiple networks, I. Blockmodels of roles and positions. *American Journal of Sociology, 81,* 730-780.

Wolfram, S. (1983). Statistical mechanics of cellular automata. *Reviews of Modern Physics, 55,* 601-644.

Wolfram, S. (1984). Universality and complexity in cellular automata. *Physica D, 10,* 1-35.

Wolfram, S. (1986). Cellular automata fluids: Basic theory. *Journal of Statistical Physics, 45,* 601-644.

Wolfram, S. (1994). *Cellular automata and complexity: Collected papers.* Reading, MA: Addison-Wesley.

Zucker, L. G. (1977). The role of institutionalization in cultural persistence. *American Sociological Review, 42,* 726-743.

Chapter 15

Self-Organization, Complexity Catastrophe, and Microstate Models at the Edge of Chaos

BILL McKELVEY

Consider General Motors Corporation. GM seems like a giant sequoia tree rotting slowly from the top. Theories abound as to why: myopic management; hubris; politics; vertical integration; inefficiency; outdated plant and equipment; the Icarus Paradox (Miller, 1990), resistance to change; permanently failing organizations (Meyer & Zucker, 1989), unions; and so forth. GM is a dinosaur (Loomis, 1993) stuck in a time warp with a "gargantuan bureaucracy" (Kerwin, 1998, p. 26) that, as a high-cost producer of low-quality cars, is well off the efficiency curve. It is not that there isn't motive. The industry is very competitive, and everyone in the industry knows GM is below the curve. Furthermore, GM has spent billions trying to get back on the curve—some say it has spent more than the total asset value of Toyota.

What is not working at GM, and can organization science explain it? Like Gaul, organization science is divided into three parts: rational, natural, and open systems (Scott, 1998). The rational system view—the visible hand, as Chandler (1977)—calls it, puts the blame on managers. The natural system view—the invisible hand—tells us that the emergent structure apparently is defeating whatever good ideas the managers do come up with. The open systems view focuses on environmental effects and boundary transactions. Paradigm proliferation (Donaldson, 1995) further delineates views within Scott's broad framework. Much as one might like some of the newer paradigms, Pfeffer (1997) cautions that much of the paradigm proliferation in organization science results from fads and fashion. He quotes himself 16 years earlier, saying, "If we use relatively simpler processes and models the world will appear to be simpler and more certain. . . . We overlook the potential for finding simpler models to describe the world" (1981, p. 411). So, in this chapter, I reduce Scott's framework to four driving forces: *adaptive tension*,

AUTHOR'S NOTE: I wish to thank Joel Baum and members of the Brussels Complexity Workshop for many helpful suggestions. All errors remaining are my responsibility. Citations in this chapter follow temporal order.

self-organization (by managers or nonmanagers), *interdependency effects*, and *multilevel coevolution*.

Ironically, Pfeffer (1997) decries the dangerous liaison with economics while simultaneously calling for simplicity. The one thing that economists' penchant for mathematical models has created is a constant drive for simplicity. They focus on just a few key variables; otherwise, the mathematics becomes intractable. Following the direction of current philosophy of science, embodied in *Campbellian realism* (McKelvey, this volume), I not only follow Pfeffer and the economists in emphasizing parsimony but also take a step in the direction of a formal model-centered organization science by framing my complexity theory application to firms in terms of computational models.[1] Campbellian realism calls, in part, for scientists to coevolve the development of theory and model so as to maximize "experimental adequacy" tests—the theory predicts model behavior, and the model allows testing of the intricacies of the theory.

The second section of this chapter develops two topics. *Self-organization theory* states that if the level of adaptive tension falls outside a region defined by the chaos theorists' "critical values" (Cramer, 1993),[2] the resulting complexity field will not support the emergence of structures necessary for constructive adaptation. *Complexity catastrophe theory* states that if the conditions of complexity catastrophe exist, Friedman's (1953) natural selection–based constrained maximization or Campbell's blind-variation-selection-and-retention (BVSR) processes may function properly and yet fail to produce the kinds of intrafirm behavior necessary for survival and growth in a selectionist competitive context. Together, these theories state that (a) critical value effects create emergent structure in the middle range of adaptive tension and (b) complexity effects on the flat and jagged extremes of rugged landscapes combine to produce a nonlinear inverted U effect on organizational performance relative to adaptive tension and complexity.

The chapter's third section illustrates how to set up the groundwork for testing experimental adequacy. The model frameworks come from Kauffman (1993). I draw on both his Boolean statistical mechanics and his $NK[C]$ model. I conclude that (a) self-organization and complexity catastrophe theories offer useful insights into the prolonged poor performance of large complex organizations such as GM, and (b) computational modeling approaches offer a basis for testing the experimental adequacy of scientific theories pertaining to complexity theory applications to firms.

Complexity Catastrophe at the Edge of Chaos

Self-organization at the edge of chaos and complexity catastrophe involves both downward and upward causality. The interplay between downward and upward causation arises frequently in Campbell's writing (1974a, 1981, 1988b, 1990, 1994). It is also a constant source of debate in biological evolution (Eldredge, 1995). Paleontologists and ecologists emphasize downward causation (Stanley, 1979; Gould, 1983; Eldredge, 1985; Pianka, 1994), whereas the selfish gene folks emphasize upward causation (Williams, 1966, 1970; Maynard Smith, 1975; Dawkins, 1976; Kimura, 1983). The clash of selectionist causal paths is growing in organization science (McKelvey, 1997) and is evident in many chapters in this volume. Is emergent order in an industry—the kinds of firms surviving—the result of the ecological selection of firms or the competitive selection of individuals and ideas within firms that combine to create successful firms? Although the debate rages in biology (Eldredge, 1995), cooler heads argue that the production of "order" that is favorably selected ecologically (downward causation) is the result of BVSR processes boiling up from within (upward causation) (Kauffman, 1993; Depew & Weber, 1995). Lewontin (1974) said that it is the interactive context that counts in biology. Campbell makes the same point for sociocultural systems and the epistemology of knowledge. Baum and Singh (1994), Van de Ven and Poole (1995), and Hunt and Aldrich (1998) recognize multilevel causation in organizations.

What about the interactive context of GM? Friedman uses selectionist theory to suggest that successful firms behave "*as if* they were seeking rationally to maximize their expected returns" (1953, p. 22). Apparently, GM is not doing this. What it takes to compete effectively in the automobile business is reasonably transparent these days, and the usefulness of performance incentive packages for executives is also well known. Because GM has been failing for two decades, why hasn't it been fixed? Following Friedman, the application of natural selection theory *inside* firms suggests that only those managers who are successful in maximizing rational expectations would survive and move up, and therefore GM *should* have just as many good managers as any other large firm and be just as able to maximize its returns. The implication is instead that the selection process of good individuals and ideas within GM has broken down. Why? Madsen, Mosakowski, and Zaheer (this volume) suggest one reason: Internal BVSR has failed.

A second possibility is that BVSR is working but that complexity effects thwart it. Two fundamental ideas from complexity theory may go a long way toward explaining GM's malaise. One idea boils down to the proper management of adaptive tension, and the second idea focuses on the proper management of coevolutionary interdependencies. Causality goes like this: By operating on these two basic parameters, managers "seed the clouds" by unleashing the natural forces in firms that produce adaptive self-organization and by inhibiting the buildup of complexity catastrophe. Self-organization is a strong force augmenting BVSR in a rapidly changing competitive context. Complexity catastrophe is a strong force thwarting BVSR. Although risking oversimplification, these two theories let me stay well within Pfeffer's simplicity standard.

Self-organization theory, initiated by Prigogine and colleagues (Prigogine, 1962, 1980; Nicolis & Prigogine, 1977, 1989; Prigogine & Stengers, 1984), holds that adaptive tension "critical values" (a) create fundamentally different kinds of complexity fields, (b) give rise to different bases for explaining complexity phenomena, and (c) frame a particular kind of complexity "at the edge of chaos" in which emergent self-organized structures leading to significant adaptive change will occur. This theory implies that adaptive tension

within GM must be outside the critical value levels needed to foster self-organized adaptive response.

Complexity catastrophe theory, promulgated by Kauffman and colleagues (mostly summarized in Kauffman, 1993), holds that complex interdependencies within entities may accumulate to thwart selectionist effects by altering the adaptive landscape to produce the conditions of complexity catastrophe. This view implies that BVSR may be working effectively within GM but that complexity effects create conditions in which the selected agents or ideas are little better than those selected against.

Skeptical readers knowing that Prigogine's theory stems from nonlinear thermodynamics and that Kauffman's theory comes from biology may question whether these theories are relevant to firms and organization science. To be sure, the compatibility of underlying assumptions is critical and cannot be dismissed; nevertheless, space precludes discussion of the following points:

1. There is reason to believe that the assumptions of stochastically idiosyncratic microstates—particles in physics, molecules in chemistry, genetic material and cells in biology, actors in economics, and activities in value chains (Porter, 1985) or organizational processes (Mackenzie, 1986)—apply as much in organization science as they do in modern natural sciences. This point, following from the conflation of modern natural science with the ontological assumptions of relativists and postmodernists (Schwartz & Ogilvy, 1979; Lincoln, 1985; Chia, 1996), is one I have argued at length elsewhere (McKelvey 1997, 1998b).

2. A growing body of relevant literature describes the microstate basis of complexity theory and justifies the application of complexity and chaos theory to organization science (see, for example, treatments by Stacey, 1992, 1995, 1996; Zimmerman and Hurst, 1993; Levy, 1994; Merry, 1995; Thiétart and Forgues 1995; McKelvey 1997, 1998a, in press; Baum and Silverman, in press). A forthcoming special issue of *Organization Science* discusses complexity theory applications to organizations, not to mention supportive arguments in a host of new books appearing recently, such as Eve, Horsfall, and Lee (1997), Brown and Eisenhardt (1998), Byrne (1998), Cilliers (1998), and Lissack and Gunz (in press).

3. Arguments supporting formal models in organization science are already well established. These models further develop the implications of complexity theory, or other subjects such as organizational learning and adaptation, in organization science and have sound epistemological and scientific bases (McKelvey, 1998a, this volume, in press). Computational models are also increasingly used to further theory development in organization science (March, 1991; Carley, 1994, 1995, forthcoming; Prietula & Carley, 1994; Bruderer & Singh, 1996; Carley & Svoboda, 1996; Levinthal, 1997a, 1997b; Levinthal & Warglien, 1997; Rivkin, 1997; Lomi & Larsen, this volume). Empirical testing of model behavior is beginning in experimental organizations (Carley, 1996) and real-world firms (Cheng & Van de Ven, 1996; Sorenson, 1997).

Complexity Theory

Over the past 35 years, complexity theory has become a broad-ranging interdisciplinary subject, as demonstrated in the books by Anderson, Arrow, and Pines (1988), Nicolis and Prigogine (1989), Kaye (1993), Mainzer (1994), Favre, Guitton, Guitton, Lichnerowicz, and Wolff (1995), Nadel and Stein (1995), Belew and Mitchell (1996), and Arthur, Durlauf, and Lane (1997). The study of "complex adaptive systems" (Cowan, Pines, & Meltzer, 1994) focuses its modeling activities on how stochastic idiosyncratic microstate events, whether particles, molecules, genes, neurons, human agents, or firms, self-organize into emergent aggregate structure. My rather narrow treatment here focuses on emergent dissipative structures, adaptive landscapes, critical values, complexity catastrophe, and agent-based computational modeling. The traditional way sciences have dealt with the stochastic microstate assumption is with statistical mechanics (Gibbs, 1902; Tolman, 1938; Weidlich & Haag, 1983; Aoki, 1996). In the second half of the 20th century, complexity theory has emerged as an alternative method of explaining phenomena given a stochastic microstate assumption (McKelvey, 1997). Instead of using the statistical mechanics artifice of taking an average (of stochastic idiosyncratic microstate movements) so as to then continue in the manner of an exact

science, complexity theory accepts and builds on random idiosyncratic nonlinear behavior. In the following subsections, I divide complexity theory into (a) emergent dissipative structures, (b) critical value effects, and (c) complexity effects on adaptive landscapes.

Emergent Dissipative Structures

Complexity theory departs from classical Newtonian deterministic laws about the conservation of motion and conservation of energy as represented by the first law of thermodynamics. Given the second law of thermodynamics, that all ordered states eventually dissipate (via entropy) into disordered states, complexity theory emphasizes dissipative dynamical systems created or maintained by negentropy and eroded by entropy (Nicolis & Prigogine, 1989; Mainzer, 1994). Negentropic effects, which create or maintain order in the form of new structure, and entropic (energy dissipation) order-destroying effects within any structure form the heart of complexity theory.[3]

"[Newtonian] physics deals with an invented, simplified world. This is how it derives its strength, this is why it works so well" (Cohen & Stewart, 1994, p. 12). This idealized view of physics mirrors the "semantic conception of theories" in modern philosophy of science (see Suppe, 1977, 1989; Thompson, 1989). It is predicated on the belief that the universe is "algorithmically compressible" into simple rule explanations (Barrow, 1991, p. 15). But how do phenomena appear, absent the invented, idealized, simplified world of 19th century physics? Offering a view based on Kolmogorov's K-complexity theory (Kolmogorov, 1965), Cramer (1993) defines complexity "as the logarithm of the number of ways that a system can manifest itself or as the logarithm of the number of possible states of the system: $K = \log N$, where K is the complexity and N is the number of possible, distinguishable states" (p. 210). For a parallel view of the "algorithmic information content" of complex bit strings, see Gell-Mann (1994, chap. 2). Cramer then identifies three levels of complexity, depending on how much information is necessary to describe the complexity. These are defined in Table 15.1, section 1a.

TABLE 15.1 Some Complexity Theory Definitions

1a: Definition of Kinds of Complexity by Cramer (1993)

Subcritical complexity exists when the amount of information necessary to describe the system is less complex than the system itself. Thus a rule, such as $F = ma = md^2s/dt^2$ is much simpler in information terms than trying to describe the myriad states, velocities, and acceleration rates pursuant to understanding the force of a falling object. "Systems exhibiting subcritical complexity are strictly deterministic and allow for exact prediction" (1993, p. 213). They are also "reversible" (allowing retrodiction as well as prediction), thus making the "arrow of time" irrelevant (Eddington, 1930; Prigogine & Stengers, 1984).

At the opposite extreme is Cramer's *fundamental complexity* for which the description of a system is as complex as the system itself—the minimum number of information bits necessary to describe the states is equal to the complexity of the system. Cramer lumps chaotic and stochastic systems into this category, although deterministic chaos is recognized as fundamentally different from stochastic complexity (Morrison, 1991; Gell-Mann, 1994), because the former is "simple rule" driven and stochastic systems are random, though varying in their stochasticity.

In between, Cramer puts *critical complexity*. The defining aspect of this category is the possibility of emergent simple deterministic structures fitting subcritical complexity criteria, even though the underlying phenomena remain in the fundamentally complex category. It is here that natural forces ease the investigator's problem by offering intervening objects as "simplicity targets," the behavior of which lends itself to simple rule explanation. Cramer (1993, pp. 215-217) has a long table categorizing all kinds of phenomena according to his scheme.

1b: Definitions of Attractors by Gleick (1987)

Point attractors act as equilibrium points around which forces cause the system to oscillate away from these points, but eventually the system returns to equilibrium—traditional control-style management decision structures may act in this manner (appearing as subcritical complexity).

Periodic attractors or *limit cycles* (pendulum behavior) foster oscillation predictably from one extreme to another—recurrent shifts in the centralization and decentralization of decision making, or functional specialization vs. cross-functional integration fit here (also appearing as subcritical complexity).

If adaptive tension is raised beyond some critical value, systems may be subject to *strange attractors* in that, if plotted, they show never-intersecting, stable, low-dimensional, nonperiodic spirals and loops that are not attracted by some central equilibrium point but nevertheless appear constrained not to breach the confines of what might appear as an imaginary bottle. If they intersected, the system would be in equilibrium (Gleick, 1987, p. 140), following a point attractor. The attractor is "strange" because it "looks" like the system is oscillating around a central equilibrium point, but it isn't. Instead, as an energy importing and dissipating structure, it is responding with unpredictable self-organized structure to tensions created by imposed external conditions, such as tension between different heat gradients in the atmosphere caught between a hot earth's surface and a cold upper atmosphere, or constraints in a fluid flow at the junction of two pipes, or tension created by newly created dissipative structures, such as eddies in a turbulent fluid flow in a canyon below a waterfall, or "MBA terrorist" structural changes imposed in an attempt to make over an acquired firm.

As a metaphor, think of a point attractor as a rabbit on an elastic tether: The rabbit moves in all directions, but as it tires, it is drawn toward the middle, where it lies down to rest. Think of a strange attractor as a rabbit in a pen with a dog on the outside: The rabbit keeps running to the side of the pen opposite from the dog, but as it tires, it comes to rest in the middle of the pen. The rabbit ends up in the "middle" in either case. With the tether, the cause is the *pull* of the elastic. In the pen, the cause is *repulsion* from the dog attacking from all sides.

Complexity theorists define systems in the critical complexity category as being in a state "far from equilibrium" (Prigogine & Stengers, 1984). The key question becomes, What keeps emergent structures in states of equilibrium far above entropy, that is, in states counter to the second law of thermodynamics? Prigogine and colleagues observe that energy-importing, self-organizing, open systems create structures that in the first instance increase negentropy but nevertheless ever after become sites of energy or order dissipation, thereby accounting to the second law. Consequently, they are labeled "dissipative structures" because they are the sites where imported energy is dissipated. If energy ceases to be imported, the dissipative structures themselves eventually cease to exist. Negentropy may occur from adding energy or simply by dividing (finite) structures (Eigen & Winkler, 1981; Cohen & Stewart, 1994). Entropy occurs simply from the merging of structures. Thus, despite the wishful aspirations of Wall Street gurus and CEOs to add energy from synergy, mergers and acquisitions are mostly entropic, a classic example being the assimilation of Getty Oil into Texaco.

Self-organized dissipative structures may exhibit two key behaviors: persistence and nonlinearity. As to persistence, following Eigen's work on autocatalytic hypercycles (Eigen & Schuster, 1979), Depew and Weber (1995) observe that "the most effective way of building structure and dissipating entropy is by means of *autocatalysis*" (p. 462), wherein some agent is produced that furthers the autocatalytic process (though remaining unchanged itself), thereby leading to a positive feedback "autocatalytic cycle." Given their sensitivity to initial conditions, autocatalytic dissipative structures "are capable of generating dynamics that produce order, chaos, or complex organization at the edge of chaos" (1995, p. 462). As to nonlinearity, Depew and Weber note further that the behavior of dissipative structures is nonlinear and tends to create marked explosions or crashes of structure, a situation far from the gradualism of Darwin. They also observe that when "a system is constrained far from equilibrium [because of imported energy], macroscopic order arises not as a violation of the second law of thermodynamics but as a consequence of it" (1995, p. 464). This kind of order may appear as Cramer's subcritical complexity. Thus, self-organizing systems may come to stasis at any of the several levels of complexity. Complexity-caused self-organizing structures with auto-catalytic tendencies are now seen as a ubiquitous natural phenomenon (Cramer, 1993; Kaye, 1993; Mainzer, 1994; Favre et al., 1995) and hypothesized as broadly applicable to firms (Stacey, 1992, 1995, 1996; Zimmerman & Hurst, 1993; Levy, 1994; Thiétart & Forgues, 1995).

If such emergent structures are in some way opposed to each other, they may themselves become tension creators giving rise to still other emergent self-organized structures, or possibly chaotic behavior. Thus, as the energy gradient increases (between a more entropic equilibrium state and the "far from equilibrium" state), and the stress of maintaining the negentropic state increases, there is a likelihood that the system will oscillate between the different states, thereby creating chaotic behavior. Oscillations that traditionally were taken as variance around an equilibrium point now may be discovered to be oscillating around a strange attractor, or as bifurcated oscillations around two attractors. If the stress increases beyond some additional limit, the chaotic behavior will change to pure random behavior—no deterministic structure at all, possibly not even probability distributions. Definitions of *point*, *periodic*, and *strange* attractors are given in Table 15.1, section b. By this line of reasoning, Nicolis and Prigogine (1989), Ulanowicz (1989), and Depew and Weber (1995) use thermodynamic energy differentials to explain how the various states of complexity come to exist (see also Beck and Schlögl, 1993).

Critical Value Dynamics

"Critical values" determine when a system shifts from being explainable by the simple rules of Newtonian science, to having self-organizing capability, to behaving chaotically (Cramer, 1993). Nicolis and Prigogine (1989, chap. 1) offer an overview of the function of critical values in natural science. As an example, consider the life cycle of an atmospheric storm cell. The level of adaptive tension setting up the heat convection dynamics in a weather system is defined by the difference between the warm-to-hot surface of the earth and the cold upper atmosphere. At a low level of adaptive tension, heat is slowly transferred from air molecule to air molecule via conduction. Energetic (heated) molecules at the surface more rapidly collide with molecules just above the surface and thereby transfer their heat energy collision-by-collision to the less energetic molecules—but the molecules stay in their local area just banging around at each other. If the adaptive tension increases sufficiently, to the first critical value, some mass of air molecules, having become collectively "lighter" than other molecules, will start rising toward the upper atmosphere in bulk, thus setting up a convection current. At this critical value, clear air turbulence appears, and if the rising bulk of air is sufficiently moist, it will appear visible as clouds as it reaches the cooler upper atmosphere. The "bulk air current" is classed as an emergent structure by complexity theorists. If the adaptive tension between surface and upper atmosphere increases still further, the structures quite predictably develop as thunderstorms. Examples of other kinds of emergent structures appear in physics, chemistry, biology, and other natural sciences. Thunderstorms may be treated as isolated physical structures and are scientifically studied via scientific realist epistemology and the analytical mechanics of Newtonian science. In Prigogine's terminology (Nicolis & Prigogine, 1989, chap. 2), the storm cells are dissipative structures occurring as the result of negentropy: They are created by the energy differential between hot and cold air, and they serve to dissipate the energy of the hot surface air into the cold upper atmosphere. This accomplished, they dissipate to the point of disappearance.

Suppose the adaptive tension between hot lower air and cold upper air were to increase further, perhaps by the conflation of warm moist air from the Gulf of Mexico and a cold air front coming down from Alaska, say over Kansas. At some point, a second critical value is reached that defines "the edge of chaos." At this point, the point attractor, or the limit cycle (pendulum) attractor of a conservative reversible deterministic system, is replaced by (a) two attractors causing the system to oscillate between the two, (b) possibly several attractors, or (c) a strange attractor in which the system is confined to a limited space by forces defining behavioral extremes (limits) rather than by the attraction of a central point. In a weather system, chaotic emergent structures are things like tornadoes: The system oscillates between tornadic and nontornadic behavior.

The key propositions are as follow:

1. The sun's energy causes an adaptive tension (energy differential) between hot surface and upper atmosphere.

2. Below the first critical value, energy will dissipate via conduction among the kinetic gas particles (microstates).
3. Above the first critical value of adaptive tension, one or more convection currents or dissipative structures (storm cells) will emerge to exist in a state far from equilibrium—at the edge of chaos.
4. Above the second critical value, the dissipative structures will pass from a state "at the edge of chaos" to a state governed by deterministic chaos and multiple basins of attraction—occasional tornadoes.

Complexity Catastrophe

The notion of an adaptive landscape is attributed to Sewall Wright (1931, 1932). The landscape metaphor has subsequently retained considerable popularity among biologists, though in other disciplines *sequence*, *configuration*, or *search space* is preferred. An adaptive landscape has three elements: (a) a configuration space, (b) fitness functions, and (c) move rules that define the steps of the *adaptive walk*. As one approaches explanation from a "micro" level, the landscape or search space becomes central. As Macken and Stadler (1995) observe, Maynard Smith (1970) uses it to study protein evolution; Eigen (1971), Spiegelman (1971), and coworkers (Kramer, Mills, Cole, Nishihara, & Spiegelman, 1974) use it to investigate the *in vitro* evolution of RNA molecules; the Vienna group also uses it to study RNA adaptation (Fontana, Schnabl, & Schuster, 1989; Fontana & Schuster, 1987); and Kauffman and Weinberger (1989) introduce the idea of a tunable landscape in which complex interdependencies are allowed to affect fitness yields.

Kauffman's (1993, pp. 33-34) new wrinkle in *fitness landscapes* is that his landscapes have features causing variations in their *ruggedness*. Primarily, ruggedness is a function of the number of parts comprising the evolving organism, N, and the amount of interconnectedness among the parts, K (1993, pp. 40-54):

1. When $K = 0$, the landscape appears as gently rolling ridges coming off a towering volcano—Kilimanjaro and surrounding plains. This landscape has one very high global optimum. Kauff-

man shows that the "correlation structure" of this landscape is high; the fitness value for one neighbor is highly similar to that of other neighbors, and any move toward increased fitness will lead inexorably toward the global optimum.

2. When $K = N - 1$, the landscape is very jagged—perhaps like the modest peaks, valleys, and ridges of the Alpine Dolomite landscape, with many peaks and ridges having precipitous sides. This landscape is uncorrelated in that one kind of move in no way predicts what happens with some other move.

3. As K increases from 0 to $N - 1$, the number of optima peaks increases, the level of precipitousness increases, the correlation among fitness moves decreases, and the height of the peaks decreases.

As N and K increase, the number of fitness optima available to a player vastly increases, the level of fitness at any given optimum diminishes so that peaks are less valuable if attained, the predictability of finding a better than average fitness peak diminishes rapidly, and players more likely will be trapped on suboptimal fitness peaks. Kauffman holds that any selectionist progression toward properties that are rare in a coevolving system of entities may be overwhelmed by large numbers of mutations toward the more numerous statistically typical central tendencies of other properties composing the broader population. Three forces may suppress selection (1993, p. 25):

1. "Selection is simply too weak in the face of mutations to hold a population at small volumes of the ensemble which exhibit rare properties; hence typical properties are encountered instead."

2. "Even if selection is very strong, the population typically becomes trapped on suboptimal peaks which do not differ substantially from the average properties of the ensemble."

3. Each of the foregoing limitations on selection becomes "more powerful as the *complexity* of the entities under selection increases."

In the face of weakened selection, the "spontaneous order" resulting from the more numerous "typical" characteristics of ensembles will "shine through." "In short, this theme . . . states that much of the order in organisms may be spontaneous.

Rather than reflecting selection's successes, such order . . . may reflect selection's failure" (1993, pp. 29-30).

Given a tunable landscape, Kauffman (1993) identifies two conditions when complexity effects may thwart selectionist effects as the root cause of order in biology:

1. In a "correlated" landscape containing some clearly advantageous fitness peaks, if selection forces are weak and thus fail to hold members of a population high up on the peaks, the apparent order in the population is due to the typical properties of the majority of the population still spread around the valley. That is, "adapting systems exhibit order not *because* of selection but *despite* it" (1993, p. 35).

2. In a "rugged" landscape, the fittest members of the population exhibit characteristics little different from the entire population when the three following conditions apply: (a) as peaks proliferate, they become less differentiated from the general landscape; (b) in precipitous rugged landscapes, adaptive progression is trapped on the many suboptimal "local" peaks; and (c) strong selection forces exist.

Kauffman labels these conditions "complexity catastrophes" because one or the other inevitably happens if the "complexity of the entities under selection increases." Thus, complexity imposes an upper bound on adaptive progression via selection "when the number of parts exceeds a critical value" (1993, p. 36). The "catastrophe" is designated as such because complexity acts to thwart the selectionist process, thereby stopping progression toward improved fitness.

The items above defining the catastrophe conditions introduce two concepts central to Kauffman's thesis, "correlated" and "rugged" landscapes, which are also key determinants of his notion of tunable landscapes and which form the key elements of the NK model. N represents the number of significant components composing an adapting entity, such as a gene, chromosome, trait, or species; in our case, N could be the number of process events, units, actors, or firms, or generally the number of agents attempting to achieve higher fitness. K stands for the number of interdependencies among the agents; K can range from 0 to $N - 1$. Thus, K is a measure of the complexity of interdependencies. Kauffman argues that K causes the landscape to buckle and deform, with the result that it changes from a single dominant fitness peak at the $K = 0$ extreme to many low-level peaks at the $K = N - 1$ extreme. Kauffman defines the $K = 0$ landscape as highly correlated, whereas the $K = N - 1$ landscape is highly rugged. Rugged landscapes contain many peaks and valleys, steep slopes, and many suboptimal peaks, and they offer a greater chance of an agent being trapped on a suboptimal peak. Note that suboptimal in a land of many low peaks may not be much less than a considerably flattened global optimum, nor much higher that the surrounding plain.

Kauffman uses the *NK* model to investigate the *rate of adaptation* and *level of success* likely on a particular landscape. With tunable landscapes, one may ask how levels of complexity affect rates and levels of adaptation by altering the ruggedness of the landscape. Kauffman uses the *NK* model to answer questions pertaining to adaptive evolutionary rates in protein evolution, the crystallization theory of the origin of life, the origin of a connected metabolism, the formation of autocatalytic sets of RNA catalysts, and the evolution of genetic regulatory circuits. With the *NK[C]* model, he uses cellular automata models to explore the distortion of landscapes resulting from microlevel complexity effects on the coevolutionary dynamics between opponents, the complexity-induced percolation[4] of emergent ecological structures, and complexity-induced alterations of the landscape affecting the relative height of Nash equilibrium levels.

Complexity Effects in Firms

Critical Value Dynamics Translated to Firms

To apply the critical value idea to firms, consider a small firm recently acquired by a larger firm. With a low level of adaptive tension—below the first critical value—in which existing management stays in place and little change is imposed by the acquiring firm, there would be little reason for people in the acquired firm to create new struc-

tures, though there might be "conduction" type changes in the sense that new ideas from the acquiring firm percolate slowly from one person to another person adjacent in a network. If the acquiring firm raises adaptive tension—by setting performance objectives calling for increasing returns on investment, more market share, or other goals, or perhaps changing the top manager—but keeps the tension below the second critical value, complexity theory predicts that new structures will emerge that will lead more quickly to better performance.

Above the second critical value, complexity theory predicts chaotic behavior. Suppose the acquiring firm changes several of the acquired firm's top managers and sends in "MBA terrorists" to change the management systems "overnight"—new budgeting approaches, new information systems, new personnel procedures, promotion approaches and benefits packages, new production and marketing systems—as well as changing the acquired firm's culture and day-to-day interaction patterns. In this circumstance, two bifurcating attractors could emerge, one being an attractor for people trying to respond to the demands of the MBA terrorists and the other an attractor for people trying to resist change and hang onto the comfortable preacquisition ways of doing business.

In between the first and second critical values is the region complexity theorists refer to as at "the edge of chaos"—Cramer's critical complexity field. It is also the region where Cohen and Stewart's (1994) "emergent simplicity" concept prevails. Here, structures emerge to solve a firm's adaptive tension problems. To use the storm cell metaphor, in this region the "heat conduction" of interpersonal dynamics between communicating individuals in a value chain network is insufficient to resolve the observed adaptive tension. As a result, the equivalent of organizational storm cells consisting of "bulk" adaptive work (heat energy) flows starts in the form of formal or informal emergent structures—new network formations, new informal or formal group activities, new departments, new entrepreneurial ventures, importation of new technologies and competencies that are then embedded within the new social or formal organizational structures, and so forth. These organizational structures are the emergent "simple rule"–governed structures that Cohen and Stewart discuss. Their emergence is caused by the contextual dynamics of adaptive responses to changing environmental conditions. Having emerged, they generate work flows of a probabilistically predictable nature. For epistemological purposes, these structures may be explained using the simple rule epistemology of traditional normal science—prediction, generalization, falsification, nomic necessity,[5] experiments, and so forth. As one may see, in this region there is a confluence of both contextual (downward) and reductionist (upward) forms of causal explanation.

Besides defining the critical value concept in nature and in firms, it is important to understand how the state of a critical value might be defined by the adaptive tension experienced by a firm or one of its subunits. Although critical values in organization science are unlikely to have the precise value they appear to have in some natural sciences (Johnson & Burton, 1994), it seems likely that a probability distribution of such values will exist for individual firms and each of their subunits. I assume here that adaptive tension may not be uniform for a firm as a whole or across its single business units (SBUs).

Complexity Catastrophe Translated to Firms

Suppose a notebook computer firm and an opponent exist in a coevolutionary pocket (Porter, 1990) and that they coevolve in terms of a number of technologies (departments), N, in charge of, for example, processor and bus speed, motherboard, hard drive capacity and speed, weight, battery life, display, multimedia capability, upgradability, reliability, and service—each in the charge of, or treated as, an agent. Each firm has a level of interdependency among its agents, K, and between its agents and those in its opponent, C. *Within a firm*, each agent could be a source of a good idea (a fitness improvement) or an impediment (for example, yield on processor speed could be inhibited by a slow bus and poor heat sink). *Between firms*, coevolution could push a technology ahead because the opponent is more advanced (leading to

fitness improvement) or slow it down because the opponent is lagging.

Supposing that an agent gets a good idea from another agent within the firm, as K increases, the likely yield from the idea diminishes because of the increased probability of impediments from the increasing number of interdependencies. Eventually, the high probability of impediments from epistatic interdependencies[6] thwarts the yield from the BVSR process, leading, in Kauffman's terms, to complexity catastrophe. Increasing the number of coevolving technologies between a firm and its opponent leads to increased instability, what Kauffman terms "coupled dancing" (1993, p. 249). Although the interaction between K and C is complicated, according to Kauffman's modeling a higher C generally allows a higher K before catastrophe hits.[7] Further details about the translation of the $NK[C]$ model to firms are given in the third section of this chapter.

A Stylized Complexity Theory of Firms

Over the course of this discussion, I have applied a few key principles from complexity theory to firms. They are restated below.

Critical value dynamics from Prigogine:

1. A corporation's performance demands cause an adaptive tension (energy differential) between an SBU's current practices and what is required by the acquiring firm or the market.
2. Below the first critical value, adaptive change may occur at some minimal level within the constraints of the existing SBU process (microstates) governed by its existing organizational culture and structure.
3. Above the first critical value of adaptive tension, one or more dissipative structures (informal or formal groups or other organizing units) will emerge to exist in a state far from equilibrium.
4. Above the second critical value, the dissipative structures will pass from a region "at the edge of chaos" to a region governed by deterministic chaos and multiple basins of attraction—possibly bifurcated basins of attraction, one being the existing practices and the other being attempts to conform to the demands of the MBA terrorists sent down from corporate headquarters, or multiple

basins of attraction as people oscillate among various short-lived attempts to deal with the tension.

Complexity catastrophe from Kauffman:

5. BVSR forces are too weak in the face of industry competition for a subset of firms to hold a unique attribute; hence, typical properties pervading the industry prevail. That is, systems facing high innovation opportunities exhibit order not so much because of competitive selection but because complexity effects offer no resistance. That is, *some* complexity, by offering resistance, strengthens the BVSR process. Thus, if selection had dominated, Apple Computer's superior operating system would have prevailed. As it happened, the prevailing "typical" system of the PCs won out—not because the best was selected nor because complexity effects thwarted Apple more than any other firm.

6. Even with strong selection forces, an industry may be characterized by many suboptimal innovation opportunities that do not differ substantially from the average properties of the industry. That is, given that (a) as peaks proliferate, they become less differentiated from the general landscape; (b) in precipitous rugged landscapes, adaptive progression is trapped on the many suboptimal "local" peaks; and (c) even in the face of strong selection forces, the fittest members of the industry exhibit characteristics little different from the entire industry. Therefore, even though selection is strong, complexity effects thwart selection effects. For example, gasoline retailing may be a very competitive industry, but the minimal improvements from different additives do not give any particular firm an advantage.

These six propositions reduce complexity theory to the following two results: (a) Emergent dissipative structures appear between the first and second critical values of adaptive tension and (b) as complexity increases, selection effects are initially enhanced because the landscape has some fairly high suboptimal fitness peaks, then thwarted as too much complexity lowers the multiplying peaks to minimal levels. Adaptive success thus appears as a two-dimensional Gaussian distribution of likely performance—a single rounded hill when plotted against adaptive tension and complexity.

An Illustrative Experimental Adequacy Test

Campbellian realism, as further developed by McKelvey (this volume), defines a model-centered epistemology in which science is divided into two independent activities. In this late 1990s interpretation of effective scientific activity, Campbell (Campbell, 1988a, Paller & Campbell, 1989) and scientific realists such as Bhaskar (1975), Boyd (1991), De Regt (1994), and Aronson, Harré, and Way (1994) join semantic conception theorists (Beth, 1961; Suppes, 1962; van Fraassen, 1970, 1980; Suppe, 1977, 1989; Lloyd, 1988; Thompson, 1989) to replace the axiomatic basis of theory[8] with a "theory-model" link in which axioms may or may not be essential. The difference is illustrated in Figure 15.1. In this view, the theory-model link is "coevolutionarily" improved as theory and model are developed toward increased predictive isomorphism—"experimental adequacy." More or less in parallel, the "model-phenomena" link is also coevolutionarily developed, leading to improved "ontological adequacy"—fit with real-world phenomena. In contrast to this modern interpretation of science, organization science still attempts to develop a link directly between theory and the complex reality of the real world, also illustrated in Figure 15.1.

To conform to Campbellian realism and the thrust of the semantic conception, in what follows I show that both self-organization and complexity catastrophe theories may be formally modeled. To illustrate, I take only the first step of suggesting that computational models exist with which to develop the theory-model link. Their origin is jointly from biology, physics, and computer science.

Modeling Emergent Structure

Kauffman's *NK* model derives from physicists' spin glass models (Weinberger, 1991), a set of models used to study the energy landscape created by sets of magnetic dipoles spinning in similar or

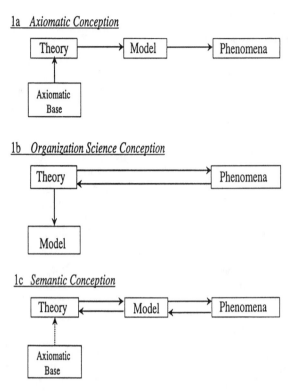

Figure 15.1. Conceptions of the Axiom-Theory-Model-Phenomena Relationship

opposite directions (Fischer & Hertz, 1993). Whereas physicists use these binary particle models to understand energy minimization, Kauffman (1993) uses them to understand how organisms, via mutations, take hill climbing "adaptive walks" to maximize fitness. A step in the walk occurs when, for example, a gene moves to a new point on the landscape by adopting a mutant form from a neighboring gene. The *NK* model is a "static" model. It is useful for answering questions about how many local optima there are, what their fitness levels are, lengths of adaptive walks, rates at which improved fitnesses are found, and so forth (see Kauffman, 1993, chap. 2).

To model emergent structure phenomena, I draw on a series of studies by Kauffman and Derrida and colleagues[9] in which they discovered parameters controlling the emergence of structure in random Boolean (binary) networks. In this modeling approach, Kauffman shifts from spin glasses to the computer scientists' *cellular automata*, focusing on *Boolean network dynamics*.[10] Spin glass models are *single change* "bit-flipping" functions in which the outcome state is based on a single randomly chosen input. Automata are *mutational functions* having 2^K inputs—that is, K binary inputs, each of which has some probabilistic effect on the Boolean outcome state (Jones, 1995). Given a binary cell function, on or off, the total number of different outcomes in an *autonomous* (closed to inputs outside the automata elements in the network) Boolean network is 2^K. Because this could be a truly vast number (2.8×10^{14} for $K = 24$), Kauffman creates a "Boolean statistical mechanics" in which fairly "exact" outcomes are created by sampling and averaging to describe the total system of elements (Gelfand & Walker, 1984; Kauffman, 1974).

For $K = 2$ inputs, there are 16 Boolean functions, shown in Figure 15.2. In this "tabular" depiction, the on-off inputs are on the edges and the outcome disposition is inside the box.[11] For game theorists, one of the inputs is a "feedback element" showing the current state of the automata element itself, but for Kauffman, inputs are determined only by the existing states of other elements in the network. The stability of a Boolean network may be upset by "minimal" or "structural" perturbations. Minimal perturbations are caused by a state flip in an input, say from on to off. Structural perturbations come from changing the outcome state of one or more Boolean function elements. In Kauffman's models, only minimal perturbations create network instability. Emergent structure in Kauffman's models could derive from two sources: *forcing functions* and *homogeneity bias*. Forcing functions occur when only one input can force the outcome state. In the "OR" function, any input with a 1 forces an outcome state of 1. With the "AND" function, any input with a 0 forces an outcome state of 0. In Figure 15.2, only the "XOR" and "IFF" functions are not forcing function on one or both inputs.[12] As the number of inputs K increases, the relative number of forcing functions decreases rapidly, dropping from 87.5% for $K = 2$ to less than 5% for $K = 4$ (Gelfand & Walker, 1984, p. 128). Homogeneity bias is created by altering the number of functions that are forcing. Thus, if the ratio of "OR" functions is increased ("OR" has three out of four values = 1), the probability of homogeneity increases. If the ratio of the "IFF" or "XOR" functions is increased, homogeneity stays the same because for them, the ratio of 1s and 0s is 50/50. In Kauffman's models, automata elements are randomly selected, meaning that both forcing and homogeneity impacts are fully randomized.

A substantial body of research bearing on random Boolean networks identifies several parameters that shift the systems from *ordered* to *complex* to *chaotic* behavior, as reviewed by Kauffman (1993, chap. 5). These networks are termed "annealed" because at each time period, the connections from other automata cells and the cell functions are randomly reassigned. As a result, there is no reason to expect them to revisit some prior state, that is, to act as a limit cycle. This is in contrast to "quenched" networks, in which connections and cell functions are randomly assigned only once, at the outset (Kauffman 1993, p. 198). In either case, there are N vertices or binary variables, K input

connections from other cells, and P (the forcing bias of the cells). As N, K, and P increase, random Boolean networks shift from *order* to *chaos*. At $K = 2$ with $P = 0.5$ (meaning no imposed forcing bias), networks show a phase shift separating order from chaos. Depending on the size of K, there is also a generalized phase shift parameter, P_c, also separating *order* from *chaos*. In the region of $K = 2$ with $P = 0.5$ or approximately at P_c, there exists a "boundary region" in which *complex emergent structure* appears.

Figure 15.3a presents a lattice, coming from Weisbuch (1991), showing two kinds of emergent structure: (a) "islands" of structure (non 1s) separated by (b) a larger "percolating frozen structure" of forced cell functions, all of which have a value of 1. In this lattice, $K = 4$ and $P = 0.2$. Although the frozen structure has been forced to a value of 1, the cells in the islands still are able to oscillate between 1 and 0. In this "ordered regime," the control parameters produce ordered behavior in the percolated structure—the "forcing" behavior at some initial cell percolates throughout the system, resulting in uniform behavior with cells in the percolated structure all in one state. That is, a small change in one cell ripples through the frozen component, producing wholesale forcing into one basin of attraction—the value 1, in this particular lattice. Alternatively, one could also see a *chaotic regime* (shown in Figure 15.3b) in which the larger "percolating chaotic structure" oscillates around long to possibly limitless limit cycles and islands are frozen on a single value where $K = 4$ and $P > P_c$ ($P_c = 0.28$). This would also result if $K > 3$ with $P > P_c$. In this circumstance, the major component would continue oscillating on the 1 and 0 values, with *order* appearing as small isolated islands frozen on one value. In terms of the NK model, ordered networks adapt more readily on less rugged landscapes, whereas chaotic systems adapt more successfully on rugged landscapes, according to Kauffman's results (1993, pp. 215-217).

Kauffman argues that at the point of the $K = 2$ with $P = 0.5$, or $K > 2$ with $P \approx P_c$ "phase shift" transitions, there exists a "liquid region" in which complex adaptive systems emerge "at the edge of chaos"—the small, isolated frozen islands in the Boolean network model. Thus, these network sys-

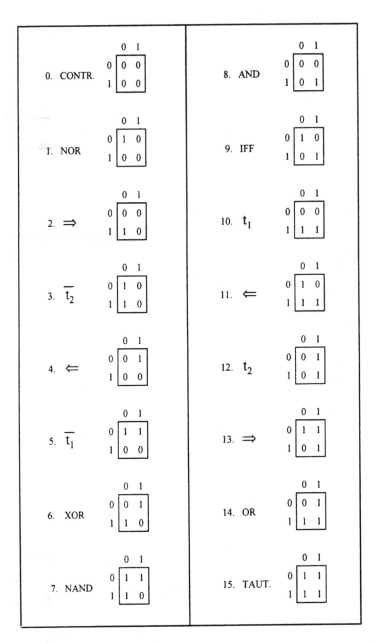

Figure 15.2. Sixteen Boolean Functions for $K = 2$ Inputs
SOURCE: Adapted from Westhoff, Yarbrough, and Yarbrough (1996, p. 12). Reproduced by permission of Princeton University Press.

tems may lie in three states: (a) the ordered regime of small, isolated frozen islands; (b) the chaotic regime of one large frozen state with a few oscillating islands remaining; or (c) the liquid region of the phase transition state where the large frozen component "melts" into some number of oscillat-

ing islands. This model thus behaves consistently with complexity theory in that it shows emergent structure when the critical values take on the instigating values.

Needless to say, complexity theory applied to biology is quite new. Using random Boolean net-

1	1	4	4	8	8	8	1	1	4	4	1	1	1	1	1
1	1	1	1	8	8	4	1	1	1	1	1	1	4	1	1
4	1	1	1	8	72	4	1	1	1	1	1	1	4	1	4
4	1	1	72	72	36	4	1	2	1	1	1	1	1	1	1
4	4	1	18	1	18	36	2	2	2	1	1	1	1	6	1
4	1	1	18	18	18	36	1	1	1	1	1	1	12	6	12
12	1	18	18	18	18	18	1	1	1	1	1	12	12	1	1
1	1	18	18	18	1	18	1	1	1	1	1	1	12	12	12
1	1	1	1	1	1	1	1	1	4	4	1	12	12	1	1
1	1	1	1	1	1	1	1	1	1	4	4	4	12	1	1
1	4	4	1	1	1	1	1	1	1	4	4	1	4	1	4
1	1	1	1	1	1	1	1	1	1	1	4	1	4	4	4
1	1	1	1	2	2	1	1	1	1	1	1	1	1	4	1
1	1	1	1	1	1	1	1	1	1	1	1	1	1	4	1
1	1	1	8	8	1	1	1	1	1	1	4	4	1	1	1
1	1	8	8	8	8	1	1	1	1	4	1	1	4	4	1

$K = 4$, $P < P_c$. Percolated ordered regime shown as 1's.

Figure 15.3a. Weisbuch's Lattice Showing an Ordered Regime
SOURCE: Reproduced from *Complex Systems Dynamics: An Introduction to Automata Networks*, Weisbuch (p. 139, Figure 10.9). Original ©1991 by Addison-Wesley for the Santa Fe Institute. Reprinted with permission of Perseus Books Publishers, a member of Perseus Books, LLC.
NOTE: $K = 4$, $P < P_c$. Percolated ordered regime shown as 1s.

works to model biological behavior is even more novel. Little of either has been applied to developing a model-centered organization science, except for a brief example given by Gelfand and Walker (1984, p. 230) in which they apply this modeling approach to managerial control systems focused on repetitive routines. Consider the following rudimentary illustration.

Imagine a firm with 20 agents (line managers, staff, and engineers) responsible for various parts of a value chain. At any given time, for any specific activity, an agent has two alternatives: make an adaptive improvement (value 1) or do nothing (value 0). In making this decision, an agent may consider a variety of inputs, from one other person or from many other people. For modeling purposes, an agent can make only a binary decision at a given time period, but obviously over many time

periods, an agent can make rather complicated adaptive moves. For modeling purposes, we limit an agent to a fixed number of input connections from other individuals, though of course in the real world he or she could have varying inputs on any given day for any specific activity. Given the cost of time and effort to communicate, along with boundedly rational abilities to process information, Simon's (1957) satisficing theory suggests that agents might typically settle for a small fixed number of information inputs for any given decision. Given that we have narrowed managerial decision making down to micro sequences of decisions on specific micro aspects of their responsibilities at any given time, the 20 agents in the model are not unreasonably simplified from real agents. With this model, then, we can alter the number of agents, alter the number of decision (cell) out-

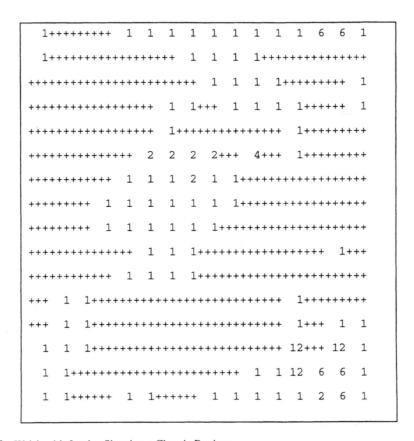

Figure 15.3b. Weisbuch's Lattice Showing a Chaotic Regime
SOURCE: Reproduced from *Complex Systems Dynamics: An Introduction to Automata Networks*, Weisbuch (p. 139, Figure 10.10). Original ©1991 by Addison-Wesley for the Santa Fe Institute. Reprinted with permission of Perseus Books Publishers, a member of Perseus Books, LLC.
NOTE: $K = 4$, $P > P_C$. The percolated chaotic regime shows as groups of three plus signs (+++) indicating cells with limit cycles too long to be measured.

comes, and alter the number of input connections they consider at any given instant. In addition, we can randomly assign each agent one from a range of cell input configurations and cell functions or rules—from the lattice defined as 2^{2^k}.

Supposing agents were limited to two inputs, the range of possible cell functions is given in Figure 15.2—16 in all. Agents could have many more inputs: They could value or weight each input differently, or they could wait until input information from other agents accumulates to some level deserving their attention. The range of cell functions thus may become limitlessly more complicated. To cope with a potentially vast number of cell inputs and functions, Kauffman (1974) introduces his "statistical mechanics ensemble model-

ing" approach. Instead of working through an entire lattice containing potentially billions of elements, he assumes that the samples drawn and averaged in the manner of statistical mechanics fairly accurately represent the mix of cell functions distributed in the entire multidimensional $2 \times 2 \times K$ /mul> N lattice. For now, let's stay with the simple $2 \times 2 \times (K = 2)$ lattice, with the parameter P ranging from 0.5 to 1.0. We may delete N because, as Stauffer (1987a, p. 791) observes, the forcing dynamic is independent of N, varying only by K and P.

Now imagine that at the time a corporation acquires a new division (SBU), each SBU value chain agent responds to two inputs from fellow agents—represented as $K = 2$. Suppose further that the

TABLE 15.2   Stauffer's Table Showing the Probability π Given p and K

p	K = 2	K = 3	K = 4
0	1	1	1
0.05	0.995	0.9892	0.9718
0.10	0.9838	0.9554	0.8770
0.15	0.9675	0.8997	0.7313
0.20	0.9488	0.8268	0.5655
0.25	0.9297	0.7440	0.4072
0.30	0.9118	0.6599	0.2739
0.35	0.8965	0.5832	0.1730
0.40	0.8848	0.5219	0.1048
0.45	0.8775	0.4824	0.0661
0.5	0.8750	0.46875	0.0536

SOURCE: Reproduced from Stauffer (1987a, p. 792) with permission of Plenum Publishing Company.

acquiring corporation imposes up to two additional inputs—represented as $K = 3$ or 4. Suppose as well that the adaptive tension imposed by the acquiring firm ranges from MBA terrorist type demands to the mildest of suggestions—represented as P. Given Prigogine's theory, consider the following question: How many corporate interdependencies (cell inputs) governing the agents of an existing SBU value chain should the acquiring firm impose, and how much forcing should they impose so as to ensure the level of emergent structure likely to optimize SBU adaptation? Below the first critical value, little change results. Above the second critical value, chaos results. In the middle are the emergent dissipative structures at the edge of chaos. Three critical value scenarios are possible.

First, a preliminary response to this question rests on some analytic results produced by Stauffer (1987a), shown in Table 15.2. The left-hand column shows P ranging from 0 to 0.5—because the probabilities are symmetric, the results for P are the same as for $1 - P$. At $P = 0.5$ (no bias toward either 1 or 0 values) and $K = 2$, these results mirror Kauffman's simulation results—the incidence of forcing cells is at a high enough probability ($\pi = 0.8750$) that forcing results. A phase transition occurs at $K = 2$. The model generates a dominant component of cells percolating throughout the network showing short oscillating cycles around a repeating state (limit cycle) attractor with a few isolated frozen islands here and there in which cells

oscillate through long, if not limitless, cycles. This is the *ordered* regime where cells in the dominant component oscillate around a quickly repeating limit cycle, not unlike a negative feedback process in a goal-directed control (machine bureaucracy) system. In terms of our acquiring firm, this means that, absent inputs from the corporate level, most of the behavior in the SBU is retained at a steady state by the governing routines and information inputs. Because forcing is independent of N, a model of SBU behavior would appear similar to the lattice shown in Figure 15.3a: There would be a minimal number of islands of emergent adaptive structure "oscillating" in attempts to improve adaptation, but most agents in the lattice would be frozen in an ordered regime continuing mostly unchanged.

Second, suppose the MBA terrorists enter the SBU and create so much adaptive tension that chaos results. This is represented in Table 15.2 by $K = 4$ (the right-hand column). Now there are four inputs to each agent or cell instead of two. One can see right away that if P remains at 0.5, π quickly reduces well below the phase transition level (which is 0.59275; Stauffer, 1987a, p. 792), at which a network becomes ordered. As a result, the network consists of a dominant *chaotic* regime in which a small perturbation starting in a cell having lengthy, or limitless, cycles between repeating states percolates throughout the system, except for a few frozen stable (low limit cycle) islands. In this case, it is oscillation that percolates. This is opposite to the stable percolation structure of the ordered regime in which cells oscillate around a quickly repeating limit cycle. This means that absent any "forcing" by the corporate center, three things happen that foster chaos: (a) a few SBU agents abandon the negative feedback process in favor of freewheeling change (oscillation) of a nonlinear positive feedback kind (that is, the limit cycle has lengthy or limitless repetition); (b) this tendency among a few agents percolates throughout the value chain to become the dominant chaotic component, though with a few isolated frozen islands showing ordered regimes; and (c) each agent responds to the four inputs with an independent, idiosyncratic, possibly limitless change process (oscillation cycle) in his or her attempt to respond to the adaptive tension raised by the MBA terrorists—or to attempt to revert to behavior existing before acquisition. The latter situation represents bifurcated chaos between two attractors—maintain the status quo or try to please the MBA terrorists. A model of SBU behavior would appear similar to the lattice in Figure 15.3b.[13]

Finally, consider the "edge of chaos" region between the first and second critical values. In the random Boolean network model, the region between the two critical values is compressed down to a very narrow slice at the phase transition. Studies (Stauffer, 1987a, 1987b; Weisbuch, 1991) show that for the $K = 3$ column, the phase transition occurs at 0.278 (within Kauffman's (1974) limits of 0.26 ± 0.02). For the $K = 4$ column, there is some disparity between the analytic method of Stauffer and the numerical method of Kauffman, depending on the kinds of automata rules used (see Hartman & Vichniac, 1986). For consistency, I will stay with Kauffman's computational number—0.26 ± 0.02—for the $K = 4$ column. The results are that the first and second critical values are compressed nearly to the same point and that P has to be lowered to 0.26 ± 0.02 to reach the threshold. Thus, the complexity theorists' "edge of chaos" kind of complexity is what Kauffman calls a liquid region at the transition point.

So, let's assume we are starting with $P = 0.5$ and the frozen dominant component is chaotic. Then, as P is lowered nearly to the 0.26 level, the frozen

percolated *chaotic* component "melts" and the model creates numerous substructures of the more ordered kind—shorter limit cycle oscillations. Oppositely, if we started with an ordered regime (P near 0) and were to raise P toward 0.26, the frozen percolated *ordered* component would melt, creating numerous substructures of the more chaotic, less ordered kind—longer limit cycles.

Ideally, one would want to expand the melting zone of the model. Critical values in firms are likely fuzzy and, given that the most interesting "action" is in the melting zone, the larger the zone is, the more one can develop the model to represent the nuances of emergent structuration in firms. Furthermore, specific automata cells may be identified that more easily represent aspects of the corporate/SBU governance relationship. Thus, cell functions could be designed to represent U-, M-, and H-form corporate/SBU governance relationships (Williamson, 1975), or cells could be designed to represent other governance and communication interdependencies between corporate general office and SBU or among different parts and levels of a value chain. Following this line of reasoning, it seems possible that a model from statistical physics, via biology, could be developed to study the liquid region of adaptive tension where critical complexity emerges, and with it emergent structures. Although I am not aware of studies already doing this, it seems logical that one could also take a "fractal" approach with the model. Thus, one could bring the main model into the "melting" zone and then, as substructures appear, they also could be forced into their own melting zones. In this way, the model would have a widened melting zone and could more subtly represent firms showing emergent dissipative structures.

Modeling Complexity Catastrophe

Kauffman (1993, p. 239) argues that his $NK[C]$ Boolean game model behaves like Boolean networks, if agent outcomes are limited to 0 or 1, the K number of interdependencies is taken as the number of inputs, and Nash equilibria in N-person games are equivalent to agents being trapped on local optima. Table 15.3 presents material defining the model's parameters and translating Kauffman's

TABLE 15.3 Defining an Adaptive Chainscape to Fit Kauffman's *NK[C]* Simulations

S	A species, *S*, which is a population, is treated as a single homogeneous entity. "Simulations of coevolving systems are carried out under the assumption that each species acts *in turn*, in the context of the current state of the other species" (Kauffman, 1993, p. 245). Kauffman's simplification of species down to a single acting entity is what makes his model applicable to my analysis of firms. Thus, *S* = number of firms.
N	The *NK* model consists of *N* sites, with each site interpreted as an independent "part" or "agent." A site for Kauffman is a protein or trait, that is, a "part." For firms, *N* could equal the number of subunits, production stations, value chain units, process events, competencies, teams, employees, and so forth.
K	Measures *internal coevolutionary density* among parts within a firm. Thus, *K* is a measure of the interdependencies among the various potentially changing parts or agents. Kauffman terms *K* a measure of *epistatic links* (1993, p. 41), that is, links that inhibit change. Because of the interdependencies, the fitness improvement (yield) from a particular change may be diminished because of fitness limitations posed by other parts. He takes a much broader view of their definition than the narrow "allele suppresser effect" typical in biology. In fact, he views the effects of multiple alleles as so complex that he relies on a random fitness function. My definition of *K* as interdependencies having suppressing effects seems well within Kauffman's usage.
C	Measures *external coevolutionary density* among parts between a pair of competing firms. The *other* member of a coevolving pair (gene or species) has a number of proteins or traits, *C*, that are *interdependent* with any mutation behavior (or lack of it) of a given focal part (protein or trait). For me, *C* represents interdependent agents/microagents between a pair of competing coevolving firms. Some number of the opponent's parts might coevolve with a given part of the focal firm.
A	The Boolean network attribute of Kauffman's model is retained by assuming that any adaptive walk an agent might make in attempting to improve its fitness is limited to a "two alternative" action, *A*—remain unchanged or adopt a change. Any more complicated decision may be reduced to a sequence of binary choices.
D	The dimensionality, *D*, of a search space/landscape/chainscape is, therefore, defined as $N(A-1)$.
w_j	Because the interdependency effects w_j are complex and unpredictable, Kauffman assigns random values between 0.0 and 1.0. Given *K* competencies w_j that are epistatically linked to w_i, the A^K fitness contributions w_j are averaged together with w_i at period $t-1$ to create a modified value of w_i at time *t*.
W, w_i	The total fitness value *W* of a chain vector is the average of all its *N* agents, $W = \frac{1}{N} \sum_{i=1}^{N} w_i$
Agent fitness	Kauffman interprets each "site" as an independent "agent." The fitness contribution of each of any particular agent's two options, $A = 0$ or 1, is randomly assigned a value ranging from 0.0 to 1.0.
One-change neighbor	For a given firm's value chain of length *N*, and given a rule of only "one change" allowed per time period for any agent trying to change toward improved *microstates* seen in a neighboring agent, there are A^N "one-change neighbor" *microagents*, each of which is different from a given microagent at only one competence point or locus, that is, in my case, 2^N neighboring microagents. Instead of a firm having *one* alternative value chain that is better on, say, 10 out of 24 competencies, each agent is defined to have 23 neighboring microagents, 10 of which are better, each differing by only one competence, and each microagent can adopt only one improvement per period. This is what creates the combinatorial search space/chainscape.
Chainscape	A "chainscape" is, thus, a multidimensional landscape consisting of a total of A^N "one-change neighbor" microagents—for Kauffman, 2^N. If $A = 2$ and $N = 24$, the landscape is a multidimensional lattice comprising 16,777,216 microstates. Within this landscape, each agent is *next to* $(A-1) \times (N-1)$ microagents, each of which may change from one time period to the next depending on changes at other microstate sites (microagents).
Adaptive walk	Evolution is defined as an adaptive walk through a chainscape where a firm improves the parts of its chain at each time period by surveying all the one-change neighboring microagents and randomly selecting one from those offering improved fitness. If none offers an improvement, the agent stays unchanged.
Epistatic links	Agents may have one or more interdependencies (epistatic links) to other agents that inhibit the fitness value of a changed competence. For example, a notebook firm's chances of improving performance reliability may be inhibited by adoption of a leading edge (unreliable) experimental competence conserving battery power, or enhanced by staying with an older, highly reliable competence in active matrix screen technology.

TABLE 15.4   Additional Notes on the Iteration Dynamics of Kauffman's *NK*[*C*] Simulations

---

1. One item that may seem awkward for my use is Kauffman's "generation," or time period. When Kauffman the biologist lets a model run 8,000 generations or so, it seems reasonable. For organizations, even 2,000 clocking cycles may seem long. Length here depends on how "micro" an adaptive walk takes place at each time period. Following Barney (1994), I focus on "micro" decisions rather than "big" decisions.

2. The distribution from which fitness values are randomly drawn could affect the outcome. Kauffman (1993, p. 44) draws his values "from the uniform interval between 0.0 and 1.0." He could have used peaked Gaussian or U-shaped distributions. Kauffman concludes that the statistical features of his landscape models are "largely insensitive to the choice made for the underlying distribution" (1993, pp. 44-45).

3. In *co*evolutionary simulations, at each time period, the actions of an agent are moderated by the effects of actions by the *C* agents/parts in the opposing firm, as well as the actions of the given firm's *K* agents.

4. In Kauffman's coevolutionary games, at each time period an agent assesses its current fitness and the fitness of *K* other internal agents, then picks a "one-change" neighbor (defined in Table 15.3) offering higher fitness, assuming that the *K* other agents do not change their action, *A*. In this game, no foresight is allowed.

5. Because there is no foresight, "in this limit of *pure strategies*, the dynamics of the myopic coevolutionary game is [*sic*] identical to that of a random Boolean network. . . . [A] steady state in this game corresponds to a *pure strategy Nash equilibrium* (Nash 1951)" (Kauffman, 1993, p. 240).

6. In Kauffman's model it is possible for Nash equilibria to occur at less than optimum fitness levels for individual agents and for the entire system. Kauffman also allows for the possibility that subgroups of agents might become "frozen" in a particular Nash equilibrium fitness level, while other agents continue to coevolve, though not necessarily to Nash equilibria at improved fitness levels.

7. Given that how each competence interacts with all the $N(A - 1)$ other competencies is very complex and unpredictable, the simulations model their statistical features by using a fitness function in which a value between 0.0 and 1.0 is randomly selected and assigned to each competence alternative.

8. Given two *co*evolving firms A and B, randomly selected values 0.0 to 1.0 are assigned to represent the effect on firm A that competencies, *C*, from firm B might have (that are epistatically linked to firm A).

9. In these models, during the course of a simulation run, the values of both *K* and *C* remain the same for all chain loci, and their effects may inhibit or enhance fitness values at any chain locus.

10. The effect of *C* is that the chainscapes of both firms 1 and 2 are mutually causal.

SOURCE: Adapted from Kauffman (1993, pp. 33-45).

NK landscape into the context of value chain competencies composed of microstates governed by microagents—a "chainscape" in which microagents governing the value chain *parts* of firms take adaptive walks. Table 15.4 offers additional notes on what happens as the model iterates through its time periods. In the *NK*[*C*] Boolean game, fitness yields are assigned to the 0 or 1 actions by drawing from a uniform distribution ranging from 0.0 to 1.0. The *K* interdependencies that might serve to modify fitness yields from an agent's actions are drawn from a fitness table in which fitness levels of each "one-change" nearest neighbor are assigned by drawing from a uniform distribution also ranging from 0.0 to 1.0. Kauffman points out that the complexity tuning effect occurs when increasing *K* reduces the height of local optima while also increasing their number. Complexity catastrophe occurs as *K* is increased. An explanation of Kauffman's modeling approach is given in Westhoff and colleagues (1996), and an illustration of their application to firms in McKelvey (1998a, in press).

In describing how *K* and *C* effects enter into the model, Kauffman says:

> For each of the *N* traits in species 2, the model will assign a random fitness between 0.0 and 1.0 for each combination of the *K* traits internal to species 2, together with all combinations of *C* traits in species 1. In short, we expand the random fitness table for each trait in species 2 such that the trait looks at its *K* internal epistatic inputs and also at the *C* external epistatic inputs from species 1. (1993, p. 244)

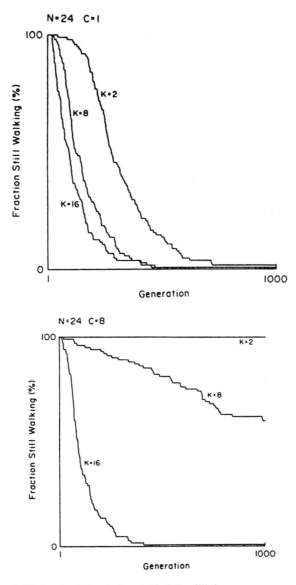

Figure 15.4. Size of *K* and *C* Related to Time to Reach Nash Equilibrium
SOURCE: Reproduced from *The Origins of Order: Self-Organization and Selection in Evolution*, Kauffman (p. 247, Figure 6.3), ©1993 by Oxford University Press. Reprinted with permission.

One might conclude from this that *K* and *C* are combined into one overall moderating effect on the fitness yield from an agent's choice to adopt a higher fitness from a nearest neighbor. Results of the models indicate otherwise. As Kauffman points out (1993, pp. 249, 254), the speed at which agents encounter Nash equilibria increases as *K* increases, and it decreases as *C* and *S* increase. Thus, in these models *K* acts as a complexity "forcing" effect in speeding up the process of reaching stable Nash equilibria at low fitness peaks, thereby bringing on complexity catastrophe. In contrast, *C* acts as a destabilizing effect, as does *S*. *K* effects are averaged as per the static single-agent *NK* model, leaving *C* and *S* effects (*S* multiplies the *C* effects) to modify fitness yields on an agent's actions independently of *K* effects. The consequence is that increasing *K* "tunes" the landscape toward more ruggedness (increased numbers of less fit local optima) and increased likelihood of agents being marooned on local optima. Increasing *C* and/or *S* prevents achieving Nash equilibrium by prolonging the "coupled dancing," as Kauffman calls it, in which opponents keep altering each other's landscapes, keep the fitness search going, and thereby prevent stabilization. The more opponents there are, the more the instability persists.

In the *NK*[*C*] model, *K* acts as a force toward increased complexity and complexity catastrophe, whereas *C* appears to act as a force away from catastrophe; that is, internal complexity leads to complexity catastrophe but external complexity leads away from catastrophe. The experiments in his Figure 6.3 (reproduced here as Figure 15.4) show that increasing *C* prolongs instability (the fraction of coupled dances not reaching Nash equilibrium). This behavior of the model is significant since because, from Kauffman's theory and the quotation above, one might easily conclude with reason that—holding *S* constant—external complexity *C* should lead to complexity catastrophe just as much as internal complexity *K* does. Kauffman's Figure 6.4 (1993, p. 248; not shown here) clearly shows this not to be true.

Kauffman experiments with the *NK*[*C*] model using various combinations of parameters, as described in the "computational experiments" below. To help readers connect these models back to Kauffman's book, I label the models by their figure or table numbers in his book (1993). Outcomes from some of the experiments are described briefly.

1. Can too many coevolutionary links among a firm's value chain competencies inhibit competitive advantage? The experiments[14] show that increasing *K* is not good, unless the opponent has a high *K* or a high *C*. If Nash equilibria are encountered, low *K* is better than high *K*, because low *K* means higher fitness peaks. As the probability of encountering Nash equilibria decreases, however—say because of an opponent's actions to raise

its *K* or *C*—the better it is to have a high *K*. If the opponent does not raise *C*, and therefore Nash equilibria occur quickly, the high *K* firm will lose its advantage. A firm's strategy with respect to number of internal coevolutionary links among value chain competencies, *K*, seems to hinge on whether the search for Nash equilibria is prolonged; that is, on whether an opponent will raise *C*.

> *Proposition 1:* In general, keeping one's internal coevolutionary interdependencies just below those of an opponent is the best strategy.

2. Can too many coevolutionary chain links between a firm and an opponent inhibit its competitive advantage? The simulations[15] show that firms having dense external coevolutionary ties with opponents (that is, high *C*s prevail) benefit from a higher upper bound on their *K* before catastrophe sets in. During the pre-Nash oscillation period, however, rapid moves by a firm are likely to have significant detrimental effects on its opponents. A "maximin" strategy suggests that a firm should target coevolutionary opponents whose *C*s match its own *K*.

> *Proposition 2a:* Absent any more pointedly aggressive strategy toward a specific opponent, a firm should attempt to equalize internal and external coevolutionary interdependencies.
>
> *Proposition 2b:* For a more targeted strategy, a firm is best off if it attacks opponents who have moderate *C*s and low *K*s, while keeping its *K* slightly higher than the *K* of its opponents, until its *K* reaches the *C* of its opponents.

Why? High *C*s allow higher *K*s—true—but lower *K*s tune the landscape toward higher fitness peaks. This produces the inverted U relation between performance and complexity.

3. Should strategists worry about possible complexity catastrophes? One of Kauffman's basic insights is the complexity catastrophe. I would like to use his findings to consider how complexity catastrophes might affect firms. The underlying question is, what is the effect of landscape ruggedness on firms? The experiments[16] show that lower levels of K create moderately rugged landscapes composed of a few high and somewhat precipitous local optima peaks. As levels of K increase, the number of peaks increases, but their height diminishes, with the result that the landscape appears less rugged, with less differentiation between the plains and the local optima peaks. The lesson for a notebook computer firm, for example, seems to be this:

> *Proposition 3:* Create a rugged landscape to heighten access to local optima having higher fitness peaks, by keeping internal coevolutionary interdependencies relatively small ($K = 2$ to 8) even though the number of value chain competencies, N, in your coevolutionary pocket, is rising.

In this section, I have shown how the second principle of complexity theory applied to firms may be appropriately modeled using Kauffman's $NK[C]$ model. I have emphasized the effects of C in raising the upper bound allowed for increasing K before complexity catastrophe sets in.[17] Raising C has the effect of moderating the slopes of the inverted U "hill" when performance is plotted against adaptive tension and complexity.

Conclusion

Two aspects of complexity theory are emphasized. First, I identify four propositions from Prigogine's (Nicolis & Prigogine, 1989) *self-organization theory* that relate the chaos theorists' critical values to different kinds of complexity. The region between the first and second critical values is identified as the complexity zone "at the edge of chaos" in which emergent structures will occur. These structures are analogous to the bulk air currents that most effectively reduce the tension between a hot earth and a cold upper atmosphere. From this analogy, I argue that there is a region between the critical values of adaptive tension that corporations may impose on acquired SBUs in which SBU adaptation and performance in a rapidly changing competitive context may be maximized as a result of emerging structures (the equivalent of bulk air currents). This complexity theory application emphasizes adaptive tension,

governance, and emergent self-organized structure in SBUs. It argues that too much or too little adaptive tension diminishes the likelihood of effective adaptation.

Second, using the notebook computer industry as an example, I translate Kauffman's (1993) *complexity catastrophe theory* to firms. This theory argues that the BVSR process may be thwarted if a firm tries to coevolve on too many interdependent value chain elements or technologies. In this theory, K, the number of interdependencies, "tunes" a firm's adaptive landscape such that too low or too high a K depresses adaptive effectiveness. Complexity catastrophe occurs when, even though the BVSR process is functioning effectively, the value chain elements favorably selected are not really any more effective than those not selected.

Both theories are then computationally modeled in an illustrative fashion. As far back as 1969, Kauffman (1969, 1974, 1993) began using random Boolean network models to explore the dynamics of emergent structure. His early studies have subsequently been pursued by Gelfand and Walker (1984), Derrida (1987), and a number of colleagues in statistical physics, particularly Stauffer (1987a, 1987b) and Weisbuch (1991). Using as an example the various levels of adaptive tension that could be imposed by an acquiring firm in governing a new SBU acquisition, I demonstrate how the parameters of the random Boolean network model fit the organizational world. Although at a primitive state of application, these models show how one could use the theory to develop the complexity theory of emergent structure in firms, depending on the critical values of adaptive tension. Using the example of coevolutionary adaptation in the notebook computer industry, I then use Kauffman's (1993) $NK[C]$ model to show how one might explore the dynamics of complexity effects on the adaptive BVSR capabilities of firms. These effects may be modeled in terms of intrafirm complexity as well as interfirm complexity. Taken together, these theory-model links suggest that firms adapt best under conditions of moderate adaptive tension and value chain complexity.

Of course, much remains to be accomplished. Not since the early exploration by Gelfand and

Walker (1984) has anyone tried to apply random Boolean networks to the study of organizational adaptation, so my use of this approach is surely primitive. Kauffman's *NK* model is seeing some application to firms on adaptive landscapes (Levinthal, 1997a, 1997b; Levinthal & Warglien, 1997; Rivkin, 1997; Sorenson, 1997). Baum (this volume) applies the *NK[C]* model at the group level within firms. McKelvey (1998a, in press) also applies the *NK[C]* at the agent level within firms. The use of the random Boolean network model is novel in my application here and undoubtedly needs further development to more readily fit complexity theory applications to firms.

Most articles in present-day organization science do not begin or end with a formal model. Perhaps not all of them should, but in top drawer sciences such as physics, biology, and economics, *many* published reports of scientific activity are centered around formal models. As developed elsewhere (McKelvey, this volume), *Campbellian realism* is very clear in the model-centeredness of its view of current epistemology. There is no doubt that current philosophy of science strongly supports Campbellian realism from three epistemological perspectives: (a) *scientific realism* (Bhaskar, 1975; Boyd, 1991; Aronson et al., 1994, De Regt, 1994), (b) the *semantic conception* (Beth, 1961; Suppes, 1962; van Fraassen, 1970; Suppe, 1977, 1989), and (c) *evolutionary epistemology* (Popper, 1963; Campbell, 1974b, 1990; Churchland & Hooker, 1985; Rescher, 1990). In the language of scientific and Campbellian realism, effective science requires tests of *experimental adequacy*. I have taken space to present the two illustrative modeling approaches to demonstrate my concern that organization science in general, and complexity applications in particular, be shifted in the direction of model-centered science.

Because of the tractability requirements of formal models, whether mathematical or computational, advanced sciences move forward in terms of theories far more parsimonious than the norm in organization science. Model-centeredness automatically drives parsimony—often more than validity concerns appear to justify. Be this as it may, parsimony characterizes sciences having far more external status, influence, and funding than organi-

zation science. Pfeffer was right on target nearly two decades ago in calling for "simpler models" (1981, p. 411). Given the dictates of models and Pfeffer's good judgment, this chapter reduces Scott's (1998) "rational, natural, and open systems" framework to four fundamental forces: *adaptive tension, self-organization* (both managerial and nonmanagerial), *interdependency effects*, and *multilevel coevolution*.

My approach has several important limitations. That complexity theory, via Prigogine's self-organization and Kauffman's catastrophe propositions, applies to firms is surely preliminary. Given the variety of agent-based models available, *spin glass* (Mézard, Parisi, & Vivasoro, 1987; Fischer & Hertz, 1993), *simulated annealing* (Aarts & Korst, 1989), *cellular automata* (Toffoli & Margolus, 1987; Weisbuch, 1991), *neural networks* (Wasserman, 1989, 1993; Müller & Reinhardt, 1990; Freeman & Skapura, 1993), *genetic algorithm* (Holland, 1975, 1995; Goldberg, 1989; Mitchell, 1996), and most recently, *population games* (Blume, 1995), there is little reason to rush into acceptance of Kauffman's Boolean statistical mechanics, Boolean network, and *NK[C]* models. Furthermore, the four fundamental forces I emphasize may not offer the best framing for 21st-century organization science. Of course, the approach described here may never pass any kind of reasonable *ontological adequacy* test, the other primary requirement of Campbellian realism.

I started with the question, Do adaptive tension, self-organization, interdependency, and coevolution contribute in any way toward explaining why dinosauric firms like General Motors languish in a state of seeming permanent failure (Meyer & Zucker, 1989)? We can come up with a long list of reasons, from unions to myopic management. For a specific firm any and all these reasons could hold. This is similar to why a plant on the side of Pikes Peak might die—no water, blown away, washed away, eaten, buried by a landslide, poisoned, hit by lightning, and so on. To form an organization science around case studies of why a corporation such as GM lives or dies is like a botanist trying to draw scientific generalizations from a study of the Pikes Peak plant. It doesn't work! According to Campbellian realism, what does work is nomic necessity and model-centeredness accompanied by effective tests of experimental and ontological adequacy. There also is Pfeffer's (1981, 1997) continued request for parsimony. With these views in mind, I zero in on just a few underlying forces, suggest a theory based on laws of the counterfactual conditional kind, and illustrate how a couple of computational models might allow experimental adequacy tests. Needless to say, the coevolution of the theory-model link is in its infancy.

Notes

1. Starbuck (1965), Cohen, March, and Olsen (1972), Carley (1991, 1994), March (1991), and Burton and Obel (1984, 1995), among others, are well ahead of me in formally modeling organizational behavior. Carley (1995) gives a review of formal modeling in organization science.

2. To be defined more fully in the next section. Below the first critical value, no structure emerges, and above the second critical value, the system becomes chaotic.

3. Schrödinger (1944) coined the term *negentropy* to refer to energy importation.

4. An emergent structure is said to "percolate" when it stretches from one edge of a network lattice to another—top to bottom, left to right, and so on (Stauffer, 1987b).

5. Nomic necessity is a requirement imposed by philosophers to protect against explanations responding to "accidental regularities" by insisting that all explanations be based on theories that include at least some laws of the "counterfactual conditional" kind, that is, "If A then B." For example, a theory purporting to offer a culture-based explanation why Japanese firms have no-layoff policies is based on the accidental regularity that "all Japanese firms have no-layoff policies." Because exceptions exist, the regularity, as stated here, is mistaken.

6. Epistatic interdependencies have an effect only if they force a lower fitness than what is "drawn" by an agent—hence, they always act to limit the fitness yield an agent otherwise might obtain from the draw.

7. Implications of Kauffman's *NK[C]* model for firms is spelled out in more detail in McKelvey (in press).

8. Thompson (1989) gives a good review of the reasons why philosophers shifted from the syntactic/axiomatic view to the semantic conception of theories.

9. Some key contributors are Kauffman (1974), Gelfand and Walker (1984), Derrida and Flyvbjerg (1986), Derrida and Pomeau (1986), Derrida and Stauffer (1986), and Derrida and Weisbuch (1987).

10. I cannot replicate Kauffman's development here. Recourse to Kauffman (1993, chap. 5) is highly recommended.

11. A very accessible description of automata is given in Westhoff, Yarbrough, and Yarbrough (1996). A more advanced introduction is given by Weisbuch (1991).

12. Weisbuch (1991, p. 11) says only functions numbered 1, 4, 7, 8, 11, and 13 are truly forcing. Other authors such as Gelfand and Walker (1984) and Westhoff and colleagues (1996) consider all but functions 6 and 9 as forcing because for these two, the outcome state depends on knowing both input states.

13. This model does not discriminate between deterministic chaos (bifurcation into two or a few attractors) and an even less structured, totally random kind of complexity where no algorithmic compression is possible.

14. Experiments in Figures 6.3 and 6.4 (Kauffman, 1993, pp. 247-249). Set $N = 24$; $C = 1, 8, 20$; $K = 2, 4, 8, 12, 16$. Allow only one random change per time period at only one (randomly selected) of the N sites (competencies); each agent chooses a new one-change neighbor if it contributes to an improved overall chain fitness. The experiments draw 100 to 200 pairs over 250+ time periods.

15. Also based on experiments shown in Figures 6.3 and 6.4 (Kauffman, 1993).

16. Experiments in Tables 2.1 and 2.2 (Kauffman, 1993, pp. 55, 56). Set $N = 8, 16, 24, 48, 96$; $K = 0$ to 95. Starting from a randomly selected firm, allow only one random change per time period at only one (randomly selected) of the N sites; each firm chooses a one-change neighbor if one of its sites is an improvement. Walks occur on 100 randomly selected landscapes with average fitness levels reported.

17. Additional experimental results from Kauffman's *NK[C]* model that are relevant to strategy in coevolutionary pockets appear in McKelvey (in press).

References

Aarts, E., & Korst, J. (1989). *Simulated annealing and Boltzmann machines.* New York: Wiley.

Anderson, P. W., Arrow, K. J., & Pines, D. (Eds.). (1988). *The economy as an evolving complex system* (Proceedings of the Santa Fe Institute, Vol. 5). Reading, MA: Addison-Wesley.

Aoki, M. (1996). *New approaches to macroeconomic modeling: Evolutionary stochastic dynamics, multiple equilibria, and externalities as mean field.* New York: Cambridge University Press.

Aronson, J. L., Harré, R., & Way, E. C. (1994). *Realism rescued.* London: Duckworth.

Arthur, W. B., Durlauf, S. N., & Lane, D. A. (Eds.). (1997). *The economy as an evolving complex system* (Proceedings of the Santa Fe Institute, Vol. 27). Reading, MA: Addison-Wesley.

Barney, J. B. (1994). Beyond individual metaphors in understanding how firms behave: A comment on game theory and prospect theory models of firm behavior. In R. P. Rumelt, D. E. Schendel, & D. J. Teece (Eds.), *Fundamental issues in strategy: A research agenda* (pp. 55-69). Boston: Harvard Business School Press.

Barrow, J. D. (1991). *Theories of everything: The quest for ultimate explanation.* New York: Fawcett Columbine.

Baum, J.A.C., & Silverman, B. S. (in press). Complexity in the dynamics of organizational founding and failure. In M. Lissack & H. Gunz (Eds.), *Managing the complex—1.* New York: Quorum.

Baum, J.A.C., & Singh, J. V. (1994). Organizations as hierarchies and evolutionary processes: Some reflections on a theory of organizational evolution. In J.A.C. Baum & J. V. Singh (Eds.), *Evolutionary dynamics of organizations* (pp. 3-22). New York: Oxford University Press.

Beck, C., & Schlögl, F. (1993). *Thermodynamics of chaotic systems.* Cambridge, UK: Cambridge University Press.

Belew, R. K., & Mitchell, M. (Eds.). (1996). *Adaptive individuals in evolving populations* (Proceedings of the Santa Fe Institute, Vol. 26). Reading, MA: Addison-Wesley.

Beth, E. (1961). Semantics of physical theories. In H. Freudenthal (Ed.), *The concept and the role of the model in mathematics and natural and social sciences* (pp. 48-51). Dordrecht, The Netherlands: Reidel.

Bhaskar, R. (1975). *A realist theory of science.* London: Leeds Books.

Blume, L. E. (1997). Population games. In W. B. Arthur, S. N. Durlauf, & D. A. Lane (Eds.), *The economy as an evolving complex system* (Proceedings of the Santa Fe Institute, Vol. 27, pp. 425-460). Reading, MA: Addison-Wesley.

Boyd, R. (1991). Confirmation, semantics, and the interpretation of scientific theories. In R. Boyd, P. Gasper, & J. D. Trout (Eds.), *The philosophy of science* (pp. 3-35). Cambridge, MA: Bradford/MIT Press.

Brown, S. L., & Eisenhardt, K. M. (1998). *Competing on the edge: Strategy as structured chaos.* Boston: Harvard Business School Press.

Bruderer, E., & Singh, J. V. (1996). Organizational evolution, learning, and selection: A genetic-algorithm-based model. *Academy of Management Journal, 39,* 1322-1349.

Burton, R. M., & Obel, B. (1984). *Designing efficient organizations: Modelling and experimentation.* New York: North-Holland.

Burton, R. M., & Obel, B. (Eds.). (1995). *Design models for hierarchical organizations: Computation, information, and decentralization.* Boston: Kluwer.

Byrne, D. (1998). *Complexity theory in the social sciences: An introduction.* London: Routledge.

Campbell, D. T. (1974a). Downward causation in hierarchically organized biological systems. In F. J. Ayala & T. Dobzhansky (Eds.), *Studies in the philosophy of biology* (pp. 179-186). London: Macmillan.

Campbell, D. T. (1974b). Evolutionary epistemology. In P. A. Schilpp (Ed.), *The philosophy of Karl Popper* (Vol. 14, pp. 413-463). La Salle, IL: Open Court.

Campbell, D. T. (1981). Levels of organization, selection, and information storage in biological and social evolution. *The Behavioral and Brain Sciences, 4,* 236-237.

Campbell, D. T. (1988a). Descriptive epistemology: Psychological, sociological, and evolutionary. In D. T. Campbell, *Methodology and epistemology for social science: Selected papers* (E. S. Overman, Ed., pp. 435-486). Chicago: University of Chicago Press.

Campbell, D. T. (1988b). A general "selection theory" as implemented in biological evolution and in social belief-transmission-with-modification in science. *Biology and Philosophy, 3,* 171-177.

Campbell, D. T. (1990). Levels of organization, downward causation, and the selection-theory approach to evolutionary epistemology. In G. Greenberg & E. Tobach (Eds.), *Theories of the evolution of knowing* (T. C. Schneirla Conference Series, Vol. 4, pp. 1-17). Hillsdale, NJ: Erlbaum.

Campbell, D. T. (1994). How individual and face-to-face-group selection undermine firm selection in organizational evolution. In J.A.C. Baum & J. V. Singh (Eds.), *Evolutionary dynamics of organizations* (pp. 23-38). New York: Oxford University Press.

Carley, K. M. (1991). Designing organizational structures to cope with communication breakdowns: A simulation model. *Industrial Crisis Quarterly, 5,* 19-57.

Carley, K. M. (1994). Sociology: Computational organization theory. *Social Science Computer Review, 12,* 611-624.

Carley, K. M. (1995). Computational and mathematical organization theory: Perspective and directions. *Computational and Mathematical Organization Theory, 1,* 39-56.

Carley, K. M. (1996). A comparison of artificial and human organizations. *Journal of Economic Behavior and Organization, 31,* 175-191.

Carley, K. M. (in press). Organizational adaptation. *Annals of Operations Research.*

Carley, K. M., & Svoboda, D. M. (1996). Modeling organizational adaptation as a simulated annealing process. *Sociological Methods and Research, 25,* 138-168.

Chandler, A. D., Jr. (1977). *The visible hand: The managerial revolution in American business.* Cambridge, MA: Belknap/Harvard University Press.

Cheng, Y., & Van de Ven, A. H. (1996). Learning the innovation journey: Order out of chaos. *Organization Science, 7,* 593-614.

Chia, R. (1996). *Organizational analysis as deconstructive practice.* Berlin: Walter de Gruyter.

Churchland, P. M., & Hooker, C. A. (Eds.). (1985). *Images of science.* Chicago: University of Chicago Press.

Cilliers, P. (1998). *Complexity and postmodernism: Understanding complex systems.* London: Routledge.

Cohen, J., & Stewart, I. (1994). *The collapse of chaos: Discovering simplicity in a complex world.* New York: Viking/Penguin.

Cohen, M. D., March, J. G., & Olsen, J. P. (1972). A garbage can model of organizational choice. *Administrative Science Quarterly, 17,* 1-25.

Cowan, G. A., Pines, D., & Meltzer, D. (Eds.). (1994). *Complexity: Metaphors, models, and reality* (Proceedings of the Santa Fe Institute, Vol. 19). Reading, MA: Addison-Wesley.

Cramer, F. (1993). *Chaos and order: The complex structure of living things* (D. L. Loewus, Trans.). New York: VCH.

Dawkins, R. (1976). *The selfish gene.* New York: Oxford University Press.

De Regt, C.D.G. (1994). *Representing the world by scientific theories: The case for scientific realism.* Tilburg, The Netherlands: Tilburg University Press.

Depew, D. J., & Weber, B. H. (1995). *Darwinism evolving: Systems dynamics and the genealogy of natural selection.* Cambridge, MA: Bradford/MIT Press.

Derrida, B. (1987). Valleys and overlaps in Kauffman's model. *Philosophical Magazine B, 56*, 917-923.

Derrida, B., & Flyvbjerg, H. (1986). Multivalley structure in Kauffman's model: Analogy with spin glasses. *Journal of Physics A: Mathematics and General, 19*, L1003-L1008.

Derrida, B., & Pomeau, Y. (1986). Random networks of automata: A simple annealed approximation. *Europhysics Letters, 1*, 45-49.

Derrida, B., & Stauffer, D. (1986). Phase transitions in two-dimensional Kauffman cellular automata. *Europhysics Letters, 2*, 739-745.

Derrida, B., & Weisbuch, G. (1987). Dynamical phase transitions in three-dimensional spin glasses. *Europhysics Letters, 4*, 657-722.

Donaldson, L. (1995). *American anti-management theories of organization.* Cambridge, UK: Cambridge University Press.

Eddington, A. (1930). *The nature of the physical world.* London: Macmillan.

Eigen, M. (1971). Self-organization of matter and the evolution of biological macromolecules. *Naturwissenschaften, 58*, 465-523.

Eigen, M., & Schuster, P. (1979). *The hypercycle: A principle of natural self-organization.* New York: Simon & Schuster.

Eigen, M., & Winkler, R. (1981). *Laws of the game: How the principles of nature govern chance.* New York: Knopf.

Eldredge, N. (1985). *Unfinished synthesis: Biological hierarchies and modern evolutionary thought.* New York: Oxford University Press.

Eldredge, N. (1995). *Reinventing Darwin.* New York: Wiley.

Eve, R. A., & Horsfall, M.E.L. (Eds.). (1997). *Chaos, complexity and sociology: Myths, models, and theories.* Thousand Oaks, CA: Sage.

Favre, A., Guitton, H., Guitton, J., Lichnerowicz, A., & Wolff, E. (1995). *Chaos and determinism* (B. E. Schwarzbach, Trans.). Baltimore: Johns Hopkins University Press.

Fischer, K. H., & Hertz, J. A. (1993). *Spin glasses.* New York: Cambridge University Press.

Fontana, W., Schnabl, W., & Schuster, P. (1989). Physical aspects of evolutionary optimization and adaptation. *Physical Review A, 40*, 3301-3321.

Fontana, W., & Schuster, P. (1987). A computer model of evolutionary optimization. *Biophysical Chemistry, 26*, 123-147.

Freeman, J. A., & Skapura, D. M. (1992). *Neural networks: Algorithms, applications, and programming techniques.* Reading MA: Addison-Wesley.

Friedman, M. (1953). *Essays in positive economics.* Chicago: University of Chicago Press.

Gelfand, A. E., & Walker, C. C. (1984). *Ensemble modeling.* New York: Marcel Dekker.

Gell-Mann, M. (1994). *The quark and the jaguar.* New York: Freeman.

Gibbs, J. W. (1902). *Elementary principles in statistical mechanics.* New Haven, CT: Yale University Press.

Gleick, J. (1987). *Chaos: Making a new science.* New York: Penguin.

Goldberg, D. E. (1989). *Genetic algorithms in search, optimization and machine learning.* Reading, MA: Addison-Wesley.

Gould, S. J. (1983). The hardening of the modern synthesis. In M. Greene (Ed.), *Dimensions of Darwinism* (pp. 71-93). Cambridge, UK: Cambridge University Press.

Hartman, H., & Vichniac, G. W. (1986). Inhomogeneous cellular automata. In E. Bienenstock, F. F. Soulié, & G. Weisbuch (Eds.), *Disordered systems and biological organization* (pp. 53-57). Heidelburg: Springer-Verlag.

Holland, J. (1975). *Adaptation in natural and artificial systems.* Ann Arbor: University of Michigan Press.

Holland, J. H. (1995). *Hidden order.* Reading, MA: Addison-Wesley.

Hunt, C. S., & Aldrich, H. E. (1998). The second ecology: Creation and evolution of organizational communities. *Research on Organizational Behavior, 20*, 267-301.

Johnson, J. L., & Burton, B. K. (1994). Chaos and complexity theory for management. *Journal of Management Inquiry, 3*, 320-328.

Jones, T. (1995). *Evolutionary algorithms, fitness landscapes and search.* Unpublished doctoral dissertation, Department of Computer Science, University of New Mexico, Albuquerque.

Kauffman, S. A. (1969). Metabolic stability and epigenesis in randomly connected nets. *Journal of Theoretical Biology, 22*, 437-467.

Kauffman, S. A. (1974). The large-scale structure and dynamics of gene control circuits: An ensemble approach. *Journal of Theoretical Biology, 44*, 167-190.

Kauffman, S. A. (1993). *The origins of order: Self-organization and selection in evolution.* New York: Oxford University Press.

Kauffman, S. A., & Weinberger, E. D. (1989). The *N-K* model of rugged fitness landscapes and its application to maturation of the immune response. *Journal of Theoretical Biology, 141*, 211-245.

Kaye, B. (1993). *Chaos & complexity.* New York: VCH.

Kerwin, K. (1998, July 27). GM: It's time to face the future. *Business Week*, pp. 26-28.

Kimura, M. (1983). *The neutral theory of molecular evolution.* Cambridge, UK: Cambridge University Press.

Kolmogorov, A. N. (1965). Three approaches to the qualitative definition of information. *Problems of Information Transmission, 1*, 4-7.

Kramer, F. R., Mills, D. R., Cole, P. E., Nishihara, T., & Spiegelman, S. (1974). Evolution *in vitro*: Sequence and phenotype of a mutant RNA resistant to ethidium bromide. *Journal of Molecular Biology, 89*, 719-736.

Levinthal, D. A. (1997a). Adaptation on rugged landscapes. *Management Science, 43*, 934-950.

Levinthal, D. A. (1997b). *The slow pace of rapid technological change: Gradualism and punctuation in technological change.* Unpublished manuscript, The Wharton School, University of Pennsylvania, Philadelphia.

Levinthal, D. A., & Warglien, M. (1997). *Landscape design: Designing for local action in complex worlds.* Unpublished manuscript, The Wharton School, University of Pennsylvania, Philadelphia.

Levy, D. (1994). Chaos theory and strategy: Theory, application and managerial implications. *Strategic Management, 15,* 167-178.

Lewontin, R. C. (1974). *The genetic basis of evolutionary change.* New York: Columbia University Press.

Lincoln, Y. S. (Ed.). (1985). *Organizational theory and inquiry.* Newbury Park, CA: Sage.

Lissack, M., & Gunz, H. (Eds.). (in press). *Managing the complex—1.* New York: Quorum.

Lloyd, E. A. (1988). *The structure and confirmation of evolutionary theory.* Princeton, NJ: Princeton University Press.

Loomis, C. J. (1993, May 3). "Dinosaurs?" *Fortune,* pp. 36-42.

Macken, C. A., & Stadler, P. F. (1995). Evolution on fitness landscapes. In L. Nadel & D. L. Stein (Eds.), *1993 lectures in complex systems* (Lectures Vol. 6, Santa Fe Institute, pp. 43-86, Santa Fe, NM). Reading, MA: Addison-Wesley.

Mackenzie, K. D. (1986). *Organizational design: The organizational audit and analysis technology.* Norwood, NJ: Ablex.

Mainzer, K. (1994). *Thinking in complexity: The complex dynamics of matter, mind, and mankind.* New York: Springer-Verlag.

March, J. G. (1991). Exploration and exploitation in organization learning. *Organization Science, 2,* 71-87.

Maynard Smith, J. (1970). Natural selection and the concept of a protein space. *Nature, 225,* 563-564.

Maynard Smith, J. (1975). *The theory of evolution* (3rd ed.). Harmondsworth, UK: Penguin.

McKelvey, B. (1997). Quasi-natural organization science. *Organization Science, 8,* 351-380.

McKelvey, B. (1998a). Complexity vs. selection among coevolutionary microstates in firms: Complexity effects on strategic organizing. *Comportamento Organizacional E Gestão, 4,* 17-59.

McKelvey, B. (1998b, January). *"Good" science from postmodernist ontology: Realism, complexity theory, and emergent dissipative structures.* Paper presented at the Non-Linearity and the Organization conference, New Mexico State University, Las Cruces.

McKelvey, B. (in press). Avoiding complexity catastrophe in coevolutionary pockets: Strategies for rugged landscapes. *Organization Science.*

Merry, U. (1995). *Coping with uncertainty: Insights from the new sciences of chaos, self-organization, and complexity.* Westport, CT: Praeger.

Meyer, M. W., & Zucker, L. G. (1989). *Permanently failing organizations.* Newbury Park, CA: Sage.

Mézard, M., Parisi, G., & Vivasoro, M. A. (1987). *Spin glass theory and beyond.* Singapore: World Scientific.

Miller, D. (1990). *The Icarus Paradox.* New York: HarperBusiness.

Mitchell, M. (1996). *An introduction to genetic algorithms.* Cambridge, MA: MIT Press.

Morrison, F. (1991). *The art of modeling dynamic systems.* New York: Wiley Interscience.

Müller, B., & Reinhardt, J. (1990). *Neural networks.* New York: Springer-Verlag.

Nadel, L., & Stein, D. L. (Eds.). (1995). *1993 lectures in complex systems* (Lectures Vol. 6, Santa Fe Institute). New York: Addison-Wesley.

Nicolis, G., & Prigogine, I. (1977). *Self-organization in non-equilibrium systems.* New York: Wiley.

Nicolis, G., & Prigogine, I. (1989). *Exploring complexity: An introduction.* New York: Freeman.

Paller, B. T., & Campbell, D. T. (1989). Maxwell and van Fraassen on observability, reality, and justification. In M. L. Maxwell & C. W. Savage (Eds.), *Science, mind, and psychology: Essays in honor of Grover Maxwell* (pp. 99-132). Lanham, MD: University Press of America.

Pfeffer, J. (1981). Four laws of organizational research. In A. Van de Ven & W. Joyce (Eds.), *Perspectives on organization design and behavior* (pp. 409-418). New York: Wiley.

Pfeffer, J. (1997). *New directions for organization theory.* New York: Oxford University Press.

Pianka, E. R. (1994). *Evolutionary ecology* (5th ed.). New York: HarperCollins.

Popper, K. R. (1963). *Conjectures and refutations.* London: Routledge & Kegan Paul.

Porter, M. E. (1985). *Competitive advantage.* New York: Free Press.

Porter, M. E. (1990). *Competitive advantage of nations.* New York: Free Press.

Prietula, M. J., & Carley, K. M. (1994). Computational organization theory: Autonomous agents and emergent behavior. *Journal of Organizational Computation, 41,* 41-83.

Prigogine, I. (1962). *Non-equilibrium statistical mechanics.* New York: Wiley Interscience.

Prigogine, I. (1980). *From being to becoming—Time and complexity in the physical sciences.* San Francisco: Freeman.

Prigogine, I., & Stengers, I. (1984). *Order out of chaos: Man's new dialogue with nature.* New York: Bantam.

Rescher, N. (Ed.). (1990). *Evolution, cognition, and realism: Studies in evolutionary epistemology.* Lanham, MD: University Press of America.

Rivkin, J. (1997, August). *Imitation of complex strategies.* Paper presented at the Academy of Management, Boston.

Schrödinger, E. (1944). *What is life: The physical aspect of the living cell.* Cambridge, UK: Cambridge University Press.

Schwartz, P., & Ogilvy, J. (1979). *The emergent paradigm: Changing patterns of thought and belief* (Analytic Report 7, Values and Lifestyle Program). Menlo Park, CA: SRI International.

Scott, W. R. (1998). *Organizations: Rational, natural, and open systems* (4th ed.). Englewood Cliffs, NJ: Prentice Hall.

Simon, H. A. (1957). Rationality and administrative decision making. In *Models of man* (pp. 196-206). New York: Wiley.

Sorenson, O. (1997). *The complexity catastrophe in the evolution in the computer industry: Interdependence and adaptability in organizational evolution.* Unpublished doctoral dissertation, Sociology Department, Stanford University.

Spiegelman, S. (1971). An approach to the experimental analysis of precellular evolution. *Quarterly Reviews of Biophysics, 4*, 213-253.

Stacey, R. D. (1992). *Managing the unknowable: Strategic boundaries between order and chaos in organizations.* San Francisco: Jossey-Bass.

Stacey, R. D. (1995). The science of complexity: An alternative perspective for strategic change processes. *Strategic Management Journal, 16*, 477-495.

Stacey, R. D. (1996). *Complexity and creativity.* San Francisco: Berrett-Koehler.

Stanley, S. M. (1979). *Macroevolution: Pattern and process.* San Francisco: Freeman.

Starbuck, W. H. (1965). Organizational growth and development. In J. G. March (Ed.), *Handbook of organizations* (pp. 451-533). Chicago: Rand McNally.

Stauffer, D. (1987a). On forcing functions in Kauffman's random Boolean networks. *Journal of Statistical Physics, 46*, 789-794.

Stauffer, D. (1987b). Random Boolean networks: Analogy with percolation. *Philosophical Magazine B, 56*, 901-916.

Suppe, F. (1977). *The structure of scientific theories* (2nd ed.). Chicago: University of Chicago Press.

Suppe, F. (1989). *The semantic conception of theories & scientific realism.* Urbana-Champaign: University of Illinois Press.

Suppes, P. (1962). Models of data. In E. Nagel, P. Suppes, & A. Tarski (Eds.), *Logic, methodology, and philosophy of science: Proceedings of the 1960 International Congress* (pp. 252-261). Stanford, CA: Stanford University Press.

Thiétart, R. A., & Forgues, B. (1995). Chaos theory and organization. *Organization Science, 6*, 19-31.

Thompson, P. (1989). *The structure of biological theories.* Albany: State University of New York Press.

Toffoli, T., & Margolus, N. (1987). *Cellular automata machines.* Cambridge, MA: MIT Press.

Tolman, R. C. (1938). *The principles of statistical mechanics.* New York: Dover.

Ulanowicz, R. E. (1989). A phenomenology of evolving networks. *Systems Research, 6*, 209-217.

Van de Ven, A. H., & Poole, M. S. (1995). Explaining development and change in organizations. *Academy of Management Review, 20*, 510-540.

van Fraassen, B. C. (1970). On the extension of Beth's semantics of physical theories. *Philosophy of Science, 37*, 325-339.

van Fraassen, B. C. (1980). *The scientific image.* Oxford, UK: Clarendon.

Wasserman, P. D. (1989). *Neural computing: Theory and practice.* New York: Van Nostrand Reinhold.

Wasserman, P. D. (1993). *Advanced methods in neural computing.* New York: Van Nostrand Reinhold.

Weidlich, W., & Haag, G. (1983). *Concepts and models of a quantitative sociology.* Berlin: Springer-Verlag.

Weinberger, E. D. (1991). Local properties of Kauffman's *N-K* model: A tunably rugged energy landscape. *Physical Review A, 44*, 6399-6413.

Weisbuch, G. (1991). *Complex systems dynamics: An introduction to automata networks* (Lecture notes Vol. 2, Santa Fe Institute, S. Ryckebusch, Trans.). Reading, MA: Addison-Wesley.

Westhoff, F. H., Yarbrough, B. V., & Yarbrough, R. M. (1996). Modelling complexity, adaptation and evolution. *Journal of Economic Behavior and Organization, 29*, 1-25.

Williams, G. C. (1966). *Adaptation and natural selection: A critique of some current evolutionary thought.* Princeton, NJ: Princeton University Press.

Williams, M. B. (1970). Deducing the consequences of evolution: A mathematical model. *Journal of Theoretical Biology, 29*, 343-385.

Williamson, O. E. (1975). *Markets and hierarchies.* New York: Free Press.

Wright, S. (1931). Evolution in Mendelian populations. *Genetics, 16*, 97-159.

Wright, S. (1932). The roles of mutation, inbreeding, crossbreeding and selection in evolution. *Proceedings of the Sixth International Congress on Genetics, 1*, 356-366.

Zimmerman, B. J., & Hurst, D. K. (1993). Breaking the boundaries: The fractal organization. *Journal of Management Inquiry, 2*, 334-355.

Part IV

Methodology and Epistemology

Chapter 16

Donald T. Campbell's Methodological Contributions to Organization Science

MARTIN G. EVANS

Donald Campbell

Fortunately for us, Donald Campbell was a man who, at least in one respect, did not practice what he preached. In his chapter about the fish-scale view of the social sciences, he advocated that each of us stick fairly close to our knitting, but branch out a little bit into the fields of adjacent knitters (Campbell, 1969). Thus, there would be overlap like the scales of a fish—forgive the mixed metaphors—and the whole fish would be covered. Don Campbell was not like that. His work, both methodological and substantive, covered the whole fish, nay, whole schools of fishes. My aim in this chapter is more modest: I want to elucidate the impact his work has had in two areas of methodology—construct validity of measurement and causal inference. I will do this by exploring the impact of three (one for construct validity, two for causal infer-

ence) bodies of work initiated by Campbell (and his colleagues). In doing this, I will try to identify the reasons for the development of the ideas, the ways in which they have been developed and used in organization science, and future directions to be taken. Before doing that, let me demonstrate the pervasiveness of the ideas in social science generally and management in particular.

Pervasiveness of Campbell's Contributions

I did a search of the citation index since 1981, when the CD-ROM version began, to obtain the extent to which citations had accrued to these three areas of Campbell's contribution. For construct validity, I searched on the Campbell and Fiske (1959) citation. For the quasi-experimental design

AUTHOR'S NOTE: My thanks to Richard Bagozzi, Joel Baum, Whitney Berta, Bill McKelvey, and Xiao Li for their helpful comments on an earlier draft of this chapter and to Vinay Kanetkar, who has immeasurably contributed to my growth as a methodologist.

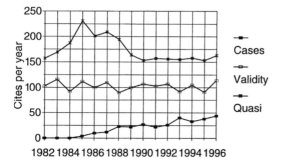

Figure 16.1. Citations in All Journals

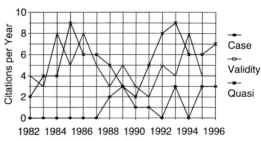

Figure 16.2. Management Citations

work, I searched on three major citations: the Campbell and Stanley (1963) presentation in Gage's handbook on research in education, the Campbell and Stanley standalone monograph (1966), and the more recent Cook and Campbell book (1979). For the casework, I searched the original appearance of the article in *Comparative Political Science* (1975), its reprint in a book of readings (Campbell, 1979), and, because the yield was very low, Robert Yin's (1984) book on case research, which was inspired by Campbell's piece. The results for all social sciences are presented in Figure 16.1. The Campbell and Fiske data are in the middle of the graph and show a steady 100 citations per year since 1981. The quasi-experimental citations are at the top of the figure and show nicely a peak at the 5-year half-life of a publication (in this case, the Cook and Campbell volume). Finally, the case work seems to be a sleeper. There were very few citations to the Campbell articles; the citation count seems to be picking up with respect to the Yin volume, published in 1984.

The situation in management is much the same—but, of course, with lower numbers and a higher year-to-year variance. Figure 16.2 shows the unstable data, but the picture can be better viewed by examining the cumulative record since 1981—shown in Figure 16.3. Again, the case-work is the least cited, despite the rise to respectability within our domain of more ethnographic methods.

I will now turn to the kind of influence each of these seminal articles has had on our field. For construct validity, my focus will be on the advances

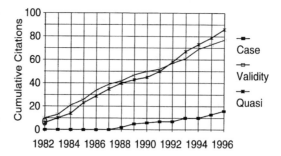

Figure 16.3. Cumulative Citations (Management Journals)

in application of the multitrait-multimethod matrix; for causal inference, I will explore the enormously influential quasi-experimental design and its—I hesitate to say—alternative, the case analysis (see also the work of Yin, 1984).

Construct Validity[1]

In the mid-1950's, the nature of psychological measurement was in a bit of a mess. Strict operationalists argued that the measure represented what it measured and nothing else, those involved in the employment testing business were simply concerned that the measure predicted some outcome of practical importance (i.e., job performance), and those with a more conceptual frame of mind argued that the measure was an indicator of a concept, of what today we would call a latent variable. The difficulty was in assessing how well that measure tapped that construct: the nature of the construct

TABLE 16.1 Typical MTMM Correlation Matrix

	SA1	*SA2*	*SS1*	*SS2*	*SM1*	*SM2*	*FA1*	*FA2*	*FS1*	*FS2*	*FM1*	*FM2*
SA1	1											
SA2	.572	1										
SS1	.615	.470	1									
SS2	.335	.438	.604	1								
SM1	.337	.255	.441	.403	1							
SM2	.164	.214	.264	.306	.377	1						
FA1	.258	.287	.316	.283	.161	.156	1					
FA2	.219	.239	.214	.203	.141	.050	.668	1				
FS1	.241	.281	.343	.401	.232	.123	.412	.282	1			
FS2	.204	.249	.290	.330	.199	.041	.379	.387	.755	1		
FM1	.156	.244	.195	.249	.269	.270	.361	.228	.418	.219	1	
FM2	.109	.155	.188	.232	.312	−.013	.236	.266	.323	.358	.596	1

SOURCE: Data are from Graham and Collins (1991).
NOTE: Shaded entries are validities. S = self-rating; F = friend rating; A = alcohol; S = smoking; M = marijuana use.

validity of the measure. A task force of the time, inspired by the American Psychological Association, tried to draw some consistency out of the prevailing confusion and argued for a variety of indicators of measure validity—face validity, content validity, predictive (or concurrent, or postdictive) validity, and construct validity. The last of those was the potential jewel in the theoretician's crown; however, ways of establishing this type of validity were still uncertain. In 1959, Campbell and Fiske suggested some ways in which construct validity could be assessed: by examining how the various constructs measured by similar and different methods could be compared. This is the famous multitrait-multimethod correlation matrix.[2] Table 16.1 presents such a matrix.

Campbell and Fiske (1959) argued that four desiderata provided the underpinnings of what they called convergent and discriminant validity. Measures of the same construct should be highly correlated (convergent), measures of different constructs should be less highly correlated (discriminant), and these differences should hold whether the constructs are measured with similar or dissimilar measures. The four criteria are as follows:

1. The correlations along the diagonals (the validities, representing the same construct measured in two or more different ways) should be high and significantly different from zero.

2. The validities (the correlations between different measures of the same constructs) should be higher than the correlations in the heterotrait-heteromethod triangles; that is, they should be higher than the intercorrelations between different constructs measured in different ways. Failure to meet this criterion suggests that there are not multiple traits.

3. The validities (the correlations between different measures of the same constructs) should be higher than the correlations in the heterotrait-monomethod triangles; that is, they should be higher than the intercorrelations between different constructs measured in the same way. Failure to meet this criterion suggests that there may be strong method factors operating.

4. The pattern of correlations is the same across each of the hetero- (or mono-) method triangles. That is, each measure of the construct behaves similarly to all other measures of the construct when placed in the nomological network of all the variables in the system analyzed.

Marsh (1989) has extended this list by arguing reasonably that a comparison of the correlations in the monomethod triangles with those in the heteromethod triangles would give further indication of the strength of the method effects. If they were higher in the monomethod triangles, then method effects might be operating.

During the first 10 years of application of the Campbell and Fiske criteria, the assessment of whether or not the desiderata were met was a judgment call based on the researcher's scanning of the matrix. This call was particularly difficult to make for the final criterion when large matrices were involved. In many analyses, this criterion was ignored. Only Evans (1969) made a crude attempt to bring quantification to bear on the analysis: He used the sign test[3] to examine the differences between the validities and the other correlations; more subtly, he used the coefficient of concordance to assess the similarity of patterns within each of the triangles (heteromethod and monomethod).[4]

The criticisms of the Campbell and Fiske (1959) approach are not with its logic, which is impeccable. Rather, the difficulties are with the application to correlation matrices of raw measures. The arguments made were that

- Differences in reliability of the measures would affect the correlations and hence the judgments of validity (Schmitt, Coyle, & Saari, 1977; Schmitt & Stults, 1986; Widaman, 1985)
- Similar effect sizes for traits and measures were needed (Althauser & Heberlein, 1970; Alwin, 1974; Marsh, 1989)

There also was concern about other assumptions implicit in the Campbell and Fiske guidelines:

- That the traits and methods contributed additively to observed scores
- The assumption that method factors were to be uncorrelated; implied by Campbell and Fiske's insistence that maximally dissimilar methods be used, an insistence violated by most investigators who usually compared, in their MTMM analyses, sets of traits measured with fairly similar pencil-and-paper trait methods

With the development of structural equation modeling and confirmatory factor analysis (Jöreskog, 1971) and the associated analytic tools (LISREL, Mx, EQS, and AMOS), more sophisticated analytic techniques reached the hands of researchers. These provided solutions to some of the problems associated with the Campbell and Fiske (1959) approach (Alwin, 1974; Campbell & O'Connell, 1967; Marsh, 1989) and have stimulated a number of alternative analytic approaches (for example, Browne, 1984; Kenny & Kashy, 1992; Marsh & Hocevar, 1988; Widaman, 1985) to provide evidence about the strength of traits or methods in a particular data set.

Bagozzi and colleagues (1991; see also Bagozzi & Yi, 1990) have articulated most clearly the developmental history. I cite from Bagozzi et al., footnote 1:

> The ten procedures are in rough chronological order: the classic criteria of Campbell & Fiske (1959), the analysis of variance (Boruch & Wollins, 1970), confirmatory factor analysis (Werts & Linn, 1970; Jöreskog, 1974), exploratory factor analysis (Golding & Seidman, 1974), the generalized proximity function (Hubert & Baker, 1979), smallest space analysis (Levin, Montag, & Comrey, 1983), the direct product model (Browne, 1984), the second order confirmatory factor analysis model with measures loading directly on trait and methods factors (Anderson, 1985, 1987), the hierarchical confirmatory factor analysis model with measures loading indirectly on traits and methods (Marsh & Hocevar, 1988), and the first order confirmatory factor analysis model with separate factors for traits and methods and measure specificity (Kumar & Dillon, 1990). (p. 422)[5]

The ANOVA and smallest space methods of assessing convergent and discriminant validities are inappropriate because of the operations being performed on raw correlations rather than on the latent variables of interest (Schmitt & Stults, 1986). Accordingly, I will focus the remaining discussion on the confirmatory factor analysis techniques, which all try to assess convergent and discriminant validities using the latent underlying constructs.

My focus in evaluating alternative MTMM hypotheses will be on one or more of four basic analytical approaches. First, is the nested sequence of hypotheses proposed by Widaman (1985). The second analytical framework extended Widaman's framework by incorporating correlated uniqueness (Kenny & Kashy, 1992; Marsh, 1989; Marsh & Bailey, 1991); that is, models have no method effects per se but have correlated error terms of methods. I will also discuss alternatives to this (Kanetkar & Evans, 1997). The third analytic framework posits that traits and methods can be represented as second-order factors, especially when multiple indicators are available for every trait-method combination (Anderson, 1985, 1987; Marsh & Hocevar, 1988). The final analytic framework builds on the work of Campbell and O'Connell (1967) to formally represent the interaction of traits and methods (Bagozzi & Yi, 1992; Browne, 1984; Cudeck, 1988; Dudgeon, 1994; Wothke & Browne, 1990). I will discuss each in turn.

Widaman's Nested Process for Assessing MTMM Matrices

Widaman (1985) proposed an important taxonomy for exploring the MTMM matrix to identify the strength of trait factors, the strength of method factors, and the interrelations between traits and between methods. Note that this model and Marsh's (1989) model assume the independence of traits and methods. In his taxonomy, he argues for the exploration of sixteen models[6] involving the following combinations of trait factors and method factors:

Traits

1. No trait factor
2. One trait factor loading all measures
3. Several orthogonal trait factors (T)
4. Several oblique trait factors (same factors as in 3, but allowed to correlate)

Methods

A. No method factors
B. A single method factor loading all measures[7]
C. Several orthogonal method factors (M)
D. Several oblique method factors (same factors as in C, but allowed to correlate)

This gives us the 16 combinations (1A, the null model, through 4D, the model with unconstrained trait and method factors). These are shown in Table 16.2. Many of these models are nested going from the top right to bottom left of the matrix, and the null model is nested within the other models. This

provides an opportunity to test whether more complex models provide better fit than simpler models as well as providing information (through factor loadings) about the strength of the trait and methods factors. To provide formal specification of these alternative models, Widaman (1985) proposed the following:

$$\Sigma = XX^{-1} = \lambda_{tt}\Phi_{tt}\lambda_{tt}^{-1} + \lambda_{mm}\Phi_{mm}\lambda_{mm}^{-1} + \theta_\delta \ (1)$$

where

$S =$ the variance-covariance matrix formed from the X matrix of p measured variables[8] and N observations,

$\lambda_{tt} =$ the $p \times t$ matrix of factor loadings and t is the number of traits,

$\lambda_{mm} =$ the $p \times m$ matrix of factor loadings and m is the number of methods used in the study,

Φ_{tt} and $\Phi_{mm} =$ $t \times t$ and $m \times m$ matrices, respectively indicating trait and method variance-covariances, and

$\theta_\delta =$ the $p \times p$ diagonal matrix indicating trait-method combination uniqueness.

Hypotheses about construct validity and the presence or absence of trait and methods factors can be assessed by varying the parameter structure of these matrices. These are explained briefly in Table 16.2. There are five parameter matrices in Equation 1, namely, λ_{tt}, λ_{mm}, Φ_{tt}, Φ_{mm}, and θ_δ. For model specifications A to D (see above) in which there are *no* correlated uniquenesses, the θ_δ matrix is set to be diagonal.

To assess convergent validity, we would compare the fit of model 4D (correlated traits and correlated methods) with that of 1D (correlated methods only); if all the variation can be explained by the methods factors, then there is little evidence for convergent validity of the traits. Evidence for discriminant validity would flow from comparing models with a single trait (or with orthogonal traits) and those with correlated traits (e.g., comparing 2D with 4D or 3D with 4D)—a well-fitting model with a single trait would show no evidence of discriminant validity, a well-fitting model with orthogonal traits would show the highest discriminant validity, and intermediate solutions with correlated traits

TABLE 16.2 Taxonomy and Model Specification for MTMM Data

Trait Structure	A	B	C	D	E
1	1A: Null model θ_δ diagonal All other matrices 0	1B: 1 method factor Λ_{mm} is $p \times 1$ Φ_{mm} is 1×1 $\Lambda_{tt} = 0$ $\Phi_{tt} = 0$	1C: M uncorrelated method factors Λ_{mm} is $p \times m$ Φ_{mm} is diagonal $\Lambda_{tt} = 0$ $\Phi_{tt} = 0$	1D: M correlated method factors Λ_{mm} is $p \times m$ Φ_{mm} is $M \times m$ $\Lambda_{tt} = 0$ $\Phi_{tt} = 0$	1E: Correlated method errors θ_δ is block diagonal $\Lambda_{tt} = 0$ $\Phi_{tt} = 0$
2	2A: 1 trait factor $\Lambda_{mm} = 0$ $\Phi_{mm} = 0$ Λ_{tt} is $p \times 1$ Φ_{tt} is 1×1	2B: 2 general factors Λ_{mm} is $p \times 1$ Φ_{mm} is $p \times 1$ Λ_{tt} is $p \times 1$ Φ_{tt} is 1×1	2C: 1 general trait and M uncorrelated method factors Λ_{mm} is $p \times m$ Φ_{mm} is diagonal Λ_{tt} is $p \times 1$ Φ_{tt} is 1×1	2D: 1 general trait and M correlated method factors Λ_{mm} is $p \times m$ Φ_{mm} is $m \times m$ Λ_{tt} is $p \times 1$ Φ_{tt} is 1×1	2E: 1 general trait and correlated method errors θ_δ is block diagonal Λ_{tt} is $p \times 1$ Φ_{tt} is $p \times 1$
3	3A: T uncorrelated trait factors $\Lambda_{mm} = 0$ $\Phi_{mm} = 0$ Λ_{tt} is $p \times t$ Φ_{tt} is diagonal	3B: T uncorrelated trait factors and 1 method factor Λ_{mm} is $p \times 1$ Φ_{mm} is 1×1 Λ_{tt} is $p \times t$ Φ_{tt} is diagonal	3C: T uncorrelated trait and M uncorrelated method factors Λ_{mm} is $p \times m$ Φ_{mm} is diagonal Λ_{tt} is $p \times t$ Φ_{tt} is diagonal	3D: T uncorrelated trait and M correlated method factors Λ_{mm} is $p \times m$ Φ_{mm} is $m \times m$ Λ_{tt} is $p \times 1$ Φ_{tt} is diagonal	3E: T uncorrelated and correlated method errors θ_δ is block diagonal Λ_{tt} is $p \times t$ Φ_{tt} is diagonal
4	4A: T correlated trait factors $\Lambda_{mm} = 0$ $\Phi_{mm} = 0$ Λ_{tt} is $p \times t$ Φ_{tt} is $t \times t$	4B: T correlated trait factors and 1 method factor Λ_{mm} is $p \times 1$ Φ_{mm} is 1×1 Λ_{tt} is $p \times t$ Φ_{tt} is $t \times t$	4C: T correlated trait and M uncorrelated method factors Λ_{mm} is $p \times m$ Φ_{mm} is diagonal Λ_{tt} is $p \times t$ Φ_{tt} is $t \times t$	4D: T correlated trait and M correlated method factors Λ_{mm} is $p \times m$ Φ_{mm} is $m \times m$ Λ_{tt} is $p \times t$ Φ_{tt} is $t \times t$	4E: T correlated trait and correlated method errors θ_δ is block diagonal Λ_{tt} is $p \times t$ Φ_{tt} is $t \times t$

SOURCE: Adapted from Marsh (1989).
NOTE: Model specifications A to D require that matrix θ_δ be diagonal.

would be subject to a judgment call depending on the size of the correlations.

Critiques of Widaman

Marsh (1989) has argued that the hierarchical nesting is not as neat as Widaman supposes. As stated by Byrne and Goffin (1994), Marsh (1989; Marsh & Bailey, 1991) has argued that methods factors also can represent trait variance, and if this is so, nested comparisons as suggested by Widaman (1985) may not be justified.

Marsh (1989) suggests that when traits can be represented by a second-order factor, there may be confounding between models. Specifically, model 3B uncorrelated traits and a single method may represent a general trait and unique traits rather than what is assumed in Widaman's parameterization. Therefore, if this model fits as well as model 4C (correlated traits and uncorrelated methods), it may be difficult to distinguish between them. Although Marsh's logic is correct if inferences are drawn just from these two models, an examination of the fit of other models in Widaman's matrix will settle the matter. The question at issue is how we distinguish between the following two states of nature:

1. Traits are uncorrelated, but there is a single method factor.
2. Traits are correlated, but there are uncorrelated methods factors.

These can be distinguished if one compares model 3B (uncorrelated traits and one method factor, which might be a general trait) with model 4B (correlated traits and one method factor, which will not be a general trait factor because this is now captured in the correlations between the trait factors). If there is an improved fit going from 3B to 4B, then the single methods factor is *not* an ersatz second-order trait factor, so that other comparisons with model 3B can be made with confidence. If the model fit does not improve and there are high loadings on the single trait factor, then Marsh's concerns may be in order. This, however, will be an issue to be addressed on a case-by-case basis.

An additional problem with Widaman's hierarchical model is a practical one: Most researchers have established that there is great difficulty in getting satisfactory solutions to real empirical data. Cases abound in which correlations greater than unity between latent variables are produced or variances in error terms are negative. To cope with these problems, Marsh (1989) proposed an alternative solution: correlated uniquenesses rather than the assessment of methods factors per se.

Correlated Uniqueness

Marsh and Bailey (1991) argue that the method factor models C and D are too restricted. The implication of the constraints in these models is that the tests are congeneric. They argue for a less restrictive model, Model E, in which the method effects are assessed by examining the correlated uniquenesses, which represent the correlation between two variables measured with the same method after removing trait effects. This is described in the final column of Table 16.2.

Kanetkar and Evans (1997) have shown that many of the difficulties associated with the failure of empirical estimates may be due to the minimal number of items used in the analyses (mainly simulations). Marsh and his associates tend to follow the conventional rules of thumb in their simulations; that is, analyze at least three traits and three methods and have at least three indicators for each trait and for each method. These rules, however, are predicated on the notion that each indicator is of complexity 1; that is, it loads on just one factor. The analyses we are working on have to violate that assumption: Each item is associated with both a trait *and* a method—at least in the more complicated models. Thus, new rules must be developed. In our simulations (where input data were based on models 4C, 4D, and 4E), we used two indicators for each trait-method pair. When Kanetkar and I did this in a series of simulations, we had no difficulty in getting convergence with all the models, and the correct model usually had the best fit to the data.

Turning to real data, Kanetkar and I encountered greater difficulty. Few studies have sufficient indicators for each trait-method combination. Many

TABLE 16.3 Item Structure for the Job Satisfaction Study

Type of Satisfaction	Interview	Observation	Checklist	Total
General satisfaction	5	2	0	7
Challenge satisfaction	0	2	6	8
Total	5	4	6	15

TABLE 16.5 Item Structure for the Immoral Behavior Study

	Self	Friend	Total
Alcohol	2	2	4
Smoking	2	2	4
Marijuana	2	2	4
Total	6	6	6

TABLE 16.4 Item Structure for the Job Characteristics Data

Characteristic	Interview	Observation	Checklist	Total
Task	0	3	2	5
Challenge	0	4	3	7
Feedback	0	3	1	4
Variety	0	3	2	5
Autonomy	0	4	3	7
Total	0	17	11	28

studies have quite unbalanced sets of indicators. In a single study, one concept may have seven indicators spanning two methods, and another may have five indicators spanning three methods. With Kanetkar, I am reanalyzing three data sets of this kind (Kanetkar & Evans, 1997). They are drawn from Glick, Jenkins, and Gupta (1986; two covariance matrices: job satisfaction and job characteristics) and Graham and Collins (1991; one covariance matrix). The number of items tapping each method-trait combination is shown in Tables 16.3, 16.4, and 16.5. The results of our analyses are shown in Tables 16.6 through 16.11. For the satisfaction data, with two facets (general and chal-

TABLE 16.6 Comparison of the Standardized Parameter Estimates for Six Alternative MTMM Models

	Model Specification					
Measure	3C	4C	3D	4D	3E	4E
GS11	−0.631	−0.805	0.258	−0.702	0.788	0.625
GS12	0.514	0.581	−0.317	0.473	−0.704	−0.419
GS13	−0.702	−0.653	0.724	−0.423	0.656	0.386
GS14	−0.669	−0.651	0.496	−0.473	0.367	0.418
GS15	0.084	0.445	−0.176	0.388	−0.060	−0.350
GS01	−0.092	−0.197	0.037	−0.380	0.087	0.346
GS02	0.137	0.211	−0.071	0.353	0.142	−0.324
CSC1	0.750	0.736	−0.055	0.735	0.353	0.845
CSC2	0.779	0.807	0.101	0.827	0.325	0.958
CSC3	0.503	0.573	−0.427	0.556	0.240	0.695
CSC4	0.797	0.793	−0.170	0.787	0.217	0.850
CSC5	0.408	0.444	−0.386	0.433	0.109	0.436
CSC6	0.548	0.594	−0.299	0.585	0.227	0.675
CS01	0.075	0.180	0.006	0.356	0.124	0.321
CS02	−0.116	−0.224	−0.012	−0.384	−0.339	−0.348
Correlation	—	−0.798	—	0.958	—	0.954

SOURCE: Results are based on Glick, Jenkins, and Gupta's (1986) satisfaction measures.
NOTE: GS11 to GS15 measured general satisfaction using interview, and GS01 to GS02 measured the same construct using observational methods. CSC1 to CSC6 measured challenge satisfaction using card sort method, and CS01 to CS02 measured the same construct using observational methods.

TABLE 16.7 Comparison of Goodness-of-Fit Indicators for 19 Alternative MTMM Models

Model	χ^2	*Goodness-of-Fit Indicator*					Comments
		df	Adjusted GFI	AIC	RMSEA	ECVI	
1A	4271.9	105	0.252	4061.9	0.280	8.470	—
2A	2194.1	90	0.437	2014.1	0.215	4.441	—
3A	2397.4	90	0.497	2217.4	0.225	4.841	—
4A	2118.7	89	0.491	1940.7	0.212	4.297	—
2B	363.1	75	0.838	213.1	0.087	0.898	—
3B	419.1	75	0.864	269.1	0.095	1.008	—
4B	210.6	74	0.916	62.6	0.060	0.602	—
1C	765.8	89	0.765	587.8	0.122	1.633	—
2C	230.2	75	0.090	80.2	0.064	0.636	—
3C	468.1	75	0.850	318.1	0.101	1.104	—
4C	212.5	74	0.915	64.5	0.061	0.605	—
1D	548.1	86	0.853	376.1	0.103	1.217	—
2D	124.1	72	0.949	−19.9	0.038	0.439	Two parameters unidentified
3D	116.4	72	0.953	−27.6	0.035	0.424	—
4D	116.6	71	0.952	−25.4	0.036	0.429	—
1E	481.8	74	0.839	333.8	0.104	1.135	—
2E	93.7	59	0.953	−24.3	0.034	0.433	One parameter on the boundary
3E	436.7	59	0.824	318.7	0.112	1.108	Two parameters on the boundary
4E	91.4	58	0.953	−24.6	0.034	0.432	One parameter on the boundary

SOURCE: Data are from Glick, Jenkins, and Gupta (1986), using covariance matrix of two traits related to satisfaction.

lenge) measured with three methods (interview, observation, and check list), model 4D with correlated traits and methods fits the data well. For the job characteristics data, none of the models fit well. Again Model 4D (correlated traits and correlated methods) was the best-fitting model involving traits. For the deviant behavior analysis, Model 4C, with correlated traits and orthogonal methods, best fit the data.

There is one remaining problem with all these methods in one specific situation, in which different informants are asked the same questions about a person or object. That is when supervisors rate employees on a number of performance dimensions and these are compared with ratings by peers and by the employee himself, or when different informants provide information on different organizational characteristics. The error term in these measures includes both measure specific variance and random variance[9] (Kumar & Dillon, 1990). One solution to this problem has been to use second-order factor analysis (Anderson, 1985, 1987; see below) or to add measure specific factors to the

standard MTMM Widaman-type analysis. To do this, specific item factors are included in the analysis alongside the methods factors (in this case, informants) and the trait factors. Only the data set provided by Graham had these characteristics (multiple informants, common questions). Kanetkar and I, however, were unable to get convergence for this model (even after equating the loadings for each specific variance).

Second Order Factors

Anderson (1985, 1987) has suggested a second-order factor analytic model to deal with the specific variance issue. In this model, several items tap each construct, but the constructs are modeled as higher-level factors and each item is modeled as a lower-level factor with several informants responding to the item, so that each first-level factor has several indicators. As well as assessing convergent (loadings on the factors) and discriminant (correlations between the factors) validity, it is also possible to assess the specific variance associated with each

TABLE 16.8 Comparison of the Standardized Parameter Estimates for Four Alternative MTMM Models

	Model Specification			
Measures	*3C*	*4C*	*3D*	*4D*
TiC1	−0.038	0.051	−0.037	−0.037
TiC2	0.022	0.059	0.023	0.028
TiO1	−0.288	0.659	−0.288	−0.281
TiO2	−0.842	−0.267	−0.841	−0.826
TiO3	−0.787	−0.225	−0.787	−0.790
CoC1	−0.086	−0.348	−0.076	−0.164
CoC2	−0.145	−0.439	−0.129	−0.226
CoC3	−0.130	−0.419	−0.115	−0.193
CoO1	−0.489	−0.915	−0.472	−0.578
CoO2	−0.320	−0.873	−0.308	−0.421
CoO3	−0.471	−0.903	−0.455	−0.548
CoO4	0.441	0.889	0.425	0.524
TfC1	−0.034	−0.007	−0.036	−0.052
TfO1	0.780	0.652	0.779	0.795
TfO2	0.871	0.855	0.871	0.843
TfO3	0.385	0.178	0.385	0.443
VaC1	−0.156	−0.228	−0.137	−0.130
VaC2	0.213	0.311	0.199	0.204
VaO1	−0.211	−0.872	−0.216	−0.369
VaO2	0.328	0.886	0.329	0.378
VaO3	−0.230	−0.869	−0.237	−0.360
AuC1	−0.096	−0.359	−0.081	−0.440
AuC2	−0.110	0.384	−0.091	−0.560
AuC3	−0.068	−0.162	−0.056	−0.475
AuO1	−0.271	−0.865	−0.270	−0.044
AuO2	−0.290	−0.856	−0.285	−0.057
AuO3	0.254	0.816	0.249	0.0421
AuO4	−0.384	−0.794	−0.379	−0.017

SOURCE: Results are based on Glick, Jenkins, and Gupta (1986).
NOTE: TiC1 and TiC2 measured task identity using card sort, TiO1 to TiO3 measured the same construct using observation, CoC1 to CoC3 measured complexity using card sort, CoO1 to CoO4 measured the same construct using observation, TfC1 measured task feedback, TfO1 to TfO3 measured task feedback using observation, VaC1 and VaC2 measured variety using card sort, VaO1 to VaO3 measured the same construct using observation, AuC1 to AuC3 measured autonomy using card sort, and AuO1 to AuO4 measured the same construct using observations.

question. Unfortunately, Kumar and Dillon (1990) suggest a major problem with the procedure: There is an untestable (because it is a function of the algebra of the covariances) constraint on the ratio of specific variance to trait variance. This makes it impossible to tell whether a model fits badly because of violation of the constraint or the failure to achieve convergent and discriminant validity.

An alternative parameterization of a second-order model involves creating trait method units as the first factor and then loading these onto the second-order pure trait factors and methods factors. Once again, according to Bagozzi and colleagues (1991), these have even more restrictive constraints (see Table 16.12) than the Anderson parameterization.

Multiplicative Models
of the Methods and Traits

Quite early in the development of the MTMM perspective, Campbell and O'Connell (1967, 1982) argued that traits and methods might interact in their influence on measures. In other words, the correlation between two traits might be inflated because of method correlations when there is a strong relationship between traits, but this would not occur when traits are less highly correlated. Technicians have developed a technique for assessing this: Direct product models. In such models, instead of assessing method and trait effects in a linear fashion, one assesses the direct (or Kronecker) product of the trait and method covariances (see Bagozzi et al., 1991, for further details).

Unanswered Questions

Table 16.12 summarizes these alternative ways of testing MTMM matrices. Recent work in our field suggests that researchers are using the confirmatory factor analysis methods of exploring construct validity in the development of new constructs—though much of the cited literature concerns reanalysis of old matrices using more modern methods; see Bagozzi and colleagues (1991) and Bagozzi and Yi (1990) for reanalyses of organizationally relevant data. In the development of new constructs, the techniques usually are applied appropriately, with good attempts to model second-order factors when the construct is likely to have that structure. In one case, however, I found the initial conceptualizations quite inadequate (Spreitzer, 1995).[10] As Fiske and Campbell bewail in their 1992 article, it doesn't seem as though the constructs we are developing are much better.

TABLE 16.9 Comparison of Goodness-of-Fit Indicators for 19 Alternative MTMM Models

Model	χ^2	df	Adjusted GFI	AIC	RMSEA	ECVI	Comments
1A	13930.8	378	0.105	13174.9	0.266	27.540	—
2A	4561.9	350	0.446	3861.9	0.154	9.214	—
3A	4032.5	350	0.542	3332.5	0.144	8.172	—
4A	2263.5	340	0.661	1583.5	0.106	4.731	—
2B	3063.9	322	0.544	2419.9	0.130	6.382	—
3B	1847.4	322	0.708	1203.4	0.097	3.987	—
4B	1319.5	312	0.788	695.5	0.080	2.990	—
1C	4064.0	350	0.503	3364.0	0.145	8.234	—
2C	2292.0	322	0.655	1648.0	0.110	4.863	—
3C	1292.7	322	0.814	648.7	0.077	2.895	—
4C	992.3	312	0.837	368.3	0.066	2.346	One parameter on the boundary
1D	3861.6	349	0.508	3163.6	0.141	7.840	—
2D	2289.0	321	0.654	1647.0	0.110	4.861	—
3D	1104.5	321	0.831	462.5	0.069	2.529	—
4D	888.3	311	0.857	266.3	0.061	2.145	—
1E	522.8	187	0.873	148.8	0.060	1.944	—
2E	211.6	159	0.926	−96.4	0.028	1.468	One parameter on the boundary
3E	460.5	159	0.864	142.5	0.061	1.938	Estimated parameters not significant
4E	189.7	149	0.932	−184.0	1.446	1.446	One parameter on the boundary

SOURCE: Data are from Glick, Jenkins, and Gupta (1986), using a covariance matrix of five traits related to job characteristics.

TABLE 16.10 Comparison of the Standardized Parameter Estimates for Six Alternative MTMM Models

Measures	3C	4C	3D	4D	3E	4E
Sa1	−0.403	−0.196	−0.745	−0.338	0.303	0.429
Sa2	−0.573	−0.262	−0.274	−0.741	0.303	0.478
Ss1	−0.125	−0.251	−0.126	−0.180	0.337	0.558
Ss2	−0.248	−0.348	−0.240	−0.282	0.591	0.608
Sm1	0.184	0.266	0.184	0.254	0.185	−0.538
Sm2	0.222	0.197	0.219	0.225	−0.460	0.047
Fa1	−0.061	−0.876	0.043	−0.146	0.151	0.484
Fa2	−0.090	−0.756	0.003	−0.133	0.247	0.410
Fs1	−0.880	−0.928	−0.846	−0.918	0.311	0.590
Fs2	−0.647	−0.835	−0.625	−0.639	0.229	0.538
Fm1	0.923	0.918	0.910	0.856	−0.100	0.402
Fm2	0.513	0.708	0.507	0.580	0.364	0.607
Correlation (a,s)	—	0.508	—	0.268	—	0.890
Correlation (a,m)	—	−0.450	—	−0.239	—	0.518
Correlation (s,m)	—	−0.473	—	−0.364	—	0.649

SOURCE: Data are from Graham and Collins (1991), using a correlation matrix for three traits related to use of alcohol, smoking, and marijuana.
NOTE: Sa1 to Sm2 measured self-report about alcohol (a), smoking (s), and marijuana (m) usage, respectively. Fa1 to Fm2 measured friend's assessment about the same behavior.

TABLE 16.11 Comparison of Goodness-of-Fit Indicators for 19 Alternative MTMM Models

Model	χ^2	df	*Goodness-of-Fit Indicator* Adjusted GFI	AIC	RMSEA	ECVI	Comments
1A	2734.0	66	0.357	2602.0	0.271	5.025	—
2A	1302.2	54	0.606	1194.2	0.205	2.462	—
3A	1336.4	54	0.550	1228.4	0.208	2.524	—
4A	1057.8	51	0.588	955.8	0.190	2.028	—
2B	829.7	42	0.679	745.7	0.185	1.646	Starting values provided
3B	531.5	42	0.749	447.5	0.145	1.102	Two estimates on the boundary
4B	392.0	39	0.797	314.0	0.128	0.860	Two estimates on the boundary
1C	996.7	54	0.705	888.7	0.178	1.905	—
2C	725.0	42	0.768	398.5	0.138	1.4553	One parameter on the boundary
3C	482.5	42	0.768	398.5	0.138	1.013	One parameter on the boundary
4C	307.9	39	0.843	229.9	0.112	0.706	—
1D	881.2	53	0.726	775.2	0.169	1.698	—
2D	585.3	41	0.746	503.3	0.156	1.204	One parameter on the boundary
3D	400.5	41	0.799	318.5	0.126	0.868	Two parameters on the boundary
4D	328.1	38	0.820	252.1	0.118	0.747	One parameter on the boundary
1E	282.0	36	0.844	210.0	0.112	0.671	—
2E	132.3	24	0.882	84.3	0.091	0.443	One parameter linear combination
3E	172.3	24	0.847	124.3	0.106	0.515	Three parameters linear combination
4E	100.5	21	0.896	58.5	0.083	0.396	One parameter linear combination

SOURCE: Data are from Graham and Collins (1991), using a correlation matrix of three traits related to use of alcohol, smoking, and marijuana.

One major question is not really addressed in all this technical work on the MTMM matrix: What next? What do you do if you have methods effects in your measurement model? The answer is to use the method variables as control variables in subsequent analyses. This will partial out the effects of methods and provide a more adequate test of your underlying theoretical models. Only in the Glick and colleagues (1986) study has such a tack been taken.

In conclusion to this section, despite the potential problems associated with some of the methods, we can improve our assessment of the MTMM matrices, but nothing replaces careful a priori conceptualization and operationalization. I would continue to examine the hierarchically nested sets of models advocated by Widaman, supplemented with the correlated uniquenesses model of Marsh.

I now turn to Campbell's second great methodological contribution to organizational science: his work on the unraveling of causal relationships. His work, with his colleagues Julian Stanley and Tom Cook, on quasi-experimentation has made an enduring impression on our field.

The Quasi-Experimental Revolution

The initial impetus for Campbell's writings in this domain came from the field of educational reform. Many attempts were being made to develop new programs for teaching, such as the new math, phonics, and whole language instruction. Only educators are more vulnerable to fads than are managers.

It is, I think, fair to say that experimental research in organizational settings was at its height in the 1970s. This was the time of the peak of the Quality of Working Life movement (QWL), when a federally (U.S.) funded set of national demonstration projects to improve work quality required, as part of their mandate, careful formal

TABLE 16.12 Models and Associated Problems for Assessing MTMM

Technique	Structure of Model and Comparisons Made	Assumptions	Problems
Classic criteria of Campbell and Fiske (1959)	Correlation matrices. Compare relative size of correlations. Examine patterns through coefficient of concordance (Bagozzi, Yi, & Phillips, 1991; Evans, 1969).	Trait and method factors have independent linear effects All traits are equally affected by method factors There are no correlations between methods There are no correlations between traits and methods (Schmitt & Stults, 1986)	The comparison of correlations with measures of differential reliability may result in incorrect inferences being drawn
Confirmatory factor analysis (Jöreskog, 1971; Werts & Linn, 1970; Widaman, 1985)	LISREL type models that are nested. They include none, one, or many traits and/or methods (see Figure 16.1)	Trait and method factors have additive linear effects Trait and method factors are not correlated	Possible lack of Identification if all measures are tau-equivalent (Graybill, 1961; Kenny & Kashy, 1992) Inability to distinguish between general method and general traits in some models (is it a first-order method or a second-order trait?) (Marsh, 1989) Confounding of measure-specific variance and random variance (Kumar & Dillon, 1990)
Second-order confirmatory factor analysis model with measures loading directly on trait and methods factors (Anderson, 1987)		Trait and method factors have additive linear effects Trait and method factors are not correlated	Ratio of trait variance to measure specificity is the same for all measures (Kumar & Dillon, 1990) Confounding of measure-specific variance and random variance (Kumar & Dillon, 1990)
Hierarchical confirmatory factor analysis model with measures loading indirectly on traits and methods (Marsh & Hocevar, 1988)		Trait and method factors have additive linear effects Trait and method factors are not correlated	Same proportion of trait to method variance in each pair Same proportion of trait to specific variance in each pair Same proportion of method to specific variance in each pair (Bagozzi, Yi, & Phillips, 1991) Confounding of measure-specific variance and random variance (Kumar & Dillon, 1990)

(continued)

TABLE 16.12 Continued

Technique	Structure of Model and Comparisons Made	Assumptions	Problems
Marsh's (1989) extension to models involving correlated uniquenesses	No trait factor estimated. All methods models (none, one, many) can be compared. Methods are assessed by correlations in the θδ matrix.	Trait and method factors have additive linear effects Trait and method factors are not correlated	Confounding of measure-specific variance and random variance (Kumar & Dillon, 1990)
First-order confirmatory factor analysis model with separate factors for traits and methods and measure specificity (Kumar & Dillon, 1990)	Similar to Widaman (1985) but with additional latent variables for each specific question. Only useful when same questions are asked of different informants; not useful when different scale items are used in different methods.		Requires more than one indicator of each method, and same indicators found across methods Possible overfitting of models resulting in estimation problems
Expanded indicators of trait-method combinations (Kanetkar & Evans, 1997)	Multiple indicators of each trait-method combination.	Trait and method factors have additive linear effects Trait and method factors are not correlated	Requires at least three indicators for each method-trait combination Possible overfitting of models resulting in estimation problems
Direct product model (Browne, 1984)	Kronecker product of traits and methods to assess the potential interactions between traits and methods identified by Campbell and O'Connell (1982).	Trait and method factors have multiplicative effects	Unable to untangle trait and methods effect

evaluation—for example, the outstanding work of the Tavistock group at the Rushton mine and the evaluation reported by Goodman, Conlon, Epple, and Fidler (1979).

In organizational settings, managers and employees have a pragmatic interest in understanding "what works" in terms of human resources, organizational design, or even reengineering interventions. On the other hand, managerial scholars have an overlapping, though not identical, interest in testing their theories about organizational design and human behavior. These interests are overlapping rather than identical because of the different values underlying the positions. In a real sense, they match two underlying philosophies about the nature of causation: the activity theory and the essentialist theory (Cook & Shadish, 1994). In the former, one is interested merely in whether a change has taken place and, to a lesser extent, whether it can be generalized to other situations; in the latter, one is interested in *why* the change occurred. The leads to rather different emphases being placed on the types of threats to validity that may occur. Managers are interested in events bringing about change that can be replicated in other situations; researchers are more interested in the internal validity of the study: Did the particular stimulus bring about change, or were there alternative causes for the change? Similarly, the manager is more interested in putting together a package of stimuli that bring about the change, whereas the researcher wants to explore with some precision how the components of that package might work. I will explore some implications of this difference later. Both, however, wish to distinguish real change from "accidental regularities" (McKelvey, this volume). That is why experimentation and quasi-experimentation are so important to both managers and researchers.

Cook and Campbell (1979) identify four major areas in which research might be problematic: statistical conclusion validity (i.e., lack of power in the test, inappropriate manipulations, poor reliability in the measures), construct validity (i.e., is the measure or manipulation doing what it is supposed to?, see above), internal validity (are there alternative causes for the observed effects?: This is where the authors develop lists of potential alternative

causes such as history and maturation), and external validity (will the effect generalize to other situations?; potential barriers to this include selection and test-treatment interactions). As in most areas of science, the investigator has to make a series of trade-offs. The things one does to improve one kind of validity often weaken another kind.

Over the past 15 years—since the invention of the on-line citation index—the work of Campbell and his associates (Campbell & Stanley, 1963, 1966; Cook & Campbell, 1979) has been cited more than 180 times in the core journals *Administrative Science Quarterly*, *Journal of Applied Psychology*, *Academy of Management Journal*, *Academy of Management Review*, and *Personnel Psychology Organizational Behavior and Human Decision Processes* and its predecessor, *Organizational Behavior and Human Performance*. The questions I posed to a subset of these data were these: What kinds of design issues were being discussed? Was the discussion invoking a fundamental consideration of how a study might be defined, or was it offering a post hoc justification for what was done? (We've all done that in response to a reviewer—or was it merely an honorific nod to the great and the good?) Finally, what kinds of designs are typically used? This leads to the associated question of What have we learned or forgotten? Perhaps I should start with the issue of the commonly used designs together with a brief discussion of their strengths and weaknesses, then deal with the comments made by authors about those designs and end with the lessons for the future. To answer these questions, I examined all cited articles for the years 1986-1995. This subset included about 70 articles, nearly all of them empirical.

Table 16.13 presents the data relevant to this question about the most commonly used designs. The strongest designs, off-on-off designs, regression discontinuity designs, and the Solomon four-group design (Solomon, 1949) are not much used by those citing Campbell and his associates.[11] As well as a large number of cross-sectional studies, two designs predominate: the pretest-posttest design (22 out of 65) and the posttest-only design (23 out of 65). Most of these designs incorporate control (randomized) or comparison (nonrandomized

TABLE 16.13 Types of Study Citing
Quasi-Experimental Books Over the Past 10 Years

Time series	2	
Intra-individual	1	
Event history	1	
Pretest-posttest		
No control	4	
Random control	1	
Comparison	9	
Two or more treatments, random	0.5	
Two or more treatments, comparison	4.5	
With extra analyses		4
Alternative measures	2	
Multiple treatment and multiple		
dependent variables	1	
Cross section	11	
Solomon four-group	1	
Regression discontinuity	1	
Treatment off/treatment on/treatment off		
design		
No control	2	
Control	0	
Comparison	3	
Posttest only		
No control	1	
Control, random	5	
Multiple treatments, random	5	
Comparison, nonrandom	2	
Multiple comparisons, nonrandom	5	
With added analyses		4
Multiple treatment and multiple dependent	1	
variables		
Multiple studies	2	
Total	65	

groups): Only four of the pretest-posttest designs lack such comparisons; the corresponding figure for the posttest-only design is one. Some have additional controls in the way of additional dependent variables (in addition to the dependent variable of interest) to assess the differential impact of an intervention. The combination makes these quite strong designs. There are, however, some issues to be discussed.

With respect to the pretest-posttest design, there was very little concern about the influence of pretesting on the efficacy of the intervention. Nearly all the studies using comparison groups had both pretest and posttest for all conditions. None used the quasi-experimental analogue to the Solomon four-group design described by Evans (1975), in which some subjects in each of the treatment and comparison conditions are randomly assigned to get and not to get the pretest measure. This enables the researcher to examine possible interactions between pretest and treatment, though, as always, at some cost: Either the expense of the study is increased as more subjects have to be surveyed, or the statistical power of the tests is reduced. In such a design, there is also the possibility of communication, between those pretested and those not, that might nullify the potential differential effect of pretesting. Whether or not this procedure is necessary depends on the potential reactivity of pretesting. In those studies using institutionally gathered records such as attendance data (e.g., Frayne & Latham, 1987), the danger of reactive pretesting is minimal. When the pretests are attitudinal data, however, the danger is higher. In such cases, it is the package (of intervention coupled with the pretest) that can be generalized to other situations and not just the intervention alone. This is a critical issue for the practitioner in terms of the question What made a difference here?

Most of the posttest-only studies had randomized treatments, and only one had no control at all. Where there were nonrandomized assignments to treatments, some (though not all) investigators took care to carry out supplementary analyses to rule out selection effects.

In two cases, investigators carried out a series of studies—sometimes reported in a single paper, sometimes over the course of a multiyear research program—to triangulate their answers to a particular problem. These involved moving from laboratory to field or enlarging a pretest-posttest design so that the control group became a second experimental group. Such multifaceted designs increase our confidence in the results reported.

An interesting issue that has arisen in the training literature concerns the circumstances in which a one-group posttest-only design is adequate. The argument is made that as practitioners are interested in is whether or not some group of trainees has reached proficiency or not, where proficiency is defined as meeting or exceeding some cutoff level on a standard test of performance. This answers a different question from that of whether or not the new level of proficiency was caused by the training (Sackett & Mullen, 1993). They argue that it is necessary to assess change only when one is interested in answering different questions: whether a new training program is effective or not, or the more complicated question of whether the new training program is better than the current program or than no training. In the second case, some kind of comparison group is essential; in the first case, a pretest-posttest-only design will tell whether or not there has been change and may be able to tell us whether the change is due to the training. Sackett and Mullen argue that the pretest-posttest-only design may be the *best* design to use for establishing whether or not a training program caused the increase in performance. Why? Because of statistical power issues: If the groups of employees are limited in number, the power of the full experimental design (with comparison groups) may not have sufficient statistical power (see also Arvey, Cole, Hazucha, & Hartanto, 1985). They argue that alternative means can be used to rule out factors such as history and maturation. One of these alternatives is cleverly delineated by Haccoun and Hamtiaux (1994). They explore the use of nonrelevant dependent variables as the provider of baseline data and compare the efficacy of these baseline data with a classical control group. They find equally strong inferences about the success of the program could be drawn from either set of comparisons. This design, then, proves useful when sample size considerations rule out the use of more complicated designs.

I will now turn to the comments made by investigators. I am interested in knowing whether the research design was carefully articulated *ab initio* with a careful consideration of the relevant threats for that situation, or whether most discussion was

TABLE 16.14 Comments Associated With These Studies

Ex ante	
Sampling issues for relevance	3
Triangulate	1
Justifying the design	6
Statistical issues	2
Ex post	
Multiple heterogeneous samples	1
Monomethod out ruled	1
Construct validity	3
Multiple issues	2
Justifying null on basis of careful theory	1
No placebo	1
Ethical issues	1
Honorifics	
Artifactual interactions not plausible	1
Historical context	1
External validity is a question	5
Inferential issues	4
Lots of little studies = external validity	3
Theoretical advantages of the regression discontinuity design	1
Power in ANCOVA, ANOVA, etc.	1
Method for dealing with missing data in pretest-posttest studies	1
A call for the experimental analysis of questionnaires	1
Total	40

post hoc, assessing a single threat that seemed plausible or, the cynical might argue, was drawn to the author's attention by a reviewer.

In Table 16.14, I show the data related to what kinds of issues are discussed in the papers citing one or more of the three major sources of information on quasi-experimental design. Many of the citations refer only to the design and not to any reasoning for the choice of that design in the particular situation being explored. This means that such designs have become institutionalized in our literature and little explanation is required. To me, this signals that the worst fears of Campbell and Stanley about the grids they provided have been realized, a fear that was echoed by Sackett and Mullen (1993):

Campbell and Stanley's (1963) famous table which summarized with "+," "−," and "?" the degree to which various designs controlled the various threats to internal validity contained a footnote that tends to disappear when the table is reprinted or modified: "It is with extreme reluctance that these summary tables are presented because they are apt to be 'too helpful.' . . . It is against the spirit of this presentation to create uncomprehended fears of, or confidence in, specific designs." (p. 620)

The essence of good design—for us, for Sackett and Mullen, and for Campbell and his colleagues—is thought and diagnosis. Absent a careful rationale, the adoption of a particular design is a reflex action rather than the consequence of a carefully thought out testing of alternatives—at least as described in the literature. The 20% of studies that do discuss their choice of design ex ante—that is, before they describe their procedures, measures, and results—tend to talk about four things. Most members of this group provide a full discussion of the design, with some attempt to anticipate the threats and develop an appropriate design. Others talk only about issues related to the sample. That is, they discuss problems of selecting a sample that is appropriate for the research question that they are addressing; this is most prevalent when the unit of analysis is the organization. Finally, a number of people are concerned about monomethod bias and discuss how they went about triangulating their data to avoid this.

A second set of citations to these three books were piecemeal comments made by authors ex post, and these authors may have been responding to reviewers' queries about a particular threat to validity. In these citations, authors presented, in the discussion section of their papers, a logical argument about why a particular threat was ruled out. Only a few papers specified that their design out ruled a variety of alternatives; rather, they argued that a particular threat was ruled out or that a particular type of validity was established. Several argued for the external validity of their work, usually based on the sample; one justified technique on ethical grounds.

The third set of citations also appeared after the analysis and results section but tended to be either admissions of a potential threat or throwaway assertions not based on logic or data. The comments here on external validity admitted that their samples might not generalize. Several producers of single small-scale laboratory experiments cited Cook and Campbell's (1979) comment that cumulating a large number of heterogeneous experiments was the way to develop external validity, with the implication that their study was a useful addition to the pool.

These data are, I think, somewhat discouraging. I would say that here is little up-front concern with the particular design issues faced in a particular research situation. The development of new site-specific threats does not appear to be taken seriously despite the warnings of Cook and Campbell and of Cook and Shadish (1994).

The kind of in-depth discussion exemplified in the theoretical article by Sackett and Mullen (1993), in the empirical piece by Haccoun and Hamtiaux (1994), and in the multi-article studies of Campion and his associates (Campion, 1988; Campion & McClelland, 1993) of the pros and cons of each design decision was what I found most missing in the literature that I surveyed.

What Have We Forgotten?

Although the absence of commentary in many of the papers examined makes this issue difficult to assess, it seems to me that we have forgotten two major issues. First, we have forgotten Hawthorne and the issue of sensitization. Barling, Weber, and Kelloway (1996) argue that their treatment and control groups differed on two dimensions: getting training versus not getting training, and not getting training and getting transformational leadership training. Thus, they argue that the differences could be, though are unlikely to be, caused by just getting training rather than by the particular training delivered. They argue that in future studies, the control group should be given "placebo" training to rule out this threat. The design they used is fairly commonplace, and it is rare that placebo designs are used. I believe that our inferences would be enhanced if this strategy were used where feasible.

Second, we are quite good about dealing with concerns of immediate external validity; in other words, samples are drawn, controls are used, and covariate analyses are employed, so that we have some confidence that generalization to other units of the same type in the same organization can be ensured. External validity, however, is broader—it is about generalizability to other contexts and other places. Here, I think we do less well. We do not really consider whether or not the success of a managerial intervention may or may not be contingent on a host of organization-specific characteristics. Organizational scientists have been less interested in these kinds of context effects that might affect the more global external validity of their findings; that is, the intervention may work because it occurs within the organizational context of a particular firm—a context that is characterized by the presence or absence of trust, of particular patterns of task interdependence, or by particular levels of environmental uncertainty. Johns (1993) has argued that organizational context may affect the receptivity to adopting innovations developed elsewhere. I take the position that organizational context may affect the efficacy of innovations that have demonstrated success elsewhere even if they are adopted.

A second threat to the broader generalization is the selection problem. Schneider (1983) has argued that different people are attracted to and remain in different kinds of organizations, so that programs that work in one place may not work elsewhere. This is a concern strongly articulated by Cronbach (1982) in the education domain. I will deal with each in turn.

Constraints on Efficacy

Two streams of research show some support for the position that efficacy of adoption may be affected by organizational characteristics. The first is the empirical work of Peters and his associates (O'Connor et al., 1984; Peters, O'Connor, & Rudolf, 1980; Peters, Chassie, Lindholm, O'Connor, & Kline, 1982; Peters, Fisher, & O'Connor, 1982; Phillips & Freedman, 1984) on the effect of organizational resource availability on a number of relationships between organizational variables; the second is the theoretical attack of James and his associates (James, Demaree, Mulaik, & Ladd,

1992) on the lack of situational thinking in the work on validity generalization.

Peters and O'Connor have argued that most models of organizational behavior—motivation, leadership, goal setting—are based on the assumption that the employees involved have adequate resources (information, equipment and materials, finances, collegial help, task ability, time, supportive work environment) to do the things expected of them. This might be extended to a position that many organizational interventions will work well only in the presence of resource adequacy. Of course, some interventions (training, team building) are designed specifically to ameliorate the absence of these resources, but my argument would be that these programs will be effective only when the other resources are in place. In other words, in munificent settings, organizational interventions work; in impoverished settings, they do not. This is not a new idea. The earliest and most dramatic example is found in the work of Harris and Fleishman (1955), who found that leadership training was successful only when the trainees returned to organizational environments that supported their newly acquired behaviors.

The second set of ideas comes from James and colleagues (1992), who were theorizing in the context of understanding validity generalization. They argue compellingly that variation in individual (and presumably organizational) performance is much more likely when organizations have what they call a nonrestrictive climate (which is characterized by high confidence in employees, valuing achievement, desiring employees to reach potential, decentralized decision making, low standardization of work procedures, merit-based reward systems, and innovative approaches to problem solving) than when the organization has a highly restrictive climate (characterized by low confidence in employees, distrust of employee motives, devaluing of individual decisions and individual differences, centralized decision making, high formalization of communication, high standardization of work procedures, satisficing performance standards, non–merit-based pay systems, and programmed approaches to problem solving).[12] Any intervention that succeeds well in a less restrictive climate may fail dismally if tried in a more restrictive climate. It will fail because of constraints on behavior that will not permit individuals to deploy the skills that they have developed in the program. The converse is not necessarily the case. Some programs that prove successful in the restrictive climate will also prove successful in the less restrictive climate; other programs, which rely for their success on the climate engendered by the restrictions, will be unsuccessful in the less restrictive climate.

Selection Effects

Organizational scientists, who are mainly interested in the results of training programs or other managerial interventions (Quality Circles, TQM, reengineering) are really concerned with local selection problems.[13] That is, the intervention usually is provided to an intact group—a work group, a department, a plant—so that selection effects of either a gross kind (such as the intervention being given to the poorest performing employees, who then improve as they regress toward the mean) or a more subtle kind (ex post matching of members of the intact groups so that both regress toward their respective means) may occur. Most analysts do a good job of controlling for such effects, through analysis of covariance for the first problem and avoidance of ex post matching. A larger selection issue is still moot. Will these results generalize to different kinds of people in different organizations?

Theorists are divided on this question. On one hand, Schneider (1983) and others argue that different kinds of organizations attract and retain different kinds of people, so that these differences have to be taken into account when assessing the transportability of an intervention developed in one company to another. On the other hand, it can be argued that this assumption of "sorting" assumes a freer labor market than currently exists and a fuller set of information among those choosing organizations. These are not very realistic assumptions: People usually do not have complete knowledge of the characteristics of the firms that they are joining. Schneider's response to this argument would be that the socialization mechanisms of the firm provide the homogeneity among individuals neces-

sary to provide some constraint on the portability of programs. Program and evaluation replication across sites with known, and differing, characteristics will help us to answer these questions.

In conclusion to this section, quasi-experimental designs are used frequently in organization science, though the field survey is still the most popular approach.[14] Most designers implicitly adopt one or other of the stronger designs proposed by Campbell and his associates. They appear to do this, however, in a nonreflective way. Very few studies combine designs in interesting ways to rule out threats. Generalizability to other organizations—either because of organizational constraints or individual differences—remains a critical issue for organizational scientists to address.

Case Research

In the realm of positivistic social science,[15] where most will recognize that I dwell, case research has long been recognized as a technique for identifying good ideas. That is, vivid examples of unusual behavior impress themselves upon the investigator's notice. These vivid examples lead to the investigator designing a more positivistic study to test the hunches that he or she has spun, as a means of identifying the causes of that interesting observation.

Expanding on this view, Eisenhardt (1989a) suggests that cases can be used as theory *building* techniques. This means something more than the generation of good ideas: The painstaking research that is used to describe a case can be employed to develop a full-fledged theoretical framework. This is done through a combination of (a) within-case analysis, (b) contrasting the current case with prior literature, and (c) comparing multiple cases.[16]

In Eisenhardt's view, this requires the investigator to start as the ideal tabula rasa (blank slate) upon which the ideas generated from the data are inscribed, integrated, and challenged. In other words, the investigator should enter the field site with no theoretical conceptions about what is important or what the interdependencies are among variables. There are a couple of problems with this position. First, the tabula rasa is difficult to achieve. Most of us, at some level, have hidden assumptions that are difficult to remove. These affect our implied frame of reference and the ease with which information is noticed and incorporated. I prefer the position taken by Argyris (1960), who argues that the role of the researcher is to be as explicit as possible about her or his theory and its underlying assumptions. Only then can the researcher search out, with equal frequency, opportunities to support and to refute those theories: The tabula rasa cannot engage in refutation.

Eisenhardt's (1989a) article also reflects the tension between the need for guided inquiry and the need to be open to new, unanticipated information. Eisenhardt argues for an atheoretical frame for the initial steps of the theory yet also argues for choosing concepts for specific focus that have been identified in earlier theories as important variables to be understood in attacking the research questions. There is difficulty in balancing these two positions, yet a conscious awareness of them has the potential for providing the kind of theoretical innovation that Eisenhardt calls for.

Idea generation and theory building are *not* the ways in which Campbell (1979) views the case study. Rather, he views it as a technique for theory testing. In this chapter, he makes a partial retraction of his dismissive treatment of the case study in his quasi-experimental design writings. He is unapologetic in his concern that inferring causality requires comparative analysis. Although this can be most rigorously achieved through pretest-posttest designs and experimental versus comparison groups, he concedes that a similar effect can be obtained by examining the pattern of dependent variable changes that occur in a particular situation or follow from a particular intervention. He is crystal clear that such a pattern has to be predicted a priori from a comprehensive theoretical position and that each derivation has to be deduced carefully and logically from that framework. Only through the a priori anticipation of a pattern of results and the a postiori matching of that pattern can we be reasonably sure that we are not observing "accidental regularities." Campbell, for reasons outlined below, nevertheless would prefer the investigator to make a formal comparison between two groups, a position that has been elaborated by Yin (1984),

who argues for the importance of comparative case research.

The problems with the analysis of a single case are well known:

- It is still difficult, despite the multiple dependent variables, to unambiguously assign causality to particular interventions or situations rather than to others of the multiple independent variables that are operating; strong theory helps, alternative theoretical predictions about additional independent variables help even more
- Perceptual processes lead the researcher to be able to assimilate information and ideas that are consistent with her or his frame of reference much more easily than ideas that are inconsistent. This means that the investigator has to be on guard continually to ensure that he or she actively seeks out counterexamples to the theory being tested
- Selection of the site in which to carry out the research may bias the findings in favor of the theory

These concerns led to Yin's (1984) suggestion that comparative case analysis was a more appropriate way of undertaking qualitative research than just analyzing the single case. This brings us back to the key desideratum of comparison as the essence of determining causality. Comparison can occur between different cases at the same point in time, or (as we shall see below) the same case proceeding over time.

I found about 16 citations to the work on case analysis in the core organizational literature. About five were merely honorific. I also found, however, that the multiple case/multiple indicator approach has been used in three ways in the organizational literature:

- A priori to select situations in which to write cases to ensure that contrasts across dimensions of theoretical interest are available (e.g., Eisenhardt's [1989b] examination of decision-making processes in high technology firms). Six out of 16 citations to this work had this pattern.
- A postiori in a "grounded theory" mode to understand organizational processes (e.g., the second part of Mintzberg, Raisinghani, and Theoret [1976]). Four citations had this pattern.
- A postiori (and very rarely) to test theory. Only two citations took this stance.[17] One, Ross and Staw

(1993), used a careful examination of the temporal unfolding for the pattern matching of the independent variables, based on earlier theorizing and research (Ross & Staw, 1986) on escalating commitment. The other study, Gilbert (1989), was an examination of the impact of the union status of a firm (union versus nonunion) on the effectiveness of the implementation of quality of working life programs. In this article, she carefully articulated each of the steps of the implementation process (from initial idea to final outcomes). She then developed indicators for the successful completion of each step. The case descriptions were then analyzed as to whether the step had been successfully completed or not. Finally, these success ratings were compared for the set of union and nonunion firms.

Many of the critics (Knights & McCabe, 1998) and proponents (Larsson, 1993) of case survey research seem to miss the important levels of analysis issue: that the information gathered from a single case is very different from the information garnered from a series of comparisons between cases. Knights and McCabe argue that case surveys are misguided because the theoretical insights are constructed through the interaction between the investigator and her research site. The more formal comparison of cases, or perhaps the expectation that this comparison is to occur, will undermine this process. This argument, though, is based on the insights gathered on the basic case; it is irrelevant to the question of the insights gathered from a comparison between cases. Here, surely the question is an empirical one: Are generalizations possible? Are the theoretical constructions a function of the investigator or the site? These kinds of questions can be answered (Campbell, 1975, 1979; Hirschman, 1986; Lincoln & Guba, 1985) through the use of multiple investigators and multiple informants. Larsson (1993) is equally confused about the levels of analysis issue. He argues that case surveys provide triangulation of quantitative and qualitative methods (Jick, 1979). This is not the case: The qualitative work has occurred at the single-case level of analysis. The quantitative work occurs at case comparison level. Yes, two methodologies are being used, but not to deal with the same data. Qualitative methods generate the data for input to the quantitative methods.

Just as Eisenhardt (1989a) provides good suggestions for the best practices in theory-generating case surveys, so Larsson (1993) provides good rules for performing theory-testing research. He carefully delineates the requirements for undertaking a case survey on previously existing cases and traces the decisions that have to be made by the investigator.

1. Theoretical domain. The domain of inquiry has to be bounded carefully; that is, case survey research, unlike case research, has to be guided by a very specific research question. Without this specificity, the researcher has little to guide him or her as to which studies should be included and which not.
2. Criteria for including studies. As with meta-analysis, there is some controversy about the use of research quality as a criterion for inclusion. Yin and Yates's (1974) study of urban decentralization (cited in Larsson, 1993) excluded posttest-only studies. Larsson (1989) included only studies that provided sufficient detail on the issues about which he was concerned. An alternative would be to include all studies and then examine whether study quality was associated with reported outcomes. Criteria for inclusion also can include such factors as year of study, industry, and publication status. The important rule is to be explicit about the criteria and describe the criteria in the report.
3. Breadth of search. It is important to be explicit about how the search was conducted, whether the search was confined to published research, whether it was geographically constrained (e.g., European studies only), and whether it was temporally constrained, even if only by the availability of electronic resources.
4. The choice of variables. This will be determined primarily by the research question; however, the availability of the data in the case report may limit the kinds of variables that are available for study. Most case surveyors have to deal with the fact that there will be differential availability of data across different studies surveyed. The absence of data should be coded and can be analyzed in the quantitative analysis (Cohen & Cohen, 1983, chap. 7).
5. Coding the variables. A variety of issues are raised here: the complexity of the coding scheme, the number of raters, the confidence in the rating, and the interrater reliability. As with all variables, the nature of the data will determine the coding scheme used. Some data (say, a firm's SIC code)

will be nominal; other data will be continuous. With continuous data, there is a trade-off between simplicity and sensitivity. One or two categories will be easy for coders to classify, yet subtle differences will be lost. More than five or six will result in the coders having difficulty deciding on the correct coding. Most investigators have used about four or five categories together with the "no information" category. It is important to use multiple coders to assess the accuracy of the coding. In the ideal case, multiple coders will be used for all the cases. Where this is not possible, a sample of the cases should be coded by multiple coders. A second way of estimating the accuracy of this inference is to ask the author of the original case to record agreement with the assigned codes. Note that this process involves assessing the accuracy of inferences from the written case, not the accuracy of what went into the case (that is, the validity of the data gathered by the original investigator). One estimate of the validity of the original data in each case can be obtained by asking the original participants in the case whether or not the case is an accurate representation of their world (Miller & Friesen, 1977).

6. Criteria for judging the adequacy of the data. I would suggest that the criteria suggested by the more positivist case researchers (e.g., Hirschman, 1986; Lincoln & Guba, 1985) are still appropriate.[18]

   a. Credibility. This is akin to internal validity. Does the picture painted by the case writer conform to the reality "on the ground?" Sharing the case with the members of the field site and exploring the discrepancies between what the writer says and what the actors perceive will—on the assumption that the actors are interested in reporting an accurate picture of their world reported—produce a more accurate and credible picture.

   b. Transferability. This is akin to generalizability or external validity; that is, is the picture painted in on research site generalizable to others. It is here that the case survey method is strong. It provides multiple cases that can be compared. In these comparisons, the boundary conditions of the theories can be assessed and contingency theories developed if transferability is low.

   c. Dependability. This is the analogue to reliability. It has to be assessed at two levels. First, would one or more investigators draw similar information from the study's informants? Multiple investigators on each case would be worthwhile. Second, and more easily, do different raters code the same data in similar ways? This is the classical interrater reliability to which most investigators adhere.

   d. Confirmability. The analogue here is toward objectivity. The question is whether the biases of the investigator are distorting the picture painted in the case. The test would be whether investigators with different frames of reference would draw an essentially similar interpretation from the same data.

Campbell's (1975, 1979) ideas about the case study as having multiple degrees of freedom have found little application in the organizational science. Only Ross and Staw (1993) have employed this technique. The extensions of the ideas, developed by Yin (1984), are—if not flourishing—beginning to take hold in our field. Further work on identifying bodies of case research, such as those used by Mintzberg and colleagues (1976), would be useful. They would provide the grist for the case surveyors' mill.

Conclusion: *Si Monumentum Requiris, Circumspice*[19]

Donald Campbell has touched our field(s) deeply. His scope has ranged from anthropology through attitude theory, cognition, ethnocentrism and stereotyping (both cultural and scientific), evolutionary thought, leadership, persuasion, and the development of scientific insight. Through it all is the common thread of understanding the way the world works. To enhance this understanding, Campbell focused on the issues addressed here, including how to ensure that we had an accurate understanding. This led him first to the issues of construct validity, later to the issues of designing evaluation studies for real-world settings, and finally to how to improve the yield from case study research.

Where should we go next? First, with respect to multitrait-multimethod research, there is too much methodological research around the methods of MTMM and not enough research that focuses on using MTMM to develop new measures and refine old measures. In undertaking this work, I think it is time to move forward and analyze new data sets rather than working on more refined analyses of old data sets. What we really need in this area is conceptual refinement of the measures. This will involve a cyclical process between item development and item analysis until measures of sufficient robustness have been identified for all our constructs of interest. This is a long agenda. In doing this work, following the experience of Kanetkar and Evans (1997), I encourage the use of multiple items tapping each method-trait pair. This is necessary to obtain acceptable solutions from confirmatory factor analyses. The incorporation of time into investigations (using an extension of the multiplicative model methods developed by Cudeck, 1988) will allow us to assess the stability of the traits effects and method effects over time (test-retest reliability). Second, our substantive analyses must model both the substantive relationships of interest and the method effects we uncover. The logic followed by Glick and his associates (1986) in looking at the incremental fit for a model including both substance and methods over a model that included only methods effects is appropriate.

My previous discussion of the quasi-experimental design literature suggested that we need to be much more deliberate in our choice, or at least the reporting, of the appropriate design. Too many of us provide a "throwaway" citation to the quasi-experimental literature rather than think through the appropriate design based on a clear-sighted assessment of the relevant threats to validity. There is a lesson here for dissertation advisers and journal referees. The logic of the rationale for the design should be spelled out. As I stated earlier, placebo groups rarely are used; we are satisfied with treatment groups and control groups. The sources of difference, however, include not only the treatment but also the fact that there has been a treatment. Placebos add to the expense of a study, but if referees and editors do not insist on their presence (or at least the presence of a convincing rationale for their absence), then they will not be included. Along with this clear threat to internal validity, the question of external validity rarely is addressed. At the risk of being overprescriptive (Pfeffer, 1993), some information about the environmental and

organizational context in which the study was performed is essential. This should include information about the time of the study; the economic, industry, and geographic position of the firm; the organization's size, basic structure, and dominant technologies; and the kinds of internal cultural variables (even if they are only assessed impressionistically) identified as important by James and colleagues (1992). If these types of variables are routinely included in all our research reports, it will be much easier to explore the kinds of questions raised here in secondary analysis. Each study then is a different case that is amenable to case survey analysis using the methods outlined by Larsson (1993).

Notes

1. This section is heavily based on my work with Vinay Kanetkar (Kanetkar & Evans, 1997).

2. Ironically, despite his efforts, Campbell could not get his ideas incorporated into the formal APA guidelines (Campbell, 1960; Fiske & Campbell, 1992).

3. In retrospect, this was too lenient a criterion. Most analysts today argue that not more than 5% of the correlations in either the heteromethod or monomethod triangles should be higher than the validity correlations.

4. Marsh (1993) has compared average correlations in the heterotrait-heteromethod triangles with the average validities and the average correlations in the heterotrait-monomethod triangles. Bagozzi, Yi, and Phillips (1991) appear to have rediscovered the use of the coefficient of concordance for testing the fourth criterion (see also Byrne & Goffin, 1993).

5. Since that time, an additional method, covariance component analysis (Kiers, Takane, & Ten Berge, 1996; Wothke, 1996), has been developed for the assessment of additive models. See Bagozzi, Yi, and Nassen (in press) for an illustration of this (and other) models.

6. Bagozzi and Yi (1991) suggest examining only four models: the null model (1A), a trait-only model (4A), a methods-only model (1D), and a model with both traits and methods (4D).

7. Combinations 2A and 1B are indistinguishable. Note also that it is not possible to perform nested tests between any pair of models with labels 2 and 3 or B and C because they have the same number of parameters to be estimated.

8. Note that p is equal to $m \times t \times n$ where n is the number of variables for each trait-method combination.

9. This issue does not arise when different scales of measurement are used by different raters. In such a case, there is no common question used across the measures.

10. Looking at her conceptualization of empowerment, the concepts seemed very similar to those developed by Hackman and Oldham (1975) as psychological states in the job design literature. No attempt was made to perform discriminant validity with these two sets of concepts.

11. A second analysis of recent issues of our core journals, looking at all contributions, confirmed this assessment.

12. Again, the proviso holds that any intervention designed to change the organization from the more restrictive climate to the less restrictive climate (and for symmetry in the other direction) is not included in what follows.

13. Economists also worry about "sorting bias"—that is, that people select themselves into particular situations. For example, a major concern has been the impact of unionization on wages. There is considerable difficulty in analyzing this question because (a) different kinds of people select themselves into union firms and (b) different kinds of firms elect to have, or are forced to have, unionized employees. This results in great difficulty in specifying the causal factors that affect the wage differentials between unionized and nonunionized workers. Heckman (1980) has made attempts to solve this—two-stage least squares—but other analysts are not convinced of his solutions (Ashenfelter & Card, 1985). (Both articles are cited in Cook and Shadish, 1994.)

14. Mitchell (1985) has made some sensible suggestions for undertaking field research, based on considerations analogous to those expressed by Campbell and his colleagues.

15. Or perhaps (see McKelvey, this volume, in press) I have been following the scientific realism philosophy without quite realizing it.

16. Interestingly, in a response to Dyer and Wilkins's (1991) critique of the superficiality of her approach, Eisenhardt (1991) argues that this is *exactly* what many of the "single-case" studies praised by Dyer and Wilkins actually did. The investigators compared groups within the sites, they looked at how different rules were enforced (note the similarity to Cook and Campbell's (1979, p. 127) multiple manipulation design), and they examined how similar events were interpreted.

17. Another five citations to case surveys were found in Larsson (1993); only three of these were organizational in scope, the others concerned public policy issues. One just provided descriptive data, and the other two did provide theory testing using similar techniques to those used by Gilbert (1989).

18. By 1990, Lincoln had moved away from this position and thrown off the vestiges of positivism in her criteria. The criteria of a good case study are as follow: (a) It provides a "fair" picture of the situation. This is based on the assumption that different actors in the case will have different interests, different levels of power, and different attitudes; the role of the case writer is to portray these accurately. This is similar to, but more than, credibility in the prior criteria. (b) That the case would contribute, in four ways, to the "states of being" of the actors. It would improve their self-understanding (ontological authenticity), it would improve their knowledge of other people's positions (educative authenticity), it would improve their desire to take action to change their situation (catalytic authenticity), and it would improve their skills and abilities for taking such action (tactical authenticity). These criteria are very much in the spirit of "action research."

19. "If you seek his monument, look [or at least read] about you." This is the epitaph of another Renaissance man, Christopher Wren.

References

Althauser, R. P., & Heberlein, T. A. (1970). Validity and the multitrait-multimethod matrix. In E. F. Borgatta & W. Bohrnstedt (Eds.), *Sociological methodology 1970* (pp. 151-169). San Francisco: Jossey-Bass.

Alwin, D. F. (1974). Approaches to the interpretations of relationships and the multitrait-multimethod matrix. In H. L. Costner (Ed.), *Sociological methodology 1973-74* (pp. 79-105).San Francisco: Jossey-Bass.

Anderson, J. C. (1985). A measurement model to assess measure-specific factors in multiple-informant research. *Journal of Marketing Research, 22,* 86-92.

Anderson, J. C. (1987). An approach for confirmatory measurement and structural equation modeling of organizational properties. *Management Science, 33,* 9-31.

Argyris, C. (1960). *Understanding organizational behavior,* Homewood, IL: Dorsey.

Arvey, R. D., Cole, D, A., Hazucha, J. F., & Hartanto, F. M. (1985). Statistical power of training evaluation designs. *Personnel Psychology, 38,* 493-507.

Ashenfelter, O., & Card, D. (1985). Using the longitudinal structure of earnings to estimate the effect of training programs. *Review of Economic Statistics, 67,* 648-660.

Bagozzi, R. P., & Yi, Y. (1990). Assessing method variance in multitrait-multimethod matrices: The case of self-reported affect and perceptions at work. *Journal of Applied Psychology, 75,* 547-560.

Bagozzi, R. P., & Yi, Y. (1991). Multitrait-multimethod matrices in consumer research. *Journal of Consumer Research, 17,* 426-439.

Bagozzi, R. P., & Yi, Y. (1992). Testing hypotheses about methods, traits, and communalities in the direct-product model. *Applied Psychological Measurement, 16,* 373-380.

Bagozzi, R. P., Yi, Y., & Nassen, K. D. (in press). Representation of measurement error in marketing variables: Review of approaches and extension to three-facet designs. *Journal of Econometrics.*

Bagozzi, R. P., Yi, Y., & Phillips, L. W. (1991). Assessing construct validity in organizational research. *Administrative Science Quarterly, 36,* 421-458.

Barling, J., Weber, T., & Kelloway, E. K. (1996). Effects of transformational leadership training on attitudinal and financial outcomes: A field experiment. *Journal of Applied Psychology, 81,* 827-832.

Boruch, R. F., & Wollins, L. (1970). A procedure for estimation of trait method and error variance attributable to a measure. *Educational and Psychological Measurement, 30,* 547-574.

Browne, M. W. (1984). The decomposition of multitrait-multimethod matrices. *British Journal of Mathematical and Statistical Psychology*, *37*, 1-21.

Byrne, B., & Goffin, R. D. (1993). Modeling MTMM data from additive and multiplicative covariance structures: An audit of construct validity concordance. *Multivariate Behavioral Research*, *28*, 67-96.

Campbell, D. T. (1960). Recommendations for APA test standards regarding construct, trait, or discriminant validity. *American Psychologist*, *15*, 546-553.

Campbell, D. T. (1969). Ethnocentrism of disciplines and the fish-scale model of omniscience. In M. Sherif & C. W. Sherif (Eds.), *Interdisciplinary relationships in the social sciences* (pp. 328-348). Chicago: Aldine.

Campbell, D. T. (1975). "Degrees of freedom" and the case study. *Comparative Political Science*, *8*, 178-193.

Campbell, D. T. (1979). "Degrees of freedom" and the case study. In T. D. Cook & C. S. Reichardt (Eds.), *Qualitative and quantitative methods in evaluation research* (Sage Research Progress Series in Evaluation, Vol. 1. pp. 49-67). Beverly Hills, CA: Sage.

Campbell, D. T., & Fiske, D. W. (1959). Convergent and discriminant validation by multitrait-multimethod matrix. *Psychological Bulletin*, *56*, 81-105.

Campbell, D. T., & O'Connell, E. J. (1967). Method factors in multitrait-multimethod matrices: Multiplicative rather than additive. *Multivariate Behavioral Research*, *2*, 409-426.

Campbell, D. T., & O'Connell, E. J. (1982). Methods as diluting trait relationships rather than adding irrelevant systematic variance. In D. Brinberg & L. H. Kidder (Eds.), *New directions for methodology of social and behavioral science: Forms of validity in research* (pp. 93-111). San Francisco: Jossey-Bass.

Campbell, D. T., & Stanley, J. C. (1963). Experimental and quasi-experimental designs for research on teaching. In N. L. Gage (Ed.), *Handbook of research on teaching* (pp. 171-246). Chicago: Rand McNally.

Campbell, D. T., & Stanley, J. C. (1966). *Experimental and quasi-experimental designs for research.* Chicago: Rand McNally.

Campion, M. A. (1988). Interdisciplinary approaches to job design: A constructive replication with extensions. *Journal of Applied Psychology*, *73*, 467-481.

Campion, M. A., & McClelland, C. (1993). Follow-up and extension of the interdisciplinary costs and benefits of enlarged jobs. *Journal of Applied Psychology*, *78*, 339-351.

Cohen, J. P., & Cohen, P. (1983). *Applied multiple regression/correlation analysis for the behavioral sciences* (2nd ed.). Hillsdale, NJ: Erlbaum.

Cook, T. D., & Campbell, D. T. (1979). *Quasi-experimentation: Design and analysis issues for field settings.* Chicago: Rand McNally.

Cook, T. D., & Shadish, W. R. (1994). Social experiments: Some developments over the past fifteen years. *Annual Review of Psychology*, *45*, 545-580.

Cronbach, L. J. (1982). *Designing evaluations of educational and social programs.* San Francisco: Jossey-Bass.

Cudeck, R. (1988). Multiplicative models and MTMM matrices. *Journal of Educational Statistics*, *13*, 131-147.

Dudgeon, P. (1994). A reparameterization of the restricted factor analysis model for multitrait-multimethod matrices. *British Journal of Mathematical and Statistical Psychology*, *47*, 283-308.

Dyer, W. G., & Wilkins, A. L. (1991). Better stories, not better constructs, to generate better theory: A response to Eisenhardt. *Academy of Management Review*, *16*, 613-619.

Eisenhardt, K. M. (1989a). Building theories from case study research. *Academy of Management Review*, *14*, 532-550.

Eisenhardt, K. M. (1989b). Making fast strategic decisions in high-velocity environments. *Academy of Management Journal*, *32*, 543-576.

Eisenhardt, K. M. (1991). Better stories and better constructs. *Academy of Management Review*, *16*, 620-623.

Evans, M. G. (1969). Convergent and discriminant validities between the Cornell Job Descriptive Index and a measure of goal attainment. *Journal of Applied Psychology*, *53*, 102-106.

Evans, M. G. (1975). Opportunistic organizational research: The role of patch-up designs. *Academy of Management Journal*, *18*, 98-108.

Fiske, D. W., & Campbell, D. T. (1992). Citations do not solve problems. *Psychological Bulletin*, *112*, 393-395.

Frayne, C. A., & Latham, G. P. (1987). Applications of social learning theory to employee self-management of attendance. *Journal of Applied Psychology*, *72*, 387-392.

Gerbing, D. W., & Anderson, J. C. (1987). Improper solutions in the analysis of covariance matrices: Their interpretability and a comparison of alternative respecifications. *Psychometrika*, *52*, 99-111.

Gilbert, B. (1989). The impact of union involvement on the design and introduction of Quality of Working Life. *Human Relations*, *42*, 1057-1078.

Glick, W. H., Jenkins, D. G., & Gupta, N. (1986). Method versus substance: How strong are underlying relationships between job characteristics and attitudinal outcomes. *Academy of Management Journal*, *29*, 441-484.

Golding, S. L., & Seidman, E. (1974). Analysis of multitrait-multimethod matrices: A two step principal components procedure. *Multivariate Behavioral Research*, *9*, 479-496.

Goodman, P. S., Conlon, E., Epple, D., & Fidler, E. (1979). *Assessing organizational change: The Rushton quality of work experiment.* London: Tavistock.

Graham, J. W., & Collins, N. L. (1991). Controlling correlational bias via confirmatory factor analysis of MTMM data. *Multivariate Behavioral Research*, *26*, 607-629.

Graybill, F. A. (1961). *An introduction to linear statistical models.* New York: McGraw-Hill.

Haccoun, R. R., & Hamtiaux, T. (1994). Optimizing knowledge tests for inferring learning acquisition levels in single group training evaluation designs: The Internal Referencing Strategy. *Personnel Psychology*, *47*, 593-604.

Hackman, J. R., & Oldham, G. R. (1975). Development of the Job Diagnostic Survey. *Journal of Applied Psychology*, *60*, 159-170.

Harris, E. F., & Fleishman, E. A. (1955). Human relations training and the stability of leadership patterns. *Journal of Applied Psychology, 39,* 20-25.

Heckman, J. J. (1980). Sample selection bias as a specification error. In E. W. Stromsdorfer & G. Farkas (Eds.), *Evaluation studies review annual* (Vol. 5, pp. 61-76). Beverly Hills, CA: Sage.

Hirschman, E. C. (1986). Humanistic inquiry in marketing research: Philosophy, method and criteria. *Journal of Marketing Research, 23,* 237-249.

Hubert, L. J., & Baker, F. B. (1979). A note on analyzing the multitrait-multimethod matrix: An analysis of a generalized proximity function comparison. *British Journal of Mathematical and Statistical Psychology, 32,* 179-184.

James, L. R., Demaree, R. G., Mulaik, S. A., & Ladd, R. T. (1992). Validity generalization in the context of situational models. *Journal of Applied Psychology, 77,* 3-14.

Jick, T. D. (1979). Mixing qualitative and quantitative methods: Triangulation in action. *Administrative Science Quarterly, 24,* 602-611.

Johns, G. (1993). Constraints on the adoption of psychology-based personnel practices: Lessons from organizational innovation. *Personnel Psychology, 46,* 569-592.

Jöreskog, K. G. (1971). Statistical analysis of sets of congeneric tests. *Psychometrika, 36,* 109-133.

Kanetkar, V., & Evans, M. G. (1997). *Confirmatory factor analysis of multitrait-multimethod matrices: The effects of misspecification on estimates, solutions, and goodness-of-fit indicators.* Unpublished manuscript, Rotman School of Management, University of Toronto.

Kenny, D. A., & Kashy, D. A. (1992). Analysis of multitrait-multimethod matrix by confirmatory factor analysis. *Psychological Bulletin, 112,* 165-172.

Kiers, H.A.L., Takane, Y., & Ten Berge, J.M.F. (1996). The analysis of multitrait-multimethod matrices via constrained component analysis. *Psychometrika, 61,* 601-628.

Knights, D., & McCabe, D. (1998). What happens when the phone goes wild: Staff, stress, and spaces for escape in a BPR telephone banking work regime. *Journal of Management Studies, 35,* 164-194.

Kumar, A., & Dillon, W. R. (1990). On the use of confirmatory measurement models in the analysis of multiple-informant reports. *Journal of Marketing Research, 27,* 102-111.

Larsson, R. (1989). *Organizational integration of mergers and acquisitions: A case survey of realization of synergy potentials.* Lund, Sweden: Lund University Press.

Larsson, R. (1993). Case survey methodology: Quantitative analysis of patterns across case studies. *Academy of Management Journal, 36,* 1515-1546.

Levin, J., Montag, I., & Comrey, A. L. (1983). Comparison of multitrait-multimethod, factor, and smallest space analysis on personality scale data. *Psychological Reports, 53,* 591-596.

Lincoln, Y. S. (1990). The making of a constructionist: A remembrance of transformations past. In E. Guba (Ed.), *The paradigm dialog* (pp. 67-87). Newbury Park, CA: Sage.

Lincoln, Y. S., & Guba, E. G. (1985). *Naturalistic inquiry.* Beverly Hills, CA: Sage.

Marsh, H. W. (1989). Confirmatory factor analysis of multitrait-multimethod data: Many problems and a few solutions. *Applied Psychological Measurement, 13,* 335-361.

Marsh, H. W. (1993). Multitrait-multimethod analysis: Inferring each trait-method combination with multiple indicators. *Applied Measurement in Education, 6*(1), 49-81.

Marsh, H. W., & Bailey, M. (1991). Confirmatory factor analysis of multitrait-multimethod data: A comparison of alternative models. *Applied Psychological Measurement, 15,* 47-70.

Marsh, H. W., & Hocevar, D. (1988). A new, more powerful approach to multitrait-multimethod analyses: Application of second order confirmatory factor analysis. *Journal of Applied Psychology, 73,* 107-117.

Miller, D., & Friesen, P. H. (1977). Strategy making in context: Ten empirical archetypes. *Journal of Management Studies, 14,* 253-280.

Mintzberg, H., Raisinghani, D., & Theoret, A. (1976). The structure of "unstructured" decision processes. *Administrative Science Quarterly, 21,* 246-275.

Mitchell, T. R. (1985). An evaluation of the validity of correlational research conducted in organizations. *Academy of Management Review, 10,* 192-205.

O'Connor, E. J., Peters, L. H., Pooyan, A., Weekley, J., Frank, B., & Erenkranz, B. (1984). Situational constraints effects on performance, affective reactions, and turnover: A field replication. *Journal of Applied Psychology, 69,* 663-672.

Peters, L. H., Chassie, M. B., Lindholm, L. R., O'Connor, E. J., & Kline, C. R. (1982). The joint influences of situational constraints and goal setting on performance and affective outcomes. *Journal of Management, 8,* 7-20.

Peters, L. H., Fisher, C. D., & O'Connor, E. J. (1982). The moderating effect of situational control of performance variance on the relationship between individual differences and performance. *Personnel Psychology, 35,* 609-622.

Peters, L. H., O'Connor, E. J., & Rudolf, C. J. (1980). The behavioral and affective consequences of performance-relevant situational variables. *Organizational Behavior and Human Decision Processes, 25,* 79-96.

Pfeffer, J. (1993). Barriers to the advance of organizational science: Paradigm development as a dependent variable. *Academy of Management Review, 18,* 599-620.

Phillips, J. S., & Freedman, S. M. (1984). Situational performance constraints, task characteristics, and their relationship with motivation and satisfaction. *Journal of Management, 3,* 321-331.

Ross, J., & Staw, B. M. (1986). Expo 86: An escalation prototype. *Administrative Science Quarterly, 31,* 274-297.

Ross, J., & Staw, B. M. (1993). Organizational escalation and exit: Lessons from the Shoreham nuclear power plant. *Administrative Science Quarterly, 36,* 701-732.

Sackett, P. R., & Mullen, E. J. (1993). Beyond formal experimental design: Towards an expanded view of the training evaluation process. *Personnel Psychology, 46,* 613-627.

Schmitt, N., Coyle, B. W., & Saari, B. B. (1977). A review and critique of analyses of multitrait-multimethod matrices. *Multivariate Behavioral Research, 13,* 447-478.

Schmitt, N., & Stults, D. M. (1986). Methodological review: Analysis of multitrait-multimethod matrices. *Applied Psychological Measurement, 10,* 1-22.

Schneider, B. J. (1983). Interactional psychology and organizational behavior. In L. L. Cummings & B. M. Staw (Eds.), *Research in organizational behavior* (Vol. 5, pp. 1-31). Greenwich, CT: JAI.

Solomon, R. L. (1949). An extension of the control group design. *Psychological Bulletin, 46,* 137-150.

Spreitzer, G. M. (1995). Psychological empowerment in the work place: Dimensions, measurement, and validation. *Academy of Management Journal, 38,* 1442-1465.

Werts, C. E., & Lin, R. L. (1970). Path analysis: Psychological examples. *Psychological Bulletin, 74,* 193-212.

Widaman, K. F. (1985). Hierarchically nested covariance structure models for multitrait-multimethod data. *Applied Psychological Measurement, 9,* 1-26.

Wothke, W. (1996). Models for multitrait-multimethod matrix analysis. In G. A. Marcoulides & R. E. Schumacher (Eds.), *Advanced structural equation modeling* (pp. 7-56). Mahwah, NJ: Erlbaum.

Wothke, W., & Browne, M. W. (1990). The direct product model for the MTMM matrix parameterized as a second order factor analysis model. *Psychometrika, 55,* 255-262.

Yin, R. K. (1984). *Case study research: Design and methods.* Beverly Hills, CA: Sage.

Yin, R. K., & Yates, D. (1974). *Street level governments: Assessing decentralization and urban services* (R-1527-NSF). Santa Monica, CA: RAND.

Chapter 17

What Can Management Researchers Learn From Donald Campbell, the Philosopher?

An Exercise in Hermeneutics

MARGARETHA HENDRICKX

That Donald Campbell was a fine social scientist is beyond dispute, but that he was also a cutting edge philosopher is apparently less well appreciated among management researchers. Browsing through the philosophy journals and books in a humanities library or bookshop, we find many articles and book chapters praising Campbell as one of the ground-breaking philosophers of biology. Campbell was a major contributor to the stream of philosophy called evolutionary epistemology (EE). Today, a more than 1,100-item bibliography exists on this view of knowledge construction (Cziko & Campbell, 1997), investigating its implications for areas of research ranging from the emergence of consciousness in the animal kingdom (Heyes, 1987) to the nutritional origin of sensory receptors in photo-bacteria (Wächtershäuser, 1987). Belgian philosopher Callebaut (1993) uses Campbell as a model to illustrate how contemporary philosophers work. A review of the management literature, however, will uncover few references to either Campbell's philosophical papers in general or his work on *hermeneutics*, the philosophical approach Campbell explored increasingly during the later part of his life.

The purpose of this chapter is twofold: to investigate the hermeneutical dimension in Campbell's work and to show how Campbell's own work, read from a hermeneutically informed approach, takes on a richer meaning: Campbell was attempting to make sense of the moral implications of neo-Darwinism. For the purpose of illustration, I examine the essay Campbell delivered at the 1992 Conference on Evolutionary Organizational Dynamics at New York University, "How Individual and Face-to-Face Group Selection Undermine Firm Selection in Organizational Evolution" (Campbell, 1994a), hereafter called the New York essay. Briefly, in this essay Campbell investigated the conditions that undermine firm longevity. I first read the New York essay without attending to the philosophical dimension in Campbell's work. Read from this angle, Campbell appears to argue that groups are ontologically real, that it is important to understand firm-level selection as well as individual and face-to-face group selection given that lower-level selection processes may undermine higher-level ones: Selection at individual and face-to-face group levels may lead to firm-level dysfunction. Then I reread the New York essay through the lens of *philosophical hermeneutics*. This lens reveals that, rather than believing that groups really exist out there, deep down Campbell was attempting to make sense of the "nihilistic" neo-Darwinian implication that human beings are selfish (on average). The opening argument of the New York essay about ontologically real groups was his first, but not last, attempt to make sense of this view of humanity and its implications for firm longevity. Moreover, Campbell believed we need a better understanding of how individuals relate to one another—face-to-face interactions—and not so much "real" groups. We then may realize that the idea of biologically induced opportunism is primarily a manufactured fact.

1. Philosophical Hermeneutics: A Tool to Cope With Interpretive Dilemmas

Broadly speaking, philosophical hermeneutics evokes a dialogue focused on understanding what it means to be *interpretive*[1] human beings (Crusius, 1991). From a historical viewpoint, hermeneutical philosophers were at first primarily interested in uncovering the knowledge embedded in the Scriptures (Palmer, 1969). For example, which interpretive strategy allows us to recover the true meaning of Matthew 4:1-11, Luke 4:1-13, and Mark 1:12-13, stating that, when Jesus went out into the

wilderness to pray, the devil set out to tempt Him? How should we interpret the word "devil"? Is it a good idea to think of this word as a sign corresponding to a real entity out there? Or should we view the concept of the devil as a fiction constructed for a specific purpose? Should we first study the worldview in which Matthew, Luke, and Mark were reasoning before deciding how to interpret their Gospels? What does it mean to live in a world inhabited by devils and demons? (I use this example given that Donald Campbell himself was puzzled by the ideas of evil, original sin, and temptation, as discussed in part 3 of this chapter.)

During the quest for the true interpretation of the Scriptures, it became clear that interpretive processes and issues span many additional activities beyond biblical interpretation itself. The field of hermeneutics therefore gradually modified its scope. Although it was originally equivalent to biblical exegesis, over time it identified itself with philology, the science of linguistic understanding, the methodology of the study of interpretive beings (the social sciences), and, today, philosophical hermeneutics, the study of interpretation in its most elementary form (Crusius, 1991). Given that the focus of this chapter is on philosophical hermeneutics, I limit my discussion to this type of hermeneutics. (The appendix contains a brief discussion of the other types and how they are different from philosophical hermeneutics.)

Hermeneutical philosophers (e.g., Bernstein, 1983; Gadamer, 1960/1975; Heidegger, 1927/1962) contend that ontological questions must be addressed at the same time as epistemological issues. Epistemological questions are questions about "the nature and derivation of knowledge, the scope of knowledge, and the reliability of claims to knowledge" (Flew, 1984, p. 109). Ontological questions, on the other hand, are questions about existence, our own existence and the existence of the entities we perceive to be in the environment. In the above paragraph, I pointed out the issues that arise when we attempt to make sense of the Scriptures. Another widely discussed interpretive conundrum is Niels Bohr's complementarity thesis.

Why did Bohr (1928, 1934) articulate a thesis of complementarity to make sense of the contradictions between classical and quantum mechanics?

How should we interpret Bohr's arguments for this thesis that we may use "apparently conflicting models in mutually exclusive domains of experience" (Polkinghorne, 1993, pp. 446-447)? Did Bohr attempt to make clear that the randomly moving "electrons" postulated by quantum mechanics are really out there and that, via a complex set of arguments and mathematical equations, we are able to express quantum properties in terms of macroscopic observable instruments? Or is there, as hermeneutical philosophers argue, an ontological dimension that we first need to address? What are the ontological implications of arguing that randomly moving electrons exist behind macroscopic observable phenomena? What does this view imply about beings? Did Bohr equate free will with randomly inspired actions? Did Bohr believe that human beings are nothing more than stochastic atomic machines, and was he trying to explain that this view allows one to overcome the inconsistencies between classical and quantum mechanics? Or was Bohr unwilling to make this ontological statement of human beings and the universe? Was he intrigued by the role that language plays during the initiation of scientists and theory development, as MacKinnon (1996) argues? Did Bohr formulate a complementarity thesis in his attempts to reconcile the incommensurable vocabularies of classical Newtonian and quantum mechanics? Did he believe we need to view the quantum postulate as a helpful linguistic device to organize the thought processes of experimental physicists while they are figuring out the properties of matter?[2]

We must ask similar questions when we read Campbell's work. For example, what did Campbell (1994a) attempt to communicate when he stated that ontologically real groups may undermine firm longevity? Did he want us to do research on causal group-level and firm-level forces? Or did he view this argument as a trial-and-error schema to organize our thoughts on the social processes that take place in companies and their effect on long-term performance?

The need for philosophical hermeneutics is especially great when we deal with texts that have special authority and function as decision-making guides, as in the case of a sacred text, a legal code, or even an article in the *Academy of Management Executive*. Every text, whether published in the Scriptures, *Physics Review*, *Nature*, *Metaphysics*, or *Strategic Management Journal*, presents such choices of interpretation. Philosophical hermeneutics helps us characterize these choices and understand what is at stake.

At face value, it may seem that we may study and interpret the ontological status of entities such as demons, atoms, groups, and firms *independently from* studying our own ontological status, as if it is possible to gather knowledge about the "objects" in the environment independently from gathering knowledge about ourselves. Philosophical hermeneutics questions this surface approach to ontology. It argues that how we view the existence of objects in the extra-mental world is *a function of* how we frame our own existence and relationship with the environment. (By "extra-mental reality," I mean the world as it exists independently from how an individual perceives it.) Our perception of the outside world is a function of how we perceive our own position in and relationship with the phenomena—in the past, present, and future. We, therefore, need a better understanding of the reference frames[3] we use to make sense of this relationship and the extent to which these frames confuse us or help us clarify and focus our thought processes—especially if we want to develop a proper understanding of the processes taking place in the world.

Philosophical hermeneutics makes the following three arguments. First, it is possible to identify two frames of reference with which to make sense of questions of interpretation: a God's Eye frame and a participant frame. Second, the God's Eye frame tends to have a mind-closing effect. It reinforces dogmatic argumentation and, therefore, promotes conflict and intolerance. As such, the God's Eye frame *is not* an attractive way to make sense of the world. Instead, it is preferable that we *all* eventually reason in a participant frame of reference. Third, given the problematic nature of the God's Eye frame, we need a better understanding of issues of framing, that is, the difference between God's Eye and participant frames of reference.

One way to clarify these three arguments is by invoking the hypothetical construct of "Mr. Jones."

Mr. Jones is a researcher who has not paid attention to the philosophical literature on framing. He does not realize that he has a tendency to oscillate between God's Eye and participant modes of reasoning and that he takes a different approach to research depending on the frame of reference in which he works. Given that this chapter is written in the context of management and organization studies, I set up Mr. Jones as a management researcher, but the arguments developed next apply to any type of institutionalized discourse.

The God's Eye View of Reading a Text

Broadly speaking, the God's Eye view is a way of reasoning that implies that certain individuals are in privileged positions to discover Deep Truth about the universe. As Putnam[4] (1981) puts it, in the God's Eye view

> the world consists of some fixed totality of extra-mental objects [as described in physics]. There is exactly one true and complete description of "the way the world is." Truth involves some sort of correspondence relation between words or thought-signs and external things and sets of things. (p. 49)

The God's Eye way of reasoning is depicted in Figure 17.1a. The person with the magnifying glass is a management researcher—Mr. Jones—who is investigating a specific managerial issue, for example, how the performance of quite successful companies sometimes declines. He thinks of himself as a value-neutral observer who studies the real essences of these firms. Arrow 1 represents the supposed correspondence relation between thought signs, symbolized by a researcher standing on the moon, and the phenomena in the extra-mental reality, as symbolized by the globe. Arrow 2 stands for the relation between thought-signs and linguistic signs, symbolized by a book. Arrow 3 represents the relation between linguistic signs and extra-mental phenomena.[5]

The God's Eye view of the world reinforces the idea that we must evaluate our scientific beliefs and texts as if they are approximate photographs of the phenomena under investigation. Plato was one of the first to suggest that human knowledge be treated as a crude and imperfect picture of "Ideal Forms." French philosopher René Descartes gave this view a "scientific" foundation. He literally interpreted the human eye as a lens of what, today, we call a photo camera in *Optics* (1637/1967) and his *Treatise on Man* (completed in 1633 and posthumously published in 1662[6]). Pushing this metaphor to the limit leads to the idea that it is fruitful to treat linguistic signs as if they are imprecise pictures of the phenomena in the outside world. Indeed, philosopher Ludwig Wittgenstein attempted to articulate such a picture theory of language in his *Tractatus Logico-Philosophicus* (1921/1961).

The God's eye point of view inspires Mr. Jones to think of his relationship with phenomena under investigation as one of the sides of a triangle (Figure 17.1b). He functions in this triangle as a (very complicated) mirror. His research activities may be broken down in primarily three tasks, "observing," "describing," and "verifying." First, he *inductively* observes what is happening in the world. The reflected photons fall on his eyes' retinas and induce an electron cascade that leads to the creation of photograph-like images of the phenomena in his brain. Via a very complex set of biochemical and neurological reactions, these images are translated in patterns of dots on paper or digital signals stored on a computer disk: Mr. Jones describes what he observes in the world. He then generalizes his empirical findings in hypotheses and *deductively* tests (and observes) whether the postulated relations hold true.

This triangular reasoning squeezes Mr. Jones out of the world, so to speak. He believes that, with proper training, he is capable of transcending his own subjectivity, as if he was able to turn his values and preferences off as easily as he turns his computer on to write up his research findings. It is the job, the duty, of Mr. Jones to publish articles with "true" descriptions of what happens in corporations. He believes that it is possible to obtain the value-neutral state of mind of an outsider and draw an imaginary line—the dotted box in Figure 17.1a—detaching him from the phenomena under study. He perceives his relationship with these as independent of time, space, and mind, as if he is like God. Mr. Jones appears capable of mentally

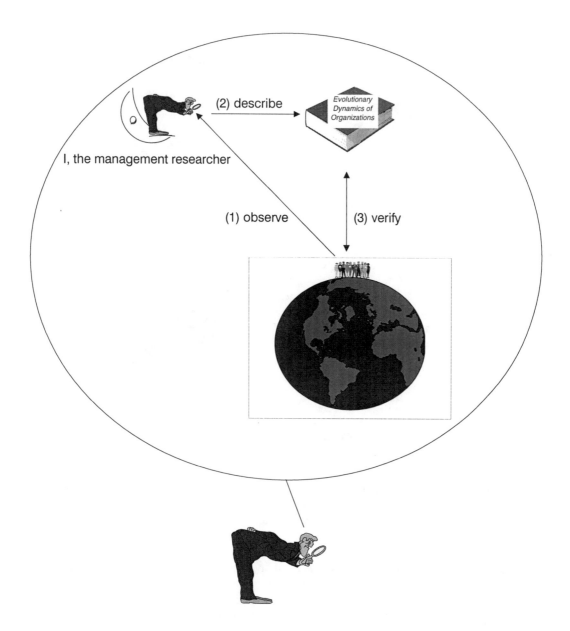

Figure 17.1a. Mr. Jones in a God's Eye Mode of Reasoning

stepping outside his own existence and examining organizational phenomena "from above"—like a bird. He believes that what he *sees* is the way the phenomena in the extra-mental world *are*.

The God's Eye worldview sets up a scientific text as if it is equivalent to a snapshot of a certain area of the world at a certain point in time—the researcher acts like a video camera. A scientific text has only one photograph-like interpretation, as if one could freeze it in time and space to bring out its one true meaning. When Mr. Jones reads Campbell's New York essay, he uses the same decision

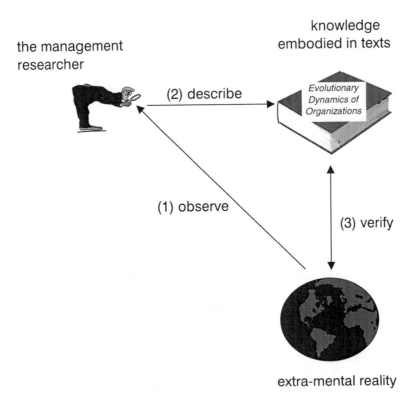

the management
researcher

knowledge
embodied in texts

Evolutionary
Dynamics of
Organizations

(2) describe

(1) observe

(3) verify

extra-mental reality

Figure 17.1b. Schematic Presentation of a God's Eye Frame of Reference: Triangular Reasoning

rules he would use to study photographic images. Just like he holds a photograph next to the real phenomenon to determine the photograph's "truth" or "falsehood," he treats a text as if he somehow is able to determine unambiguously whether its content is true or false. He tacitly evaluates whether each sentence Campbell wrote is approximately true or false. He wonders whether the ideas communicated by Campbell's text are mirrorlike reflections of the real world. Is the author really thinking what he wrote down? Do the words on paper really correspond to his thoughts (Arrow 2)? Are his thoughts truthful representations of the extra-mental phenomena (Arrow 1)? In other words, the God's Eye frame of reference misleads us to believe that problems of misinterpretation are not a serious concern; if a researcher is in the correct frame of mind, he should be able to discover the one true meaning of a text. Indeed, phi-

losophers in the logical positivist and analytical tradition attempted to develop a linguistic system that ensured a proper use of analytic (logical) and synthetic (empirical) statements and that would minimize the use of vague terms and ambiguously derived inferences. They hoped this linguistic system would solve the problem of misinterpretation (Abel, 1953).

In summary, a God's Eye point of view suggests:

Proposition 1a: It is a good idea to evaluate a scholarly publication in the same way that you would evaluate a photograph.

Proposition 2a: It is a good idea to give the reading process the same ontological status as the activities of a computer scanner.

Proposition 3a: Textual interpretation is not a serious concern; philosophers of language and cognitive scientists eventually will solve this problem.

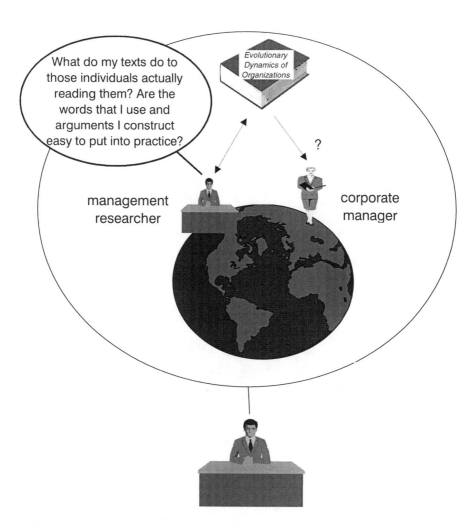

Figure 17.2a. Mr. Jones in a Participant Mode of Reasoning

To summarize, a God's Eye view portrays the reading of scientific texts as an automated, mechanical activity like that in a photovoltaic cell. It downplays the creative and subjective aspects of reading. It removes "Donald Campbell" and "you" from it. It misleadingly gives the impression that the true meaning of a text eventually will emerge as long as enough competent individuals read the same text; the development of intersubjective agreement helps us determine its truth content, and though some of us may experience difficulties overcoming subjective tendencies, these biases, on average, do not create a serious problem. Thus, the God's Eye views deceptively suggests that we, as management researchers, need not worry about the possibility of misinterpretation as long as we make sure to use accurate and precise language.

The Participant View of Reading a Text

A participant frame of reference sets up a human being as the product of and an active participant in the human community he attempts to study and understand.[7] Figure 17.2a illustrates the participant frame. Mr. Jones now thinks of himself as a participant in a discourse about ways to help companies

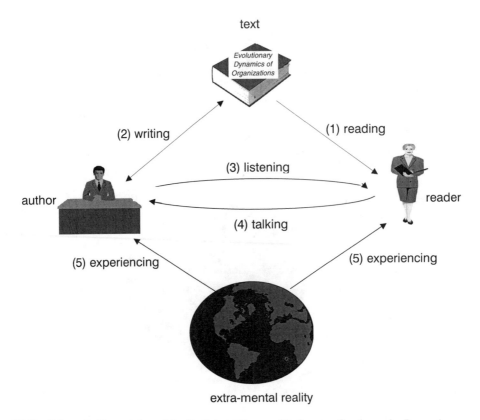

Figure 17.2b. Schematic Presentation of the Participant Frame of Reference: Quadrangular Reasoning

succeed in the long run. He perceives himself as a voice in a universal conversation, in which the various points of view of actual persons reflect their various interests and purposes (Putnam, 1981, pp. 49-50). One of these purposes is to find the most clarifying lens with which to discover the degree of effectiveness of managers' actions and thoughts.

In the participant worldview, a management researcher explicitly acknowledges that he is the product of a certain history and culture. Thus, Mr. Jones realizes that he knows as much as he learned from the books that he read, the experiences he underwent, and the conversations in which he participated. He has come to terms with the subjective nature of what he knows and understands the futility of attempting to reason in a value-neutral way. (It is literally inconceivable.) Instead, Mr. Jones talks openly about his research values and investigates whether they make sense after all. Mr. Jones

attempts to understand whether or not his espoused values are the values he *actually* uses in his research. He also wants to know the extent to which his values in use are consistent with values benefiting the human species[8] as a whole (Campbell, 1979, p. 39; 1982a, pp. 333-334). His values motivate him (Campbell, 1993b, p. 36). He looks upon his research questions as issues with practical consequences for him, his neighbors, and the top management teams he studies.

To answer questions such as these, Mr. Jones reasons in terms of a quadrangle, as depicted in Figure 17.2b. He views himself as a corner of this quadrangle, either as a reader or as an author, with "the Other" in the opposite corner. The text and the extra-mental reality mark the third and fourth connecting points. So, compared to the God's Eye view, where the Other is either an onlooker like Mr. Jones or, alternatively, someone down there to be observed—Figure 17.1a—the participant frame of reference does not classify readers and writers as a function of whether they know less or more; rather, it implies that they know something different.

The participant view explicitly sets up a text as a mental lens. It is an instrument we craft (Booth, Colomb, & Williams, 1995). It fulfills two functions, bridging the space and time separating human minds and providing a focusing device. "Text" is something that stands between us and the outside world. It stands between a writer and his readers. Its purpose is to focus our thoughts and bring the thoughts of the author into focus. The arrows in Figures 17.2a and 17.2b stand for reading, writing, listening, talking, and experiencing. No arrow links the text with the extra-mental reality because the text is *never* positioned next to the reality. The participant frame reminds us that we never hold a text next to the phenomenon and estimate its truth content in the same way as we would evaluate that type of content in a photograph of—say—the Eiffel Tower. In other words, in a participant frame of reference, it becomes meaningless to evaluate a text as a function of its truth or falsity. As Putnam (1981) states it, what God's Eye researchers call "truth" is some sort of warranted acceptability, "some sort of ideal coherence of our beliefs with each other and with our experience *as those experiences are themselves represented in our belief system*—and not correspondence with extra-mental or discourse-independent 'states of affairs.' " (pp. 49-50).

American philosopher John Dewey elaborated the "lens" view of texts and beliefs. I took the words "photograph" and "mental glasses" from his work. Wittgenstein also contributed to making this distinction. As mentioned above, in the earlier part of his life, Wittgenstein attempted to develop a picture theory of language by studying the extent to which the logical form of a linguistic system corresponds with the world it represents. He very publicly abandoned this project in the later part of his philosophical career in favor of a more nominalist view of language in his *Philosophical Investigations* and *Blue and Brown Books*, posthumously published in 1953 and 1958, respectively.

Note that there exist two ways in which we may use the lens concept. One way is to think of this concept as the lens of a photo camera. In this view,

we are inspired to evaluate our knowledge and beliefs as snapshots taken from a particular angle, as stated in Proposition 2a. The second way is to imagine the concept of "lens" as denoting a pair of eyeglasses an optician is crafting for a person with poor vision, a microscope to study the bacteria in a drop of saliva, or a telescope to study the stars in the sky. In this second meaning, the mental lens is something that stands between us and the world. As Dewey put it:

> The thinking process does not go on endlessly in terms of itself, but seeks outlet through reference to particular experiences. It is tested by this reference; not, however, as if a theory could be tested by directly comparing it with facts—an obvious impossibility— but through use in facilitating commerce with facts. It is tested as *glasses* are tested; things are looked at through the medium of specific meanings to see if thereby they assume a more orderly and clearer aspect, if they are less blurred and obscure. (1916, p. 198; cited in Morgenbesser, 1977, p. xvii; emphasis added)

So, we have a paradigmatic change in the meaning attached to the words "text," "belief," "human mind," and "knowledge." Table 17.1 summarizes this Kuhnian shift[9] in meaning. How you view the knowledge communicated in a text is a function of the interpretive frame in which you reason. The God's Eye frame sets you up in a triangle and makes you more likely to treat a scientific text as a descriptive photograph of that specific area of the world you are "objectively" observing and describing. It makes you believe there is only "one" correct interpretation of a text (the one that is consistent with *your* knowledge of the fundamental nature of the universe). To state it in exaggerated terms, the God's Eye view sets up the researcher as a Cartesian machine. He has the function of a digital photo camera; his eyes act like a lens of such a camera. His brain is the mechanism that runs the camera. As such, the text is conceptualized as a crude photograph. It communicates knowledge about the way the world is in the same way as a photograph taking by a weather satellite records the development and movement of tropical storms. By continuously comparing the text with the real world, the God's Eye frame confusingly gives the

TABLE 17.1 Comparison Between the God's Eye and Participant Frames of Reference With a Special Emphasis on Reading

	God's Eye View of the World	*Participant View of the World*
How researchers conceptualize their relationship with the phenomena under study	A side of a triangle with the text and the world in the other corners.	A side in a quadrangle; the other corners are marked by the text, the world, and the imagined human being with whom the researcher is communicating.
Assumptions about the role of the researcher/author	Cartesian machine; digital photo camera.	Optician; lens crafter.
Scientific text, concept	Crude photograph of the extra-mental reality.	Mental lens to bring our thoughts about the extra-mental world into focus.
Purpose of creating a scientific text	Develop approximately true descriptions of organizational phenomena. To make sure that everyone knows the truth.	Develop mental lenses to help managers better cope with firm-specific phenomena. To solve problems that eventually make a life/death difference.
Problem of misinterpretation	Can be solved as long as we all use clear and precise language.	Is a human characteristic that humans need to learn to cope with.
The role of hermeneutics	The study of linguistic principles that help us uncover the true meaning of the text.	Speeds up the knowledge construction process; the better we understand where the author comes from, the easier it becomes to appreciate how our viewpoints differ from his and how to proceed from there.
Reading a scientific text	A quantum-driven mirroring operation. Photons fall on the text and are reflected on the reader's retina. The optical nerve sends a set of impulses to the brain. Certain neural processes in the brain allow the reader to evaluate whether the sentences read are true or false.	Attempt to reconstruct the frame of reference of the author. Understand how his frame of reference is different from ours, and, based on an appreciation of these differences, attempt to understand what the author is attempting to communicate.
Choice among competing interpretations of the same text	Choose the one that is most true.	Our frame of reference determines the decision rule of choice to cope with competing interpretations. Choose the most charitable.
Existence of contradictions in a text	Does not really address it. Ideally, the meaning of a text should be self-evident.	Inherent characteristic of a text. By-product of the negotiation game.
Historical origin	Galileo Galilei (1564-1642), René Descartes (1596-1650), Gottfried Wilhelm Leibniz (1646-1716), Gottlob Frege (1848-1925), Bertrand Russell (1872-1970), Ludwig Wittgenstein (1889-1951) in the earlier part of his life	Charles Darwin (1809-1882), William James (1842-1910), John Dewey (1859-1952), Wittgenstein (1889-1951) in the later part of his life

impression that we move toward developing true descriptions of the world. It makes us believe that we must compare our thoughts and actions with these true scientific texts to find out which of our beliefs are true or false; doing so ensures that we eventually approach the truth. The God's Eye frame gives the impression that uncertainty may be eliminated in the long run. (As I elaborate later, this last implication makes the God's Eye frame problematic.)

From a participant point of view, on the other hand, this question about knowledge is a function of the frame of reference in which you reason. If you think of yourself as a corner in a quadrangle, you are more likely to treat a text as a lens to focus someone else's thinking and bring that person's thoughts into focus. The participant view sets up the researcher as an optician; he crafts lenses/texts to make his customers see better. Beliefs also are evaluated as lenses. We, human beings, have the ability to be self-conscious. We have the capability to take a step backward and evaluate our thoughts as a function of their effectiveness: We are capable of seeing "through" our own thoughts and investigate whether the world looks more muddled or more clear according to our thoughts and actions.

Appreciating the difference in connotation between these two uses of the term "lens"—and how they imply different meanings for associated words such as "text," "belief," and "mind"—is important, yet the management and organizations literature rarely clarifies the difference between these two meanings of the word "lens." For example, Putnam, Phillips, and Chapman (1996) set a lens up as "a screen that *filters*, protects, shields, and guides transmission . . . an eye that scans, sifts, and relays" (p. 380), something that selects and distorts—like the specialty lenses of a camera; that is, the Cartesian approach.

Also Poole and Van de Ven (1989) do not indicate whether they view a theory as a lens or as a photograph. They discuss a theory as something standing between the researcher and the phenomena he studies, like a lens: "Theories always constrain the theorist's field of vision: one of the canons of good theory construction is to recognize these limitations" (p. 563). At the same time, Poole

and Van de Ven use photo camera-like imagery. For example, in the next paragraph they state, "The researcher develops a 'trained incapacity' to appreciate aspects not mentioned in her or his theory. As this progression toward consistency continues, the theory becomes more and more 'perfect,' with less and less correspondence to the multifaceted reality it seeks to portray." This is equivalent to stating that it is better to take theoretical snapshots from many different angles—even if the snapshots are inconsistent with one another—rather than strive to develop one perfect photograph that portrays just one facet of the reality. As if management researchers are in the business of taking pictures of the organizational phenomena. As if the head of a researcher operates like a digital photo camera. In other words, they do not address the possibility that a carefully crafted "perfect" lens actually may bring problems into focus and broaden the reader's horizon rather than closing it off.

Allison (1971) and Bartlett and Ghoshal (1993), on the other hand, use the term "lens" in Dewey's (1916) sense. They make a clear distinction between the phenomena under investigation and the theories or models that stand as a lens between the researcher (or manager) and the phenomena. These lenses

> highlight the partial emphasis of each framework— what each magnifies and what it leaves out. Each concentrates on one class of variables, in effect, relegating other important factors to a *ceteris paribus* clause. The models can therefore be understood as building blocks in a larger model of the determinants of outcomes. (Allison, 1963, p. 275)

The theory either distorts or brings the relevant issues into focus. The responsibility of researchers is to continuously investigate the potential for distortions and remove them once discovered.

Interpretation as a Negotiation Game

The participant frame of reference conceives of a text as the product of a language negotiation game (Mauws & Phillips, 1995; Wittgenstein, 1953, 1958). It highlights 13 aspects of the text reading process not really emphasized in the God's Eye view.[10] First, the participant view explicitly stresses that the author is not just writing *about* something, he is also writing *for* a particular audience. There is always "the Other." Campbell had a reader, or a group of readers, in mind when he penned papers such as the New York essay. He wrote papers to clarify the thought processes of one or another of his audiences. To understand what Campbell was attempting to communicate in his New York essay, therefore, we first need to first figure out which "Other" he had in mind when he wrote that text. *Who* was Campbell negotiating with in his mind as he wrote this essay? *How* did Campbell conceptualize his audience? Was Campbell "talking" to those already agreeing with him, and did he want to rally support for the argument that everyone disagreeing with him was wrong? Or was Campbell's target audience everyone interested in the problems he was attempting to understand? (I address these questions, and others posed below, later in this chapter.)

Second, the text qua lens is as effective as the vocabularies, grammars, and rhetorical sophistication of its readers. The extent to which a reader is trained and accustomed to pay attention to the historical nature of vocabularies, grammars, and rhetorical styles determines how likely he is to uncover historical nuances and the sociocultural context within which an author was writing. What did certain words mean at the time Campbell first used them? Did these words *still* have that same meaning in 1992 at the conference on evolutionary organizational dynamics in New York? When the text was published in 1994? Today? Or did these words undergo a Kuhnian meaning shift? What happened that these words became associated with a different meaning? Also, which words had negative and positive meanings for Campbell? Do they still have the same connotations today?

Third, how readers make sense of the text is a function of their own a priori framework. Just as the author is a member of a discourse community and works within a framework and set of rules that guide his construction of arguments, readers also work within an a priori framework that is partially influenced by the interlocking discourse communities to which they belong. This framework acts like a focusing device and tacitly guides readers'

interpretation of the text, downplaying certain passages, increasing attention to others, and treating certain passages as "correct" and "important" and others as "ambiguous," "incorrect," and "unimportant."

Fourth, the text is as good as the discourse rules that mediate the negotiating process between the author and his readers. Broadly speaking, authors and readers may negotiate in terms of "true/false" or "problem-solving" rules. Do we need to read Campbell's text as if he is giving a description of how the world works? Or should we first uncover the problem that Campbell decided to investigate? Should we investigate the solution that Campbell offers to cope with this problem and whether that is the best solution after all?

In summary, these four aspects of the participant frame of reference suggest the following:

Proposition 1b: An author writes not just about a phenomenon but also for an audience.

Proposition 2b: An author constructs his text in an a priori conceived frame of reference.

Proposition 3b: A reader makes sense of a text within the context of his own a priori conceived frame of reference.

Proposition 4b: A text is as good as the discourse rules that mediate the negotiating process between an author and his readers.

Fifth, in a way, academic discourse is like the new product development process. Management researchers design and manufacture knowledge (Knorr-Retina, 1981). They act like opticians, developing and refining mental lenses to help managers organize and focus their thoughts.[11] For example, consider a Black & Decker chain saw. Whether or not a chain saw functions properly is determined by both its producers and its users (Von Hippel, 1988). For a chain saw to be effective, both manufacturers and users need to have certain levels of specific skills. If design engineers focus only on developing the sharpest saw to cut wood with minimum effort and ignore usage and safety issues, do-it-yourselfers are likely to cut off their fingers, hands, or feet. With a saw designed to maximize safety features, however, do-it-yourselfers who are convinced they do not need to read the enclosed instructions to operate the chain saw also may get into trouble. Similarly, whether or not a management text works properly depends on how *both* management researchers and managers conceive of one another. They need to work together to understand how to create and effectively use texts.

Sixth, scientific text production is a problem-coping activity. To continue with the new product development metaphor, the customer has a need, a problem if you like. It is cold; her family needs shelter. The development of chain saws helps her cope with this problem. She is now able to more effectively build houses and cut wood to put in the fireplace. Thus, engineers designed this tool to help users *cope* with a problem. The tool does not make the problem go away; instead, it helps us, human beings, cope with it successfully. In the same way, irrespective of how meticulously authors choose their words and arguments, the problem of misinterpretation remains. Carefully crafted texts help us cope with that problem.

The participant frame sets up the dialogue between a management researcher and his readers as a problem-coping activity (Popper, 1979, pp. 241-245). A scientific text comes into existence for one of two reasons: Either the author is attempting to point out a problem and persuade others that this problem is real and may have disastrous consequences if we keep on ignoring it, or the author is attempting to communicate a solution, a particular way of coping with this problem.

Seventh, just as the design engineers at the chain saw company need to develop and implement procedures to test the safety of the chain saw models they design, management researchers need to develop heuristics to minimize the unintended effects of the theories they manufacture. One such heuristic is the metaphor of *a pair of mental spectacles*. It helps us attach a practicable and operational meaning to the idea of a mental lens. Either spectacles are properly designed so the user notices a speeding car approaching, or they are of the inappropriate strength, so that the user's eyes become irritated and it is just too late when he realizes the car is actually speeding in his direction. A text is a tool to organize your thoughts and help you cope with environmental ambiguities. Either the text is of the correct "strength," gradually bringing the

issue discussed into focus and improving your understanding of it, or the text is of an incorrect strength (either too strong or too weak), putting the issue discussed out of focus, and confusing and irritating you. You get a headache reading that text, and the world appears to be more complicated afterward.

Eighth, the metaphor of a scientific text as a set of mental spectacles suggests that a management researcher should think of herself as an optician. She needs to create clear and practicable texts. She needs to consider whether the texts she writes ultimately will help managers cope more effectively with extra-mental problems or, alternatively, they contain such abstract arguments that few will find use for them. She needs to ensure that her texts do not create misleading impressions with possibly disastrous consequences. For example, we would not want to create mental spectacles giving users the impression that an approaching car is a mile away when in reality it is much closer. Nor would we want to create the mental equivalent of a pair of spectacles that gives readers (and managers) the illusion that a truck is about to hit them while in reality no such thing is about to happen. We want our texts to bring to the foreground the most important issues while relegating to the background unimportant and irrelevant ones.

Ninth, once we think of a text as if it is a mental lens, we realize that management-oriented texts should conceptualize the problem of misinterpretation as something that managers need to learn to cope with rather than believing that they can solve it or assume it away. Texts remind managers that they cannot remove the problem of misinterpretation in the same way that we cannot prevent winter from arriving. Thus, the most general criterion that every text needs to pass is that it should help the reader cope with the problem of misinterpretation; at a minimum, a text should present this problem as nonsolvable. We cannot write a research paper as if its message is obvious and self-evident. A scholarly paper cannot contain imagery reinforcing a God's Eye view of the world—that it is acceptable to reason as if we are capable of knowing what happened on the First Day of the universe, as if our knowledge *is* unquestionable. Thus, a text cannot contain a "voice of God" rhetorical style or

God's Eye view concepts and arguments, that is, symbolic imagery suggesting that the solutions to problems are obvious and self-evident. It should not mislead us to believe that the problem of mis-interpretation is something we eventually will eradicate in the same way as we controlled small-pox.

In summary, in addition to the foregoing Propo-sitions 1b-4b, the participant frame suggests the following:

Proposition 5b: The metaphor of new product devel-opment is a suitable one to make sense of the relationship between readers and authors.

Proposition 6b: Scientific text production is a prob-lem-coping activity.

Proposition 7b: Various aspects of text production and usage need to be evaluated in the same way as you would evaluate a pair of glasses and how it is crafted.

Proposition 8b: A management researcher needs to think of her job as analogous to that of an optician.

Proposition 9b: Every text should, one way or an-other, emphasize that misinterpretation is a prob-lem that we need to learn to cope with *and not* one that we can solve.

In contrast with the God's eye view, the partici-pant frame requires us to give up our "quest for certainty" (Dewey, 1929b). In the same way that it is impossible to evaluate a pair of glasses as a function of its truth-content—you never ask your optician whether your contact lenses are true—it becomes impossible to evaluate a text as a function of its one and true meaning. At best, we realize that our interpretation of a text is incomplete. We will never be able to state that we discovered its "true meaning" in the same way that a pair of contact lenses does not have an absolute use. Given that it is impossible to completely eliminate the possibil-ity of misinterpretation, we always have to make a leap of faith when reading a text. We have to believe we share something human with the author—what-ever that human element may be. Within the philo-sophical literature and the literature on practical logic, this act of trust is better known as the princi-ple of charity (Davidson, 1973-1974, p. 19; Fisher, 1988, pp. 17-18, 22; Quine, 1960, p. 59). The prin-ciple of charity explicitly presupposes that it is impossible to fix problems of misinterpretation. In every text—even in the best of physical science (Campbell 1986, 1991b, p. 592)—readers may find a set of sentences that are inconsistent with their views, and with which they may disagree. A reader's opinion of the author, then, determines whether she will treat these inconsistencies as iso-lated cases or as an indication that the entire paper is wrong. If a reader is positively predisposed to-ward the author, she is more likely to conclude that she is dealing with a slip of the pen. If, in contrast, the reader questioned the author's authority and qualifications before even picking up his paper, she is much more likely to treat these inconsistencies as indications that the author is dumb or confused. Thus, there is an act of faith involved when we make sense of a text. We must have faith in the author's intelligence and good intentions. This act of faith plays an especially important role when we discover incompatible arguments in the same text.

Proposition 10b: Interpreting requires an act of faith in a rationality that the 5.4 billion members of the human species share.

It is more difficult to grasp these issues from a God's Eye frame. This frame gives us the impres-sion that "truth" is somehow obvious and easily discovered—at least, if we search for it. It does not acknowledge that equally rational people may be reasoning in a different frame of reference. Conse-quently, from a God's Eye frame, when an author writes something that conflicts with what we hold to be true, there must be something wrong with that author. The God's Eye frame of reference makes for less charitable readers.

Given that the participant frame of reference explicitly brings to the foreground that the frame-work in which we reason guides us while we make sense of a text, it allows us to make sense of this phenomenon. Thus, the participant frame suggests that a reader who classifies authors as a function of their brilliance—or stupidity—may be reasoning in a God's Eye view of the world. At the same time, it reminds us, as readers, of the difficulty of nego-tiating a vocabulary that appeals to multiple audi-ences. The participant frame makes us put more effort into understanding where the author is coming from and what he is attempting to communicate.

Thus, with respect to the questions raised in the context of proposition 4b, the negotiation rules that link authors with their readers are a function of the frame of reference the reader is living in when she is reading a text. In a God's Eye view, a reader is more likely to employ a true/false rule. In a participant frame, on the other hand, a reader is more likely to adopt a problem-coping rule to make sense of a text. She is more likely to wonder which problem the author is struggling with.

The problem of the God's Eye frame of reference—the reason that philosophers such as Putnam critique it—is that it does not really address issues of interpretation given that it downplays the active negotiation during the reading and writing of a text. It inspires the belief that we, humans, can obtain the know-how to solve problems of misinterpretation and negotiation by developing a formal logical scientific language. The God's Eye frame wants us to believe that, if we all work very hard on this project, we eventually will develop such a timeless language and the hermeneutical problem will go away, as if it is in principle possible to stop time and organize an intercontinental conference among all scientists in the world and decide once and forever the meaning attached to every scientific concept and argument. For example, the 17th century mathematician Gottfried Leibniz (1679/1956) believed he could develop a *characteristica universalis*—a universal system of characters that would be able to express all human thoughts. It would solve the problem of misinterpretation and the religious wars that were dividing Europe at that time (Styazhkin, 1969, pp. 61-70; Toulmin, 1990, pp. 100-103). The ideal candidate language was symbolic logic. This idea was not farfetched given that, writing less than 60 years earlier, in 1623, Galileo Galilei had declared in *The Assayer* (1623/1960) that

> Philosophy is written in this grand book—I mean the universe—which stands continually open to our gaze, but it cannot be understood unless one first learns to comprehend the language and interpret the characters in which it is written. It is written in the language of mathematics, and it characters are triangles, circles, and other geometrical figures, without which it is humanly impossible to understand a single word of it. (pp. 183-184).

In the 17th century, it was generally believed that "God had infused certain men (such as Adam and Moses) with scientific knowledge, which was passed on to successive generations intact. Even Newton, in his historical musings, employed a static model, maintaining that his *Principia* [1687] was a recovery of wisdom known to the ancients" (Richards, 1987, p. 560). So, this preference for mathematics and logic was consistent with the zeitgeist.

About two centuries later, mathematician Gottlieb Frege, who is considered the founding father of modern mathematical logic, gave this project of constructing a universal and timeless language additional impetus when he invented the quantifier and variable construction to formalize general expressions such as "Caesar conquered Gaul" in logic (Veatch, 1954, pp. 3-13). Russell and Wittgenstein (in the earlier part of his career) continued the project of developing a timeless picture language that would allow us to better understand the logically true nature of the universe and eventually eradicate disagreement and resultant violence and war. The first requisite was to develop an unambiguous logical system, free of contradictions. Mathematician-philosopher David Hilbert then claimed that the only foundation necessary for mathematics was its formalization and the proof that the system produced is consistent. In 1931, mathematical logician Kurt Gödel showed that the consistency of arithmetic cannot be proved within the system itself, thus demonstrating the impossibility of achieving part of the Hilbert program. Gradually, more and more problems were discovered in the project of developing a paradox-free, timeless formal language. The emerging consensus among today's philosophers is that W. A. Quine gave the final blow to this project in his article "Two Dogmas of Empiricism" (1951). In 1960, Quine published his "indeterminacy of radical translations" thesis: A sentence always can be properly regarded as meaning a multitude of different things. In that same book, he articulated the principle of charity as discussed in proposition 10b. The meaning attached to a particular word is continuously renegotiated and never crystal clear, as Wittgenstein also had argued in his later years.[12] We *must* learn how to be charitable (Davidson, 1973-1974, p. 19).

Thus, Putnam and an increasing number of other philosophers question the God's Eye view of the world because it presents a misleading and problematic view of issues of misinterpretation. The God's Eye view inspires us to treat the problem of misinterpretation as something that we are capable of solving; issues of interpretation are not a serious hurdle in research. The neglect of problems of interpretation is not an issue if you study tables and chairs, apples falling from a tree, or humans jumping from the roof of a seven-floor building; however, once we deal with metaphysical, invisible concepts such as "evil demon," "egoism," "atom," and "ontologically real groups," we need to be more sensitive to problems of misinterpretation. The insensitivity of researchers to the possibility of misinterpretation may form a more serious problem than how to keep "selfish" researchers honest (Hull, 1988). To conclude that researchers are selfish, we first must conclude that neo-Darwinian theories may be unambiguously interpreted and translated into psychology theories. As the contemporary literature on evolutionary psychology indicates (Nicholson, 1997, pp. 1057-1059), it is unlikely that this perfect translation ever will take place.

At issue here is the relation between issues of interpretation and dogmatic reasoning. (A dogma is defined as "a belief held unquestioningly and with undefended certainty" [Blackburn, 1994, p. 109]). If you believe that the problem of misinterpretation somehow can be fixed, you implicitly accept that the truth about the outside world somehow is self-evident: When rational people with complete information look at the same phenomena, they must reach identical conclusions that need not be scrutinized; given that these people are rational, their conclusions must be logically coherent and, hence, correct. In reality, however, we cannot exclude the possibility that these logically supported conclusions are quite biased. Thus, we always should keep our conclusions open for revision; we

should continuously question them. If, however, we (misleadingly) believe that the problem of misinterpretation can be fixed, we will be less likely to take such a critical attitude toward our own conclusions. We will be more likely to take them as givens, as if we can safely assume that our decision rules are based on unquestionably true principles. As such, we begin treating our beliefs as dogma: We accept them without question (there is no need to scrutinize them given that they are based on true premises). In reality, however, we have arbitrarily taken them as given.[13] Thus, the God's Eye frame is problematic because it inspires us to treat arbitrarily constructed dogmas as obvious (and hence unquestionable) truths. Individuals reasoning in a God's Eye frame have more difficulties with revising taken-for-granted beliefs that turn out to be questionable on second thought. (See Booth, 1974, for a more elaborate discussion of the problems arising from dogmatic reasoning. For an argument against dogmatism in the context of management research, see Mahoney, 1993).

This brings us to the participant frame of reference. In this frame, a scientific language is one of the many, continuously renegotiated vocabularies. There is nothing privileged about the vocabulary of scientists (Rorty, 1981). That science is successful has more to do with the extent to which scientists are skilled social negotiators (Campbell, 1993a) than with the degree to which the scientific language and associated decision rules are truly timeless and unambiguously accurate and precise. Whereas the God's Eye frame puts its money on the development of a pure paradox-free linguistic system, the participant frame emphasizes the quality of communicative acts and dialogue.

To ensure arguments of reasonable quality, linguistic signs need to meet the following three criteria. First, linguistic signs need to be constructed in such a way that we can relatively easily relate them to human experiences. Experience is the source of all knowledge (Dewey, 1929a); thus, concepts and arguments need to be anchored in the *present*. They need to relate to issues we make sense of today. This is what Popper (1962/1992) attempted to express with his arguments for falsifiability: We better not develop arguments when we know in advance we never will obtain the knowledge needed to test them. For example, we cannot argue that the underlying nature of the universe *is* random, paradoxical, or ambiguous. It is *impossible* to test whether our inability to discern nonparadoxical regularities at the subatomic level is proof of the stochastic nature of the universe (Hacking, 1990) or, alternatively, that these difficulties indicate that we are still ignorant in many ways. It is relatively easy to understand what the sign "ignorance" brings into focus: We have to read and think a bit more. It is much more difficult to use the idea that the universe *is* random and paradoxical as a guide for practical decision making. Does it mean that chance may undermine your decisions? What would we be communicating with such an argument? Thus we need to question the God's Eye reference frame because its implications are likely to create confusion and, hence, problems. It puts researchers in a nonhuman position. It presupposes knowledge of what happened during the first second of the universe's existence (see note 13). We would have to think of "science as a transcendental activity, one that could best be conducted by sending teams of observers to hover over Earth" (Cronbach, 1986, p. 83). Such an approach requires us to reason as if we can step outside our skin—something we cannot experience.

Second, concepts and arguments must not choke the conversation. We must construct them in a way that does not reinforce dogmatic reasoning. The only justification of dogmatic ways of reasoning is the argument that others must blindly believe and accept what you say. In the limit, you can always claim that you somehow *know* what happened during the first second on the First Day of the universe. The implicit assumption at the basis of a dogmatic argument is that the Creator designed the world in such a way as to give rise to individuals like you (who somehow are capable of grasping what the Creator had in mind when starting up the universe).[14] Your colleagues must passively trust that you have good reasons to make arguments like these. At this point, your colleagues will terminate the conversation or question your credentials. In either case, the dialogue has been interrupted.

Third, a reader must be able to put concepts and arguments into practice without having to appeal to a wide range of additional presuppositions. One of the elements of philosophical hermeneutics is an emphasis on practical judgment—Aristotle's phronesis (Gadamer, 1960; Bernstein, 1983). Arguments and concepts should be such that we evaluate them as a function of their operational consequences. If an argument is so abstract that we are unsure how managers may operationalize it, this is a red flag indicating that the argument may be nonsensical from a practicable point of view. Thus, we should think twice before introducing abstract arguments. It is impossible to operationalize them without invoking additional assumptions. They do not meet the condition of entitativity (Campbell, 1973, pp. 1050-1051; reprinted in Campbell, 1989, p. 154).

Proposition 11b: Concepts and arguments need to connect with human experiences.

Proposition 12b: Concepts and arguments need to be designed so as to guarantee the continuation of the dialogue; arguments cannot be dogmatic.

Proposition 13b: Concepts and arguments need to reinforce practical judgment.

To summarize, by arguing that ontological questions hang together with epistemological ones, hermeneutics points out that we must address how we view our relationship with the outside world—a side in a triangle? a quadrangle?—before we can decide which entities exist and use texts to justify these decisions. Every individual has to answer this question for him- or herself. Although it is impossible to force someone to address this issue, nevertheless, we still may point out that there is something strange and confusing about the God's Eye approach to research. We need to understand Putnam's (1981) arguments in this spirit. Putnam is not arguing that there "exist" individuals reasoning in a God's Eye frame of reference. Instead, he believes that it is a way of reasoning that we easily may slip in, but that nevertheless is problematic. Thus, Putnam's arguments need to be treated as lenses. He focuses our thoughts on the issue of framing: It is preferable to reason in a participant frame as opposed to a God's Eye frame of reference.

Figure 17.3a. Research From a Traditional Cartesian Point of View

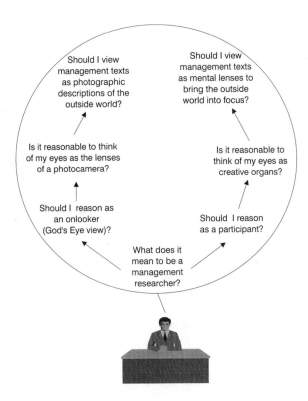

Figure 17.3b. Research From a Philosophical Hermeneutics Point of View

The practical implications of philosophical hermeneutics are illustrated in Figures 17.3a and 17.3b. Figure 17.3a presents research according to traditional Cartesian epistemology. This approach treats epistemological questions independently from ontological ones. A researcher working in this tradition is not specifically required or inspired to address ontological questions, or trained to deal with them. He will at once take a particular epistemological viewpoint and do research from there. Figure 17.3b presents research from a philosophical hermeneutics point of view. In this approach, we explicitly address ontological questions at the same time as epistemological ones.

2. Campbell and Philosophical Hermeneutics

Starting in the 1970s, Campbell began developing an active interest in hermeneutics. It was one of his undergraduate students who brought hermeneutics to his attention. As Campbell put it in his 1977 William James Lectures,

I have been lucky all my teaching career to have students, most often undergraduates, highly concerned for my education, eager both to correct error and to bring me up to date on the intellectual currents that are stimulating them. At Northwestern, their tutorials and reading assignments have exposed me to existentialism, phenomenology, structuralism, dialectics and, most puzzling of all, hermeneutics. How could a doctrine about the exegesis of archaic religious texts provide an epistemology usable in science? Under the guiding rule that where there's smoke there's fire, or that intelligent people are not stupid and therefore must be getting at something (a rule I often reluctantly apply), I've tried to puzzle out how this could be. (1988, p. 478)

One of the hermeneutical issues that particularly caught Campbell's imagination was the extent to which trust in a shared rationality plays a role in textual interpretation (1988, p. 477) and interpretive acts in general (1978, p. 187; Campbell & Paller, 1989, pp. 234-236). To underline the importance of trust, he invented the slogan "omnifallibilist trust" (Cook & Campbell, 1986). Campbell noticed a connection between willingness to "trust" and the principle of charity as elaborated in the work of W. V. Quine, a philosopher he greatly admired—see also proposition 10b. Thus, Campbell viewed the hermeneutical literature as a source of arguments that justify the belief in shared rationality even if we cannot offer a scientific foundation for this belief (Cook & Campbell, 1986). He developed a checklist of hermeneutical principles of his own (e.g., 1991b, 1995), which he called "validity-seeking hermeneutics." He even went so far as to reinterpret his own research on cultural differences in optical illusions as an enactment of the principle of charity (e.g., 1986, p. 111; 1991b, pp. 594; 1996).

Campbell never played an active role in the hermeneutical movement at the same level as he did in the philosophical school of thought called evolutionary epistemology (EE). He never cited the work of Heidegger, who laid the groundwork for philosophical hermeneutics, emphasizing instead the contributions of Schleiermacher, Dilthey, Habermas, and Weber (see the appendix to this chapter for a brief discussion of the views of these hermeneutical philosophers). He explicitly stated that he was more interested "in hermeneutic methodology rather than assumptions about human nature" (1991b, p. 594). It is also debatable whether Campbell fully understood philosophical hermeneutics. He explicitly acknowledged that his knowledge of this literature was incomplete (1991b): "I feel sure that in that vast literature there are many other hermeneutic principles, but I do not recollect encountering such a list (This is a request for help)" (p. 589).

We have reason to believe, nevertheless, that Campbell was in the process of taming the idea of philosophical hermeneutics. Initially, he judged Gadamer to be "in net, an ontological nihilist," a Weberian ideal-type category that he had invented to classify researchers and philosophers believing in nothing (1991b, p. 588). However, he added that the hermeneutical literature had frustrated him,[15] that he was "not prepared to cite chapter and verse" and that perhaps ontological nihilism is an ideal type with no occupants, not even the "paradigm theorists [Kuhn and his disciples] of education and the social sciences." Indeed, Campbell (1995, pp. 22-23) appropriated Gadamer's "interpretive horizon" and dropped his accusations of nihilism altogether. Instead, he proposed hermeneutics as the successor philosophy of positivism.

3. An Exercise in Hermeneutics: Applying the Principle of Charity

Given the prominence of the principle of charity in a hermeneutical worldview, I illustrate how this principle works. As Campbell very succinctly explained, the principle of charity comes into play when a reader encounters an argument inconsistent with her own views. It is tempting, then, to put the paper or book down, and to conclude that the author was dumb, confused, or a dilettante. The principle of charity counters this temptation and instructs us to make an effort to translate the ideas of the author into our own worldview and vocabulary. As Quine (1960) puts it,

> The maxim of translation underlying all this is that assertions startingly [*sic*] false on the face of them are likely to turn on hidden differences of language. The maxim is strong enough in all of us to swerve us even from the homophonic method that is so fundamental to the very acquisition and use of one's mother tongue. (p. 59)

We translate the troubling passage in such a way that we bring to the surface the conditions under which we would agree with the arguments of the author: Which one of our own taken-for-granted assumptions do we need to alter to align our views with those of the author? While we raise this question, we may find that we disagree with the author because he built his arguments on a set of taken-for-granted assumptions different from what we consider acceptable. In other words, our disagreement with the author is motivated by a collective ignorance: we did not pay enough attention to each other's set of background assumptions. So, our misunderstanding is not based on incommensurable idiosyncrasies.

To illustrate how the principle of charity works, I interpret Campbell's arguments for *ontologically real groups*. I primarily focus on Campbell's New

York essay. I first read this essay from a superficial perspective without paying attention to Campbell's philosophical work. In that case, this essay looks like an invitation to research the effects of ontologically real groups in corporations. Then I read the New York essay from a philosophical hermeneutics–informed perspective. Now, I come to view Campbell as a problem-coper. He is attempting to figure out how to make sense of the problem of cooperation in the face of selfish behavior. I discover that I Campbell has three different options to deal with this problem, and that the textual evidence does not really indicate which option Campbell prefers. So, as a reader, I also must choose: I must decide how to interpret these ambiguities in Campbell's work. I can choose between a God's Eye way of handling these ambiguities and a participant approach.

In the God's Eye approach, I could conclude that the world *is* paradoxical (Rescher, 1987): It is difficult to make sense of Campbell's texts because texts mirror a paradoxical reality; texts *are* ambiguous and *have* multiple meanings. Then I would be making a nonfalsifiable dogmatic statement about the extra-mental reality. As elaborated in Proposition 12b, it is impossible to find out whether the world is really paradoxical or whether you use this argument to cover up your own ignorance. Moreover, this argument acts like a confusing lens. It suggests that it is all right to nurture ignorance and accept paradoxes rather than use them as an inducement to reexamine taken-for-granted assumptions (the process that Argyris and Schön (1974) call double-loop learning). So, I would not be a very charitable reader if I were to conclude that Campbell had given up on coping with inconsistencies.

As I will argue below, the participant frame of reference points us in a different direction: Campbell was struggling with a genuine problem. He was searching for words to express his thoughts on the moral implications of neo-Darwinism. He was writing to open up a dialogue about troublesome moral assumptions that we use during theory development and research without necessarily realizing it. Campbell's texts contain several ambiguous and contradictory passages given that he was experimenting with various words and arguments in his search to articulate his intuitions in the clearest way. He was in the process of clarifying his own thought processes.

As indicated in part 1 of this chapter, I believe that we, as authors, all somehow are working in a participant frame of reference (at least, I am). If we use concepts and arguments that resonate with a God's Eye view of the world, this is not because we dogmatically believe in such a view, but rather because we do not reflect enough on how our words and rhetorical style reinforce one or the other worldview. Thus, I choose to interpret Campbell as a problem-coper. I eliminate those interpretations implying that Campbell was working in a God's Eye frame of reference.

To summarize, the hermeneutical exercise below illustrates how the meaning of a text is never self-evident. We always have to make a leap of faith and must choose whether or not to be charitable.

Surface Interpretation (God's Eye Approach)

"Groups are real!" Campbell wrote in the New York essay in 1992. In the same sentence, he cited his own work on this topic published in 1958. At first, Campbell's position seems quite clear. It is worthwhile to study groups and organizations in their own right. Perhaps, one day in the 1950s, Campbell had a flash of insight and said to himself something like this: "Eureka! Herbert Spencer was right. Ontologically distinct groups really exist out there in society, and we in social psychology better continue to develop and refine theories to make sense of them. Groups and organizations have properties of their own that cannot be fully grasped by just studying the individuals that make up these groups and organizations. Let's write a paper on how the boundaries of these organizations are formed, and where these boundaries begin and leave off."

The "groups are real" interpretation of the New York essay seems even more justified when we read Campbell's arguments about *downward causation*. One of his most concise summaries of this argument is this:

> Where natural selection operates through life and death at a higher level of organization, the laws of the higher level selective system determine in part the distribution of lower level events and substances. Description of intermediate-level phenomena is not completed by describing its possibility and implementation in lower level terms. Its presence, prevalence, or distribution (all needed for the complete explanation of biological phenomena) will often require reference to laws at a higher level of organization as well. Paraphrasing Point 1, for biology, all processes at the lower levels of a hierarchy are restrained by, and act in conformity to, the laws of the higher levels. (1990b, p. 4)

Figure 17.4 visualizes this argument. One way to grasp the essence of downward causation is to contrast it with the idea of *upward causation*— Point 1 in the quotation above. Upward causation implies that all processes at the higher levels of organization are restrained by and act in conformity to the laws of lower levels, including the levels of subatomic physics (Campbell, 1990b, p. 4). This argument is sometimes also called explanatory reductionism (Mayr, 1982, pp. 60-62). Broadly speaking, at least nine levels of complex organization are identified (Mohr, 1989, p. 138): the subatomic particle, the atom, the molecule, the macromolecule, the unicellular organism or cellular organelle, the cell of the multicellular organism, the organ, the individual, and the group. The atomic properties of molecules have an upward effect on the aggregations of molecules, the higher levels of biological organization. The behavior of the higher-level entities must be explained in terms of the behavior of the lower-level entities. Although the upward causation argument may seem obvious today and too trivial to mention, we should keep in mind that leading evolutionary biologists such as Mayr (1982, pp. 60-62) question the generality of this argument.[16]

As elaborated in the quotation above, the *downward causation* argument suggests that the higher-level system also affects the behavior at the lower level of organization, especially in living systems (Pattee, 1973). In spite of the widespread interest in hierarchies, however, one is still rather uncertain about the classification of hierarchies and their special attributes (Mayr, 1982, p. 64). For example, although it is generally agreed that level eight, the individual level, has a downward causal effect on

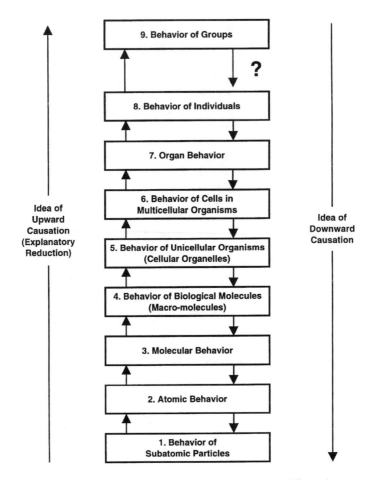

Figure 17.4. Visual Presentation of the Arguments for Upward and Downward Causation

the lower levels in the hierarchy, it is less certain whether level nine, the group, also has downward effects. It is actively debated whether groups and group behavior are qualitatively distinct from individuals and interpersonal behavior, and whether different and additional concepts are required to analyze groups (Hogg, 1995a, p. 270).

It is in this context that the "groups are real" movement manifests itself in sociology, social psychology, evolutionary biology, and philosophy of biology. The scholars in this movement argue that we *do* have reason to believe that groups have properties that go beyond the individual human beings making up the group; to completely understand the behavior of an individual, we first must

study the characteristics of the crowd or society to which the individual belongs. Groups make individuals do things they never would have done on their own. In biology, Wynne-Edwards (1962) usually is credited with having introduced this argument. In sociology, Durkheim often is viewed as the founding father of "groups are real" research, given that he introduced the notion of "collective forces" in *Suicide, a Study of Sociology* (1897/ 1951, p. 309; cited in Hacking, 1990, p. 177).

Collective tendencies have a reality of their own; they are forces as real as cosmic forces, though of another sort; they, likewise, affect the individual from without, though through other channels. The proof that the reality of collective tendencies is no less than that of cosmic forces is that this reality is demonstrated in the same way, by the uniformity of effects.

When an individual commits suicide, it is *not* because of his individual desires or lack thereof, but because of "suicidogenetic currents" operating at the societal level; different societies produce different rates of suicide.[17] In the same way that we must study groups to identify average characteristics and behaviors of the individuals making them up, "groups are real" scholars, like Durkheim, argue that the study of populations of ontologically *real* groups or societies is required to comprehend the characteristics and behaviors of these supra-individual entities, that is, those causal forces acting on individuals.

Reading Campbell's New York essay at the surface suggests that he is part of the above-discussed movement. His position has the following two characteristics. First, he explicitly rejects the idea of group selection in the biological evolution of vertebrates (1972, 1979, 1982b, 1983). Although he used this argument (1965a) to make sense of group conflict and the willingness of males to sacrifice their life for their nations, he changed his mind after reading the 1966 work by the biologist Williams (Campbell, 1972):

> What I now wish to revise is the source of these dispositions. In greater continuity with the mainstream of social psychological thought, I now believe that these self-sacrificial dispositions, including especially the willingness to risk death in warfare, are in man a product of a social indoctrination, which is counter to rather than supported by genetically transmitted behavioral traits. (p. 23)

Second, he believed that these social forces exist independently from biological forces and actually "can override biological evolution and lead individuals to do things that are biologically stupid in terms of *individual* inclusive fitness." Social evolution counters "individual selfish tendencies which biological evolution has continued to select as a result of genetic competition among the cooperators" (1975b, p. 1115). Given that Boyd and Richerson (1985) made a similar argument, Camp-

bell cites them in support of his position (e.g., 1991c, p. 96; 1994a, pp. 27-29; Campbell & Specht, 1985, p. 38).

Figure 17.5 summarizes Campbell's surface position on the existence of ontologically real groups. A superficial reading of Campbell's New York essay indicates that management researchers had better investigate the conditions favoring individual and face-to-face group selection as opposed to firm-level selection, especially when the individual and group selection processes tend to erode firm-level innovations: "firm-level adaptations will be under continual undermining pressures from individual and face-to-face group preferences" (Campbell, 1994a, p. 38).

Hermeneutically Informed Interpretation (Participant Approach)

Reading the New York essay from a hermeneutic perspective, however, an entirely different interpretation emerges. According to propositions 5b-8b, we must conceptualize Campbell's text as a mental lens to help in comprehending and coping with problems. Such a "problem-coping view" of Campbell's work requires us to identify the problem that he was fascinated by *before* attempting to make sense of his texts. We need not look far to grasp the problem that was puzzling Campbell. In the fourth paragraph of his New York essay (1994a), he states:

> Methodological individualism dominates our neighboring field of economics, much of sociology, and all of psychology's excursions into organization theory. This is the dogma that all human social group processes are to be explained by laws of individual behavior—that groups and social organizations have no ontological reality—that where used, references to organizations, and so on, are but convenient summaries of individual behavior. So pervasive is this dogma that even in a group of social scientists focused on laws of social organization (such as those represented in this book and in the exciting conference it represents) adhere to it, or at least have not self-consciously rejected it. To get into the issues of this chapter we must reject methodological individualism as an a priori assumption, make the issue an empirical one, and take the position that groups, human social organiza-

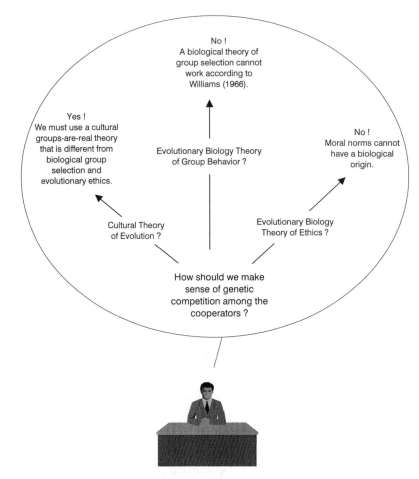

Figure 17.5. Surface Interpretation of Campbell's "Groups Are Real" Arguments

tions, *might be* ontologically real, with laws not de-rivable from individual psychology. Indeed, some principles of organizational form cannot be in any sense attributes of individual persons. One of my favorite early papers (Campbell, 1958) explicitly sides with that strident minority of sociologists who assert that "Groups are real!" even though it finds human organizations "fuzzier" than stones or white rats. (pp. 23-24)

It is clear that Campbell did not like methodo-logical individualism, but he does not give us any clues as to why. In the paragraph quoted above, however, he indicates that there is a problem with individual psychology. To appreciate what is at fault with methodological individualism, we must

first discover what is wrong with individual psy-chology. Campbell gave no references to the litera-ture on individual psychology with which he has a problem. We need to read on.

At this point, we must choose among two inter-pretive directions. We could conclude that Camp-bell implies that there is something wrong with *every* theory of individual psychology that has ever been written. Furthermore, no matter how much effort psychologists put into their work, we may safely conclude that a satisfactory theory of indi-vidual psychology will never be achieved. Certain aspects of economic and social reality, such as cooperation, simply cannot be understood by studying how individuals' schemas are constructed and how these schemas are used to make sense of and guide their relationships with the extra-mental world. Campbell therefore concluded that the only reasonable alternative is to adopt the concept of "ontologically real groups."

Alternatively, we could assume that Campbell believed something is wrong with *some* theories of individual psychology, and he was searching for words to expose the weaknesses of these theories to us. In this latter interpretation, an important objective is to discredit problematic theories. If Campbell used strong and dramatic language, it is because he was getting carried away in his zeal to rally support for his ideas and not because he intended to discredit *every* theory of individual psychology.

Indeed, in his earlier work, Campbell made quite clear which theories of individual psychology he had a problem with: those *normatively* grounded in the neo-Darwinian theory of evolutionary biology (1975b; Campbell & Specht, 1985, pp. 35-36). Neo-Darwinism implies that the gene (or groups of genes) is the unit of selection (Dawkins, 1976). Certain "selfish" genes induce behavior that makes it more likely that these genes are present in a higher number in the next generation: You exist today because your ancestors had fewer moral hesitations about behaving selfishly than their fellow human beings. If we push this neo-Darwinian argument to the limit, we must conclude that our ancestors were genetically programmed to choose those moral norms that enhanced their own genetic fitness; thus, there is no need to feel guilty about behaving selfishly yourself. Campbell had a problem with this line of reasoning that what is, biologically, is therefore morally good. He called it "ethically unjustified normative biologism." He considered this type of reasoning "nihilistic" (see especially Campbell, 1979).

As a social human being, Campbell believed there is more to being human than acting out a selfish genetic program. From a scientific viewpoint, however, Campbell thought he had to accept neo-Darwinian arguments to avoid rejecting biological evolution. Thus, it appears that Campbell developed his "groups are real" arguments *not* for the "surface" reason that groups exist and therefore deserve study, but rather to neutralize the moral implications of neo-Darwinism that he considered

unacceptable. Indeed, according to the New York essay (1994a):

> Accepting the dogma of *no biological group selection of human traits*, I (Campbell 1975b, 1979, 1982b, 1983, 1991c) have attributed the capacity of organized human beings for ultrasociality to cultural evolution. I have argued that the culturally evolved moral norms are predominantly preaching against the very sort of personality that biological individual selection would produce—tendencies for selfish and nepotistic cheating on the social contract, free-riding and free-loading on the altruistic products of others, etc. (p. 26)

The answers to the questions raised in the context of propositions 1b and 2b—Which audience is Campbell addressing? What meaning do Campbell's words have?—now become clear. Campbell's primary audience are those individuals puzzled by normative biologism. Campbell's arguments need to be situated in the dialogue investigating how to deal with the conflict between commonsense ethics and biologically inspired ethical systems. Campbell is tickling our mind. He wants us to reflect on these issues of egoism and nepotism. He does not want us to blindly accept them as scientific facts. With respect to the question raised in the context of proposition 2b, Campbell used the words "selfishness" and "self-sacrifice" in the context of violence and warfare. These words had a vivid meaning for him. He did not use them as stylized facts that are easy to tract mathematically.

Let us now take a second look at the dilemma facing Campbell—how to make sense of cooperation without having to reject Darwinism. On the surface, it may seem that the only option available to Campbell was to argue for a (blind) variation-selection-retention analogy of ontologically real groups—a variation of his 1965b chapter.[18] In reality, however, Campbell had three possible research agendas from which to choose, outlined in Figure 17.6. The first option, A, was to conclude that neo-Darwinian biologists were misusing the word "theory." The word "theory" is usually employed to denote "a statement of relations among concepts within a set of boundary assumptions and constraints" (Bacharach, 1989, p. 496). Thus, a

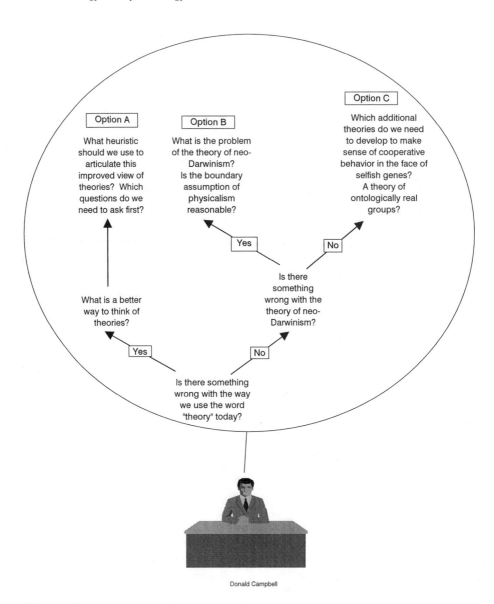

Figure 17.6. Donald Campbell's Dilemma

theory is mainly a linguistic construct, consisting of nothing more than words uttered in a conversation or black dots printed on paper. How the theory "connects" with the extra-mental reality is a function of the epistemology a researcher endorses. It is one of the many boundary assumptions constraining a theory. As indicated in the introduction, Campbell made important contributions to EE (e.g.,1974b). Because "evolutionary" epistemol-ogy is different from traditional Cartesian episte-mology, a theory of Darwinism consistent with EE must be different from one conceived in a tradi-tional epistemological worldview.

Traditional epistemology tried to answer the problem of knowledge without presuming any knowledge in the process. It pursued questions of knowledge independent from ontological ques-tions. The end result was skepticism. EE, on the other hand, deliberately begs questions about the possibility of knowledge. It assumes that knowledge *is* possible. In addition, it brings ontological questions into the epistemological conversation. We make "hypothetically ontological" statements when articulating epistemological viewpoints (Campbell, 1974c, p. 141; 1987, p. 165). For example, an individual arguing for EE implicitly makes a statement about himself as a biological knowing creature emerging from an evolutionary process of trial and error elimination *and not* a descendant of Adam and Eve or the designed end product of an evolutionary process started by the Creator himself. The argument that we *cannot* pursue epistemology independent from ontology is also at the basis of philosophical hermeneutics as discussed in part 1 of this chapter.

Given that Campbell was one of the founders of EE, we would expect him to have been in the process of sketching a new meaning for the concept "theory" that takes this new view of the relation between ontology and epistemology into account—if he had not developed it already.

Campbell's second option, B, was to conclude there was something wrong with the neo-Darwinian theory of natural selection. In this view, there would be nothing wrong with the concept of theory in and of itself, but there might be something wrong with certain elements of neo-Darwinism. For example, evolution might be punctuated with bursts of mutations and then periods of stabilization (Eldredge & Gould, 1972) rather than the gradual accumulation of mutations, as Darwin originally proposed.

The third option available to Campbell, C, was to conclude that humanity needs a separate theory for the study of cooperation. According to this third option, there would be nothing wrong with the concept of "theory" or the neo-Darwinian view of evolution. The theory of neo-Darwinism may be kept in its entirety—the selfish gene *is* the unit of selection; human beings *are* selfish and nepotistic (on average). To cover the full spectrum of human behavior, we need to complement the neo-Darwinian theory of evolution with additional theories to make sense of those aspects of human behavior that cannot be explained by neo-Darwinism itself. As discussed above, neo-Darwinism does

not adequately explain self-sacrificing and moral behavior; therefore, the additional theory would have to make sense of this type of action.

On the surface, it appears that Campbell chose option C. He explicitly accepted a hard-line neo-Darwinism and the principle of downward causation (e.g., 1974a; Campbell & Paller, 1989, p. 232), and he clarified on several occasions that his theory of cultural evolution describes a set of phenomena that act independently from those elaborated in theories of biological evolution (e.g., 1972, 1979, 1982b, 1983).

Just because Campbell tentatively explored option C, however, does not mean it was his final choice, as the tension in the following paragraph reveals:

> Even though the primary message of my chapter requires a continual ongoing conflict between behaviors that optimize organized groups and behaviors that optimize an individual's personal and nepotistic interest (which I pose as a conflict between the products of biological and cultural evolution), I do not want to deny that our biological evolutionary history, way back to its prehuman primate roots, has been increasingly social, and that our biological human nature contains innate adaptations furthering some forms of sociality (possibly the products of biological group selection). (1994a, p. 29)

Here, it appears that Campbell was not content with the "conflict between the products of biological and cultural evolution." He reluctantly wondered whether or not it is possible to develop a theory of evolution in which the cultural and biological forces are not at odds with one another. For example, one of the newer approaches in evolutionary biology is the study of the evolution and adaptive value of cognitive capabilities in animals (e.g., Bechtel, 1993). This research question resonates well with Campbell's (1990b) arguments about the evolution of problem-solving strategies—from non-mnemonic problem solving in blue-green algae, bacteria, and protozoa to scientific problem solving in the higher primates. Thus, possibly, Campbell was contemplating option B, the development of a theory of biological evolution that explicitly makes sense of the evolution of cognition and behavior in itself; that is without reduction into genetics. Rereading Campbell's work reveals indeed that he wrote extensively on the importance of creativity. In the New York essay, he stated:

> Not at all do I deny the importance of creative thought. . . . Certainly when we come to business firm–level adaptations, creative thought rather than blind chance will most often be the source of the group-level variations upon which selection of firms operates. I have expanded natural-selection analogies into a general selection theory, and from this expanded perspective, the occurrence of intelligent planning as a source of group-level adaptations is not in conflict with our shared evolutionary perspective. (1994a, p. 31)

This quotation clarifies that Campbell viewed creativity as fundamentally different from stochastic processes—the random tautomerizations of electrons in the DNA molecules controlling gene expression in the brain. That the issue of creativity played an important part in the worldview of Campbell also can be derived from his complaint that inadequate attention had been paid to his work on creativity: "Too frequently, I have been misread as *denying* creativity" (1990a, p. 9).

We also find passages, albeit not in the New York essay, indicating that Campbell pursued option A, the development of a new conception of the word "theory." He called his own epistemological position "hypothetical realism" (1959; 1993a, p. 89). He argued that this position has all along been consistent with an antirealism *both* for scientific beliefs and ordinary individual perception (Campbell, 1993a, p. 89; Campbell & Paller, 1989, p. 234). This argument is not surprising given that Campbell, in the earlier part of his career, demonstrated that visual perception is culturally biased (e.g., Segall, Campbell, & Herskovits, 1966).

The curious thing is that once you take the hypothetical and contingent nature of "groups are real" arguments into account, you will find that Campbell weakened his own arguments about the realness of groups. For example, consider the introductory paragraph in the New York essay. Why did Campbell write "*might* be ontologically real" instead of "are ontologically real"? Why did he bother italicizing "might"? Did he have second thoughts about committing himself to this argu-

ment? He did not add an italicized "might" to the other arguments in his New York essay. The following paragraph (Campbell, 1994b, p. 148) also is intriguing:

> In 1958, I published a paper that remains a favorite of mine. It is a contribution to the "groups are real" literature, using the Gestalt principles of perceptual organization to relativize the concepts of thing or entity even for physical-object exemplifications. This relativization allows, and provides imperfect criteria for, positing "real" ontological status for some social organizations.

Is Campbell suggesting here that we need to interpret the "groups are real" argument as a schema to organize our thought processes about organizational phenomena *and not* a "real" entity some of us are capable of measuring, studying, and testing?

In summary, it is possible to derive the following five interpretations from the foregoing contradictions in Campbell's New York essay, as outlined in Figure 17.7:

1. Campbell was not really sure which one of the three options A, B, or C he should pursue. He was "frustrated."
2. Campbell was deliberately ambiguous about his viewpoints on neo-Darwinism, selfish/opportunistic conceptions of managers, the ontological reality of groups, and the meaning of the word "theory." He believed contradictions invoke creative thought and prevent the freezing of thinking and premature closing of the minds of his readers (Poole & Van de Ven, 1989; Starbuck, 1988).
3. Campbell was searching for a new way to make sense of the word "theory," consistent with his arguments for an evolutionary epistemology (option A).
4. Campbell believed we need a better conception of what it means to be human than what neo-Darwinism offers (option B).
5. Campbell believed that it is impossible to reject the theory of neo-Darwinism; therefore, in order to make sense of cooperative behavior, neo-Darwinism needs to be complemented with theories of social behavior, for example, theories that postulate that groups are ontologically real (option C).

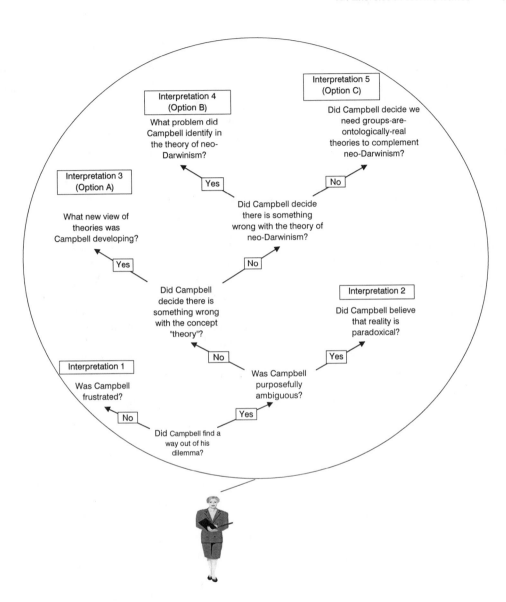

Figure 17.7. The Dilemma of a Campbell Scholar

Applying the Principle of Charity to Campbell's Own Work

How should we interpret Campbell's New York essay? Which one of the five interpretations should we choose? Campbell is not here anymore, so we cannot ask him. Even if we could ask him and he confirmed our choice, we cannot exclude the possibility that Campbell is just eagerly performing his "duty to the dialectic processes of scholarship," encouraging younger scholars to publish their work (1991a, p. 166).

At face value, it looks like we need to choose interpretation 1. Our discussion indicates a level of ambiguity in Campbell's work. On one hand, he seems to be promoting the "groups are real" argument, but at the same time, he downplays his own argument by italicizing "might" in the New York essay and calling it a "relativization" (Campbell, 1994b, p. 149). If we were to choose interpretation 1, we could find additional evidence that Campbell was flip-flopping between positions. On one hand, Campbell (1991c) rejects the idea that moral intuitions may have a biological origin, but at the same time, he himself makes the conceptual leap from selfish genes replicating themselves inside bodies to selfish behavior by the "whole" bodies themselves. He even makes this leap with respect to nepotism. In the New York essay, he writes "I find that I use [the biological] term [inclusive fitness] as a substitute for *self-interest,* as a sociobiological expansion of self-interest to include nepotism" (1994a, p. 25). How could Campbell question the argument that our morals have a biological origin and at the same time state that he uses biological terms as a substitute for moral concepts such as self-interest and nepotism?

Another inconsistency is his treatment of the correspondence *theory* of truth. Campbell explicitly rejects this definition of truth (1991b, pp. 588-589; 1994b, p. 128). At the same time, he argues that we must strive for a correspondence *goal* of truth, that we still may maintain a "correspondence definition of the meaning of "truth" (Campbell & Paller, 1989, p. 252). Now, how can you, as a scientist, claim that the goal of science is to get closer to the truth and, at the same time, argue that it is impossible to measure whether theories correspond to reality? Either you believe you can measure the extent to which theories correspond to phenomena under investigation, or you believe you cannot. You cannot make both arguments at the same time.

This brings us to interpretation 2: that Campbell deliberately added contradictions to his papers. Maybe Campbell believed that the reality *is* paradoxical, and he included a few inconsistent statements in every paper to remind readers of the intrinsic ambiguities in the outside world and its "buzzing, booming confusion." In this second interpretation, Campbell would be working within the postmodern tradition that contradictions and inconsistencies are a sign of our times: We need to learn to accept contradictions rather than worry about them. This interpretation is not very plausible. Campbell himself never wrote a paper stating

that paradoxes may have pedagogical value (Morgan, 1988). In addition, this second interpretation is not very interesting. The outside world is already complex and ambiguous in itself. It is difficult enough to make sense of this world; it is easy enough to articulate paradoxical statements by accident. It would be counterproductive to complicate sense-making processes by adding additional layers of contradictory statements on purpose. This brings us back to interpretation 1: Is Campbell frustrated? Has he given up on making sense of genetic competition among the cooperators?

When we investigate the above identified interpretive dilemma through the lenses of hermeneutical philosophy, an entirely different answer unfolds. How you interpret the work of Donald Campbell is a function of your frame of reference. You may choose among two reference frames, a God's Eye frame or a participant frame. Are you reading the work of Campbell from the perspective of an onlooker—as if you are standing outside the universe in the shoes of the Creator? If you are, you would be justified in concluding that the New York essay gives a muddle-headed impression. It contains several contradictory statements.

Or are you reading Campbell's work as a participant in an ongoing dialogue attempting to understand what it means to be human? The participant view inspires you to reason as if you are situated in a quadrangle. The text acts as a pair of mental glasses focusing how the author experienced the phenomena. You need to think of Donald Campbell as an optician, a lens crafter. He was in the process of crafting improved mental lenses to focus your thoughts on "hypothetically normative" heuristics to guide social interactions. He was searching for words to communicate his ideas.

If we then apply the principle of charity and assume that Campbell was on the same track as his favorite philosophers, and we read his work again, we find many passages indicating that interpretation 3 (option A) is the most valid one. When we make epistemology evolutionary, we must also develop an evolutionary conception of the word "theory." In Campbell's words, we cannot treat the word "theory" as if it is a clairvoyant picture of the reality. For example, we cannot interpret the neo-Darwinian theory of biological evolution in a literal way, as a natural fact: "It is obvious that the direct invocation of biological evolution to justify *scientific* beliefs has to be given up" (Campbell & Paller 1989, p. 232). Although Campbell does not communicate it in exactly my words, it looks like he was in the process of articulating a view of theories as manufactured instruments, mental lenses. He was "looking" through the theories he encountered and investigating whether these theories clarified his thoughts or, alternatively, confused him. For example, when Campbell "looked through" the theory of neo-Darwinian evolution, he noticed that it contradicted many of common-sense notions of ethics. As he illustrated in his 1975 presidential address at the meeting of the American Psychological Association in Chicago, Campbell was not someone who easily dismissed common sense. Rather, he used the extent to which our theories are consistent with or contradict our commonsense "recipes for living" as a test for the cross-validity of these theories and a stepping-stone to develop new theories (1978, pp. 186-187, 192). In this view, his arguments about cultural forces are an attempt to make sense of the contradictions between commonsense wisdom and scientific wisdom.

At the same time that Campbell was attempting to make sense of the contradictions between our moral norms in use and the norms predicted by neo-Darwinism, he also was in the process of constructing an epistemology that would overcome the contradictions between science and common sense without completely rejecting one or the other viewpoint—evolutionary epistemology (EE). In the 1970s, he discovered philosophical hermeneutics, or validity-seeking hermeneutics as he called it. He realized that both hermeneutics and EE reject the separation of ontological from epistemological questions. We all make ontological statements about humans as knowers when we argue for a particular epistemological position. EE sets up researchers as members of a biological community—an intercommunicating gene pool—emerging in an evolutionary process of trial and error elimination. Hermeneutics inspires us to think of researchers as individuals having faith in the rationality they share with the other members of their human community. By 1992, Campbell had four

publications on the importance of validity-seeking hermeneutics. Two more would follow. It looks, therefore, like he was working through the hermeneutical literature at the time he was preparing the New York essay; he was in the middle of sorting out his thoughts on how to use hermeneutics as a guide for practicable research.

In this interpretation, it would be unfair to interpret Campbell as dogmatically defending the "groups are ontologically real" argument—interpretation 5 (option C). Even though some still may consider this argument a valid explanation (e.g., Walsh, 1995, p. 286), it is hard to ignore the problematic nature of this argument. Perhaps, the immediate problem is the difficulty, if not impossibility, of connecting this argument to human experiences—proposition 11b. It is *by definition* impossible to test whether a causal group force or a supernatural force is making an individual act in a particular way. If group forces really are out there, they are also acting on us, the researchers. What we retrospectively call "free will" (Bourgeois, 1984) in reality is a "group force" guiding our behavior. To test this argument, we would have to step outside our own existence, hang in outer space, and then look down to observe the group forces in action to become inspired on how to test them—which is impossible.

A second problem is that, to make this research approach credible, we need to prove in a nonhuman way that cultural group forces really operate out there. For example, you could claim that the Creator revealed in a dream that some of the choices of researchers are guided by a still-to-be-identified transcendental force. (Descartes used a "dream" argument to make his materialistic philosophy more palatable.) But how can an argument appealing to the supernatural guide practical decision making? How can arguments like these promote informed discussion—proposition 12b? Would it not be simpler to study schemas (Fiske & Morling, 1995, pp. 489-494) and how they influence the social identity of an individual (Hogg, 1995b)? Third, most of us learned about "groups are real" forces from the literature, that is, by reading "texts." In this view, we need to evaluate "groups are real" arguments as a function of their textual qualities—we could evaluate them as if they were mental lenses crafted by researchers/opticians. This brings to the foreground that, as far as we know, human beings created this argument. The interesting and puzzling question then is why we would construct arguments that a priori state there must be limits to what we, researchers, are able to comprehend and do, and at the same time state that it is impossible to know these limits? Arguments like these are not very practicable—proposition 13b. Might it not be better to just consider these arguments artifacts, abandoned thought experiments inherited from the past?

Given Campbell's continued emphasis that all theories are potentially open to revision, the more charitable interpretation is that Campbell himself was in the process of revising his position in the "groups are real" movement. Campbell formulated his "groups are ontologically real" arguments in the earlier part of his career—his first publication on this issue was in 1958. He wrote most of his papers on hermeneutics later in life—he mentioned hermeneutics for the first time in his 1977 William James lectures. So, it is reasonable to surmise that Campbell was in the process of switching to a worldview informed by philosophical hermeneutics at the time he wrote the New York essay. In this view, the inconsistencies in Campbell's texts surface as accidental by-products of his struggle to find the right words to articulate a new conception of the word "theory" and, based on that, a new conception of what it means to be human that moves beyond neo-Darwinian explanations of selfish behavior. The interpretation that Campbell was about to abandon the "groups are real" position seems even more credible given that a large number of today's social psychologists decided to opt out of the formal controversy about the need for supraindividual constructs (Hogg, 1995a, pp. 269-270).

Discussion, Conclusion, and Implications

With this chapter, I present an exercise in philosophical hermeneutics and, at the same time, make a call to add it to the tool kit of management researchers. I analyze the paper Campbell presented at the 1992 New York conference on orga-

nizational evolution—the "New York essay"—to illustrate the need to pay more attention to philosophical hermeneutics. Although Campbell did not discuss hermeneutics specifically in that essay, he wrote it at the same time he reiterated elsewhere (1995, p. 19; 1996) that hermeneutics is a promising philosophical approach to develop "a new consensus on the theory of science." Somehow, the researchers attending the 1992 conference did not take up this call for more serious research on the value of hermeneutics for management studies— none of the chapters in *Evolutionary Dynamics of Organizations* (Baum & Singh, 1994), or most of the others in this volume for that matter, mentions the role that hermeneutics plays in Campbell's work. The editors' introduction and McKelvey's chapter on "Campbellian realism" are exceptions.

At least two things can be learned from studying Campbell the philosopher. The first lesson is to develop a more sophisticated understanding of hermeneutics. Campbell was explicit in his excitement about this stream in philosophy. He even requested help to come up with a better checklist than the one he developed (Campbell, 1991b, p. 589). Once you take Campbell's interest in hermeneutics seriously, you discover that there is indeed an "Interpretive Turn" taking place in philosophy (Hiley, Bohman, & Shusterman, 1991; see the appendix for more details). As discussed in part 1 of this chapter, the core idea of philosophical hermeneutics is that we all must ask ontological questions together with epistemological ones. At face value, it may seem that ontological questions are questions about the objects in the outside world. In reality, they are questions about how we make sense of our own existence and our relationship with the entities that make up the environment. Our perception of these entities is a function of how we perceive our own position in the world. We may choose from at least two frames of reference to make sense of our existence and relationships, a God's Eye and a participant frame. Each of these frames gives a different meaning to the process of studying a scholar's work—the environmental entities called "text." In the God's Eye frame, we become inspired to treat the text as a crude photograph of the content of the mind of the author that itself contains a set of digitalized photo negatives of the outside reality. This frame downplays our own subjective input in the reading process. In the participant frame, we engage in an imaginary dialogue with the author. The text acts as a lens bringing into focus what the author is attempting to communicate as well as our own thoughts.

Philosophical hermeneutics foregrounds the continuous imaginary negotiation taking place between readers and authors. These linguistic negotiations—Campbell (1993a, p. 89) called them social negotiations—determine the meanings we attach to words and arguments. For these negotiations to take place, however, we first must assume that authors possess the same type of rationality as we do. This is expressed in proposition 10b. It is in our best interest—assuming we want the conversation to continue—to view the authors we read and people with whom we carry on discourse as equally rational. We cannot assume a priori that authors lack the capability, or background knowledge, to communicate something substantive. If we search for it, we will always find a passage that, at face value, sounds rather preposterous or illogical, but that cannot in itself be grounds to completely dismiss a viewpoint. If we do not include *every* voice in the conversation, we run the risk of leaving out those that turn out to make a significant difference after all. Given that in many cases the authors are dead, or too busy to spend time with you to explain what they mean by word so-and-so—alternatively, you may not have that kind of time—every text will contain a residual level of ambiguity. When you encounter opaque passages, you never will be able to prove beyond reasonable doubt that the author was not confused or "stupid," to use Campbell's favorite word. Instead, you first must believe in a shared rationality. You must have faith that the Other is as rational as you.

The growing recognition of the value of philosophical hermeneutics emerges out of the realization that it is impossible to construct timeless criteria to decide in advance that a viewpoint is so unimportant that you should not bother reading about it and attempting to understand it, or that you may officially label it "irrelevant" (Rorty, 1987, p. 39). We never can exclude the possibility that our ignorance makes us misinterpret the words of an author. Alternatively, getting a better understanding of dissenting viewpoints allows us to notice weaknesses in our own educational systems. Said differently, we need to think of these arguments as lenses and not as statements of facts. What is the most interesting lens? Is it one that a priori assumes that it is acceptable to categorize authors as a function of whether or not they are too muddle-headed to be communicating something substantive? Or is it one that assumes a shared rationality and that inspires you to treat the ambiguities you encounter in a text as opportunities for furthering the dialogue? Which of the two lenses is best suited to cope with ignorance?

This brings us to the second lesson: what it means to practice philosophical hermeneutics. While constructing this interpretation of Campbell's later philosophical work, we go twice through a hermeneutical exercise—that is, how to be charitable interpreters. The first hermeneutical exercise is Campbell's New York essay. How should you interpret this essay? Did Campbell want to convince you to continue the study of ontologically real groups—interpretation 5 (option C)? Or was Campbell trying to persuade you to develop a more sophisticated understanding of the linguistic signs, "epistemology" and "theory," a process that may lead to an interpretation of biological evolution not requiring the assumption of selfishness and nepotism—interpretation 3 (option A)? Stated differently, did Campbell think that the chapter on human egoism is closed, that evolutionary biology has *proven* that human beings *are* selfish and nepotistic (on average) and the most honest act is to accept that and develop social institutions to control the selfish activities of humans? Or was Campbell in the process of figuring out that this argument about egoism is a cultural artifact that we inherited from the religious literature on original sin? Given the opportunity, would he rewrite the New York essay and encourage management researchers to investigate the connection between scientific and religious practices and use the insights generated by that activity to study the factors promoting firm longevity? Although Campbell did not state the latter conclusion explicitly, it looks like it would just have been a matter of time for him to have published such an argument. For example, Campbell (1975b) argued that traditional religious moral teaching may act as a better source of commonsense recipes for living than psychology and psychiatry. He also stated,

> One way of achieving that epistemic humility would be to try to translate religious truths into modern metaphors. It seems desirable that sympathetic social scientists study those religious scriptures, parables, commandments, prayers, affirmations, sermons, etc. that are suspected of having a message worth preserving, and attempt to restate them in metaphors consistent with the scientific world image. Many will deal with human nature, and these should be relatively easy to translate. Others will present supra-individual social system truths, and for these we as yet have no generally accepted social science concepts. (1991c, p. 93)

If we combine this statement with Campbell's arguments about the subjective element in knowledge construction (1984, p. 28), that theories are underdetermined (1978, p. 188; 1991b, p. 589), and his many references to Knorr-Retina's (1981) *The Manufacture of Knowledge* (e.g., 1982a, p. 327; 1984, p. 31; 1986, p. 118; 1993a, p. 89; Holzner, Campbell, & Shahidullah, 1985, p. 309), it looks like it would have been just a matter of time for Campbell to have pointed out that religious truths are also manufactured and that, unfortunately, a few of them are not very enlightening. In that view, the arguments for biological selfishness/opportunism possibly are inspired by the theological fascination for the notions of evil and sin, and they are, just like these theological arguments, fabrications of the mind.

Which interpretation of Campbell's work you choose depends on your frame of reference and how you apply the principle of charity. If you believe that people are selfish on average and that the idea of sin is historically real, then you are more likely to interpret several of Campbell's works (1975a, 1975b, 1991c) as evidence that Campbell believed in some form of sin and evil himself. In that view, you probably accept the various arguments about nepotism and selfishness in the New York essay as universal truths. You probably agree with Campbell that we must warn "firms" that there exist "selfish groups" that vicariously undermine firm-level implementations. If, on the other

hand, you view these arguments about sin as fiction that even some of the early Christians found puzzling—if God is good and omnipotent, why would He send a serpent to tempt Adam and Eve; why would He make us pay for their missteps? (Pagels, 1988)—then you may be more likely to choose interpretation 3 (option A), or possibly interpretation 4 (option B). In that case, you would view the New York essay as a crude call for a better understanding of how human beings relate to one another—the study of face-to-face groups.

The second hermeneutical exercise, then, is Campbell's appropriation of philosophical hermeneutics. Campbell took a first stab at articulating what this philosophy stands for. He was explicit about the incompleteness of his own understanding. Thus, if you want to dismiss philosophical hermeneutics, it is easy do so. You could conclude that hermeneutics deals with minor interpretive details that serious management researchers with which do not need to concern themselves and that Campbell's excitement about hermeneutics was exaggerated. Alternatively, you may interpret Campbell's work on validity-seeking hermeneutics as a signal of an important turn in Campbell's own philosophical thinking. As discussed in the paragraph above, the interpretation you favor is a function of the extent to which you apply the principle of charity.

Once you appropriate this principle, you may find that many others express their excitement about having discovered hermeneutics. Perhaps the following quotation, taken from Kuhn (1977, p. xii; cited in Rorty, 1979, p. 323, and Bernstein, 1983, p. 31), most clearly summarizes the maxim of hermeneutically informed research.

> When reading the works of an important thinker, look first for the apparent absurdities in the text and ask yourself how a sensible person could have written them. When you find an answer, I continue, when those passages make sense, then you may find that more central passages, ones you previously thought you understood, have changed their meaning.

Adding philosophical hermeneutics to our tool kit and paying it the same level of attention that we give to statistical and mathematical techniques offers the prospect of developing improved understanding of who we are, and who and what we are studying. We interpret the texts in our field in different ways because we come from different backgrounds and, hence, have different levels of ignorance. Disagreement about how to make sense of a management paper or book brings this ignorance into focus. A better understanding of what it means to be human may help us better cope with ignorance. It may lead to improved communication among authors and readers and a speedier process of moving ideas from their early academic origins into enlightened managerial practice.

Appendix:
What Is Philosophical Hermeneutics?

Given that the term *hermeneutics* has several different meanings and that, to my knowledge, these variations in hermeneutics have not been discussed in the context of management studies, I briefly clarify what *philosophical hermeneutics* stands for and how it is different from other approaches to hermeneutics. The following discussion of hermeneutics is adapted from part I of Palmer (1969) and chapter 1 of Crusius (1991).

From a historical perspective, philosophical hermeneutics is primarily a European and, to some extent, even a German philosophical school of thought. It was practiced independently from analytical and logical empiricist philosophy. Over the last 10 years, however, post-analytical and post-logical empiricist philosophers have rediscovered hermeneutics as a unique philosophical approach that may help address their conundrums. This development is sometimes referenced as the "Interpretive Turn" (e.g., Hiley et al., 1991).

The core of philosophical hermeneutics is that it questions a traditional epistemology and philosophy of science approach. Since René Descartes, philosophy (of science) has been preoccupied with epistemological problems. Its basic questions are "How do we come to know anything?" and "How can be sure of what we claim to know?" So conceived, Cartesian epistemology sets up management research as a search for knowledge of what happens in companies and markets. It ignores, however, the question we must raise prior to studying knowledge: "What does it mean to be a being?"—an ontological question. There is nothing to know and hence no problem of knowledge without "beings"—someone capable of knowledge, something to know about. Ontological questions therefore must be asked at the same time as epistemological questions. Said differently, we can address ontological questions in two ways. We can assume that the questions about the ontology of the environment can be asked independently of questions about our own ontology—the God's Eye view of ontology. Or we can assume that our answers to questions about the ontology of the outside world are a function of how we address the question of our own ontology. The arguments about frame of reference are introduced in the conversation for this purpose: to allow people to understand that their perceptions of their own existence affect their perception of the phenomena in the outside world. Martin Heidegger—in *Being and Time* (1927/ 1962)—generally is recognized as having pointed out the importance of ontological questions about our selves. He also provided the impetus for Hans-Georg Gadamer's extensive development of philosophical hermeneutics in *Truth and Method* (1960/1975).

To fully grasp what philosophical hermeneutics stands for, it is necessary to realize that there are at least four *other* ways in which the word "hermeneutics" has been used (Crusius, 1991, pp. 3-6; Palmer, 1969, pp. 33-45). In its first meaning, hermeneutics is biblical interpretation, a theory of biblical exegesis. For example, how should a minister interpret those passages where Luke, Matthew, and John talk about Jesus' confrontation with the devil? In its second meaning, it is philological methodology. What is the philological origin of the words "devil" and "Satan?" What other meanings have these words independent of the Scriptures? In its third meaning, it becomes the science of all linguistic understanding. Friedrich Schleiermacher (1819/1977) believed it would be possible to develop a set of universally applicable rules to uncover the true meaning of any text—not just the Scriptures. In the fourth meaning, then, it is a methodological foundation for the social sciences. William Dilthey (1926/1988), a biographer of Schleiermacher, argued that because human beings are different from the entities studied in physics, we need a special "historical" methodology to study human actions. This fourth usage of the word "hermeneutics" is similar to Weber's *Verstehen*.

Philosophical hermeneutics differs from biblical, philological, scientific, and social science methodology hermeneutics in its view of the status of interpretation. As Crusius (1991, p. 5) puts it, interpretation is not primarily a science—or art, if you prefer—that is, the special discipline of priests, constitutional lawyers, or professors. Rather, it is human "being," our mode of existence in the world. That is, hermeneutics does not come into play only when intersubjective understanding fails, as in the case of the Protestant and Roman Catholic Church Fathers. It is not only an instrument for overcoming or preventing misunderstanding, as it was for Schleiermacher. It is not just the enabling discipline of the human sciences, as it was for Dilthey. Rather, *interpretation* constitutes the

world in which we exist. We always find ourselves in the midst of interpretations carried by sounds traveling in the air, texts in books sitting on bookshelves, and habits we have inherited from the past. We need to become more conscious, therefore, of the interpretive heuristics we use.

This brief discussion of hermeneutics hardly does justice to the growing literature on interpretive issues. For example, I did not discuss Paul Ricoeur's contribution to hermeneutical philosophy or the widely publicized Habermas-Gadamer controversy (Ingram, 1980). I also did not situate Derrida's position that texts do not project stable linguistic meaning, but operate as fluidly changing networks in conjunction with shifting intertextual relations with other texts, in ways that mirror shifting social convention and disguises.

Notes

1. There are many similarities between philosophical hermeneutics and Weick's *Sense-Making in Organizations* (1995). For example, both use the words "interpretation" and "sense-making." There are also important differences. Perhaps the most obvious difference is situated in how Weick clarifies the word "interpretation." He suggests that the word "connotes an activity that is more detached and passive than the activity of sense making" and that "when people discuss interpretation, it is usually assumed that an interpretation is necessary and that the object to be interpreted is evident" (Weick, 1995, p. 14). Philosophical hermeneutics attaches a much broader meaning to the term "interpretation": being *is* interpreting (Crusius, 1991). In this hermeneutical view, if interpretation is perceived to be a passive process, this has more to do with the attitude of the interpreting individual than with the interpretive process itself.

2. Bohr expressed on several occasions that physicists must be agnostic and not try to explain what the Creator had in mind while starting up the universe (Loder & Neidhardt, 1996, p. 285). It is unlikely, therefore, that he wanted us to view the thesis of complementarity as a natural causal law linking macroscopic Newtonian properties with quantum-level properties. Instead, he proposed the thesis of complementarity as a heuristic device to make sense of the inconsistencies between Newtonian and quantum mechanics (Loder & Neidhardt, 1996; MacKinnon, 1996). One such inconsistency is the relationship between a quantum object as a wave and as a particle, two classical concepts that are mutually exclusive in both classical and quantum theory. The experimental detection of a particle is usually its location at a point in space (e.g., on a photographic plate) at a particular time. A wave, on the other hand, is defined

in terms of wavelength and frequency, which are related to the momentum and energy, the conservation of which is the basis of causality.

An additional problem is that Newtonian and quantum mechanics are the product of two incompatible philosophical systems (Faye, 1991). Newton believed he was describing the universe as created by God, as if, he, Isaac Newton, could imagine what God was doing during the first second of the universe. This belief acted as an assumption in his mental model: He presupposed a strict and immutable separation between the means of observation—the observer—and the object under study. Newton thus endorsed an epistemology that the researcher can step outside his existence and study the universe from a God's Eye point of view. From that position, a researcher should be able to discover the true nature of the universe and the true causal forces governing change.

The theory of relativity, on the other hand, explicitly presupposes that it is impossible to ascribe properties to objects independently of the experimental setups in which they make themselves known. The theory of relativity shows that the properties described by the classical Newtonian concepts are not absolute, but are relative to a frame of reference selected by the subject (Faye, 1991, pp. 169-170). Thus, quantum mechanics is based on an epistemology that presumes the researchers to be an insider—a part of the detecting instrument—and not an outsider.

We must view the complementarity thesis, therefore, as an attempt to overcome inconsistencies in a practicable way. To be sure, to this day physicists are not sure what to make of the inconsistencies between quantum mechanics and Newtonian mechanics and Bohr's answer to these paradoxes (Beller, 1993; MacKinnon, 1996, p. 270).

3. Throughout the chapter, I use the terms "reference frame," "frame," "view," "worldview," and "viewpoint" interchangeably to denote what social psychologists call a "schema"—a cognitive structure that organizes an individual's knowledge about an object, person, or situation, including knowledge about attributes and relationships among those attributes (Fiske & Morling, 1995).

4. I primarily quote from Hilary Putnam's (1981) *Reason, Truth, and History* in this chapter, but one should keep in mind that other philosophers such as John Dewey, Richard Rorty, Michael Dummett, and Floyd Merrell made similar arguments. For a historical review of arguments against the God's Eye view, see Linsky (1997, pp. 128-132).

5. As students of Popper may realize, Figures 17.1a-b, 17.2a-b, 17.3a-b, and 17.5-17.7 are visual presentations of Karl Popper's Three World View. The globe symbolizes World 1, the material world as discussed in theories of physics, chemistry, and biology. The human figures symbolize World 2, the world of mental states and processes. The book stands for World 3, the emergent world of products of the human mind. For more details, see Popper (1979, 1994) and Popper and Eccles (1977/1993).

6. In *Treatise on Man*, Descartes developed his now famous machine theory of living creatures. He decided not to publish this work after he heard of the trouble that the Roman Catholic Church had caused Galileo. For a historically informed discussion of Descartes' machine views on vision, see Smith (1976, pp. 170-174) and Wolf-Devine (1993).

7. Philosophy literature offers several terms to denote the participant worldview, such as the internal view (Putnam, 1981, p. 50) and the pragmatists' worldview (Putnam, 1981, p. 50; 1995; Rorty, 1982, pp. xiii-xlvii). I choose the term "participant"—which Bernstein (1983) also extensively uses—because this term neutralizes the us-vs.-them or insider-vs.-outsider dichotomy that is implicit in the God's Eye frame.

8. The term "human species" is used here for the following reason. One of the core insights of philosophical hermeneutics (and postmodernism) is that we need to give up the quest for certainty: It is humanly impossible to develop an indubitable foundation of rational criteria that can be used to resolve disputes of any kind. We will never obtain certainty; we will never be able to exclude the possibility that *we* (and not the others) are wrong. This raises the question whether it is still meaningful to strive for consensus: If it is impossible to develop a set of timeless criteria of rationality, we cannot use agreement and consensus as a measure of progress toward truth. For all we know, the consenting group may have been brainwashed by a particular theory like the German citizens of the 1930s and 1940s who used evolutionary biology to justify their racial policies and genocide (Lerner, 1992). Thus, if consensus in itself cannot be a measure of rational progress toward truth, we cannot exclude the possibility that arguments in favor of consensus are part of a political scheme that has nothing to do with getting access to true knowledge in itself. For reasons like these, researchers such as Cannella and Paetzold (1994) and Van Maanen (1995a, 1995b; Elsbach, 1994) argue *against consensus.* In their view, we need to think of academia as consisting of several communities, each developing its own body of theories and text. If the views of these communities conflict, so be it. No community—no matter how many members it has, no matter how much these members agree among themselves—has the right to question, judge, or condemn the views of other communities.

I believe we do not need to go that far and reject the idea of consensus in its entirety. Biology offers a justification for consensus. The biological species concept developed by Mayr (1963) stresses that species have a reality and an internal genetic cohesion owing to the historically evolved genetic program that is shared by all members of the species. According to this concept, then, the members of a species constitute a reproductive community. They draw from the same large intercommunicating gene pool. They form a set of groups of interbreeding natural populations that are reproductively isolated from other species (Mayr, 1992, p. 17). In this view, as long as human beings are able to reproductively mix their genes with one another, there is no reason to believe that they can form academic communities with norms of rationality that are incommensurable with one another. Said differently, Cannella, Paetzold, and Van Maanen's position would make sense only if we could establish that the various discourse communities in management are reproductively isolated. As long as we cannot establish this condition, we must accept a shared rationality. It is in this spirit that I use the term "human species" rather than "society" or "culture."

One could object that, as a the human genome sequencing project approaches completion, it should be possible to develop genetic markers for irrationality in the same way as one claims to have developed such genetic markers for schizophrenia. As Oyama (1985), Lerner (1992), and many others indicate, however, the implicit assumption in this model is that we can unambiguously separate genetic from environmental influences. Such a model would block the study of how the *interactions* between genes and their cellular context determines what happens to the individual—which is problematic. A second problem is the role of researchers in such studies. Which criteria would exclude the possibility that researchers rather than their research subjects are irrational? The case of Nazi research practices indicates that this problem is real and not imagined. It is more productive, therefore, to presume that the members of the human species share the same rationality, however defined.

9. Many similarities exist between Kuhn's (1962/1970) *The Structure of Scientific Revolutions* and philosophical hermeneutics, as Kuhn himself acknowledges (e.g., 1977, pp. xiii-xv). It should be stated, however, that the field of philosophy (as well as management) is still divided about the merits and contributions of Kuhn's work. On one hand are those who claim that Kuhn promoted mob psychology (Scheffler, 1967, p. 81) and that he presented a relativistic position that he recanted at a later point in time when he realized how nonsensical it was (Hunt, 1990, pp. 2-5; 1992, p. 89). On the other are those who claim that we must first become familiar with existential, phenomenological, and hermeneutical philosophy to fully grasp the significance of Kuhn's work. In the view of this latter group, the claim that Kuhn's *The Structure of Scientific Revolutions* is an argument for relativism (in the pejorative meaning of the word) indicates that the author of that claim is reasoning in a God's Eye view (Rorty, 1987, p. 41) and is unsure how to act like a charitable interpreter.

10. Many of the arguments presented in this section are also present in the writings of French philosopher Jacques Derrida (1967/1973, 1967/1976, 1967/1978). For a collection of essays on how to interpret the work of Derrida, see Madison (1993).

11. Space limitations prevent me from properly discussing the complete philosophical context of the arguments for a participant frame of reference and against a God's Eye frame of reference. There exist connections with pragmatism and constructivism. Pragmatism shares with philosophical hermeneutics a concern with practice: We should not cognitively divorce theory development from the situation in which the resultant theories are applied or implemented; a commitment to develop practicable theories should guide our philosophical choices and resultant preferences for management theories. Pragmatism is a primarily American philosophy that was developed about 100 years ago by Charles Peirce, William James, and John Dewey and is now experiencing a revival. See Rorty

(1979, 1982) for more details on the link between hermeneutics and pragmatism.

Constructivism is a movement in mathematics and science education, and curriculum design in general which holds that "knowledge is not passively received either through the senses or by way of communication, but is actively built up by the cognising subject" (von Glasersfeld, 1988, p. 83), as a result of an a priori conceived frame of reference interacting with the individual's sensory inputs. Constructivists reject "objectivist" teaching traditions in which it is the teacher's responsibility to map a reality or structure onto the mind of a student by controlling the learning process to progress toward previously determined outcomes. Instead, constructivists argue that students live in a particular mental model that they use to make sense of experiences and the information they are confronted with during the learning process. Individuals more easily learn and change their mental models when the presented information is linked to their existing mental models. Constructivism and philosophical hermeneutics share an interest in understanding the role of mental models in sense making. Whereas philosophical hermeneutics addresses the relationship between mental models and ontological issues, constructivism focuses on developing teaching methods that take into account the mental model in which a student lives. Steffe and Gale's 1995 book contains a collection of essays on the core tenets of constructivism. For a bibliography on constructivism, see Selden and Selden (1996).

12. This historically informed review of the demise of the picture theory of language is taken from Romanos (1983). See also Block (1981) for a more general discussion of the philosophy of Ludwig Wittgenstein.

13. The problem of the arbitrariness of the choice of presuppositions is also known as the problem of infinite regress. The arguments for a participant way of reasoning are based on the presupposition that it is futile to attempt to understand what happened during that very first fraction of time of the existence of the universe—what Ferris (1988, p. 413) calls the 10^{-43} second ABT interval of time (where ABT stands for "after the beginning of time"). Aristotle was one of the first philosophers to point out that this line of reasoning would lead to an infinite regress problem (Toulmin & Goodfield, 1965, pp. 31-32, 42-45): We could always subdivide that first fraction of time further, or we could ask what happened in the fraction of a second of time before it. We eventually begin to feel like a fly zooming around in a fly-bottle (Wittgenstein, 1953). For a discussion of the problem of infinite regress in the context of management research, see Collis (1994).

14. A reviewer of this paper wondered why I capitalized words such as First Day, First Second, Creator and God given that, as he said, they are just metaphors. Indeed, from a surface reading it might seem that the participant view reinforces atheism. *This surface interpretation is incorrect.* As discussed in the opening section of this chapter, hermeneutics came into existence as a discipline attempting to unravel the messages communicated in the Scriptures. The question that these hermeneutical philosophers inevitably had to address is whether it is meaningful to reason as if we can imagine what happened on

the First Day of the universe independent of whether we take a religious or scientific approach to answering this question. Although the scope of hermeneutics broadened to include many additional interpretive acts that have nothing to do with religion in itself, the hermeneutical enterprise nevertheless remains linked with theology.

Although from a surface viewpoint it may seem that science promotes atheism, the history of the relation between science and theology is more nuanced. Science emerged out of natural theology. Scientists such as Isaac Newton (see note 2) viewed their theories as rational justifications for the existence of God and how He had created the world. Newton ascribed the arrangement of the planets to the aesthetic considerations that had weighted with God (Brooke, 1996, p. 8). Thus, whereas science may be secular in practice, from an intellectual viewpoint it is not necessarily so. Theologians, philosophers, and scientists are exploring the extent to which science and religion may coexist (e.g., Richardson & Wildman, 1996).

In this dialogue, it makes more sense to stay away from atheism and take a middle of the road approach such as agnosticism or apophatic theology. Agnosticism, which means literally "not-knowism," is used here in strong meaning (Sutherland, 1993). In this meaning it implies that one "does not believe that there *can be* knowledge of a God who transcends this world. . . . We could no more know that God does not exist, than that God does exist" (1993, p. 15). In this view, an agnostic would refuse to engage in conversations about the existence of God given that this conversation topic is impossible to settle: None of the conversation partners has personally met God or knows someone who did. The only pieces of "evidence" we have of the existence of God are texts, and it is impossible to decide whether these texts should be interpreted literally or metaphorically. This strong-form agnosticism should be differentiated from a weaker meaning in which agnosticism stands for the "belief that we do not have sufficient reason to affirm or deny God's existence" (1993, p. 15). In this weaker meaning, atheism is equally plausible as theism. Someone might conclude from the fact that they do not have sufficient reason to affirm the existence of God, that disbelief in God is the appropriate attitude. In strong-form agnosticism, on the other hand, atheism is not an option because the question about the existence of God is never asked.

Apophaticism is a term used to refer to a particular style of theology, which stresses that God cannot be known in terms of human categories (Winters, 1998). Apophatic (which derives from the Greek *apophasis*, "negation" or "denial") approaches to theology are especially associated with the monastic tradition of the Eastern Orthodox church.

Given that these so-called middle of the road type of viewpoints do not explicitly deny the existence of God, the arguments in this chapter about the "Creator," "God," "First Day," and so on are not purely metaphorical. I therefore capitalize these terms.

15. Campbell expressed here a frustration that probably everyone learning about hermeneutics experiences sooner or later. From a superficial perspective, it is easy to be shocked by the rejection of certainty implicit in philosophical hermeneutics, and to feel compelled to write articles and books to save science and humanity from the nihilistic implications of some forms of philosophical hermeneutics. For example, when Cambridge University decided to confer an honorary doctorate to Jacques Derrida, one of the intellectual heirs of Gadamer, "some of the most eminent names in academic philosophy, including Sydney's Professor David Armstrong, Harvard's Willard van Orman Quine and Yale's Ruth Barcan Marcus" unsuccessfully campaigned against this decision (Rothwell, 1992a, 1992b). They believed that Derrida's work represented an antiphilosophical (unprofessional) attack on the values of reason, truth, and scholarship. Similarly, Donaldson (1992) and Beyer (1992) felt compelled to critique the Wittgensteinian notion of a language game elaborated by Astley and Zammutto (1992). Donaldson (1992) called it a management approach "in which students are told that any problem can be licked by dreaming up a sufficiently ambiguous set of words to bedazzle the stakeholders—Voodoo Management or Management by Mumbo Jumbo" (p. 464). As Campbell himself acknowledged, however, the more you study hermeneutics, the more you come to realize that the accusations of ontological nihilism are misleading.

16. See Hoyningen-Huene and Wuketits (1989) and Charles and Lennon (1992) for a review of the idea of reductionism and its problems.

17. See Hacking (1990, pp. 170-179) for a historical introduction to Durkheim's "collective tendencies are real" arguments.

18. In this chapter, Campbell presented a (blind) variation-selection-retention analogy to make sense of sociocultural evolution. He also applied this analogy to the study of creative thought (1974c). The three essentials of this analogy are (a) the occurrence of *variations*: heterogeneous, haphazard, "blind," but in any event variable (the mutation process in organic evolution and the exploratory responses in learning); (b) consistent *selection* criteria: selective elimination, propagation and retention (differential survival of certain mutants in organic evolution, and differential reinforcement of certain responses in learning); and (c) a mechanism for the preservation, duplication, or *propagation* and *retention* of the positively selected variants (the rigid duplication process of the DNA in viruses, prokaryotes, plants, and animals; memory in learning). In management, this analogy has been applied to make sense of the emergence of new organizational forms (e.g., Aldrich, 1979), internal corporate venturing in diversified corporations (Burgelman, 1983), and the emergence of new strategic initiatives (Burgelman, 1991), to give a few examples.

References

Abel, T. (1953). The operation called "Verstehen." In H. Feigl & M. Brodbeck (Eds.), *Readings in the philosophy of science* (pp. 677-687). New York: Appleton-Century-Crofts.

Aldrich, H. E. (1979). *Organizations and environment.* Englewood Cliffs, NJ: Prentice Hall.

Allison, G. T. (1971). *Essence of decision: Explaining the Cuban Missile Crisis.* Boston: Little, Brown and Company.

Argyris, C., & Schön, D. (1974). *Theory in practice.* San Francisco: Jossey-Bass.

Astley, W. G., & Zammutto, R. F. (1992). Organization science, managers, and language games. *Organization Science, 3*(4), 443-460.

Bacharach, S. B. (1989). Organizational theories: Some criteria for evaluation. *Academy of Management Review, 14*(4), 496-515.

Bartlett, C. A., & Ghoshal, S. (1993). Beyond the M-form: Toward a managerial theory of the firm. *Strategic Management Journal, 14*(Winter Special Issue), 23-46.

Baum, J.A.C., & Singh, J. V. (1994). *Evolutionary dynamics of organizations.* Cambridge, MA: Oxford University Press.

Bechtel, W. (1993). Decomposing intentionality: Perspectives on intentionality drawn from language research with two species of chimpanzees. *Biology and Philosophy, 8,* 1-32.

Beller, M. (1993). Einstein and Bohr's rhetoric of complementarity. In M. Beller, J. Renn, & R. S. Cohen (Eds.), *Einstein in context* (pp. 241-256). New York: Cambridge University Press

Bernstein, R. J. (1983). *Beyond objectivism and relativism: Science, hermeneutics, and praxis.* Philadelphia: University of Pennsylvania Press.

Beyer, J. M. (1992). Metaphors, misunderstandings, and mischief: A commentary. *Organization Science, 3*(4), 467-472.

Blackburn, S. (1994). *The Oxford dictionary of philosophy.* Oxford, UK: Oxford University Press.

Block, I. (1981). *Perspectives on the philosophy of Wittgenstein.* Cambridge, MA: MIT Press.

Bohr, N. (1928). The quantum postulate and the recent developments in atomic theory. *Science, 121,* 580-590.

Bohr, N. (1934). *Atomic theory and the description of nature.* Cambridge, UK: Cambridge University Press.

Booth, W. C. (1974). *Modern dogma and the rhetoric of assent.* Notre Dame, IN: University of Notre Dame Press.

Booth, W. C., Colomb, G. C., & Williams, J. M. (1995). *The craft of research.* Chicago: University of Chicago Press.

Bourgeois, L. J., III. (1984). Strategic management and determinism. *Academy of Management, 9*(4), 586-596.

Boyd, R., & Richerson, P. J. (1985). *Culture and the evolutionary process.* Chicago: University of Chicago Press.

Brooke, E.J.H. (1996). Science and theology in the Enlightenment. In W. M. Richardson & W. J. Wildman (Eds.), *Religion & science: History, method, dialogue* (pp. 7-28). New York: Routledge.

Burgelman, R. A. (1983). A process model of internal corporate venturing in the diversified major firm. *Administrative Science Quarterly, 28,* 223-244.

Burgelman, R. A. (1991). Intra-organizational ecology of strategy making and organizational adaptation: Theory and field research. *Organization Science, 2*(3), 239-262.

Callebaut, W. (1993). *Taking the naturalistic turn or how real philosophy of science is done.* Chicago: University of Chicago Press.

Campbell, D. T. (1958). Common fate, similarity, and other indices of the status of aggregates of persons as social entities. *Behavioral Sciences, 3*(1), 220-228.

Campbell D. T. (1959). Methodological suggestions for a comparative psychology of knowledge processes. *Inquiry, 2*(3), 152-182.

Campbell, D. T. (1965a). Ethnocentric and other altruistic motives. In D. Levine (Ed.), *The Nebraska Symposium on Motivation* (pp. 283-311). Lincoln: University of Nebraska Press.

Campbell, D. T. (1965b). Variation, selection, and retention in socio-cultural evolution. In H. R. Barringer, G. I. Blanksten, & R. W. Mack (Eds.), *Social change in developing areas: A reinterpretation of evolutionary theory* (pp. 19-48). Cambridge, MA: Schenkman.

Campbell, D. T. (1972). On the genetics of altruism and the counter-hedonic components in human culture. *Journal of Social Issues, 28*(3), 21-37.

Campbell, D. T. (1973). Ostensive instances and entitativity in language learning. In W. Gray & D. Rizzo (Eds.), *Unity through diversity: A festschrift for Ludwig von Bertalanffy* (pp. 1043-1047). New York: Gordon and Breach.

Campbell, D. T. (1974a). "Downward causation" in hierarchically organized biological systems. In F. Ayala & T. Dobzhansky (Eds.), *Studies in the philosophy of biology* (pp. 179-186). London: Macmillan.

Campbell, D. T. (1974b). Evolutionary epistemology. In P. A. Schilpp (Ed.), *The philosophy of Karl Popper* (pp. 413-463). La Salle, IL: Open Court.

Campbell, D. T. (1974c). Unjustified variation and selective retention in scientific discovery. In F. Ayala & T. Dobzhansky (Eds.), *Studies in the philosophy of biology* (pp. 139-161). London: Macmillan.

Campbell, D. T. (1975a). The conflict between social and biological evolution and the concept of original sin. *Zygon, 10,* 234-249.

Campbell, D. T. (1975b). On the conflicts between biological and social evolution and between psychology and moral tradition. *American Psychologist, 30*(4), 1103-1126.

Campbell, D. T. (1978). Qualitative knowing in action research. In M. Brenner, P. Marsh, & M. Brenner (Eds.), *The social contexts of method* (pp. 184-209). New York: St. Martin's.

Campbell, D. T. (1979). Comments on the sociobiology of ethics and moralizing. *Behavioral Science, 24,* 37-45.

Campbell, D. T. (1982a). Experiments as arguments. *Knowledge: Creation, Diffusion, Utilization, 3,* 327-337.

Campbell, D. T. (1982b). Legal and primary-group social controls. *Journal of Social and Biological Structures, 5*(4), 431-438.

Campbell, D. T. (1983). The two distinct routes beyond kin selection to ultra-sociality: implications for the humanities and social science. In D. L. Bridgeman (Ed.), *The nature of pro-social development: Interdisciplinary theories and strategies* (pp. 11-41). New York: Academic Press.

Campbell, D. T. (1984). Can we be scientific in applied social science? *Evaluation Studies Annual Review, 9,* 26-48.

Campbell, D. T. (1986). Science's social system of validity enhancing collective belief change and the problems of social science. In D. W. Fiske & R. A. Shweder (Eds.), *Metatheory in social science: Pluralism and subjectivities* (pp. 108-135). Chicago: University of Chicago Press.

Campbell, D. T. (1987). Neurological embodiments of belief and the gaps in the fit of phenomena to noumena. In A. Shimony & D. Nails (Eds.), *Naturalistic epistemology* (pp. 165-192). Dordrecht, The Netherlands: D. Reidel.

Campbell, D. (1988). Descriptive epistemology: Psychological, sociological, and evolutionary. (From the William James Lectures of 1977). In E. S. Overman (Ed.), *Methodology and epistemology: Selected papers by Donald Campbell* (pp. 435-486). Chicago: University of Chicago Press.

Campbell, D. (1989). Models of language learning and their implications for social constructionist analyses of scientific belief. In S. Fuller, M. De Mey, T. Shinn, & S. Woolgar (Eds.), *The cognitive turn, sociological and psychological perspectives on science* (pp. 153-158). Dordrecht, The Netherlands: Kluwer Academic.

Campbell, D. T. (1990a). Epistemological roles for selection theory. In N. Rescher (Ed.), *Evolution, cognition, and realism: Studies in evolutionary epistemology* (pp. 1-20). Lanham, MD: University Press of America.

Campbell, D. T. (1990b). Levels of organization, downward causation, and the selection-theory approach to evolutionary epistemology. In E. Tobach & G. Greenberg (Eds.), *Theories of evolution and knowing* (pp. 1-18). Hillsdale, NJ: Lawrence Erlbaum.

Campbell, D. T. (1991a). Autopoetic evolutionary epistemology and internal selection. *Journal of Social and Biological Structures*, *14*(2), 166-173.

Campbell, D. T. (1991b). Coherentist empiricism, hermeneutics, and the commensurability of paradigms. *International Journal of Educational Research*, *15*(6), 587-597.

Campbell, D. T. (1991c). A naturalistic theory of archaic moral orders. *Zygon*, *26*(1), 91-114.

Campbell, D. T. (1993a). Plausible co-selection of belief by referent: All the "objectivity" that is possible. *Perspectives on Science*, *1*(1), 88-108.

Campbell, D. T. (1993b). Systematic errors to be expected of the social scientist on the basis of a general psychology of cognitive bias. In P. D. Blanck (Ed.), *Interpersonal expectations: Theory, research and applications* (pp. 25-41). New York: Cambridge University Press.

Campbell, D. T. (1994a). How individual and face-to-face-group selection undermine firm selection in organizational evolution. In J.A.C. Baum & J. V. Singh (Eds.), *Evolutionary dynamics of organizations* (pp. 23-38). New York: Oxford University Press.

Campbell, D. T. (1994b). The social psychology of scientific validity: An epistemological perspective and a personalized history. In W. R. Shadish & S. Fuller (Eds.), *The social psychology of science* (pp. 124-161). New York: Guilford.

Campbell, D. T. (1995). The post-positivist, non-foundational, hermeneutic epistemology exemplified in the works of Donald W. Fiske. In P. E. Shrout & S. T. Fiske (Eds.), *Personality research, methods and theory: A festschrift honoring Donald W. Fiske* (pp. 13-27). Hillsdale, NJ: Lawrence Erlbaum.

Campbell, D. T. (1996). Can we overcome world-view incommensurability/relativity in trying to understand the other? In R. Jessor, A. Colby, & R. A. Shweder (Eds.), *Ethnography and human development* (pp. 153-172). Chicago: University of Chicago Press.

Campbell, D. T., & Paller, B. T. (1989). Extending evolutionary epistemology to "justifying" scientific beliefs (a sociological rapprochement with a fallibilist perceptual foundationalism?) In K. Hahlweg & C. A. Hooker (Eds.), *Issues in evolutionary epistemology* (pp. 231-257). Albany: State University of New York Press.

Campbell, D. T., & Specht, J. C. (1985). Altruism: Biology, culture and religion. *Journal of Social and Clinical Psychology*, *3*(1), 33-42.

Cannella, A. A., & Paetzold, R. L. (1994). Pfeffer's barriers to advance of organizational science: A rejoinder. *Academy of Management Review*, *19*(2), 331-341.

Charles, D., & Lennon, K. (1992). *Reduction, explanation and realism.* New York: Clarendon.

Collis, D. J. (1994). Research note: How valuable are organizational capabilities? *Strategic Management Journal*, *15*(Special issue), 143-152.

Cook, T. D., & Campbell, D. T. (1986). The causal symptoms of quasi-experimental practice. *Synthese*, *68*, 141-180.

Cronbach, L. (1986). Social inquiry for and by Earthlings. In D. W. Fiske & R. A. Shweder (Eds.), *Metatheory in social science: Pluralism and subjectivities* (pp. 83-107). Chicago: University of Chicago Press.

Crusius, T.W.W. (1991). *A teacher's introduction to philosophical hermeneutics.* Urbana, IL: National Council of Teachers of English.

Cziko, G. A., & Campbell, D. T. (1997). *Selection theory bibliography* [World Wide Web page]. Retrieved September 30, 1998 from the World Wide Web: http://www.ed.uiuc.edu/facstaff/g-cziko/stb/

Davidson, D. (1973-1974). On the very idea of a conceptual scheme. *Proceedings of the American Philosophical Association*, *47*, 5-20.

Dawkins, R. (1976). *The selfish gene.* Oxford, UK: Oxford University Press.

Derrida, J. (1973). *Speech and phenomena: And other essays on Husserl's theory of signs* (D. B. Allison, Trans.). Evanston, IL: Northwestern University Press. (Original work published 1967)

Derrida, J. (1976). *Of grammatology* (G. C. Spivak, Trans.). Baltimore, MD: Johns Hopkins University Press. (Original work published 1967)

Derrida, J. (1978). *Writing and difference* (A. Bass, Trans.). London, UK: Routledge. (Original work published 1967)

Descartes, R.. (1967). *Discourse on method, optics, geometry, and meteorology* (P. J. Olscamp, Trans.). Indianapolis: Bobbs-Merrill. (Original work published 1637)

Descartes, R. (1972). *Treatise of man.* (T. S. Hall, Trans.). Cambridge, MA: Harvard University Press. (Original work published 1662)

Dewey, J. (1916). *Essays in experimental logic*. Chicago: Chicago University Press.

Dewey, J. (1929a). *Experience and nature*. London: Allen & Unwin.

Dewey, J. (1929b). *Quest for certainty: A study of the relation of knowledge and action*. New York: Minton, Balch.

Dilthey, W. (1988). *Introduction to the human sciences: An attempt to lay a foundation for the study of society and history* (R. J. Betanzos, Trans.). Detroit, MI: Wayne State University Press. (Original work published 1926)

Donaldson, L. (1992). Managing beyond games: A comment. *Organization Science, 3*(4), 461-466.

Durkheim, E. (1951). *Suicide, a study in sociology* (J. A. Spaulding & G. Simpson, Trans.). Glencoe, IL: Free Press. (Original work published 1897)

Eldredge, N., & Gould, S. J. (1972). Punctuated equilibria: An alternative to phyletic gradualism. In T. J. Schopf (Ed.), *Models in paleobiology* (pp. 82-115). San Francisco: Freeman, Cooper.

Elsbach, K. D. (1994, Winter). An interview with John Van Maanen. *Organization and Management Theory Division Newsletter*, pp. 1-6.

Faye, J. (1991). *Niels Bohr: His heritage and legacy*. Dordrecht, The Netherlands: Kluwer Academic.

Ferris, T. (1988). *Coming of age in the Milky Way*. New York: Anchor/Doubleday.

Fisher, A. (1988). *The logic of real arguments*. New York: Cambridge University Press.

Fiske, S. T., & Morling, B. A. (1995). Schema. In A.S.R. Manstead & M. Hewstone (Eds.), *The Blackwell encyclopedia of social psychology* (pp. 489-494). Cambridge, MA: Blackwell.

Flew, A. (1984). *A dictionary of philosophy*. New York: St. Martin's.

Gadamer, H.-G. (1975). *Truth and method* (G. Barden & J. Cumming, Eds.). London: Sheed & Ward. (Original work published 1960)

Galilei, G. (1960). The assayer (S. Drake, Trans.). In *The controversy on the comets of 1618* (S. Drake and C. D. O'Malley, Trans., pp. 151-336). Philadelphia: University of Pennsylvania Press. (Original work published 1623)

Hacking, I. (1990). *The taming of chance*. New York: Cambridge University Press.

Heidegger, M. (1962). *Being and time* (J. MacQuarrie & E. Robinson, Trans.). London: SMC Press. (Original work published 1927)

Heyes, C. M. (1987). Cognizance of consciousness in the study of animal knowledge. In W. G. Callebaut & R. Pinxten (Eds.), *Evolutionary epistemology: A multiparadigm program* (pp. 105-138). Dordrecht, The Netherlands: D. Reidel.

Hick, J. (1963). *The philosophy of religion*. Englewood Cliffs, NJ: Prentice Hall.

Hiley, D. R., Bohman, J. F., & Shusterman, R. (1991). *The interpretive turn: Philosophy, science, culture*. Ithaca, NY: Cornell University Press.

Hogg, M. A. (1995a). Group processes. In A.S.R. Manstead & M. Hewstone (Eds.), *The Blackwell encyclopedia of social psychology* (pp. 269-274). Cambridge, MA: Blackwell.

Hogg, M. A. (1995b). Social identity theory. In A.S.R. Manstead & M. Hewstone (Eds.), *The Blackwell encyclopedia of social psychology* (pp. 555-560). Cambridge, MA: Blackwell.

Holzner B., Campbell, D. T., & Shahidullah, M. (1985). The comparative study of science and the sociology of scientific validity. *Knowledge: Creation, Diffusion, Utilization, 6*(4), 307-328.

Hoyningen-Huene, P., & Wuketits, F. M. (1989). *Reductionism and systems theory in the life sciences: Some problems and perspectives*. Dordrecht, The Netherlands: Kluwer Academic.

Hull, D. (1988). *Science as a process: An evolutionary account of the social and conceptual development of science*. Chicago: University of Chicago Press.

Hunt, S. D. (1990). Truth in marketing theory and research. *Journal of Marketing, 54*(July), 1-15.

Hunt, S. D. (1992). For reason and realism in marketing. *Journal of Marketing, 56*(April), 89-102.

Ingram, D. B. (1980). *Truth, method, and understanding in the human sciences: The Gadamer/Habermas controversy*. Unpublished doctoral dissertation, University of California, San Diego.

Knorr-Retina, K. (1981). *The manufacture of knowledge: An essay on the constructivist and contextual nature of science*. Oxford, UK: Pergamon.

Kuhn, T. S. (1970). *The structure of scientific revolutions*. Chicago: University of Chicago Press. (Original work published 1962)

Kuhn, T. S. (1977). *The essential tension*. Chicago: University of Chicago Press.

Leibniz, G. (1956). On the general characteristic. In *Philosophical papers and letters: A selection* (L. E. Loemke, Trans. and Ed., pp. 339-350). Chicago: University of Chicago Press. (Original work published 1679)

Lerner, R. M. (1992). *Final solutions: Biology, prejudice and genocide*. University Park: Pennsylvania State University Press.

Linsky, B. (1997). Metaphysics II (1945 to the present). In J. V. Canfield (Ed.), *Philosophy of meaning, knowledge and value in the twentieth century* (pp. 108-133). London: Routledge.

Loder, J. E., & Neidhardt, W. J. (1996). Barth, Bohr, and dialectic. In W. M. Richardson & W. J. Wildman (Eds.), *Religion & science: History, method, dialogue* (pp. 271-289). New York: Routledge.

MacKinnon, E. (1996). Complementarity. In W. M. Richardson & W. J. Wildman (Eds.), *Religion & science: History, method, dialogue* (pp. 255-270). New York: Routledge.

Madison, G. M. (1993). *Working through Derrida*. Evanston, IL: Northwestern University Press.

Mahoney, J. T. (1993). Strategic management and determinism: Sustaining the conversation. *Journal of Management Studies, 30*(August), 173-191.

Mauws, M. K., & Phillips, N. (1995). Understanding language games. *Organization Science, 6*(3), 322-334.

Mayr, E. (1963). *Animal species and evolution.* Cambridge, MA: Harvard University Press.

Mayr, E. (1982). *The growth of biological thought: Diversity, evolution and inheritance.* Cambridge, MA: The Belknap Press of Harvard University Press.

Mayr, E. (1992). Species concepts and their application. In M. Ereshefsky (Ed.), *The units of evolution: Essays on the nature of species* (pp. 15-26). Cambridge, MA: MIT Press.

Mohr, H. (1989). Is the program of molecular biology reductionistic? In P. Hoyningen-Huene & F. M. Wuketits (Eds.), *Reductionism and systems theory in the life sciences: Some problems and perspectives* (pp. 137-161). Dordrecht, The Netherlands: Kluwer Academic.

Morgan, G. (1988). Teaching MBAs transformational thinking. In R. E. Quinn & K. S. Cameron (Eds.), *Paradox and transformation: Toward a theory of change in organization and management* (pp. 237-248). Cambridge, MA: Ballinger.

Morgenbesser, S. (1977). *Dewey and his critics: Essays from the Journal of Philosophy* (Selected, with an introduction by S. Morgenbesser). New York: The Journal of Philosophy, Inc.

Nicholson, N. (1997). Evolutionary psychology: Toward a new view of human nature and organizational society. *Human Relations, 9,* 1053-1078.

Oyama, S. (1985). *The ontogeny of information: Developmental systems and evolution.* New York: Cambridge University Press.

Pagels, E. (1988). *Adam, Eve, and the serpent.* New York: Vintage Books.

Palmer, R. E. (1969). *Hermeneutics: Interpretation theory in Schleiermacher, Dilthey, Heidegger, and Gadamer.* Evanston, IL: Northwestern University Press.

Pattee, H. H. (1973). *Hierarchy Theory: The challenge of complex systems.* New York: George Braziller.

Polkinghorne, J. (1993). Physical science and Christian thought. In A. E. McGrath (Ed.), *The Blackwell encyclopedia of modern Christian thought* (pp. 443-448). Oxford, UK: Blackwell.

Poole, M. S., & Van de Ven, A. H. (1989). Using paradox to build management and organization theories. *Academy of Management Review, 14*(4), 562-578.

Popper, K. R. (1992). *Conjectures and refutations.* London: Routledge and Kegan Paul. (Original work published 1962)

Popper, K. R. (1979). *Objective knowledge: An evolutionary approach.* Oxford, UK: Clarendon.

Popper, K. R. (1994). *Knowledge and the body-mind problem: In defense of interaction* (M. A. Notturno, Ed.). London: Routledge and Kegan Paul.

Popper, K. R., & Eccles, J. C. (1993). *The self and its brain.* London: Routledge and Kegan Paul. (Original work published 1977)

Putnam, H. (1981). *Reason, truth, and history.* Cambridge, UK: Cambridge University Press.

Putnam, H. (1995). *Pragmatism: An open question.* Cambridge, MA: Blackwell.

Putnam, L. L., Phillips, N., & Chapman, P. (1996). Metaphors of communication and organization. In S. R. Clegg, C. Hardy, & W. R. Nord (Eds.), *Handbook of organization studies* (pp. 375-409). Thousand Oaks, CA: Sage.

Quine, W. V. (1951). Two dogmas of empiricism. *Philosophical Review, 60,* 20-46.

Quine, W. V. (1960). *Word and object.* Cambridge, MA: MIT Press.

Rescher, N. (1987). *The strife of systems: An essay on the grounds and implications of philosophical diversity.* Pittsburgh, PA: University of Pittsburgh Press.

Richards, R. J. (1987). *Darwin and the emergence of evolutionary theories of mind and behavior.* Chicago: University of Chicago Press.

Richardson, W. M., & Wildman, W. J. (Eds.). (1996). *Religion & science: History, method, dialogue.* New York: Routledge.

Romanos, G. D. (1983). *Quine and analytic philosophy.* Cambridge, MA: Bradford.

Rorty, R. (1979). *Philosophy and the mirror of nature.* Princeton, NJ: Princeton University Press.

Rorty, R. (1981). Method, social science, and social hope. *The Canadian Journal of Philosophy, 11,* 569-588.

Rorty, R. (1982). *Consequences of pragmatism (essays: 1972-1980).* Minneapolis: University of Minnesota Press.

Rorty, R. (1987). Science as solidarity. In J. S. Nelson, A. Megill, & D. N. McCloskey (Eds.), *The rhetoric of the human sciences* (pp. 38-52). Madison: University of Wisconsin Press.

Rothwell, N. (1992a, May 20). Honor served in Derrida affair. *Australian Higher Education Supplement,* pp. 13, 20.

Rothwell, N. (1992b, May 13). Those dons and the Derrida to-do. *Australian Higher Education Supplement,* p. 13.

Scheffler, I. (1967). *Science and subjectivity.* Indianapolis: Bobbs-Merrill.

Schleiermacher, F.D.E. (1977). *Hermeneutics: The handwritten manuscripts by F.D.E. Schleiermacher* (H. Kimmeerle, Ed., J. Duke and J. Forstman, Trans.). Missoula, MT: Scholars Press. (Original work published 1819)

Segall, M. H., Campbell, D. T., & Herskovits, M. J. (1966). *The influence of culture on visual perception.* Indianapolis: Bobbs-Merrill.

Selden, A., & Selden, J. (1996). *The Mathematical Association of America Online: Constructivism. [World Wide Web page].* Retrieved September 30, 1998 from the World Wide Web: http://www.maa.org/t_and_l/sampler/construct.html

Smith, C.U.M. (1976). *The problem of life: An essay in the origins of biological thought.* London: Macmillan.

Starbuck, W. H. (1988). Surmounting our human limitations. In R. E. Quinn & K. S. Cameron (Eds.), *Paradox and transformation: Toward a theory of change in organization and management* (pp. 19-64). Cambridge, MA: Ballinger.

Steffe, L. P., & Gale, J. (1995). *Constructivism in education.* Hillsdale, NJ: Lawrence Erlbaum.

Styazhkin, N. I. (1969). *History of mathematical logic from Leibniz to Peano.* Cambridge, MA: MIT Press.

Sutherland, S. (1993). Atheism. In A. E. McGrath (Ed.), *The Blackwell encyclopedia of modern Christian thought* (pp. 15-20). Oxford, UK: Blackwell.

Toulmin, S. (1990). *Cosmopolis: The hidden agenda of modernity.* New York: Free Press.

Toulmin, S., & Goodfield, J. (1965). *The discovery of time.* Chicago: University of Chicago Press.

Van Maanen, J. (1995a). Fear and loathing in organization studies. *Organization Science, 6*(6), 687-692.

Van Maanen, J. (1995b). Style as theory. *Organization Science, 6*(1), 133-143.

Veatch, H. (1954). *Realism and nominalism revisited.* Milwaukee, WI: Marquette University Press.

von Glasersfeld, E. (1988). The reluctance to change a way of thinking. *Irish Journal of Psychology, 9,* 83-90.

Von Hippel, E. (1988). *The sources of innovation.* New York: Oxford University Press.

Wächtershäuser, G. (1987). Light and life: On the nutritional origins of sensory perception. In G. Radnitzky & W. W. Bartley III (Eds.), *Evolutionary epistemology, theory of rationality, and the sociology of knowledge* (pp. 121-138). La Salle, IL: Open Court.

Walsh, J. P. (1995). Managerial and organizational cognition: Notes from a trip down memory lane. *Organization Science, 6*(3), 280-317.

Weick, K. (1995). *Sense-making in organizations.* Thousand Oaks, CA: Sage.

Williams, G. C. (1966). *Adaptation and natural selection.* Princeton, NJ: Princeton University Press.

Winters, J. (1998). *Saying nothing about no-thing: Apophatic theology in the classical world* [World Wide Web page]. Retrieved September 30, 1998, from the World Wide Web: http://www.interlog.com/winters/my.papers/apophatic.html

Wittgenstein, L. (1953). *Philosophical investigations* (G.E.M. Anscombe, Trans.). New York: Macmillan.

Wittgenstein, L. (1958). *Preliminary studies for the "philosophical investigations" generally known as the blue and brown books.* Oxford, UK: Blackwell.

Wittgenstein, L. (1961). *Tractatus logico-philosophicus* (D. F. Pears & B. F. McGuinness, Trans.). Atlantic Highlands, NJ: Humanities Press International. (Original work published 1921)

Wolf-Devine, C. (1993). *Descartes on seeing: Epistemology and visual perception.* Carbondale: Southern Illinois University Press.

Wynne-Edwards, V. C. (1962). *Animal dispersion in relation to social behavior.* Edinburgh: Oliver & Boyd.

Chapter 18

Toward a Campbellian Realist Organization Science

BILL McKELVEY

For nearly four decades, Don Campbell's epistemology has responded to four enduring dilemmas:

1. How to build a postpositivist science that maintains the "goal of objectivity" in science (1974b) without forcing metaphysical terms out of theories and out of science in favor of operationalist observable terms?

2. How to develop a selectionist evolutionary epistemology that does not steer scientists toward Comtean positivism, instrumentalism, naïve realism, or operationalism at the expense of theory terms less detectable or more metaphysical in nature (1974b)?

3. How to build an objectivist postrelativist epistemology that incorporates the dynamics of science changing over time without abandoning the goal of objectivity (1988a)?

4. How to develop an objectivist epistemology while remaining sensitive to the differing perceptions, interpretations, and social constructions of individual scientists and scientific communities (1988a)?

Campbell's search for resolution drove him to become a "critical, hypothetical, corrigible scientific realist" (1988a, pp. 444-445). As he himself admitted many times, and as his work suggests so clearly, he also became *an avowed evolutionary epistemologist*. Scientific realism resolved the first dilemma. Evolutionary epistemology abrogated the third one, and Campbell's later conflation of evolutionary epistemology with hermeneutics nullified the fourth. In all of his writing, however, Campbell seems not have returned to the second one. One purpose of this chapter is to resolve the second dilemma.

Assuming that Campbell's dilemmas are resolved and his epistemology at least preliminarily completed—realizing that no epistemology is ever finished—Campbell offers a useful message for organization science. His *Campbellian realism* provides the foundation for an objective organization science that denies neither the epistemological dynamics uncovered by historical relativists such as Hanson (1958), Kuhn (1962), and Feyerabend

AUTHOR'S NOTE: I wish to thank Martin Evans for many helpful comments and Margaretha Hendrickx for many philosophical insights and suggestions, as well as considerable coaching. Needless to say, all remaining errors and oversights are my responsibility. Citations in this chapter follow temporal order.

(1975) nor the sociology of knowledge developed by interpretists and social constructionists (Bloor, 1976; Burrell & Morgan, 1979; Brannigan, 1981; Shapin & Schaffer, 1985; Latour & Woolgar, 1986; Nickles, 1989). Campbell's epistemology and the broader scientific realist and evolutionary epistemologies upon which he draws suggest that the current paradigm war between organizational positivists (Pfeffer, 1982, 1993, 1995; Donaldson 1985, 1996) and relativists (Lincoln, 1985; Lincoln & Guba, 1985; Reed & Hughes, 1992; Perrow, 1994; Van Maanen 1995a, 1995b; Alvesson & Deetz, 1996; Burrell, 1996; Chia, 1996) is philosophically uninformed, archaic, and dysfunctional.

Does it matter that organization scientists are philosophically archaic? Indeed it does. Pfeffer (1993) presents data showing that multiparadigm disciplines are given low status in the broader scientific community, with a variety of negative consequences. Donaldson (1995) counts 15 paradigms already, and Prahalad and Hamel (1994) call for even more, as do Clegg, Hardy, and Nord (1996). As Campbell (1995) notes, the physical and biological sciences are held in high esteem because they hold to the goal of objectivity in science: The use of an objective external reality serves as the ultimate criterion variable for winnowing out inferior theories and paradigms. Relativist programs, on the other hand, in principle tolerate as many paradigms as there are socially constructed perspectives and interpretations. Hughes (1992) says, "The naivety of reasoned certainties and reified objectivity, upon which organization theory built its positivist monuments to modernism, is unceremoniously jettisoned [and] these articles of faith are unlikely to form the axioms of any rethinking or new theoretical directions" (p. 297). If he is correct, organization science is destined to proliferate even more paradigms and sink to even lower status—surely an unattractive outcome. Campbellian realism provides a way out of this downward spiral. A dynamic objectivist organization science that does not deny a social constructionist sociology of knowledge *is* possible. Surely this is a message that would delight many organization scientists.

Campbell's intense interest in scientific realism and evolutionary epistemology makes little sense

absent a realization that he was well aware that philosophers had abandoned both the Received View[1] and historical relativism by 1970. The epitaph appeared as Suppe's *The Structure of Scientific Theories* in 1977. I begin with a painfully brief review of the essential arguments causing the abandoning. I then turn to a discussion of some aspects of scientific realism that seem most relevant to social science, social construction of knowledge, organization science, and the realist direction Campbell takes. My next discussion shows how the conflation of current scientific realist literature and Campbell's selectionist evolutionary epistemology resolves the four dilemmas. I conclude with a statement of Campbell's message for organization scientists.

I. The Positivist and Relativist Failures[2]

Campbell (1988a) favors an "ontological realism" emphasizing external reality as the ultimate criterion variable against which to test theories. He uses "ontological nihilism" to describe the more radical ontological relativisms following from Kuhn (1962) and Feyerabend (1975) and earlier subjectivists (Natanson, 1963). Less radical but nevertheless *ontologically weak* semantic and epistemological relativisms define numerous subjectivist programs constituting the "culture science" that Perrow (1994) points to as most relevant for organization science, such as interpretism, social constructionism, and postmodernism. Campbell's ontological realism reflects his interest in an objectivist postpositivist epistemology. His development of evolutionary epistemology reflects his continuing interest in the dynamics of how sciences change in their search for improved verisimilitude in observation and explanation without abandoning objectivist ontological realism.

Campbell's scientific realism and evolutionary epistemology develop in parallel with an emerging consensus among philosophers that positivism and relativism are flawed constructions. Campbell's dilemma is to produce a dynamic objectivist epistemology while avoiding the Charybdis of operationalism and the Scylla of an ontologically weak relativism.

A. The Failure of Positivism

The word "positivist," like the word "bourgeois," has become more of a derogatory epithet than a useful descriptive concept, and consequently has been largely stripped of whatever agreed meaning it may once have had. (Giddens, 1974, p. ix)

In fact, "positivism" has both strong and weak points, and how it is defined has evolved. Positivists worry about the fundamental dilemma of science: how to conduct truth-tests of theories, given that many of their constituent terms are unobservable and unmeasurable, seemingly unreal, and thus beyond the direct firsthand sensory experience of investigators. The term *positivism* was coined by August Comte. He attempted to avoid the dilemma by disallowing into science terms not directly apparent to the human senses. Comte claimed that the goal of science is prediction based only on observable terms (Audi, 1995, p. 147).

Following Newtonian mechanics, German *mechanistic materialism* held that "existence obeys, in its origin, life, and decay, mechanical laws inherent in things themselves, discarding every kind of super-naturalism and idealism in the exploration of natural events" (Suppe, 1977, p. 8, quoting Büchner, 1855). It rests on empirical inquiry rather than philosophical speculation, a view in which there is no doubt that a real objective world exists. Materialism gave way to the neo-Kantian view that "science is concerned to discover the general forms of structures of sensations; the knowledge science yields of the 'external worlds' is seen as webs of logical relations which are not given, but rather exemplified in sensory experience" (Suppe, 1977, p. 9). Thus, science discovers not only the structure of matter but also the *logic* of the interrelations among the phenomena. This view had become the dominant philosophy of the German scientific community by 1900. By the mid-19th century, Hegel's philosophy of "the identity of reason and reality" dominated. It proclaimed that only "reason" is "real," denying the existence of tangible entities such as earth, water, and fire.

The world is purely perception, a matter of the mind!

Mach added the notion that scientific statements must be *empirically verifiable*, resulting in *neopositivism*. The excesses of Mach's approach, which included a rejection of mathematics, subsequently were denied, resulting in a *modified positivism* (Whitehead & Russell, 1910-1913) that still held to verifiability as a basis of ensuring truth but included mathematics as an appropriate expression of scientific laws. During the ensuing decade, the main elements of the *Received View* developed; they were published in Carnap's (1923) first publication. It formally stated the tenets of *logical positivism*, because it included mathematical, theoretical, and observational languages as well as the separation of theory and observation terms.

By 1910, the Vienna Circle, a group of Germans trained in logic, mathematics, and physics meeting at the University of Vienna, accepted the task of considering how to respond to (a) Hegelian idealism; (b) scientists' beliefs in mechanistic materialism; (c) neo-Kantian sensory experiencing of the external world; (d) Machian neopositivism's emphasis of verification, and finally the crowning blows; (e) Planck's quantum mechanics; and (f) Einstein's theory of special relativity, the last two of which violated determinism, sensory relevance, and verificationism. Their official manifesto, *The Scientific World View: The Vienna Circle*, was published in 1929.[3] It further defined *logical positivism*.

Responding to the philosophical dilemma, logical positivists founded their epistemology on axiomatic theories, using terms comprising three languages: "(1) logical and mathematical terms; (2) theoretical terms; and (3) observation terms" (Suppe, 1977, p. 12). Theory terms are unreal, abbreviated representations of phenomena described by the observation terms. *Correspondence rules* (C-rules) ensure that theoretical terms are linked explicitly to observation terms. The Vienna Circle held that theory terms are unreal and, thus, theoretical explanations of causality are also unreal, leading to the view that theories may be interpreted only as *instrumental summaries* of empirical results (Boyd, 1991; Hunt, 1991; pp. 276-277). The "scientific truth" in theory terms is ascertained via verification in observation terms. Logical positivists attempted to clarify the language of science by expunging metaphysical terms not amenable to direct sensory testing and by insisting that logic terms be verified as to cognitive meaning and truth, thereby "ridding it [science] of meaningless assertions by means of the verifiability principle and reconstructing it through formal logic into a precise, ideal language" (Hunt, 1991; p. 271).

In his classic statement, Schlick (1932-1933/1991) focused on the seeming impossibility of ever knowing whether the external world is different from the metaphysical or transcendent reality of the human senses, that is, cognitive construction or interpretation. In his view, the only way to tell if some datum is real or not is to take it away and see if there is a difference. Thus, if I sit once and the chair is there, and if I sit again and the chair is not there and I fall, I may conclude the chair is real. This is what Schlick refers to as a *testable difference*.

Subsequently, Braithwaite (1953), Nagel (1956, 1961), and Hempel (1965) evolved an epistemology focusing on *laws*, *explanation*, and *theory*, known as *logical empiricism*.[4] It replaced logical positivism by the mid-20th century. The logical empiricists immediately encountered a problem with the verifiability principle, because for a law to be verified, it must be empirically proved universally true for all times at all places, an impossibility. Consequently, verifiability was abandoned, to be replaced by a somewhat relaxed *testability criterion* that all propositions have to be amenable to some measure of empirical test, a view eventually championed by Popper (1959) as his *falsifiability principle*. This modification finally admitted that theory terms could never be directly "verified" empirically.

In responding to the fundamental dilemma, the logical empiricists attempted to deal with the problems identified with the logical positivists' strict separation of theory and observation terms via the use of C-rules. How could there be an "unreal" theory term explicitly defined via C-rules without having the theory term simply be the result of an observable measure of some sort? This would become an *operationalist's* treatment of theory: It is whatever is measured (Hempel, 1954). It created

the "theoretician's dilemma:" (a) If all theory terms can be explicitly defined by reduction to observation terms, then theory terms are unnecessary; and (b) If theory terms cannot be explicitly defined and related to observation terms, they are surely unnecessary because they are meaningless (Hempel, 1965, p. 186). Furthermore, if theory terms are isomorphic to operational measures, there is no possibility of using the theory to predict new phenomena, as yet unmeasured.

It is clear that the term "positivism" is now obsolete among modern philosophers of science (Rescher, 1970, 1987; Devitt, 1984; Nola, 1988; Suppe, 1989; Hunt, 1991; Aronson, Harré, & Way, 1994; de Regt, 1994). Many key ingredients of positivism nevertheless still remain in good standing among scientific realists, such as theory terms, observation terms, tangible observables and unobservables, intangible and metaphysical terms, auxiliary hypotheses, causal explanation, empirical reality, testability, incremental corroboration and falsification, and generalizable lawlike statements (as shown in Table 18.1). The *legacy* of the Received View in Table 18.1 is *ontologically strong*, in the sense that it posits an external reality and that successive scientific discoveries and theories over time more and more correctly describe and explain this reality: Reality acts as a strong external criterion variable against which scientific theories are held accountable.

B. Relativism

Many scholars interpret historical relativism as antithetical to positivism. Thus, historical relativism "made scientific knowledge a social phenomenon in which science became a subjective and, to varying degrees, an irrational enterprise" (Suppe, 1977, p. 705). Nola (1988) separates relativism into three kinds:

> 1. "Ontological relativism is the view that what exists, whether it be ordinary objects, facts, the entities postulated in science, etc., exists only relative to some relativizer, whether that be a person, a theory or whatever" (p. 11): *ontologically nihilistic*.

TABLE 18.1 Basic Tenets of Organization Science Remaining From Positivism

1. The truth or falsity of a statement cannot be determined solely by recourse to axiomatic formalized mathematical or logical statements without reference to empirical reality.
2. Analytic (logic) and synthetic (empirical fact) statements are both essential elements of any scientific statement, though not always jointly present.
3. Theory and observation terms are not strictly separate; they may shift from one categorization to the other or may satisfy both categorizations simultaneously.
4. Theory terms do have antecedent meaning independent of observation terms.
5. Theoretical language invariably is connected to observation language through the use of auxiliary statements and theories, lying outside the scope of the theory in question, which may or may not be well developed or even stated.
6. The meaning of theoretical terms may be defined by recourse to analogies or iconic models.
7. Procedures for connecting theories with phenomena must specify causal sequence and experimental connections; experimental connections must include all methodological details.
8. Theories may or may not be axiomatizable or formalizable.
9. It is meaningless to attempt to derive formalized syntactical statements from axioms devoid of semantic interpretation.
10. Formalization is an increasingly desirable element of organization science, approaching the state of being necessary though not sufficient.
11. Static semantic interpretation of formalized syntactical statements is not sufficient, given the dynamic nature of scientific inquiry.
12. The "lawlike" components of theories contain statements in the form of generalized counterfactual conditionals, "If A, then B," and theories gain importance as they become more generalizable.
13. Lawlike statements must have empirical reference; otherwise, they are tautologies.
14. Lawlike statements must have "nomic" necessity, meaning that the statement or finding that "If A, then B" is interesting only if a theory purports to explain the relationship between A and B; that is, "If A, then B" cannot be the result of an accident.
15. The theory purporting to explain "If A, then B" must be a systematically related set of statements embedded in a broader set of theoretical discourse interesting to organization scientists, which is to say that empirical findings not carefully connected to lawlike statements are outside scientific discourse.
16. Some number of the statements constituting a theory must consist of lawlike generalizations.
17. Theoretical statements must be of a form that is empirically testable.

SOURCE: The first 11 tenets come from Suppe's summary (1977, p. 117); the remaining 6 come from Hunt (1991, pp. 107-117).

2. Epistemological relativisms may allege that (a) what is known or believed is relativized to individuals, cultures, or frameworks; (b) what is perceived is relative to some incommensurable paradigm; (c) there is no general theory of scientific method, form of inquiry, or rule of reasoning or evidence that has privileged status. Instead, they are variable with respect to times, persons, cultures, and frameworks (pp. 16-18): *ontologically very weak.*

3. Semantic relativism holds that truth and falsity are "relativizable to a host of items from individuals to cultures and frameworks. What is relativized is variously sentences, statements, judgements or beliefs" (p. 14): *ontologically weak.*

Nola observes that Hanson, Kuhn, and Feyerabend espouse both semantic and epistemological relativism. Relativisms[5] familiar to organization science range across all three kinds, that is, from

ontological nihilism to ontological weakness. Campbell clearly considers himself a semantic relativist in addition to being an ontological realist (Campbell & Paller, 1989).

It is important to recognize (a) that historical relativism does put science in motion, as it were, shifting philosophical thinking from the static Received View to the dynamics of how scientific communities shift from one *Weltanschauung* (worldview) to another; and (b) that relativism is *ontologically weak* in the sense that perceptions, interpretations and social constructions, and epistemologies diminish the strength of external reality to act as an external criterion variable guiding truth-testing, and therefore seemingly antithetical to Campbell's ontological realism. Even so, in the last decade of his writing, Campbell folded some of the dynamic aspects of relativism into his brand of realism. Consequently, it is important to discriminate between elements of relativism remaining in good standing and strands that have been abandoned. By Suppe's (1977) analysis, key historical relativists are Toulmin (1953, 1961), Bohm (1957), Hanson (1958), Kuhn (1962, 1970, 1977), and Feyerabend (1962, 1970, 1975). Because Toulmin sets the stage and Kuhn has been the most influential on organizational scientists, I outline their main ideas, followed by a brief critique.

Toulmin notes that a regularity such as "light travels in a straight line" is an "ideal of natural order" that does not need explanation. If light bends, however, this is an irregularity needing explanation—hence the search for a law. Theories are to explain, not necessarily to predict. Toulmin claims that theories are neither true nor false: They are simply representations of phenomena that may be more or less fruitful in allowing a theorist to answer questions about irregularities.

> Scientific theories thus are formulated, judged, maintained, and developed relative to a *Weltanschauung* which includes the changed meanings attached to terms after they undergo a language shift resulting from their incorporation into the theory, ideals of natural order, and presumptions which determine what are counted as significant facts, what questions the scientist asks, the assumptions which underlie his theorizing, and the standards by which he assesses the fruitfulness of the theory. This *Weltanschauung* is dynamically evolving, and may change as the theory undergoes development. (Suppe, 1977, p. 132)

That the *Weltanschauung* may evolve in interaction with developing theories is what gives relativism its dynamic character and is what clearly sets it apart from the Received View, which holds that theories evolve from formalized axiomatic reduction—which is necessarily static (Suppe, 1977, p. 114).

Kuhn is surely the most influential relativist. Following Toulmin, Kuhn builds on the idea of *Weltanschauungen*, which both see as dynamically evolving. The fundamental difference is that in Toulmin's framework, the *Weltanschauung* changes incrementally in a gradualist fashion, whereas in Kuhn's view *Weltanschauung* dynamics consist of long periods of relative stability, termed *normal science*, broken intermittently by

paradigm shifts. Paradigm is Kuhn's term for *Weltanschauung*. Unfortunately, as Masterman (1970) points out, "paradigm" has some 21 different meanings in Kuhn's 1962 book. Shapere (1964, p. 385) complains, "In short, anything that allows science to accomplish anything can be a part of (or somehow involved in) a paradigm." Hence, Kuhn (1977) substitutes a more narrowly defined *disciplinary matrix* for paradigm.

In Kuhn's view, science evolves through long periods of convergent "normal puzzle"-solving activities punctuated infrequently by paradigm shifts. Normal science is carried out by scientists sharing a common "disciplinary matrix," acquired through apprenticeship. The matrix defines the shared exemplars of good scientific activity, core values, and methods. The matrix constitutes the *Weltanschauung*. Communities with different exemplars and different conceptual perspectives see the world and conduct their science differently; consequently, there is no "neutral" observation language and incommensurability results, preventing members of one *Weltanschauung* from being able to communicate with and evaluate the work of those following a different paradigm. Eventually, an accumulation of anomalies causes a paradigm shift.

As Suppe (1977) notes, complaints against Kuhn's framework are legion. First is the problem of the 21 definitions of the term *paradigm*, as already noted. Second, many disagree that a correct reading of scientific history offers any indication of disjunctive shifts between normal puzzle solving and revolution. Third, others complain that under Kuhn's framework, science becomes irrational and subjective, leaving it with no objective or independent basis of resolving disputes—"an antiempirical idealism" (Suppe, 1977, p. 151). Fourth, meanings of terms may not in fact change just because disciplinary matrices shift.

Critique

Suppe elaborates four specific arguments against relativism,[6] as follow.

1. *Objectivity.* The strong form of relativism (ontological nihilism)—that objects, facts, and properties are colored by the nature of the theory

held by an observer—is rejected by Scheffler (1967) as being no different from Hegelian idealism, in which all objects in the world are perceptions and "in the mind." Suppe notes, however, that Toulmin, Hanson, Kuhn, Feyerabend, and Bohm all accept a weaker form—that objects, facts, and properties, as they exist, are independent of an observer but that the nature of objects, facts, and properties thought to be observed by an individual might indeed be determined by the influence of the *Weltanschauung*.[7] The weak form also fails, however, because *Weltanschauungen* do not exist for reasons of history, meaning-variance, and uniformity.

2. *Historical accuracy*. Toulmin's view that *Weltanschauungen* changed gradually with the accumulation of ideals of natural order, theories, and laws appears more accurate than Kuhn's view that normal science is punctuated by occasional revolutions, caused by a crisis of anomalies. Hull (1975) says, "The periods which he [Kuhn] had previously described as pre-paradigm contained paradigms not that different from those of normal science. . . . [N]or does normal science alternate with revolutionary science; both are taking place all the time. Sometimes a revolution occurs without any preceding state of crisis" (p. 397). Laudan (1977) concludes, "virtually every major period in the history of science is characterized both by the co-existence of numerous competing paradigms, with none exerting hegemony over the field, and by the persistent and continuous manner in which the foundational assumptions of every paradigm are debated within the scientific community. . . . Kuhn can point to no major science in which paradigm monopoly has been the rule, nor in which foundational debate has been absent" (pp. 74, 151; taken from Hunt, 1991, p. 326).

3. *Meaning-variance*. One of the claims of the historical relativists is that as a field shifts from one *Weltanschauung* to another, the meanings of all the underlying theory terms also change. The implication of this is that there are consequently no common terms to use in making comparative evaluations of the different *Weltanschauungen* as to truth. Suppe (1977, pp. 199-208) first shows that the strong form preferred by Feyerabend and Bohm—that "any change in theory alters the mean-

ings of all the terms in the theory"—is untenable. He observes that no historical relativist has established that *any* change, even a major one, in any theory changes *all* the terms.

Suppe then argues why a weaker form preferred by Toulmin, Kuhn, and Hanson—that "meanings of terms in theories are determined partially by the principles of the theory"—also is untenable and undermines as well the conclusion that *Weltanschauung* are incommensurable. First, it is untenable because theories are constantly reformulated to generate propositions fitting particular empirical circumstances for deductive tests. If such reformulations are taken as substantive changes in a theory, with constituent terms all changing as well, then attempts to create general theory that might apply to more than one phenomenon—such as gravitational force applied to bending light rays, falling bodies, or orbital mechanics—would constitute changes in the meanings of terms and thus would presume that every application of the gravity force constitutes a new *Weltanschauung*, which seems ridiculous on its face. Second, once it is agreed that only *some* elements of a theory might change and thus only *some* terms might change meaning, the opposite is true, that *some* terms will *not* change in meaning, suggesting that the *Weltanschauungen* are not incommensurable—common terms may allow comparative analyses.[8] Third, theories are not simply "linguistic formulations" in the sense that they change just because terms, as linguistic entities, change. Theories are not thought to change if translated from English to French. Suppe extends this argument to include what appear to be "translations" within one language, as a scientific community moves from, say, Newtonian theory to Einsteinian theory. Thus, even though the linguistic structure of a theory might change, the meanings of many of its terms might not change at all, leaving the theories semantically commensurable though seemingly linguistically incommensurable.

The availability of many cross-paradigm terms is illustrated in the *Handbook of Organization Studies* (Clegg et al., 1996). It contains chapters falling into the positivist, interpretist, and postmodernist disciplinary matrices, yet the obvious presumption of the editors is that the terms used in each chapter share meaning across matrices; otherwise, the editors are in the awkward position of having "edited" a book much of which they do not understand.

4. *Weltanschauung uniformity.* A *Weltanschauung* typically is a complex framework supposedly emerging from the collective beliefs of a scientific community. These beliefs are the result of years of training and of exemplars such as textbooks, apprenticeships, research programs, and journal articles, and course are composed of all the relevant theory language of principles and terms, various theory formulations, experimental methods, and so on—truly a complex multifaceted belief system. Suppose that each individual is somewhat different by virtue of being trained at different places, apprenticing to different mentors, and studying different books and articles. If the individuals are somewhat different, it seems unlikely that a uniform *Weltanschauung* would emerge. Inasmuch as a *Weltanschauung* belief system is complex, it is unlikely that a paradigm shift from one paradigm to another would necessarily involve all elements of a complex belief system. Thus, for any given paradigm shift, some number of beliefs, theories, terms, and definitions would remain unchanged among some number of *Weltanschauung* members, thus undermining incommensurability.

Suppe (1977, pp. 217-221), concludes that (a) historical relativists deserve credit for alerting us to the dynamics of how science progresses and (b) the idea that scientific communities possess incommensurable *Weltanschauungen* is false. It follows that the "different province" idea mentioned by Perrow (1994) has been rejected by philosophers. Consequently, the *Weltanschauung* approach not only is *not* a contender as an accepted epistemology, but it also cannot be used to debunk the tenets Suppe concludes still remain intact from the Received View. Thus, there is reason to reject the view that organizations and organization science are somehow limited to a "culture science" that is incommensurable with the legacy of the Received View.

II. Scientific Realism

Although positivism failed, the problem remains: how to conduct truth-testing given a mixture of metaphysical and observable terms while also avoiding naïve realism or operationalism? Although the disjunctive paradigm shift and incommensurability aspects of relativism failed, the question remains: how to deal with changing science and how to produce an objectivist epistemology given the influence of socially constructed and thus totally metaphysical or idealist scientific conceptions of phenomena. Campbell's solution is to combine scientific realism, evolutionary epistemology, and hermeneutics. Although Campbell's epistemology depends on scientific realism, I believe it is fair to conclude that his scholarly roots in the scientific realist literature are not as well delineated as one might like—the best being Paller and Campbell (1989). The credibility of Campbell's message would be strengthened, I believe, if the connection was further elucidated. Consequently, in this section I review a few critical scientific realist developments directly supporting his approach.

Scientific realists adhere to the premise "that the long term success of a scientific theory gives reason to believe that something like the entities and structure postulated by the theory actually exists" (McMullin, 1984, p. 26)—a statement that is still considered at the heart of scientific realism (Hunt, 1991; de Regt, 1994). Philosophers' fundamental concerns over how best to ascertain the truth of scientific theories have truly metamorphosed from the Received View, past the postpositivist teachings of Hanson, Kuhn, and Feyerabend, and on into scientific realism. In fact, there is currently a vigorous discourse about scientific realism, little of which appears to have penetrated into organization science. This is despite the fact that scientific realism is the most widely accepted reconstructed logic among current philosophers of science (Boyd, 1991; Aronson, et al., 1994; de Regt, 1994; Wright, 1997).[9]

Before 1980, scientific realism typically was a *convergent epistemological realism*, holding that

(1) "mature" scientific theories are approximately true; (2) the concepts in these theories genuinely refer [to empirical phenomena]; (3) successive theories in a domain will retain the ontology of their predecessors; (4) truly referential theories will be "successful;" and, conversely, (5) "successful" theories will

TABLE 18.2 Boyd's Elements of Scientific Realism

1. "Theoretical terms" in scientific theories (i.e., nonobservational terms) should be thought of as putatively referring (to phenomena) expressions; scientific theories should be interpreted "realistically."
2. Scientific theories, interpreted realistically, are confirmable *and in fact often confirmed* as approximately true by ordinary scientific evidence interpreted in accordance with ordinary methodological standards.
3. The historical progress of mature sciences is largely a matter of successively more accurate approximations to the truth about both observable and unobservable phenomena. Later theories typically build on the (observational and theoretical) knowledge embodied in previous theories.
4. The reality that scientific theories describe is largely independent of scientists' thoughts or theoretical comments.

SOURCE: Adapted from Boyd (1983, p. 45).

TABLE 18.3 Laudan's Arguments Against Scientific Realism

1. There is no historical evidence showing that whether a theory's central terms "refer" to real phenomena or not is related to success.
2. The notion of "approximate truth" is too vague to permit one to judge whether its laws would be empirically successful or not.
3. Realists have no explanation for why many theories that lack approximate truth and real-world reference are nevertheless successful—quantum theory being the classic example.
4. Early "approximate truths" in early theories often are not preserved in later theories.
5. The realist argument based on reference and approximation as the basis of truth ignore the anti-realist's main objection—that explanatory success corresponds to truth.
6. The standard of approximative improvement is irrelevant—a theory should not have to explain how or why earlier rivals worked.
7. If an early theory is false, it is nonsensical to expect a later improvement based on the earlier falsity to be an improvement on truth.
8. Realists have not demonstrated that other nonrealist theories are inadequate to explain the success of a science.

SOURCE: Paraphrased from Laudan (1981).

contain central terms that refer. (Anderson, 1988, p. 403; based on Laudan, 1981)

Boyd (1983) also advocates the approximationist/convergent approach in his description of scientific realism (shown in Table 18.2). The approximationist view was convincingly debunked by Laudan in a widely cited article (1981). He accused 1970s realists of depending too naïvely on a process of convergence toward theories thought to have higher truth value. He said this is nothing other than the notorious "fallacy of affirming the consequent." To state that the theory "the sun goes around the earth" is true because I see the sun rise every morning is an example of this fallacy. Some details of Laudan's logic are presented in Table 18.3.

Scientific realism's early aura of accomplishment during the 1970s ended with another key antirealist event—the publishing of van Fraassen's very influential book *The Scientific Image* (1980) (Derksen, 1994). Van Fraassen develops a strong argument for his antirealist *constructive empiricism*, key elements of which are listed in Table 18.4. In a penetrating critique, he debunked the root premise of the realists, that theory terms other than those directly observable could be truth-tested and considered both real and true, as being unnecessary. In his view, a theory may become successful, be adopted, and be believed in as empirically adequate without one having to take the additional step of believing it is true and its terms real.

Paller and Campbell (1989) define their "hypothetical realism" to counter both these attacks, arguing that "evolutionary epistemology argues against it [epistemological realism], as against naïve, direct, and clairvoyant realisms" (p. 121). First, they connect hypothetical realism to Pop-

TABLE 18.4 Van Fraassen's Constructive Empiricism

---

1. "Science aims to give us theories which are empirically adequate: and acceptance of a theory involves as belief only that it is empirically adequate. . . . I shall call it constructive empiricism. . . . [A] theory is empirically adequate if what it says about observable things and events in this world is true. . . . [A] little more precisely: such a theory has at least one model that all the actual phenomena fit inside" (p. 12; italics not reproduced) "[It] concerns actual phenomena: what does happen, and not, what would happen under different circumstances" (p. 60).

2. "The syntactic picture of a theory identifies it with a body of theorems. . . . This should be contrasted with the alternative of presenting a theory in the first instance by identifying a class of structures as its models. . . . The models occupy centre stage" (p. 44).

3. To present a theory is to specify a family of structures, its *models*, and secondly, to specify certain parts of those models (the empirical *substructures*) as candidates for the direct representation of observable phenomena. The structures which can be described in experimental and measurement reports we can call *appearances*: the theory is empirically adequate if it has some model such that all appearances are isomorphic to empirical substructures of that model" (p. 64).

4. "With this new [model-centered, semantic] picture of theories in mind, we can distinguish between two epistemic attitudes we can take up toward a theory. We can assert it to be true (i.e., to have a model which is a faithful replica, in all detail, of our world), and call for belief; or we can simply assert its empirical adequacy, calling for acceptance as such. In either case we stick our necks out: empirical adequacy goes far beyond what we can know at any given time. (All the results of measurement are not in; they will never all be in; and in any case, we won't measure everything that can be measured.) Nevertheless there is a difference: the assertion of empirical adequacy is a great deal weaker than the assertion of truth, and the restraint to acceptance delivers us from metaphysics" (pp. 68-69).

5. "It is philosophers, not scientists (as such), who are realists or empiricists, for the difference in views is not about what exists but about what science is" (van Fraassen, 1985, p. 255, note 6).

SOURCE: All quotations are from van Fraassen (1980) unless otherwise specified.

---

per's (1959) *epistemologically fallibilist realism* and Popper's slogan, "we do not know; we can only guess" (p. 278)—which Popper later called *metaphysical realism*. Next, they connect hypothetical realism to Polanyi's (1958) "hidden reality" by drawing on his argument "that the data do not compel belief in scientific theories and entities and that the duty of scientists is to strive for theories that describe that reality" (Paller & Campbell, 1989, p. 120). Most important, they then connect hypothetical realism to Bhaskar's (1975/1997) "transcendental realism." Finally, they claim that Laudan accepts their view as outside the range of his critique.

Bhaskar's Transcendental Realism

I have three specific reasons for starting with Bhaskar. First, the main themes of Bhaskar seem to have survived the van Fraassen attack and remain central to the most recent development by Harré (Aronson et al., 1994), one of the earliest tillers of the scientific realism field (Harré, 1961, 1970). Second, Bhaskar is particularly important to organization scientists because his realism in-

cludes elements of neo-Kantian transcendental idealism and the social construction of science. He says, "epistemological relativism in this sense [that scientific progress depends on social constructions] is the handmaiden of ontological realism and must be accepted" (1975/1997, p. 249). The Kuhnian developmental paradigm is central to his conception of scientific realism (p. 193). Third, Paller and Campbell (1989, p. 120) note that Bhaskar's transcendental realism fits with Campbell's critical hypothetical realism. Campbell places himself centrally between the ontologically strong and weak camps, saying "I am an epistemological relativist, but I am not an ontological nihilist" (1988a, p. 447). The record is clear that Campbell draws about equally from realism (1989a, 1990a; Paller & Campbell, 1989) and relativism (Campbell, 1989b, 1991, 1995) in pursuing his selectionist epistemology. In the light of this, I briefly outline Bhaskar's argument, taking it to be a combined realist/relativist approach particularly well suited for organization science.

"There is in science a characteristic kind of dialectic in which a regularity is identified, a plausible explanation for it is invented and the reality

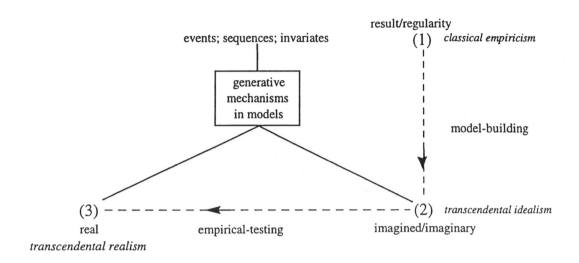

Figure 18.1. Bhaskar's Depiction of the Logic of Scientific Discovery
SOURCE: Graphically reconstructed from Diagram 3.1 in Bhaskar (1975, p. 145). Used with permission of Verso.

of the entities and processes postulated in the explanation is then checked" (Bhaskar, 1975/1997, p. 145). This logic of scientific discovery is diagrammed in Figure 18.1. The quotation describes Comtean positivism, what Bhaskar terms *classical empiricism*, in which intangible and unmeasurable terms are avoided in favor of observable instrumental relations between factual events. In this view, science is reduced to "facts and their conjunctions. Thus science becomes a kind of epiphenomenon of nature" (p. 25). Bhaskar says that classical empiricist epistemology holds for closed systems but falls apart in open systems where the many uncontrolled influences minimize the likelihood of an unequivocal determination of a counterfactual such as "If *A*, then *B*." "It is only if I have grounds for supposing that the system in which the mechanism acts is closed that the prediction of the consequent event is deductively justified" (p. 103).

In Stage 1 of Figure 18.1, Bhaskar makes a clear distinction between developing theory based on identified *regularities*—which could be accidental—and experimentally contrived *invariances* in which repeated experiments produce an outcome regularity by manipulating what is hypothesized to be an underlying force, process, mechanism, or

structure. Contrived invariances better fit the counterfactual conditional basis of lawlike statements about generative forces that might seldom if ever be discernible naturally in complex open systems (like organizations) because of the many countervailing influences. Bhaskar then notes that both Stages 2 and 3 lead to the development of conceptual representations of posited underlying generative forces such as structures and processes in the form of iconic[10] or formal (mathematical or computational) models.

Initially, the mental models of *transcendental idealists* and *transcendental realists* both contain "imagined" (Bhaskar's term, p. 145) conceptual, intangible, and unmeasurable theory terms. The difference is that for idealists, they remain forever intangible, interpreted, socially constructed, metaphysical, and *unreal*, whereas for realists the better detection of theoretical terms, repeated experiments, and other kinds of empirical research that are requirements for moving from Stage 2 to Stage 3 eventually give cause to believe that what were initially imagined metaphysical terms and entities become *real*. Thus, transcendental idealists, reflecting Hegelian and neo-Kantian idealism, historical relativism (Hanson, 1958; Kuhn, 1962;

Feyerabend, 1975), and interpretive social construction (Brannigan, 1981; Taylor, 1985; Munévar, 1991; Masters, 1993), see models as artificial constructs.

Bhaskar notes, however, that although models may be independent of particular scholars, they are not independent of human activity in general. The natural world becomes a construction of the human mind and of a scientific community (1975/1997, pp. 27, 148-167). He says that transcendental realists regard

> objects of knowledge [in the models] as the structures and mechanisms that generate phenomena; and the knowledge as produced in the social activity of science. These objects are neither phenomena (empiricism) nor human constructs imposed upon the phenomena (idealism), but real structures which endure and operate independently of our knowledge, our experience and the conditions which allow us access to them. Against empiricism the objects of knowledge are structures, not events; against idealism, they are intransitive. (p. 25)

Bhaskar (1975/1997, p. 25) takes an "updated dynamized" version of Kant's famous *transcendental argument* that reason and experience presume a priori objectively valid phenomena (Audi, 1995, p. 808). "Intransitive objects of knowledge are in general invariant to our knowledge of them: they are the real things and structures, mechanisms and processes, events and possibilities of the world" (p. 22). *Intransitive* means that objects of scientific discovery exist independently of human perceptions, interpretations, and social constructions, and by *structured*, Bhaskar means they are "distinct from the patterns of events that occur" (p. 35). Further elaborated, structures are underlying forces that may occur independently of observed regularities and may not be observable or measurable except via contrived experiments and the creation of invariances.

Bhaskar's diagram offers a choice between two flow conceptions. "Regularity" flow begins at Stage 1 with Comtean positivism, in which science is limited to stating relations among intransitive measurable empirical *Realm 1*[11] regularities. Next comes Stage 2 and the recognition that science includes *Realm 3* theory terms representing under-

lying causes, which relativists now take as transitive idealistic conceptions that are unreal and unique to observers or perhaps scientific communities. Finally comes Stage 3, with the recognition that science includes Realm 3 conceptions that are real in that they do indeed represent intransitive natural underlying causal forces. "Invariance" flow, the preferred view, starts with the bifurcation between experimentally contrived invariances and identified event regularities. Terms in models purporting to represent the underlying natural causal forces reflect *simultaneously* both Stage 2 (cognitive [idealistic] concepts of underlying mechanisms that are transitive, reflecting the idea of science as a "process-in-motion" [Bhaskar, 1975/1997, p. 146]) and Stage 3 (approximations of intransitive real underlying forces). In the invariance flow view, four fundamental aspects of science are highlighted: (a) creation of counterfactual experimental invariances, (b) creation of iconic or formal models containing at least some Realm 3 terms representing underlying causal mechanisms, (c) recognition that science consists of process-in-motion that creates transitive theory terms, and (d) recognition that scientific realism is based on theory terms that are successively improved approximations of intransitive real underlying causal mechanisms.

Fallibilist Realism

Bhaskar's analysis shows that scientific realism describes a process in which theoretical terms and entities initially imagined, interpreted, or socially constructed eventually are held accountable for truth content with respect to an objective reality via experiments and other kinds of empirical research. Bhaskar clearly supports Campbell's conflation of realism and relativism. Remaining to be supported is Campbell's "fallibilist realism." This calls for further analysis of the nature of truth-testing and further delineation of the relation between truth-testing and the Realms of terms.

Giere (1985), a *convergent realist*, accepts the model-centeredness of van Fraassen's proposed epistemology[12] but distinguishes between observability (Realm 1) and detectability (Realm 2). Van Fraassen accepts detection if humans could get repositioned so the detection instrument was unnecessary—thus, the moons of Jupiter are observable, though from Earth they are detectable only with an instrument, whereas quarks can never be observed by humans. This puts the basis of belief on human capabilities—we can travel to the stars but cannot shrink down to see quarks. Should the basis of truth rest on human physiology or travel capabilities? No. Giere and others (Churchland, 1979; Shapere, 1982) accept belief based on detection, and by adding experimental manipulation we may include Hacking (1983) and Harré (1986). Devitt (1991) suggests that van Fraassen's argument provides the grounds for its own defeat, as follows: The arguments van Fraassen makes to support constructive empiricism, which are that (a) research findings give information about Realm 1 objects and (b) research findings give information about unobserved observables via detection (Realm 2), defeat his thesis that research experience does not give information about unobservables. De Regt says, "Since van Fraassen admits that the gathered information about Realm 1 and Realm 2 entities is uncertain, the embarrassing question arises why experience cannot, in a risky way, inform us about unobservables" (1994, p. 110).

Devitt (1984, p. 128) concludes that even van Fraassen would surely have to accept a "weak form of scientific realism." Supposing, for example, that we view only human footprints in the sand (no person in sight), the weak form holds that some unobservable entity X made the footprints and therefore we have the right to believe in the truth of a theory using X—as real—to explain the footprints, but we have no right to believe that a human being made them—it could have been a robot. Derksen (1994) also argues that this form can be defended because one can have epistemic reasons for believing in unobservables as real (something unreal cannot make real footprints) even though we cannot make the stronger claim that a specific kind of X actually exists. Thus, "we can have reasons for believing that a theoretical entity X [i.e., an unobservable] is an—acceptable—candidate for reality, worthy to be taken seriously" (p. 23).

De Regt's (1994, pp. 279-280) "negative argument for scientific realism" is as follows:

1. Many scientific beliefs are based on epistemologically founded rationality; that is, scientists do not have beliefs about the world that are not based on some argument.
2. By insisting on only empirical adequacy, van Fraassen denies the existence of epistemic rationality.
3. Scientists are not prepared to give up on all rational scientific beliefs.
4. Thus, van Fraassen's constructive empiricism is implausible.
5. Therefore, scientific realism gains plausibility.

Possibly the negative argument is not any stronger than the weak argument. De Regt ends his book with a "strong argument for scientific realism," as paraphrased in Table 18.5. In de Regt's flow of science, incremental inductions systematically reduce belief in the less truthlike theories in favor of those having high verisimilitude (truthlikeness). Successful theories, defined as those that are instrumentally reliable, therefore incorporate higher verisimilitude. The likelihood of underdetermined and thus potentially false theories remaining, and of including Realm 3 terms, is minimal. At any given time, the inductive process leads to *probable* knowledge about Realm 3 terms, which warrants *tentative* belief in the existence of the Realm 3 terms—putting scientific realism on a more plausible foundation than van Fraassen's constructive empiricism. De Regt's "strong argument" is clearly a *fallibilist realism*—note how many times "probability" appears.

The meaning of plausibility and verisimilitude is fleshed out by Aronson, Harré, and Way (AHW) (1994). Building on van Fraassen's model-centered conception of science, they develop their *plausibility thesis*, key tenets of which are shown in Table 18.6. As does Bhaskar (1975/1997, chap. 1), AHW argue that plausibility stems from both the experimental[13] and the ontological adequacy of a model. Verisimilitude and plausibility increase as a function of both (a) improved experimental adequacy of a model to predict or retrodict and (b) improved ontological adequacy of a model to represent (refer to) phenomena defined as within the scope of a theory. Scientific progress is based on the increasingly close relationship between accurate representation of reality, on one hand, and

TABLE 18.5 De Regt's Strong Argument for Scientific Realism

1. A *plausible* distinction exists between Realm 1 (observable) and Realm 3 (unobservable) terms, as viewed by scientists.
2. This distinction is epistemologically relevant. Realm 3 terms (and the explanations constructed from them) are, thus, limited to more cautious claims.
3. The true/false dichotomy is replaced by "truthlikeness" (Popper's verisimilitude), and degrees or *probabilities* of truthlikeness. "Probabilism is the 'new' paradigm."
4. Current scientific theories are considered instrumentally reliable in that they incorporate highly *probable* knowledge concerning Realm 1 terms.
5. These theories are the result of incremental inductions eliminating theories with lower *probability* truthlikeness.
6. Many of the highly *probable* theories remaining postulate and depend on the existence of Realm 3 terms.
7. Underdetermination remains a risk because there are infinitely many ontologically interesting, probably wrong, but empirically equivalent (at any given time) alternative theories (analogous to few equations with many unknowns).
8. The chance that the postulated Realm 3 terms do not exist (are not real—and thus the theory/explanation is based on terms whose truth value can never be ascertained) is present but negligible.
9. "Therefore, inductive arguments in science lead to *probable* knowledge concerning unobservables; one is epistemologically warranted to *tentatively* (at any given time) believe in the existence of the specified unobservables; scientific realism is *more plausible* than [van Fraassen's] constructive empiricism."

SOURCE: Liberally paraphrased, with some quotations, from de Regt (1994, p. 284).

prediction and measurement, on the other. Thus, Figure 18.2, reproduced from Aronson, Harré, and Way (AHW), shows the relation between (a) scientific progress defined as better predictions and manipulations (*experimental adequacy*)—defined as predictions suggested by a theory *P* compared to experimentally created invariances (results) *B*; and (b) making the model more representative (*ontological adequacy*)—defined as a model's representation of phenomenon *T* compared to what the phenomenon is like in reality, *A*. It shows two possible dynamics. First, the dotted line toward the origin shows progress in the *quest for increased truth* as a function of <u>both</u> experimental and ontological adequacy. Second, the *veil of perception* depicting the level of observability of the terms constituting the theory may move from Realm 3 to Realm 1 independently of where the dotted line "level of truth" is. AHW then state their *principle of epistemic invariance*, which holds that "the epistemological situation remains the same for observables and unobservables alike," whether the state of observability is in Realms 1, 2 or 3 (1994, p. 194).

Although van Fraassen (1980) challenges scientific realism, his model-centered view of science (confirmed as the semantic conception by Beth, 1961; Suppes, 1962; Lloyd, 1988; Suppe, 1989;

and Thompson, 1989), underlies de Regt's and AHW's support of Campbell's hypothetical realism. First, Bhaskar sets up the model development process in terms of experimentally manipulated invariances—as opposed to observed regularities. He differentiates between (a) the creation of a transcendental idealist model as an incrementally improved socially constructed representation of a transitive reality—based on individually interpreted, socially constructed, and imagined knowledge of reality; and (b) the creation of a transcendental realist iconic or formal model, which progressively more accurately and successfully (in terms of accuracy of predictions) represents intransitive reality. Second, van Fraassen develops a model-centered epistemology and sets up experimental adequacy as the only reasonable and relevant truthlikeness criterion. Third, accepting the model-centered view and experimental adequacy, AHW add ontological adequacy so as to create a scientific realist epistemology. In their view, models are judged as having a higher probability of truthlikeness if they are experimentally adequate in terms of a theory leading to predictions testing out experimentally, and ontologically adequate if terms of the model's structures accurately represent that portion of reality deemed within the scope of the theory. In recognizing the fundamental dif-

TABLE 18.6 Aronson, Harré, and Way's Plausibility Thesis

1. "A theory . . . [must consist of lawlike statements] capable of yielding more or less correct predictions and retrodictions, the familiar criterion of 'experimental[a] adequacy' " (p. 191).
2. The lawlike statements of a theory must also be "based on a model . . .which expresses the common ontology accepted by the community" (p. 191), which is to say, the model must relatively accurately represent that portion of the phenomena defined by the scope of the theory—that is, ontological adequacy.
3. "Taken together, increasing experimental adequacy and ontological adequacy [which increase plausibility] are inductive grounds for a claim of increasing verisimilitude" (p. 191).
4. "The content of a theory consists of a pair of models . . ., that is, both the descriptive [ontological adequacy] and the explanatory [experimental adequacy] model" (p. 193) should represent the phenomena. Ideally, as a science progresses, the pair of models would merge into one model.
5. "The verisimilitude of a theory is nothing other than its content: that is, of the model or models of which that content consists" (p. 193).
6. The juxtaposition of both experimental and ontological adequacy minimizes underdetermination.
7. "The key to our defense of our revised form of convergent realism is the idea that realism can be open to test by experimental considerations" (p. 194).
8. "When it comes to gathering evidence for our beliefs, *the epistemological situation remains the same for observables and unobservables alike*, no matter whether we are dealing with observables [Realm 1], possible observables [Realm 2] or unobservables [Realm 3]" (p. 194).
9. "The increase in accuracy of our predictions and measurements is a function of how well the models upon which the theories we use to make these predictions and measurements depict nature" (p. 194).
10. "Scientific progress serves as a measure of the extent our theories are getting closer to the truth" (p. 194).
11. "Convergent realism is not necessarily committed to using verisimilitude to *explain* scientific progress, it is committed to the view that there is a functional *relationship* between the two, that as our theories are getting closer to the truth we are reducing the error of our predictions and measurements *and vice versa*" (pp. 194-195).
12. "The relationship between theory and prediction, on the one hand, and between nature and the way it behaves, on the other, remains the same as we move from observables to possible observables to unobservables in principle" (p. 196).

SOURCE: Paraphrased and quoted from Aronson, Harré, and Way (1994).
a. As explained in note 13, I have substituted "experimental" for "empirical" to avoid confusion.

ferentiation between experimental and ontological adequacy, AHW mirror Bhaskar's move away from an epistemic-driven ontology to an ontology viewed independently of epistemology. They also set up the independence between movement toward improved truthlikeness and the designation of whether the terms are Realm 3 or Realm 1.

Finally, de Regt develops a "strong argument" for scientific realism building on the probabilist paradigm, recognizing that instrumentally reliable theories leading to highly probable knowledge consist of a *succession of eliminative inductions*[14] that reduce the probability of underdetermination to negligible proportions. This supports the idea that instrumentally reliable inductive arguments based on observables leads to similar quality arguments based on unobservables, thus agreeing with AHW's view of the independence of (a) movement toward truthlikeness and (b) movement from Realm 1 to Realm 3 terms or entities. Hence, the

realist view that at any given time, one is "epistemologically warranted to *tentatively* believe in the existence of the specified unobservables" (de Regt, 1994, p. 284). As defined here, the *new* convergent realism is more plausible than van Fraassen's constructive empiricism, because the latter insists that scientists abandon scientifically rational beliefs pertaining to the tentative reality of terms included in theories shown over time to be instrumentally reliable in producing highly probable knowledge about Realm 3 entities (terms) in the context of constant movement from Realm 1 to Realm 3.

Boyd (1983) concludes, and reaffirms in 1991, that scientific realism offers the only explanation for the instrumental reliability of the scientific method that itself meets the standards of scientific soundness (1991, p. 14).[15] The *new inductively plausible convergent scientific realism* also solidly supports Campbell's hypothetical realism. How

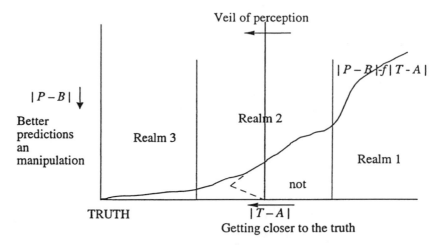

Figure 18.2. Aronson, Harré, and Way's Representation of Convergent Realism
SOURCE: Reprinted by permission of Open Court Publishing company, a division of Carus Publishing Company, Peru, IL, from *Realism Rescued* by J. L. Aronson, R. Harré, and E. C. Way (1994, p. 195). Reproduced by permission of Gerald Duckworth & Co. Ltd.

the "convergent" part actually works, over time, to produce theories having a hiy permigher probability of truth is the subject of selectionist evolutionary epistemology, a subject in which Campbell was without peer.

III. Evolutionary Epistemology

Campbell (1974b) credits Popper for introducing and developing a Darwinian selectionist evolutionary epistemology.[16] Popper's thoughts on this subject are mainly collected in his book *Conjectures and Refutations* (1963), though his earliest writing on the subject dates back to 1934. In a later book, *Objective Knowledge: An Evolutionary Approach* (1972), Popper states:

> The growth of our knowledge is the result of a process closely resembling what Darwin called "natural selection"; that is, *the natural selection of hypotheses*; our knowledge consists, at every moment, of those hypotheses which have shown their (comparative) fitness by surviving so far in their struggle for existence; a competitive struggle which eliminates those hypotheses which are unfit. From the amoeba to Einstein, the growth of knowledge is always the same: we try to solve our problems, and to obtain, by a

process of elimination, something approaching adequacy in our tentative solutions. (p. 261)

During the 25 years following Campbell's 1974b chapter, a considerable literature has emerged, including some 22 papers by Campbell and colleagues.[17] This literature broadly, and Campbell quite specifically, makes three selectionist arguments:

1. Our visual and cognitive capabilities have evolved in a manner that ensures that we as human beings perceive and mentally process the world around us accurately—otherwise, we would not have survived a dangerous and changing world;
2. The plethora of scientific ideas abounding in a socially constructed scientific community are selectively winnowed out and eventually cohere (following hermeneuticists' coherence theory[18]), such that the community evolves toward holding the most fruitful theories; and
3. The dominant and/or coherent theories held by a scientific community become fruitful (defined as successful and/or instrumentally reliable) as they are selectively and successively adapted to more closely fit with real-world entities.

Campbell's conclusion is unmistakable—that selectionist (trial-and-error) learning is the best explanation for the evolution, if not progression, of human thought and more specifically, the progression of scientific explanation. His attention in 1974 focuses mostly on showing just how pervasive is the infusion of selectionist theory into writing about creative thought, perception, and scientific explanation. As Campbell's development of selectionist evolutionary epistemology evolves, the four dilemmas emerge. I begin with a short review of how evolutionary epistemology deals with the dynamics of science. Then, in the following section, I show how the dilemmas are resolved.

A. *Epistemological Dynamics*

Hahlweg and Hooker (1989, pp. 43-44) offer an insightful summary of the arguments in favor of the centrality of selectionist epistemology to epistemological dynamics:

> From *Lorenz* [1941/1982] we take the fundamental importance of understanding the evolutionary history of an organism, capacity, or function for understanding its nature and dynamics. We also take the conclusion that an evolutionary history of cognition supports a general epistemological fallibilism, indeed, a complex fallibilism that is "penetrable," one whose structure can be theorized (fallibly), investigated and perhaps improved upon. From *Piaget* [1950/1972] we take the importance of understanding all living processes in terms of the dynamics of open-ended regulatory systems, and the basic idea that psychogenesis is an extension of embryogenesis in this sense. *Popper* [1972] taught us the importance of reversing the traditional priority between the questions "What is knowledge?" and "How does knowledge progress?," and the methodological incisiveness of fallibilism. From *Toulmin* [1972] we take the importance for any evolutionary theory of science of recognizing its historical and social dimensions, and the systematic importance of methods in relations to theories. And from *Campbell* [1974a, 1974b, 1990b] we take the fundamental role of processes of variation and selective retention to evolutionary development, in particular the power of nested hierarchies of such processes for regulatory systems development, and the importance of recognizing social context in their functioning. It has become evident that evolutionary epistemology sheds fresh light on many areas of traditional philosophy.

Campbell and Paller (1989) say that "for the epistemologist of scientific belief, the design puzzle is the presumed fit between belief and the invisible [Realm 3] world to which such belief refers" (pp. 232-233). They line up with Bhaskar (1975/1997) in noting that because "scientific beliefs are the property and product of a social system [selectionist] epistemology must include specification of social processes that would plausibly lead to the substitution of more valid belief" (Campbell & Paller, 1989, p. 233). Their sociological aspect is similar to Bhaskar's sociology of knowledge component in his transcendental idealism. The fallibilist sociology of knowledge process leads in an approximationist convergent fashion toward a more probable belief in the truth of explanations about intransitive entities—whether Realm 1, 2, or 3. Hahlweg (1989) proposes theories as maps that guide action, saying, "we select maps on the basis of their capacity to guide us to our destination. Likewise we choose to employ theories that can serve as guides to action. In doing so we indirectly select for theories that depict the genuine invariant relationships holding in the world" (pp. 70-71). His view could look instrumental, but he emphasizes that picking out theories as guides to action is tantamount to indirectly selecting true theories.

Hooker (1989) develops an *evolutionary naturalism epistemology* in which knowledge is conceived of as a "primary factor in the coordination of our responses to our environment (including now both our internal environment and the guiding of our search for more knowledge)" (p. 108). In this, he is followed by Plotkin (1993), who sees the human brain and its cognitive processing capability as the primary evolutionary adaptation through which the human species now copes with an increasingly rapidly changing environment. In this respect, the evolution of science is virtually one and the same with the evolution of the human brain, its cognitive processing, and the human species's adaptive capabilities. Hooker distinguishes between a horizontal "convergent" evolution of knowledge and a vertical "punctuated" form. Thus:

> Theories regulate the development of practices (technologies) and data structures (facts), and methods regulate the development of theories. Methods, theo-

ries, and technologies may all be refined and extended; this [horizontal evolution of knowledge] is the "normal" situation. They may also change in more radical or revolutionary ways [vertical evolution of knowledge], thereby forcing it [theoretical development] to retreat to less committed assumptions. The key to understanding scientific development is the process of ascending these theoretical and methodological hierarchies and the multiple ways in which normal science may pave the way for this. (1989, p. 109)

Hooker sees science as evolving in both convergent and punctuated ways. Popper (1972) views science as two evolutionary trees growing in the same scientific forest and at the same time. One tree, like Hooker's horizontal evolution, converges toward optimal designs "within the line" of speciation or specialization toward a specific niche—it shows more and more branches in reflecting the growth of *applied* knowledge resting on the growth of tools and instruments in ever more applied specialized and differentiated niches. The other tree, reflecting the growth of *pure knowledge* or basic research, shows a tendency toward increasing integration, fewer theories, and thus fewer and fewer major branches. Rather than an "either-or" type of horizontal (convergent) or vertical (punctuated) evolution, Popper sees it as simultaneous evolution toward many applied branches and fewer integrative theory branches. Taken together, we have *convergent*, *punctuated*, and *integrative* evolutions of science.

To summarize into Campbell's tripartite framework, a selectionist evolutionary epistemology has replaced the historical relativism of Kuhn and colleagues for the purpose of framing a dynamic epistemology. First, much of the literature from Lorenz forward has focused on the selectionist evolution of the human brain, our cognitive capabilities, and our visual senses (Campbell, 1988a), concluding that these capabilities do indeed give us accurate information about the world in which we live. Second, Campbell (1986b, 1988a, 1988b, 1989b, 1991, 1995) draws on the hermeneuticists' coherence theory in a selectionist fashion to argue that over time, members of a scientific community (as

a tribe) attach increased scientific validity to an entity as the meanings given to that entity increasingly cohere across members. This process is based on hermeneuticists' use of coherence theory to attach meaning to terms discovered in archaic religious texts. Campbell draws on the hermeneuticists' "validity-seeking" principles, such as the *hermeneutic circle* of "part-whole iterating," *omnifallibilist trust, pattern matching, increasing correspondence with increasing scope, partial proximal revision, fallibilist privileging of observations and core*, and the *principle of charity*. (Campbell's use of hermeneutics is discussed more fully in Campbell [1991] and also by Hendrickx in chapter 17 in this volume.) This is a version of the social constructionist process of knowledge validation that defines Bhaskar's transcendental idealism and sociology of knowledge components in his scientific realist account. The coherentist approach selectively winnows out the worst of the theories and thus approaches a more probable truth. If Campbell stopped here, I would place him only in the semantic relativist camp—but he does not.

Third, Campbell (1988a, 1991), Bhaskar (1975/ 1997), Hahlweg and Hooker (1989), Aronson and colleagues (1994), and others add the scientific realist component to the second part, thereby producing an ontologically strong dynamic epistemology. In this view, the coherence process within a scientific community continually develops in the context of selectionist testing for ontological validity. The socially constructed coherence enhanced theories of a scientific community are tested against an objective reality, with a winnowing out of the less ontologically correct theoretical entities. This process, consistent with the strong version of scientific realism proposed by de Regt (1994), does not guarantee "truth," but it does move science in the direction of increased verisimilitude.[19]

B. Resolving the Dilemmas

The First and Second

In the final section of his 1974 chapter, Campbell says:

The *goal of objectivity* in science is a noble one, and dearly to be cherished. It is in true worship of this goal that we remind ourselves that our current views of reality are partial and imperfect. We recoil at a view of science which recommends we give up the search for ultimate truth and settle for practical computational recipes making no pretense at truly describing [and explaining] a real world. Thus our sentiment is to reject pragmatism, utilitarian nominalism, utilitarian subjectivism, utilitarian conventionalism, or instrumentalism, in favor of a critical hypothetical realism. (1974b, p. 447)

Campbell faces the dilemma that selectionist epistemology appears to favor pragmatism, instrumentalism, and classical naïve realism when, as the above quotation indicates, he recoils at that possibility, preferring "ultimate truth" instead. The instrumental, classical empiricist view of science, dating back to Comtean positivism, defines science as focusing on predictions limited to observable (Realm 1) terms, such as "A falling rock will accelerate" or "A large firm will have more hierarchical layers showing on its organization chart." This is a problem because scientific explanation invariably includes entities (terms) from Realms 2 or 3. As a result of this dilemma, selectionist epistemology has within itself a continuance of the long-running debate about how to resolve the fundamental philosophical problem—how to conduct truth-tests in Realms 2 and 3.

Previously, I demonstrated that (a) most present-day philosophers of science adopt scientific realism as a credible replacement of positivism and its goal of an objectivist science, (b) scientific realism has withstood attacks by van Fraassen and Laudan, and (c) There is a credible epistemologically sound argument in favor of a *fallibilist* scientific realism based on the combined works of Bhaskar (1975/1997), Aronson and colleagues (1994), Derksen (1994), and de Regt (1994), among many others. Campbell's first dilemma disappears because scientific realism offers an objectivist alternative to positivism while still retaining terms and entities in Realms 1, 2, *and* 3.

In this literature and in Campbell's epistemology, fallibilism may result from three causes. Using the diagram from Aronson and colleagues

(1994), (a) we may be some distance from the origin on the "dotted line" toward truth in the sense that our theory consists of the wrong terms and logic, (b) we may have too much "metaphysicality" in the terms and entities of our theory for solid truth-tests, and (c) we may be closer to Stage 2 (socially constructed idealism) than Stage 3 (empirically based realism) in Bhaskar's diagram. Thus, at any given time we may not know quite which source of fallibilism is operating to tarnish our truth-test. Because the dynamics of selectionist evolutionary epistemology "select" to lessen all three kinds of fallibility by winnowing out the most obvious elements of fallibilism, there is slow incremental progress toward increased verisimilitude.

Given that the search for truth at any given time is independent from the metaphysicality of terms and entities, there is nothing in selectionist winnowing that inexorably pushes toward operationalism or naïve realism. Fallibilism could be as much due to operational measures that are overly narrow in meaning, are too unstable because of changing instruments, or have poor reliability and validity, as it might be to too many metaphysical entities and lack of solid measures. The crux of the matter hinges on the *quest for truth* on one hand and the *veil of perception* on the other, as depicted in Figure 18.2. Aronson and colleagues (1994) set the *quest* and the *veil* independent of each other, each being an independent cause of higher verisimilitude. The quest is now defined in terms of the "new" convergent realism, probable knowledge, the rationality of existential scientific beliefs, fallibilist eliminative inductions, and the risk that the prolonged existence of Realm 3 terms falsely postulated to be real is negligible. The veil moves independently of the quest, depending on the development of detection instruments or methods such that the quest is not held hostage by limitations that human sensory capacities might place on the where the veil might be set at any given time. The scientific realists' separation of the quest from the veil is important because this negates Campbell's concern that selectionist epistemology, as a fallibilist process of searching for truth, steers science toward Realm 1 terms. It does not. Whether to believe that Realm 3 terms are or are not real is now independent of the status of the quest for truth. The dilemma is resolved.

The Third and Fourth

An *objectivist inductively plausible convergent fallibilist scientific realism* also resolves Campbell's third and fourth dilemmas. Popper would add his term, *falsificationist*, to this string of adjectives. Scientific realism is an objectivist postpositivist epistemology that backs its way toward more probably true theories by incrementally winnowing out the worst of the theories, terms, and entities at any given time. Selective evolutionary epistemology is a well-developed literature that provides the mechanics for how convergent scientific realism changes the beliefs and theories held by scientists. Objective reality plays the role of ecological forces in evolutionary theory. The selection process imposed by the objective ecology provides an ever present context in which theories, conceptions, interpretations, social constructions, terms, and imagined entities all compete for survival.

Surviving theories are not of guaranteed Truth. The search for Truth with a capital T died along with positivism. Surviving theories are more fruitful, presumably, because they have more verisimilitude or more instrumental reliability. Thus the theory "The sun rises because it goes around the earth" is very reliable but we now know it is false. The theory "Earthquake swarms precede volcanic eruptions" has high verisimilitude but not reliability. A theory could be successful—that is, used frequently—for either reason. As Laudan (1981) points out, in the context of instrumental reliability, success does not guarantee truth; however, the relation of success with verisimilitude may be a function of a science's life cycle. If *Verisimilitude* and *Reliability* are set up as in an equation, realists would expect that *Success* would initially vary directly mostly with *R* but that as *R* asymptotes toward 100% predictability, *S* would vary more and more with *V*. If, on the other hand, *R* does not asymptote out but continues low, *S* might vary randomly with *R* but more directly with *V*. Two of the many reasons why this might be so are that (a) as fields of inquiry widen, early high *R* theories are found wanting—for 10th-century farmers, it is

irrelevant whether a theory about the sun rising is true or not, but for launching probes to Jupiter in the 20th century it makes a tremendous difference; and (b) drawing on de Regt (1994), it is irrational for scientists to knowingly accept a false theory, or to ignore the verisimilitude of a theory, and despite continuous calls for instrumentalism or pragmatism over the years most scientists still insist on thinking of theories as true or false, so the question of verisimilitude never goes away—and it is equally irrational for philosophers to ignore the rationality of scientists. Note that in the above, I did not say *S* caused *V* or that *V* caused *S*—just that they would vary directly.

Scientific realists conclude, therefore, that surviving theories have higher verisimilitude than those that do not. This view of the dynamic process does not deny the existence of interpreted theory terms or socially constructed terms, nor does it even deny the possibility that disciplinary matrices or paradigms might be incommensurable. Neither does it require that social scientists give up their favorite relativist paradigm, because all of these fit into Bhaskar's transcendental idealism, which is Stage 2 on the way to an objectivist empirically tested transcendental realism. So, unless scientists are willing to arrest scientific progress at Stage 2, by denying that some explanations of sunlight, falling rocks, earthquakes, quasars, disease, behavior, and organizational knowledge and learning have more verisimilitude than others, Campbell's epistemology, built solidly on ontological realism, resolves the third and fourth dilemmas. Epistemology is now at a point where an objectivist dynamic view of science exists, as does an objectivist epistemology that includes transcendental idealism and the many relativist paradigms.

IV. Campbellian Realist Organization Science

There could be as many different uses of *paradigm* in organization science as there are in Kuhn's 1962 book. Some authors worry deeply about the right or wrong paradigm; how many there are;

about positivism, relativism, subjectivity, and re-flexivity; about incommensurability; and perhaps about whether there is much real truth to what is taught in business schools and practiced by consultants. A few authors argue about it vociferously in the journals. Most organization researchers, like most physicists, go blissfully about their empirical work without worrying about "all that philosophical stuff"—pick a theory, propose a hypothesis, find a data set, find some results at $p < .05$, get published, get tenure, get promoted. Pfeffer (1993) says that the result of all this is a low-status science busily replicating itself with little outside influence or attention.

Much of this miasma is archaic and misinformed. Organization scientists are not positivists because they do not believe in verification and covering laws but do believe in cause and metaphysical terms. Nor are they strong-form relativists, because they do not believe in paradigm incommensurability—otherwise how could one author write about all paradigms in one textbook, and worse, think that incommensurable paradigms could be explained to students? If the paradigm war is archaic, misinformed, and vapid anyway, what added benefit does Campbell offer?

Campbellian realism is critical because elements of positivism and relativism, in fact, remain. Thus, core aspects of the underlying epistemological debate also continue. Many theory terms pertaining to organizational behavior still are in Realms 2 or 3, as this hypothesis suggests:

> Firms with <u>configurations</u> of *competence enhancing* <u>HR system attributes</u> that are <u>unique</u>, *causally ambiguous*, and *synergistic* will have *sustained competitive advantage* over firms that have <u>HR system configurations</u> that are <u>typical</u>, *causally determinate*, and *nonsynergistic* (Lado & Wilson, 1994, p. 718; my emphasis).[20]

Although the underlined terms probably are in Realm 2, it seems likely that the italicized terms may never leave Realm 3. Some would argue that even "firms" is a Realm 2 entity. Because metaphysical terms remain, the positivists' fundamental concern over how to ascertain truthlikeness also remains. The hypothesis also consists of several

lines of text, with the meaning of each word subject to individual interpretation and collective social construction, so these aspects of semantic relativism also remain.

Boiled down, the debate between objectivists and social constructionists surely continues and could still work to produce a multiparadigm organization science continuing in low status. With the debate crystallized to its essence, Campbell's epistemology offers a solution that folds into a single epistemology (a) metaphysical terms, (b) objectivist empirical investigation, (c) recognition of socially constructed meanings of terms, and (d) a dynamic process by which a multiparadigm discipline might reduce to fewer but more significant theories. Surely this is a message that organization science needs at this stage in its life cycle.

The resolution of the Campbellian dilemmas defines a *critical, hypothetical, corrigible, scientific realist selectionist evolutionary* epistemology characterized as follows:

1. A scientific realist postpositivist epistemology that maintains the goal of objectivity in science without excluding metaphysical terms and entities;
2. A selectionist evolutionary epistemology governing the winnowing out of less probable theories, terms, and beliefs in the search for increased verisimilitude that may do so without the danger of systematically replacing metaphysical terms with operationalisms;
3. A postrelativist epistemology that incorporates the dynamics of science without abandoning the goal of objectivity; and
4. An objectivist selectionist evolutionary epistemology that includes as part of its path toward increased verisimilitude the inclusion of, but also the winnowing out of, the more fallible, individual interpretations and social constructions of the meanings of theory terms comprising theories purporting to explain an objective external reality.

As I have demonstrated at least in part, the epistemological directions espoused by Campbellian realism have strong foundations and wide support in the scientific realist and evolutionary epistemology communities. Although philosophers never seem to agree exactly on anything, broad

TABLE 18.7 Suggested Elements of an Organization Science Epistemology

Organization science

1. Is an objectivist science that includes terms in all three Realms.
2. Recognizes that though the semantic meanings of all terms are subject to interpretation and social construction by individuals and the scientific community, this semantic relativism does not thwart the eventual goal of an objective though fallible search for increased verisimilitude.
3. Includes a selectionist evolutionary process of knowledge development that systematically winnows out the more fallible theories, terms, and entities over time.
4. Does not, as a result of its selectionist process, systematically favor either operational or metaphysical terms.
5. Accepts the principle that the true/false dichotomy is replaced by verisimilitude and degrees or probabilities of truthlikeness.[a]
6. Includes theories that are eventually the result of fallible incremental inductions eliminating those having less probable verisimilitude.[a]
7. Because knowledge concerning Realm 1 and 2 terms and entities is at best probable, tentative belief in the probable existence and verisimilitude of Realm 3 terms is no less truthlike than the fallible truth associated with theories comprising Realms 1 and 2 terms and entities.[a]
8. Defines theories to consist of lawlike statements having predictive elements capable of being tested for experimental adequacy.[b]
9. Insists that theories be based on (preferably formalized) models representing that portion of phenomena within the scope of the theory and subject to tests for ontological adequacy.[b]
10. Defines verisimilitude in terms of the content of its models.[b]
11. Is based on a convergent realism in which there is a functional relationship such that increased verisimilitude serves to reduce the error in measures and predictions and vice versa.[b]
12. Holds that the relation between (a) theory and prediction and (b) organizations and how they behave remains independent of whether terms and entities are in Realms 1, 2, or 3.[b]

a. Based on one of de Regt's (1994) points from Table 18.5.
b. Based on one of Aronson, Harré, and Way's (1994) points from Table 18.6.

consensus does exist that these tenets reflect what is best about current philosophy. As the debate about organization science epistemology goes forward, the points listed in Table 18.7 should be seriously considered as central elements of the field. These points combine key epistemological tenets developed by Campbell, de Regt, and Aronson and colleagues.

I would be remiss not to make a special point of the role of experiments in Campbellian realism. Experiments and what Bhaskar terms "contrived invariances" play a central role in scientific realism, as is evident in the elements of Table 18.7 attributed to de Regt and Aronson and colleagues. Campbell, needless to say, has advocated quasi-experiments for fields such as organization science for years (Cook & Campbell, 1979). The literature following from this work is described in more detail by Evans (this volume). Although I do not have space to develop the ideas of the semantic conception theorists (Beth, 1961; Suppes, 1962;

Lloyd, 1988; Suppe, 1989; Thompson, 1989), this line of epistemology, as a third ontologically strong postpositivism, places models at the center of science. Although organization scientists have been remiss in failing to draw on experimental or quasi-experimental research designs, the development of microcomputers has made computational models and computational experimental methods more accessible. Coupled with the semantic conception's positioning of models, it is now possible for organization science to become much more of an experimental science. I outline this approach elsewhere (McKelvey, 1998a, 1998b, 1998c).

A significant caveat is relevant. As I have argued elsewhere (McKelvey, 1997), organization science is *quasi-natural*. Organizational phenomena appear to result from both human intentionality and naturally emergent behavior and may have varying amounts of the reflexive component that Perrow (1994) emphasizes. The field, as Hannan and Freeman (1977) observed long ago, has made more progress in describing and understanding intentional managerial behavior than it has in developing the science of how idiosyncratic process events and other microstate levels of behavior interact to produce emergent aspects of organization structure, function, and process. Because of this imbalance, Campbellian realism serves the interests of organization scientists attempting to develop the natural side of organization science more than it might for those worried about intentionality and reflexiveness.

V. Conclusion

Now that the excesses of positivism and historical relativism have been abandoned, the discourse reduces to the age-old debate among objectivists and subjectivists, which Natanson (1963) observes goes back to Plato and Aristotle. Much of the postpositivist postrelativist philosophy of science has evolved as scientific realism and evolutionary epistemology. Campbell has built on these developments to create a *Campbellian realism* particularly relevant to organization science.

In this chapter, I first review some of the reasons why positivism and relativism were abandoned by philosophers. I then argue that the four Campbellian dilemmas bringing together objectivism, metaphysical entities, relativism, and science dynamics are resolved now that the scientific realist and evolutionary epistemology literatures are more fully developed. Given that Campbellian realism is now on a strong footing, its implications for organization science are more compelling.

In Table 18.7, I combine the message of the four resolved dilemmas with key elements of the realism set forth by de Regt (1994) and Aronson and colleagues (1994). Taken together, these elements suggest key tenets of a new organization science. These tenets allow organization science to get past the current paradigm debates in its literature. Some of this debate exists only because authors are philosophically misinformed and out of date. The debate over the verisimilitude of more specific paradigms such as contingency theory, organizational economics, population ecology, institutional theory, and the like (Donaldson, 1995) continues largely

because the scientific standards thought to guide organization science are so vague and watery that corroboration or refutation of one or another theory remains obscure. Table 18.7 sets the scientific "bar" high enough to make the research process more telling.

In addition to organization scientists being philosophically uninformed, much of the low quality and low status of organization science could simply be a result of the fact that organization science is more than two centuries younger than physics and economics. The low stature also seems to result in part from the difficulty of applying normal science methods to the study of intentional behavior, some of which may reflexively respond to the research process itself, as Perrow (1994) observes. Nevertheless, it appears that many organizational phenomena may be studied fruitfully under the guidance of the tenets suggested in Table 18.7. If organization scientists were to follow these tenets of Campbellian realism—really present-day science—there is some reason to hope that theory proliferation would diminish and the status and influence of organization science, as viewed by outsiders, would rise.

Notes

1. Putnam (1962) refers to the combination of both logical positivism and logical empiricism as the *Received View*.

2. Lengthy histories of positivism are given by Kraft (1953), Ayer (1959), and Hanfling (1981). Kraft was a founding member of the Vienna Circle. Ayer joined circa 1933. Key sources of relativism are Hanson (1958), Kuhn (1962), and Feyerabend (1975). Suppe (1977) uses some 150 pages to develop the logic underlying their abandonment. I reduce this to a few paragraphs, doing considerable injustice to the careful development of his arguments as a result. Readers questioning the arguments should take time to study Suppe's logic in its original form. There are many other critiques of course, such as Putnam (1981), Nola (1988), and Rogers (1993), not to mention critiques implicit in the development of scientific realism and evolutionary epistemology.

3. It took the form of a pamphlet titled *Wissenschaftliche Weltauffassung, Der Wiener Kreis,* Wien, Artur Wolf, 1929 (Neurath, Hahn, & Carnap, 1929/1973), later reprinted and translated.

4. Logical empiricism was a label preferred by some members of the Vienna Circle very early on, specifically, Morris (1935), Carnap (1936-1937), and Schlick (1938).

5. The category "strong forms of relativism" also includes other ontologically weak subjectivist *postpositivisms* such as ethnomethodology, historicism, radical humanism, phenomenology, semioticism, literary explication, hermeneutics, and critical theory, all of which are "post" positivist and in all of which subjective and cultural forces dominate ontological reality. Lincoln and Guba (1985, p. 7) use the term *naturalism* to encompass a similar set of postpositivist paradigms.

6. Space precludes expanding the critique beyond the basic objections outlined by Suppe to include Natanson (1963), Ravitz (1971), Stockman (1983), Taylor (1985), Nola (1988), Munévar (1991), or Masters (1993), among others.

7. Suppe's characterization is confirmed by Nola (1988).

8. To pick an example, consider the most famous so-called paradigm shift, that from Newton to Einstein. In his 1905 paper, Einstein drew mainly on the work of Faraday 70 years earlier. The reason he cited Faraday was that he (Einstein) defined the problem as how to specify a theory of relative motion for the electrodynamics of moving bodies parallel to the already existing theory of relative motion in Newtonian mechanics. By 1895, both Poincaré and H. A. Lorentz had announced principles of relativity, but to balance the equation governing the relative motion of two inertial systems, they retained the concept of ether. In contrast, because the speed of light was discovered to remain constant (Einstein, unaware of the discovery, assumed it as a principle), Einstein accommodated relativity by allowing time to change. Thus, in the Lorentz transformation equations, $t' = t$ became $t' = (t - vx/c^2)/(1 - v^2/c^2)^{1/2}$. Note that none of the terms on the right side of the equation changed meaning, only the t' term changed. What is important to note is that there would have been no reason for Einstein to do what he did if the other terms *had not remained unchanged*—a clear violation of incommensurability. The significance of relativity theory is that none of the terms changed meaning except time. In addition, the new idea appeared in a journal article in an obscure Einstein's first year of publication after his doctorate. How on earth could referees in the old paradigm accept for publication an article by an unknown author in a different, supposedly incommensurable, paradigm? This makes sense only if relativity was in fact *not* incommensurable with existing "Newtonian" thinking. See Holton (1988) for the full range of views on whether or not relativity theory was incommensurable with Maxwell, Poincaré, and Lorentz.

9. For additional evidence of support, see Popper (1956/1982), Maxwell (1962, 1970), Hesse (1963, 1974), Sellars (1963), Smart (1963), Shapere (1969), Harré (1970, 1986, 1994), McMullin (1970, 1978), Boyd (1973, 1989, 1992), MacKinnon (1979), Putnam (1982, 1987, 1990, 1993), Devitt (1984), Leplin (1984, 1986), Churchland and Hooker (1985), Hooker (1987), Rescher (1987), Nola (1988), Suppe (1989), Hunt (1991), Dummett (1992), Blackburn (1993), Derksen (1994).

10. An iconic model is one that offers a visual image such as "boxes and arrows," balls and sticks (for atoms), or a mechanical representation.

11. As my discussion proceeds, it will be convenient to use Harré's (1989) labels for kinds of terms or entities: *Realm 1*

entities are currently observable (number of employees in a firm)], *Realm 2* entities are currently unobservable but potentially detectable (process event networks in a firm), and *Realm 3* (metaphysical) entities are beyond any possibility of observation by any conception of current science (psychological need, environmental uncertainty, underlying cause). Note that they are not the same as Bhaskar's three stages.

12. My analysis of the Giere and Devitt critique closely follows that given by de Regt (1994, pp. 107-113).

13. I have substituted *experimental* in place of van Fraassen's *empirical* adequacy. As made clear by Bhaskar, philosophers prefer experimental empirical methods and nomic necessity so as to avoid accidental regularities. This fits closely with the label "Better predictions and manipulation" that AHW use in their Figure 9.1 (Figure 18.2 here). This also avoids confusion with *ontological* adequacy, which is also an empirical test of how well model structures represent the real world.

14. Section III shows that successive elimination of inductions is essentially the same as selective evolutionary epistemology.

15. For a recent review of the antirealist arguments, see Wright (1997). Despite the review, Wright holds to a "very narrow and guarded Realism" (1997, p. viii), though he does recognize that antirealism may apply in some circumstances. Suppe (1989) and Blackburn (1993) also suggest a somewhat qualified "quasi-realism." Another review of realist and antirealist arguments is Cohen, Hilpinen, and Renzong (1996).

16. Campbell prefers "selectionist evolutionary epistemology" so as to emphasize his favorite thing in the world, *blind-variation-and-selective-retention*. He emphasizes that this process underlies all inductive knowledge, increases in knowledge, and all increases in the fit of systems to their environments (1974b). Other authors such as Rescher (1987) place less emphasis on the "blind" aspect; some use evolutionary theory only to explain the development of the brain and biological bases of cognitive processes (Bradie, 1986); Lorenz (1941/1982) uses evolutionary theory to explain the biological basis of conceptual structures and categories á lá Kant; Hahlweg (1989), Callebaut (1987), and many others set language up as the genotype with scientists playing the role of phenotypes; Hooker (1995, p. 4) now embeds his *evolutionary naturalized realism* in the framework of "dynamic nonlinear self-organizing complex adaptive systems," that is, complexity theory (Prigogine & Stengers, 1984; Nicolis & Prigogine, 1989; Cowan, Pines, & Meltzer, 1994; Belew & Mitchell, 1996; Arthur, Durlauf, & Lane, 1997).

17. The literature includes a number of edited volumes (Greenberg & Tobach, 1984, 1987, 1988, 1990; Callebaut & Pinxten, 1987; Radnitzky & Bartley, 1987; Fuller, De Mey, Shinn, & Woolgar, 1989; Hahlweg & Hooker, 1989; Maxwell & Savage, 1989; Rescher, 1990), some singly authored books (Ruse, 1986; Hooker, 1987; Stich, 1990), and numerous articles including those by Campbell (1959, 1960, 1965, 1974a, 1974b, 1979, 1985, 1986a, 1986b, 1987, 1988a, 1988b, 1989a, 1989b, 1990a, 1990b, 1991, 1994, 1995), Holzner, Campbell, and Shahidullah (1985), Campbell and Paller (1989), and Paller and Campbell (1989).

18. In coherence theory, the truth of an argument is a function of how well it coheres with arguments proposed by others. Hermeneuticists agree that such a process does allow them to know the true meaning of a text beyond a shadow of a doubt.

19. For a counter view, see Stich (1990), who argues for pragmatism over selectionist explanation.

20. If one applied the Copenhagen Interpretation (Bitbol, 1996), which holds that a particle such as an electron is metaphysical because the act of detection alters its state—the Heisenberg Uncertainty Principle—one might conclude that all terms in this hypothesis are metaphysical because it is well known that the act of measuring in firms sensitizes them and thus could (it is an uncertainty) alter their state.

References

Alvesson, M., & Deetz, S. (1996). Critical theory and postmodernism approaches to organizational studies. In S. R. Clegg, C. Hardy, & W. R. Nord (Eds.), *Handbook of organization studies* (pp. 191-217). Thousand Oaks, CA: Sage.

Anderson, P. F. (1988). Relativism revidivus: In defense of critical relativism. *Journal of Consumer Research, 15*, 403-406

Aronson, J. L., Harré, R., & Way, E. C. (1994). *Realism rescued.* London: Duckworth.

Arthur, W. B., Durlauf, S. N., & Lane, D. A. (Eds.). (1997). *The economy as an evolving complex system* (Proceedings Vol. 27). Reading, MA: Addison-Wesley.

Audi, R. (Ed.). (1995). *The Cambridge dictionary of philosophy.* Cambridge, UK: Cambridge University Press.

Ayer, A. J. (1959). *Logical positivism.* Glencoe, IL: Free Press.

Belew, R. K., & Mitchell, M. (Eds.). (1996). *Adaptive individuals in evolving populations* (Proceedings of the Santa Fe Institute, Vol. 26). Reading, MA: Addison-Wesley.

Beth, E. (1961). Semantics of physical theories. In H. Freudenthal (Ed.), *The concept and the role of the model in mathematics and natural and social sciences* (pp. 48-51). Dordrecht, The Netherlands: Reidel.

Bhaskar, R. (1997). *A realist theory of science* (2nd ed.). London: Verso. (Original work published 1975)

Bitbol, M. (1996). *Schrödinger's philosophy of quantum mechanics.* Dordrecht, The Netherlands: Kluwer.

Blackburn, S. (1993). *Essays in quasi-realism.* New York: Oxford University Press.

Bloor, D. (1976). *Knowledge and social imagery.* London: Routledge and Kegan Paul.

Bohm, D. (1957). *Causality and chance in modern physics.* London: Routledge and Kegan Paul.

Boyd, R. (1973). Realism: Underdetermination and a causal theory of reference. *Noûs, 7*, 1-12.

Boyd, R. (1983). On the current status of scientific realism. *Erkenntnis, 19*, 45-90.

Boyd, R. (1989). What realism implies and what it does not. *Dialectica, 43*, 5-29.

Boyd, R. (1991). Confirmation, semantics, and the interpretation of scientific theories. In R. Boyd, P. Gasper, & J. D. Trout (Eds.), *The philosophy of science* (pp. 3-35). Cambridge, MA: Bradford/MIT Press.

Boyd, R. (1992). Constructivism, realism, and philosophical method. In J. Earman (Ed.), *Inference, explanation, and other frustrations: Essays in the philosophy of science* (pp. 131-198). Berkeley: University of California Press.

Bradie, M. (1986). Assessing evolutionary epistemology. *Biology and Philosophy, 1*, 401-459.

Braithwaite, R. B. (1953). *Scientific explanation.* Cambridge, UK: Cambridge University Press.

Brannigan, A. (1981). *The social basis of scientific discoveries.* Cambridge, UK: Cambridge University Press.

Büchner, L. F. (1855). *Kraft und Stoff.* Frankfort aum Main: Meidinger Sohn.

Burrell, G. (1996). Normal science, paradigms, metaphors, discourses and genealogies of analysis. In S. R. Clegg, C. Hardy, & W. R. Nord (Eds.), *Handbook of organization studies* (pp. 642-658). Thousand Oaks, CA: Sage.

Burrell, G., & Morgan, G. (1979). *Sociological paradigms and organizational analysis.* London: Heinemann.

Callebaut, W. (1987). Why it makes sense to extend the genotype/phenotype distinction to culture. *La Nuova Critica.*

Callebaut, W., & Pinxten, R. (Eds.). (1987). *Evolutionary epistemology: A multiparadigm program.* Dordrecht, The Netherlands: Reidel.

Campbell, D. T. (1959). Methodological suggestions from a comparative psychology of knowledge processes. *Inquiry, 2*, 152-182.

Campbell, D. T. (1960). Blind variation and selective retention in creative thought as in other knowledge processes. *Psychological Review, 67*, 380-400.

Campbell, D. T. (1965). Variation and selective retention in socio-cultural evolution. In H. R. Barringer, G. I. Blanksten, & R. W. Mack (Eds.), *Social change in developing areas: A reinterpretation of evolutionary theory* (pp. 19-48). Cambridge, MA: Schenkman.

Campbell, D. T. (1974a). "Downward causation" in hierarchically organized biological systems. In F. J. Ayala & T. Dobzhansky (Eds.), *Studies in the philosophy of biology* (pp. 179-186). London: Macmillan.

Campbell, D. T. (1974b). Evolutionary epistemology. In P. A. Schilpp (Ed.), *The philosophy of Karl Popper* (The Library of Living Philosophers, Vol. 14, pp. 413-463). La Salle, IL: Open Court.

Campbell, D. T. (1979). A tribal model of the social system vehicle carrying scientific knowledge. *Knowledge, 2*, 181-201.

Campbell, D. T. (1985). Toward an epistemologically-relevant sociology of science. *Science, Technology, & Human Values, 10*, 38-48.

Campbell, D. T. (1986a). Rationality and utility from the standpoint of evolutionary biology. *Journal of Business, 59*(Special Issue), S355-S364.

Campbell, D. T. (1986b). Science's social system of validity-enhancing collective belief change and the problems of the social sciences. In D. W. Fiske & R. A. Shweder (Eds.), *Metatheory in social science: Pluralisms and subjectivities* (pp. 108-135). Chicago: University of Chicago Press.

Campbell, D. T. (1987). Selection theory and the sociology of scientific validity. In W. Callebaut & R. Pinxten (Eds.), *Evolutionary epistemology: A multiparadigm program* (pp. 139-158). Dordrecht, The Netherlands: Reidel.

Campbell, D. T. (1988a). Descriptive epistemology: Psychological, sociological, and evolutionary. In D. T. Campbell, *Methodology and epistemology for social science: Selected papers* (E. S. Overman, Ed., pp. 435-486). Chicago: University of Chicago Press.

Campbell, D. T. (1988b). A general "selection theory" as implemented in biological evolution and in social belief-transmission-with-modification in science. *Biology and Philosophy, 3,* 171-177.

Campbell, D. T. (1989a). Being mechanistic/materialistic/realistic about the process of knowing. *Canadian Psychology, 30,* 184-185.

Campbell, D. T. (1989b). Models of language learning and their implications for social constructionist analysis of scientific beliefs. In S. Fuller, M. De Mey, T. Shinn, & S. Woolgar (Eds.), *The cognitive turn: Sociological and psychological perspectives on science* (pp. 153-158). Dordrecht, The Netherlands: Kluwer.

Campbell, D. T. (1990a). Epistemological roles for selection theory. In N. Rescher (Ed.), *Evolution, cognition, realism* (pp. 1-19). Lanham, MD: University Press of America.

Campbell, D. T. (1990b). Levels of organization, downward causation, and the selection-theory approach to evolutionary epistemology. In G. Greenberg & E. Tobach (Eds.), *Theories of the evolution of knowing* (T. C. Schneirla Conference Series, Vol. 4, pp. 1-17). Hillsdale, NJ: Erlbaum.

Campbell, D. T. (1991). Coherentist empiricism, hermeneutics, and the commensurability of paradigms. *International Journal of Educational Research, 15,* 587-597.

Campbell, D. T. (1994). How individual and face-to-face-group selection undermine firm selection in organizational evolution. In J.A.C. Baum & J. V. Singh (Eds.), *Evolutionary dynamics of organizations* (pp. 23-38). New York: Oxford University Press.

Campbell, D. T. (1995). The postpositivist, non-foundational, hermeneutic epistemology exemplified in the works of Donald W. Fiske. In P. E. Shrout & S. T. Fiske (Eds.), *Personality research, methods and theory: A festschrift honoring Donald W. Fiske* (pp. 13-27). Hillsdale, NJ: Erlbaum.

Campbell, D. T., & Paller, B. T. (1989). Extending evolutionary epistemology to "justifying" scientific beliefs (a sociological rapprochement with a fallibilist perceptual foundationalism?) In K. Hahlweg & C. A. Hooker (Eds.), *Issues in evolutionary epistemology* (pp. 231-257). New York: State University of New York Press.

Carnap, R. (1923). Über die Aufgabe der Physik und die Andwendung des Gründsatze der Einfachstheit. *Kant-Studien, 28,* 90-107.

Carnap, R. (1936-1937). Testability and meaning. *Philosophy of Science, 3,* 420-468; *4,* 1-40.

Chia, R. (1996). *Organizational analysis as deconstructive practice.* Berlin: Walter de Gruyter.

Churchland, P. M. (1979). *Scientific realism and the plasticity of mind.* Cambridge, UK: Cambridge University Press.

Churchland, P. M., & Hooker, C. A. (Eds.). (1985). *Images of science.* Chicago: University of Chicago Press.

Clegg, S. R., Hardy, C., & Nord, W. R. (Eds.). (1996). *Handbook of organization studies.* Thousand Oaks, CA: Sage.

Cohen, R. S., Hilpinen, R., & Renzong, Q. (1996). *Realism and anti-realism in the philosophy of science.* Dordrecht, The Netherlands: Kluwer.

Cook, T. D., & Campbell, D. T. (1979). *Quasi-experimentation: Design and analysis issues for field settings.* Boston: Houghton Mifflin.

Cowan, G. A., Pines, D., & Meltzer, D. (Eds.). (1994). *Complexity: Metaphors, models, and reality* (Proceedings of the Santa Fe Institute, Vol. 19). Reading, MA: Addison-Wesley.

de Regt, C.D.G. (1994). *Representing the world by scientific theories: The case for scientific realism.* Tilburg, The Netherlands: Tilburg University Press.

Derksen, A. A. (1994). Harré and his versions of scientific realism. In A. A. Derksen (Ed.), *The scientific realism of Rom Harré* (pp. 23-88). Tilburg, The Netherlands: Tilburg University Press.

Devitt, M. (1984). *Realism and truth.* Oxford, UK: Oxford University Press.

Devitt, M. (1991). *Realism and truth* (2nd ed.). Oxford, UK: Oxford University Press.

Donaldson, L. (1985). *In defence of organization theory: A reply to the critics.* Cambridge, UK: Cambridge University Press.

Donaldson, L. (1995). *American anti-management theories of organization: A critique of paradigm proliferation.* Cambridge, UK: Cambridge University Press.

Donaldson, L. (1996). *For positivist organization theory.* Thousand Oaks, CA: Sage.

Dummett, M.A.E. (1992). *The logical basis of metaphysics.* London: Duckworth.

Feyerabend, P. K. (1962). Explanation, reduction, and empiricism. In H. Feigl & G. Maxwell (Eds.), *Current issues in the philosophy of science* (pp. 28-97). New York: Holt, Rinehart & Winston.

Feyerabend, P. K. (1970). Against method: Outline of an anarchistic theory of knowledge. In M. Radnor & S. Winokur (Eds.), *Minnesota studies in the philosophy of science* (Vol. 4, pp. 17-130). Minneapolis: University of Minnesota Press.

Feyerabend, P. K. (1975). *Against method.* Thetford, UK: Lowe and Brydone.

Fuller, S., De Mey, M., Shinn, T., & Woolgar, S. (Eds.). (1989). *The cognitive turn: Sociological and psychological perspectives on science.* Dordrecht, The Netherlands: Kluwer.

Giddens, A. (Ed.). (1974). *Positivism and sociology.* London: Heinemann.

Giere, R. N. (1985). Constructive realism. In P. M. Churchland & C. A. Hooker (Eds.), *Images of science: Essays on realism and empiricism* (pp. 75-98). Chicago: University of Chicago Press.

Greenberg, G., & Tobach, E. (Eds.). (1984). *Behavioral evolution and integrative levels* (T. C. Schneirla Conference Series, Vol. 1). Hillsdale, NJ: Erlbaum.

Greenberg, G., & Tobach, E. (Eds.). (1987). *Cognition, language and consciousness: Integrative levels* (T. C. Schneirla Conference Series, Vol. 2). Hillsdale, NJ: Erlbaum.

Greenberg, G., & Tobach, E. (Eds.). (1988). *Evolution of social behavior and integrative levels* (T. C. Schneirla Conference Series, Vol. 3). Hillsdale, NJ: Erlbaum.

Greenberg, G., & Tobach, E. (Eds.). (1990). *Theories of the evolution of knowing* (T. C. Schneirla Conference Series, Vol. 4). Hillsdale, NJ: Erlbaum.

Hacking, I. (1983). *Representing and intervening.* Cambridge, UK: Cambridge University Press.

Hahlweg, K. (1989). A systems view of evolution and evolutionary epistemology. In K. Hahlweg & C. A. Hooker (Eds.), *Issues in evolutionary epistemology* (pp. 45-78). New York: State University of New York Press.

Hahlweg, K., & Hooker, C. A. (1989). I. Historical and theoretical context. In K. Hahlweg & C. A. Hooker (Eds.), *Issues in evolutionary epistemology* (pp. 23-44). Albany: State University of New York Press.

Hanfling, O. (1981). *Logical positivism.* Oxford, UK: Basil Blackwell.

Hannan, M. T., & Freeman, J. (1977). The population ecology of organizations. *American Journal of Sociology, 83,* 929-984.

Hanson, N. R. (1958). *Patterns of discovery.* Cambridge, UK: Cambridge University Press.

Harré, R. (1961). *Theories and things.* London: Sheed & Ward.

Harré, R. (1970). *The principles of scientific thinking.* London: Macmillan.

Harré, R. (1986). *Varieties of realism: A rationale for the natural sciences.* Oxford, UK: Basil Blackwell.

Harré, R. (1989). Realism, reference and theory. In A. P. Griffiths (Ed.), *Key themes in philosophy* (pp. 53-68). Cambridge, UK: Cambridge University Press.

Harré, R. (1994). Three varieties of realism. In A. A. Derksen (Ed.), *The scientific realism of Rom Harré* (pp. 5-21). Tilburg, The Netherlands: Tilburg University Press.

Hempel, C. G. (1954). A logical appraisal of operationism. *Scientific Monthly, 79,* 215-220.

Hempel, C. G. (1965). *Aspects of scientific explanation.* New York: Free Press.

Hesse, M. (1963). *Models and analogies in science.* London: Sheed & Ward.

Hesse, M. (1974). *The structure of scientific inference.* Berkeley: University of California Press.

Holton, G. (1988). *Thematic origins of scientific thought: Kepler to Einstein.* Cambridge, MA: Harvard University Press.

Holzner, B., Campbell, D. T., & Shahidullah, M. (1985). The comparative study of science and the sociology of scientific validity. *Knowledge: Creation, Diffusion, Utilization, 6,* 307-328.

Hooker, C. A. (1987). *A realist theory of science.* New York: State University of New York Press.

Hooker, C. A. (1989). Evolutionary epistemology and naturalist realism. In K. Hahlweg & C. A. Hooker (Eds.), *Issues in evolutionary epistemology* (pp. 101-150). New York: State University of New York Press.

Hooker, C. A. (1995). *Reason, regulation, and realism.* Albany: State University of New York Press.

Hughes, M. (1992). Decluding organization. In M. Reed & M. Hughes (Eds.), *Rethinking organizations: New directions in organization theory and analysis* (pp. 295-300). Newbury Park, CA: Sage.

Hull, D. (1975). Review of books by Hempel, Kuhn, and Shapere. *Systematic Zoology, 24,* 395-401.

Hunt, S. D. (1991). *Modern marketing theory: Critical issues in the philosophy of marketing science.* Cincinnati: South-Western.

Kraft, V. (1953). *The Vienna Circle* (Trans. by A. Pap). New York: Philosophical Library.

Kuhn, T. S. (1962). *The structure of scientific revolutions.* Chicago: University of Chicago Press.

Kuhn, T. S. (1970). *The structure of scientific revolutions* (2nd ed.). Chicago: University of Chicago Press.

Kuhn, T. S. (1977). Second thoughts on paradigms. In F. Suppe (Ed.), *The structure of scientific theories* (2nd ed., pp. 459-482). Urbana: University of Illinois Press.

Lado, A. A., & Wilson, M. C. (1994). Human resource systems and sustained competitive advantage: A competency-based perspective. *Academy of Management Review, 19,* 699-727.

Latour, B., & Woolgar, S. (1986). *Laboratory life: The construction of scientific facts* (2nd ed.). Princeton, NJ: Princeton University Press.

Laudan, L. (1977). *Progress and its problems.* Berkeley: University of California Press.

Laudan, L. (1981). A confutation of convergent realism. *Philosophy of Science, 48,* 19-48.

Leplin, J. (Ed.). (1984). *Scientific realism.* Berkeley: University of California Press.

Leplin, J. (1986). Methodological realism and scientific rationality. *Philosophy of Science, 53,* 31-51.

Lincoln, Y. S. (Ed.). (1985). *Organizational theory and inquiry.* Newbury Park, CA: Sage.

Lincoln, Y. S., & Guba, E. G. (1985). *Naturalistic inquiry.* Beverly Hills, CA: Sage.

Lloyd, E. A. (1988). *The structure and confirmation of evolutionary theory.* Princeton, NJ: Princeton University Press.

Lorenz, K. (1941). Kants Lehre vom apriorischen im Lichte gegenwärtiger Biologie. *Blätter für Deutsche Philosophie, 15,* 94-125. [Also reprinted as "Kant's doctrine of the a priori in the light of contemporary biology." In H. C. Plotkin (Ed.), *Learning, development, and culture* (pp. 121-143). New York: Wiley.]

MacKinnon, E. (1979). Scientific realism: The new debates. *Philosophy of Science, 46,* 501-532.

Masterman, M. (1970). The nature of a paradigm. In I. Lakatos & A. Musgrave (Eds.), *Criticism and the growth of knowl-*

edge (pp. 59-90). Cambridge, UK: Cambridge University Press.

Masters, R. D. (1993). *Beyond relativism.* Hanover, NH: University Press of New England.

Maxwell, G. (1962). The necessary and the contingent. In H. Feigl & G. Maxwell (Eds.), *Current issues in the philosophy of science* (pp. 398-404). New York: Holt, Rinehart & Winston.

Maxwell, G. (1970). Theories, perception, and structural realism. In R. G. Colodny (Ed.), *The nature and function of scientific theories: Essays in contemporary science and philosophy* (pp. 3-34). Pittsburgh: University of Pittsburgh Press.

Maxwell, M. L., & Savage, C. W. (Eds.). (1989). *Science, mind, and psychology: Essays in honor of Grover Maxwell.* Lanham, MD: University Press of America.

McKelvey, B. (1997). Quasi-natural organization science. *Organization Science, 8,* 351-380.

McKelvey, B. (1998a, June). *Can strategy be better than acupuncture? A realist/semantic conception of competence-based research.* Paper presented at the 4th International Conference on Competence-Based Management, Oslo.

McKelvey, B. (1998b). Complexity vs. Selection among coevolutionary microstates in firms: Complexity effects on strategic organizing. *Comportamento Organizacional E Gestão, 4,* 17-59.

McKelvey, B. (1998c, June). *Thwarting faddism at the edge of chaos: On the epistemology of complexity research.* Paper presented at the EIASM Workshop on Complexity and Organization, Brussels.

McMullin, E. (1970). The history and philosophy of science: A taxonomy. In H. Feigl & G. Maxwell (Eds.), *Minnesota studies in the history of science* (Vol. 5, pp. 12-67). Minneapolis: University of Minnesota Press.

McMullin, E. (1978). Structural explanation. *American Philosophical Quarterly, 15,* 139-147.

McMullin, E. (1984). A case for scientific realism. In J. Leplin (Ed.), *Scientific realism* (pp. 8-40). Berkeley: University of California Press.

Morris, C. W. (1935). The relation of the formal and empirical sciences within scientific empiricism. *Erkenntnis, 5,* 6-14.

Munévar, G. (1991). *Beyond reason: Essays on the philosophy of Paul Feyerabend.* Dordrecht, The Netherlands: Kluwer.

Nagel, E. (1956). *Logic without metaphysics.* Glencoe, IL: Free Press.

Nagel, E. (1961). *The structure of science.* New York: Harcourt, Brace.

Natanson, M. (Ed.). (1963). *Philosophy of the social sciences.* New York: Random House.

Neurath, O., Carnap, R., & Hahn, H. (1929). Wissenschaftliche Weltauffassung, Der Wiener Kreis, Wien, Artur Wolf. [Reprinted as "The scientific conception of the world: The Vienna Circle" in M. Neurath & R. S. Cohen (Eds.), *Empiricism and sociology* (1973) (pp. 301-318). Dordrecht, The Netherlands: Reidel.]

Nickles, T. (1989). Integrating the science studies disciplines. In S. Fuller, M. De Mey, T. Shinn, & S. Woolgar (Eds.), *The cognitive turn* (pp. 225-256). Dordrecht, The Netherlands: Kluwer.

Nicolis, G., & Prigogine, I. (1989). *Exploring complexity: An introduction.* New York: Freeman.

Nola, R. (1988). *Relativism and realism in science.* Dordrecht, The Netherlands: Kluwer.

Paller, B. T., & Campbell, D. T. (1989). Maxwell and van Fraassen on observability, reality, and justification. In M. L. Maxwell & C. W. Savage (Eds.), *Science, mind, and psychology: Essays in honor of Grover Maxwell* (pp. 99-132). Lanham, MD: University Press of America.

Perrow, C. (1994). Pfeffer slips. *Academy of Management Review, 19,* 191-194.

Pfeffer, J. (1982). *Organizations and organization theory.* Boston: Pitman.

Pfeffer, J. (1993). Barriers to the advancement of organizational science: Paradigm development as a dependent variable. *Academy of Management Review, 18,* 599-620.

Pfeffer, J. (1995). Mortality, reproducibility, and the persistence of styles of theory. *Organization Science, 6,* 681-686.

Piaget, J. (1950). *Introduction a l'Epistemologie Genetique, 3* vols., Paris: Presses Universitaire de France. [Also, *Principles of Genetic Epistemology,* trans. by W. Mays, London: Routledge & Kegan Paul, 1972.]

Plotkin, H. (1993). *Darwin machines and the nature of knowledge.* Cambridge, MA: Harvard University Press.

Polanyi, M. (1958). *Personal knowledge.* Chicago: University of Chicago Press.

Popper, K. R. (1959). *The logic of scientific discovery.* London: Hutchinson.

Popper, K. R. (1963). *Conjectures and refutations.* London: Routledge and Kegan Paul.

Popper, K. R. (1972). *Objective knowledge: An evolutionary approach.* Oxford, UK: Oxford University Press.

Popper, K. R. (1956/1982). Realism and the aim of science. Totowa, NJ: Rowman and Littlefield. [One of three volumes edited by W. W. Bartley III from the *Postscript to the logic of scientific discovery,* written by Popper during the years 1951-1956]

Prahalad, C. K., & Hamel, G. (1994). Strategy as a field of study: Why search for a new paradigm? *Strategic Management Journal, 15,* 5-16.

Prigogine, I., & Stengers, I. (1984). *Order out of chaos: Man's new dialogue with nature.* New York: Bantam.

Putnam, H. (1962). What theories are not. In E. Nagel, P. Suppes, & A. Tarski (Eds.), *Logic, methodology, and philosophy of science: Proceedings of the 1960 International Congress* (pp. 240-251). Stanford, CA: Stanford University Press.

Putnam, H. (1981). *Reason, truth, and history.* Cambridge, UK: Cambridge University Press.

Putnam, H. (1982). Three kinds of scientific realism. *Philosophical Quarterly, 32,* 195-200.

Putnam, H. (1987). *The many faces of realism.* La Salle, IL: Open Court.

Putnam, H. (1990). *Realism with a human face.* Cambridge, MA: Harvard University Press.

Putnam, H. (1993). *Renewing philosophy.* Cambridge, MA: Harvard University Press.

Radnitzky, G., & Bartley, W. W. III. (Eds.). (1987). *Evolutionary epistemology, rationality, and the sociology of knowledge.* La Salle, IL: Open Court.

Ravitz, J. R. (1971). *Scientific knowledge and its social problems.* Oxford, UK: Clarendon.

Reed, M., & Hughes, M. (Eds.). (1992). *Rethinking organization: New directions in organization theory and analysis.* London: Sage.

Rescher, N. (1970). *Scientific explanation.* New York: Free Press.

Rescher, N. (1987). *Scientific realism: A critical reappraisal.* Dordrecht, The Netherlands: Reidel.

Rescher, N. (Ed.). (1990). *Evolution, cognition, and realism: Studies in evolutionary epistemology.* Lanham, MD: University Press of America.

Ruse, M. (1986). *Taking Darwin seriously: A naturalistic approach to philosophy.* Oxford, UK: Blackwell.

Scheffler, I. (1967). *Science and subjectivity.* Indianapolis: Bobbs-Merrill.

Schlick, M. (1938). *Gesamelte Aufsätze.* Vienna: Gerold.

Schlick, M. (1932/1933). "Positivismus und Realismus," *Erkenntnis* III, 1-31. [Reprinted as "Positivism and Realism," (trans. by P. Heath), in R. Boyd, P. Gasper, & J. D. Trout (Eds.), *The Philosophy of Science,* Cambridge, MA: Bradford/MIT Press, pp. 23-66.]

Sellars, W. (1963). *Science, perception, and reality.* London: Routledge and Kegan Paul.

Shapere, D. (1964). The structure of scientific revolutions. *Philosophical Review, 73,* 383-394.

Shapere, D. (1969). Notes toward a post-positivistic interpretation of science. In P. Achinstein & S. F. Barker (Eds.), *The legacy of logical positivism: Studies in the philosophy of science* (pp. 115-160). Baltimore: Johns Hopkins University Press.

Shapere, D. (1982). The concept of observation in science and philosophy. *Philosophy of Science, 49,* 485-525.

Shapin, S., & Schaffer, S. (1985). *Leviathan and the air-pump.* Princeton, NJ: Princeton University Press.

Smart, J.J.C. (1963). *Philosophy and scientific realism.* London: Routledge and Kegan Paul.

Stich, S. (1990). *Fragmentation of reason.* Cambridge, MA: MIT Press.

Stockman, N. (1983). *Antipositivist theories of the sciences: Critical rationalism, critical theory and scientific realism.* Dordrecht, The Netherlands: Reidel.

Suppe, F. (1977). *The structure of scientific theories* (2nd ed.). Chicago: University of Chicago Press.

Suppe, F. (1989). *The semantic conception of theories & scientific realism.* Urbana-Champaign: University of Illinois Press.

Suppes, P. (1962). Models of data. In E. Nagel, P. Suppes, & A. Tarski (Eds.), *Logic, methodology, and philosophy of science: Proceedings of the 1960 International Congress* (pp. 252-261). Stanford, CA: Stanford University Press.

Taylor, C. (1985). Interpretation and the sciences of man. In C. Taylor, *Philosophy and the human sciences: Philosophical papers* (Vol. 2, pp. 15-57). Cambridge, UK: Cambridge University Press.

Thompson, P. (1989). *The structure of biological theories.* Albany: State University of New York Press.

Toulmin, S. (1953). *The philosophy of science: An introduction.* London: Hutchinson.

Toulmin, S. (1961). *Foresight and understanding.* London: Hutchinson.

Toulmin, S. (1972). *Human understanding* (Vol. 1). Princeton, NJ: Princeton University Press.

van Fraassen, B. C. (1980). *The scientific image.* Oxford, UK: Clarendon.

van Fraassen, B. C. (1985). Empiricism in the philosophy of science. In P. M. Churchland & C. A. Hooker (Eds.), *Images of science* (pp. 245-308). Chicago: University of Chicago Press.

Van Maanen, J. (1995a). Fear and loathing in organization studies. *Organization Science, 6,* 687-692.

Van Maanen, J. (1995b). Style as theory. *Organization Science, 6,* 133-143.

Whitehead, A., & Russell, B. (1910-1913). *Principia Mathematica* (3 vols.). Cambridge, UK: Cambridge University Press.

Wright, J. (1997). *Realism and explanatory priority.* Dordrecht, The Netherlands: Kluwer.

Appendix:
Donald T. Campbell's Curriculum Vitae

Born: November 20, 1916, Grass Lake, Michigan
Died: May 6, 1996, Bethlehem, Pennsylvania

Education:

1937	A.A.	San Bernardino Valley Union Junior College
1939	A.B.	(Psychology) University of California, Berkeley
1947	Ph.D.	(Psychology) University of California, Berkeley

Past Employment:

1941-1943	Psychologist, Research and Analysis Branch, Coordinator of Information/ Office of Strategic Services, Washington, DC
1943-1946	Ensign and Lieutenant, J.G., U.S. Navy (Reserve)
1947-1950	Assistant Professor, Psychology, Ohio State University
1950-1953	Assistant Professor, Psychology, University of Chicago
1953-1979	Associate Professor of Psychology, Northwestern University 1953-1958; Professor 1958-1973; Morrison Professor 1973-1979
1954	Visiting Associate Professor, Yale University
1965-1966	Fellow, Center for Advanced Study in the Behavioral Sciences, Stanford, CA
1968-1969	Fulbright Lecturer and Visiting Professor in Social Psychology, University of Oxford
1977	Visiting Professor, Psychology and Social Relations, Harvard University
1979-1982	New York State Board of Regents Albert Schweitzer Professor, The Maxwell School of Citizenship and Public Affairs, Syracuse University
1983-1996	University Professor of Sociology-Anthropology, Psychology and Education, Lehigh University, Bethlehem, PA

Elected Offices:

| 1966-1967 | President, Midwestern Psychological Association |

1968-1969	President, Division of Personality and Social Psychology, American Psychological Association
1968-1969	President, Division of Personality and Social Psychology, American Psychological Association
1975	President, American Psychological Association

Honors and Awards:

1965-1966	Fellow, Center for Advanced Study in the Behavioral Sciences
1969	Distinguished Scientific Contribution Award, American Psychological Association
1973	Member, National Academy of Sciences
1974	Kurt Lewin Memorial Award, Society for the Psychological Study of Social Issues
1977	William James Lecturer, Harvard University
1977	Hovland Memorial Lecturer, Yale University
1977	Myrdal Prize in Science, The Evaluation Research Society
1977	Illinois Psychological Association Distinguished Psychologist Award
1981	Award for Distinguished Contributions to Research in Education, American Educational Research Association
1985	Career Achievement Award, Eastern Evaluation Research Society
1988	Distinguished Scientist Award, Society of Experimental Social Psychology
1988	Award for Distinguished Service to Measurement, Educational Testing Service
1989	Award for Outstanding Methodological Innovator in Public Policy Studies, Policy Studies Organization
1989	William James Fellow Award, American Psychological Society
1990	Honorary Fellow, International Association for Cross-Cultural Psychology
1991	Sage Anniversary Lectureship, American Evaluation Association
1992	Member, American Philosophical Society
1992	Award for Outstanding Service to the Field of Education, College of Education, Lehigh University

Honorary Degrees:

1974	Doctor of Law, University of Michigan
1975	Doctor of Science, University of Florida
1978	Doctor of Social Sciences, Claremont Graduate School
1978	Doctor of Humane Letters, University of Chicago
1979	Doctor of Science, University of Southern California
1983	Doctor of Science, Northwestern University
1985	Doctor of Philosophy, University of Oslo

Books and Other Dedications:

Kiesler, C. A., Collins, B. E., & Miller, N. (1969). *Attitude change: A critical analysis of theoretical approaches.* New York: Wiley.

Crano, W. D., & Brewer, M. B. (1973). *Principles of research in social psychology.* New York: McGraw-Hill.

Powers, W. T. (1973). *Behavior: The control of perception.* Chicago: Aldine.

Glass, G. V, Wilson, V. L., & Gottman, J. M. (1975). *Design and analysis of time-series experiments.* Boulder: Colorado Associated University Press.

Kidder, L. H., & Stewart, V. M. (1974). *The psychology of intergroup relations: Conflict and consciousness.* New York: McGraw-Hill.

Cook, T. D., Del Rosario, M., Hennigan, K. M., Mark, M. M., & Trochim, W.M.K. (Eds.). (1978). *Evaluation studies review annual.* Beverly Hills, CA: Sage.

McCleary, R., & Hay, R. A., Jr. (1978). *Applied time series for the social sciences.* Beverly Hills, CA: Sage.

Tucker, R. K., Weaver, R. L. II, & Fink, C. B. (1981). *Research in speech communication.* Englewood Cliffs, NJ: Prentice Hall.

Rossi, P. H., & Freeman, H. E. (1982). *Evaluation: A systematic approach* (2nd ed.). Beverly Hills, CA: Sage.

Agnew, N. M., & Pyke, S. W. (1982). *The science game: An introduction to research in the behavioral sciences* (3rd ed.). Englewood Cliffs, NJ: Prentice Hall.

McMillan, J. H., & Schumacher, S. (1984). *Research in education.* Boston: Little, Brown.

Kenny, D. A. (1985). Quantitative methods for social psychology. Chapter 9 in G. Lindzey & E. Aronson (Eds.), *Handbook of social psychology* (3rd ed., pp. 487-508). New York: Random House.

Crano, W. D., & Brewer, M. B. (1986). *Principles and methods of social research.* Boston: Allyn & Bacon.

Shadish, W. R., Cook, T. D., & Levinton, L. C. (1991). *Foundations of program evaluation: Theories of practice.* Newbury Park, CA: Sage.

Caporael, L. R., & Brewer, M. B. (Eds.). (1991). *Issues in evolutionary psychology* (special issue of the *Journal of Social Sciences*), 47(3).

Festschrift:

Brewer, M. B., & Collins, B. E. (Eds.). (1981). *Scientific inquiry in the social sciences: A volume in honor of Donald T. Campbell.* San Francisco: Jossey-Bass.

Award names:

As of 1982, the Division of Personality and Social Psychology of the American Psychological Association has named its annual award "The Donald T. Campbell Award for Significant Research in Social Psychology."

As of 1983, the Policy Studies Organization initiated "The Donald Campbell Award" to be given annually to an outstanding methodological innovator in public policy studies.

Publications:

1. *The generality of a social attitude.* Unpublished doctoral dissertation, University of California, Berkeley, 1947.
2. The indirect assessment of social attitudes. *Psychological Bulletin, 47*(1), 15-38, 1950.

3. Hites, R. W., & Campbell, D. T. A test of the ability of fraternity leaders to estimate group opinion. *Journal of Social Psychology, 32*, 95-100, 1950.

4. Wyatt, D. F., & Campbell, D. T. A study of the interviewer bias as related to interviewers' expectations and own opinions. *International Journal of Opinion and Attitude Research, 4*(1), 77-83, 1950.

5. Campbell, D. T., & Mohr, P. J. The effect of ordinal position upon responses to items in a check list. *Journal of Applied Psychology, 34*(1), 62-67, 1950.

6. Campbell, D. T., & McCandless, B. R. Ethnocentrism, xenophobia and personality. *Human Relations, 4*(2), 185-192, 1951.

7. Wyatt, D. F., & Campbell, D. T. On the liability of stereotype or hypothesis. *Journal of Abnormal Social Psychology, 46*(4), 496-500, 1951.

8. On the possibility of experimenting with the "bandwagon" effect. *International Journal of Opinion and Attitude Research, 5*(2), 251-260, 1951.

9. Rinder, I. D., & Campbell, D. T. Varieties of inauthenticity. *Phylon, 3*, 270-275, 1952.

10. The Bogardus social distance scale. *Sociology and Social Research, 36*(5), 322-326, 1952.

11. Parish, J. A., & Campbell, D. T. Measuring propaganda effects with direct and indirect attitude tests. *Journal of Abnormal and Social Psychology, 48*(1), 3-9, 1953.

12. Operational delineation of "what is learned" via the transposition experiment. *Psychological Review, 61*(3), 167-174, 1954.

13. A rationale for weighting first, second, and third sociometric choices. *Sociometry, 17*, 242-243, 1954.

14. The informant in quantitative research. *American Journal of Sociology, 60*(4), 339-342, 1955.

15. Rankin, R. E., & Campbell, D. T. Galvanic skin response to Negro and white experimenters. *Journal of Abnormal and Social Psychology, 51*(1), 30-33, 1955.

16. Kidd, J. S., & Campbell, D. T. Conformity to groups as a function of group success. *Journal of Abnormal and Social Psychology, 51*(3), 390-393, 1955.

17. Clarke, R. B., & Campbell, D. T. A demonstration of bias in estimates of Negro ability. *Journal of Abnormal and Social Psychology, 51*(3), 585-588, 1955.

18. An error in some demonstrations of the superior social perceptiveness of leaders. *Journal of Abnormal and Social Psychology, 51*(3), 694-695, 1955.

19. Adaptive behavior from random response. *Behavioral Science, 1*(2), 105-110, 1956.

20. Campbell, D. T., & Burwen, L. S. Trait judgments from photographs as a projective device. *Journal of Clinical Psychology, 12*(3), 215-221, 1956.

21. Burwen, L. S., Campbell, D. T., & Kidd, J. The use of a sentence completion test in measuring attitudes towards superiors and subordinates. *Journal of Applied Psychology, 40*(4), 248-250, 1956.

22. Review of F. A. Logan et al., *Behavior theory and social science. Contemporary Psychology, 1*(9), 264-266, 1956.

23. Perception as a substitute trial and error. *Psychological Review, 63*(5), 330-342, 1956.

24. Enhancement of contrast as composite habit. *Journal of Abnormal and Social Psychology, 53*(3), 350-355, 1956.

25. *Leadership and its effects upon the group* (Ohio Studies in Personnel, Bureau of Business Research Monograph No. 83). Columbus: Ohio State University, 1956.

26. Burwen, L. S., & Campbell, D. T. The generality of attitudes towards authority and nonauthority figures. *Journal of Abnormal and Social Psychology, 54*(1), 24-31, 1957.

27. Chapman, L. J., & Campbell, D. T. Response set in the F scale. *Journal of Abnormal and Social Psychology, 54*(1), 129-132, 1957.

28. Campbell, D. T., & McCormack, T. H. Military experience and attitudes toward authority. *American Journal of Sociology, 62*(5), 482-490, 1957.

29. Campbell, D. T., & Tyler, B. B. The construct validity of work-group morale measures. *Journal of Applied Psychology, 41*(2), 91-92, 1957.

30. Campbell, D. T., & Chapman, J. P. Testing for stimulus equivalence among authority figures by similarity in trait description. *Journal of Consulting Psychology, 21*(3), 253-256, 1957.

31. A typology of tests, projective and otherwise. *Journal of Consulting Psychology, 21*(3), 207-210, 1957.

32. Factors relevant to the validity of experiments in social settings. *Psychological Bulletin, 54*(4), 297-312, 1957.

33. Burwen, L. S., & Campbell, D. T. A comparison of test scores and role-playing behavior in assessing superior vs. subordinate orientation. *Journal of Social Psychology, 46*, 49-56, 1957.

34. Chapman, L. J., & Campbell, D. T. An attempt to predict the performance of three-man teams from attitude measures. *Journal of Social Psychology, 46*, 277-286, 1957.

35. Westfall, R. L., Boyd, H. W., & Campbell, D. T. The use of structured techniques in motivation research. *Journal of Marketing, 22*, 134-139, 1957.

36. Campbell, D. T., Hunt, W. A., & Lewis, N. A. The effects of assimilation and contrast in judgments of clinical materials. *American Journal of Psychology, 70*(3), 347-360, 1957.

37. *Interrelationships among leadership criteria measures for a population of Air Force pilot cadets* (Research Report, AFPTRC-TN-57-70, ASTIA Document 131421), June 1957.

38. *Intercorrelations among leadership criteria for a population of Air Force instructors* (Research Report, AFPTRC-TN-57-90, ASTIA Document 134233), June 1957.

39. Cotton, J. W., Campbell, D. T., & Malone, R. D. The relationship between factorial composition of test items and measures of test reliability. *Psychometrika, 22*(4), 347-357, 1957.

40. Common fate, similarity, and other indices of the status of aggregates of person of social entities. *Behavioral Science, 3*(1), 14-25, 1958.

41. Campbell, D. T., Lewis, N. A., & Hunt, W. A. Context effects with judgmental language that is absolute, extensive and extra-experimentally anchored. *Journal of Social Psychology, 55*(3), 220-228, 1958.

42. Campbell, D. T., & Mehra, K. Individual differences in evaluations of group discussions as a projective measure of attitudes toward leadership. *Journal of Social Psychology, 47*, 101-106, 1958.

43. Campbell, D. T., & Shanan, J. Semantic idiosyncrasy as a method in the study of attitudes. *Journal of Social Psychology, 47*, 107-110, 1958.

44. Campbell, D. T., Hunt, W. A., & Lewis, N. A. The relative susceptibility of two rating scales to disturbances resulting from shifts in stimulus context. *Journal of Applied Psychology, 42*(4), 213-217, 1958.

45. Campbell, D. T., & Gruen, W. Progression from simple to complex as a molar law of learning. *Journal of General Psychology, 59*, 237-244, 1958.

46. Campbell, D. T., & Kral, T. P. Transposition away from a rewarded stimulus card to a nonrewarded one as a function of a shift in background. *Journal of Comparative and Physiological Psychology, 51*(5), 592-595, 1958.

47. Systematic error on the part of human links in communication systems. *Information and Control, 1*(4), 334-369, 1959.

48. Campbell, D. T., & Fiske, D. W. Convergent and discriminant validation by the multitrait multimethod matrix. *Psychological Bulletin, 56*(2), 81-105, 1959.

49. Chapman, L. J., & Campbell, D. T. The effect of acquiescence response-set upon relationships among the F scale, ethnocentrism, and intelligence. *Sociometry, 22*(2), 153-161, 1959.

50. Miller, N., & Campbell, D. T. Recency and primacy in persuasion as a function of the timing of speeches and measurements. *Journal of Abnormal and Social Psychology, 59*(1), 1-9, 1959.

51. Methodological suggestions from a comparative psychology of knowledge processes. *Inquiry, 2,* 152-182, 1959.

52. Chapman, L. J., & Campbell, D. T. Absence of acquiescence response set in the Taylor manifest anxiety scale. *Journal of Consulting Psychology, 23*(5), 465-466, 1959.

53. Small, D. O., & Campbell, D. T. The effect of acquiescence response-set upon the relationship of the F scale and conformity. *Sociometry, 23*(1), 69-71, 1960.

54. Campbell, D. T., Miller, N., & Diamond, A. L. Predisposition to identify instigating and guiding stimulus as revealed in transfer. *Journal of General Psychology, 63,* 69-74, 1960.

55. Blind variation and selective survival as a general strategy in knowledge processes. In M. C. Yovits & S. H. Cameron (Eds.), *Self-organizing systems* (pp. 205-231). Oxford, UK: Pergamon, 1960.

56. Maher, B. A., Watt, N., & Campbell, D. T. Comparative validity of two projective and two structured attitude tests in a prison population. *Journal of Applied Psychology, 44*(4), 284-288, 1960.

57. Recommendations for APA test standards regarding construct, trait, or discriminant validity. *American Psychologist, 15,* 546-553, 1960.

58. Blind variation and selective retention in creative thought as in other knowledge processes. *Psychological Review, 67*(6), 380-400, 1960.

59. Thistlethwaite, D. L., & Campbell, D. T. Regression-discontinuity analysis: An alternative to the ex post facto experiment. *Journal of Educational Psychology, 51*(6), 309-317, 1960.

60. Campbell, D. T., & Clayton, K. N. Avoiding regression effects in panel studies of communication impact. *Studies in Public Communication, 3,* 99-118, 1961.

61. Campbell, D. T., & LeVine, R. A. A proposal for cooperative cross-cultural research on ethnocentrism. *Journal of Conflict Resolution, 5*(1), 82-108, 1961.

62. Jacobs, R. C., & Campbell, D. T. The perpetuation of an arbitrary tradition through several generations of a laboratory microculture. *Journal of Abnormal and Social Psychology, 62*(3), 649-658, 1961.

63. Krantz, D. L., & Campbell, D. T. Separating perceptual and linguistic effects of context shifts upon absolute judgments. *Journal of Experimental Psychology, 62*(1), 35-42, 1961.

64. Conformity in psychology's theories of acquired behavioral dispositions. In I. A. Berg & B. M. Bass (Eds.), *Conformity and deviation* (pp. 101-142). New York: Harper, 1961.

65. The mutual methodological relevance of anthropology and psychology. In F.L.K. Hsu (Ed.), *Psychological anthropology: Approaches to culture and personality* (pp. 333-352). Homewood, IL: Dorsey, 1961.

66. Campbell, D. T., & Damarin, F. L. Measuring leadership attitudes through an information test. *Journal of Social Psychology, 55,* 159-175, 1961.

67. Renner, K. E., Maher, B. A., & Campbell, D. T. The validity of a method for scoring sentence-completion responses for anxiety, dependency and hostility. *Journal of Applied Psychology, 46,* 285-290, 1962.

68. Harvey, O. J., & Campbell, D. T. Judgments of weight as affected by adaptation range, adaptation duration, magnitude of unlabeled anchor, and judgmental language. *Journal of Experimental Psychology, 65*(1), 12-21, 1963.

69. Segall, M. H., Campbell, D. T., & Herskovits, M. J. Cultural differences in the perception of geometric illusions. *Science, 139,* 769-771, 1963.

70. Campbell, D. T., & Stanley, J. C. Experimental and quasi-experimental designs for research on teaching. In N. L. Gage (Ed.), *Handbook of research on teaching* (pp. 171-246). Chicago: Rand McNally, 1963. (Reprinted as *Experimental and quasi-experimental designs for research,* Chicago: Rand McNally, 1966)

71. Social attitudes and other acquired behavioral dispositions. In S. Koch (Ed.), *Psychology: A study of a science: Vol. 6. Investigations of man as socius* (pp. 94-172). New York: McGraw-Hill, 1963.

72. Watson, R. I., & Campbell, D. T. (Eds.). *E. G. Boring: History, psychology, and science: Selected papers.* New York: Wiley, 1963.

73. Lubetsky, J., & Campbell, D. T. Age and sex as sources of stimulus equivalence in judgments of photos and peers. *Journal of Clinical Psychology, 19*(4), 502-505, 1963.

74. From description to experimentation: Interpreting trends as quasi-experiments. In C. W. Harris (Ed.), *Problems in measuring change* (pp. 212-242). Madison: University of Wisconsin Press, 1963.

75. Distinguishing differences of perception from failures of communication in cross-cultural studies. In F.S.C. Northrop & H. H. Livingston (Eds.), *Cross-cultural understanding: Epistemology in anthropology* (pp. 308-336). New York: Harper & Row, 1964.

76. Campbell, D. T., Miller, N., Lubeteky, J., & O'Connell, E. J. Varieties of projection in trait attribution. *Psychological Monographs, 78*(592), 1-33, 1964.

77. Spear, N. E., Hill, W. F., & Campbell, D. T. Effect of unconsumed reward on subsequent alternation of choice. *Psychological Reports, 15,* 407-411, 1964.

78. Ethnocentric and other altruistic motives. In D. Levine (Ed.), *The Nebraska symposium on motivation, 1965* (pp. 283-311). Lincoln: University of Nebraska Press, 1965.

79. Hicks, J. M., & Campbell, D. T. Zero-point scaling as affected by social object, scaling method, and context. *Journal of Personality and Social Psychology, 2*(6), 793-808, 1965.

80. Variation and selective retention in socio-cultural evolution. In H. R. Barringer, G. I. Blanksten, & R. W. Mack (Eds.), *Social change in developing areas: A reinterpretation of evolutionary theory* (pp. 19-48). Cambridge, MA: Schenkman, 1965.

81. Experimental design: Quasi-experimental design. In D. L. Sills (Ed.), *International encyclopedia of the social sciences* (Vol. 5, pp. 259-263). New York: Macmillan & Free Press, 1968.

82. Miller, N., Campbell, D. T., Twedt, H., & O'Connell, E. J. Similarity, contrast, and complementarity in friendship choice. *Journal of Personality and Social Psychology, 3*(1), 3-12, 1966.

83. Campbell, D. T., & Tauscher, H. Schopenhauer, Sequin, Lubinoff, and Zehender as anticipators of Emmert's Law: With comments on the uses of eponymy. *Journal of the History of the Behavioral Sciences, 2*(1), 58-63, 1966.

84. Pattern matching as an essential in distal knowing. In K. R. Hammond (Ed.), *The psychology of Egon Brunswik* (pp. 81-106). New York: Holt, Rinehart & Winston, 1966.

85. Campbell, D. T., Kruskal, W. H., & Wallace, W. P. Seating aggregation as an index of attitude. *Sociometry, 29*(1), 1-15, 1966.

86. Webb, E. J., Campbell, D. T., Schwartz, R. D., & Sechrest, L. B. *Unobtrusive measures: Nonreactive research in the social sciences.* Chicago: Rand McNally, 1966.

87. Segall, M. H., Campbell, D. T., & Herskovits, M. J. *The influence of culture on visual perception.* Indianapolis: Bobbs-Merrill, 1966.

88. Administrative experimentation, institutional records, and nonreactive measures. In J. C. Stanley & S. M. Elam (Eds.), *Improving experimental design and statistical analysis* (pp. 257-291). Chicago: Rand McNally, 1967.

89. Stereotypes and the perception of group differences. *American Psychologist, 22*(10), 817-829, 1967.

90. Campbell, D. T., Siegman, C. R., & Rees, M. B. Direction-of-wording effects in the relationships between scales. *Psychological Bulletin, 68*(5), 293-303, 1967.

91. Campbell, D. T., & O'Connell, E. J. Methods factors in multitrait-multimethod matrices: Multiplicative rather than additive? *Multivariate Behavioral Research, 2*(4), 409-426, 1967.

92. A cooperative multinational opinion sample exchange. *Journal of Social Issues, 24*(2), 245-258, 1968.

93. Campbell, D. T., & LeVine, R. A. Ethnocentrism and intergroup relations. In R. P. Abelson, E. Aronson, W. J. McGuire, T. M. Newcomb, M. J. Rosenberg, & P. H. Tannenbaum (Eds.), *Theories of cognitive consistency: A sourcebook* (pp. 551-564). Chicago: Rand McNally, 1968.

94. Campbell, D. T., & Ross, H. L. The Connecticut crackdown on speeding: Time-series data in quasi-experimental analysis. *Law and Society Review, 3*(1), 33-53, 1968.

95. Ethnocentrism of disciplines and the fish-scale model of omniscience. In M. Sherif & C. W. Sherif (Eds.), *Interdisciplinary relationships in the social sciences* (pp. 328-348). Chicago: Aldine, 1969.

96. Rozelle, R. M., & Campbell, D. T. More plausible rival hypotheses in the cross-lagged panel correlation technique. *Psychological Bulletin, 71*(1), 74-80, 1969.

97. A phenomenology of the other one: Corrigible, hypothetical and critical. In T. Mischel (Ed.), *Human action: Conceptual and empirical issues* (pp. 41-69). New York: Academic Press, 1969.

98a. Reforms as experiments. *American Psychologist, 24*(4), 409-429, 1969.

98b. Shaver, P., & Staines, G. Problems facing Campbell's "experimenting society." *Urban Affairs Quarterly, 7*(2), 173-186, 1971.

98c. Comments on the comments by Shaver and Staines. *Urban Affairs Quarterly, 7*(2), 187-192, 1971.

98d. Legal reforms and experiments. *Journal of Legal Education, 23*(1), 217-239, 1971. (Modification of 98a)

99. Winch, R. F., & Campbell, D. T. Proof? No. Evidence? Yes. The significance of tests of significance. *American Sociologist, 4*(2), 140-143, 1969.

100. Herskovits, M. J., Campbell, D. T., & Segall, M. H. *A cross-cultural study of perception.* Indianapolis: Bobbs-Merrill, 1969. (Revised edition)

101. Prospective: Artifact and control. In R. Rosenthal & R. Rosnow (Eds.), *Artifact in behavior research* (pp. 351-382). New York: Academic Press, 1969.

102. Definitional versus multiple operationalism. *Et al., 2*(2), 14-17, 1969.

103. Werner, O., & Campbell, D. T. Translating, working through interpreters, and the problem of decentering. In R. Naroll & R. Cohen (Eds.), *A handbook of method in cultural anthropology* (pp. 398-420). Garden City, NY: Natural History Press, 1970.

104. Natural selection as an epistemological model. In R. Naroll & R. Cohen (Eds.), *A handbook of method in cultural anthropology* (pp. 51-85). Garden City, NY: Natural History Press, 1970.

105. Campbell, D. T., & LeVine, R. A. Field manual anthropology. In R. Naroll & R. Cohen (Eds.), *A handbook of method in cultural anthropology* (pp. 366-387). Garden City, NY: Natural History Press, 1970.

106. Kidder, L., & Campbell, D. T. The indirect testing of social attitudes. In G. F. Summers (Ed.), *Attitude measurement* (pp. 333-385). Chicago: Rand McNally, 1970.

107. Brewer, M. B., Campbell, D. T., & Crano, W. D. Testing a single-factor model as an alternative to the misuse of partial correlations in hypothesis-testing research. *Sociometry, 33*(1), 1-11, 1970.

108. Ross, H. L., Campbell, D. T., & Glass, G. V. Determining the social effects of a legal reform: The British "Breathalyser" crackdown of 1967. *American Behavioral Scientist, 13*(4), 493-509, 1970.

109. Considering the case against experimental evaluations of social innovations. *Administrative Science Quarterly, 15*(1), 110-113, 1970.

110. Campbell, D. T., & Erlebacher, A. How regression artifacts in quasi-experimental evaluations can mistakenly make compensatory education look harmful. In J. Hellmuth (Ed.), *Compensatory education: A national debate: Vol. 3. Disadvantaged child* (pp. 185-210). New York: Brunner/Mazel, 1970. (Reply to the replies, 221-225)

111. Campbell, D. T., & Frey, P. W. The implications of learning theory for the fade-out of gains from compensatory education. In J. Hellmuth (Ed.), *Compensatory education: A national debate: Vol. 3. Disadvantaged child* (pp. 455-463). New York: Brunner/Mazel, 1970.

112. Raser, J. R., Campbell, D. T., & Chadwick, R. W. Gaming and simulation for developing theory relevant to international relations. In A. Rapoport (Ed.), *General systems: Yearbook of the Society for General Systems Research* (Vol. 15, pp. 183-204). Ann Arbor, MI: Society for General Systems Research, 1970.

113. Brickman, P., & Campbell, D. T. Hedonic relativism and planning the good society. In M. H. Appley (Ed.), *Adaptation-level theory: A symposium* (pp. 287-304). New York: Academic Press, 1971.

114. Temporal changes in treatment-effect correlations: A quasi-experimental model for institutional records and longitudinal studies. In G. V Glass (Ed.), *Proceedings of the 1970 invitational conference on testing problems* (pp. 93-110). Princeton, NJ: Educational Testing Service, 1971.

115. Distinguished Scientific Contribution Award, 1970 [Award to D. T. Campbell, including citation, biography, and publications]. *American Psychologist, 26*(1), 77-81, 1971.

116. Measuring the effects of social innovations by means of time-series. In J. M. Tanur, F. Mosteller, W. H. Kruskal, R. F. Link, R. S. Pieters, & G. R. Rising (Eds.), *Statistics: A guide to the unknown* (pp. 120-129). San Francisco: Holden-Day, 1972.

117. LeVine, R. A., & Campbell, D. T. *Ethnocentrism: Theories of conflict, ethnic attitudes and group behavior.* New York: Wiley, 1972.

118. Crano, W. D., Kenny, D. A., & Campbell, D. T. Does intelligence cause achievement?: A cross-lagged panel analysis. *Journal of Educational Psychology, 63*(3), 258-275, 1972.

119. Herskovits, cultural relativism, and metascience. In M. J. Herskovits. *Cultural relativism* (pp. v-xxiii). New York: Random House, 1972.

120. On the genetics of altruism and the counter-hedonic components in human culture. *Journal of Social Issues, 28*(3), 21-37, 1972.

121. Webb, E. J., & Campbell, D. T. Experiments on communication effects. In I. de S. Pool, W. Schramm, F. W. Frey, N. Maccoby, & E. B. Parker (Eds.), *Handbook of communications* (pp. 938-952). Chicago: Rand McNally, 1973.

122. The social scientist as methodological servant of the experimenting society. *Policy Studies Journal, 2*(1), 72-75, 1973.

123. Ostensive instances and entitativity in language learning. In W. Gray & N. D. Rizzo (Eds.), *Unity through diversity* (Part 2, pp. 1043-1057). New York: Gordon & Breach, 1973.

124. Salasin, S. Experimentation revisited: A conversation with Donald T. Campbell. *Evaluation, 1*(1), 7-13, 1973.

125. Evolutionary epistemology. In P. A. Schilpp (Ed.), *The philosophy of Karl R. Popper* (The Library of Living Philosophers, Vol. 14, pp. 413-463). La Salle, IL: Open Court, 1974.

126. Unjustified variation and selective retention in scientific discovery. In F. J. Ayala & T. Dobzhansky (Eds.), *Studies in the philosophy of biology* (pp. 139-161). London: Macmillan, 1974.

127. "Downward causation" in hierarchically organized biological systems. In F. J. Ayala & T. Dobzhansky (Eds.), *Studies in the philosophy of biology* (pp. 179-186). London: Macmillan, 1974.

128. Riecken, H. W., Boruch, R. F., Campbell, D. T., Caplan, N., Glennan, T. K., Pratt, J., Rees, A., & Williams, W. *Social experimentation: A method for planning and evaluating social intervention.* New York: Academic Press, 1974.

129. "Degrees of freedom" and the case study. *Comparative Political Studies, 8*(2), 178-193, 1975.

130. Campbell, D. T., Boruch, R. F., Schwartz, R. D., & Steinberg, J. Confidentiality-preserving modes of access to files and to interfile exchange for useful statistical analysis. Appendix A to A. M. Rivim et al., *Protecting individual privacy in evaluation research* (A report of the Committee on Federal Agency Evaluation Research of the National Academy of Sciences, National Research Council, Washington, DC, A-1–A-25). Washington, DC: National Research Council, 1975.

131. Assessing the impact of planned social change. In G. M. Lyons (Ed.), *Social research and public policies* (pp. 3-45). Hanover, NH: The Public Affairs Center, Dartmouth College, 1975.

132. The conflict between social and biological evolution and the concept of original sin. *Zygon, 10,* 234-249, 1975.

133. Campbell, D. T., & Boruch, R. F. Making the case for randomized assignment to treatments by considering the alternatives: Six ways in which quasi-experimental evaluations in compensatory education tend to underestimate effects. In C. A. Bennett & A. Lumsdaine (Eds.), *Evaluation and experiments: Some critical issues in assessing social programs* (pp. 195-296). New York: Academic Press, 1975.

134. Reintroducing Konrad Lorenz to psychology. In R. I. Evans (Ed. & interviewer), *Konrad Lorenz: The man and his ideas* (pp. 88-128). New York: Harcourt Brace Jovanovich, 1975.

135. Tavris, C. The experimenting society: To find programs that work, government must measure its failures: A conversation with Donald T. Campbell. *Psychology Today, 9*(4), 46-56, 1975.

136. On the conflicts between biological and social evolution and between psychology and moral tradition. *American Psychologist, 30,* 1103-1126, 1975.

137. Cook, T. D., & Campbell, D. T. The design and conduct of quasi-experiments and true experiments in field settings. In M. D. Dunnette (Ed.), *Handbook of industrial and organizational research* (pp. 223-226). Chicago: Rand McNally, 1976.

138. Brewer, M. B., & Campbell, D. T. *Ethnocentrism and intergroup attitudes: East African evidence.* New York: John Wiley, 1976.

139. Focal local indicators for social program evaluation. *Social Indicators Research, 3,* 237-256, 1976.

140. Discussion comment on "the natural selection model of conceptual evolution." *Philosophy of Science, 44*(3), 502-507, 1977.

141. Keeping the data honest in the experimenting society. In H. W. Melton & J. H. David (Eds.), *Interdisciplinary dimensions of accounting for social goals and social organizations* (pp. 37-42). Columbus, OH: Grid, Inc., 1977.

142. Qualitative knowing in action research. In M. Brenner, P. Marsh, & M. Brenner (Eds.), *The social contexts of method* (pp. 184-209). London: Croom Helm, 1978. (Reprinted in D. T. Campbell [E. S. Overman, Ed.], *Methodology and epistemology for social science* [pp. 360-376]. Chicago: University of Chicago Press, 1988)

143a. Comments on the sociobiology of ethics and moralizing. *Behavioral Science, 24,* 37-45, 1979.

143b. Social morality norms as evidence of conflict between biological human nature and social system requirements. In G. S. Stent (Ed.), *Morality as a biological phenomenon* (pp. 75-92). Berlin: Dahlem Konferenzen, 1979.

144. Cook, T. D., & Campbell, D. T. *Quasi-experimentation: Design and analysis for field settings.* Chicago: Rand McNally, 1979.

145. A tribal model of the social system vehicle carrying scientific knowledge. *Knowledge, 2,* 181-201, 1979.

146. Darning up the gaps in the seamless web of scholarship. *Syracuse Scholar, 1,* 73-77, 1979-1980.

147. Social dispositions of the individual and their group functionality: Evolutionary aspects. In E. V. Shorokhova & M. I. Bobneva (Eds.), *Psychological mechanisms for the regulation of social behavior* (pp. 76-102). Moscow: Nauka, 1979. (Translated by M. I. Bobneva into Russian)

148. *Models of experiments in social psychology and applied research.* Moscow: Progress, 1980. (Translated by M. I. Bobneva into Russian)

149. Campbell, D. T., & Wertsch, J. V. Soviet perspectives on American social psychology. *Soviet Psychology, 19,* 3-11, 1980. (With introduction by guest editors)

150. Discussion with R. E. Evans. In R. E. Evans (Interviewer and Ed.), *The making of social psychology* (pp. 73-84). New York: Gardner, 1980.

151. Webb, E. J., Campbell, D. T., Schwartz, R. D., Sechrest, L., & Grove, J. B. *Nonreactive measures in the social sciences.* Boston: Houghton Mifflin, 1981. (Revision of item 86)

152. *Epistemologia evoluzionistica*. Rome: Editore Armando Armondo, 1981. (Translation and 56-page introduction by Massimo Stanzione)

153. Levels of organization, selection, and information storage in biological and social evolution. *The Behavioral and Brain Sciences*, *4*, 236-237, 1981.

154. Variation and selective retention theories of sociocultural evolution. Comments on R. N. Adams, Natural selection, energetics, and "cultural materialism." *Current Anthropology*, *22*, 603-608 and 608-609, 1981.

155. Foreword: Several invitations to several groups of readers. In J. Zeisel, *Inquiry by design: Tools for environment-behavior research* (pp. vii-x). Monterey, CA: Brooks/Cole, 1981.

156. Introduction: Getting ready for the experimenting society. In L. Saxe & M. Fine, *Social experiments: Methods for design and evaluation* (Sage Library of Social Research Vol. 131, pp. 13-18). Beverly Hills, CA: Sage, 1981.

157. Another perspective on a scholarly career. In M. B. Brewer & B. E. Collins (Eds.), *Scientific inquiry and the social sciences: A volume in honor of Donald T. Campbell* (pp. 454-486). San Francisco: Jossey-Bass, 1981.

158. Experiments as arguments. *Knowledge: Creation, Diffusion, Utilization*, *3*, 327-337, 1982.

159. Campbell, D. T., & O'Connell, E. Methods as diluting trait relationships rather than adding irrelevant systematic variance. In D. Brinberg & L. Kidder (Eds.), *New directions for methodology of social and behavioral science: Forms of validity in research* (pp. 93-111). San Francisco: Jossey-Bass, 1982.

160. Campbell, D. T., & Cecil, J. S. A proposed system of regulation for the protection of participants in low-risk areas of applied social research. In J. E. Sieber (Ed.), *The ethics of social research* (pp. 97-121). New York: Springer-Verlag, 1982.

161. The "blind-variation-and-selective-retention" theme. In J. M. Broughton & D. J. Freeman-Moir (Eds.), *The cognitive-developmental psychology of James Mark Baldwin: Current theory and research in genetic epistemology* (pp. 87-96). Norwood, NJ: Ablex, 1982.

162. Legal and primary-group social controls. *Journal of Social and Biological Structures*, *5*(4), 431-438, 1982.

163. The general algorithm for adaptation in learning, evolution, and perception. *The Behavioral and Brain Sciences*, *6*(1), 178-179, 1983. (Commentary on T. D. Johnston, *The Behavioral and Brain Sciences*, *4*, 125-173)

164. Two distinct routes beyond kin selection to ultrasociality: Implications for the humanities and social sciences. In D. L. Bridgeman (Ed.), *The nature of prosocial development: Theories and strategies* (pp. 11-41). New York: Academic Press, 1983.

165. Foreword: An informal history of the regression discontinuity design. In W.M.K. Trochim, *Research design for program evaluation: The regression-discontinuity approach* (pp. 15-43). Beverly Hills, CA: Sage, 1984.

166. Hospital and landsting as continuously monitoring social polygrams: Advocacy and warning. In B. Cronholm & L. von Knorring (Eds.), *Evaluation of mental health services programs* (pp. 13-39). Stockholm: Forskningsraadet Medicinska, 1984.

167. Campbell, D. T., & Specht, J. C. Altruism: Biology, culture, and religion. *Journal of Social and Clinical Psychology*, *3*(1), 33-42, 1984.

168. Can we be scientific in applied social science? In R. F. Conner, D. G. Altman, & C. Jackson (Eds.), *Evaluation Studies Review Annual*, *9*, 26-48, 1984.

169. Science policy from a naturalistic sociological epistemology. In P. D. Asguith & P. Kitcher (Eds.), *PSA 1984*, *2*, 14-29, 1985.

170. Foreword. In R. K. Yin, *Case study research* (pp. 7-9). Beverly Hills, CA: Sage, 1984.

171. Kenny, D. A., & Campbell, D. T. Methodological considerations in the analysis of temporal data. In K. J. Gergen & M. M. Gergen (Eds.), *Historical social psychology* (pp. 125-138). Hillsdale, NJ: Lawrence Erlbaum, 1984.

172. Toward an epistemologically-relevant sociology of science. *Science. Technology & Human Values, 10*(1), 38-48, 1985.

173. Holzner, B., Campbell, D. T., & Shahidullah, M. The comparative study of science and the sociology of scientific validity. *Knowledge: Creation, Diffusion, Utilization, 6*(4), 307-328, 1985.

174. Quasiexperimental approaches in therapeutic research. *Muscle & Nerve, 8*(6), 483-485, 1985.

175. The agenda beyond Axelrod's *The evolution of cooperation. Political Psychology, 7*(4), 793-796, 1986.

176. Ginsberg, P. Campbells in China: A conversation with the editor. *Eastern Evaluation Research Society Newsletter, 8*(1), 6- 9, 1986.

177. Rationality and utility from the standpoint of evolutionary biology. *Journal of Business, 59*(4), S355-S364, 1986. (Reprinted in R. M. Hogarth & M. W. Reder [Eds.], *Rational choice: The contrast between economics and psychology* [pp. 171-180]. Chicago: University of Chicago Press, 1987)

178. Science's social system of validity-enhancing collective belief change and the problems of the social sciences. In D. W. Fiske & R. A. Shweder (Eds.), *Metatheory in social science: Pluralisms and subjectivities* (pp. 108-135). Chicago: University of Chicago Press, 1986.

179. [Review of W. L. Wallace, *Principles of scientific sociology*]. *Ethology and Sociobiology, 7*, 135-137, 1986.

180. Watson, K. F. Programs, experiments, and other evaluations: An interview with Donald Campbell. *The Canadian Journal of Program Evaluation, 1*(1), 83-86, 1986.

181. Cook, T. D., & Campbell, D. T. The causal assumptions of quasi-experimental practice. *Synthese, 68*, 141-180, 1986.

182. Relabeling internal and external validity for applied social scientists. In W. M. Trochim (Ed.), *Advances in quasi-experimental design and analysis: New directions for program evaluation* (pp. 67-77). San Francisco: Jossey-Bass, 1986.

183. Neurological embodiments of belief and the gaps in the fit of phenomena to noumena. In A. Shimony & D. Nails (Eds.), *Naturalistic epistemology* (pp. 165-192). Dordrecht, The Netherlands: D. Reidel, 1987.

184. Selection theory and the sociology of scientific validity. In W. Callebaut & R. Pinxten (Eds.), *Evolutionary epistemology: A multiparadigm program* (pp. 139-158). Dordrecht, The Netherlands: D. Reidel, 1987.

185. Campbell, D. T., Heyes, C. M., & Callebaut, W. G. Evolutionary epistemology bibliography. In W. Callebaut & R. Pinxten (Eds.), *Evolutionary epistemology: A multiparadigm program* (pp. 405-431). Dordrecht, The Netherlands: D. Reidel, 1987.

186. Guidelines for monitoring the scientific competence of preventive intervention research centers: An exercise in the sociology of scientific validity. *Knowledge: Creation, Diffusion, Utilization, 8*(3), 389-430, 1987.

187. Problems for the experimenting society in the interface between evaluation and service providers. In S. L. Kagan, D. R. Powell, B. Weissbourd, & E. F. Zigler (Eds.), *America's family support programs: Perspectives and prospects* (pp. 345-351). New Haven, CT: Yale University Press, 1987.

188. Ross, A. O. [Interview with D. T. Campbell]. In *Personality: The scientific study of complex human behavior* (pp. 184-185). New York: Holt, Rinehart & Winston, 1987.

189. Assessing the impact of programs, facilities, policies, and regulations. In He Zhao Fa (Ed.), *Uses of sociology: An international conference sponsored by the Sociology Department, Zhonashan University* (pp. 184-198). Guangzhou: Zhongshan University Press, 1987.

190. Foreword. In Philip Brickman et al., *Commitment, conflict, and caring* (pp. vii-x). Englewood Cliffs, NJ: Prentice Hall, 1987.

191. A general "selection theory" as implemented in biological evolution and in social belief-transmission-with-modification in science. *Biology & Philosophy, 3*(2), 171-177, 1988.

192. Preface. In M. Sherif, O. J. Harvey, B. J. White, W. R. Hood, & C. W. Sherif, *Intergroup conflict and cooperation: The robber's cave experiment* (pp. xiii-xxi). Middletown, CT: Wesleyan University Press, 1988.

193. Provocation on reproducing perspectives: Part 5. *Social Epistemology, 2*(2), 189-192, 1988.

194. Popper and selection theory: Response. *Social Epistemology, 2*(4), 371-377, 1988.

195. *Methodology and epistemology for social science: Selected papers* (E. S. Overman, Ed.). Chicago: University of Chicago Press, 1988.

196. Uncritical adaptationism criticized [Review of John Dupre, (Ed.), *The latest on the best: Essays on evolution and optimality*]. *Contemporary Psychology, 34*(2), 128-129, 1989.

197. Fragments of the fragile history of psychological epistemology and theory of science. In B. Gholson, W. R. Shadish, R. A. Neimeyer, & A. C. Houts (Eds.), *Psychology of science: Contributions to metascience* (pp. 21-46). New York: Cambridge University Press, 1989.

198. In memoriam: Milton Rokeach, 1918-1988. *Public Opinion Quarterly, 53*, 258-261, 1989.

199. Honoring Nevitt Sanford [Review of Mervin B. Freedman (Ed.), *Social change and personality: Essays in honor of Nevitt Sanford*]. *Contemporary Psychology, 34*(10), 944-945, 1989.

200. Being mechanistic/materialistic/realistic about the process of knowing. *Canadian Psychology, 30*(2), 184-185, 1989.

201. Paller, B. T., & Campbell, D. T. Maxwell and van Fraassen on observability, reality, and justification. In M. L. Maxwell & C. W. Savage (Eds.), *Science, mind and psychology: Essays in honor of Grover Maxwell* (pp. 99-132). Lanham, MD: University Press of America, 1989.

202. Campbell, D. T., & Paller, B. T. Extending evolutionary epistemology to "justifying" scientific beliefs: A sociological rapprochement with a fallibilist perceptual foundationalism? In K. Hahlweg & C. A. Hooker (Eds.), *Issues in evolutionary epistemology* (pp. 231-257). Albany: State University of New York Press, 1989.

203. Braverman, M. T., & Campbell, D. T. Facilitating the development of health promotion programs: Recommendations for researchers and funders. In M. T. Brayerman (Ed.), *Evaluating health promotion programs* (pp. 5-18). San Francisco: Jossey-Bass, 1989.

204. Kenny, D. A., & Campbell, D. T. On the measurement of stability in overtime data. *Journal of Personality, 57*(2), 445-481, 1989.

205. Models of language learning and their implications for social-constructionist analyses of scientific belief. In S. Fuller, M. De Mey, T. Shinn, & S. Woolgar (Eds.), *The cognitive turn: Sociological and psychological perspectives on science* (pp. 153-158). Dordrecht, The Netherlands: Kluwer Academic, 1989.

206. Erkenntnistheorie evolutionare. In H. Seiffert & G. Radnitzky (Eds.), *Handlexikon zur Wissenschaftstheorie* (pp. 61-62). Munchen: Ehrenwirth, 1989.

207. Levels of organization, downward causation, and the selection-theory approach to evolutionary epistemology. In G. Greenberg & E. Tobach (Eds.), *Theories of the evolution of knowing* (T. C. Schneirla Conference Series, Vol. 4, pp. 1-17). Hillsdale, NJ: Lawrence Erlbaum, 1990.

208. Asch's moral epistemology for socially shared knowledge. In I. Rock (Ed.), *The legacy of Solomon Asch: Essays in cognition and social psychology* (pp. 39-55). Hillsdale, NJ: Lawrence Erlbaum, 1990.

209. Epistemological roles for selection theory. In N. Rescher (Ed.), *Evolution, cognition, realism* (pp. 1-19). Lanham, MD: University Press of America, 1990.

210. Toedter, L. J., Lasker, J. N., & Campbell, D. T. The comparison group problem in bereavement studies and the retrospective pretest. *Evaluation Review, 14*(1), 75-90, 1990.

211. Cziko, G. A., & Campbell, D. T. Comprehensive evolutionary epistemology bibliography. *Journal of Social and Biological Structures, 13*(1), 41-82, 1990.

212. Campbell, D. T., et al. *Head Start research and evaluation: Blueprint for the future. Recommendations of the Advisory Panel for the Head Start Evaluation Design Project.* Washington, DC: Department of Health and Family Services, 1990.

213. Methodological supplement. In *Final Report of the Head Start Evaluation Design Project* (pp. 1-19). Washington, DC: Department of Health and Family Services, 1990.

214. The Meehlian corroboration-verisimilitude theory of science. *Psychological Inquiry, 1*(2), 142-147, 1990.

215. Campbell, D. T., & Reichardt, C. S. Problems in assuming the comparability of pretest and posttest in autoregressive and growth models. In R. E. Snow & D. E. Wiley (Eds.), *Improving inquiry in social science: A volume in honor of Lee J. Cronbach* (pp. 201-219). Hillsdale, NJ: Lawrence Erlbaum, 1991.

216. A naturalistic theory of archaic moral orders. *Zygon, 26*(1), 91-114, 1991.

217. Cook, T. D., Campbell, D. T., & Peracchio, L. Quasi experimentation. In M. D. Dunnette & L. M. Hough (Eds.), *Handbook of industrial and organizational psychology* (Vol. 1, pp. 491-576). Palo Alto, CA: Consulting Psychologists Press, 1991.

218. Autopoetic evolutionary epistemology and internal selection. *Journal of Social and Biological Structures, 14*(2), 166-173, 1991.

219. Coherentist empiricism, hermeneutics, and the commensurability of paradigms. *International Journal of Educational Research, 15*(6), 587-597, 1991.

220. Methods for the experimenting society. *Evaluation Practice, 12*(3), 223-260, 1991.

221. Miro, M., & Pelechano, V. Entrevista con Donald T. Campbell. *Psicologemas, 5*(9), 139-151, 1991.

222. Fiske, D. W., & Campbell, D. T. Citations do not solve problems. *Psychological Bulletin, 112*(3), 393-395, 1992.

223. Rosenwein, R. E., & Campbell, D. T. Mobilization to achieve collective action and democratic majority/plurality amplification. *Journal of Social Issues, 48*(2), 125-138, 1992.

224. Plausible coselection of belief by referent: All the "objectivity" that is possible. *Perspectives on Science, 1*(1), 88-108, 1993.

225. The social psychology of scientific validity: An epistemological perspective and a personalized history. In W. R.Shadish & S. Fuller (Eds.), *The social psychology of science* (pp. 124-161). New York: Guilford, 1993.

226. Systematic errors to be expected of the social scientist on the basis of a general psychology of cognitive bias. In P. D. Blanck (Ed.), *Interpersonal expectations: Theory, research, and applications* (pp. 25-41). New York: Cambridge University Press, 1993.

227. Systems theory and social experimentation. In S. A. Umpleby & V. N. Sadovsky (Eds.), *Reconstructing knowledge and action: Systems theory in the United States and the Soviet Union.* New York: Hemisphere, 1994.

228. Quasi-experimental research designs in compensatory education. In E. M. Scott (Ed.), *Evaluating intervention strategies for children and youth at risk,* 1994.

229. Distinguishing between pattern-in-perception due to the knowing mechanisms and pattern plausibly attributable to the referent. In E. Carvallo (Ed.), *Nature, cognition, and system* (Vol. 3). Amsterdam, The Netherlands: Kluwer. 1994.

230. How individual and face-to-face-group selection undermine firm selection in organizational evolution. In J.A.C. Baum & J. V. Singh (Eds.), *Evolutionary dynamics of organizations* (pp. 23-38). New York: Oxford University Press, 1994.

231. The postpositivist, non-foundational, hermeneutic, coherentist epistemology exemplified in the works of Donald W. Fiske. In P. E. Shrout & S. T. Fiske (Eds.), *Advances in personality research, methods and theory: A festschrift honoring Donald W. Fiske* (pp. 13-27). Hillsdale, NJ: Erlbaum, 1994.

232. Introduction: Toward a sociology of scientific validity. In K. M. Kim, *Explaining scientific consensus* (pp. x-xx). New York: Guilford, 1994.

233. Retrospective and prospective on program impact assessment. *Evaluation Practice*, *15*(3), 291-298, 1994.

Posthumous Publications (as of 8/19/98):

234. Wu, P., & Campbell, D. T. Extending latent variable LISREL analyses of the 1969 Westinghouse Head Start evaluation to blacks and full year whites. *Evaluation and Program Planning*, *19*(3), 183, 1996

235. Can we overcome world-view incommensurability/relativity in trying to understand the other? In R. Jessor, A. Colby, & R. A. Shweder (Eds.), *Ethnography and human development* (pp. 153-172). Chicago: University of Chicago Press, 1996.

236. Regression artifacts in time-series and longitudinal data. *Evaluation and Program Planning*, *19*(4), 377-389, 1996.

237. Unresolved issues in measurement validity: An autobiographical overview. *Psychological Assessment*, *8*, 1996.

238. The perceptual constancies as a general epistemological model. In K. R. Fischer & F. Stadler (Eds.), *Wahrnehmungund Gegenstandswerk: Zum Lebenswerk von Egon Brunswik* (pp. 175-176). Vienna: Springer-Verlag, 1997.

239. From evolutionary epistemology via selection theory to a sociology of scientific validity. *Evolution and Cognition*, *3*(1), 5-38, 1997.

240. Campbell, D. T., & Russo, J. (Ed.). *Social experimentation* [collected papers]. Thousand Oaks, CA: Sage, 1999.

Forthcoming:

Campbell, D. T., & Kenny, D. *A primer on regression artifacts.* New York: Guilford.

Russo, J. (Ed.). *Social measurement* [collected papers]. Thousand Oaks, CA: Sage.

Posthumous Book Dedications:

Jessor, R., Colby, A., & Shweder, R. A. (Eds.). *Ethnography and human development.* Chicago: University of Chicago Press, 1996.

Chelimsky, E., & Shadish, W. (Eds.). *Evaluation for the 21st century: A handbook.* Thousand Oaks, CA: Sage, 1997.

Dunn, W. (Ed.). *Policy Studies Review Annual: Vol. 11. The experimenting society: Essays in memory of Donald T. Campbell.* New Brunswick, NJ: Transaction Publishers, 1998.

Baum, J.A.C., & McKelvey, B. (Eds.). *Variations in organization science: In honor of Donald T. Campbell.* Thousand Oaks, CA: Sage, 1999.

Heyes, C., & Hull, D. (Eds.). *Donald T. Campbell's contributions to philosophy of science.* In preparation.

Author Index

Subject Index

Action, interpreting networks of, 246-247
  centrality, 247
  cliques, 246, 271
  clusters, 246, 271
  density, 247
  reachability, 246-247
Action, patterns of, 237, 238
  analyzing, 241
  institutions as, 239
  See also Sequential data
Actions, network of, 238
  as models of routines, 241
  compared to traditional social networks, 238-239
  example, 240-241
  mapping, 241-243
  process grammars and, 239
  reasons for, 238-241
  routines as, 238
  using in organizational theory, 247-251
  See also Narrative positivism
Actions, relations between, 242. *See also* Sequential
  adjacency
Adaptation, 190-191
Adaptive landscape, 285, 302
Adaptive tension, 279, 302
  critical values, 281
Agency theorists, 65, 119
Agency theory, 6, 119, 126, 191
Agent-based adaptive learning models, 7
Aggregation problem, 255
Altruism, 20, 26-27
  versus egoism, 26
American Psychological Association, 313, 369
Antinomy, 23-24, 27
Attractors:
  definitions, 283

periodic, 283, 284
point, 283, 284, 285
strange, 283, 284, 285
Axiom-Theory-Model-Phenomena relationship, 289-290

Baldwin effect, 24
Bandwagon effects, 39, 43, 159
Benchmarking, 80, 86-87, 238
Blind variation, 79-80, 84, 89, 95, 238
  characteristics of effective, 81-85
  concept of, 81-84
  need for multiple failures, 84-85
  requirement for multiple variations, 84
  See also Blind variation, sources of;
    Blind-variation-and-selective-retention (BVSR);
    Organizational copying
Blind variation, sources of, 85-86
  diffusion, 85
  rational selection, 86
  selective propagation of temporal variations, 85-86
Blind-variation-and-selective-retention (BVSR), 2, 8, 10,
  20, 21-23, 31, 35-36, 89, 238, 280, 281, 288, 301
  basic ideas, 81-82
  creativity and, 25
  environment, 28
  equiprobability, 83
  major components, 22
  processes, 280
  randomness, 83
  statistical independence, 83-84
  unrestrainedness, 83
  See also Blind variation; Organizational copying
Boolean network dynamics, 290
Boolean networks, 290-291, 296, 301, 302
  random, 291-292

About the Contributors

Howard E. Aldrich (PhD, University of Michigan) is Kenan Professor of Sociology, Director of the Industrial Relations Curriculum, Director of the Sociology Graduate Studies Program, and Adjunct Professor of Business at the University of North Carolina, Chapel Hill (e-mail: howard_aldrich@unc.edu; www.unc.edu/~healdric/). He has published more than 100 articles on organizations, entrepreneurship, evolutionary theory, ethnic relations, and organizational strategy. He is the author or coauthor of four books: *Organizations and Environments* (1979), *Population Perspectives on Organizations* (1986), *Organizations Evolving* (forthcoming), and *Ethnic Entrepreneurs: Immigrant Business in Industrial Societies (1990; with Roger Waldinger and Robin Ward).*

Philip Anderson (PhD, Columbia University) is Associate Professor of Business Administration at the Amos Tuck School of Business, Dartmouth College (e-mail: philip.anderson@dartmouth.edu). His research interests include processes of technical evolution, managing during industrial transformations, venture capital dynamics, and competitive strategy. He is coauthor of *Managing Strategic Innovation and Change: A Collection of Readings* (with Michael L. Tushman) and *Inside the Kaisha:*

De-Mystifying Japanese Business Behavior (with Noboru Yoshimura), which was named 1997 Booz Allen & Hamilton/Financial Times Global Business Book of the Year for Industry Analysis/Business Context. His articles have appeared in the *Harvard Business Review*, *Research Technology Management, Academy of Management Executive*, *Administrative Science Quarterly*, and *Academy of Management Journal*.

Joel A. C. Baum (PhD, Organizational Behavior, University of Toronto) is Professor of Strategy and Organization at the J. L. Rotman School of Management (with a cross-appointment to the Department of Sociology), University of Toronto (e-mail: baum@mgmt.utoronto.ca; www.mgmt.utoronto.ca/~baum). Studying economic phenomena from the point of view of a sociologist, he is concerned with how institutions, interorganizational relations, and managers shape patterns of competition and cooperation among firms, organizational founding and failure, and industry evolution. His recent publications include two series of articles. One, coauthored with Helaine J. Korn, appearing in the *Academy of Management Journal* and *Strategic Management Journal*, examines antecedents to and consequences of multimarket competition. The other, with Paul Ingram, appearing in *Strategic*

Management Journal, Administrative Science Quarterly, and *Management Science*, explores the dynamics of organizational and interorganizational learning. With Jitendra V. Singh, he coedited *Evolutionary Dynamics of Organizations* (1994). He is editor-in-chief of *Advances in Strategic Management* and a member of the editorial board of *Administrative Science Quarterly*.

Martin G. Evans (PhD, Yale University) is Professor of Organizational Behavior at the J. L. Rotman School of Management, University of Toronto (e-mail: evans@mgmt.utoronto.ca). He has been exploring issues in, around, and about organizations for more than 30 years. His most recent work includes an examination of the structure of IQ, the implications of evolutionary psychology for management, and the career implications of downsizing. Recent publications include articles in *Managerial and Decision Economics*, *Academy of Management Executive*, and *Academy of Management Journal*. He has always been interested in issues of methodology and causal inference and has published in these areas since 1969.

David N. Grazman is Assistant Professor of Health Administration and Public Administration at the University of Southern California (e-mail: grazman@usc.edu). He has a general interest in organizational change, and his research efforts to date have focused on the privatization of health care systems as well as the development and coordination of service delivery systems whose clients, such as the elderly, have multiple health and social service needs. He holds a PhD in Business Administration (Management and Organization) from the University of Minnesota and a master's degree in Public Policy from Harvard University.

Margaretha Hendrickx is a doctoral candidate in Strategic Management at the Krannert School of Management, Purdue University (e-mail: Margaretha_Hendrickx@mgmt.purdue.edu). Before joining the Krannert PhD program, she was part of a research group at Purdue dedicated to isolating transposable DNA sequences in maize and using this system to map the maize genome. She has degrees in plant molecular genetics, bio-

chemistry, and agricultural engineering from Purdue University and the State University of Ghent, Belgium. The inconsistencies and contradictions between research approaches in physics, engineering, biology, and social sciences spawned her interest in philosophy and the philosophy of science. Her work will appear in *Strategic Management Journal*.

Paul Ingram is Associate Professor of Management at the Columbia Business School, Columbia University (e-mail: pi17@columbia.edu; www.columbia.edu/~pi17). His current research interests include the role of the state in organizational theory, the influence of ideology on organizations, and the causes and effects of ties between competing organizations. Recent publications include articles in *Management Science* and *Advances in Strategic Management*. He received an MS and a PhD in Organizational Theory from Cornell University.

Amy L. Kenworthy is a doctoral candidate in Organizational Behavior at the Kenan-Flagler Business School, University of North Carolina, Chapel Hill (e-mail: kenworta@icarus.bschool.unc.edu). Her current dissertation-related research is focused on the longitudinal relationships among entrepreneurs' self-set goals, entrepreneurs' evaluative perceptions of their goals, and performance. Additional research interests include cross-cultural comparisons of entrepreneurs, service learning as a pedagogical tool, and negotiation.

Erik R. Larsen (PhD, Copenhagen Business School) is Reader in management and systems in the Department of Management Systems and Information, City University Business School, London (e-mail: E.R.Larsen@city.ac.uk). His current interests include electricity deregulation, nonlinear dynamics, and computational organizational theory. With D. Bunn, he recently coedited *Systems Modeling for Energy Policy*. His book *Organizations and Strategy: Dynamics and Processes* (with Alessandro Lomi) will appear in the Sage Strategy Series in the year 2000.

Alessandro Lomi (PhD, Cornell University) is Associate Professor of Organization Theory and Behavior at the School of Economics of the University of Bologna, Italy (e-mail: alx@economia.unibo.it). His current research interests include the analysis of interorganizational networks, ecological models of organizations, and computational organization theory. With Erik Larsen, he recently published articles in the *Journal of the Operational Research Society* and the *Journal of Computational and Mathematical Organization Theory*.

Tammy L. Madsen is Assistant Professor of Strategy and Organization at the Edwin L. Cox School of Business, Southern Methodist University (e-mail: tmadsen@mail.cox.smu.edu). Her current research integrates strategy and evolutionary theory to examine the reciprocal interactions between intrafirm evolutionary processes and firm outcomes and the effects of institutional change (deregulation) on firm evolution and competitive dynamics. She received her MS in Management from the University of Southern California and her PhD in Strategy and Organization from UCLA. Beginning in August, 1999, she will be Assistant Professor in the Management Department at the Leavey School of Business and Administration, Santa Clara University.

Bill McKelvey (PhD, Sloan School of Management at MIT) is Professor of Strategic Organizing at the Anderson School at UCLA (e-mail: mckelvey@anderson.ucla.edu). He has authored one book, *Organizational Systematics* (1982), and is preparing another, *Restructuring the Science of Socio-Economic Systems*. Current publications focus on human and social aspects of competitive strategy, organization design, epistemology of organization science, micro/macrocoevolutionary theory and method, organizational process microstate rate dynamics, knowledge-flow dynamics, complexity theory and emergent structure, and computational methods involving adaptive learning models.

Danny Miller (PhD, Management, McGill University) is Research Professor at Ecole des Hautes Etudes Commerciales, Montreal, Canada, and a Visiting Research Scholar at Columbia University (e-mail: danny.miller@hec.ca). His research fo-

cuses on organizational evolution, strategic themes and strategy integration, competitive weaponry, and top management effects. His most recent work appears in the *Academy of Management Journal*, *Strategic Management Journal*, *Social Forces*, and *Journal of Management*.

Anne S. Miner (PhD, Stanford University) is Associate Professor in the Management and Human Resources Department, Business School, University of Wisconsin–Madison (e-mail: asminer@facstaff.wisc.edu). Her research focuses on population- and organizational-level learning, with an emphasis on strategy. She has published related work in *Administrative Science Quarterly*, *Academy of Management Review*, *Academy of Management Journal*, *Organization Science*, *Research in Organizational Behavior*, and the *American Sociological Review*. She is currently exploring these topics in the context of international technology and technology entrepreneurship. She serves as an Associate Editor at *Management Science* and teaches the strategic management of technology.

Elaine Mosakowski received her PhD from the University of California, Berkeley, in Management. Her research interests lie at the nexus of strategic management and organization theory. A general theme in her work involves strategic and organizational choices under high levels of uncertainty. Her recent work has addressed the following questions: How should firms organize in an industry in which most transactions are speculative? If managers do not understand the factors that contribute to their success or failure, how can they make strategic decisions? What is the role of managerial choice in generating firm rents?

Atul Nerkar is Assistant Professor of Management at the Graduate School of Business, Columbia University (e-mail: aan19@columbia.edu). His current research focuses on the determinants of technological competence of firms. He is examining the above in the context of pharmaceutical, chemical, and optical disc industries with specific emphasis on the patent portfolios of firms and the evolutionary process underlying their development. He received his PhD in Strategic Management in 1997 from the Wharton School, University of Pennsylvania.

Brian T. Pentland (PhD, Organization Studies, Sloan School of Management at MIT) is Assistant Professor in the School of Labor and Industrial Relations at Michigan State University (e-mail: brian.pentland@ssc.msu.edu). His primary interest is in the relationship between work and technology, although he also has been developing techniques for business process modeling and the sequential analysis of qualitative data. His publications have appeared in *Administrative Science Quarterly, Organization Science, Accounting, Organizations and Society, Technology Studies*, and *Accounting, Management and Information Technologies*. He is a member of the editorial boards of *Administrative Science Quarterly* and *Accounting, Management and Information Technologies*.

Sri Raghavan is a doctoral candidate in the Management Department at the University of Wisconsin–Madison. His research interests include interorganizational imitation processes as well as organizational creativity and innovation. His current work focuses on the types and combinations of imitation processes that occur in organizations and their impact on organizational innovation. Prior to his current doctoral education, he obtained graduate degrees in economics and political science.

Hayagreeva Rao is Associate Professor at Goizueta Business School and the Department of Sociology, Emory University (e-mail: hayagreeva_rao@bus.emory.edu). His research studies the social foundations of economic outcomes, analyzing how institutional and ecological processes lead to the creation, transformation, and extinction of organizational structures. His recent publications include an article in the *American Journal of Sociology*. He serves on the editorial boards of *Administrative Science Quarterly, Academy of Management Review*, and *Organization Science*.

Peter W. Roberts is Assistant Professor of Strategy at the Graduate School of Industrial Administration at Carnegie Mellon University (e-mail:

proberts@andrew.cmu.edu). His research, which has appeared in the *Academy of Management Review* and *Strategic Management Journal*, focuses on issues related to organizational and competitive dynamics. Before joining the faculty at Carnegie Mellon, he completed a PhD in Organizational Analysis at the University of Alberta and held a faculty position at the Australian Graduate School of Management in Sydney, Australia.

Elaine Romanelli is Associate Professor of Strategy and Director of the Global Entrepreneurship Studies Program in the McDonough School of Business at Georgetown University (e-mail: romanele@gunet.georgetown.edu). Her research focuses on processes of organizational change, as well as the role of new businesses in the development and transformation of industries and regions. She has published articles in *Administrative Science Quarterly, Academy of Management Journal, Annual Review of Sociology, Organization Science*, and *Research in Organizational Behavior*. She received her AB degree in English Literature from the University of California, Berkeley, and her MBA and PhD degrees in Management from Columbia University.

Lori Rosenkopf (PhD, Management of Organizations, Columbia University) is Assistant Professor of Management at the Wharton School of the University of Pennsylvania (e-mail: rosenkopf@wharton.upenn.edu). Her research focuses on the coevolution of technology and organization. Two current efforts examine how firms' knowledge-building strategies shape technological evolution and how interorganizational linkages facilitate knowledge building between firms. Recent publications include articles in *Industrial and Corporate Change* and *Organization Science*.

Jitendra V. Singh is Professor of Management and Vice Dean–International Academic Affairs at the Wharton School of the University of Pennsylvania (e-mail: singhj@wharton.upenn.edu). His current research concerns organizational evolution and change. He has published numerous articles in leading management journals and currently serves on the editorial boards of *Asia Pacific Journal of*

Management, Strategic Management Journal, Journal of Business Venturing, and *Organization Science*. He also has edited two books: *Organizational Evolution: New Directions* (1990) and *Evolutionary Dynamics of Organizations* (coedited with Joel A. C. Baum, 1994). He received his PhD from Stanford Business School. His earliest education was in natural and mathematical sciences. He earned his BS from Lucknow University, India, and an MBA from the Indian Institute of Management, Ahmedabad, India. He is also an avid, albeit occasional, poet.

Andrew H. Van de Ven (PhD, University of Wisconsin) is Vernon H. Heath Professor of Organizational Innovation and Change in the Carlson School of Management of the University of Minnesota (e-mail: avandeve@csom.umn.edu; www.csom.umn.edu/wwwpages/faculty/vandeven/ahvhome.htm). He is currently conducting a real-time longitudinal study of the changes unfolding in Minnesota's health care physicians, organizations, and industry. He is the coauthor of two forthcoming books: *The Innovation Journey* and *Studying Organizational Change and Development: Theory and Methods*. He serves in an editorial capacity for *Organization Science, Academy of Management Review, Journal of Business Venturing*, and *Human Resources Management Journal*. He is also series coeditor for *Management of Innovation and Change* and *Foundations of Organizational Science*. He is 1999 Vice President and Program Chair of the Academy of Management.

Srilata Zaheer (PhD, Sloan School of Management, MIT) is Associate Professor of Strategic Management and Organization at the Carlson School of Management, University of Minnesota (e-mail: szaheer@csom.umn.edu). Her current research interests include the impact of globalization on organizations, firm competitive advantage from networks in time and space, and learning and legitimacy in multinational enterprises. Recent publications include articles in *Management Science*, and *Strategic Management Journal*.